FPGA PROTOTYPING BY VHDL EXAMPLES

FPGA PROTOTYPING BY VHDL EXAMPLES

Xilinx Spartan™-3 Version

Pong P. Chu
Cleveland State University

A JOHN WILEY & SONS, INC., PUBLICATION

Published by John Wiley & Sons, Inc., Hoboken, New Jersey.
Published simultaneously in Canada.

For general information on our other products and services or for technical support, please contact our Customer Care Department within the United States at (800) 762-2974, outside the United States at (317) 572-3993 or fax (317) 572-4002.

Wiley also publishes its books in a variety of electronic formats. Some content that appears in print may not be available in electronic format. For information about Wiley products, visit our web site at www.wiley.com.

Library of Congress Cataloging-in-Publication Data:

Chu, Pong P., 1959–
FPGA prototyping by VHDL examples / Pong P. Chu.
p. cm.
Includes bibliographical references and index.
ISBN 978-0-470-18531-5 (cloth : alk. paper)
1. Field programmable gate arrays—Design and construction. 2. Prototypes, Engineering. 3.VHDL (Computer hardware description language) I. Title.
TK7895.G36C485 2008
621.39'5—dc22 2007029063

10 9 8 7 6 5 4 3 2 1

To my parents, Chia-Chi and Chi-Te, my wife, Lee, and my daughter, Patricia

CONTENTS

PREFACE

HDL (hardware description language) and *FPGA* (field-programmable gate array) devices allow designers to quickly develop and simulate a sophisticated digital circuit, realize it on a prototyping device, and verify operation of the physical implementation. As these technologies mature, they have become mainstream practice. We can now use a PC and an inexpensive FPGA prototyping board to construct a complex and sophisticated digital system. This book uses a "learning by doing" approach and illustrates the FPGA and HDL development and design process by a series of examples. A wide range of examples is included, from a simple gate-level circuit to an embedded system with an 8-bit soft-core microcontroller and customized I/O peripherals. All examples can be synthesized and physically tested on a prototyping board.

Focus and audience

Focus The main focus of this book is on the effective derivation of hardware, not the syntax of HDL. Instead of explaining every language construct, the book is limited to a small synthesizable subset and uses about a dozen code templates to provide the skeletons of various types of circuits. These templates are general and can easily be integrated to construct a large, complex system. Although this approach limits the "freedom" of syntactic expression, it will not prevent us from developing innovative hardware architecture. Because of the generality and flexibility of HDL, the same circuit can usually be described by a wide variety of language constructs and coding styles. Many of these codes are intended for modeling. They may lead to unnecessarily complex hardware implementation and sometimes cannot be synthesized at all. The template approach actually forces us to think more about hardware and develop a good coding practice for synthesis. Since we are more interested in hardware, it is more beneficial to spend time on developing 10 different hardware architectures with the same code template rather than describing the same circuit with 10 different versions of codes.

There are two popular HDLs, *VHDL* and *Verilog*. Both languages are used widely and are IEEE standards. This book uses VHDL, and a separate book with a similar title uses Verilog. Despite the drastic syntactic differences in the two languages, their capabilities are very similar, particularly for our purposes. After we comprehend the design practice and coding methodology in one language, learning the other language is rather straightforward.

Although the book is intended for beginning designers, the examples follow strict design guidelines and prepare readers for future endeavors. The coding and design practice is "forward compatible," which means that:

- The same practice can be applied to large design in the future.
- The same practice can aid other system development tasks, including simulation, timing analysis, verification, and testing.
- The same practice can be applied to ASIC technology and different types of FPGA devices.
- The code can be accepted by synthesis software from different vendors.

In summary, the book is a hands-on, hardware-centric text that involves *minimal HDL overhead* and follows good design and coding practice to achieve *maximal forward comparability*.

Audience and perquisites The book contains three major parts: basic digital circuits, peripheral modules, and embedded microcontroller. The intended audience is students in an introductory or advanced digital system design course as well as practicing engineers who wish to learn FPGA- and HDL-based development. For the materials in the first two parts, readers need to have a basic knowledge of digital systems, usually a required course in electrical engineering and computer engineering curricula. For the materials in the third part, prior exposure to assembly language programming will be helpful.

Logistics

Although a major goal of this book is to teach readers to develop software-independent and device-neutral HDL codes, we have to choose a software package and a prototyping board to synthesize and implement the design examples. The synthesis software and FPGA devices from Xilinx, a leading manufacture in this area, are used in the book.

Software The synthesis software used in the book is the Web version of the Xilinx *ISE* package. The functionality is of this version is similar to that of the full version but supports only a limited number of devices. Most introductory development boards use FPGA devices from the inexpensive Spartan-3 family. Since the Web version supports the Spartan-3 device, it fits our need. The simulation software used in the book is the starter version of Mentor Graphics' *ModelSim XE III* package. It is a customized edition of *ModelSim*. Both software packages are free and can be downloaded from Xilinx's Web site.

FPGA prototyping board This book is prepared to be used with several entry-level FPGA prototyping boards manufactured by Digilent Inc., including the *Spartan-3 Starter*, *Nexys-2*, and *Basys* boards, all of which contain a Spartan-3/3E FPGA device and have similar I/O peripherals. The design examples in the book are based on the Spartan-3 Starter board (or simply the *S3 board*), but most of them can be used directly in other boards as well. The applicability of the HDL codes is summarized below.

- **Spartan-3 Starter 3 (S3) board**. The S3 board contains all the peripherals and no additional accessory module is needed. All HDL codes and discussions can be applied to this board directly.
- **Nexys-2 board**. The Nexys-2 board is a newer board, which contains a larger FPGA device and a larger memory chip. Its peripherals are similar to those in the S3 board. There are two differences. First, the "color depth" of its VGA interface is expanded from 3 bits to 8 bits. The the output of the VGA interface circuits discussed in Chapters 12 and 13 needs to be modified accordingly. Second, it contains a more sophisticated external memory device. Although the device can be configured as an asynchronous SRAM, the timing characteristics is different from that of the S3 board's memory device, and thus the HDL codes for the memory controller in Chapter 10 cannot be used directly. However, the same design principle can be applied to construct a new controller.
- **Basys board**. The Basys board is a simpler board. It lacks the RS-232 connector. To implement the UART module and the serial interface discussed in Chapter 7, we need Digilent's *RS-232 converter peripheral module*. The Basys board has no external memory devices, and thus the discussion of the memory controller in Chapter 10 is not applicable.
- **Other FPGA boards**. Most peripherals discussed in this book are de facto industrial standards, and the corresponding HDL codes can be used as long as a board provides proper analog interface circuits and connectors. Except for the Xilinx-specific portions, the codes can be applied to the boards based on the FPGA devices from other manufacturers as well.

PC Accessories The design examples include interfaces to several PC peripheral devices. A keyboard, a mouse, and a VGA monitor are required for the respective modules, and a "straight-through" serial cable (the most commonly used type) is required for the UART module. These accessories are widely available and can probably be obtained from an old PC.

Book organization

The book is divided into three major parts. Part I introduces the elementary HDL constructs and their hardware counterparts, and demonstrates the construction of a basic digital circuit with these constructs. It consists of six chapters:

- Chapter 1 describes the skeleton of an HDL program, basic language syntax, and logical operators. Gate-level combinational circuits are derived with these language constructs.
- Chapter 2 provides an overview of an FPGA device, prototyping board, and development flow. The development process is demonstrated by a tutorial on Xilinx ISE synthesis software and a tutorial on Mentor Graphics ModelSim simulation software.
- Chapter 3 introduces HDL's relational and arithmetic operators and routing constructs. These correspond to medium-sized components, such as comparators, adders, and multiplexers. Module-level combinational circuits are derived with these language constructs.

- Chapter 4 covers the codes for memory elements and the construction of "regular" sequential circuits, such as counters and shift registers, in which the state transitions exhibit a regular pattern.
- Chapter 5 discusses the construction of a finite state machine (FSM), which is a sequential circuit whose state transitions do not exhibit a simple, regular pattern.
- Chapter 6 presents the construction of an FSM with data path (FSMD). The FSMD is used to implement register transfer (RT) methodology, in which the system operation is described by data transfers and manipulations among registers.

Part II applies the techniques from Part I to design an array of peripheral modules for the prototyping board. Each chapter covers the development, implementation, and verification of an individual peripheral. These modules can be incorporated to a larger project. Part II consists of seven chapters:

- Chapter 7 discusses the design of a universal asynchronous receiver and transmitter (UART), which provides a serial link to receive and transmit data via the prototyping board's RS-232 port.
- Chapter 8 covers the design of a keyboard interface, which reads scan code from a keyboard. The keyboard is connected via the prototyping board's PS2 port.
- Chapter 9 covers the design of a mouse interface, which obtains the button and movement information from a mouse. The mouse is also connected via the prototyping board's PS2 port.
- Chapter 10 discusses the implementation and timing issues of a memory controller. The controller is used to read data from and write data to the two static random access memory (SRAM) devices on the S3 board.
- Chapter 11 discusses the inference and application of Spartan-3 device-specific components. The focus is on the FPGA's internal memory blocks and the digital clock management (DCM) circuit.
- Chapter 12 presents the design and implementation of a video controller. The discussion covers the generation of video synchronization signals and shows the construction of simple bit- and object-mapped graphical interface. The monitor is connected to the prototyping board's VGA port.
- Chapter 13 continues development of the video controller. The discussion illustrates the construction of text interface and general tile-mapped scheme.

Part III introduces an FPGA-based soft-core microcontroller, known as *PicoBlaze*, and demonstrates the integration of a general-purpose processor and customized circuit. It includes four chapters:

- Chapter 14 provides an overview of the organization and instruction set of PicoBlaze.
- Chapter 15 introduces the basic assembly programming and provides an overview of the development process.
- Chapter 16 discusses PicoBlaze's I/O feature and illustrates the procedure to derive customized circuits to interface other I/O peripherals.
- Chapter 17 discusses PicoBlaze's interrupt capability and demonstrates the construction of a customized interrupt-handling circuit.

In addition to regular chapters, the appendix summarizes and lists all code templates.

Special marks$^{Xilinx\ specific}$ While the examples of this book are implemented on a Xilinx-based prototyping board and the codes are synthesized by Xilinx ISE software, we try to make the HDL codes device-independent and software-neutral as much as possible. Most discussions and codes can be applied to different target devices and different synthesis software as well. However, certain codes or device features are unique to Xilinx ISE software or Spartan-3 FPGA devices. We use the *Xilinx specific* superscript, as in the heading of this section, to indicate that the discussion in the corresponding section or chapter is unique to Xilinx.

Similarly, we use marginal notes, such as the one shown on the outer edge, to indicate that the discussion in the paragraph is unique to Xilinx. This note indicates that the code or design is no longer portable and needs to be revised when a different software package or target device is used. **Xilinx specific**

Instructional use

The book can be a good companion text for an introductory digital systems course or an advanced project-oriented course. In an introductory digital systems course, the book supplies the lab portion of the curriculum. The chapters in Part I basically follow the sequence of a typical curriculum and can be presented along with regular lectures. One or two peripheral modules can be selected as case studies, and corresponding experiments can be used as term projects.

In an advanced project-oriented course, the book provides a base for independent projects. The materials in Part I should be treated as an overview or refresher, which provides a general background on HDL, synthesis, and FPGA boards. Some modules in Part II can be used to demonstrate the design of more complex circuits. These modules can also be considered as building blocks (i.e., IPs) or subsystems to be integrated into final projects. The PicoBlaze microcontroller in Part III can be used as general-purpose processor if an embedded-system type of project is desired.

Companion Web site

An accompanying Web site (`http://academic.csuohio.edu/chu_p/rtl`) provides additional information, including the following materials:

- Errata
- Code templates
- HDL code listing and relevant files
- Links to synthesis and simulation software
- Links to referenced materials
- Additional project ideas

Errata The book is self-prepared, which means that the author has produced all aspects of the text, including illustrations, tables, code listings, indexing, and formatting. As errors are always bound to happen, the accompanying Web site provides an updated errata sheet and a place to report errors.

P. P. CHU

Cleveland, Ohio
October 2007

ACKNOWLEDGMENTS

The author would like to express his gratitude to Professor George L. Kramerich for his encouragement and help.

The author also thanks John Wiley & Sons, Inc. for giving permission to use Figures 3.1, 3.2, 4.2, 4.10, 4.11, and 6.5 from my text *RTL Hardware Design Using VHDL: Coding for Efficiency, Portability, and Scalability*, and Xilinx, Inc. for giving permission to use Figures 2.3 and 8.3 from the *Spartan-3 Starter Kit Board User Guide*.

P. P. Chu

PART I

BASIC DIGITAL CIRCUITS

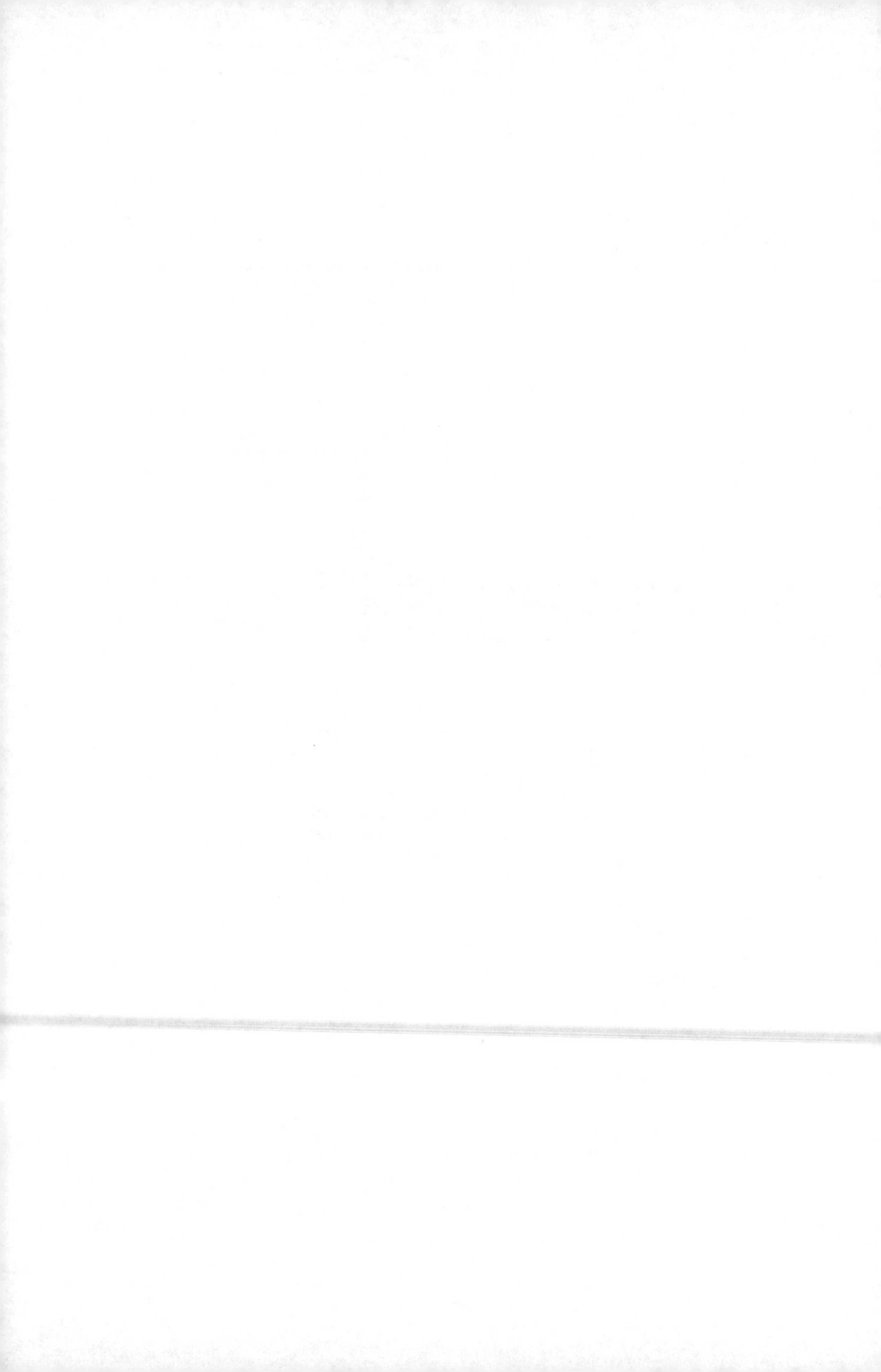

CHAPTER 1

GATE-LEVEL COMBINATIONAL CIRCUIT

1.1 INTRODUCTION

VHDL stands for "VHSIC (very high-speed integrated circuit) hardware description language." It was originally sponsored by the U.S. Department of Defense and later transferred to the IEEE (Institute of Electrical and Electronics Engineers). The language is formally defined by IEEE Standard 1076. The standard was ratified in 1987 (referred to as VHDL 87), and revised several times. This book mainly follows the revision in 1993 (referred to as VHDL 93).

VHDL is intended for describing and modeling a digital system at various levels and is an extremely complex language. The focus of this book is on hardware design rather than the language. Instead of covering every aspect of VHDL, we introduce the key VHDL synthesis constructs by examining a collection of examples. Detailed VHDL coverage may be explored through the sources listed in the Bibliography.

In this chapter, we use a simple comparator to illustrate the skeleton of a VHDL program. The description uses only logical operators and represents a gate-level combinational circuit, which is composed of simple logic gates. In Chapter 3, we cover the more sophisticated VHDL operators and constructs and examine module-level combinational circuits, which are composed of intermediate-sized components, such as adders, comparators, and multiplexers.

Table 1.1 Truth table of a 1-bit equality comparator

input $i0\ i1$	output eq
0 0	1
0 1	0
1 0	0
1 1	1

1.2 GENERAL DESCRIPTION

Consider a 1-bit equality comparator with two inputs, `i0` and `i1`, and an output, `eq`. The `eq` signal is asserted when `i0` and `i1` are equal. The truth table of this circuit is shown in Table 1.1.

Assume that we want to use basic logic gates, which include *not*, *and*, *or*, and *xor* cells, to implement the circuit. One way to describe the circuit is to use a sum-of-products format. The logic expression is

$$eq = i0 \cdot i1 + i0' \cdot i1'$$

One possible corresponding VHDL code is shown in Listing 1.1. We examine the language constructs and statements of this code in the following subsections.

Listing 1.1 Gate-level implementation of a 1-bit comparator

```
library ieee;
use ieee.std_logic_1164.all;
entity eq1 is
   port(
      i0, i1: in std_logic;
      eq: out std_logic
   );
end eq1;

architecture sop_arch of eq1 is
   signal p0, p1: std_logic;
begin
   -- sum of two product terms
   eq <= p0 or p1;
   -- product terms
   p0 <= (not i0) and (not i1);
   p1 <= i0 and i1;
end sop_arch;
```

1.2.1 Basic lexical rules

VHDL is case insensitive, which means that upper- and lowercase letters can be used interchangeably, and free formatting, which means that spaces and blank lines can be inserted freely. It is good practice to add proper spaces to make the code clear and to associate special meaning with cases. In this book, we reserve uppercase letters for constants.

An *identifier* is the name of an object and is composed of 26 letters, digits, and the underscore (_), as in i0, i1, and data_bus1_enable. The identifier must start with a letter.

The comments start with -- and the text after it is ignored. In this book, the VHDL keywords are shown in boldface type, as in **entity**, and the comments are shown in italics type, as in

```
-- this is a comment
```

1.2.2 Library and package

The first two lines,

```
library ieee;
use ieee.std_logic_1164.all;
```

invoke the std_logic_1164 package from the ieee library. The package and library allow us to add additional types, operators, functions, etc. to VHDL. The two statements are needed because a special data type is used in the code.

1.2.3 Entity declaration

The entity declaration

```
entity eq1 is
   port(
      i0, i1: in std_logic;
      eq: out std_logic
   );
end eq1;
```

essentially outlines the I/O signals of the circuit. The first line indicates that the name of the circuit is eq1, and the port section specifies the I/O signals. The basic format for an I/O port declaration is

```
signal_name1, signal_name2, ... : mode data_type;
```

The mode term can be **in** or **out**, which indicates that the corresponding signals flow "into" or "out of" of the circuit. It can also be **inout**, for bidirectional signals.

1.2.4 Data type and operators

VHDL is a *strongly typed language*, which means that an object must have a data type and only the defined values and operations can be applied to the object. Although VHDL is rich in data types, our discussion is limited to a small set of predefined types that are suitable for synthesis, mainly the std_logic type and its variants.

std_logic type The std_logic type is defined in the std_logic_1164 package and consists of nine values. Three of the values, '0', '1', and 'Z', which stand for logical 0, logical 1, and high impedance, can be synthesized. Two values, 'U' and 'X', which stand for "uninitialized" and "unknown" (e.g., when signals with '0' and '1' values are tied together), may be encountered in simulation. The other four values, '-', 'H', 'L', and 'W', are not used in this book.

A signal in a digital circuit frequently contains multiple bits. The std_logic_vector data type, which is defined as an array with elements of std_logic, can be used for this purpose. For example, let a be an 8-bit input port. It can be declared as

```
a: in std_logic_vector(7 downto 0);
```

We can use term like a(7 **downto** 4) to specify a desired range and term like a(1) to access a single element of the array. The array can also be declared in ascending order:

```
a: in std_logic_vector(0 to 7);
```

We generally avoid this format since it is more natural to associate the MSB with the leftmost position.

Logical operators Several logical operators, including **not**, **and**, **or**, and **xor**, are defined over the std_logic_vector and std_logic data type. Bit-wise operation is used when an operator is applied to an object with the std_logic_vector data type. Note that the **and**, **or**, and **xor** operators have the same precedence and we need to use parentheses to specify the desired order of evaluation, as in

```
(a and b) or (c and d)
```

1.2.5 Architecture body

The architecture body,

```
architecture sop_arch of eq1 is
   signal p0, p1: std_logic;
begin
   -- sum of two product terms
   eq <= p0 or p1;
   -- product terms
   p0 <= (not i0) and (not i1);
   p1 <= i0 and i1;
end sop_arch;
```

describes operation of the circuit. VHDL allows multiple bodies associated with an entity, and thus the body is identified by the name sop_arch ("sum-of-products architecture").

The architecture body may include an optional declaration section, which specifies constants, internal signals, and so on. Two internal signals are declared in this program:

```
signal p0, p1: std_logic;
```

The main description, encompassed between **begin** and **end**, contains three *concurrent statements*. Unlike a program in C language, in which the statements are executed sequentially, concurrent statements are like circuit parts that operate in parallel. The signal on the left-hand side of a statement can be considered as the output of that part, and the expression specifies the circuit function and corresponding input signals. For example, consider the statement

```
eq <= p0 or p1;
```

It is a circuit that performs the or operation. When p0 or p1 changes its value, this statement is activated and the expression is evaluated. The new value is assigned to eq after the default propagation delay.

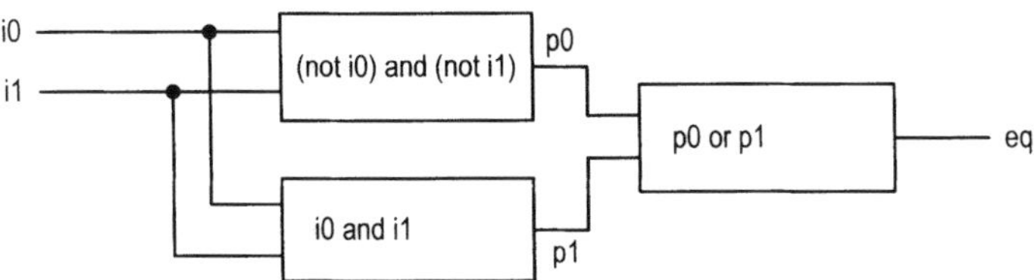

Figure 1.1 Graphical representation of a comparator program.

The graphical representation of this program is shown in Figure 1.1. The three circuit parts represent the three concurrent statements. The connections among these parts are implicitly specified by the signal and port names. The order of the concurrent statements is clearly irrelevant and the statements can be rearranged arbitrarily.

1.2.6 Code of a 2-bit comparator

We can expand the comparator to 2-bit inputs. Let the input be a and b and the output be aeqb. The aeqb signal is asserted when both bits of a and b are equal. The code is shown in Listing 1.2.

Listing 1.2 Gate-level implementation of a 2-bit comparator

```
library ieee;
use ieee.std_logic_1164.all;
entity eq2 is
   port(
      a, b: in std_logic_vector(1 downto 0);
      aeqb: out std_logic
   );
end eq2;

architecture sop_arch of eq2 is
   signal p0,p1,p2,p3: std_logic;
begin
   -- sum of product terms
   aeqb <= p0 or p1 or p2 or p3;
   -- product terms
   p0 <= ((not a(1)) and (not b(1))) and
         ((not a(0)) and (not b(0)));
   p1 <= ((not a(1)) and (not b(1))) and (a(0) and b(0));
   p2 <= (a(1) and b(1)) and ((not a(0)) and (not b(0)));
   p3 <= (a(1) and b(1)) and (a(0) and b(0));
end sop_arch;
```

The a and b ports are now declared as a two-element std_logic_vector. Derivation of the architecture body is similar to that of a 1-bit comparator. The p0, p1, p2, and p3 signals represent the results of the four product terms, and the final result, aeqb, is the logic expression in sum-of-products format.

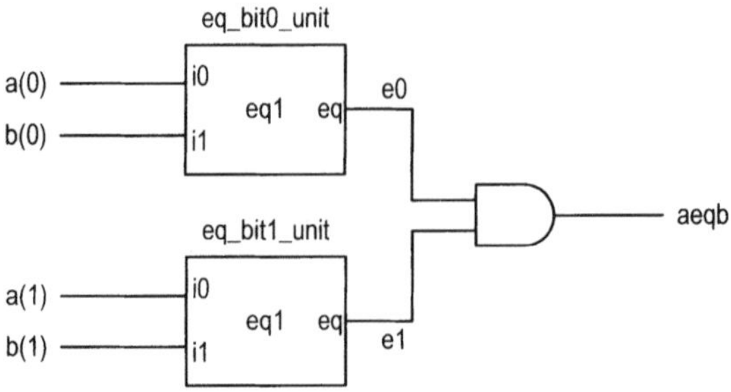

Figure 1.2 Construction of a 2-bit comparator from 1-bit comparators.

1.3 STRUCTURAL DESCRIPTION

A digital system is frequently composed of several smaller subsystems. This allows us to build a large system from simpler or predesigned components. VHDL provides a mechanism, known as *component instantiation*, to perform this task. This type of code is called *structural description*.

An alternative to the design of the 2-bit comparator of Section 1.2.6 is to utilize the previously constructed 1-bit comparators as the building blocks. The diagram is shown in Figure 1.2, in which two 1-bit comparators are used to check the two individual bits and their results are fed to an and cell. The aeqb signal is asserted only when the two bits are equal.

The corresponding code is shown in Listing 1.3. Note that the entity declaration is the same and thus is not included.

Listing 1.3 Structural description of a 2-bit comparator

```
architecture struc_arch of eq2 is
   signal e0, e1: std_logic;
begin
   -- instantiate two 1-bit comparators
   eq_bit0_unit: entity work.eq1(sop_arch)
      port map(i0=>a(0), i1=>b(0), eq=>e0);
   eq_bit1_unit: entity work.eq1(sop_arch)
      port map(i0=>a(1), i1=>b(1), eq=>e1);
   -- a and b are equal if individual bits are equal
   aeqb <= e0 and e1;
end struc_arch;
```

The code includes two component instantiation statements, whose syntax is:

```
unit_label: entity lib_name.entity_name(arch_name)
   port map(
      formal_signal=>actual_signal,
      formal_signal=>actual_signal,
      . . .
   );
```

The first portion of the statement specifies which component is used. The unit_label term gives a unique id for an instance, the lib_name term indicates where (i.e., which library) the component resides, and the entity_name and arch_name terms indicate the names of the entity and architecture. The `arch_name` term is optional. If it is omitted, the last compiled architecture body will be used. The second portion is port mapping, which indicates the connection between *formal signals*, which are I/O ports declared in a component's entity declaration, and *actual signals*, which are the signals used in the architecture body.

The first component instantiation statement is

```
eq_bit0_unit: entity work.eq1(sop_arch)
   port map(i0=>a(0), i1=>b(0), eq=>e0);
```

The `work` library is the default library in which the compiled entity and architecture units are stored, and `eq1` and `sop_arch` are the names of the entity and architecture defined in Listing 1.1. The port mapping reflects the connections shown in Figure 1.2. The component instantiation statement is also a concurrent statement and represents a circuit that is encompassed in a "black box" whose function is defined in another module.

This example demonstrates the close relationship between a block diagram and code. The code is essentially a textual description of a schematic. Although it is a clumsy way for humans to comprehend a diagram, it puts all representations into a single HDL framework. The Xilinx ISE package includes a simple schematic editor utility that can perform schematic capture in graphic format and then convert the diagram into an HDL structural description.

Xilinx specific

The component instantiation statement is added in VHDL 93. Older codes may use the mechanism in VHDL 87, in which a component must first be declared (i.e., made known) and then used. The code in this format is shown in Listing 1.4.

Listing 1.4 Structural description with VHDL-87

```
architecture vhd_87_arch of eq2 is
   -- component declaration
   component eq1
      port(
         i0, i1: in std_logic;
         eq: out std_logic
      );
   end component;
   signal e0, e1: std_logic;
begin
   -- instantiate two 1-bit comparators
   eq_bit0_unit: eq1   -- use the declared name, eq1
      port map(i0=>a(0), i1=>b(0), eq=>e0);
   eq_bit1_unit: eq1   -- use the declared name, eq1
      port map(i0=>a(1), i1=>b(1), eq=>e1);
   -- a and b are equal if individual bits are equal
   aeqb <= e0 and e1;
end vhd_87_arch;
```

Note that the original clause,

```
eq_bit0_unit: entity work.eq1(sop_arch)
```

is replaced by a clause with the declared component name

```
eq_bit0_unit: eq1
```

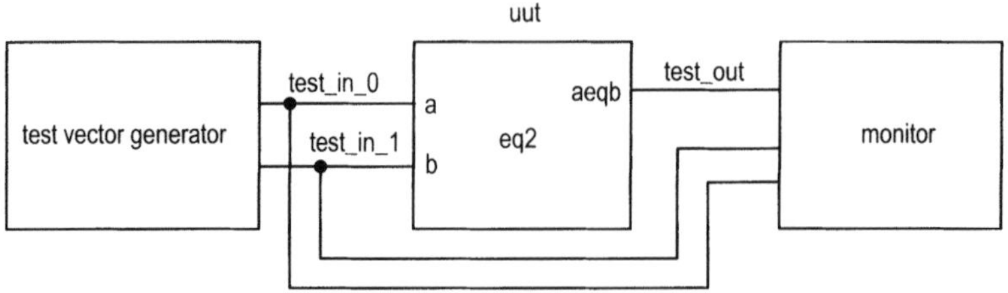

Figure 1.3 Testbench for a 2-bit comparator.

1.4 TESTBENCH

After code is developed, it can be *simulated* in a host computer to verify the correctness of the circuit operation and can be *synthesized* to a physical device. Simulation is usually performed within the same HDL framework. We create a special program, known as a *testbench*, to mimic a physical lab bench. The sketch of a 2-bit comparator testbench program is shown in Figure 1.3. The `uut` block is the unit under test, the `test vector generator` block generates testing input patterns, and the `monitor` block examines the output responses.

A simple testbench for the 2-bit comparator is shown in Listing 1.5.

Listing 1.5 Testbench for a 2-bit comparator

```
library ieee;
use ieee.std_logic_1164.all;
entity eq2_testbench is
end eq2_testbench;

architecture tb_arch of eq2_testbench is
   signal test_in0, test_in1: std_logic_vector(1 downto 0);
   signal test_out: std_logic;
begin
   -- instantiate the circuit under test
   uut: entity work.eq2(struc_arch)
      port map(a=>test_in0, b=>test_in1, aeqb=>test_out);
   -- test vector generator
   process
   begin
      -- test vector 1
      test_in0 <= "00";
      test_in1 <= "00";
      wait for 200 ns;
      -- test vector 2
      test_in0 <= "01";
      test_in1 <= "00";
      wait for 200 ns;
      -- test vector 3
      test_in0 <= "01";
      test_in1 <= "11";
      wait for 200 ns;
      -- test vector 4
```

```
        test_in0 <= "10";
        test_in1 <= "10";
        wait for 200 ns;
        -- test vector 5
        test_in0 <= "10";
        test_in1 <= "00";
        wait for 200 ns;
        -- test vector 6
        test_in0 <= "11";
        test_in1 <= "11";
        wait for 200 ns;
        -- test vector 7
        test_in0 <= "11";
        test_in1 <= "01";
        wait for 200 ns;
    end process;
end tb_arch;
```

The code consists of a component instantiation statement, which creates an instance of a 2-bit comparator, and a process statement, which generates a sequence of test patterns.

The process statement is a special VHDL construct in which the operations are performed sequentially. Each test pattern is generated by three statements. For example,

```
        -- test vector 2
        test_in0 <= "01";
        test_in1 <= "00";
        wait for 200 ns;
```

The first two statements specify the values for the `test_in0` and `test_in1` signals, and the third indicates that the two values will last for 200 ns.

The code has no monitor. We can observe the input and output waveforms on a simulator's display, which can be treated as a "virtual logic analyzer." The simulated timing diagram of this testbench is shown in Figure 2.16.

Writing code for a comprehensive test vector generator and a monitor requires detailed knowledge of VHDL and is beyond the scope of this book. This listing can serve as a testbench template for other combinational circuits. We can substitute the `uut` instance and modify the test patterns according to the new circuit.

1.5 BIBLIOGRAPHIC NOTES

A short bibliographic section appears at the end of each chapter to provide some of the most relevant references for further exploration. A comprehensive bibliography is included at the end of the book.

VHDL is a complex language. *The Designer's Guide to VHDL* by P. J. Ashenden provides detailed coverage of the language's syntax and constructs. The author's *RTL Hardware Design Using VHDL: Coding for Efficiency, Portability, and Scalability* provides a comprehensive discussion on developing effective, synthesizable codes. The derivation of the testbench for a large digital system is a difficult task. *Writing Testbenches: Functional Verification of HDL Models, 2nd edition*, by J. Bergeron focuses on this topic.

1.6 SUGGESTED EXPERIMENTS

At the end of each chapter, some experiments are suggested as exercises. The experiments help us to better understand the concepts and provide a hands-on opportunity to design and debug actual circuits.

1.6.1 Code for gate-level greater-than circuit

Develop the HDL codes in Experiment 2.9.1. The code can be simulated and synthesized after we complete Chapter 2.

1.6.2 Code for gate-level binary decoder

Develop the HDL codes in Experiment 2.9.2. The code can be simulated and synthesized after we complete Chapter 2.

CHAPTER 2

OVERVIEW OF FPGA AND EDA SOFTWARE

2.1 INTRODUCTION

Developing a large FPGA-based system is an involved process that consists of many complex transformations and optimization algorithms. Software tools are needed to automate some of the tasks. We use the Web version of the Xilinx *ISE* package for synthesis and implementation, and use the starter version of Mentor Graphics *ModelSim XE III* package for simulation. In this chapter, we give a brief overview of the FPGA device and the S3 prototyping board, and provide short tutorials for the two software packages to "jump-start" the learning process.

2.2 FPGA

2.2.1 Overview of a general FPGA device

A *field programmable gate array* (FPGA) is a logic device that contains a two-dimensional array of generic logic cells and programmable switches. The conceptual structure of an FPGA device is shown in Figure 2.1. A logic cell can be configured (i.e., *programmed*) to perform a simple function, and a programmable switch can be customized to provide interconnections among the logic cells. A custom design can be implemented by specifying the function of each logic cell and selectively setting the connection of each programmable switch. Once the design and synthesis is completed, we can use a simple adaptor cable to download the desired logic cell and switch configuration to the FPGA device and obtain the

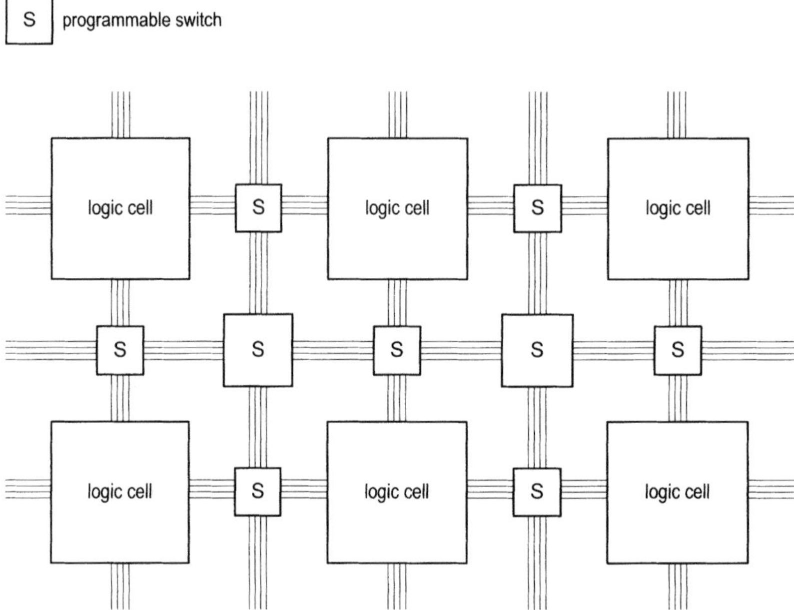

Figure 2.1 Conceptual structure of an FPGA device.

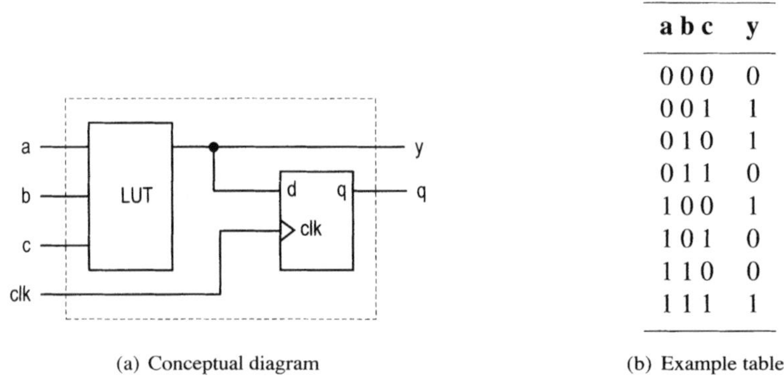

a b c	y
0 0 0	0
0 0 1	1
0 1 0	1
0 1 1	0
1 0 0	1
1 0 1	0
1 1 0	0
1 1 1	1

(a) Conceptual diagram

(b) Example table

Figure 2.2 Three-input LUT-based logic cell.

custom circuit. Since this process can be done "in the field" rather than "in a fabrication facility (fab)," the device is known as *field programmable*.

LUT-based logic cell A logic cell usually contains a small configurable combinational circuit with a D-type flip-flop (D FF). The most common method to implement a configurable combinational circuit is a *look-up table* (LUT). An n-input LUT can be considered as a small 2^n-by-1 memory. By properly writing the memory content, we can use the LUT to implement any n-input combinational function. The conceptual diagram of a three-input LUT-based logic cell is shown in Figure 2.2(a). An example of three-input LUT implementation of $a \oplus b \oplus c$ is shown in Figure 2.2(b). Note that the output of the LUT can be used directly or stored to the D FF. The latter can be used to implement sequential circuits.

Macro cell Most FPGA devices also embed certain *macro cells* or *macro blocks*. These are designed and fabricated at the transistor level, and their functionalities complement the general logic cells. Commonly used macro cells include memory blocks, combinational multipliers, clock management circuits, and I/O interface circuits. Advanced FPGA devices may even contain one or more prefabricated processor cores.

2.2.2 Overview of the Xilinx Spartan-3 devices

This book uses Xilinx Spartan-3 family FPGA devices. Based on the ratio between the number of logic cells and the I/O counts, the family is further divided into several subfamilies. Our discussion applies to all the subfamilies.

Logic cell, slice, and CLB The most basic element of the Spartan-3 device is a *logic cell* (LC), which contains a four-input LUT and a D FF, similar to that in Figure 2.2. In addition, a logic cell contains a carry circuit, which is used to implement arithmetic functions, and a multiplexing circuit, which is used to implement wide multiplexers. The LUT can also be configured as a 16-by-1 static random access memory (SRAM) or a 16-bit shift register.

To increase flexibility and improve performance, eight logic cells are combined together with a special internal routing structure. In Xilinx terms, two logic cells are grouped to form a *slice*, and four slices are grouped to form a *configurable logic block* (CLB).

Macro cell The Spartan-3 device contains four types of macro blocks: combinational multiplier, *block RAM*, *digital clock manager* (DCM), and *input/output block* (IOB). The combinational multiplier accepts two 18-bit numbers as inputs and calculates the product. The block RAM is an 18K-bit synchronous SRAM that can be arranged in various types of configurations. A DCM uses a digital-delayed loop to reduce clock skew and to control the frequency and phase shift of a clock signal. An IOB controls the flow of data between the device's I/O pins and the internal logic. It can be configured to support a wide variety of I/O signaling standards.

Devices in the Spartan-3 subfamily Althopugh Spartan-3 FPGA devices have similar types of logic cells and macro cells, their densities differ. Each subfamily contains an array of devices of various densities. The numbers of LCs, block RAMs, multipliers, and DCMs of the devices from the Spartan-3 subfamily are summarized in Table 2.1.

2.3 OVERVIEW OF THE DIGILENT S3 BOARD

The Digilent S3 board is based on a Spartan-3 device (usually an XC3S200) and has an array of built-in peripherals. The simplified layouts of the board are shown in Figure 2.3(a) and (b). The main components and connectors are as follows:

1. Xilinx Spartan-3 XC3S200 FPGA device (XC3S200FT256)
2. 2M-bit Xilinx XCF02S platform flash configuration PROM
3. Jumper to select the configuration source
4. Two 256K-by-16 asynchronous SRAM devices (ISSI IS61LV25616AL-10T).

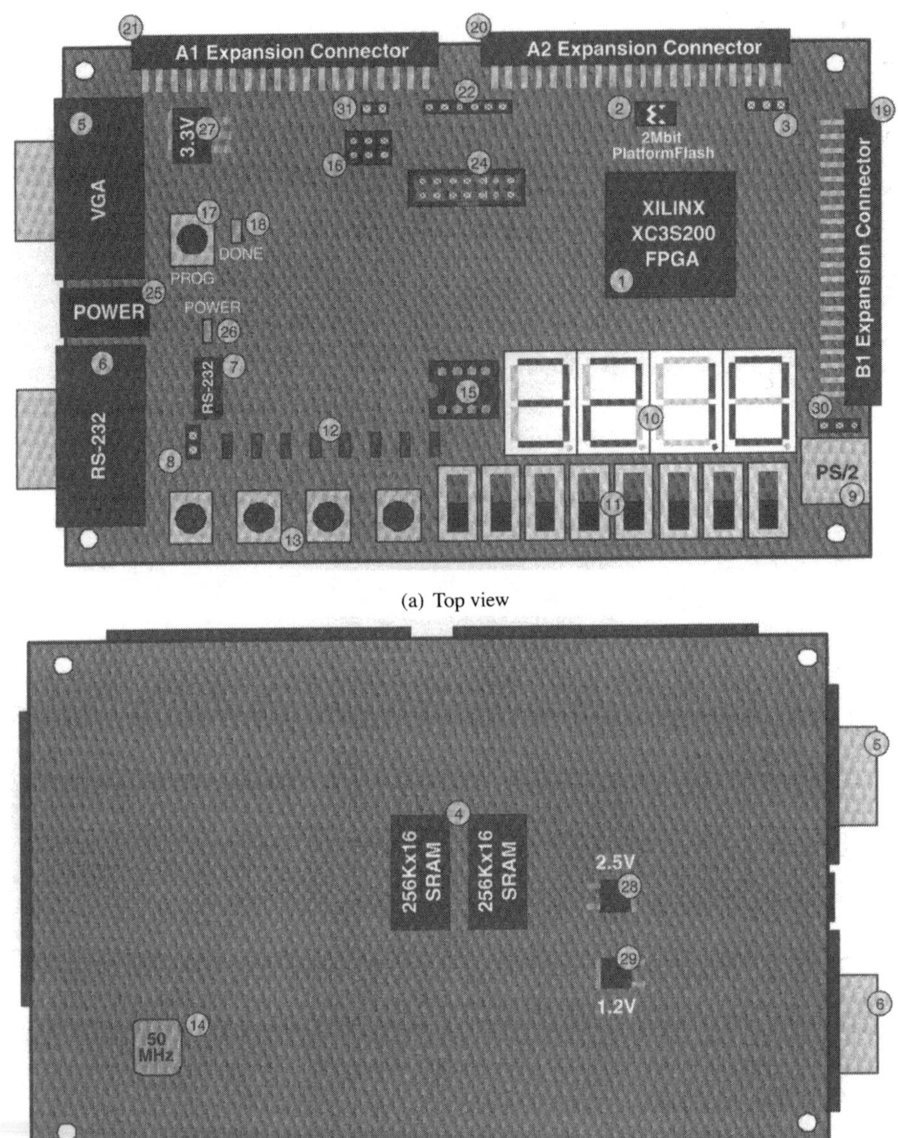

(a) Top view

(b) Bottom view

Figure 2.3 Layout of an S3 board. (Courtesy of Xilinx, Inc. © Xilinx, Inc. 1994–2007. All rights reserved.)

Table 2.1 Devices in the Spartan-3 family

Device	Number of LCs	Number of block RAMs	Block RAM bits	Number of multipliers	Number of DCMs
XC3S50	1,728	4	72K	4	2
XC3S200	4,320	12	216K	12	4
XC3S400	8,064	16	288K	16	4
XC3S1000	17,280	24	432K	24	4
XC3S1500	29,952	32	576K	32	4
XC3S2000	46,080	40	720K	40	4
XC3S4000	62,208	96	1,728K	96	4
XC3S5000	74,880	104	1,872K	104	4

5. VGA display port
6. RS-232 serial port
7. RS-232 transceiver/voltage-level convertor
8. Second RS-232 transmit and receive channel
9. PS/2 mouse/keyboard port
10. Four-digit seven-segment LED display
11. Eight slide switches
12. Eight discrete LED outputs
13. Four momentary-contact pushbutton switches
14. 50-MHz crystal oscillator clock source
15. Socket for an auxiliary crystal oscillator clock source
16. Jumper to select an FPGA configuration mode
17. Pushbutton switch to force FPGA reconfiguration
18. LED to indicate whether the FPGA is successfully configured
19. 40-pin expansion connector 1 (labeled B1)
20. 40-pin expansion connector 2 (labeled A2)
21. 40-pin expansion connector 3 (labeled A1)
22. JTAG connector for Digilent download cable.
23. Digilent low-cost download cable (included in the S3 kit but not shown in Figure 2.3)
24. JTAG port (to be used with the Xilinx Parallel Cable IV and MultiPRO Desktop Tool, which are not included in the S3 kit)
25. Power connector for an unregulated 5-V power supply (included in the S3 kit)
26. Power-on LED indicator
27. 3.3-V voltage regulator
28. 2.5-V voltage regulator
29. 1.2-V voltage regulator
30. Selector for PS2 port voltage supply (3.3 or 5 V)

2.4 DEVELOPMENT FLOW

The simplified development flow of an FPGA-based system is shown in Figure 2.4. To facilitate further reading, we follow the terms used in the Xilinx documentation. The left portion of the flow is the refinement and programming process, in which a system is transformed from an abstract textual HDL description to a device cell-level configuration

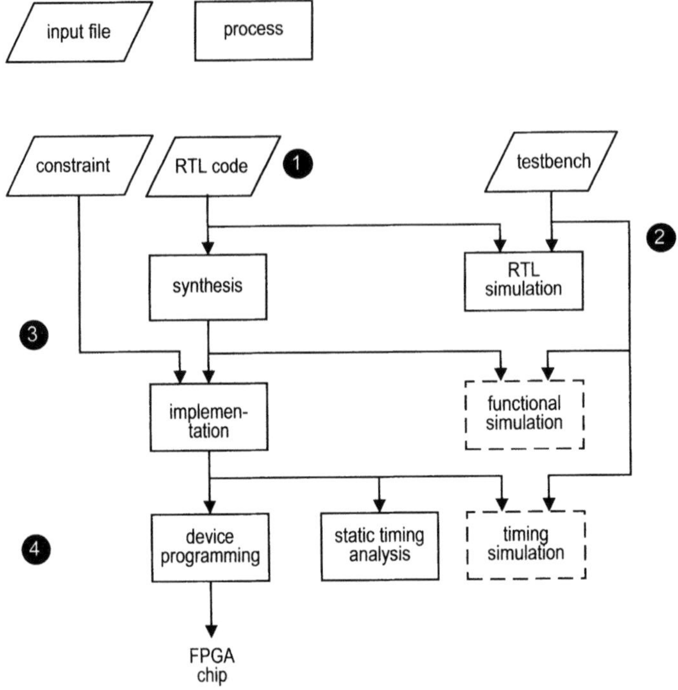

Figure 2.4 Development flow.

and then downloaded to the FPGA device. The right portion is the validation process, which checks whether the system meets the functional specification and performance goals. The major steps in the flow are:

1. Design the system and derive the HDL file(s). We may need to add a separate constraint file to specify certain implementation constraints.
2. Develop the testbench in HDL and perform *RTL simulation*. The RTL term reflects the fact that the HDL code is done at the register transfer level.
3. Perform *synthesis* and *implementation*. The synthesis process is generally known as *logic synthesis*, in which the software transforms the HDL constructs to generic gate-level components, such as simple logic gates and FFs. The *implementation* process consists of three smaller processes: translate, map, and place and route. The *translate process* merges multiple design files to a single netlist. The *map process,* which is generally known as *technology mapping*, maps the generic gates in the netlist to FPGA's logic cells and IOBs. The *place and route process*, which is generally known as *placement and routing*, derives the physical layout inside the FPGA chip. It places the cells in physical locations and determines the routes to connect various signals. In the Xilinx flow, *static timing analysis*, which determines various timing parameters, such as maximal propagation delay and maximal clock frequency, is performed at the end of the implementation process.
4. Generate and download the programming file. In this process, a configuration file is generated according to the final netlist. This file is downloaded to an FPGA device serially to configure the logic cells and switches. The physical circuit can be verified accordingly.

The optional *functional simulation* can be performed after synthesis, and the optional *timing simulation* can be performed after implementation. Functional simulation uses a synthesized netlist to replace the RTL description and checks the correctness of the synthesis process. Timing simulation uses the final netlist, along with detailed timing data, to perform simulation. Because of the complexity of the netlist, functional and timing simulation may require a significant amount of time. If we follow good design and coding practices, the HDL code will be synthesized and implemented correctly. We only need to use RTL simulation to check the correctness of the HDL code and use static timing analysis to examine the relevant timing information. Both functional and timing simulations can be omitted from the development flow.

2.5 OVERVIEW OF THE XILINX ISE PROJECT NAVIGATOR

Xilinx ISE (integrated software environment) controls all aspects of the development flow. *Project Navigator* is a graphical interface for users to access software tools and relevant files associated with the project. We use it to launch all development tasks except ModelSim simulation. The discussion in this section and the tutorial in the next section are based on ISE WebPack version 8.2.

The default ISE window is shown in Figure 2.5. It is divided into four subwindows:

- *Sources window* (top left): hierarchically displays the files included in the project
- *Processes window* (middle left): displays available processes for the source file currently selected
- *Transcript window* (bottom): displays status messages, errors, and warnings
- *Workplace window* (top right): contains multiple document windows (such as HDL code, report, schematic, and so on) for viewing and editing

Each subwindow may be resized, moved, docked, or undocked. The default layout can be restored by selecting View ≻ Restore. Note that a subwindow may contain multiple pages. The tabs at the bottom are used to select the desired page.

Sources window The sources window is used mainly to display files associated with the current project. A typical source window, which corresponds to the design of Listing 2.2, is shown in Figure 2.6. The top drop-down list, labeled Sources for:, specifies the current design view. The `synthesis/implementation` view should be selected since we use ISE only for synthesis and implementation,

There are three tabs at the bottom, labeled Sources, Snapshots, and Libraries. The Sources tab displays the project name, the FPGA device specified, and user documents and design files. The modules are displayed according to the internal design hierarchy. In Figure 2.6, the `eq2` and `eq1` entities reflect the hierarchy of Listing 2.2. The `eq2` module also includes the `eq_s3.ucf` file, which specifies the constraints of the design. We can open a file in the workplace window by double-clicking the corresponding module. A *top-level module* icon can be placed next to a module, as in the `eq2` module, to invoke synthesis and implementation for this particular module.

The Snapshots tab displays project's "snapshots," which are copies of previously stored project files. The Libraries tab shows all libraries associated with the project.

Processes window The processes window displays the processes available. The display is *context sensitive* and the available processes are based on source type selected in the sources window. For example, the `eq2` module, which is set as the top-level module,

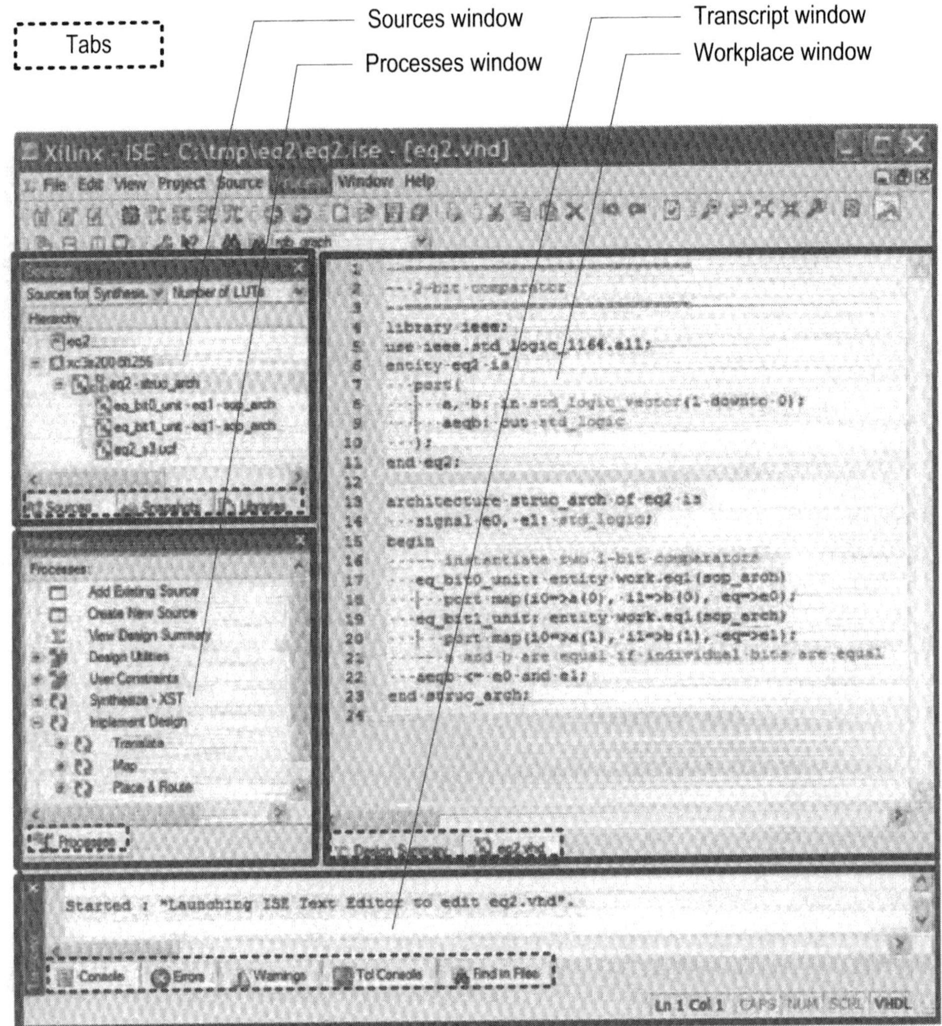

Figure 2.5 Typical ISE window.

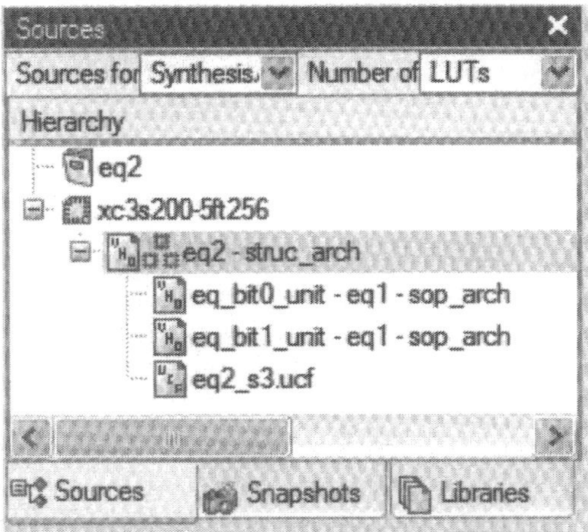

Figure 2.6 Typical source window.

is selected in Figure 2.6. The available processes are displayed in the processes window, as shown in Figure 2.7. Some processes may also contain several subprocesses. We can initiate a process by clicking on the corresponding icon. ISE incorporates the "auto make" technology, which automatically runs the processes necessary to get to the desired step. For example, when we initiate the Generate Programming File process, ISE automatically invokes the Synthesize and Implement Design processes since file generation is dependent on the implementation result, which, in turn, is dependent on the synthesis result.

Transcript window The transcript window is used to display the progress of a process and relevant messages. The Console page displays errors, warnings, and information messages. An error is signified by a red X mark next to the message and a warning is signified by a yellow ! mark. The Warnings and Errors pages display only warning and error messages.

Workplace window The workplace window is for users to view and edit various types of files. We use it to perform two main tasks. The first task is to view and edit the HDL and constraint files. The default editor is the *ISE Text Editor*, which is a simple text editor with features to assist creation of the HDL code. The second task is to check the design summary and various reports.

2.6 SHORT TUTORIAL ON ISE PROJECT NAVIGATOR

Xilinx ISE consists of an array of software tools, but detailed discussion of their use is beyond the scope of this book. We present a short tutorial in this section to illustrate the basic development process. There are four major steps:

1. Create the design project and HDL codes.
2. Create a testbench and perform RTL simulation.
3. Add a constraint file and synthesize and implement the code.
4. Generate and download the configuration file to an FPGA device.

These steps follow the general development flow discussed in Section 2.4.

We use the 2-bit comparator discussed in Chapter 1 in the tutorial. The codes are repeated in Listings 2.1 and 2.2.

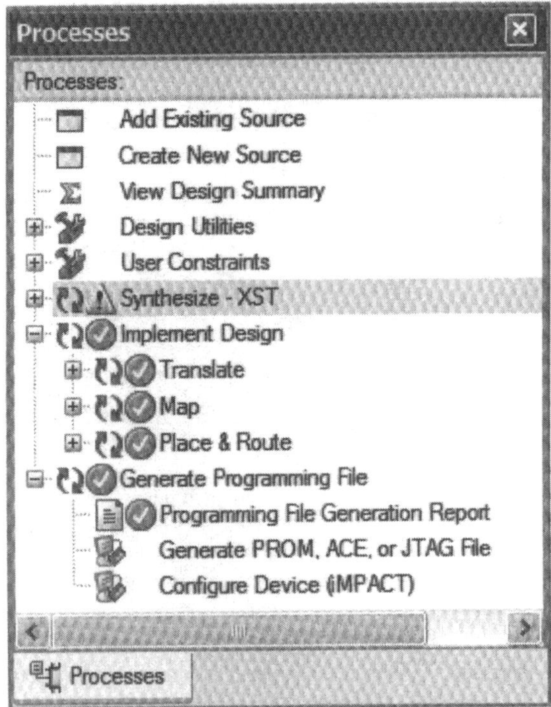

Figure 2.7 Typical processes window.

Listing 2.1 Gate-level implementation of a 1-bit comparator

```
library ieee;
use ieee.std_logic_1164.all;
entity eq1 is
   port(
      i0, i1: in std_logic;
      eq: out std_logic
   );
end eq1;

architecture sop_arch of eq1 is
   signal p0, p1: std_logic;
begin
   -- sum of two product terms
   eq <= p0 or p1;
   -- product terms
   p0 <= (not i0) and (not i1);
   p1 <= i0 and i1;
end sop_arch;
```

Listing 2.2 Structural description of a 2-bit comparator

```
library ieee;
use ieee.std_logic_1164.all;
entity eq2 is
```

```
    port(
        a, b: in std_logic_vector(1 downto 0);
        aeqb: out std_logic
    );
end eq2;

architecture struc_arch of eq2 is
    signal e0, e1: std_logic;
begin
    -- instantiate two 1-bit comparators
    eq_bit0_unit: entity work.eq1(sop_arch)
        port map(i0=>a(0), i1=>b(0), eq=>e0);
    eq_bit1_unit: entity work.eq1(sop_arch)
        port map(i0=>a(1), i1=>b(1), eq=>e1);
    -- a and b are equal if individual bits are equal
    aeqb <= e0 and e1;
end struc_arch;
```

2.6.1 Create the design project and HDL codes

There are three tasks in this step:

- Create a project.
- Add or create HDL files.
- Check the HDL syntax.

Create a project An ISE project contains basic information of a design, which includes the source files and a target device. A new project can be created as follows:

1. Select Start ≻ All Programs ≻ Xilinx ISE ≻ Project Navigator (or wherever ISE resides) to launch the ISE project navigator.
2. In Project Navigator, select File ≻ New Project. The New Project Wizard - Create New project dialog appears. Enter the project name as `eq2` and the location, and verify that `HDL` is selected in the Top-level Source Type field. Click Next.
3. The New Project Wizard - Device Properties dialog appears. We need to enter the desired target device in this dialog. This information can be found in FPGA board manual or by checking the marking on the top of the FPGA chip. For a typical S3 board, select the following:
    - Product Category: `All`
    - Family: `Spartan3`
    - Device: `XC3S200`
    - Package: `FT256`
    - Speed: `-4`

   We also need to verify that the Xilinx XST software is selected for synthesis:
    - Synthesis Tool: `XST (VHDL/Verilog)`
4. Click Next a few times to go through the remaining dialogs and then click Finish to complete the creation.

After a project is created, we can create or add the relevant HDL files and a constraint file.

Create a new HDL file If a file does not exist, we must create a new source file. The procedure to create a new HDL file is:

1. Select Project ≻ New Source. The New Source Wizard - Select Source Type dialog appears. Select VHDL Module and type the file name, eq2. Click Next.
2. The next dialog appears. This dialog allows us to enter port names. These names are then later embedded in the HDL code. Enter the I/O port information according to Listing 2.2. Click Next.
3. Click Finish and a new HDL text editor window appears in the workplace window. The software automatically generates the HDL skeleton, which includes a comment header, library clauses, an entity declaration, and an empty architecture body.
4. By default, ISE version 8.2 generates the following library clauses:

   ```
   use IEEE.STD_LOGIC_ARITH.ALL;
   use IEEE.STD_LOGIC_UNSIGNED.ALL
   ```

   The two libraries are not IEEE standard and should be replaced with

   ```
   use ieee.numeric_std.all;
   ```

   This issue is explained in Section 3.2.2.
5. Use the editor to enter the HDL code in Listing 2.2 and save the file.
6. Repeat the process to create another file for the code in Listing 2.1.

Add existing files If a file already exists, it can be added to the project as follows:

1. Select Project ≻ Add Source. A dialog window appears.
2. Go to the desired directory and select the desired files. Click Open and a new dialog appears.
3. Click OK to complete the addition. These files now appear in the sources window of the project navigator.

Check the code syntax After completing a new HDL file, we need to check the syntax of the code:

1. Select the desired file in the source window.
2. In the processes window, click the + icon next to Synthesize to expand the process hierarchy.
3. Double-click the Check Syntax process.

The bottom transcript displays the progress of the process and reports errors and warnings, which are started with a red X and yellow ! marks. Double-clicking the message leads to the offending line in the file. We can correct the problem, save the file, and repeat the syntax checking process until all syntax errors are eliminated.

2.6.2 Create a testbench and perform the RTL simulation

The testbench functions as a virtual lab bench. It consists of the HDL module to be tested and a code segment to generate the stimulus. The RTL simulation verifies operation of the HDL module in the host computer. ISE contains a built-in ISE simulator and can launch the *ModelSim* simulator manufactured by Mentor Graphics Corporation. Since the latter is more robust and versatile, we use it in the book. Although ModelSim can be invoked from ISE Project Navigator, we treat it as an individual software tool and illustrate its use in Section 2.7.

2.6.3 Add a constraint file and synthesize and implement the code

There are three tasks in this step:

- Add a constraint file.
- Perform synthesis and implementation.
- Check the design summary.

Add a constraint file *Constraints* are certain conditions imposed on the synthesis and implementation processes. For our purposes, the main type of constraint is the pin assignment of a top-level I/O port and the minimal clock rate. During the implementation process, an I/O signal of the top-level module must be mapped to a physical pin of the FPGA device. Since the peripherals' I/O signals are already permanently connected to the designated FPGA's pins on the prototyping board, we must ensure that the signals are mapped to the corresponding pins. The other type of constraint is about timing, which specifies the minimal clock frequency to facilitate the oscillator of the board.

The constraint information is stored in a text file with an extension of .ucf (for the user constraint file). In the eq2 circuit, we can connect the a and b ports to four switches and the aeqb port to an LED to verify the physical operation of the circuit. For the S3 board, the corresponding pins are F12, G12, H14, H13, and K12. The constraint file becomes

```
# 4 slide switches
NET "a<0>"  LOC = "F12"  ;  # switch 0
NET "a<1>"  LOC = "G12"  ;  # switch 1
NET "b<0>"  LOC = "H14"  ;  # switch 2
NET "b<1>"  LOC = "H13"  ;  # switch 3
# led
NET "aeqb"  LOC = "K12"  ;  # led 0
```

Note that the # sign is used for a comment and the text after it is ignored. This file must be added to the design in the sources window.

There are several ISE tools to specify and generate the constraint file. Since all of our experiments are done in the same prototyping board, the constraints (i.e., pin assignment and clock frequency) remain the same. A constraint template file that includes all connected I/O peripheral signals of the S3 board is provided in the Appendix. One easy method to create a constraint file is simply to copy and edit the template file according to the I/O port names of the current design. The procedure to create the .ucf file for the eq2 circuit is:

1. Copy the template constraint file and rename it eq2_s3.ucf.
2. Follow the procedure in Section 2.6.1 to add the new constraint file to the eq2 module in the sources window.
3. Select the constraint file.
4. In the processes window, click the + icon next to User Constraints to expand the process hierarchy.
5. Double-click the Edit Constraints (Text) process to launch the ISE text editor.
6. Rename the I/O names as needed and then delete the unused pin assignments.
7. Save the file.

The default option of ISE version 8.2 only allows the pin assignments of the existing top-level I/O ports. If unused pin assignments are not deleted from the ucf template, error messages will be generated. We can override the default option as follows:

1. Select the top-level HDL file.
2. Right-click the Implement Design process in the processes window and then select Properties... from the menu. A dialog window appears.
3. In the dialog window, check the Allow Unmatched LOC Constraints option and then click OK.

After this option is turned on, we can use the same ucf template for all designs as long as the same I/O port names are kept in the top-level module, and we don't need to edit the ucf file each time.

Perform synthesis and implementation Invoking the synthesis and implementation procedure is very simple:

1. Select the module to be synthesized and make sure that it is designated as the top-level module (with a green square next to the module icon).
2. Double-click the Implement Design process in the processes window.
3. Although the syntax is checked earlier, the code may contain constructs that cannot be synthesized or may lead to poor implementation (such as a combinational loop). The error and warning messages are displayed in the console tab of the transcript window.
4. Correct the problems and repeat the simulation and synthesis processes if needed.

Check the design summary As the project progresses, a report is generated in each process. These reports and key statistics are summarized in a design summary window. We can check the size of the resulting circuit (in terms of the numbers of slices, FFs, and LUTs) and, for a sequential circuit, check whether the clock rate meets the timing constraints. The summary can be invoked by double-clicking the View Design Summary process in the processes window. The summary for the eq2 circuit is shown in Figure 2.8. We can check the use of slices, LUTs, and so on, in the Device Utilization Summary portion. A more detailed report can be invoked by clicking the corresponding link.

2.6.4 Generate and download the configuration file to an FPGA device

The last step is to generate the configuration file and download the file to the FPGA device. There are three tasks in this step:

- Connect the download cable.
- Generate the configuration file.
- Download the configuration file.

The S3 kit comes with a parallel-port JTAG download cable, and the following discussion is based on this cable. The procedures for other cables are similar and detailed instructions can be found in their manuals.

Connect the download cable The procedure to prepare the board is as follows:

1. Make sure that the *PROM* and the *Mode* jumpers (labeled 3 and 16 in Figure 2.3) are in their default setting (as the board is shipped).
2. Connect the power cable.
3. Connect one end of the download cable to the parallel port of a PC and connect the other end to the JTAG port (labeled 22 in Figure 2.3) on the S3 board.

Generate the configuration file Generating a configuration file is very straightforward:

1. Make sure that the top-level module is selected in the source window.
2. Click Generate Programming File in the processes window.

After this process is completed, a configuration file, eq2.bit, is generated.

EQ2 Project Status			
Project File:	eq2.ise	**Current State:**	Placed and Routed
Module Name:	eq2	• **Errors:**	No Errors
Target Device:	xc3s200-5ft256	• **Warnings:**	No Warnings
Product Version:	ISE, 8.1i	• **Updated:**	Sun Jan 21 18:04:45 2007

Device Utilization Summary				
Logic Utilization	**Used**	**Available**	**Utilization**	**Note(s)**
Number of 4 input LUTs	1	3,840	1%	
Logic Distribution				
Number of occupied Slices	1	1,920	1%	
Number of Slices containing only related logic	1	1	100%	
Number of Slices containing unrelated logic	0	1	0%	
Total Number of 4 input LUTs	1	3,840	1%	
Number of bonded IOBs	5	173	2%	
Total equivalent gate count for design	6			
Additional JTAG gate count for IOBs	240			

Performance Summary			
Final Timing Score:	0	**Pinout Data:**	Pinout Report
Routing Results:	All Signals Completely Routed	**Clock Data:**	Clock Report
Timing Constraints:	All Constraints		

Detailed Reports					
Report Name	**Status**	**Generated**	**Errors**	**Warnings**	**Infos**
Synthesis Report	Current	Sat Jan 20 22:22:32 2007	0	0	0
Translation Report	Current	Sat Jan 20 22:22:46 2007	0	0	0
Map Report	Current	Sat Jan 20 22:23:00 2007	0	0	2 Infos
Place and Route Report	Current	Sat Jan 20 22:23:18 2007	0	0	1 Info
Static Timing Report	Current	Sat Jan 20 22:23:30 2007	0	0	2 Infos
Bitgen Report					

Figure 2.8 Design summary.

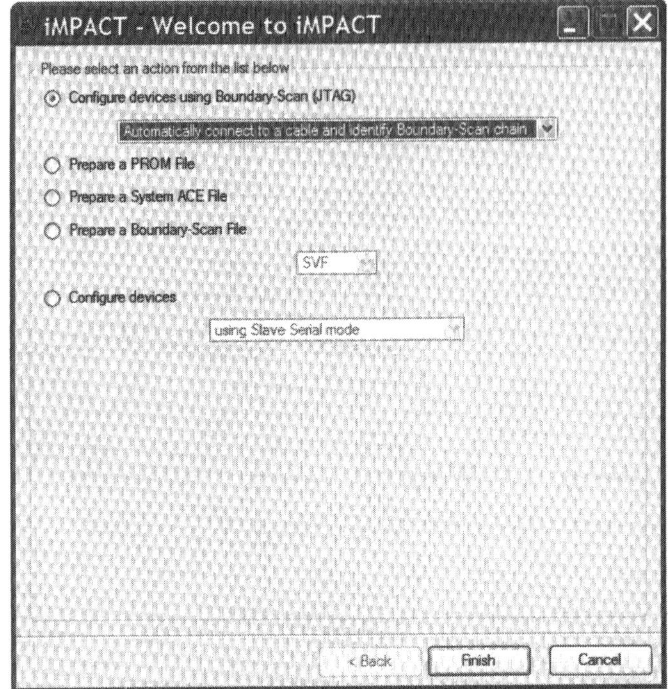

Figure 2.9 iMPACT welcome dialog.

Download the configuration file Downloading the configuration file to an FPGA device is done by a software tool known as *iMPACT*, which can be invoked from ISE Project Navigator. The procedure is

1. In the processes window, click the + sign to expand the Generate Programming File hierarchy.
2. Double-click the Configure Device (iMPACT) process. The Welcome to iMPACT dialog appears, as shown in Figure 2.9. Check Configure devices using Boundary-Scan (JTAG) and verify that Automatically connect to a cable and identify Boundary-Scan chain is selected in the drop-down list. Click Finish.
3. If a message indicating that two devices are found is displayed, click OK to continue.
4. The main iMPACT window, along with the Assign New Configuration File dialog, appears, as shown in Figure 2.10. The devices connected to the JTAG chain on the board should be detected and displayed.
5. Select the eq2.bit file and click Open to assign this configuration file to the xc3s200 device in the JTAG chain.
6. If a warning message appears, ignore it and click OK.
7. Select Bypass to skip the other device.
8. Right-click on the xc3s200 device image, and select Program .... The Programming Properties dialog opens. Click OK to program the device.
9. The Program Succeeded message appears when the downloading process is completed.

Now the FPGA device is configured and we can test the circuit with the switches and observe the output LED.

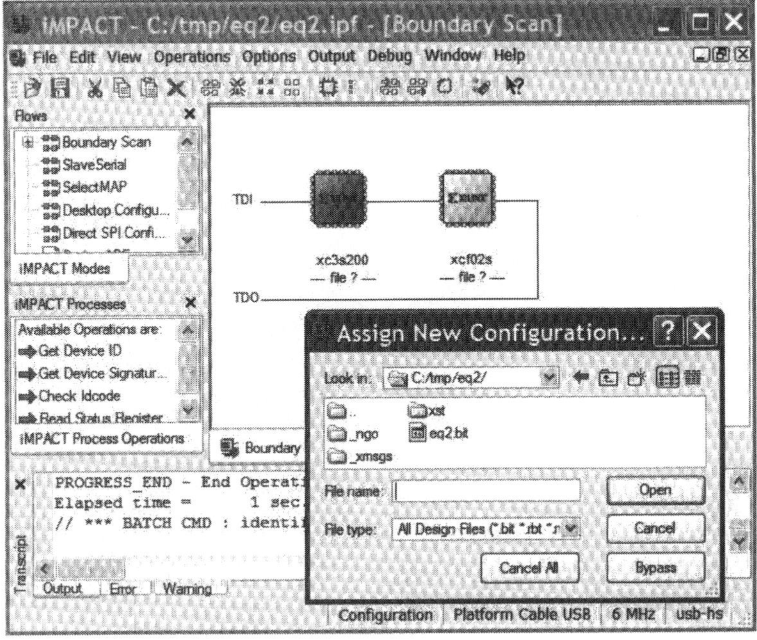

Figure 2.10 iMPACT main window.

An alternative way to configure the FPGA is to download the configuration file to a PROM and load the configuration file from the PROM. More information may be found in the sources cited in the Bibliographic section.

2.7 SHORT TUTORIAL ON THE MODELSIM HDL SIMULATOR

The ModelSim software is an HDL simulator manufactured by Mentor Graphics Corporation and can run independently without ISE. The discussion in this section is based on ModelSim XE III Starter version 6.0d.

The default ModelSim window is shown in Figure 2.11. It is divided into three subwindows: Transcript window (bottom), Workspace window, and multiple document interface (MDI) window. The Workspace window displays information on the current process. The bottom tab is used to select the desired process page, which can be Project, Library, Sim, and so on. The Transcript window keeps track of command history and messages. It can also be used as a command-line interface to enter ModelSim commands. The MDI window is an area to display HDL text, waveform, and so on. The bottom tab selects the desired pages.

Each subwindow may be resized, moved, docked, or undocked. Additional windows may appear for some operations. The default layout can be restored by selecting Window ≻ Initial Layout.

We present a short tutorial in this section to illustrate the basic simulation process. There are three steps:

1. Prepare a simulation project.
2. Compile the HDL codes.
3. Perform a simulation and examine the waveform.

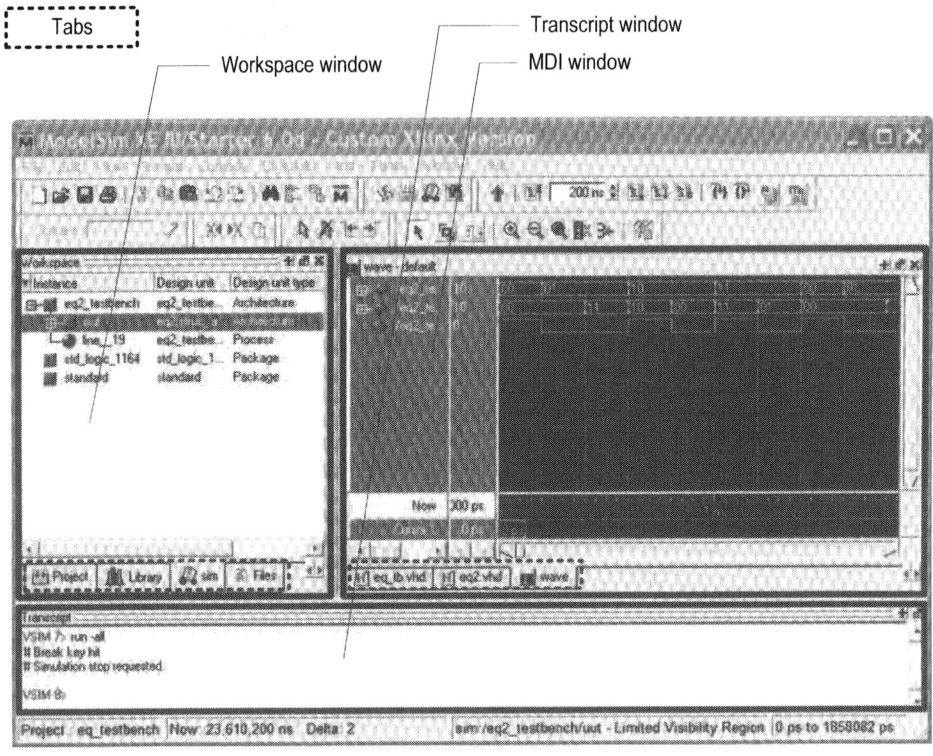

Figure 2.11 Typical ModelSim window.

We use the 2-bit comparator testbench discussed in Chapter 1 for the tutorial, and the code is repeated in Listing 2.3. An additional assertion statement,

```
assert false
   report "Simulation Completed"
   severity failure;
```

is added to the end of the process. It generates an "artificial failure" and stops the simulation.

Listing 2.3 Testbench of a 2-bit comparator

```
library ieee; use ieee.std_logic_1164.all;
entity eq2_testbench is
end eq2_testbench;

architecture tb_arch of eq2_testbench is
   signal test_in0, test_in1: std_logic_vector(1 downto 0);
   signal test_out: std_logic;
begin
   -- instantiate the circuit under test
   uut: entity work.eq2(struc_arch)
      port map(a=>test_in0, b=>test_in1, aeqb=>test_out);
   -- test vector generator
   process
```

```
   begin
      -- test vector 1
      test_in0 <= "00";
      test_in1 <= "00";
      wait for 200 ns;
      -- test vector 2
      test_in0 <= "01";
      test_in1 <= "00";
      wait for 200 ns;
      -- test vector 3
      test_in0 <= "01";
      test_in1 <= "11";
      wait for 200 ns;
      -- test vector 4
      test_in0 <= "10";
      test_in1 <= "10";
      wait for 200 ns;
      -- test vector 5
      test_in0 <= "10";
      test_in1 <= "00";
      wait for 200 ns;
      -- test vector 6
      test_in0 <= "11";
      test_in1 <= "11";
      wait for 200 ns;
      -- test vector 7
      test_in0 <= "11";
      test_in1 <= "01";
      wait for 200 ns;
      -- terminate simulation
      assert false
         report "Simulation Completed"
         severity failure;
   end process;
end tb_arch;
```

Prepare a simulation project A ModelSim simulation project consists of the library definition and a collection of HDL files. A testbench is an HDL program and can be created by using the ISE text editor, as discussed in Section 2.6.1. Alternatively, ModelSim also has a built-in editor. We assume that all HDL files are already constructed. The procedure to create a project is as follows:

1. Select Start ≻ All Programs ≻ ModelSim XE III 6.0d ≻ ModelSim (or wherever ModelSim resides) to launch the ModelSim program.
2. Select File ≻ New ≻ Project and the Create Project dialog appears, as shown in Figure 2.12(a). Enter the project name as `eq_testbench`, select the project location, and set Default Library Name to `work`. Click OK. A blank Project page appears in the main window and the Add items to the project dialog appears, as shown in Figure 2.12(b).
3. In the Add items to the project dialog, click Add Existing File and add the necessary HDL files. Click OK. The project tab appears in the workplace subwindow and displays the selected files, as shown in Figure 2.13.

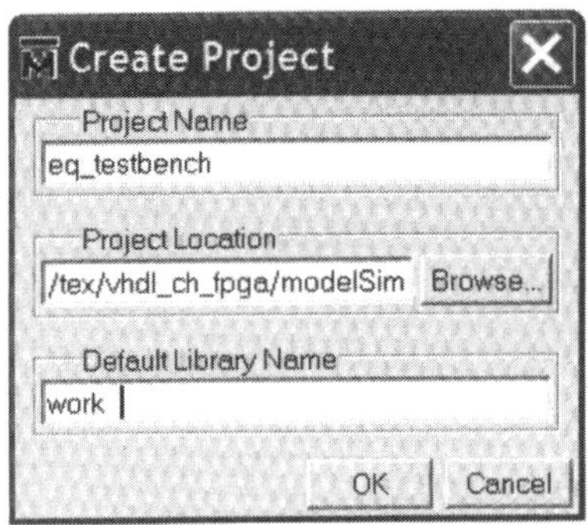

(a) `Create Project` dialog

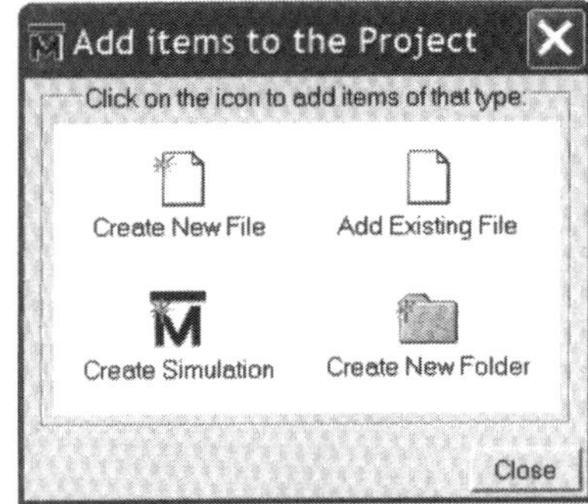

(b) `Add items` dialog

Figure 2.12 New project dialogs.

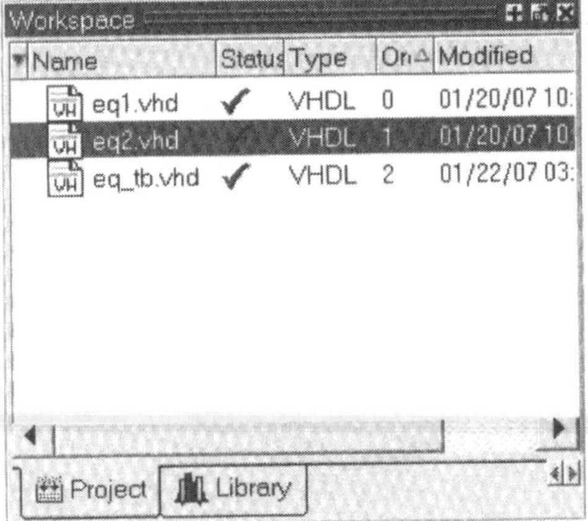

Figure 2.13 Project tab of the workplace panel.

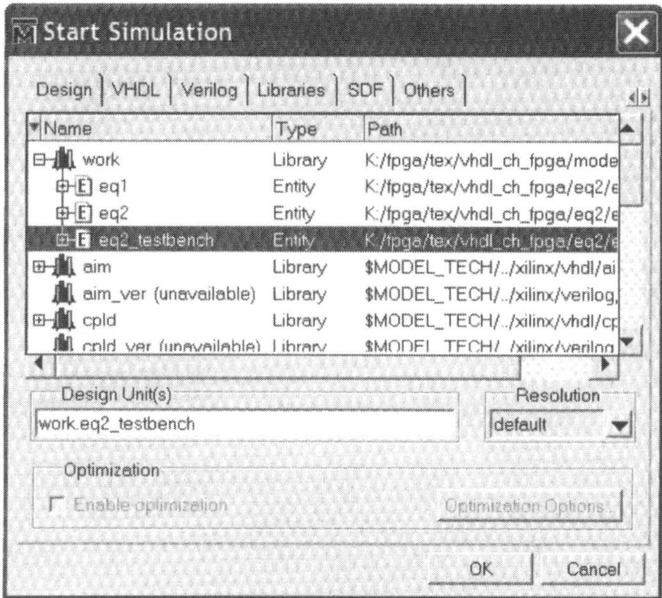

Figure 2.14 Simulate dialog.

Compile the HDL code The *compile* term here means to convert the HDL code into ModelSim internal format. In VHDL, the compiling is done on the *design unit* basis. Each entity and architecture is considered as one design unit. The procedure is:

1. Highlight the `eq1` file and right-click the mouse. Select Compile ≻ Compile Selected. Note that the compiling should be started from the modules at the bottom of the design hierarchy. The progress and messages are displayed in the transcript window.
2. If the file contains no syntactical error, a check mark shows up. Otherwise, an X mark shows up. Click the red error line in the transcript window to locate the errors. Correct the problems, save the file, and recompile the file.
3. Repeat the preceding steps to compile the `eq2` file and then the `eq_tb` file.

Perform a simulation and examine the waveform After compiling the testbench and corresponding files, we can perform the simulation and examine the resulting waveform. This corresponds to running the circuit in a virtual lab bench and checking the waveform in a virtual logic analyzer. The procedure is:

1. Select Simulate ≻ Simulate and the Simulate dialog appears.
2. In the Design tab, find and expand the work library, which is the one defined when we create the project. All compiled units are displayed, as shown in Figure 2.14.
3. Load `eq2_testbench` by double-clicking the corresponding icon. The sim tab appears in the workplace window and the corresponding page displays the structure of the `eq2_testbench` module, as shown in Figure 2.15. An object window, which contains the signals in the selected module, may also appear.
4. Highlight the uut unit and right-click the mouse. Select Add ≻ Add to Wave. This adds all the signals of the uut unit to the waveform page. The waveform page appears in the MDI window.
5. If necessary, rearrange the signals order and set them to proper format (decimal, hex, and so on.).

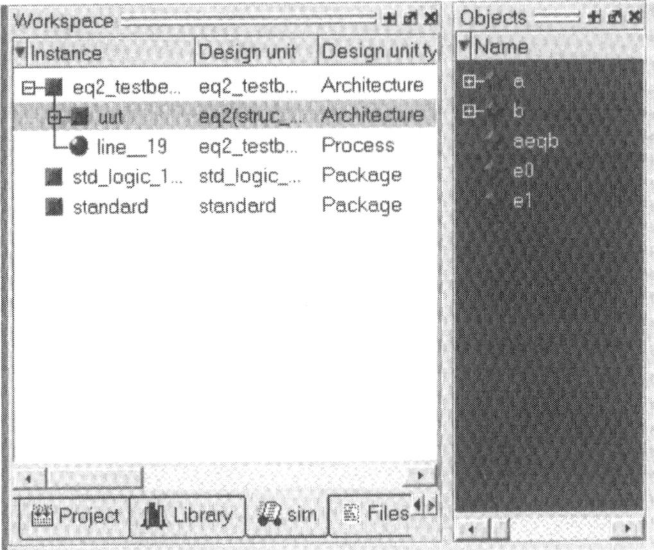

Figure 2.15 Sim panel of the workplace panel.

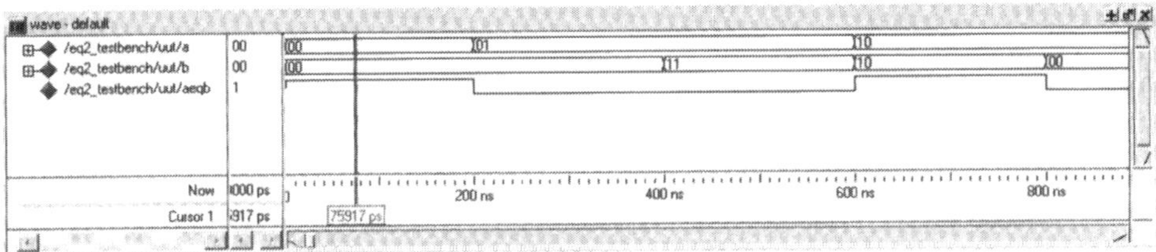

Figure 2.16 Waveform window.

6. Select Simulate ≻ Run. There are several commands to control the simulation: Restart (restart the simulation), Run (run the simulation one step), Continue run (resume the run from the interrupt), Run All (run the simulation forever), and Break (break the simulation). These commands are also shown as icons at the top of the window.
7. The waveform window displays the simulated result, shown in Figure 2.16. We can scroll the window, zoom in, or zoom out to check the correctness of the design.

2.8 BIBLIOGRAPHIC NOTES

Both Xilinx ISE and Mentor Graphics ModelSim are complex software packages, and their documentation exceeds several thousand pages. Most documentation can be accessed via the Help menu. ISE has a short 30-page tutorial, *ISE 8.1i Quick Start Tutorial*, and a more comprehensive 170-page tutorial, *ISE In-Depth Tutorial*. ModelSim also has a similar tutorial, *ModelSim Tutorial*. These tutorials provide an overview on all features of the software package. Relevant information for the Spartan-3 device can be found in its data sheets, *DS099 Spartan-3 FPGA Family: Complete Data Sheet*, which includes the detailed

Table 2.2 Truth table of a 2-to-4 decoder with enable

input			output
en	*a*(1)	*a*(0)	*bcode*
0	–	–	0000
1	0	0	0001
1	0	1	0010
1	1	0	0100
1	1	1	1000

explanation on the logic cells and macro cells. *The Design Warrior's Guide to FPGAs* by Clive Maxfield provides a comprehensive review of FPGA-related issues. The detailed layout and I/O connectors of the S3 board can be found in *Spartan-3 Starter Kit Board User Guide*. Information on other prototyping boards can be found in their manuals.

2.9 SUGGESTED EXPERIMENTS

2.9.1 Gate-level greater-than circuit

The greater-than circuit compares two inputs, a and b, and asserts an output when a is greater than b. We want to create a 4-bit greater-than circuit from the bottom up and use only gate-level logical operators. Design the circuit as follows:

1. Derive the truth table for a 2-bit greater-than circuit and obtain the logic expression in the sum-of-products format. Based on the expression, derive the HDL code using only logical operators.
2. Derive a testbench for the 2-bit greater-than circuit. Perform a simulation and verify the correctness of the design.
3. Use four switches as the inputs and one LED as the output. Synthesize the circuit and download the configuration file to the prototyping board. Verify its operation.
4. Use the 2-bit greater-than circuits and 2-bit equality comparators and a minimal number of "glue gates" to construct a 4-bit greater-than circuit. First draw a block diagram and then derive the structural HDL code according to the diagram.
5. Derive a testbench for the 4-bit greater-than circuit. Perform a simulation and verify the correctness of the design.
6. Use eight switches as the inputs and one LED as the output. Synthesize the circuit and download the configuration file to the prototyping board. Verify its operation.

2.9.2 Gate-level binary decoder

An n-to-2^n binary decoder asserts one of 2^n bits according to the input combination. The functional table of a 2-to-4 decoder with an enable signal is shown in Table 2.2. We want to create several decoders using only gate-level logical operators. The procedure is as follows:

1. Determine the logic expressions for the 2-to-4 decoder with enable and derive the HDL code using only logical operators.
2. Derive a testbench for the decoder. Perform a simulation and verify the correctness of the design.

3. Use two switches as the inputs and four LEDs as the outputs. Synthesize the circuit and download the configuration file to the prototyping board. Verify its operation.
4. Use the 2-to-4 decoders to derive a 3-to-8 decoder. First draw a block diagram and then derive the structural HDL code according to the diagram.
5. Derive a testbench for the 3-to-8 decoder. Perform a simulation and verify the correctness of the design.
6. Use three switches as the inputs and eight LEDs as the outputs. Synthesize the circuit and download the configuration file to the prototyping board. Verify its operation.
7. Use the 2-to-4 decoders to derive a 4-to-16 decoder. First draw a block diagram and then derive the structural HDL code according to the diagram.
8. Derive a testbench for the 4-to-16 decoder. Perform a simulation and verify the correctness of the design.

CHAPTER 3

RT-LEVEL COMBINATIONAL CIRCUIT

3.1 INTRODUCTION

The gate-level circuits discussed in Chapter 1 utilize simple logical operators to describe gate-level design, which is composed of simple logic cells. In this chapter, we examine the HDL description of module-level circuits, which are composed of intermediate-sized components, such as adders, comparators, and multiplexers. Since these components are the basic building blocks used in *register transfer methodology*, it is sometimes referred to as RT-level design. We first discuss more sophisticated VHDL operators and routing constructs and then demonstrate the RT-level combinational circuit design through a series of examples.

3.2 RT-LEVEL COMPONENTS

In addition to the logical operators, relational operators and several arithmetic operators can also be synthesized automatically. These operators correspond to intermediate-sized module-level components, such as comparators and adders. We examine these operators in this section and also cover miscellaneous synthesis-related VHDL constructs. Tables 3.1 and 3.2 summarize the operators and their applicable data types used in this book.

Table 3.1 Operators and data types of VHDL-93 and IEEE `std_logic_1164` package

Operator	Description	Data type of operands	Data type of result
`a ** b`	exponentiation	`integer`	`integer`
`a * b`	multiplication		
`a / b`	division	*integer type for constants and*	
`a + b`	addition	*array boundaries, not synthesis*	
`a - b`	subtraction		
`a & b`	concatenation	1-D array, element	1-D array
`a = b`	equal to	any	`boolean`
`a /= b`	not equal to		
`a < b`	less than	scalar or 1-D array	`boolean`
`a <= b`	less than or equal to		
`a > b`	greater than		
`a >= b`	greater than or equal to		
not `a`	negation	`boolean`, `std_logic`,	same as operand
`a` **and** `b`	and	`std_logic_vector`	
`a` **or** `b`	or		
`a` **xor** `b`	xor		

Table 3.2 Overloaded operators and data types in the IEEE `numeric_std` package

Overloaded operator	Description	Data type of operands	Data type of result
`a * b`	arithmetic	`unsigned`, `natural`	`unsigned`
`a + b`	operation	`signed`, `integer`	`signed`
`a - b`			
`a = b`			
`a /= b`			
`a < b`	relational	`unsigned`, `natural`	`boolean`
`a <= b`	operation	`signed`, `integer`	`boolean`
`a > b`			
`a >= b`			

Table 3.3 Type conversions between `std_logic_vector` and numeric data types

Data type of `a`	To data type	Conversion function/type casting
`unsigned`, `signed`	`std_logic_vector`	`std_logic_vector(a)`
`signed`, `std_logic_vector`	`unsigned`	`unsigned(a)`
`unsigned`, `std_logic_vector`	`signed`	`signed(a)`
`unsigned`, `signed`	`integer`	`to_integer(a)`
`natural`	`unsigned`	`to_unsigned(a, size)`
`integer`	`signed`	`to_signed(a, size)`

3.2.1 Relational operators

Six relational operators are defined in the VHDL standard: = (equal to), /= (not equal to), < (less than), <= (less than or equal to), > (greater than), and >= (greater than or equal to). These operators compare operands of the same data type and return a value of the `boolean` data type. In this book, we don't use the `boolean` data type directly, but embed it in routing constructs. This is discussed in Sections 3.3 and 3.5. During synthesis, comparators are inferred for these operators.

3.2.2 Arithmetic operators

In the VHDL standard, arithmetic operations are defined for the `integer` data type and for the `natural` data type, which is a subtype of `integer` containing zero and positive integers. We usually prefer to have more control in synthesis and define the exact number of bits and format (i.e., signed or unsigned). The IEEE `numeric_std` package is developed for this purpose. In this book, we use the `integer` and `natural` data types for constants and array boundaries but not for synthesis.

IEEE numeric_std package The IEEE `numeric_std` package adds two new data types, `unsigned` and `signed`, and defines the relational and arithmetic operators over the new data types (known as *operator overloading*). The `unsigned` and `signed` data types are defined as an array with elements of the `std_logic` data type. The array is interpreted as the binary representation of unsigned or signed integers. We have to add an additional use statement to invoke the package:

```
library ieee;
use ieee.std_logic_1164.all;
use ieee.numric_std.all;   -- invoke numeric_std package
```

The synthesizable overloaded operators are summarized in Table 3.2.

Multiplication is a complicated operation, and synthesis of the multiplication operator * depends on synthesis software and target device technology. Xilinx Spartan-3 FPGA family contains prefabricated combinational multiplier blocks. The Xilinx XST software can infer these blocks during synthesis, and thus the multiplication operator can be used in HDL code. The XCS200 device of the S3 board consists of twelve 18-by-18 multiplier blocks. While the synthesis of the multiplication operator is supported, we need to be aware of the limitation on the number and input width of these blocks and use them with care.

Xilinx specific

Type conversion Because VHDL is a strongly typed language, `std_logic_vector`, `unsigned`, and `signed` are treated as different data types even when all of them are defined as an array with elements of the `std_logic` data type. A *conversion function* or *type casting* is needed to convert signals of different data types. The conversion is summarized in Table 3.3. Note that the `std_logic_vector` data type is not interpreted as a number and thus cannot be converted directly to an integer, and vice versa.

The following examples illustrate the common mistakes and remedies for type conversion. Assume that some signals are declared as follows:

```
library ieee;
use ieee.std_logic_1164.all;
use ieee.numeric_std.all;
. . .
signal s1, s2, s3, s4, s5, s6: std_logic_vector(3 downto 0);
```

```
signal u1, u2, u3, u4, u5, u6, u7: unsigned(3 downto 0);
. . .
```

Let us first consider the following assignment statements:

```
u1 <= s1;   -- not ok, type mismatch
u2 <= 5;    -- not ok, type mismatch
s2 <= u3;   -- not ok, type mismatch
s3 <= 5;    -- not ok, type mismatch
```

They are all invalid because of type mismatch. The right-hand-side expression must be converted to the data type of the left-hand-side signal:

```
u1 <= unsigned(s1);        -- ok, type casting
u2 <= to_unsigned(5,4);    -- ok, conversion function
s2 <= std_logic_vector(u3);    -- ok, type casting
s3 <= std_logic_vector(to_unsigned(5,4));  -- ok
```

Note that two type conversions are needed for the last statement.

Let us consider statements that involve arithmetic operations. The following statements are valid since the + operator is defined with the `unsigned` and `natural` types in the IEEE `numeric_std` package.

```
u4 <= u2 + u1;   -- ok, both operands unsigned
u5 <= u2 + 1;    -- ok, operands unsigned and natural
```

On the other hand, the following statements are invalid since no overloaded arithmetic operation is defined for the `std_logic_vector` data type:

```
s5 <= s2 + s1;  -- not ok, + undefined over the types
s6 <= s2 + 1;   -- not ok, + undefined over the types
```

To fix the problem, we must convert the operands to the `unsigned` (or `signed`) data type, perform addition, and then convert the result back to the `std_logic_vector` data type. The revised code becomes

```
s5 <= std_logic_vector(unsigned(s2) + unsigned(s1));  -- ok
s6 <= std_logic_vector(unsigned(s2) + 1);             -- ok
```

Nonstandard arithmetic packages There are several non-IEEE arithmetic packages, which are `std_logic_arith`, `std_logic_unsigned`, and `std_logic_signed`. The `std_logic_arith` package is similar to the `numeric_std` package. The other two packages do not introduce any new data type but define overloaded arithmetic operators over the `std_logic_vector` data type. This approach eliminates the need for data conversion. Although using these packages seems to be less cumbersome initially, it is not good practice since these packages are not a part of IEEE standards and may introduce a compatibility problem in the long run. We do not use these packages in this book.

3.2.3 Other synthesis-related VHDL constructs

Concatenation operator The concatenation operator, &, combines segments of elements and small arrays to form a large array. The following example illustrates its use:

```
signal a1: std_logic;
signal a4: std_logic_vector(3 downto 0);
signal b8, c8, d8: std_logic_vector(7 downto 0);
```

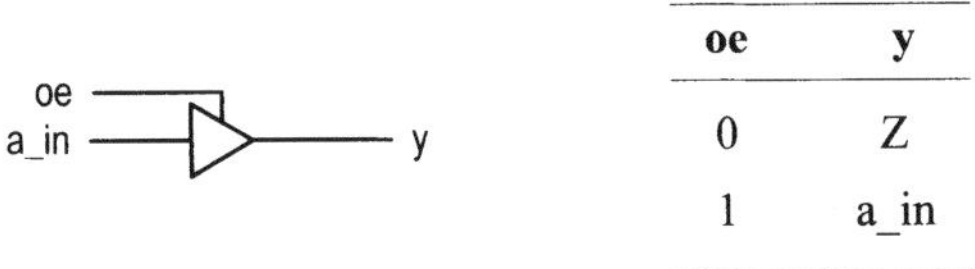

oe	y
0	Z
1	a_in

Figure 3.1 Symbol and functional table of a tri-state buffer.

```
. . .
b8 <= a4 & a4;
c8 <= a1 & a1 & a4 & "00";
d8 <= b8(3 downto 0) & c8(3 downto 0);
```

Implementation of the concatenation operator involves reconnection of the input and output signals and only requires "wiring."

One major application of the & operator is to perform shifting operations. Although both VHDL standard and `numeric_std` package define shift functions, they sometimes cannot be synthesized automatically. The & operator can be used for shifting a signal for a fixed amount, as shown in the following example:

```
signal a: std_logic_vector(7 downto 0);
signal rot, shl, sha: std_logic_vector(7 downto 0);
. . .
-- rotate a to right 3 bits
rot <= a(2 downto 0) & a(8 downto 3);
-- shift a to right 3 bits and insert 0 (logic shift)
shl <= "000" & a(8 downto 3);
-- shift a to right 3 bits and insert MSB
-- (arithmetic shift)
sha <= a(8) & a(8) & a(8) & a(8 downto 3);
```

An additional routing circuit is needed if the amount of shifting is not fixed. The design of a barrel shifter is discussed in Section 3.7.3.

'Z' value of std_logic The `std_logic` data type has a value of `'Z'`, which implies *high impedance* or an open circuit. It is not a normal logic value and can only be synthesized by a *tri-state buffer*. The symbol and function table of a tri-state buffer are shown in Figure 3.1. Operation of the buffer is controlled by an enable signal, `oe` ("output enable"). When it is `'1'`, the input is passed to output. On the other hand, when it is `'0'`, the y output appears to be an open circuit. The code of the tri-state buffer is

```
y <= a_in when oe='1' else 'Z';
```

The most common application for a tri-state buffer is to implement a *bidirectional port* to better utilize a physical I/O pin. A simple example is shown in Figure 3.2. The `dir` signal controls the direction of signal flow of the `bi` pin. When it is '0', the tri-state buffer is in the high-impedance state and the `sig_out` signal is blocked. The pin is used as an input port and the input signal is routed to the `sig_in` signal. When the `dir` signal is '1', the pin is used as an output port and the `sig_out` signal is routed to an external circuit. The HDL code can be derived according to the diagram:

```
entity bi_demo is
   port(
```

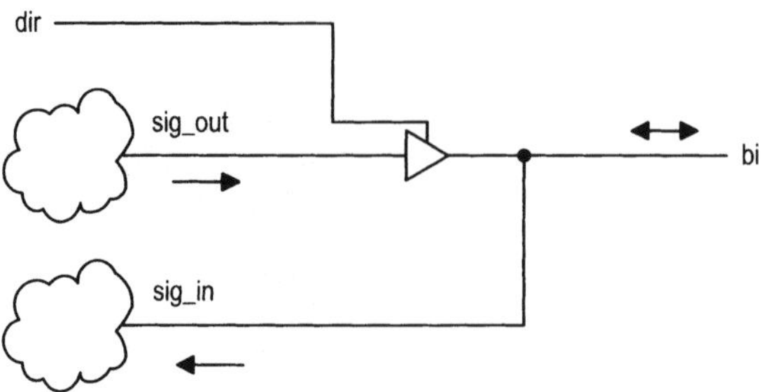

Figure 3.2 Single-buffer bidirectional I/O port.

```
      bi: inout std_logic;
      . . .
   )
begin
   sig_out <= output_expression;
   . . .
   some_signal <= expression_with_sig_in;
   . . .
   bi <= sig_out when dir='1' else 'Z';
   sig_in <= bi;
   . . .
```

Note that the mode of the `bi` port must be declared as **inout** for bidirectional operation.

Xilinx specific

For a Xilinx Spartan-3 device, a tri-state buffer exists only in the I/O block (IOB) of a physical pin. Thus, the tri-state buffer can only be used for I/O ports that are mapped to the physical pins of an FPGA device.

3.2.4 Summary

Because of the nature of a strongly typed language, the data type frequently confuses a new VHDL user. Since this book is focused on synthesis, only a small set of data types and operators are needed. Their uses can be summarized as follows:

- Use the `std_logic` and `std_logic_vector` data types in entity port declaration and for the internal signals that involve no arithmetic operations.
- Use the 'Z' value only to infer a tri-state buffer.
- Use the IEEE `numeric_std` package and its `unsigned` or `signed` data types for the internal signals that involve arithmetic operation.
- Use the data type casting or conversion functions in Table 3.3 to convert signals and expressions among the `std_logic_vector` and various numerical data types.
- Use VHDL's built-in `integer` data type and arithmetic operators for constant and array boundary expressions, but not for synthesis (i.e., not used as a data type for a signal).
- Embed the result of a relational operation, which is in the `boolean` data type, in routing constructs (discussed in Section 3.3).
- Use a user-defined two-dimensional data type for two-dimensional storage array (discussed in Section 4.2.3).

- Use a user-defined *enumerate data type* for the symbolic states of a finite state machine (discussed in Chapter 5).

3.3 ROUTING CIRCUIT WITH CONCURRENT ASSIGNMENT STATEMENTS

The *conditional signal assignment* and *selected signal assignment* statements are concurrent statements. Their behaviors are somewhat like the if and case statements of a conventional programming language. Instead of being executed sequentially, these statements are mapped to a routing network during synthesis.

3.3.1 Conditional signal assignment statement

Syntax and conceptual implementation The simplified syntax of a conditional signal assignment statement is

```
signal_name <= value_expr_1 when boolean_expr_1 else
                value_expr_2 when boolean_expr_2 else
                  . . .
                value_expr_n;
```

The Boolean expressions are evaluated successively in turn until one is found to be `true` and the corresponding value expression is assigned to the signal. The `value_expr_n` is assigned if all Boolean expressions are evaluated to be `false`.

The conditional signal assignment statement implies a cascading priority routing network. Consider the following statement:

```
r <= a + b + c when m = n else
     a - b     when m > n else
     c + 1;
```

The routing is done by a sequence of 2-to-1 multiplexers. The diagram and truth table of a 2-to-1 multiplexer are shown in Figure 3.3(a), and the conceptual diagram of the statement is shown in Figure 3.3(b). It the first Boolean condition (i.e., `m=n`) is `true`, the result of `a+b+c` is routed to `r`. Otherwise, the data connected to the 0 port is passed to `r`. We need to trace the path along the 0 port and check the next Boolean condition (i.e., `m>n`) to determine whether the result of `a-b` or `c+1` is routed to the output.

Note that all the Boolean expressions and value expressions are evaluated concurrently. The values from the Boolean circuits set the selection signals of the multiplexers to route the desired value to the output. The number of cascading stages increases proportionally to the number of when-else clauses. A large number of when-else clauses will lead to a long cascading chain and introduce a large propagation delay.

Examples We use two simple examples to demonstrate use of the conditional signal assignment statement. The first example is a priority encoder. The priority encoder has four requests, `r(4)`, `r(3)`, `r(2)`, and `r(1)`, which are grouped as a single 4-bit `r` input, and `r(4)` has the highest priority. The output is the binary code of the highest-order request. The function table is shown in Table 3.4. The HDL code is shown in Listing 3.1.

Listing 3.1 Priority encoder using a conditional signal assignment statement

```
library ieee;
use ieee.std_logic_1164.all;
```

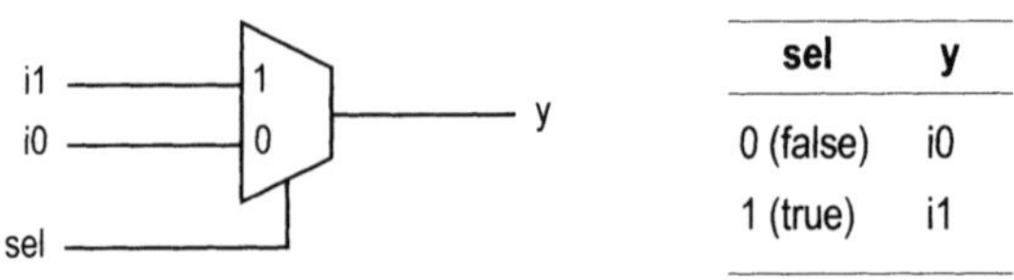

sel	y
0 (false)	i0
1 (true)	i1

(a) Diagram of a 2-to-1 multiplexer

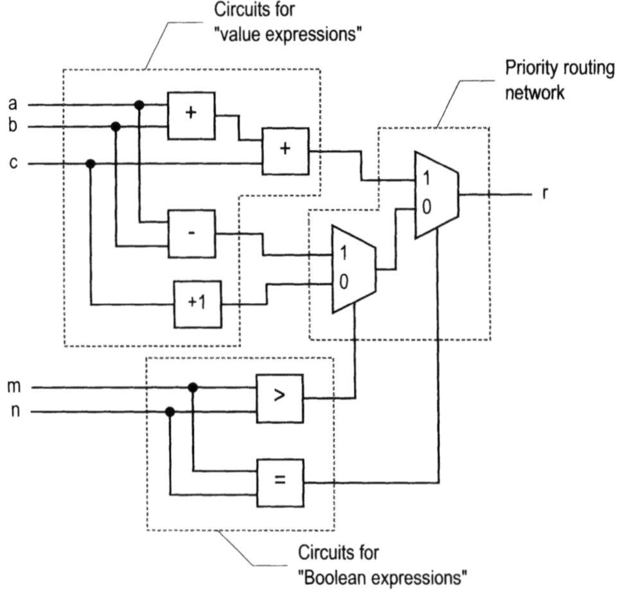

(b) Diagram of a conditional signal assignment statement

Figure 3.3 Implementation of a conditional signal assignment statement.

Table 3.4 Function table of a four-request priority encoder

input `r`	**output** `pcode`
1 – – –	100
0 1 – –	011
0 0 1 –	010
0 0 0 1	001
0 0 0 0	000

Table 3.5 Truth table of a 2-to-4 decoder with enable

input			output
en	a(1)	a(0)	y
0	–	–	0000
1	0	0	0001
1	0	1	0010
1	1	0	0100
1	1	1	1000

```
entity prio_encoder is
   port(
      r: in std_logic_vector(4 downto 1);
      pcode: out std_logic_vector(2 downto 0)
   );
end prio_encoder;

architecture cond_arch of prio_encoder is
begin
   pcode <= "100" when (r(4)='1') else
            "011" when (r(3)='1') else
            "010" when (r(2)='1') else
            "001" when (r(1)='1') else
            "000";
end cond_arch;
```

The code first checks the r(4) request and assigns "100" to pcode if it is asserted. It continues to check the r(3) request if r(4) is not asserted and repeats the process until all requests are examined.

The second example is a binary decoder. An n-to-2^n binary decoder asserts 1 bit of the 2^n-bit output according to the input combination. The functional table of a 2-to-4 decoder is shown in Table 3.5. The circuit also has a control signal, en, which enables the decoding function when asserted. The HDL code is shown in Listing 3.2.

Listing 3.2 Binary decoder using a conditional signal assignment statement

```
library ieee;
use ieee.std_logic_1164.all;
entity decoder_2_4 is
   port(
      a: in std_logic_vector(1 downto 0);
      en: in std_logic;
      y: out std_logic_vector(3 downto 0)
   );
end decoder_2_4;

architecture cond_arch of decoder_2_4 is
begin
   y <= "0000" when (en='0') else
        "0001" when (a="00") else
        "0010" when (a="01") else
```

```
        "0100" when (a="10") else
        "1000";    -- a="11"
end cond_arch;
```

The code first checks whether en is not asserted. If the condition is `false` (i.e., en is `'1'`), it tests the four binary combinations in sequence.

3.3.2 Selected signal assignment statement

Syntax and conceptual implementation The simplified syntax of a selected signal assignment statement is

```
with sel select
   sig <= value_expr_1 when choice_1,
          value_expr_2 when choice_2,
          value_expr_3 when choice_3,
          . . .
          value_expr_n when others;
```

The selected signal assignment statement is somewhat like a case statement in a traditional programming language. It assigns an expression to a signal according to the value of the `sel` signal. A choice (i.e., `choice_i`) must be a valid value or a set of valid values of `sel`. The choices have to be *mutually exclusive* (i.e., no value can be used more than once) and *all inclusive* (i.e., all values must be used). In other words, all possible values of `sel` must be covered by one and only one choice. The reserved word, **others**, is used in the end to cover unused values. Since the `sel` signal usually has the `std_logic_vector` data type, the **others** term is always needed to cover the unsynthesizable values (`'X'`, `'U'`, etc.).

The selected signal assignment statement implies a multiplexing structure. Consider the following statement:

```
signal sel: std_logic_vector(1 downto 0);
. . .
with sel select
   r <= a + b + c    when "00",
        a - b        when "10",
        c + 1        when others;
```

For synthesis purposes, the `sel` signal can assume four possible values: "00", "01", "10", and "11". It implies a 2^2-to-1 multiplexer with `sel` as the selection signal. The diagram and functional table of the 2^2-to-1 multiplexer are shown in Figure 3.4(a), and the conceptual diagram of the statement is shown in Figure 3.4(b). The evaluated result of `a+b+c` is routed to `r` when `sel` is "00", the result of `a-b` is routed when `sel` is "10", and the result of `c+1` is routed when `sel` is "01" or "11".

Again, note that all value expressions are evaluated concurrently. The `sel` signal is used as the selection signal to route the desired value to the output. The width (i.e., number of input ports) of the multiplexer increases geometrically with the number of bits of the `sel` signal.

Example We use the same encoder and decoder circuits to illustrate use of the selected signal assignment statement. The code for the priority encoder is shown in Listing 3.3. The entity declaration is identical to that in Listing 3.1 and is omitted.

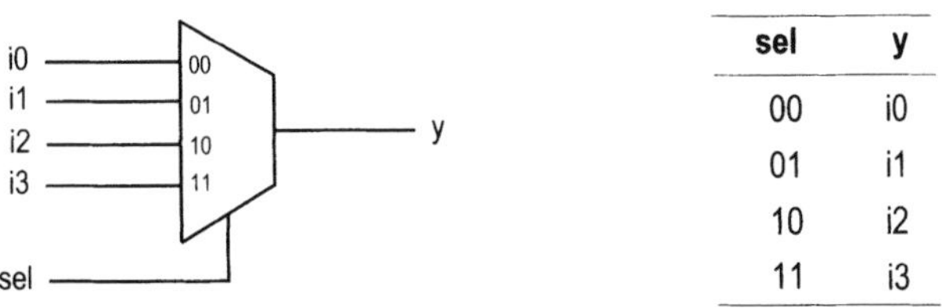

sel	y
00	i0
01	i1
10	i2
11	i3

(a) Diagram and functional table of a 4-to-1 multiplexer

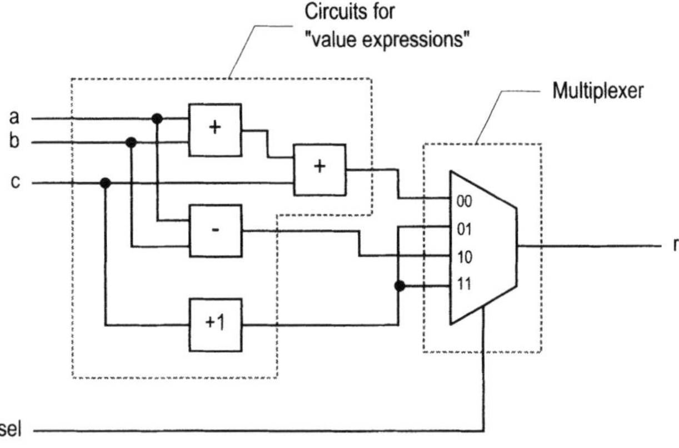

(b) Diagram of a selected signal assignment statement

Figure 3.4 Implementation of a selected signal assignment statement.

Listing 3.3 Priority encoder using a selected signal assignment statement

```
architecture sel_arch of prio_encoder is
begin
   with r select
      pcode <= "100" when "1000"|"1001"|"1010"|"1011"|
                          "1100"|"1101"|"1110"|"1111",
               "011" when "0100"|"0101"|"0110"|"0111",
               "010" when "0010"|"0011",
               "001" when "0001",
               "000" when others;    -- r="0000"
end sel_arch;
```

The code exhaustively lists all possible combinations of the `r` signal and the corresponding output values. Note that the | symbol is used if the choice is more than one value.

The code for the 2-to-4 decoder is shown in Listing 3.4.

Listing 3.4 Binary decoder using a selected signal assignment statement

```
architecture sel_arch of decoder_2_4 is
   signal s: std_logic_vector(2 downto 0);
begin
   s <= en & a;
   with s select
      y <= "0000" when "000"|"001"|"010"|"011",
           "0001" when "100",
```

```
            "0010" when "101",
            "0100" when "110",
            "1000" when others;    -- s="111"
end sel_arch;
```

We concatenate en and a to form a 3-bit signal, s, and use it as the selection signal. The remaining code again exhaustively lists all possible combinations and the corresponding output values.

3.4 MODELING WITH A PROCESS

3.4.1 Process

To facilitate system modeling, VHDL contains a number of *sequential statements*, which are executed in sequence. Since their behavior is different from that of a normal concurrent circuit model, these statements are encapsulated inside a *process*. A process itself is a concurrent statement. It can be thought of as a black box whose behavior is described by sequential statements.

Sequential statements include a rich variety of constructs, but many of them don't have clear hardware counterparts. A poorly coded process frequently leads to unnecessarily complex implementation or cannot be synthesized at all. Detailed discussion of sequential statements and processes is beyond the scope of this book. For synthesis, we restrict the use of the process to two purposes:

- Describe routing structures with *if* and *case* statements.
- Construct templates for memory elements (discussed in Chapter 4).

The simplified syntax of a process with a sensitivity list is

```
process(sensitivity_list)
begin
   sequential statement;
   sequential statement;
   . . .
end process;
```

The `sensitivity_list` is a list of signals to which the process responds (i.e., is "sensitive to"). For a combinational circuit, all the input signals should be included in this list. The body of a process is composed of any number of sequential statements.

3.4.2 Sequential signal assignment statement

The simplest sequential statement is a *sequential* signal assignment statement. The simplified syntax is

```
    sig <= value_expression;
```

The statement must be encapsulated inside a process.

Although its syntax is similar to that of a simple *concurrent* signal assignment statement, the semantics are different. When a signal is assigned multiple times inside a process, only the last assignment takes effect. For example, the code segment

```
process(a,b)
begin
```

```
      c <= a and b;
      c <= a or b;
   end process;
```

is the same as

```
   process(a,b)
   begin
      c <= a or b;
   end process;
```

On the other hand, if they are concurrent signal assignment statements, as in

```
      -- not within a process
      c <= a and b;
      c <= a or b;
```

the code infers an and cell and an or cell, whose outputs are tied together. It is not allowed in most device technology and thus is a design error.

The semantics of assigning a signal multiple times inside a process is subtle and can sometimes be error-prone. Detailed explanations can be found in the references cited in the Bibliographic section. We use multiple assignments only to avoid unintended memory, as discussed in Section 3.5.4.

3.5 ROUTING CIRCUIT WITH IF AND CASE STATEMENTS

If and *case* statements are two other commonly used sequential statements. In synthesis, they can be used to describe routing structures.

3.5.1 If statement

Syntax and conceptual implementation The simplified syntax of an if statement is

```
   if boolean_expr_1 then
      sequential_statements;
   elsif boolean_expr_2 then
      sequential_statements;
   elsif boolean_expr_3 then
      sequential_statements;
   . . .
   else
      sequential_statements;
   end if;
```

It has one *then branch*, one or more optional *elsif branches*, and one optional *else branch*. The Boolean expressions are evaluated sequentially until an expression is evaluated as `true` or the else branch is reached, and the statements in the corresponding branch will be executed.

An if statement and a concurrent conditional signal assignment statement are somewhat similar. The two statements are equivalent if each branch of the if statement contains only a single sequential signal assignment statement. For example, the previous statement

```
   r <= a + b + c when m = n else
        a - b     when m > 0 else
        c + 1;
```

can be rewritten as

```
process(a,b,c,m,n)
begin
   if m = n then
      r <= a + b + c;
   elsif m > 0 then
      r <= a - b;
   else
     r <= c + 1;
   end if;
end;
```

As in a conditional signal assignment statement, the if statement infers a similar priority routing structure during synthesis.

Example The codes of the same priority encoder and written with an if statement are shown in Listings 3.5 and 3.6. They are similar to those in Listings 3.1 and 3.2. Note that the if statement must be encapsulated inside a process.

Listing 3.5 Priority encoder using an if statement

```
architecture if_arch of prio_encoder is
begin
   process(r)
   begin
      if (r(4)='1') then
         pcode <= "100";
      elsif (r(3)='1')then
         pcode <= "011";
      elsif (r(2)='1')then
         pcode <= "010";
      elsif (r(1)='1')then
         pcode <= "001";
      else
         pcode <= "000";
      end if;
   end process;
end if_arch;
```

Listing 3.6 Binary decoder using an if statement

```
architecture if_arch of decoder_2_4 is begin
   process(en,a)
   begin
      if (en='0') then
         y <= "0000";
      elsif (a="00") then
         y <= "0001";
      elsif (a="01")then
         y <= "0010";
      elsif (a="10")then
         y <= "0100";
      else
         y <= "1000";
```

```
      end if;
   end process;
end if_arch;
```

3.5.2 Case statement

Syntax and conceptual implementation The simplified syntax of a case statement is

```
case sel is
   when choice_1 =>
      sequential statements;
   when choice_2 =>
      sequential statements;
   . . .
   when others =>
      sequential statements;
end case;
```

A case statement uses the `sel` signal to select a set of sequential statements for execution. As in a selected signal assignment statement, a choice (i.e., `choice_i`) must be a valid value or a set of valid values of `sel`, and the choices have to be mutually exclusive and all inclusive. Note that the **others** term at the end covers the unused values.

A case statement and a concurrent selected signal assignment statement are somewhat similar. The two statements are equivalent if each branch of the case statement contains only a single sequential signal assignment statement. For example, the previous statement

```
with sel select
   r <= a + b + c   when "00",
        a - b       when "10",
        c + 1       when others;
```

can be rewritten as

```
process(a,b,c,sel)
begin
   case sel is
      when "00" =>
         r <= a + b + c;
      when "10" =>
         r <= a - b;
      when others =>
         r <= c + 1;
   end case;
end;
```

As in a selected signal assignment statement, the case statement infers a similar multiplexing structure during synthesis.

Example The codes of the same priority encoder and decoder written with a case statement are shown in Listings 3.7 and 3.8. As in Listings 3.3 and 3.4, the codes exhaustively lists all possible input combinations and the corresponding output values.

Listing 3.7 Priority encoder using a case statement

```
architecture case_arch of prio_encoder is
begin
   process(r)
   begin
      case r is
         when "1000"|"1001"|"1010"|"1011"|
              "1100"|"1101"|"1110"|"1111" =>
            pcode <= "100";
         when "0100"|"0101"|"0110"|"0111" =>
            pcode <= "011";
         when "0010"|"0011" =>
            pcode <= "010";
         when "0001" =>
            pcode <= "001";
         when others =>
            pcode <= "000";
      end case;
   end process;
end case_arch;
```

Listing 3.8 Binary decoder using a case statement

```
architecture case_arch of decoder_2_4 is
   signal s: std_logic_vector(2 downto 0);
begin
   s <= en & a;
   process(s)
   begin
      case s is
         when "000"|"001"|"010"|"011" =>
            y <= "0001";
         when "100" =>
            y <= "0001";
         when "101" =>
            y <= "0010";
         when "110" =>
            y <= "0100";
         when others =>
            y <= "1000";
      end case;
   end process;
end case_arch;
```

3.5.3 Comparison to concurrent statements

The preceding subsections show that the simple if and case statements are equivalent to the conditional and selected signal assignment statements. However, an if or case statement allows *any number* and *any type* of sequential statements in their branches and thus is more flexible and versatile. Disciplined use can make the code more descriptive and even make a circuit more efficient.

This can be illustrated by two code segments. First, consider a circuit that sorts the values of two input signals and routes them to the `large` and `small` outputs. This can be done by using two conditional signal assignment statements:

```
large <= a when a > b else
         b;
small <= b when a > b else
         a;
```

Since there are two relation operators (i.e., two >) in code, synthesis software may infer two greater-than comparators. The same function can be coded by a single if statement:

```
process(a,b)
begin
   if a > b then
      large <= a;
      small <= b;
   else
      large <= b;
      small <= a;
   end if;
end;
```

The code consists of only a single relational operator.

Second, let us consider a circuit that routes the maximal value of three input signals to the output. This can be clearly described by nested two-level if statements:

```
process(a,b,c)
begin
   if (a > b) then
      if (a > c) then
         max <= a;
      else
         max <= c;
      end if;
   else
      if (b > c) then
         max <= b;
      else
         max <= c;
      end if;
   end if;
end process;
```

We can translate the if statement to a "single-level" conditional signal assignment statement:

```
max <= a when ((a > b) and (a > c)) else
       c when (a > b) else
       b when (b > c) else
       c;
```

Since no nesting is allowed, the code is less intuitive. If concurrent statements must be used, a better alternative is to describe the circuit with three conditional signal assignment statements:

```
signal ac_max, bc_max: std_logic;
. . .
```

```
ac_max <= a when (a > c) else
          c;
bc_max <= b when (b > c) else
          c;
max <= ac_max when (a > b) else
       bc_max;
```

3.5.4 Unintended memory

Although a process is flexible, a subtle error in code may infer incorrect implementation. One common problem is the inclusion of intended memory in a combinational circuit. The VHDL standard specifies that a signal will *keep its previous value* if it is not assigned in a process. During synthesis, this infers an internal state (via a closed feedback loop) or a memory element (such as a latch).

To prevent unintended memory, we should observe the following rules while developing code for a combinational circuit:

- Include all input signals in the sensitivity list.
- Include the else branch in an if statement.
- Assign a value to every signal in every branch.

For example, the following code segment tries to generate a greater-than (i.e., gt) and an equal-to (i.e., eq) output signal:

```
process(a)                -- b missing from sensitivity list
begin
   if (a > b) then        -- eq not assigned in this branch
      gt <= '1';
   elsif (a = b) then     -- gt not assigned in this branch
      eq <= '1';
   end if;                -- else branch is omitted
end process;
```

Although the syntax is correct, it violates all three rules. For example, gt will keep its previous value when the a>b expression is `false` and a latch will be inferred accordingly. The correct code should be

```
process(a,b)
begin
   if (a > b) then
      gt <= '1';
      eq <= '0';
   elsif (a = b) then
      gt <= '0';
      eq <= '1';
   else
      gt <= '0';
      eq <= '0';
   end if;
end process;
```

Since multiple sequential signal assignment statements are allowed inside a process, we can correct the problem by assigning a default value in the beginning:

```
process(a,b)
begin
   gt <= '0';            -- assign default value
   eq <= '0';
   if (a > b) then
      gt <= '1';
   elsif (a = b) then
      eq <= '1';
   end if;
end process;
```

The gt and eq signals assume '0' if they are not assigned a value later. As discussed earlier, assigning a signal multiple times inside a process can be error-prone. For synthesis, this should not be used in other context and should be considered as shorthand to satisfy the "assigning all signals in all branches" rule.

3.6 CONSTANTS AND GENERICS

3.6.1 Constants

HDL code frequently uses constant values in expressions and array boundaries. One good design practice is to replace the "hard literals" with symbolic constants. It makes code clear and helps future maintenance and revision. The constant declaration can be included in the architecture's declaration section, and it syntax is

```
constant const_name: data_type := value_expression;
```

For example, we can declare two constants as

```
constant DATA_BIT: integer := 8;
constant DATA_RANGE: integer := 2**DATA_BIT - 1;
```

The constant expression is evaluated during preprocessing and thus requires no physical circuit. In this book, we use capital letters for constants.

The use of a constant can best be explained by an example. Assume that we want to design an adder with the carry-out bit. One way to do it is to extend the input by 1 bit and then perform regular addition. The MSB of the summation becomes the carry-out bit. The code is shown in Listing 3.9.

Listing 3.9 Adder using a hard literal

```
library ieee;
use ieee.std_logic_1164.all;
use ieee.numeric_std.all;
entity add_w_carry is
   port(
      a, b: in std_logic_vector(3 downto 0);
      cout: out std_logic;
      sum: out std_logic_vector(3 downto 0)
   );
end add_w_carry;

architecture hard_arch of add_w_carry is
   signal a_ext, b_ext, sum_ext: unsigned(4 downto 0);
```

```
begin
    a_ext <= unsigned('0' & a);
    b_ext <= unsigned('0' & b);
    sum_ext <= a_ext + b_ext;
    sum <= std_logic_vector(sum_ext(3 downto 0));
    cout <= sum_ext(4);
end hard_arch;
```

The code is for a 4-bit adder. Hard literals, such as 3 and 4, are used for the ranges, as in `unsigned(4 downto 0)` and `sum_ext(3 downto 0)`, and the MSB, as in `sum_ext(4)`. If we want to revise the code for an 8-bit adder, these literals have to be modified manually. This will be a tedious and error-prone process if the code is complex and the literals are referred to in many places.

To improve the readability, we can use a symbolic constant, N, to represent the number of bits of the adder. The revised architecture body is shown in Listing 3.10.

Listing 3.10 Adder using a constant

```
architecture const_arch of add_w_carry is
    constant N: integer := 4;
    signal a_ext, b_ext, sum_ext: unsigned(N downto 0);
begin
    a_ext <= unsigned('0' & a);
    b_ext <= unsigned('0' & b);
    sum_ext <= a_ext + b_ext;
    sum <= std_logic_vector(sum_ext(N-1 downto 0));
    cout <= sum_ext(N);
end const_arch;
```

The constant makes the code easier to understand and maintain.

3.6.2 Generics

VHDL provides a construct, known as a *generic*, to pass information into an entity and component. Since a generic cannot be modified inside the architecture, it functions somewhat like a constant. A generic is declared inside an entity declaration, just before the port declaration:

```
entity entity_name is
    generic(
        generic_name: data_type := default_values;
        generic_name: data_type := default_values;
        . . .
        generic_name: data_type := default_values
    )
    port(
        port_name: mode data_type;
        . . .
    );
end entity_name;
```

For example, the previous adder code can be modified to use the adder width as a generic, as shown in Listing 3.11.

Listing 3.11 Adder using a generic

```
library ieee;
use ieee.std_logic_1164.all;
use ieee.numeric_std.all;
entity gen_add_w_carry is
5    generic(N: integer:=4);
   port(
      a, b: in std_logic_vector(N-1 downto 0);
      cout: out std_logic;
      sum: out std_logic_vector(N-1 downto 0)
10   );
end gen_add_w_carry;

architecture arch of gen_add_w_carry is
   signal a_ext, b_ext, sum_ext: unsigned(N downto 0);
15 begin
   a_ext <= unsigned('0' & a);
   b_ext <= unsigned('0' & b);
   sum_ext <= a_ext + b_ext;
   sum <= std_logic_vector(sum_ext(N-1 downto 0));
20   cout <= sum_ext(N);
end arch;
```

The N generic is declared in line 5 with a default value of 4. After N is declared, it can be used in the port declaration and architecture body, just like a constant.

If the adder is later used as a component in other code, we can assign the desired value to the generic in component instantiation. This is known as *generic mapping*. The default value will be used if generic mapping is omitted. Use of the generic in component instantiation is shown below.

```
signal a4, b4, sum4: unsigned(3 downto 0);
signal a8, b8, sum8: unsigned(7 downto 0);
signal a16, b16, sum16: unsigned(15 downto 0);
signal c4, c8, c16: std_logic;
. . .
-- instantiate 8-bit adder
adder_8_unit: work.gen_add_w_carry(arch)
   generic map(N=>8)
   port map(a=>a8, b=>b8, cout=>c8, sum=>sum8));
-- instantiate 16-bit adder
adder_16_unit: work.gen_add_w_carry(arch)
   generic map(N=>16)
   port map(a=>a16, b=>b16, cout=>c16, sum=>sum16));
-- instantiate 4-bit adder
-- (generic mapping omitted, default value 4 used)
adder_4_unit: work.gen_add_w_carry(arch)
   port map(a=>a4, b=>b4, cout=>c4, sum=>sum4));
```

A generic provides a mechanism to create *scalable code*, in which the "width" of a circuit can be adjusted to meet a specific need. This makes code more portable and encourages design reuse.

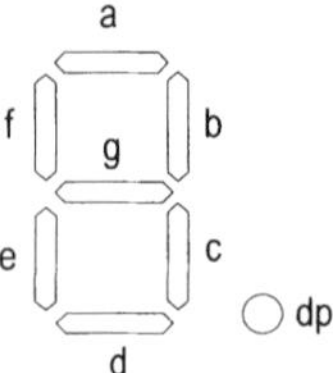

(a) Diagram of a seven-segment LED display

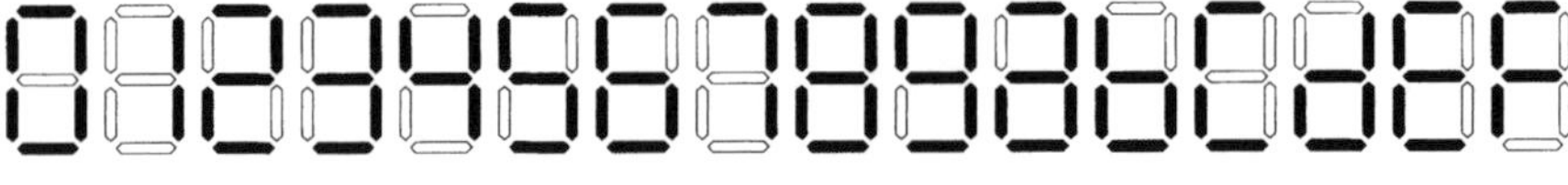

(b) Hexadecimal digit patterns

Figure 3.5 Seven-segment LED display and hexadecimal patterns.

3.7 DESIGN EXAMPLES

3.7.1 Hexadecimal digit to seven-segment LED decoder

The sketch of a seven-segment LED display is shown in Figure 3.5(a). It consists of seven LED bars and a single round LED decimal point. On the prototyping board, the seven-segment LED is configured as active low, which means that an LED segment is lit if the corresponding control signal is '0'.

A hexadecimal digit to seven-segment LED decoder treats a 4-bit input as a hexadecimal digit and generates appropriate LED patterns, as shown in Figure 3.5(b). For completeness, we assume that there is also a 1-bit input, dp, which is connected directly to the decimal point LED. The LED control signals, dp, a, b, c, d, e, f, and g, are grouped together as a single 8-bit signal, sseg. The code is shown in Listing 3.12. It uses one selected signal assignment statement to list all the desired patterns for the seven LSBs of the sseg signal. The MSB is connected to dp.

Listing 3.12 Hexadecimal digit to seven-segment LED decoder

```
library ieee;
use ieee.std_logic_1164.all;
entity hex_to_sseg is
   port(
      hex: in std_logic_vector(3 downto 0);
      dp: in std_logic;
      sseg: out std_logic_vector(7 downto 0)
   );
end hex_to_sseg;

architecture arch of hex_to_sseg is
begin
   with hex select
      sseg(6 downto 0) <=
         "0000001" when "0000",
         "1001111" when "0001",
```

```
            "0010010" when "0010",
            "0000110" when "0011",
            "1001100" when "0100",
            "0100100" when "0101",
            "0100000" when "0110",
            "0001111" when "0111",
            "0000000" when "1000",
            "0000100" when "1001",
            "0001000" when "1010", --a
            "1100000" when "1011", --b
            "0110001" when "1100", --c
            "1000010" when "1101", --d
            "0110000" when "1110", --e
            "0111000" when others; --f
   sseg(7) <= dp;
end arch;
```

There are four seven-segment LED displays on the prototyping board. To save the number of FPGA chip's I/O pins, a time-multiplexing scheme is used. The block diagram of the time-multiplexing module, `disp_mux`, is shown in Figure 3.6(a). The inputs are `in0`, `in1`, `in2`, and `in3`, which correspond to four 8-bit seven-segment LED patterns, and the outputs are `an`, which is a 4-bit signal that enables the four displays individually, and `sseg`, which is the shared 8-bit signal that controls the eight LED segments. The circuit generates a properly timed enable signal and routes the four input patterns to the output alternatively. The design of this module is discussed in Chapter 4. For now, we just treat it as a black box that takes four seven-segment LED patterns, and instantiate it in the code.

Testing circuit We use a simple 8-bit increment circuit to verify operation of the decoder. The sketch is shown in Figure 3.6(b). The `sw` input is the 8-bit switch of the prototyping board. It is fed to an incrementor to obtain `sw+1`. The original and incremented `sw` signals are then passed to four decoders to display the four hexadecimal digits on seven-segment LED displays. The code is shown in Listing 3.13.

Listing 3.13 Hex-to-LED decoder testing circuit

```
library ieee;
use ieee.std_logic_1164.all;
use ieee.numeric_std.all;
entity hex_to_sseg_test is
   port(
      clk: in std_logic;
      sw: in std_logic_vector(7 downto 0);
      an: out std_logic_vector(3 downto 0);
      sseg: out std_logic_vector(7 downto 0)
   );
end hex_to_sseg_test;

architecture arch of hex_to_sseg_test is
   signal inc: std_logic_vector(7 downto 0);
   signal led3, led2, led1, led0: std_logic_vector(7 downto 0);
begin
   -- increment input
   inc <= std_logic_vector(unsigned(sw) + 1);
```

(a) Block diagram of an LED time-multiplexing module

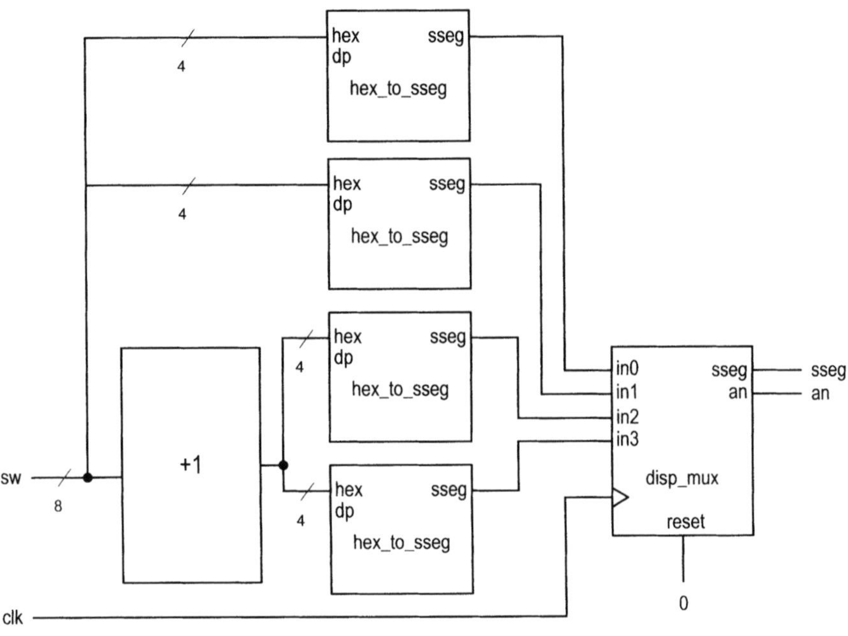

(b) Block diagram of a decoder testing circuit

Figure 3.6 LED time-multiplexing module and decoder testing circuit.

```
    -- instantiate four instances of hex decoders
    -- instance for 4 LSBs of input
    sseg_unit_0: entity work.hex_to_sseg
       port map(hex=>sw(3 downto 0), dp =>'0', sseg=>led0);
    -- instance for 4 MSBs of input
    sseg_unit_1: entity work.hex_to_sseg
       port map(hex=>sw(7 downto 4), dp =>'0', sseg=>led1);
    -- instance for 4 LSBs of incremented value
    sseg_unit_2: entity work.hex_to_sseg
       port map(hex=>inc(3 downto 0), dp =>'1', sseg=>led2);
    -- instance for 4 MSBs of incremented value
    sseg_unit_3: entity work.hex_to_sseg
       port map(hex=>inc(7 downto 4), dp =>'1', sseg=>led3);

    -- instantiate 7-seg LED display time-multiplexing module
    disp_unit: entity work.disp_mux
       port map(
          clk=>clk, reset=>'0',
          in0=>led0, in1=>led1, in2=>led2, in3=>led3,
          an=>an, sseg=>sseg);
end arch;
```

We can follow the procedure in Chapter 2 to synthesize and implement the circuit on the prototyping board. Note that the disp_mux.vhd file, which contains the code for the time-multiplexing module, and the ucf constraint file must be included in the Xilinx ISE project during synthesis.

3.7.2 Sign-magnitude adder

An integer can be represented in *sign-magnitude* format, in which the MSB is the sign and the remaining bits form the magnitude. For example, 3 and −3 become "0011" and "1011" in 4-bit sign-magnitude format.

A sign-magnitude adder performs an addition operation in this format. The operation can be summarized as follows:

- If the two operands have the same sign, add the magnitudes and keep the sign.
- If the two operands have different signs, subtract the smaller magnitude from the larger one and keep the sign of the number that has the larger magnitude.

One possible implementation is to divide the circuit into two stages. The first stage sorts the two input numbers according to their magnitudes and routes them to the max and min signals. The second stage examines the signs and performs addition or subtraction on the magnitude accordingly. Note that since the two numbers have been sorted, the magnitude of max is always larger than that of min and the final sign is the sign of max.

The code is shown in Listing 3.14, which realizes the two-stage implementation scheme. For clarity, we split the input number internally and use separate sign and magnitude signals. A generic, N, is used to represent the width of the adder. Note that the relevant magnitude signals are declared as unsigned to facilitate the arithmetic operation, and type conversions are performed at the beginning and end of the code.

Listing 3.14 Sign-magnitude adder

```
library ieee;
use ieee.std_logic_1164.all;
use ieee.numeric_std.all;
entity sign_mag_add is
   generic(N: integer:=4);  -- default 4 bits
   port(
      a, b: in std_logic_vector(N-1 downto 0);
      sum: out std_logic_vector(N-1 downto 0)
   );
end sign_mag_add;

architecture arch of sign_mag_add is
   signal mag_a, mag_b: unsigned(N-2 downto 0);
   signal mag_sum, max, min: unsigned(N-2 downto 0);
   signal sign_a, sign_b, sign_sum: std_logic;
begin
   mag_a <= unsigned(a(N-2 downto 0));
   mag_b <= unsigned(b(N-2 downto 0));
   sign_a <= a(N-1);
   sign_b <= b(N-1);
   -- sort according to magnitude
   process(mag_a,mag_b,sign_a,sign_b)
   begin
      if mag_a > mag_b then
         max <= mag_a;
         min <= mag_b;
         sign_sum <= sign_a;
      else
         max <= mag_b;
         min <= mag_a;
         sign_sum <= sign_b;
      end if;
   end process;
   -- add/sub magnitude
   mag_sum <= max + min when sign_a=sign_b else
              max - min;
   --form output
   sum <= std_logic_vector(sign_sum & mag_sum);
end arch;
```

Testing circuit We use a 4-bit sign-magnitude adder to verify the circuit operation. The sketch of the testing circuit is shown in Figure 3.7. The two input numbers are connected to the 8-bit switch, and the sign and magnitude are shown on two seven-segment LED displays. Two pushbuttons are used as the selection signal of a multiplexer to route an operand or the sum to the display circuit. The rightmost even-segment LED shows the 3-bit magnitude, which is appended with a '0' in front and fed to the hexadecimal to seven-segment LED decoder. The next LED displays the sign bit, which is blank for the plus sign and is lit with a middle LED segment for the minus sign. The two LED patterns are then fed to the time-multiplexing module, disp_mux, as explained in Section 3.7.1. The code is shown in Listing 3.15.

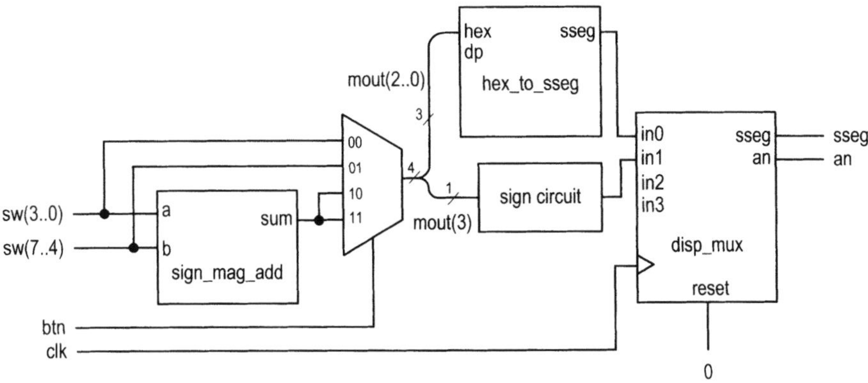

Figure 3.7 Sign-magnitude adder testing circuit.

Listing 3.15 Sign-magnitude adder testing circuit

```
library ieee;
use ieee.std_logic_1164.all;
use ieee.numeric_std.all;
entity sm_add_test is
   port(
      clk: in std_logic;
      btn: in std_logic_vector(1 downto 0);
      sw: in std_logic_vector(7 downto 0);
      an: out std_logic_vector(3 downto 0);
      sseg: out std_logic_vector(7 downto 0)
   );
end sm_add_test;

architecture arch of sm_add_test is
   signal sum, mout, oct: std_logic_vector(3 downto 0);
   signal led3, led2, led1, led0: std_logic_vector(7 downto 0);
begin
   -- instantiate adder
   sm_adder_unit: entity work.sign_mag_add
      generic map(N=>4)
      port map(a=>sw(3 downto 0), b=>sw(7 downto 4),
               sum=>sum);

   -- 3-to-1 mux to select a number to display
   with btn select
      mout <= sw(3 downto 0) when "00",   -- a
              sw(7 downto 4) when "01",   -- b
              sum when others;            -- sum

   -- magnitude displayed on rightmost 7-seg LED
   oct <= '0' & mout(2 downto 0);
   sseg_unit: entity work.hex_to_sseg
      port map(hex=>oct, dp=>'0', sseg=>led0);
   -- sign displayed on 2nd 7-seg LED
```

```
   led1 <= "11111110" when mout(3)='1' else -- middle bar
           "11111111";                       -- blank
   -- other two 7-seg LEDs blank
   led2 <= "11111111";
   led3 <= "11111111";

   -- instantiate display multiplexer
   disp_unit: entity work.disp_mux
      port map(
         clk=>clk, reset=>'0',
         in0=>led0, in1=>led1, in2=>led2, in3=>led3,
         an=>an, sseg=>sseg);
end arch;
```

3.7.3 Barrel shifter

Although VHDL has built-in shift functions, they sometimes cannot be synthesized automatically. In this subsection, we examine an 8-bit barrel shifter that rotates an arbitrary number of bits to right. The circuit has an 8-bit data input, a, and a 3-bit control signal, amt, which specifies the amount to be rotated. The first design uses a selected signal assignment statement to exhaustively list all combinations of the amt signal and the corresponding rotated results. The code is shown in Listing 3.16.

Listing 3.16 Barrel shifter using a selected signal assignment statement

```
library ieee;
use ieee.std_logic_1164.all;
entity barrel_shifter is
   port(
      a: in std_logic_vector(7 downto 0);
      amt: in std_logic_vector(2 downto 0);
      y: out std_logic_vector(7 downto 0)
   );
end barrel_shifter ;

architecture sel_arch of barrel_shifter is
begin
   with amt select
      y<= a                           when "000",
         a(0) & a(7 downto 1)         when "001",
         a(1 downto 0) & a(7 downto 2) when "010",
         a(2 downto 0) & a(7 downto 3) when "011",
         a(3 downto 0) & a(7 downto 4) when "100",
         a(4 downto 0) & a(7 downto 5) when "101",
         a(5 downto 0) & a(7 downto 6) when "110",
         a(6 downto 0) & a(7) when others; -- 111
end sel_arch;
```

While the code is straightforward, it will become cumbersome when the number of input bits increases. Furthermore, a large number of choices implies a wide multiplexer, which makes synthesis difficult and leads to a large propagation delay. Alternatively, we can construct the circuit by stages. In the nth stage, the input signal is either passed directly to output or rotated right by 2^n positions. The nth stage is controlled by the nth bit of the amt signal. Assume that the 3 bits of amt are $m_2m_1m_0$. The total rotated amount after three stages is $m_2 2^2 + m_1 2^1 + m_0 2^0$, which is the desired rotating amount. The code for this scheme is shown in Listing 3.17.

Listing 3.17 Barrel shifter using multi-stage shifts

```
architecture multi_stage_arch of barrel_shifter is
   signal s0, s1: std_logic_vector(7 downto 0);
begin
   -- stage 0, shift 0 or 1 bit
   s0 <= a(0) & a(7 downto 1) when amt(0)='1' else
         a;
   -- stage 1, shift 0 or 2 bits
   s1 <= s0(1 downto 0) & s0(7 downto 2) when amt(1)='1' else
         s0;
   -- stage 2, shift 0 or 4 bits
   y <= s1(3 downto 0) & s0(7 downto 4) when amt(2)='1' else
        s1;
end multi_stage_arch ;
```

Testing circuit To test the circuit, we can use the 8-bit switch for the a signal, three pushbutton switches for the amt signal, and the eight discrete LEDs for output. Instead of deriving a new constraint file for pin assignment, we create a new HDL file that wraps the barrel shifter circuit and maps its signals to the prototyping board's signals. The code is shown in Listing 3.18.

Listing 3.18 Barrel shifter testing circuit

```
library ieee;
use ieee.std_logic_1164.all;
use ieee.numeric_std.all;
entity shifter_test is
   port(
      sw: in std_logic_vector(7 downto 0);
      btn: in std_logic_vector(2 downto 0);
      led: out std_logic_vector(7 downto 0)
   );
end shifter_test;

architecture arch of shifter_test is
begin
   shift_unit: entity work.barrel_shifter(multi_stage_arch)
      port map(a=>sw, amt=>btn, y=>led);
end arch;
```

3.7.4 Simplified floating-point adder

Floating point is another format to represent a number. With the same number of bits, the range in floating-point format is much larger than that in signed integer format. Although VHDL has a built-in floating-point data type, it is too complex to be synthesized automatically.

		sort	align	add/sub	normalize
eg. 1	+0.54E3	-0.87E4	-0.87E4	-0.87E4	-0.87E4
	-0.87E4	+0.54E3	+0.05E4	+0.05E4	+0.05E4
				-0.82E4	-0.82E4
eg. 2	+0.54E3	-0.55E3	-0.55E3	-0.55E3	-0.55E3
	-0.55E3	+0.54E3	+0.54E3	+0.54E3	+0.54E3
				-0.01E3	-0.10E2
eg. 3	+0.54E0	-0.55E0	-0.55E0	-0.55E0	-0.55E0
	-0.55E0	+0.54E0	+0.54E0	+0.54E0	+0.54E0
				-0.01E0	-0.00E0
eg. 4	+0.56E3	+0.56E3	+0.56E3	+0.56E3	+0.56E3
	+0.52E3	+0.52E3	+0.52E3	+0.52E3	+0.52E3
				+1.07E3	+0.10E4

Figure 3.8 Floating-point addition examples.

Detailed discussion of floating-point representation is beyond the scope of this book. We use a simplified 13-bit format in this example and ignore the round-off error. The representation consists of a sign bit, s, which indicates the sign of the number (1 for negative); a 4-bit exponent field, e, which represents the exponent; and an 8-bit significand field, f, which represents the significand or the fraction. In this format, the value of a floating-point number is $(-1)^s * .f * 2^e$. The $.f * 2^e$ is the magnitude of the number and $(-1)^s$ is just a formal way to state that "s equal to 1 implies a negative number." Since the sign bit is separated from the rest of the number, floating-point representation can be considered as a variation of the sign-magnitude format.

We also make the following assumptions:

- Both exponent and significand fields are in unsigned format.
- The representation has to be either normalized or zero. *Normalized representation* means that the MSB of the significand field must be '1'. If the magnitude of the computation result is smaller than the smallest normalized nonzero magnitude, $0.10000000 * 2^{0000}$, it must be converted to zero.

Under these assumptions, the largest and smallest nonzero magnitudes are $0.11111111 * 2^{1111}$ and $0.10000000 * 2^{0000}$, and the range is about 2^{16} (i.e., $\frac{0.11111111*2^{1111}}{0.10000000*2^{0000}}$).

Our floating-point adder design follows the process of adding numbers manually in scientific notation. This process can best be explained by examples. We assume that the widths of the exponent and significand are 2 and 1 digits, respectively. Decimal format is used for clarity. The computations of several representative examples are shown in Figure 3.8. The computation is done in four major steps:

1. *Sorting*: puts the number with the larger magnitude on the top and the number with the smaller magnitude on the bottom (we call the sorted numbers "big number" and "small number").
2. *Alignment*: aligns the two numbers so they have the same exponent. This can be done by adjusting the exponent of the small number to match the exponent of the big

number. The significand of the small number has to shift to the right according to the difference in exponents.

3. *Addition/subtraction*: adds or subtracts the significands of two aligned numbers.
4. *Normalization*: adjusts the result to normalized format. Three types of normalization procedures may be needed:
   - After a subtraction, the result may contain leading zeros in front, as in example 2.
   - After a subtraction, the result may be too small to be normalized and thus needs to be converted to zero, as in example 3.
   - After an addition, the result may generate a carry-out bit, as in example 4.

Our binary floating-point adder design uses a similar algorithm. To simplify the implementation, we ignore the rounding. During alignment and normalization, the lower bits of the significand will be discarded when shifted out. The design is divided into four stages, each corresponding to a step in the foregoing algorithm. The suffixes, 'b', 's', 'a', 'r', and 'n', used in signal names are for "big number," "small number," "aligned number," "result of addition/subtraction," and "normalized number," respectively. The code is developed according to these stages, as shown in Listing 3.19.

Listing 3.19 Simplified floating-point adder

```
library ieee;
use ieee.std_logic_1164.all;
use ieee.numeric_std.all;
entity fp_adder is
   port (
      sign1, sign2: in  std_logic;
      exp1, exp2: in  std_logic_vector(3 downto 0);
      frac1, frac2: in  std_logic_vector(7 downto 0);
      sign_out: out std_logic;
      exp_out: out std_logic_vector(3 downto 0);
      frac_out: out std_logic_vector(7 downto 0)
   );
end fp_adder ;

architecture arch of fp_adder is
   -- suffix b, s, a, n for
   --        big, small, aligned, normalized number
   signal signb, signs: std_logic;
   signal expb, exps, expn: unsigned(3 downto 0);
   signal fracb, fracs, fraca, fracn: unsigned(7 downto 0);
   signal sum_norm: unsigned(7 downto 0);
   signal exp_diff: unsigned(3 downto 0);
   signal sum: unsigned(8 downto 0); --one extra for carry
   signal lead0: unsigned(2 downto 0);
begin
   -- 1st stage: sort to find the larger number
   process (sign1, sign2, exp1, exp2, frac1, frac2)
   begin
      if (exp1 & frac1) > (exp2 & frac2) then
         signb <= sign1;
         signs <= sign2;
         expb <= unsigned(exp1);
         exps <= unsigned(exp2);
```

```
         fracb <= unsigned(frac1);
         fracs <= unsigned(frac2);
      else
         signb <= sign2;
         signs <= sign1;
         expb <= unsigned(exp2);
         exps <= unsigned(exp1);
         fracb <= unsigned(frac2);
         fracs <= unsigned(frac1);
      end if;
   end process;

   -- 2nd stage: align smaller number
   exp_diff <= expb - exps;
   with exp_diff select
      fraca <=
         fracs                                when "0000",
         "0"        & fracs(7 downto 1) when "0001",
         "00"       & fracs(7 downto 2) when "0010",
         "000"      & fracs(7 downto 3) when "0011",
         "0000"     & fracs(7 downto 4) when "0100",
         "00000"    & fracs(7 downto 5) when "0101",
         "000000"   & fracs(7 downto 6) when "0110",
         "0000000" & fracs(7)             when "0111",
         "00000000"                       when others;

   -- 3rd stage: add/subtract
   sum <= ('0' & fracb) + ('0' & fraca) when signb=signs else
          ('0' & fracb) - ('0' & fraca);

   -- 4th stage: normalize
   -- count leading 0s
   lead0 <= "000" when (sum(7)='1') else
            "001" when (sum(6)='1') else
            "010" when (sum(5)='1') else
            "011" when (sum(4)='1') else
            "100" when (sum(3)='1') else
            "101" when (sum(2)='1') else
            "110" when (sum(1)='1') else
            "111";
   -- shift significand according to leading 0
   with lead0 select
      sum_norm <=
         sum(7 downto 0)                     when "000",
         sum(6 downto 0) & '0'              when "001",
         sum(5 downto 0) & "00"             when "010",
         sum(4 downto 0) & "000"            when "011",
         sum(3 downto 0) & "0000"           when "100",
         sum(2 downto 0) & "00000"          when "101",
         sum(1 downto 0) & "000000"         when "110",
         sum(0) &             "0000000" when others;

   -- normalize with special conditions
```

```
    process(sum,sum_norm,expb,lead0)
    begin
       if sum(8)='1' then -- w/ carry out; shift frac to right
          expn <= expb + 1;
          fracn <= sum(8 downto 1);
       elsif (lead0 > expb) then  -- too small to normalize;
          expn <= (others=>'0');  -- set to 0
          fracn <= (others=>'0');
       else
          expn <= expb - lead0;
          fracn <= sum_norm;
       end if;
    end process;

    -- form output
    sign_out <= signb;
    exp_out <= std_logic_vector(expn);
    frac_out <= std_logic_vector(fracn);
end arch;
```

The circuit in the first stage compares the magnitudes and routes the big number to the signb, expb, and fracb signals and the smaller number to the signs, exps, and fracs signals. The comparison is done between exp1&frac1 and exp2&frac2. It implies that the exponents are compared first, and if they are the same, the significands are compared.

The circuit in the second stage performs alignment. It first calculates the difference between the two exponents, which is expb-exps, and then shifts the significand, fracs, to the right by this amount. The aligned significand is labeled fraca. The circuit in the third stage performs sign-magnitude addition, similar to that in Section 3.7.2. Note that the operands are extended by 1 bit to accommodate the carry-out bit.

The circuit in the fourth stage performs normalization, which adjusts the result to make the final output conform to the normalized format. The normalization circuit is constructed in three segments. The first segment counts the number of leading zeros. It is somewhat like a priority encoder. The second segment shifts the significands to the left by the amount specified by the leading-zero counting circuit. The last segment checks the carry-out and zero conditions and generates the final normalized number.

Testing circuit The floating-point adder has two 13-bit input operands. Since the prototyping board has only one 8-bit switch and four 1-bit pushbuttons, it cannot provide enough number of physical inputs to test the circuit. To accommodate the 26 bits of the floating-point adder, we must create a testing circuit and assign constants or duplicated switch signals to the adder's input operands. An example is shown in Listing 3.20. It assigns one operand as constant and uses duplicated switch signals for the other operand. The addition result is passed to the hexadecimal decoders and the sign circuit and is shown on the seven-segment LED display.

Listing 3.20 Floating-point adder testing circuit

```
library ieee;
use ieee.std_logic_1164.all;
use ieee.numeric_std.all;
entity fp_adder_test is
   port(
```

```
      clk: in std_logic;
      sw: in std_logic_vector(7 downto 0);
      btn: in std_logic_vector(3 downto 0);
      an: out std_logic_vector(3 downto 0);
      sseg: out std_logic_vector(7 downto 0)
   );
end fp_adder_test;

architecture arch of fp_adder_test is
   signal sign1, sign2: std_logic;
   signal exp1, exp2: std_logic_vector(3 downto 0);
   signal frac1, frac2: std_logic_vector(7 downto 0);
   signal sign_out: std_logic;
   signal exp_out: std_logic_vector(3 downto 0);
   signal frac_out: std_logic_vector(7 downto 0);
   signal led3, led2, led1, led0:
          std_logic_vector(7 downto 0);
begin
   -- set up the fp adder input signals
   sign1 <= '0';
   exp1 <= "1000";
   frac1<= '1' &  sw(1) & sw(0) & "10101";
   sign2 <= sw(7);
   exp2 <= btn;
   frac2 <= '1' & sw(6 downto 0);

   -- instantiate fp adder
   fp_add_unit: entity work.fp_adder
      port map(
         sign1=>sign1, sign2=>sign2, exp1=>exp1, exp2=>exp2,
         frac1=>frac1, frac2=>frac2,
         sign_out=>sign_out, exp_out=>exp_out,
         frac_out=>frac_out
      );

   -- instantiate three instances of hex decoders
   -- exponent
   sseg_unit_0: entity work.hex_to_sseg
      port map(hex=>exp_out, dp=>'0', sseg=>led0);
   -- 4 LSBs of fraction
   sseg_unit_1: entity work.hex_to_sseg
      port map(hex=>frac_out(3 downto 0),
               dp=>'1', sseg=>led1);
   -- 4 MSBs of fraction
   sseg_unit_2: entity work.hex_to_sseg
      port map(hex=>frac_out(7 downto 4),
               dp=>'0', sseg=>led2);
   -- sign
   led3 <= "11111110" when sign_out='1' else -- middle bar
           "11111111";                       -- blank

   -- instantiate 7-seg LED display time-multiplexing module
   disp_unit: entity work.disp_mux
```

```
      port map(
         clk=>clk, reset=>'0',
         in0=>led0, in1=>led1, in2=>led2, in3=>led3,
         an=>an, sseg=>sseg
      );
end arch;
```

3.8 BIBLIOGRAPHIC NOTES

The Designer's Guide to VHDL by P. J. Ashenden provides detailed coverage on the VHDL constructs discussed in this chapter, and the author's *RTL Hardware Design Using VHDL: Coding for Efficiency, Portability, and Scalability* discusses the coding and optimization schemes and gives additional design examples.

3.9 SUGGESTED EXPERIMENTS

3.9.1 Multi-function barrel shifter

Consider an 8-bit shifting circuit that can perform rotating right or rotating left. An additional 1-bit control signal, `lr`, specifies the desired direction.

1. Design the circuit using one rotate-right circuit, one rotate-left circuit, and one 2-to-1 multiplexer to select the desired result. Derive the code.
2. Derive a testbench and use simulation to verify operation of the code.
3. Synthesize the circuit, program the FPGA, and verify its operation.
4. This circuit can also be implemented by one rotate-right shifter with pre- and post-reversing circuits. The reversing circuit either passes the original input or reverses the input bitwise (for example, if an 8-bit input is $a_7a_6a_5a_4a_3a_2a_1a_0$, the reversed result becomes $a_0a_1a_2a_3a_5a_5a_6a_7$). Repeat steps 2 and 3.
5. Check the report files and compare the number of logic cells and propagation delays of the two designs.
6. Expand the code for a 16-bit circuit and synthesize the code. Repeat steps 1 to 5.
7. Expand the code for a 32-bit circuit and synthesize the code. Repeat steps 1 to 5.

3.9.2 Dual-priority encoder

A dual-priority encoder returns the codes of the highest or second-highest priority requests. The input is a 12-bit `req` signal and the outputs are `first` and `second`, which are the 4-bit binary codes of the highest and second-highest priority requests, respectively.

1. Design the circuit and derive the code.
2. Derive a testbench and use simulation to verify operation of the code.
3. Design a testing circuit that displays the two output codes on the seven-segment LED display of the prototyping board, and derive the code.
4. Synthesize the circuit, program the FPGA, and verify its operation.

3.9.3 BCD incrementor

The binary-coded-decimal (BCD) format uses 4 bits to represent 10 decimal digits. For example, 259_{10} is represented as "0010 0101 1001" in BCD format. A BCD incrementor adds 1 to a number in BCD format. For example, after incrementing, "0010 0101 1001" (i.e., 259_{10}) becomes "0010 0110 0000" (i.e., 260_{10}).

1. Design a three-digit 12-bit incrementor and derive the code.
2. Derive a testbench and use simulation to verify operation of the code.
3. Design a testing circuit that displays three digits on the seven-segment LED display and derive the code.
4. Synthesize the circuit, program the FPGA, and verify its operation.

3.9.4 Floating-point greater-than circuit

A floating-point greater-than circuit compares two floating-point numbers and asserts output, `gt`, when the first number is larger than the second number. Assume that the two numbers are represented in the format discussed in Section 3.7.4.

1. Design the circuit and derive the code.
2. Derive a testbench and use simulation to verify operation of the code.
3. Design a testing circuit and derive the code.
4. Synthesize the circuit, program the FPGA, and verify its operation.

3.9.5 Floating-point and signed integer conversion circuit

A number may need to be converted to different formats in a large system. Assume that we use the 13-bit format in Section 3.7.4 for the floating-point representation and the 8-bit `signed` data type for the integer representation. An integer-to-floating-point conversion circuit converts an 8-bit integer input to a normalized, 13-bit floating-point output. A floating-point-to-integer conversion circuit reverses the operation. Since the range of a floating-point number is much larger, conversion may lead to the underflow condition (i.e., the magnitude of the converted number is smaller than "00000001") or the overflow condition (i.e., the magnitude of the converted number is larger than "01111111").

1. Design an integer-to-floating-point conversion circuit and derive the code.
2. Derive a testbench and use simulation to verify operation of the code.
3. Design a testing circuit and derive the code.
4. Synthesize the circuit, program the FPGA, and verify its operation.
5. Design a floating-point-to-integer conversion circuit. In addition to the 8-bit integer output, the design should include two status signals, `uf` and `of`, for the underflow and overflow conditions. Derive the code and repeat steps 2 to 4.

3.9.6 Enhanced floating-point adder

The floating-point adder in Section 3.7.4 discards the lower bits when they are shifted out (it is known as *round to zero*). A more accurate method is to *round to the nearest even*, as defined in the *IEEE Standard for Binary Floating-Point Arithmetic* (IEEE Std 754). Three extra bits, known as the *guard*, *round*, and *sticky bits*, are required to implement this method. If you learned floating-point arithmetic before, modify the floating-point adder in Section 3.7.4 to accommodate the round-to-the-nearest-even method.

CHAPTER 4

REGULAR SEQUENTIAL CIRCUIT

4.1 INTRODUCTION

A sequential circuit is a circuit with *memory*, which forms the *internal state* of the circuit. Unlike a combinational circuit, in which the output is a function of input only, the output of a sequential circuit is a function of the input and the internal state. The *synchronous design methodology* is the most commonly used practice in designing a sequential circuit. In this methodology, all storage elements are controlled (i.e., synchronized) by a global clock signal and the data is sampled and stored at the rising or falling edge of the clock signal. It allows designers to separate the storage components from the circuit and greatly simplifies the development process. This methodology is the most important principle in developing a large, complex digital system and is the foundation of most synthesis, verification, and testing algorithms. All of the designs in the book follow this methodology.

4.1.1 D FF and register

The most basic storage component in a sequential circuit is a D-type flip-flop (D FF). The symbol and function table of a positive edge-triggered D FF are shown in Figure 4.1(a). The value of the `d` signal is sampled at the rising edge of the `clk` signal and stored to FF. A D FF may contain an asynchronous reset signal to clear the FF to '0'. Its symbol and function table are shown in Figure 4.1(b). Note that the reset operation is independent of the clock signal.

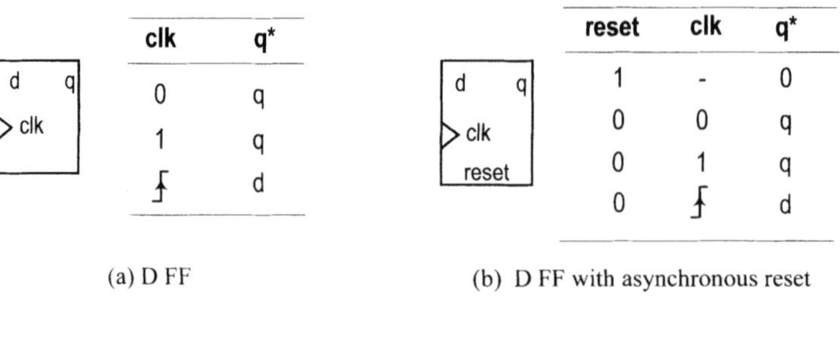

clk	q*
0	q
1	q
⨍	d

(a) D FF

reset	clk	q*
1	-	0
0	0	q
0	1	q
0	⨍	d

(b) D FF with asynchronous reset

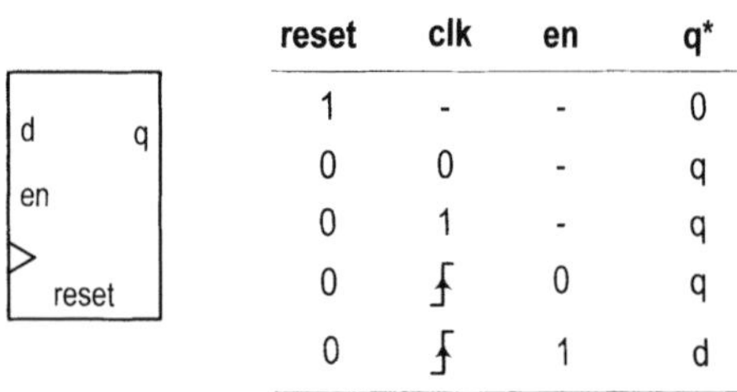

reset	clk	en	q*
1	-	-	0
0	0	-	q
0	1	-	q
0	⨍	0	q
0	⨍	1	d

(c) D FF with synchronous enable

Figure 4.1 Block diagram and functional table of a D FF.

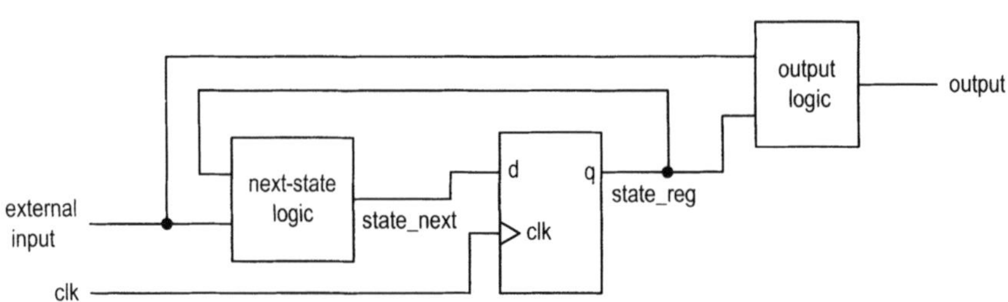

Figure 4.2 Block diagram of a synchronous system.

The three main timing parameters of a D FF are T_{cq} (clock-to-q delay), T_{setup} (setup time), and T_{hold} (hold time). T_{cq} is the time required to propagate the value of d to q at the rising edge of the clock signal. The d signal must be stable around the sampling edge to prevent the FF from entering the metastable state. T_{setup} and T_{hold} specify the time intervals before or after the sampling edge.

A D FF provides 1-bit storage. A collection of D FFs can be grouped together to store multiple bits and is known as a *register*.

4.1.2 Synchronous system

Block diagram The block diagram of a synchronous system is shown in Figure 4.2. It consists of the following parts:

- *State register*: a collection of D FFs controlled by the same clock signal

- *Next-state logic*: combinational logic that uses the external input and internal state (i.e., the output of register) to determine the new value of the register
- *Output logic*: combinational logic that generates the output signal

Maximal operating frequency One of the most difficult design aspects of a sequential circuit is to ensure that the system timing does not violate the setup and hold time constraints. In a synchronous system, the storage components are grouped together and treated as a single register, as shown in Figure 4.2. We need to perform timing analysis on only one memory component.

The timing of a sequential circuit is characterized by f_{max}, *the maximal clock frequency*, which specifies how fast the circuit can operate. The reciprocal of f_{max} specifies T_{clock}, the minimal clock period, which can be interpreted as the interval between two sampling edges of the clock. To ensure correct operation, the next value must be generated and stabilized within this interval. Assume that the maximal propagation delay of next-state logic is T_{comb}. The minimal clock period can be obtained by adding the propagation delays and setup time constraint of the closed loop in Figure 4.2:

$$T_{clock} = T_{cq} + T_{comb} + T_{setup}$$

and the maximal clock rate is the reciprocal:

$$f_{max} = \frac{1}{T_{clock}} = \frac{1}{T_{cq} + T_{comb} + T_{setup}}$$

Timing constraint in Xilinx ISE$^{Xilinx\ specific}$ During synthesis, Xilinx software will analyze the synthesized circuit and show f_{max} in a report. We can also specify the desired operating frequency as a synthesis constraint, and the synthesis software will try to obtain a circuit to satisfy this requirement (i.e., a circuit whose f_{max} is equal to or greater than the desired operating frequency). For example, if we use the 50-MHz (i.e., 20-ns period) oscillator on the prototyping board as the clock source, f_{max} of a sequential circuit must exceed this frequency (i.e., the period must be smaller than 20 ns). The following lines can be added to the constraint file:

```
NET "clk" TNM_NET = "clk";
TIMESPEC "TS_clk" = PERIOD "clk" 20 ns HIGH 50 %;
```

This indicates that the `clk` signal has a maximal period of 20 ns (i.e., 50 MHz) and a duty cycle of 50%.

After synthesis, we can check the relevant timing information by invoking the View Design Summary process from the ISE's Processes window. The Timing Constraints section shows whether the imposed constraints are met, and the Static Timing Report section provides more detailed timing information.

4.1.3 Code development

Our code development follows the basic block diagram in Figure 4.2. The key is to separate the memory component (i.e., the register) from the system. Once the register is isolated, the remaining portion is a pure combinational circuit, and the coding and analysis schemes discussed in previous chapters can be applied accordingly. While this approach may make the code a little bit more cumbersome at times, it helps us to better visualize the circuit architecture and avoid unintended memory and subtle mistakes.

Based on the characteristics of the next-state logic, we divide sequential circuits into three categories:

- *Regular sequential circuit*. The state transitions in the circuit exhibit a "regular" pattern, as in a counter or shift register. The next-state logic is constructed primarily by a predesigned, "regular" component, such as an incrementor or shifter.
- *FSM*. The state transitions in the circuit do not exhibit a simple, repetitive pattern. The next-state logic is constructed by "random logic" and synthesized from scratch. It should be called a random sequential circuit, but is commonly known as an FSM (*finite state machine*).
- *FSMD*. The circuit consists of a regular sequential circuit and an FSM. The two parts are known as a *data path* and a *control path*, and the complete circuit is known as an FSMD (*FSM with data path*). This type of circuit is used to implement an algorithm represented by *register-transfer* (RT) methodology, which describes system operation by a sequence of data transfers and manipulations among registers.

The three types of circuits are discussed in this and two subsequent chapters.

4.2 HDL CODE OF THE FF AND REGISTER

Describing storage components in HDL is a subtle procedure, and there are many ways to do it. In fact, one common problem encountered by a new HDL user is the inference of unintended latches and buffers. Instead of covering all possible forms of syntactic descriptions, we introduce the code segments for several commonly used memory components. Since our development process separates the register and the combinational circuit, these components are sufficient for all designs in this book. The components are:

- D FF
- Register
- Register file

4.2.1 D FF

We consider three types of D FFs:

- D FF without asynchronous reset
- D FF with asynchronous reset
- D FF with synchronous enable

The first two are the most basic memory components and can be found in the library of any device technology. The third can be constructed from a simple D FF. We include the code since it is a frequently used memory component and can be mapped to the FF of the Spartan-3 device's logic cell.

D FF without asynchronous reset The function table of a D FF is shown in Figure 4.1(a) and the code is shown in Listing 4.1.

Listing 4.1 D FF without asynchronous reset

```
library ieee;
use ieee.std_logic_1164.all;
entity d_ff is
   port(
      clk: in std_logic;
```

```
      d: in std_logic;
      q: out std_logic
   );
end d_ff;

architecture arch of d_ff is
begin
   process(clk)
   begin
      if (clk'event and clk='1') then
         q <= d;
      end if;
   end process;
end arch;
```

The rising edge is checked by the `clk'event and clk='1'` expression, which represents that there is a change in the `clk` signal (i.e., an "event") and the new value is '1'. If this condition is `true`, the value of `d` is stored to `q`, and if this condition is `false`, `q` keeps its previous value (i.e., memorizes the value sampled earlier). Note that only the `clk` signal is included in the sensitive list. This is consistent with the fact that the `d` signal is sampled only at the rising edge of the `clk` signal, and change in its value does not trigger any immediate response.

D FF with asynchronous reset A D FF may contain an asynchronous reset signal, as shown in the function table of Figure 4.1(b). The signal clears the D FF to '0' any time and is not controlled by the clock signal. It actually has a higher priority than the regularly sampled input. Using an asynchronous reset signal violates the synchronous design methodology and thus should be avoided in normal operation. Its major application is to perform system initialization. For example, we can generate a short reset pulse to force a system to an initial state after turning on the power. The code for a D FF with asynchronous reset is shown in Listing 4.2.

Listing 4.2 D FF with asynchronous reset

```
library ieee;
use ieee.std_logic_1164.all;
entity d_ff_reset is
   port(
      clk, reset: in std_logic;
      d: in std_logic;
      q: out std_logic
   );
end d_ff_reset;

architecture arch of d_ff_reset is
begin
   process(clk,reset)
   begin
      if (reset='1') then
         q <='0';
      elsif (clk'event and clk='1') then
         q <= d;
      end if;
```

```
   end process;
end arch;
```

Note that the `reset` signal is included in the sensitivity list, and its condition is checked before the rising-edge condition.

D FF with synchronous enable A D FF may include an additional control signal, en, to enable the FF to sample the input value. Its symbol and functional table are shown in Figure 4.1(c). Note that the en signal is examined only at the rising edge of the clock and thus is synchronous. If it is not asserted, the FF keeps its previous value. The code is shown in Listing 4.3.

Listing 4.3 One-process coding style for a D FF with synchronous enable

```
library ieee;
use ieee.std_logic_1164.all;
entity d_ff_en is
   port(
      clk, reset: in std_logic;
      en: in std_logic;
      d: in std_logic;
      q: out std_logic
   );
end d_ff_en;

architecture arch of d_ff_en is
begin
   process(clk,reset)
   begin
      if (reset='1') then
         q <='0';
      elsif (clk'event and clk='1') then
         if (en='1') then
            q <= d;
         end if;
      end if;
   end process;
end arch;
```

The enabling feature of this D FF is useful in maintaining synchronism between a fast subsystem and a slow subsystem. For example, assume that the operation rates of a fast and a slow subsystem are 50 MHz and 1 MHz. Instead of using a derived 1-MHz clock to drive the slow subsystem, we can generate a periodic enable tick that is asserted one clock cycle every 50 clock cycles. The slow subsystem is disabled (i.e., keep the previous state) for the remaining 49 clock cycles. The same scheme can also be applied to eliminate a gated clock signal.

Since the enable signal is synchronous, this circuit can be constructed by a regular D FF and simple next-state logic. The code is shown in Listing 4.4, and its block diagram is shown in Figure 4.3.

Listing 4.4 Two-segment coding style for a D FF with synchronous enable

```
architecture two_seg_arch of d_ff_en is
   signal r_reg, r_next: std_logic;
```

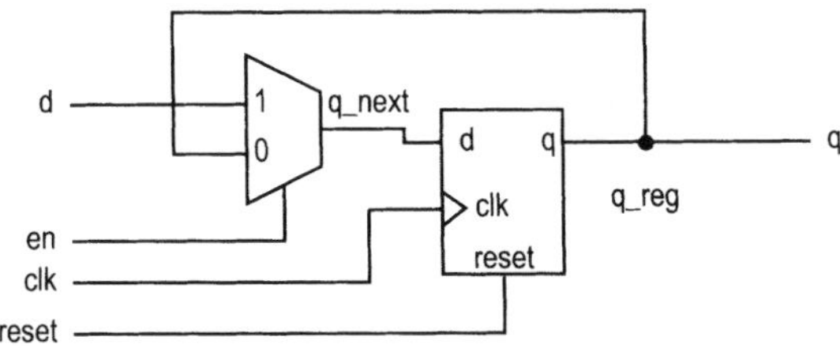

Figure 4.3 D FF with synchronous enable.

```
begin
   -- D FF
   process(clk,reset)
   begin
      if (reset='1') then
         r_reg <='0';
      elsif (clk'event and clk='1') then
         r_reg <= r_next;
      end if;
   end process;
   -- next-state logic
   r_next <= d when en ='1' else
             r_reg;
   -- output logic
   q <= r_reg;
end two_seg_arch;
```

For clarity, we use suffixes `_next` and `_reg` to emphasize the next input value and the registered output of an FF. They are connected to the d and q signals of a D FF. The earlier one-process code can be considered as shorthand for this more explicit description.

4.2.2 Register

A register is a collection of D FFs that are controlled by the same clock and reset signals. Like a D FF, a register can have an optional asynchronous reset signal and a synchronous enable signal. The code is identical to that of a D FF except that the array data type, `std_logic_vector`, is needed for the relevant input and output signals. For example, an 8-bit register with asynchronous reset is shown in Listing 4.5.

Listing 4.5 Register

```
library ieee;
use ieee.std_logic_1164.all;
entity reg_reset is
   port(
      clk, reset: in std_logic;
      d: in std_logic_vector(7 downto 0);
      q: out std_logic_vector(7 downto 0)
   );
end reg_reset;

```

```
architecture arch of reg_reset is
begin
   process(clk,reset)
   begin
      if (reset='1') then
         q <=(others=>'0');
      elsif (clk'event and clk='1') then
         q <= d;
      end if;
   end process;
end arch;
```

Note that the expression (**others**=>'0') means that all elements are assigned to '0' and is equivalent to "00000000" in this case.

4.2.3 Register file

A register file is a collection of registers with one input port and one or more output ports. The write address signal, w_addr, specifies where to store data, and the read address signal, r_addr, specifies where to retrieve data. The register file is generally used as fast, temporary storage. The code for a parameterized 2^W-by-B register file is shown in Listing 4.6. Two generics are defined in this design. The W generic specifies the number of address bits, which implies that there are 2^W words in the file, and the B generic specifies the number of bits in a word.

Listing 4.6 Parameterized register file

```
library ieee;
use ieee.std_logic_1164.all;
use ieee.numeric_std.all;
entity reg_file is
   generic(
      B: integer:=8; -- number of bits
      W: integer:=2  -- number of address bits
   );
   port(
      clk, reset: in std_logic;
      wr_en: in std_logic;
      w_addr, r_addr: in std_logic_vector (W-1 downto 0);
      w_data: in std_logic_vector (B-1 downto 0);
      r_data: out std_logic_vector (B-1 downto 0)
   );
end reg_file;

architecture arch of reg_file is
   type reg_file_type is array (2**W-1 downto 0) of
        std_logic_vector(B-1 downto 0);
   signal array_reg: reg_file_type;
begin
   process(clk,reset)
   begin
      if (reset='1') then
         array_reg <= (others=>(others=>'0'));
```

```
      elsif (clk'event and clk='1') then
         if wr_en='1' then
            array_reg(to_integer(unsigned(w_addr))) <= w_data;
         end if;
      end if;
   end process;
   -- read port
   r_data <= array_reg(to_integer(unsigned(r_addr)));
end arch;
```

The code includes several new features. First, since no built-in two-dimensional array is defined in the `std_logic_1164` package a user-defined array-of-array data type, `reg_file_type`, is introduced. It is first defined by a type statement and is then used by the `array_reg` signal. Second, a signal is used as an index to access an element in the array, as in `array_reg(..w_addr..)`. Although the description is very abstract, Xilinx software recognizes this language construct and can derive the correct implementation accordingly. The `array_reg(...) <= ...` and `... <= array_reg(...)` statements infer decoding and multiplexing logic, respectively.

Some applications may need to retrieve multiple data words at the same time. This can be done by adding an additional read port:

```
r_data2 <= array_reg(to_integer(unsigned(r_addr_2)));
```

4.2.4 Storage components in a Spartan-3 device$^{Xilinx\ specific}$

In a Spartan-3 device, each logic cell contains a D FF with asynchronous reset and synchronous enable. These D FFs basically constitute the register of Figure 4.2. Since a logic cell also contains a four-input LUT, it will be wasteful if the cell is just used simply as 1 bit of a massive storage. The Spartan-3 device also has distributed RAM (random access memory) and block RAM modules, and they can be used for larger storage requirements. These modules can be configured for synchronous operation, and their characteristics are somewhat like a restricted version of the register file. The configuration and inference of these modules are discussed in Chapter 11.

4.3 SIMPLE DESIGN EXAMPLES

We illustrate the construction of several simple, representative sequential circuits in this section.

4.3.1 Shift register

Free-running shift register A free-running shift register shifts its content to the left or right by one position in each clock cycle. There is no other control signal. The code for an N-bit free-running shift-right register is shown in Listing 4.7.

Listing 4.7 Free-running shift register

```
library ieee;
use ieee.std_logic_1164.all;
entity free_run_shift_reg is
```

```
   generic(N: integer := 8);
   port(
      clk, reset: in std_logic;
      s_in: in std_logic;
      s_out: out std_logic
   );
end free_run_shift_reg;

architecture arch of free_run_shift_reg is
   signal r_reg: std_logic_vector(N-1 downto 0);
   signal r_next: std_logic_vector(N-1 downto 0);
begin
   -- register
   process(clk,reset)
   begin
      if (reset='1') then
         r_reg <= (others=>'0');
      elsif (clk'event and clk='1') then
         r_reg <= r_next;
      end if;
   end process;
   -- next-state logic (shift right 1 bit)
   r_next <= s_in & r_reg(N-1 downto 1);
   -- output
   s_out <= r_reg(0);
end arch;
```

The next-state logic is a 1-bit shifter, which shifts r_reg right one position and inserts the serial input, s_in, to the MSB. Since the 1-bit shifter involves only reconnection of the input and output signals, no real logic is needed. Its propagation delay represents the smallest possible T_{comb}, and the corresponding f_{max} represents the highest clock rate that can be achieved for a given device technology.

Universal shift register A universal shift register can load parallel data, shift its content left or right, or remain in the same state. It can perform parallel-to-serial operation (first loading parallel input and then shifting) or serial-to-parallel operation (first shifting and then retrieving parallel output). The desired operation is specified by a 2-bit control signal, ctrl. The code is shown in Listing 4.8.

Listing 4.8 Universal shift register

```
library ieee;
use ieee.std_logic_1164.all;
entity univ_shift_reg is
   generic(N: integer := 8);
   port(
      clk, reset: in std_logic;
      ctrl: in std_logic_vector(1 downto 0);
      d: in std_logic_vector(N-1 downto 0);
      q: out std_logic_vector(N-1 downto 0)
   );
end univ_shift_reg;

architecture arch of univ_shift_reg is
```

```
   signal r_reg: std_logic_vector(N-1 downto 0);
   signal r_next: std_logic_vector(N-1 downto 0);
begin
   -- register
   process(clk,reset)
   begin
      if (reset='1') then
         r_reg <= (others=>'0');
      elsif (clk'event and clk='1') then
         r_reg <= r_next;
      end if;
   end process;
   -- next-state logic
   with ctrl select
    r_next <=
      r_reg                        when "00", --no op
      r_reg(N-2 downto 0) & d(0)   when "01", --shift left;
      d(N-1) & r_reg(N-1 downto 1) when "10", --shift right;
      d                            when others; -- load
   -- output
   q <= r_reg;
end arch;
```

The next-state logic uses a 4-to-1 multiplexer to select the desired next value of the register. Note that the LSB and MSB of d (i.e., d(0) and d(N-1)) are used as serial input for the shift-left and shift-right operations.

In a Xilinx Spartan-3 device, a logic cell's 4-input LUT is implemented by a 16-by-1 SRAM. The same SRAM can also be configured as a cascading chain of sixteen 1-bit SRAM cells, which resembles a 16-bit shift register. This can be used to construct certain forms of shift register and leads to very efficient implementation.

Xilinx specific

4.3.2 Binary counter and variant

Free-running binary counter A free-running binary counter circulates through a binary sequence repeatedly. For example, a 4-bit binary counter counts from "0000", "0001", . . ., to "1111" and wraps around. The code for a parameterized N-bit free-running binary counter is shown in Listing 4.9.

Listing 4.9 Free-running binary counter

```
library ieee;
use ieee.std_logic_1164.all;
use ieee.numeric_std.all;
entity free_run_bin_counter is
   generic(N: integer := 8);
   port(
      clk, reset: in std_logic;
      max_tick: out std_logic;
      q: out std_logic_vector(N-1 downto 0)
   );
end free_run_bin_counter;

architecture arch of free_run_bin_counter is
```

Table 4.1 Function table of a universal binary counter

syn_clr	load	en	up	q*	**Operation**
1	–	–	–	00···00	synchronous clear
0	1	–	–	d	parallel load
0	0	1	1	q+1	count up
0	0	1	0	q-1	count down
0	0	0	–	q	pause

```
   signal r_reg: unsigned(N-1 downto 0);
   signal r_next: unsigned(N-1 downto 0);
begin
   -- register
   process(clk,reset)
   begin
      if (reset='1') then
         r_reg <= (others=>'0');
      elsif (clk'event and clk='1') then
         r_reg <= r_next;
      end if;
   end process;
   -- next-state logic
   r_next <= r_reg + 1;
   -- output logic
   q <= std_logic_vector(r_reg);
   max_tick <= '1' when r_reg=(2**N-1) else '0';
end arch;
```

The next-state logic is an incrementor, which adds 1 to the register's current value. By definition of the + operator in the IEEE numeric_std package, the operation implicitly wraps around after the r_reg reaches "1...1". The circuit also consists of an output status signal, max_tick, which is asserted when the counter reaches the maximal value, "1...1" (which is equal to $2^N - 1$).

The max_tick signal represents a special type of signal that is asserted for a single clock cycle. In this book, we call this type of signal a *tick* and use the suffix _tick to indicate a signal with this property. It is commonly used to interface with the enable signal of other sequential circuits.

Universal binary counter A universal binary counter is more versatile. It can count up or down, pause, be loaded with a specific value, or be synchronously cleared. Its functions are summarized in Table 4.1. Note the difference between the reset and syn_clr signals. The former is asynchronous and should only be used for system initialization. The latter is sampled at the rising edge of the clock and can be used in normal synchronous design. The code for this counter is shown in Listing 4.10.

Listing 4.10 Universal binary counter

```
library ieee;
use ieee.std_logic_1164.all;
use ieee.numeric_std.all;
entity univ_bin_counter is
```

```
   generic(N: integer := 8);
   port(
      clk, reset: in std_logic;
      syn_clr, load, en, up: in std_logic;
      d: in std_logic_vector(N-1 downto 0);
      max_tick, min_tick: out std_logic;
      q: out std_logic_vector(N-1 downto 0)
   );
end univ_bin_counter;

architecture arch of univ_bin_counter is
   signal r_reg: unsigned(N-1 downto 0);
   signal r_next: unsigned(N-1 downto 0);
begin
   -- register
   process(clk,reset)
   begin
      if (reset='1') then
         r_reg <= (others=>'0');
      elsif (clk'event and clk='1') then
         r_reg <= r_next;
      end if;
   end process;
   -- next-state logic
   r_next <= (others=>'0') when syn_clr='1' else
             unsigned(d)    when load='1' else
             r_reg + 1      when en ='1' and up='1' else
             r_reg - 1      when en ='1' and up='0' else
             r_reg;
   -- output logic
   q <= std_logic_vector(r_reg);
   max_tick <= '1' when r_reg=(2**N-1) else '0';
   min_tick <= '1' when r_reg=0 else '0';
end arch;
```

The next-state logic follows the function table and uses a conditional signal assignment to prioritize the desired operations.

Mod-m counter A mod-m counter counts from 0 to $m - 1$ and wraps around. A parameterized mod-m counter is shown in Listing 4.11. It has two generics. One is M, which specifies the limit, m, and the other is N, which specifies the number of bits needed and should be equal to $\lceil \log_2 M \rceil$. The code is shown in Listing 4.11, and the default value is for a mod-10 counter.

Listing 4.11 Mod-m counter

```
library ieee;
use ieee.std_logic_1164.all;
use ieee.numeric_std.all;
entity mod_m_counter is
   generic(
      N: integer := 4;     -- number of bits
      M: integer := 10     -- mod-M
   );
```

```
   port(
      clk, reset: in std_logic;
      max_tick: out std_logic;
      q: out std_logic_vector(N-1 downto 0)
   );
end mod_m_counter;

architecture arch of mod_m_counter is
   signal r_reg: unsigned(N-1 downto 0);
   signal r_next: unsigned(N-1 downto 0);
begin
   -- register
   process(clk,reset)
   begin
      if (reset='1') then
         r_reg <= (others=>'0');
      elsif (clk'event and clk='1') then
         r_reg <= r_next;
      end if;
   end process;
   -- next-state logic
   r_next <= (others=>'0') when r_reg=(M-1) else
             r_reg + 1;
   -- output logic
   q <= std_logic_vector(r_reg);
   max_tick <= '1' when r_reg=(M-1) else '0';
end arch;
```

The next-state logic is constructed by a conditional signal assignment statement. If the counter reaches M-1, the new value is cleared to 0. Otherwise, it is incremented by 1.

Inclusion of the N parameter in the code is somewhat redundant since its value depends on M. A more elegant way is to define a function that calculates N from M automatically. In VHDL, this can be done by creating a user-defined *function* in a *package* and invoking the package before the entity declaration. This is beyond the scope of this book and the details may be found in the references cited in the Bibliographic section.

4.4 TESTBENCH FOR SEQUENTIAL CIRCUITS

A testbench is a program that mimics a physical lab bench, as discussed in Section 1.4. Developing a comprehensive testbench is beyond the scope of this book. We discuss a simple testbench for the previous universal binary counter in this section. It can serve as a template for other sequential circuits. The code for the testbench is shown in Listing 4.12.

Listing 4.12 Testbench for a universal binary counter

```
library ieee;
use ieee.std_logic_1164.all;

entity bin_counter_tb is
end bin_counter_tb;

architecture arch of bin_counter_tb is
```

```
   constant THREE: integer := 3;
   constant T: time := 20 ns; -- clk period
   signal clk, reset: std_logic;
   signal syn_clr, load, en, up: std_logic;
   signal d: std_logic_vector(THREE-1 downto 0);
   signal max_tick, min_tick: std_logic;
   signal q: std_logic_vector(THREE-1 downto 0);
begin
   --**************************
   -- instantiation
   --**************************
   counter_unit: entity work.univ_bin_counter(arch)
      generic map(N=>THREE)
      port map(clk=>clk, reset=>reset, syn_clr=>syn_clr,
               load=>load, en=>en, up=>up, d=>d,
               max_tick=>max_tick, min_tick=>min_tick, q=>q);

   --**************************
   -- clock
   --**************************
   -- 20 ns clock running forever
   process
   begin
      clk <= '0';
      wait for T/2;
      clk <= '1';
      wait for T/2;
   end process;
   --**************************
   -- reset
   --**************************
   -- reset asserted for T/2
   reset <= '1', '0' after T/2;

   --**************************
   -- other stimulus
   --**************************
   process
   begin
      --**************************
      -- initial input
      --**************************
      syn_clr <= '0';
      load <= '0';
      en <= '0';
      up <= '1';  -- count up
      d <= (others=>'0');
      wait until falling_edge(clk);
      wait until falling_edge(clk);
      --**************************
      -- test load
      --**************************
      load <= '1';
```

```
d <= "011";
wait until falling_edge(clk);
load <= '0';
-- pause 2 clocks
wait until falling_edge(clk);
wait until falling_edge(clk);
--************************
-- test syn_clear
--************************
syn_clr <= '1';  -- clear
wait until falling_edge(clk);
syn_clr <= '0';
--************************
-- test up counter and pause
--************************
en <= '1'; -- count
up <= '1';
for i in 1 to 10 loop -- count 10 clocks
   wait until falling_edge(clk);
end loop;
en <='0';
wait until falling_edge(clk);
wait until falling_edge(clk);
en <='1';
wait until falling_edge(clk);
wait until falling_edge(clk);
--************************
-- test down counter
--************************
up <= '0';
for i in 1 to 10 loop -- run 10 clocks
   wait until falling_edge(clk);
end loop;
--************************
-- other wait conditions
--************************
-- continue until q=2
wait until q="010";
wait until falling_edge(clk);
up <= '1';
-- continue until min_tick changes value
wait on min_tick;
wait until falling_edge(clk);
up <= '0';
wait for 4*T;  -- wait for 80 ns
en <= '0';
wait for 4*T;
--************************
-- terminate simulation
--************************
assert false
   report "Simulation Completed"
 severity failure;
```

```
   end process ;
end arch;
```

The code consists of a component instantiation statement, which creates an instance of a 3-bit counter, and three segments, which generate a stimulus for clock, reset, and regular inputs. Since operation of a synchronous system is synchronized by a clock signal, we define a constant with the built-in data type `time` for the clock period:

```
constant T: time := 20 ns; -- clk period
```

The clock generation is specified by a process:

```
process
begin
   clk <= '0';
   wait for T/2;
   clk <= '1';
   wait for T/2;
end process;
```

The `clk` signal is assigned between '0' and '1' alternatively, and each value lasts for half a period. Note that the process has no sensitivity list and repeats itself forever.

The reset stimulus involves one statement,

```
reset <= '1', '0' after T/2;
```

It indicates that the `reset` signal is set to '1' initially and changed to '0' after half a period. The statement represents the "power-on" condition, in which the `reset` signal is asserted momentarily to clear the system to the initial state. Note that, by default, the `'U'` value (for uninitialized), not `'0'`, is assigned to a signal with the `std_logic` type. Using a short reset pulse is a good mechanism to perform system initialization.

The last process statement generates a stimulus for other input signals. We first test the load and clear operations and then exercise counting in both directions. The final **assert** `false` statement forces the simulator to terminate simulation, as discussed in Section 2.7.

For a synchronous system with positive edge-triggered FFs, an input signal must be stable around the rising edge of the clock signal to satisfy the setup and hold time constraints. One easy way to achieve this is to change an input signal's value during the '1'-to-'0' transition of the `clk` signal. The `falling_edge` function of the `std_logic_1164` package checks this condition, and we can use it in a wait statement:

```
wait until falling_edge(clk);
```

Note that each statement represents a new falling edge, which corresponds to the advancement of one clock cycle. In our template, we generally use this statement to specify the progress of time. For multiple clock cycles, we can use a loop statement:

```
for i in 1 to 10 loop -- count 10 clocks
   wait until falling_edge(clk);
end loop;
```

There are other useful forms of wait statements, as shown at the end of the process. We can wait until a special condition, such as "when q is equal to 2",

```
wait until q="010";
```

or wait until a signal changes, such as

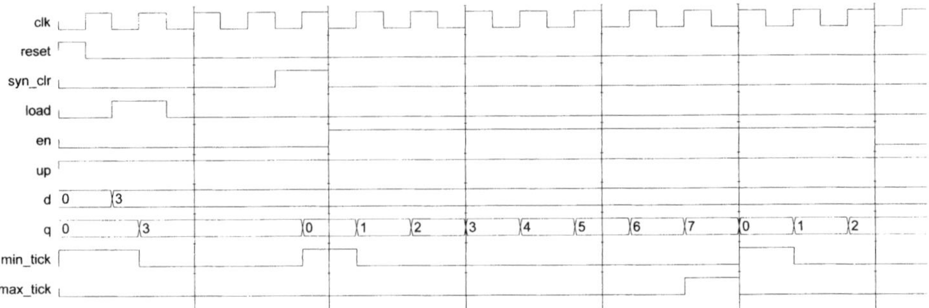

Figure 4.4 Testbench waveform.

```
wait on min_tick;
```

or wait for an absolute time, such as

```
wait for 4*T;  -- wait for 4 clock periods
```

If an input signal is modified after these statements, we need to make sure that the input change does not occur at the rising edge of the clock. An additional

```
wait until falling_edge(clk);
```

statement should be added when needed.

We can compile the code and perform simulation. Part of the simulated waveform is shown in Figure 4.4.

4.5 CASE STUDY

After examining several simple circuits, we discuss the design of more sophisticated examples in this section.

4.5.1 LED time-multiplexing circuit

The S3 board has four seven-segment LED displays, each containing seven bars and one small round dot. To reduce the use of FPGA's I/O pins, the S3 board uses a time-multiplexing sharing scheme. In this scheme, the four displays have their individual enable signals but share eight common signals to light the segments. All signals are active-low (i.e., enabled when a signal is '0'). The schematic of displaying '3' on the rightmost LED is shown in Figure 4.5. Note that the enable signal (i.e., an) is "1110". This configuration clearly can enable only one display at a time. We can *time-multiplex* the four LED patterns by enabling the four displays in turn, as shown in the simplified timing diagram in Figure 4.6. If the refreshing rate of the enable signal is fast enough, the human eye cannot distinguish the on and off intervals of the LEDs and perceives that all four displays are lit simultaneously. This scheme reduces the number of I/O pins from 32 to 12 (i.e., eight LED segments plus four enable signals) but requires a time-multiplexing circuit. Two variations of the circuit are discussed in the following subsections.

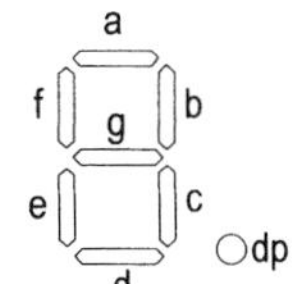

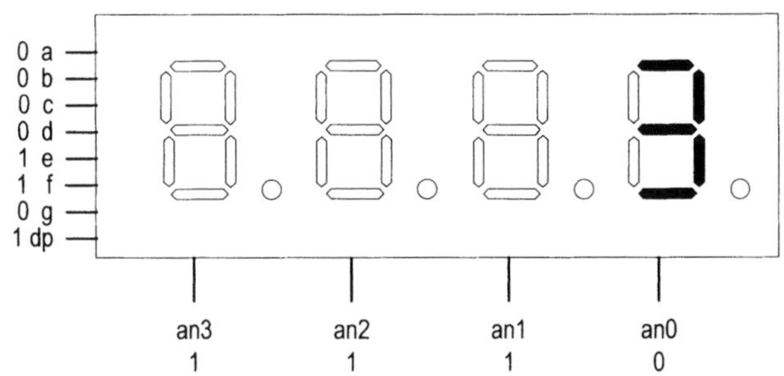

Figure 4.5 Time-multiplexed seven-segment LED display.

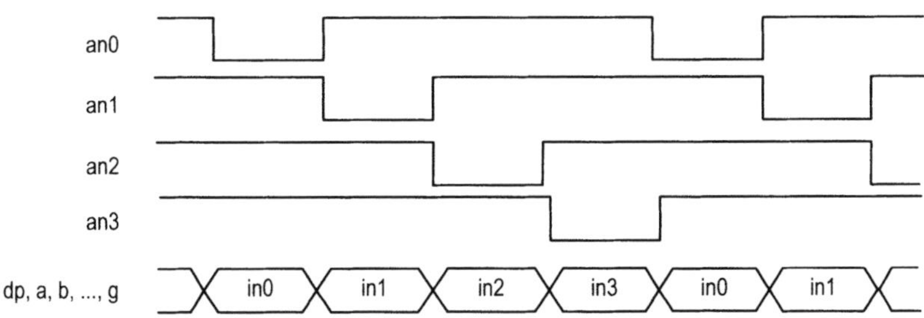

Figure 4.6 Timing diagram of a time-multiplexed seven-segment LED display.

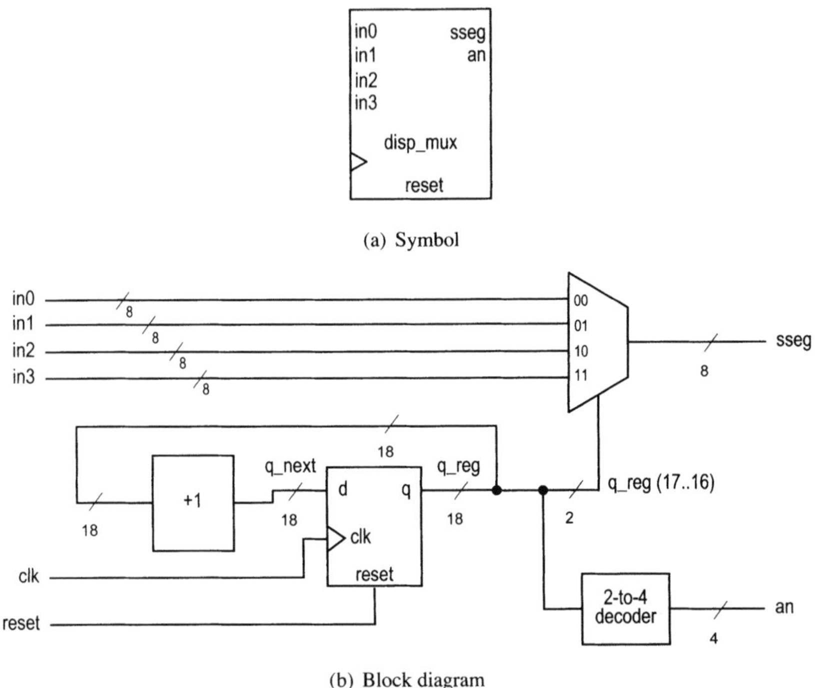

Figure 4.7 Symbol and block diagram of a time-multiplexing circuit.

Time multiplexing with LED patterns The symbol and block diagram of the time-multiplexing circuit are shown in Figure 4.7. It takes four seven-segment LED patterns, `in3`, `in2`, `in1`, and `in0`, and passes them to the output, `sseg`, in accordance with the enable signal.

The refresh rate of the enable signal has to be fast enough to fool our eyes but should be slow enough so that the LEDs can be turned on and off completely. The rate around the range 1000 Hz should work properly. In our design, we use an 18-bit binary counter for this purpose. The two MSBs are decoded to generate the enable signal and are used as the selection signal for multiplexing. The refreshing rate of an individual bit, such as `an(0)`, becomes $\frac{50M}{2^{16}}$ Hz, which is about 800 Hz. The code is shown in Listing 4.13.

Listing 4.13 LED time-multiplexing circuit with LED patterns

```
library ieee;
use ieee.std_logic_1164.all;
use ieee.numeric_std.all;
entity disp_mux is
   port(
      clk, reset: in std_logic;
      in3, in2, in1, in0: in std_logic_vector(7 downto 0);
      an: out std_logic_vector(3 downto 0);
      sseg: out std_logic_vector(7 downto 0)
   );
end disp_mux ;
```

```
architecture arch of disp_mux is
   -- refreshing rate around 800 Hz (50MHz/2^16)
   constant N: integer:=18;
   signal q_reg, q_next: unsigned(N-1 downto 0);
   signal sel: std_logic_vector(1 downto 0);
begin
   -- register
   process(clk,reset)
   begin
      if reset='1' then
         q_reg <= (others=>'0');
      elsif (clk'event and clk='1') then
         q_reg <= q_next;
      end if;
   end process;

   -- next-state logic for the counter
   q_next <= q_reg + 1;

   -- 2 MSBs of counter to control 4-to-1 multiplexing
   -- and to generate active-low enable signal
   sel <= std_logic_vector(q_reg(N-1 downto N-2));
   process(sel,in0,in1,in2,in3)
   begin
      case sel is
         when "00" =>
            an <= "1110";
            sseg <= in0;
         when "01" =>
            an <= "1101";
            sseg <= in1;
         when "10" =>
            an <= "1011";
            sseg <= in2;
         when others =>
            an <= "0111";
            sseg <= in3;
      end case;
   end process;
end arch;
```

We use the testing circuit in Figure 4.8 to verify operation of the LED time-multiplexing circuit. It uses four 8-bit registers to store the LED patterns. The registers use the same 8-bit switch as input but are controlled by individual enable signal. When we press a button, the corresponding register is enabled and the switch pattern is loaded to that register. The code is shown in Listing 4.14.

Listing 4.14 Testing circuit for time multiplexing with LED patterns

```
library ieee;
use ieee.std_logic_1164.all;
use ieee.numeric_std.all;
entity disp_mux_test is
   port(
```

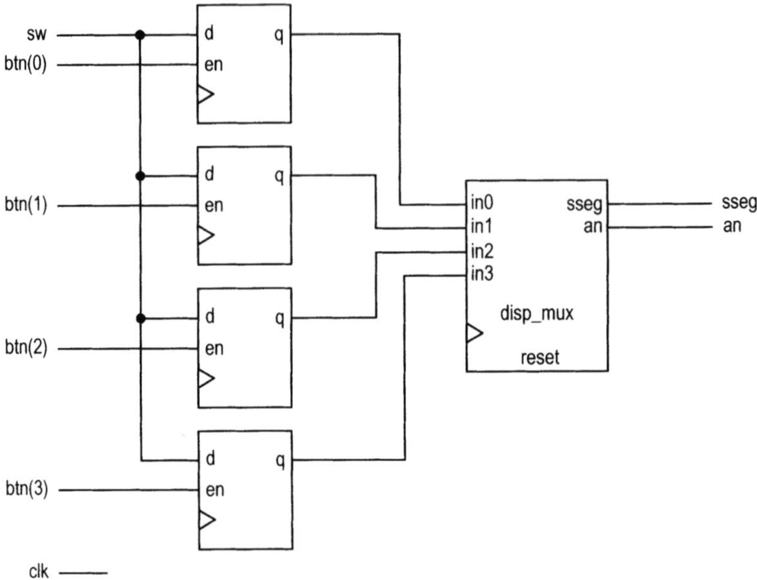

Figure 4.8 LED time-multiplexing testing circuit.

```
      clk: in std_logic;
      btn: in std_logic_vector(3 downto 0);
      sw: in std_logic_vector(7 downto 0);
      an: out std_logic_vector(3 downto 0);
      sseg: out std_logic_vector(7 downto 0)
   );
end disp_mux_test;

architecture arch of disp_mux_test is
   signal d3_reg, d2_reg: std_logic_vector(7 downto 0);
   signal d1_reg, d0_reg: std_logic_vector(7 downto 0);
begin
   disp_unit: entity work.disp_mux
      port map(
         clk=>clk, reset=>'0',
         in3=>d3_reg, in2=>d2_reg, in1=>d1_reg,
         in0=>d0_reg, an=>an, sseg=>sseg);
   -- registers for 4 led patterns
   process (clk)
   begin
      if (clk'event and clk='1') then
         if (btn(3)='1') then
            d3_reg <= sw;
         end if;
         if (btn(2)='1') then
            d2_reg <= sw;
         end if;
         if (btn(1)='1') then
            d1_reg <= sw;
```

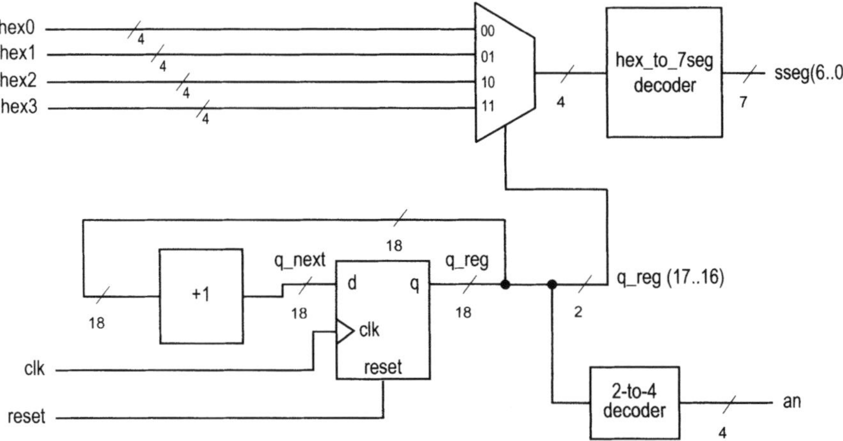

Figure 4.9 Block diagram of a hexadecimal time-multiplexing circuit.

```
            end if;
            if (btn(0)='1') then
               d0_reg <= sw;
            end if;
         end if;
      end process;
   end arch;
```

Time multiplexing with hexadecimal digits The most common application of a seven-segment LED is to display a hexadecimal digit. The decoding circuit is discussed in Section 3.7.1. To display four hexadecimal digits with the previous time-multiplexing circuit, four decoding circuits are needed. A better alternative is first to multiplex the hexadecimal digits and then decode the result, as shown in Figure 4.9.

This scheme requires only one decoding circuit and reduces the width of the 4-to-1 multiplexer from 8 bits to 5 bits (i.e., 4 bits for the hexadecimal digit and 1 bit for the decimal point). The code is shown in Listing 4.15. In addition to clock and reset, the input consists of four 4-bit hexadecimal digits, `hex3`, `hex2`, `hex1`, and `hex0`, and four decimal points, which are grouped as one signal, `dp_in`.

Listing 4.15 LED time-multiplexing circuit with hexadecimal digits

```
library ieee;
use ieee.std_logic_1164.all;
use ieee.numeric_std.all;
entity disp_hex_mux is
   port(
      clk, reset: in std_logic;
      hex3, hex2, hex1, hex0: in std_logic_vector(3 downto 0);
      dp_in: in std_logic_vector(3 downto 0);
      an: out std_logic_vector(3 downto 0);
      sseg: out std_logic_vector(7 downto 0)
   );
end disp_hex_mux ;
```

```
architecture arch of disp_hex_mux is
   -- each 7-seg led enabled (2^18/4)*25 ns (40 ms)
   constant N: integer:=18;
   signal q_reg, q_next: unsigned(N-1 downto 0);
   signal sel: std_logic_vector(1 downto 0);
   signal hex: std_logic_vector(3 downto 0);
   signal dp: std_logic;
begin
   -- register
   process(clk,reset)
   begin
      if reset='1' then
         q_reg <= (others=>'0');
      elsif (clk'event and clk='1') then
         q_reg <= q_next;
      end if;
   end process;

   -- next-state logic for the counter
   q_next <= q_reg + 1;

   -- 2 MSBs of counter to control 4-to-1 multiplexing
   sel <= std_logic_vector(q_reg(N-1 downto N-2));
   process(sel,hex0,hex1,hex2,hex3,dp_in)
   begin
      case sel is
         when "00" =>
            an <= "1110";
            hex <= hex0;
            dp <= dp_in(0);
         when "01" =>
            an <= "1101";
            hex <= hex1;
            dp <= dp_in(1);
         when "10" =>
            an <= "1011";
            hex <= hex2;
            dp <= dp_in(2);
         when others =>
            an <= "0111";
            hex <= hex3;
            dp <= dp_in(3);
      end case;
   end process;
   -- hex-to-7-segment led decoding
   with hex select
      sseg(6 downto 0) <=
         "0000001" when "0000",
         "1001111" when "0001",
         "0010010" when "0010",
         "0000110" when "0011",
         "1001100" when "0100",
```

```
            "0100100" when "0101",
            "0100000" when "0110",
            "0001111" when "0111",
            "0000000" when "1000",
            "0000100" when "1001",
            "0001000" when "1010", --a
            "1100000" when "1011", --b
            "0110001" when "1100", --c
            "1000010" when "1101", --d
            "0110000" when "1110", --e
            "0111000" when others; --f
   -- decimal point
   sseg(7) <= dp;
end arch;
```

To verify operation of this circuit, we define the 8-bit switch as two 4-bit unsigned numbers, add the two numbers, and show the two numbers and their sum on the four-digit seven-segment LED display. The code is shown in Listing 4.16.

Listing 4.16 Testing circuit for time multiplexing with hexadecimal digits

```
library ieee;
use ieee.std_logic_1164.all;
use ieee.numeric_std.all;
entity hex_mux_test is
   port(
      clk: in std_logic;
      sw: in std_logic_vector(7 downto 0);
      an: out std_logic_vector(3 downto 0);
      sseg: out std_logic_vector(7 downto 0)
   );
end hex_mux_test;

architecture arch of hex_mux_test is
   signal a, b: unsigned(7 downto 0);
   signal sum: std_logic_vector(7 downto 0);
begin
   disp_unit: entity work.disp_hex_mux
      port map(
         clk=>clk, reset=>'0',
         hex3=>sum(7 downto 4), hex2=>sum(3 downto 0),
         hex1=>sw(7 downto 4), hex0=>sw(3 downto 0),
         dp_in=>"1011", an=>an, sseg=>sseg);
   a <= "0000" & unsigned(sw(3 downto 0));
   b <= "0000" & unsigned(sw(7 downto 4));
   sum <= std_logic_vector(a + b);
end arch;
```

Simulation consideration Many sequential circuit examples in the book operate at a relatively slow rate, as does the enable pulse of the LED time-multiplexing circuit. This can be done by generating a single-clock enable tick from a counter. An 18-bit counter is used in this circuit:

```
   constant N: integer:=18;
```

```
signal q_reg, q_next: unsigned(N-1 downto 0);
. . .
q_next <= q_reg + 1;
```

Because of the counter's size, simulating this type of circuit consumes a significant amount of computation time (i.e., 2^{18} clock cycles for one iteration). Since our main interest is in the multiplexing part of the code, most simulation time is wasted. It is more efficient to use a smaller counter in simulation. We can do this by modifying the constant statement

```
constant N: integer:=4;
```

when constructing the testbench. This requires only 2^4 clock cycles for one iteration and allows us to better exercise and observe the key operations.

Instead of using a constant statement and modifying code between simulation and synthesis, an alternative is to define a generic for the relevant parameter. During instantiation, we can assign different values for simulation and synthesis.

4.5.2 Stopwatch

We consider the design of a stopwatch in this subsection. The watch displays the time in three decimal digits, and counts from 00.0 to 99.9 seconds and wraps around. It contains a synchronous clear signal, `clr`, which returns the count to 00.0, and an enable signal, `go`, which enables and suspends the counting. This design is basically a BCD (binary-coded decimal) counter, which counts in BCD format. In this format, a decimal number is represented by a sequence of 4-bit BCD digits. For example, 139_{10} is represented as "0001 0011 1001" and the next number in sequence is 140_{10}, which is represented as "0001 0100 0000".

Since the S3 board has a 50-MHz clock, we first need a mod-5,000,000 counter that generates a one-clock-cycle tick every 0.1 second. The tick is then used to enable counting of the three-digit BCD counter.

Design I Our first design of the BCD counter uses a cascading structure of three decade (i.e., mod-10) counters, representing counts of 0.1, 1, and 10 seconds, respectively. The decade counter has an enable signal and generates a one-clock-cycle tick when it reaches 9. We can use these signals to "hook" the three counters. For example, the 10-second counter is enabled only when the enable tick of the mod-5,000,000 counter is asserted and both the 0.1- and 1-second counters are 9. The code is shown in Listing 4.17.

Listing 4.17 Cascading description for a stopwatch

```
library ieee;
use ieee.std_logic_1164.all;
use ieee.numeric_std.all;
entity stop_watch is
   port(
      clk: in std_logic;
      go, clr: in std_logic;
      d2, d1, d0: out std_logic_vector(3 downto 0)
   );
end stop_watch;

architecture cascade_arch of stop_watch is
   constant DVSR: integer:=5000000;
```

```
   signal ms_reg, ms_next: unsigned(22 downto 0);
   signal d2_reg, d1_reg, d0_reg: unsigned(3 downto 0);
   signal d2_next, d1_next, d0_next: unsigned(3 downto 0);
   signal d1_en, d2_en, d0_en: std_logic;
   signal ms_tick, d0_tick, d1_tick: std_logic;
begin
   -- register
   process(clk)
   begin
      if (clk'event and clk='1') then
         ms_reg <= ms_next;
         d2_reg <= d2_next;
         d1_reg <= d1_next;
         d0_reg <= d0_next;
      end if;
   end process;

   -- next-state logic
   -- 0.1 sec tick generator: mod-5000000
   ms_next <=
      (others=>'0') when clr='1' or
                         (ms_reg=DVSR and go='1') else
      ms_reg + 1 when go='1' else
      ms_reg;
   ms_tick <= '1' when ms_reg=DVSR else '0';
   -- 0.1 sec counter
   d0_en <= '1' when ms_tick='1' else '0';
   d0_next <=
      "0000" when (clr='1') or (d0_en='1' and d0_reg=9) else
      d0_reg + 1 when d0_en='1' else
      d0_reg;
   d0_tick <= '1' when d0_reg=9 else '0';
   -- 1 sec counter
   d1_en <= '1' when ms_tick='1' and d0_tick='1' else '0';
   d1_next <=
      "0000" when (clr='1') or (d1_en='1' and d1_reg=9) else
      d1_reg + 1 when d1_en='1' else
      d1_reg;
   d1_tick <= '1' when d1_reg=9 else '0';
   -- 10 sec counter
   d2_en <=
      '1' when ms_tick='1' and d0_tick='1' and d1_tick='1' else
      '0';
   d2_next <=
      "0000" when (clr='1') or (d2_en='1' and d2_reg=9) else
      d2_reg + 1 when d2_en='1' else
      d2_reg;

   -- output logic
   d0 <= std_logic_vector(d0_reg);
   d1 <= std_logic_vector(d1_reg);
   d2 <= std_logic_vector(d2_reg);
end cascade_arch;
```

Note that all registers are controlled by the same clock signal. This example illustrates how to use a one-clock-cycle enable tick to maintain synchronicity. An inferior approach is to use the output of the lower counter as the clock signal for the next stage. Although it may appear to be simpler, it violates the synchronous design principle and is a very poor practice.

Design II An alternative for the three-digit BCD counter is to describe the entire structure in a nested if statement. The nested conditions indicate that the counter reaches .9, 9.9, and 99.9 seconds. The code is shown in Listing 4.18.

Listing 4.18 Nested if-statement description for a stopwatch

```
architecture if_arch of stop_watch is
   constant DVSR: integer:=5000000;
   signal ms_reg, ms_next: unsigned(22 downto 0);
   signal d2_reg, d1_reg, d0_reg: unsigned(3 downto 0);
   signal d2_next, d1_next, d0_next: unsigned(3 downto 0);
   signal ms_tick: std_logic;
begin
   -- register
   process(clk)
   begin
      if (clk'event and clk='1') then
         ms_reg <= ms_next;
         d2_reg <= d2_next;
         d1_reg <= d1_next;
         d0_reg <= d0_next;
      end if;
   end process;

   -- next-state logic
   -- 0.1 sec tick generator: mod-5000000
   ms_next <=
      (others=>'0') when clr='1' or
                      (ms_reg=DVSR and go='1') else
      ms_reg + 1 when go='1' else
      ms_reg;
   ms_tick <= '1' when ms_reg=DVSR else '0';
   -- 3-digit incrementor
   process(d0_reg,d1_reg,d2_reg,ms_tick,clr)
   begin
      -- default
      d0_next <= d0_reg;
      d1_next <= d1_reg;
      d2_next <= d2_reg;
      if clr='1' then
         d0_next <= "0000";
         d1_next <= "0000";
         d2_next <= "0000";
      elsif ms_tick='1' then
         if (d0_reg/=9) then
            d0_next <= d0_reg + 1;
         else        -- reach XX9
            d0_next <= "0000";
```

```
            if (d1_reg/=9) then
               d1_next <= d1_reg + 1;
            else     -- reach X99
               d1_next <= "0000";
               if (d2_reg/=9) then
                  d2_next <= d2_reg + 1;
               else -- reach 999
                  d2_next <= "0000";
               end if;
            end if;
         end if;
      end if;
   end process;
   -- output logic
   d0 <= std_logic_vector(d0_reg);
   d1 <= std_logic_vector(d1_reg);
   d2 <= std_logic_vector(d2_reg);
end if_arch;
```

Verification circuit To verify operation of the stopwatch, we can combine it with the previous hexadecimal LED time-multiplexing circuit to display the output of the watch. The code is shown in Listing 4.19. Note that the first digit of the LED is assigned to 0 and the go and `clr` signals are mapped to two buttons of the S3 board.

Listing 4.19 Testing circuit for a stopwatch

```
library ieee;
use ieee.std_logic_1164.all;
entity stop_watch_test is
   port(
      clk: in std_logic;
      btn: in std_logic_vector(3 downto 0);
      an: out std_logic_vector(3 downto 0);
      sseg: out std_logic_vector(7 downto 0)
   );
end stop_watch_test;

architecture arch of stop_watch_test is
   signal d2, d1, d0: std_logic_vector(3 downto 0);
begin
   disp_unit: entity work.disp_hex_mux
      port map(
         clk=>clk, reset=>'0',
         hex3=>"0000", hex2=>d2,
         hex1=>d1, hex0=>d0,
         dp_in=>"1101", an=>an, sseg=>sseg);

  watch_unit: entity work.stop_watch(cascade_arch)
     port map(
        clk=>clk, go=>btn(1), clr=>btn(0),
        d2 =>d2, d1=>d1, d0=>d0 );
end arch;
```

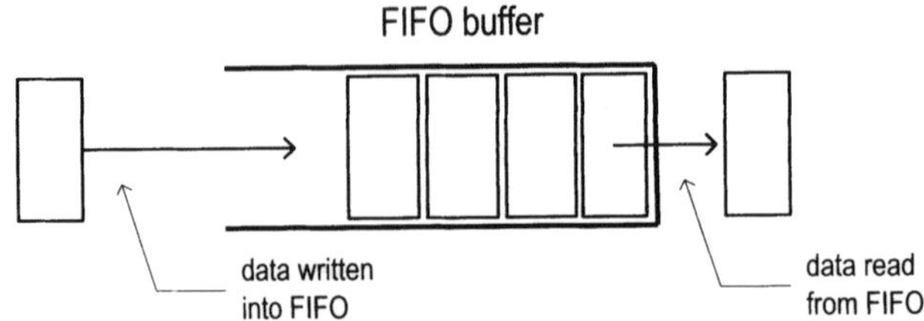

Figure 4.10 Conceptual diagram of a FIFO buffer.

4.5.3 FIFO buffer

A FIFO (first-in-first-out) buffer is an "elastic" storage between two subsystems, as shown in the conceptual diagram of Figure 4.10. It has two control signals, `wr` and `rd`, for write and read operations. When `wr` is asserted, the input data is written into the buffer. The read operation is somewhat misleading. The head of the FIFO buffer is normally always available and thus can be read at any time. The `rd` signal actually acts like a "remove" signal. When it is asserted, the first item (i.e., head) of the FIFO buffer is removed and the next item becomes available.

FIFO buffer is a critical component in many applications and the optimized implementation can be quite complex. In this subsection, we introduce a simple, genuine circular-queue-based design. More efficient, device-specific implementation can be found in the Xilinx literature.

Circular-queue-based implementation One way to implement a FIFO buffer is to add a control circuit to a register file. The registers in the register file are arranged as a circular queue with two pointers. The *write pointer* points to the head of the queue, and the *read pointer* points to the tail of the queue. The pointer advances one position for each write or read operation. The operation of an eight-word circular queue is shown in Figure 4.11.

A FIFO buffer usually contains two status signals, `full` and `empty`, to indicate that the FIFO is full (i.e., cannot be written) and empty (i.e., cannot be read), respectively. One of the two conditions occurs when the read pointer is equal to the write pointer, as shown in Figure 4.11(a), (f), and (i). The most difficult design task of the controller is to derive a mechanism to distinguish the two conditions. One scheme is to use two FFs to keep track of the empty and full statuses. The FFs are set to '1' and '0' during system initialization and then modified in each clock cycle according to the values of the `wr` and `rd` signals. The code is shown in Listing 4.20.

Listing 4.20 FIFO buffer

```
library ieee;
use ieee.std_logic_1164.all;
use ieee.numeric_std.all;
entity fifo is
   generic(
      B: natural:=8; -- number of bits
      W: natural:=4 -- number of address bits
   );
   port(
      clk, reset: in std_logic;
      rd, wr: in std_logic;
```

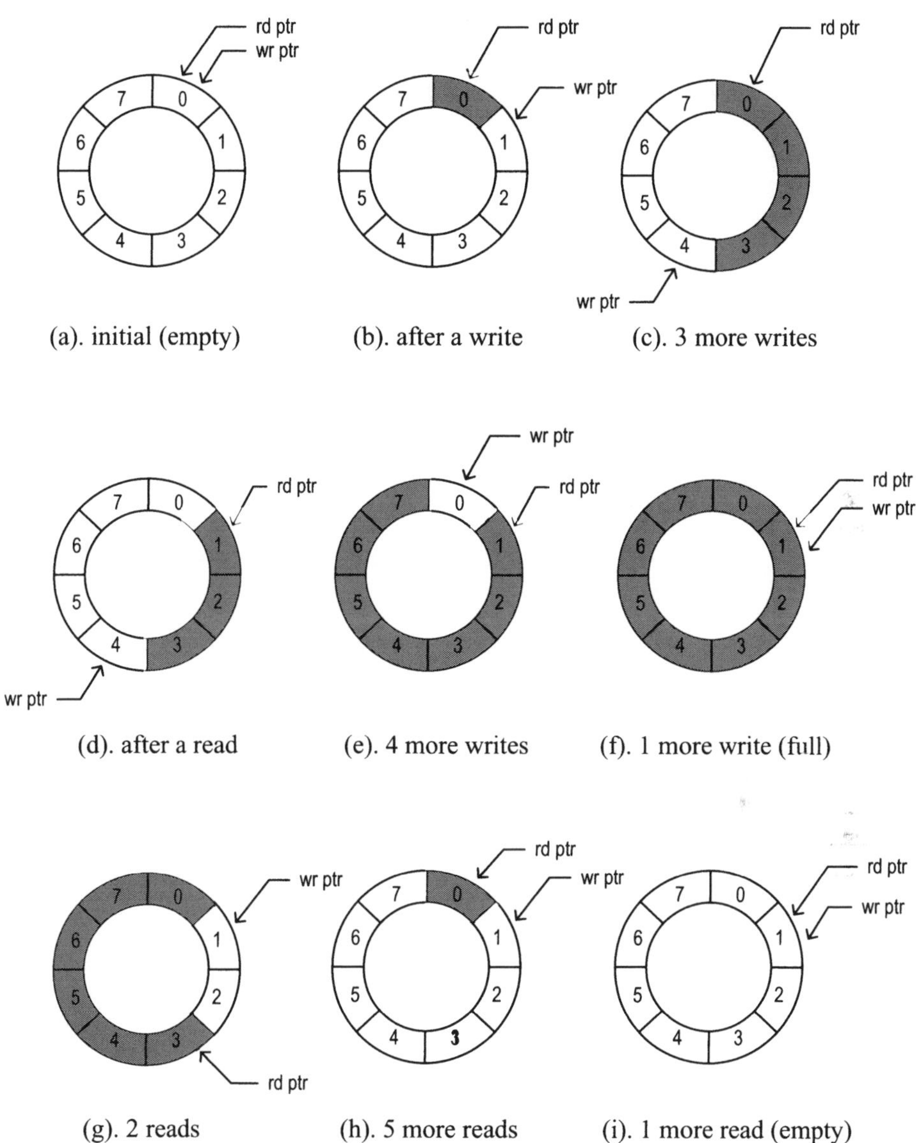

Figure 4.11 FIFO buffer based on a circular queue.

```
      w_data: in std_logic_vector (B-1 downto 0);
      empty, full: out std_logic;
      r_data: out std_logic_vector (B-1 downto 0)
   );
end fifo;

architecture arch of fifo is
   type reg_file_type is array (2**W-1 downto 0) of
        std_logic_vector(B-1 downto 0);
   signal array_reg: reg_file_type;
   signal w_ptr_reg, w_ptr_next, w_ptr_succ:
      std_logic_vector(W-1 downto 0);
   signal r_ptr_reg, r_ptr_next, r_ptr_succ:
      std_logic_vector(W-1 downto 0);
   signal full_reg, empty_reg, full_next, empty_next:
          std_logic;
   signal wr_op: std_logic_vector(1 downto 0);
   signal wr_en: std_logic;
begin
   --=================================================
   -- register file
   --=================================================
   process(clk,reset)
   begin
     if (reset='1') then
        array_reg <= (others=>(others=>'0'));
     elsif (clk'event and clk='1') then
        if wr_en='1' then
           array_reg(to_integer(unsigned(w_ptr_reg)))
                 <= w_data;
        end if;
     end if;
   end process;
   -- read port
   r_data <= array_reg(to_integer(unsigned(r_ptr_reg)));
   -- write enabled only when FIFO is not full
   wr_en <= wr and (not full_reg);

   --=================================================
   -- fifo control logic
   --=================================================
   -- register for read and write pointers
   process(clk,reset)
   begin
      if (reset='1') then
         w_ptr_reg <= (others=>'0');
         r_ptr_reg <= (others=>'0');
         full_reg <= '0';
         empty_reg <= '1';
      elsif (clk'event and clk='1') then
         w_ptr_reg <= w_ptr_next;
         r_ptr_reg <= r_ptr_next;
         full_reg <= full_next;
```

```
         empty_reg <= empty_next;
      end if;
   end process;

   -- successive pointer values
   w_ptr_succ <= std_logic_vector(unsigned(w_ptr_reg)+1);
   r_ptr_succ <= std_logic_vector(unsigned(r_ptr_reg)+1);

   -- next-state logic for read and write pointers
   wr_op <= wr & rd;
   process(w_ptr_reg,w_ptr_succ,r_ptr_reg,r_ptr_succ,wr_op,
           empty_reg,full_reg)
   begin
      w_ptr_next <= w_ptr_reg;
      r_ptr_next <= r_ptr_reg;
      full_next <= full_reg;
      empty_next <= empty_reg;
      case wr_op is
         when "00" => -- no op
         when "01" => -- read
            if (empty_reg /= '1') then -- not empty
               r_ptr_next <= r_ptr_succ;
               full_next <= '0';
               if (r_ptr_succ=w_ptr_reg) then
                  empty_next <='1';
               end if;
            end if;
         when "10" => -- write
            if (full_reg /= '1') then -- not full
               w_ptr_next <= w_ptr_succ;
               empty_next <= '0';
               if (w_ptr_succ=r_ptr_reg) then
                  full_next <='1';
               end if;
            end if;
         when others => -- write/read;
            w_ptr_next <= w_ptr_succ;
            r_ptr_next <= r_ptr_succ;
      end case;
   end process;
   -- output
   full <= full_reg;
   empty <= empty_reg;
end arch;
```

The code is divided into a register file and a FIFO controller. The controller consists of two pointers and two status FFs. Its next-state logic examines the `wr` and `rd` signals and takes actions accordingly. For example, let us consider the "10" case, which implies that only a write operation occurs. The status FF is checked first to ensure that the buffer is not full. If this condition is met, we advance the write pointer by one position and clear the empty status FF. Storing one extra word to the buffer may make it full. This happens if the new write pointer "catches" the read pointer, which is expressed by the `w_ptr_succ=r_ptr_reg` expression.

Verification circuit The verification circuit examines the operation of a 2^4-by-3 FIFO buffer. We use three switches to generate the input data and use two buttons for the `wr` and `rd` signals. The 3-bit readout and the `full` and `empty` status signals are displayed in five discrete LEDs. Because of bounces of the mechanical contact, a debouncing circuit is needed to generate a clean, one-clock-cycle tick. The debouncing module, named `debounce`, is discussed in Section 5.9 but for now can be treated as a predesigned module. The original button inputs are `btn(0)` and `btn(1)`, and the debounced signals are `db_btn(0)` and `db_btn(1)`. The code is shown in Listing 4.21.

Listing 4.21 Testing circuit for a FIFO buffer

```
library ieee;
use ieee.std_logic_1164.all;
entity fifo_test is
   port(
      clk, reset: in std_logic;
      btn: std_logic_vector(1 downto 0);
      sw: std_logic_vector(2 downto 0);
      led: out std_logic_vector(7 downto 0)
   );
end fifo_test;

architecture arch of fifo_test is
   signal db_btn: std_logic_vector(1 downto 0);
begin
   -- debouncing circuit for btn(0)
   btn_db_unit0: entity work.debounce(fsmd_arch)
      port map(clk=>clk, reset=>reset, sw=>btn(0),
               db_level=>open, db_tick=>db_btn(0));
   -- debouncing circuit for btn(1)
   btn_db_unit1: entity work.debounce(fsmd_arch)
      port map(clk=>clk, reset=>reset, sw=>btn(1),
               db_level=>open, db_tick=>db_btn(1));
   -- instantiate a 2^2-by-3 fifo
   fifo_unit: entity work.fifo(arch)
      generic map(B=>3, W=>2)
      port map(clk=>clk, reset=>reset,
               rd=>db_btn(0), wr=>db_btn(1),
               w_data=>sw, r_data=>led(2 downto 0),
               full=>led(7), empty=>led(6));
   -- disable unused leds
   led(5 downto 3)<=(others=>'0');
 end arch;
```

4.6 BIBLIOGRAPHIC NOTES

The bibliographic information for this chapter is similar to that for Chapter 3.

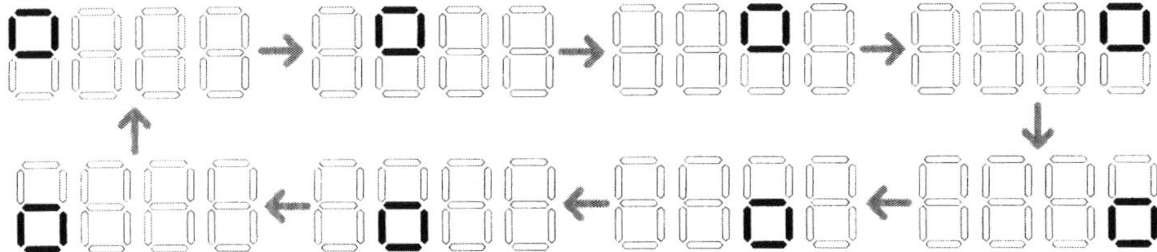

Figure 4.12 Pattern for Experiment 4.7.3.

4.7 SUGGESTED EXPERIMENTS

4.7.1 Programmable square wave generator

A programmable square wave generator is a circuit that can generate a square wave with variable on (i.e., logic '1') and off (i.e., logic '0') intervals. The durations of the intervals are specified by two 4-bit control signals, `m` and `n`, which are interpreted as unsigned integers. The on and off intervals are `m`∗100 ns and `n`∗100 ns, respectively (recall that the period of the S3 onboard oscillator is 20 ns). Design a programmable square wave generator circuit. The circuit should be completely synchronous. We need a logic analyzer or oscilloscope to verify its operation.

4.7.2 PWM and LED dimmer

The duty cycle of a square wave is defined as the percentage of the on interval (i.e., logic '1') in a period. A PWM (pulse width modulation) circuit can generate an output with variable duty cycles. For a PWM with 4-bit resolution, a 4-bit control signal, `w`, specifies the duty cycle. The `w` signal is interpreted as an unsigned integer and the duty cycle is $\frac{w}{16}$.

1. Design a PWM circuit with 4-bit resolution and verify its operation using a logic analyzer or oscilloscope.
2. Modify the LED time-multiplexing circuit to include the PWM circuit for the `an` signal. The PWM circuit specifies the percentage of time that the LED display is on. We can control the perceived brightness by changing the duty cycle. Verify the circuit's operation by observing 1 bit of `an` on a logic analyzer or oscilloscope.
3. Replace the LED time-multiplexing circuit of Listing 4.19 with the new design and use the lower 4 bits of the 8-bit switch to control the duty cycle. Verify operation of the circuit. It may be necessary to go to a dark area to see the effect of dimming.

4.7.3 Rotating square circuit

In a seven-segment LED display, a square pattern can be created by enabling the a, b, f, and g segments or the c, d, e, and g segments. We want to design a circuit that circulates the square patterns in the four-digit seven-segment LED display. The clockwise circulating pattern is shown in Figure 4.12. The circuit should have an input, `en`, which enables or pauses the circulation, and an input, `cw`, which specifies the direction (i.e., clockwise or counterclockwise) of the circulation.

Design the circuit and verify its operation on the prototyping board. Make sure that the circulation rate is slow enough for visual inspection.

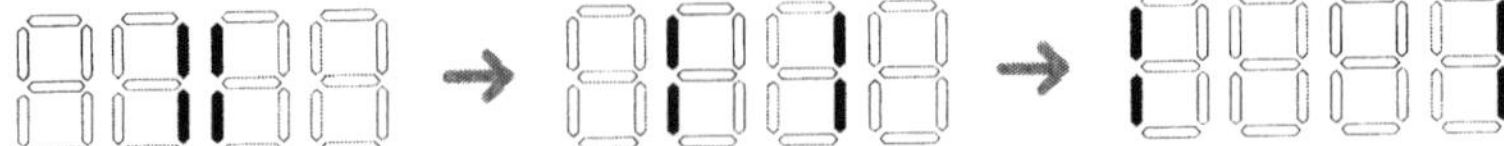

Figure 4.13 Pattern for Experiment 4.7.4.

4.7.4 Heartbeat circuit

We want to create a "heartbeat" for the prototyping board. It repeats the simple pattern in the four-digit seven-segment display, as shown in Figure 4.13, at a rate of 72 Hz. Design the circuit and verify its operation on the prototyping board.

4.7.5 Rotating LED banner circuit

The prototyping board has a four-digit seven-segment LED display, and thus only four symbols can be displayed at a time. We can show more information if the data is rotated and moved continuously. For example, assume that the message is 10 digits (i.e., "0123456789"). The display can show the message as "0123", "1234", "2345", . . ., "6789", "7890", . . ., "0123". The circuit should have an input, `en`, which enables or pauses the rotation, and an input, `dir`, which specifies the direction (i.e., rotate left or right).

Design the circuit and verify its operation on the prototyping board. Make sure that the rotation rate is slow enough for visual inspection.

4.7.6 Enhanced stopwatch

Modify the stopwatch with the following extensions:

- Add an additional signal, up, to control the direction of counting. The stopwatch counts up when the up signal is asserted and counts down otherwise.
- Add a minute digit to the display. The LED display format should be like `M.SS.D`, where `D` represents 0.1 second and its range is between 0 and 9, `SS` represents seconds and its range is between 00 and 59, and `M` represents minutes and its range is between 0 and 9.

Design the new stopwatch and verify its operation with a testing circuit.

4.7.7 Stack

A stack is a last-in-first-out buffer in which the last stored data is retrieved first. Storing a data word to a stack is known as a *push* operation, and retrieving a data word from a stack is known as a *pop* operation. The I/O signals of a stack are similar to those of a FIFO buffer except that we generally use the `push` and `pop` signals in place of the `wr` and `rd` signals. Design a stack using a register file and verify its operation with a testing circuit similar to the one in Listing 4.21.

CHAPTER 5

FSM

5.1 INTRODUCTION

An FSM (finite state machine) is used to model a system that transits among a finite number of internal states. The transitions depend on the current state and external input. Unlike a regular sequential circuit, the state transitions of an FSM do not exhibit a simple, repetitive pattern. Its next-state logic is usually constructed from scratch and is sometimes known as "random" logic. This is different from the next-state logic of a regular sequential circuit, which is composed mostly of "structured" components, such as incrementors and shifters.

In this chapter, we provide an overview of the basic characteristics and representation of FSMs and discuss the derivation of HDL codes. In practice, the main application of an FSM is to act as the controller of a large digital system, which examines the external commands and status and activates proper control signals to control operation of a *data path*, which is usually composed of regular sequential components. This is known as an FSMD (finite state machine with data path) and is discussed in Chapter 6.

5.1.1 Mealy and Moore outputs

The basic block diagram of an FSM is the same as that of a regular sequential circuit and is repeated in Figure 5.1. It consists of a state register, next-state logic, and output logic. An FSM is known as a *Moore machine* if the output is only a function of state, and is known as a *Mealy machine* if the output is a function of state and external input. Both types of output may exist in a complex FSM, and we simply refer to it as containing a Moore output and

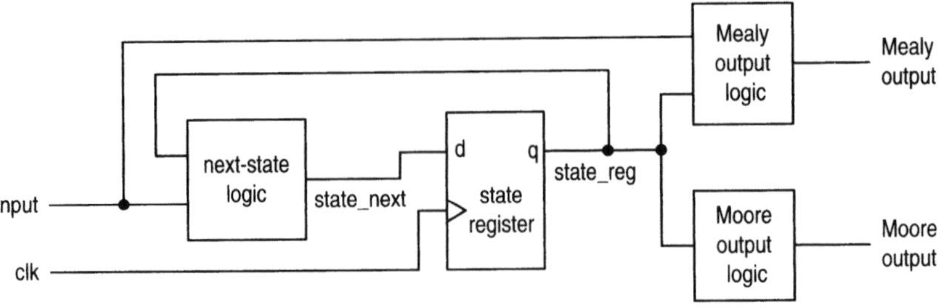

Figure 5.1 Block diagram of a synchronous FSM.

Mealy output. The Moore and Mealy outputs are similar but not identical. Understanding their subtle differences is the key for a controller design. The example in Section 5.3.1 illustrates the behaviors and constructions of the two types of outputs.

5.1.2 FSM representation

An FSM is usually specified by an abstract *state diagram* or *ASM chart* (algorithmic state machine chart), both capturing the FSM's input, output, states, and transitions in a graphical representation. The two representations provide the same information. The FSM representation is more compact and better for simple applications. The ASM chart representation is somewhat like a flowchart and is more descriptive for applications with complex transition conditions and actions.

State diagram A state diagram is composed of *nodes*, which represent states and are drawn as circles, and annotated *transitional arcs*. A single node and its transition arcs are shown in Figure 5.2(a). A logic expression expressed in terms of input signals is associated with each transition arc and represents a specific condition. The arc is taken when the corresponding expression is evaluated `true`.

The Moore output values are placed inside the circle since they depend only on the current state. The Mealy output values are associated with the conditions of transition arcs since they depend on the current state and external input. To reduce clutter in the diagram, only asserted output values are listed. The output signal takes the default (i.e., unasserted) value otherwise.

A representative state diagram is shown in Figure 5.3(a). The FSM has four states, two external input signals (i.e., `a` and `b`), one Moore output signal (i.e., `y1`), and one Mealy output signal (i.e., `y0`). The `y1` signal is asserted when the FSM is in the `s2` or `s3` state. The `y0` signal is asserted when the FSM is in the `s0` state and the `a` and `b` signals are "11".

ASM chart An ASM chart is composed of a network of ASM blocks. An *ASM block* consists of one *state box* and an optional network of *decision boxes* and *conditional output boxes*. A representative ASM block is shown in Figure 5.2(b).

A state box represents a state in an FSM, and the asserted Moore output values are listed inside the box. Note that it has only one exit path. A decision box tests the input condition and determines which exit path to take. It has two exit paths, labeled `T` and `F`, which correspond to the `true` and `false` values of the condition. A conditional output box lists asserted Mealy output values and is usually placed after a decision box. It indicates that the listed output signal can be activated only when the corresponding condition in the decision box is met.

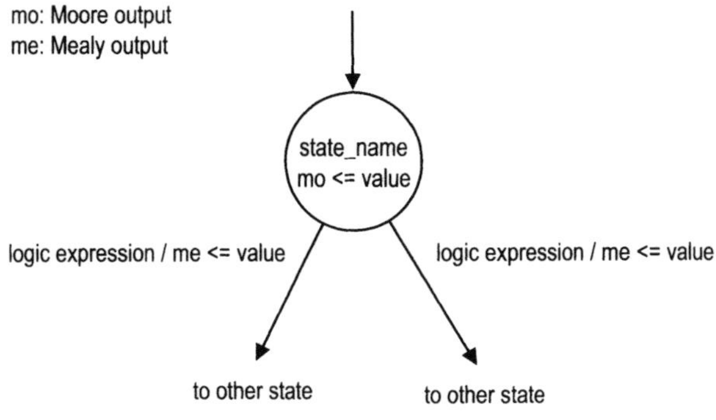

(a) Node

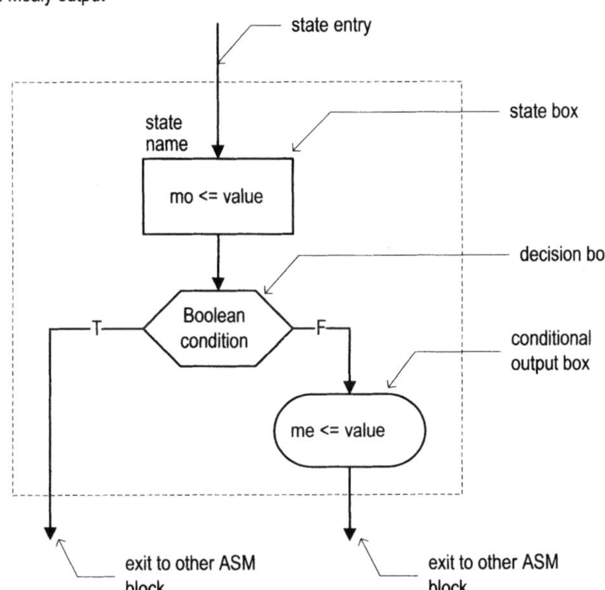

(b) ASM block

Figure 5.2 Symbol of a state.

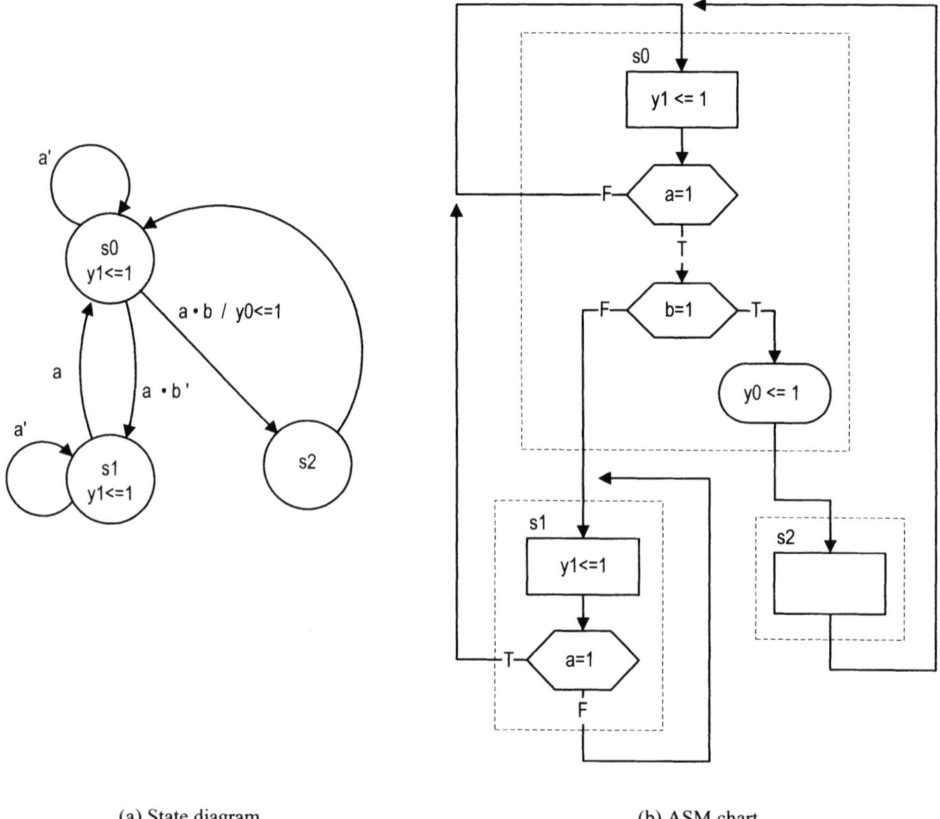

(a) State diagram

(b) ASM chart

Figure 5.3 Example of an FSM.

A state diagram can easily be converted to an ASM chart, and vice versa. The corresponding ASM chart of the previous FSM state diagram is shown in Figure 5.3(b).

5.2 FSM CODE DEVELOPMENT

The procedure of developing code for an FSM is similar to that of a regular sequential circuit. We first separate the state register and then derive the code for the combinational next-state logic and output logic. The main difference is the next-state logic. For an FSM, the code for the next-state logic follows the flow of a state diagram or ASM chart.

For clarity and flexibility, we use the VHDL's *enumerated data type* to represent the FSM's states. The enumerated data type can best be explained by an example. Consider the FSM of Section 5.1.2, which has three states: s0, s1, and s2. We can introduce a user-defined enumerated data type as follows:

```
type eg_state_type is (s0, s1, s2);
```

The data type simply lists (i.e., *enumerates*) all symbolic values. Once the data type is defined, it can be used for the signals, as in

```
signal state_reg, state_next: eg_state_type;
```

During synthesis, software automatically maps the values in an enumerated data type to binary representations, a process known as *state assignment*. Although there is a mechanism to perform this manually, it is rarely needed.

The complete code of the FSM is shown in Listing 5.1. It consists of segments for the state register, next-state logic, Moore output logic, and Mealy output logic.

Listing 5.1 FSM example

```
library ieee;
use ieee.std_logic_1164.all;
entity fsm_eg is
   port(
      clk, reset: in std_logic;
      a, b: in std_logic;
      y0, y1: out std_logic
   );
end fsm_eg;

architecture mult_seg_arch of fsm_eg is
   type eg_state_type is (s0, s1, s2);
   signal state_reg, state_next: eg_state_type;
begin
   -- state register
   process(clk,reset)
   begin
      if (reset='1') then
         state_reg <= s0;
      elsif (clk'event and clk='1') then
         state_reg <= state_next;
      end if;
   end process;
   -- next-state logic
   process(state_reg,a,b)
```

```
   begin
      case state_reg is
         when s0 =>
            if a='1' then
               if b='1' then
                  state_next <= s2;
               else
                  state_next <= s1;
               end if;
            else
               state_next <= s0;
            end if;
         when s1 =>
            if (a='1') then
               state_next <= s0;
            else
               state_next <= s1;
            end if;
         when s2 =>
            state_next <= s0;
      end case;
   end process;
   -- Moore output logic
   process(state_reg)
   begin
      case state_reg is
         when s0|s2 =>
            y1 <= '0';
         when s1 =>
            y1 <= '1';
      end case;
   end process;
   -- Mealy output logic
   process(state_reg,a,b)
   begin
      case state_reg is
         when s0 =>
            if (a='1') and (b='1') then
              y0 <= '1';
            else
              y0 <= '0';
            end if;
         when s1 | s2 =>
            y0 <= '0';
      end case;
   end process;
end mult_seg_arch;
```

The key part is the next-state logic. It uses a case statement with the `state_reg` signal as the selection expression. The next state (i.e., `state_next` signal) is determined by the current state (i.e., `state_reg`) and external input. The code for each state basically follows the activities inside each ASM block of Figure 5.3(b).

An alternative code is to merge next-state logic and output logic into a single combinational block, as shown in Listing 5.2.

Listing 5.2 FSM with merged combinational logic

```
architecture two_seg_arch of fsm_eg is
   type eg_state_type is (s0, s1, s2);
   signal state_reg, state_next: eg_state_type;
begin
   -- state register
   process(clk,reset)
   begin
      if (reset='1') then
         state_reg <= s0;
      elsif (clk'event and clk='1') then
         state_reg <= state_next;
      end if;
   end process;
   -- next-state/output logic
   process(state_reg,a,b)
   begin
      state_next <= state_reg;  -- default back to same state
      y0 <= '0';    -- default 0
      y1 <= '0';    -- default 0
      case state_reg is
         when s0 =>
            if a='1' then
               if b='1' then
                  state_next <= s2;
                  y0 <= '1';
               else
                  state_next <= s1;
               end if;
            -- no else branch
            end if;
         when s1 =>
            y1 <= '1';
            if (a='1') then
               state_next <= s0;
            -- no else branch
            end if;
         when s2 =>
            state_next <= s0;
      end case;
   end process;
end two_seg_arch;
```

Note that the default output values are listed at the beginning of the code.

The code for the next-state logic and output logic follows the ASM chart closely. Once a detailed state diagram or ASM chart is derived, converting an FSM to HDL code is almost a mechanical procedure. Listings 5.1 and 5.2 can serve as templates for this purpose.

Xilinx specific Xilinx ISE includes a utility program called *StateCAD*, which allows a user to draw a state diagram in graphical format. The program then converts the state diagram to HDL code. It is a good idea to try it first with a few simple examples to see whether the generated code and its style are satisfactory, particularly for the output signals.

5.3 DESIGN EXAMPLES

5.3.1 Rising-edge detector

The rising-edge detector is a circuit that generates a short, one-clock-cycle pulse (we call it a *tick*) when the input signal changes from '0' to '1'. It is usually used to indicate the onset of a slow time-varying input signal. We design the circuit using both Moore and Mealy machines, and compare their differences.

Moore-based design The state diagram and ASM chart of a Moore machine–based edge detector are shown in Figure 5.4. The `zero` and `one` states indicate that the input signal has been '0' and '1' for awhile. The rising edge occurs when the input changes to '1' in the `zero` state. The FSM moves to the `edge` state and the output, `tick`, is asserted in this state. A representative timing diagram is shown at the middle of Figure 5.5. The code is shown in Listing 5.3.

Listing 5.3 Moore machine–based edge detector

```
library ieee;
use ieee.std_logic_1164.all;
entity edge_detect is
   port(
      clk, reset: in std_logic;
      level: in std_logic;
      tick: out std_logic
   );
end edge_detect;

architecture moore_arch of edge_detect is
   type state_type is (zero, edge, one);
   signal state_reg, state_next: state_type;
begin
   -- state register
   process(clk,reset)
   begin
      if (reset='1') then
         state_reg <= zero;
      elsif (clk'event and clk='1') then
         state_reg <= state_next;
      end if;
   end process;
   -- next-state/output logic
   process(state_reg,level)
   begin
      state_next <= state_reg;
      tick <= '0';
      case state_reg is
```

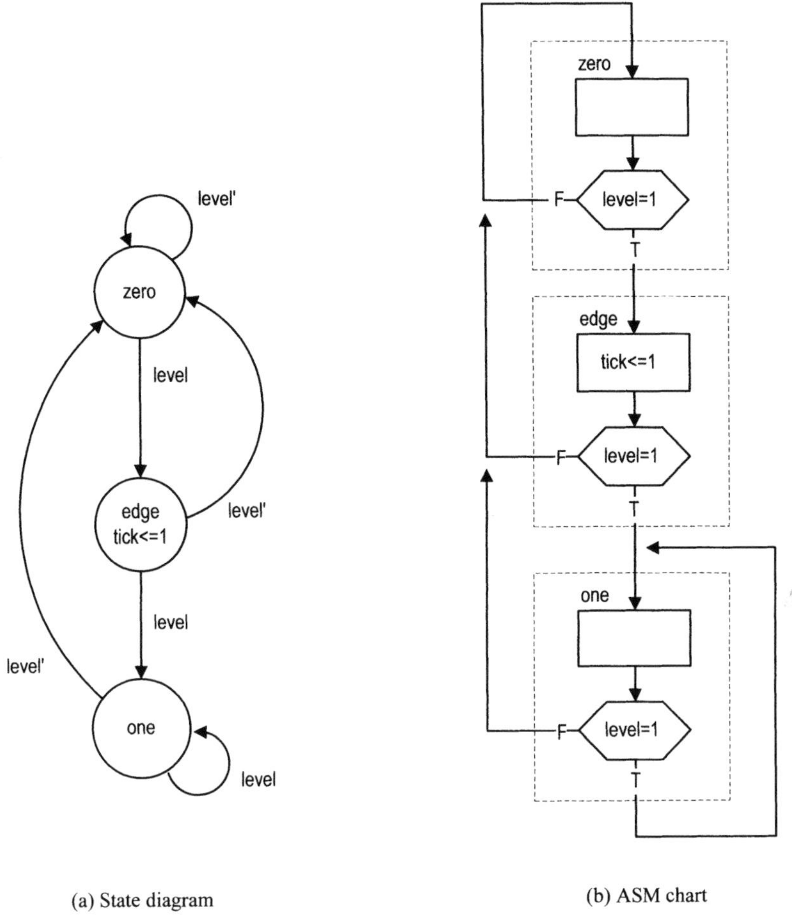

(a) State diagram

(b) ASM chart

Figure 5.4 Edge detector based on a Moore machine.

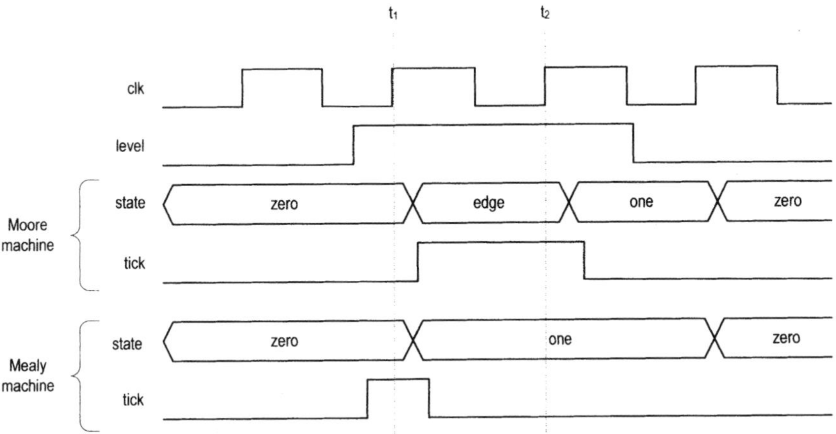

Figure 5.5 Timing diagram of two edge detectors.

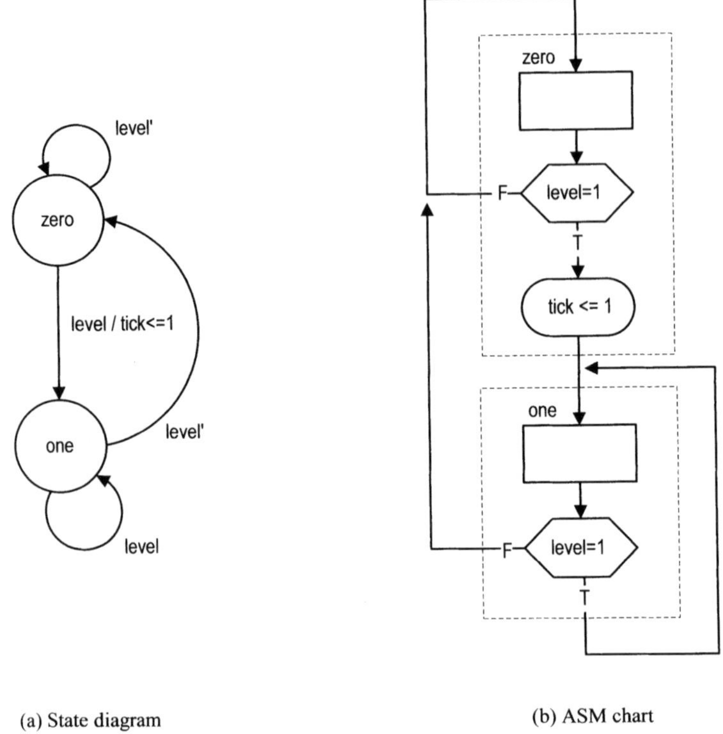

(a) State diagram

(b) ASM chart

Figure 5.6 Edge detector based on a Mealy machine.

```
            when zero=>
               if level= '1' then
                  state_next <= edge;
               end if;
            when edge =>
               tick <= '1';
               if level= '1' then
                  state_next <= one;
               else
                  state_next <= zero;
               end if;
            when one =>
               if level= '0' then
                  state_next <= zero;
               end if;
         end case;
      end process;
   end moore_arch;
```

Mealy-based design The state diagram and ASM chart of a Mealy machine–based edge detector are shown in Figure 5.6. The `zero` and `one` states have similar meaning. When the FSM is in the `zero` state and the input changes to '1', the output is asserted

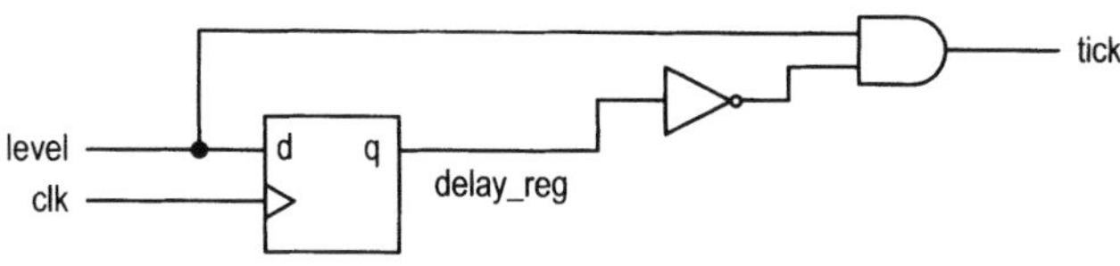

Figure 5.7 Gate-level implementation of an edge detector.

immediately. The FSM moves to the one state at the rising edge of the next clock and the output is deasserted. A representative timing diagram is shown at the bottom of Figure 5.5. Note that due to the propagation delay, the output signal is still asserted at the rising edge of the next clock (i.e., at t_1). The code is shown in Listing 5.4.

Listing 5.4 Mealy machine–based edge detector

```
architecture mealy_arch of edge_detect is
   type state_type is (zero, one);
   signal state_reg, state_next: state_type;
begin
   -- state register
   process(clk,reset)
   begin
      if (reset='1') then
         state_reg <= zero;
      elsif (clk'event and clk='1') then
         state_reg <= state_next;
      end if;
   end process;
   -- next-state/output logic
   process(state_reg,level)
   begin
      state_next <= state_reg;
      tick <= '0';
      case state_reg is
         when zero=>
            if level= '1' then
               state_next <= one;
               tick <= '1';
            end if;
         when one =>
            if level= '0' then
               state_next <= zero;
            end if;
      end case;
   end process;
end mealy_arch;
```

Direct implementation Since the transitions of the edge detector circuit are very simple, it can be implemented without using an FSM. We include this implementation for comparison purposes. The circuit diagram is shown in Figure 5.7. It can be interpreted that the output is asserted only when the current input is '1' and the previous input, which is stored in the register, is '0'. The corresponding code is shown in Listing 5.5.

Listing 5.5 Gate-level implementation of an edge detector

```
architecture gate_level_arch of edge_detect is
   signal delay_reg: std_logic;
begin
   -- delay register
   process(clk,reset)
   begin
      if (reset='1') then
         delay_reg <= '0';
      elsif (clk'event and clk='1') then
         delay_reg <= level;
      end if;
   end process;
   -- decoding logic
   tick <= (not delay_reg) and level;
end gate_level_arch;
```

Although the descriptions in Listings 5.4 and 5.5 appear to be very different, they describe the same circuit. The circuit diagram can be derived from the FSM if we assign '0' and '1' to the `zero` and `one` states.

Comparison Whereas both Moore machine– and Mealy machine–based designs can generate a short tick at the rising edge of the input signal, there are several subtle differences. The Mealy machine–based design requires fewer states and responds faster, but the width of its output may vary and input glitches may be passed to the output.

The choice between the two designs depends on the subsystem that uses the output signal. Most of the time the subsystem is a synchronous system that shares the same clock signal. Since the FSM's output is sampled only at the rising edge of the clock, the width and glitches do not matter as long as the output signal is stable around the edge. Note that the Mealy output signal is available for sampling at t_1, which is one clock cycle faster than the Moore output, which is available at t_2. Therefore, the Mealy machine–based circuit is preferred for this type of application.

5.3.2 Debouncing circuit

The slide and pushbutton switches on the prototyping board are mechanical devices. When pressed, the switch may bounce back and forth a few times before settling down. The bounces lead to glitches in the signal, as shown at the top of Figure 5.8. The bounces usually settle within 20 ms. The purpose of a debouncing circuit is to filter out the glitches associated with switch transitions. The debounced output signals from two FSM-based design schemes are shown in the two bottom parts of Figure 5.8. The first design scheme is discussed in this subsection and the second scheme is left as an exercise in Experiment 5.5.2. A better alternative FSMD-based scheme is discussed in Section 6.2.1.

An FSM-based design uses a free-running 10-ms timer and an FSM. The timer generates a one-clock-cycle enable tick (the `m_tick` signal) every 10 ms and the FSM uses this information to keep track of whether the input value is stabilized. In the first design scheme, the FSM ignores the short bounces and changes the value of the debounced output only after the input is stabilized for 20 ms. The output timing diagram is shown at the middle of Figure 5.8. The state diagram of this FSM is shown in Figure 5.9. The `zero` and `one` states indicate that the switch input signal, `sw`, has been stabilized with '0' and '1' values.

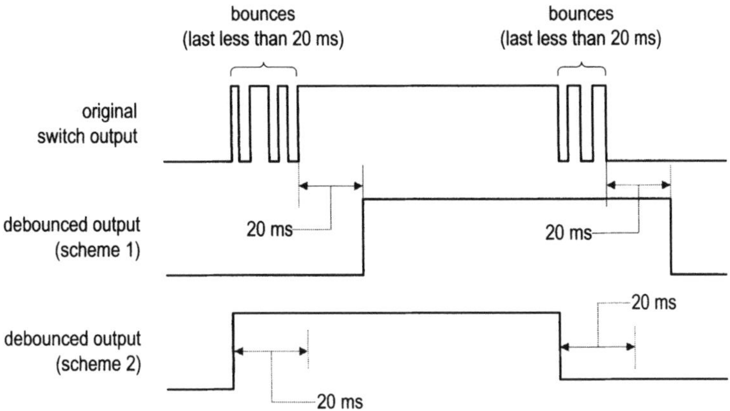

Figure 5.8 Original and debounced waveforms.

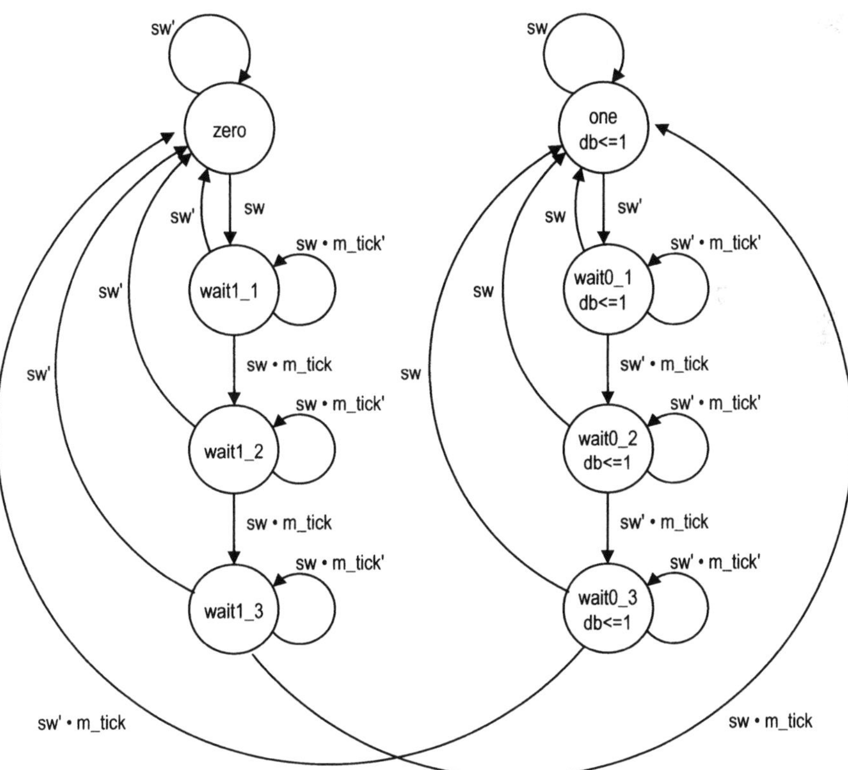

Figure 5.9 State diagram of a debouncing circuit.

Assume that the FSM is initially in the zero state. It moves to the wait1_1 state when sw changes to '1'. At the wait1_1 state, the FSM waits for the assertion of m_tick. If sw becomes '0' in this state, it implies that the width of the '1' value does not last long enough and the FSM returns to the zero state. This action repeats two more times for the wait1_2 and wait1_3 states. The operation from the one state is similar except that the sw signal must be '0'.

Since the 10-ms timer is free-running and the m_tick tick can be asserted at any time, the FSM checks the assertion three times to ensure that the sw signal is stabilized for at least 20 ms (it is actually between 20 and 30 ms). The code is shown in Listing 5.6. It includes a 10-ms timer and the FSM.

Listing 5.6 FSM implementation of a debouncing circuit

```
library ieee;
use ieee.std_logic_1164.all;
use ieee.numeric_std.all;
entity db_fsm is
   port(
      clk, reset: in std_logic;
      sw: in std_logic;
      db: out std_logic
   );
end db_fsm;

architecture arch of db_fsm is
   constant N: integer:=19;   -- 2^N * 20ns = 10ms
   signal q_reg, q_next: unsigned(N-1 downto 0);
   signal m_tick: std_logic;
   type eg_state_type is (zero,wait1_1,wait1_2,wait1_3,
                          one,wait0_1,wait0_2,wait0_3);
   signal state_reg, state_next: eg_state_type;
begin
   --=====================================
   -- counter to generate 10ms tick
   -- (2^19 * 20ns)
   --=====================================
   process(clk,reset)
   begin
      if (clk'event and clk='1') then
         q_reg <= q_next;
      end if;
   end process;
   -- next-state logic
   q_next <= q_reg + 1;
   --output tick
   m_tick <= '1' when q_reg=0 else
             '0';
   --=====================================
   -- debouncing FSM
   --=====================================
   -- state register
   process(clk,reset)
   begin
```

```
      if (reset='1') then
         state_reg <= zero;
      elsif (clk'event and clk='1') then
         state_reg <= state_next;
      end if;
   end process;
   -- next-state/output logic
   process(state_reg,sw,m_tick)
   begin
      state_next <= state_reg; --default: back to same state
      db <= '0';    -- default 0
      case state_reg is
         when zero =>
            if sw='1' then
               state_next <= wait1_1;
            end if;
         when wait1_1 =>
            if sw='0' then
               state_next <= zero;
            else
               if m_tick='1' then
                  state_next <= wait1_2;
               end if;
            end if;
         when wait1_2 =>
            if sw='0' then
               state_next <= zero;
            else
               if m_tick='1' then
                  state_next <= wait1_3;
               end if;
            end if;
         when wait1_3 =>
            if sw='0' then
               state_next <= zero;
            else
               if m_tick='1' then
                  state_next <= one;
               end if;
            end if;
         when one =>
            db <='1';
            if sw='0' then
               state_next <= wait0_1;
            end if;
         when wait0_1 =>
            db <='1';
            if sw='1' then
               state_next <= one;
            else
               if m_tick='1' then
                  state_next <= wait0_2;
               end if;
```

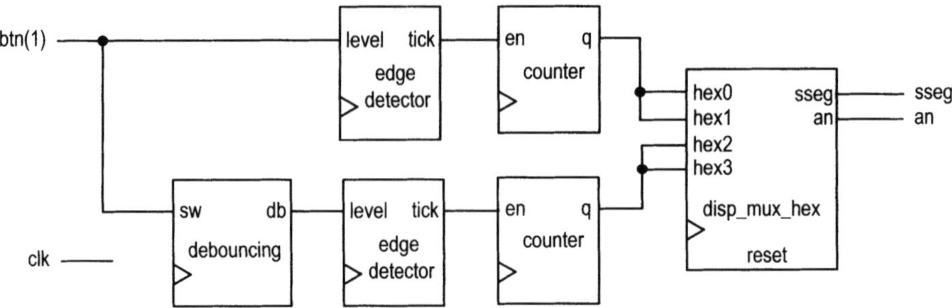

Figure 5.10 Debouncing testing circuit.

```
            end if;
         when wait0_2 =>
            db <='1';
            if sw='1' then
               state_next <= one;
            else
               if m_tick='1' then
                  state_next <= wait0_3;
               end if;
            end if;
         when wait0_3 =>
            db <='1';
            if sw='1' then
               state_next <= one;
            else
               if m_tick='1' then
                  state_next <= zero;
               end if;
            end if;
      end case;
   end process;
end arch;
```

5.3.3 Testing circuit

We use a bounce counting circuit to verify operation of the rising-edge detector and the debouncing circuit. The block diagram is shown in Figure 5.10. The input of the verification circuit is from a pushbutton switch. In the lower part, the signal is first fed to the debouncing circuit and then to the rising-edge detector. Therefore, a one-clock-cycle tick is generated each time the button is pressed and released. The tick in turn controls the enable input of an 8-bit counter, whose content is passed to the LED time-multiplexing circuit and shown on the left two digits of the prototyping board's seven-segment LED display. In the upper part, the input signal is fed directly to the edge detector without the debouncing circuit, and the number is shown on the right two digits of the prototyping board's seven-segment LED display. The bottom counter thus counts one desired 0-to-1 transition as well as the bounces.

The code is shown in Listing 5.7. It basically uses component instantiation to realize the block diagram.

Listing 5.7 Verification circuit for a debouncing circuit and rising-edge detector

```
library ieee;
use ieee.std_logic_1164.all;
use ieee.numeric_std.all;
entity debounce_test is
   port(
      clk: in std_logic;
      btn: in std_logic_vector(3 downto 0);
      an: out std_logic_vector(3 downto 0);
      sseg: out std_logic_vector(7 downto 0)
   );
end debounce_test;

architecture arch of debounce_test is
   signal q1_reg, q1_next: unsigned(7 downto 0);
   signal q0_reg, q0_next: unsigned(7 downto 0);
   signal b_count, d_count: std_logic_vector(7 downto 0);
   signal btn_reg, db_reg: std_logic;
   signal db_level, db_tick, btn_tick, clr: std_logic;
begin
   --==================================================
   -- component instantiation
   --==================================================
   -- instantiate hex display time-multiplexing circuit
   disp_unit: entity work.disp_hex_mux
      port map(
         clk=>clk, reset=>'0',
         hex3=>b_count(7 downto 4), hex2=>b_count(3 downto 0),
         hex1=>d_count(7 downto 4), hex0=>d_count(3 downto 0),
         dp_in=>"1011", an=>an, sseg=>sseg);
   -- instantiate debouncing circuit
   db_unit: entity work.db_fsm(arch)
      port map(
         clk=>clk, reset=>'0',
         sw=>btn(1), db=>db_level);

   --==================================================
   -- edge detection circuits
   --==================================================
   process(clk)
   begin
      if (clk'event and clk='1') then
         btn_reg <= btn(1);
         db_reg <= db_level;
      end if;
   end process;
   btn_tick <= (not btn_reg) and btn(1);
   db_tick <= (not db_reg) and db_level;

   --==================================================
```

```
-- two counters
--=============================================
clr <= btn(0);
process(clk)
begin
   if (clk'event and clk='1') then
      q1_reg <= q1_next;
      q0_reg <= q0_next;
   end if;
end process;
-- next-state logic for the counter
q1_next <= (others=>'0') when clr='1' else
           q1_reg + 1 when btn_tick='1' else
           q1_reg;
q0_next <= (others=>'0') when clr='1' else
           q0_reg + 1 when db_tick='1' else
           q0_reg;
--output
b_count <= std_logic_vector(q1_reg);
d_count <= std_logic_vector(q0_reg);
end arch;
```

The seven-segment display shows the accumulated numbers of 0-to-1 edges of bounced and debounced switch input. After pressing and releasing the pushbutton switch several times, we can determine the average number of bounces for each transition.

5.4 BIBLIOGRAPHIC NOTES

The bibliographic information for this chapter is similar to that for Chapter 3.

5.5 SUGGESTED EXPERIMENTS

5.5.1 Dual-edge detector

A dual-edge detector is similar to a rising-edge detector except that the output is asserted for one clock cycle when the input changes from 0 to 1 (i.e., rising edge) and 1 to 0 (i.e., falling edge).

1. Design the circuit based on the Moore machine and draw the state diagram and ASM chart.
2. Derive the HDL code based on the state diagram of the ASM chart.
3. Derive a testbench and use simulation to verify operation of the code.
4. Replace the rising detectors in Section 5.3.3 with dual-edge detectors and verify their operations.
5. Repeat steps 1 to 4 for a Mealy machine–based design.

5.5.2 Alternative debouncing circuit

One problem with the debouncing design in Section 5.3.2 is the delayed response of the onset of a switch transition. An alternative is to react to the first edge in the transition and

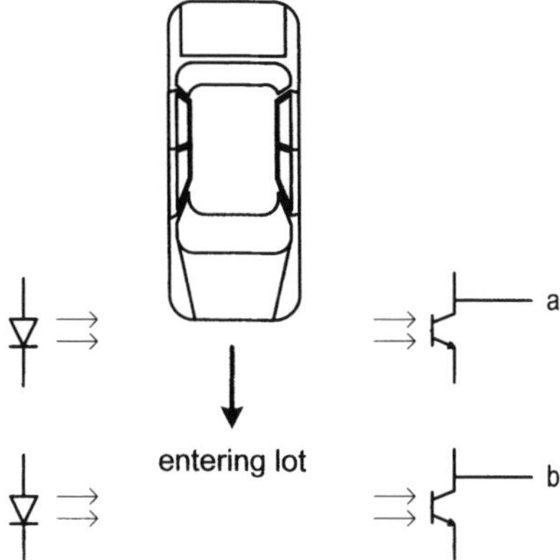

Figure 5.11 Conceptual diagram of gate sensors.

then wait for a small amount of time (at least 20 ms) to have the input signal settled. The output timing diagram is shown at the bottom of Figure 5.8. When the input changes from '0' to '1', the FSM responds immediately. The FSM then ignores the input for about 20 ms to avoid glitches. After this amount of time, the FSM starts to check the input for the falling edge. Follow the design procedure in Section 5.3.2 to design the alternative circuit.

1. Derive the state diagram and ASM chart for the circuit.
2. Derive the HDL code.
3. Derive the HDL code based on the state diagram and ASM chart.
4. Derive a testbench and use simulation to verify operation of the code.
5. Replace the debouncing circuit in Section 5.3.3 with the alternative design and verify its operation.

5.5.3 Parking lot occupancy counter

Consider a parking lot with a single entry and exit gate. Two pairs of photo sensors are used to monitor the activity of cars, as shown in Figure 5.11. When an object is between the photo transmitter and the photo receiver, the light is blocked and the corresponding output is asserted to '1'. By monitoring the events of two sensors, we can determine whether a car is entering or exiting or a pedestrian is passing through. For example, the following sequence indicates that a car enters the lot:

- Initially, both sensors are unblocked (i.e., the `a` and `b` signals are "00").
- Sensor a is blocked (i.e., the `a` and `b` signals are "10").
- Both sensors are blocked (i.e., the `a` and `b` signals are "11").
- Sensor a is unblocked (i.e., the `a` and `b` signals are "01").
- Both sensors becomes unblocked (i.e., the `a` and `b` signals are "00").

Design a parking lot occupancy counter as follows:

1. Design an FSM with two input signals, `a` and `b`, and two output signals, `enter` and `exit`. The `enter` and `exit` signals assert one clock cycle when a car enters and one clock cycle when a car exits the lot, respectively.
2. Derive the HDL code for the FSM.

3. Design a counter with two control signals, `inc` and `dec`, which increment and decrement the counter when asserted. Derive the HDL code.
4. Combine the counter and the FSM and LED multiplexing circuit. Use two debounced pushbuttons to mimic operation of the two sensor outputs. Verify operation of the occupancy counter.

CHAPTER 6

FSMD

6.1 INTRODUCTION

An FSMD (finite state machine with data path) combines an FSM and regular sequential circuits. The FSM, which is sometimes known as a *control path*, examines the external commands and status and generates control signals to specify operation of the regular sequential circuits, which are known collectively as a *data path*. The FSMD is used to implement systems described by *RT (register transfer) methodology*, in which the operations are specified as data manipulation and transfer among a collection of registers.

6.1.1 Single RT operation

An RT operation specifies data manipulation and transfer for a single destination register. It is represented by the notation

$$\mathrm{r}_{\mathrm{dest}} \leftarrow f(\mathrm{r}_{\mathrm{src1}}, \mathrm{r}_{\mathrm{src2}}, \ldots, \mathrm{r}_{\mathrm{srcn}})$$

where $\mathrm{r}_{\mathrm{dest}}$ is the destination register, $\mathrm{r}_{\mathrm{src1}}$, $\mathrm{r}_{\mathrm{src2}}$, and $\mathrm{r}_{\mathrm{srcn}}$ are the source registers, and $f(\cdot)$ specifies the operation to be performed. The notation indicates that the contents of the source registers are fed to the $f(\cdot)$ function, which is realized by a combinational circuit, and the result is passed to the input of the destination register and stored in the destination register at the next rising edge of the clock. Following are several representative RT operations:

- `r1` $\leftarrow 0$. A constant 0 is stored in the `r1` register.
- `r1` $\leftarrow$ `r1`. The content of the `r1` register is written back to itself.

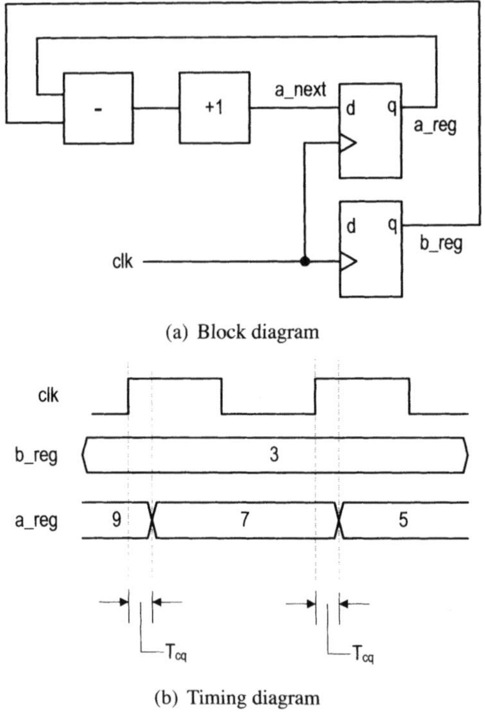

(a) Block diagram

(b) Timing diagram

Figure 6.1 Block and timing diagrams of an RT operation.

- `r2` ← `r2 >> 3`. The `r2` register is shifted right three positions and then written back to itself.
- `r2` ← `r1`. The content of the `r1` register is transferred to the `r2` register.
- `i` ← `i` + 1. The content of the `i` register is incremented by 1 and the result is written back to itself.
- `d` ← `s1` + `s2` + `s3`. The summation of the `s1`, `s2`, and `s3` registers is written to the `d` register.
- `y` ← `a*a`. The a squared is written to the y register.

A single RT operation can be implemented by constructing a combinational circuit for the $f(\cdot)$ function and connecting the input and output of the registers. For example, consider the `a` ← `a-b+1` operation. The $f(\cdot)$ function involves a subtractor and an incrementor. The block diagram is shown in Figure 6.1(a). For clarity, we use the `_reg` and `_next` suffixes to represent the input and output of a register. Note that an RT operation is synchronized by an embedded clock. The result from the $f(\cdot)$ function is not stored to the destination register until the next rising edge of the clock. The timing diagram of the previous RT operation is shown in Figure 6.1(b).

6.1.2 ASMD chart

A circuit based on the RT methodology specifies which RT operations should be executed in each step. Since an RT operation is done in a clock-by-clock basis, its timing is similar to a state transition of an FSM. Thus, an FSM is a natural choice to specify the sequencing

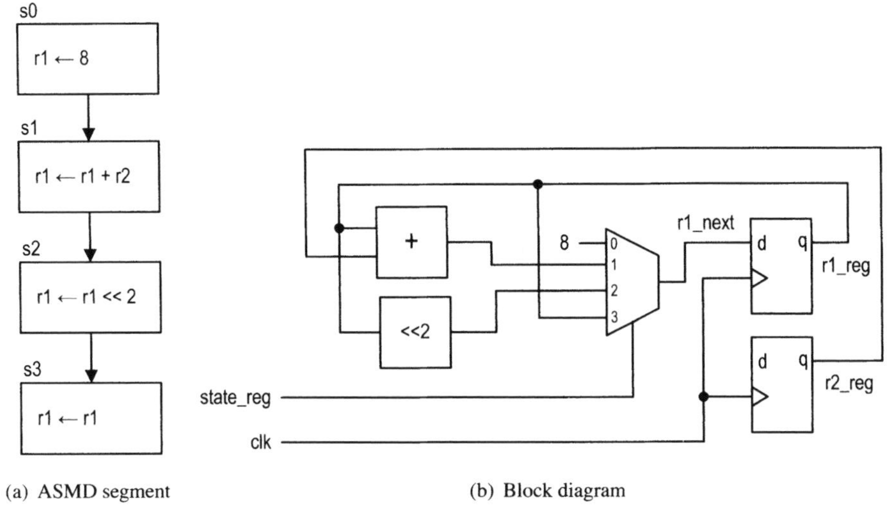

(a) ASMD segment

(b) Block diagram

Figure 6.2 Realization of an ASMD segment.

of an RT algorithm. We extend the ASM chart to incorporate RT operations and call it an *ASMD* (ASM with data path) chart. The RT operations are treated as another type of activity and can be placed where the output signals are used.

A segment of an ASMD chart is shown in Figure 6.2(a). It contains one destination register, `r1`, which is initialized with 8, added with content of the `r2` register, and then shifted left two positions. Note that the `r1` register must be specified in each state. When `r1` is not changed, the `r1` ← `r1` operation should be used to maintain its current content, as in the `s3` state. In future discussion, we assume that `r` ← `r` is the default RT operation for the `r` register and do not include it in the ASMD chart. Implementing the RT operations of an ASMD chart involves a multiplexing circuit to route the desired next value to the destination register. For example, the previous segment can be implemented by a 4-to-1 multiplexer, as shown in Figure 6.2(b). The current state (i.e., the output of the state register) of the FSM controls the selection signal of the multiplexer and thus chooses the result of the desired RT operation.

An RT operation can also be specified in a conditional output box, as the `r2` register shown in Figure 6.3(a). Depending on the `a>b` condition, the FSMD performs either `r2` ← `r2+a` or `r2` ← `r2+b`. Note that all operations are done in parallel inside an ASMD block. We need to realize the `a>b`, `r2+a`, and `r2+b` operations and use a multiplexer to route the desired value to `r2`. The block diagram is shown in Figure 6.3(b).

6.1.3 Decision box with a register

The appearance of an ASMD chart is similar to that of a normal flowchart. The main difference is that the RT operation in an ASMD chart is controlled by an embedded clock signal and the destination register is updated *when the FSMD exits the current ASMD block*, but not within the block. The `r` ← `r-1` operation actually means that:

- `r_next <= r_reg - 1;`
- `r_reg <= r_next` at the rising edge of the clock (i.e., when the FSMD exits the current block).

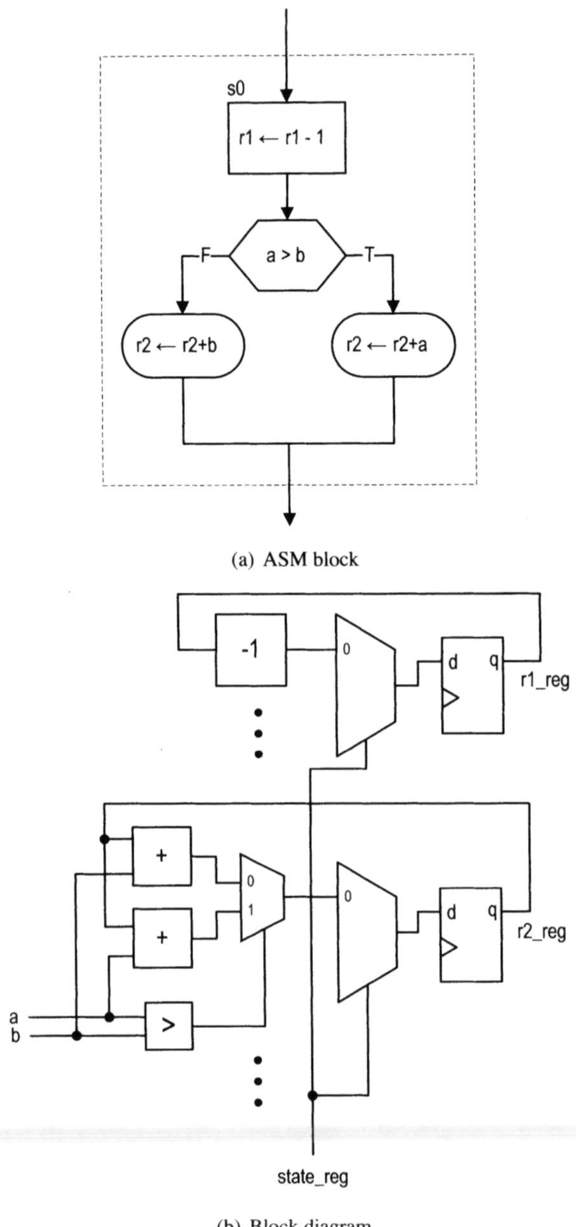

(a) ASM block

(b) Block diagram

Figure 6.3 Realization of an RT operation in a conditional output box.

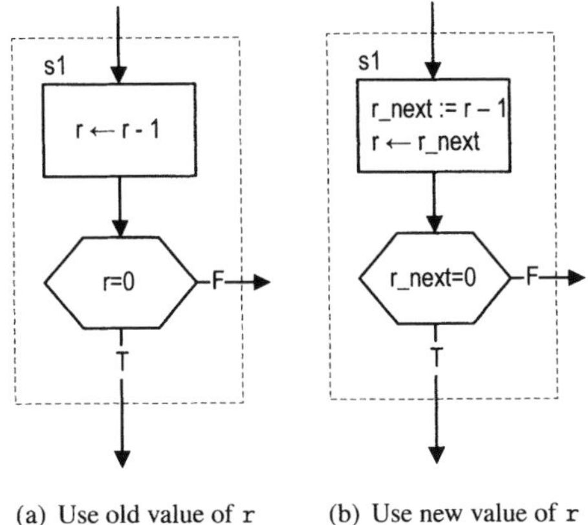

(a) Use old value of r (b) Use new value of r

Figure 6.4 ASM block affected by a delayed store.

This "delayed store" may introduce subtle errors when a register is used in a decision box. Consider the FSMD segment in Figure 6.4(a). The `r` register is decremented in the state box and used in the decision box. Since the `r` register is not updated until the FSMD exits the block, the old content of `r` is used for comparison in the decision box. If the new value of `r` is desired, we should use the output of the combinational logic (i.e., `r_next`) in the decision box (i.e., replace the `r=0` expression with `r_next=0`), as shown in Figure 6.4(b). Note that we use the := notation, as in `r_next:=r-1`, to indicate the immediate assignment of `r_next`.

Block diagram of an FSMD The conceptual block diagram of an FSMD is divided into a data path and a control path, as shown in Figure 6.5. The data path performs the required RT operations. It consists of:

- *Data registers*: store the intermediate computation results
- *Functional units*: perform the functions specified by the RT operations
- *Routing network*: routes data between the storage registers and the functional units

The data path follows the `control` signal to perform the desired RT operations and generates the `internal status` signal.

The control path is an FSM. As a regular FSM, it contains a state register, next-state logic, and output logic. It uses the external `command` signal and the data path's `status` signal as the input and generates the `control` signal to control the data path operation. The FSM also generates the `external status` signal to indicate the status of the FSMD operation.

Note that although an FSMD consists of two types of sequential circuits, both circuits are controlled by the same clock, and thus the FSMD is still a synchronous system.

6.2 CODE DEVELOPMENT OF AN FSMD

We use an improved debouncing circuit to demonstrate derivation of the FSMD code. Although the debouncing circuit in Section 5.3.2 uses an FSM and a timer (which is a regular sequential circuit), it is not based on the RT methodology because the two units are running independently and the FSM has no control over the timer. Since the 10-ms enable

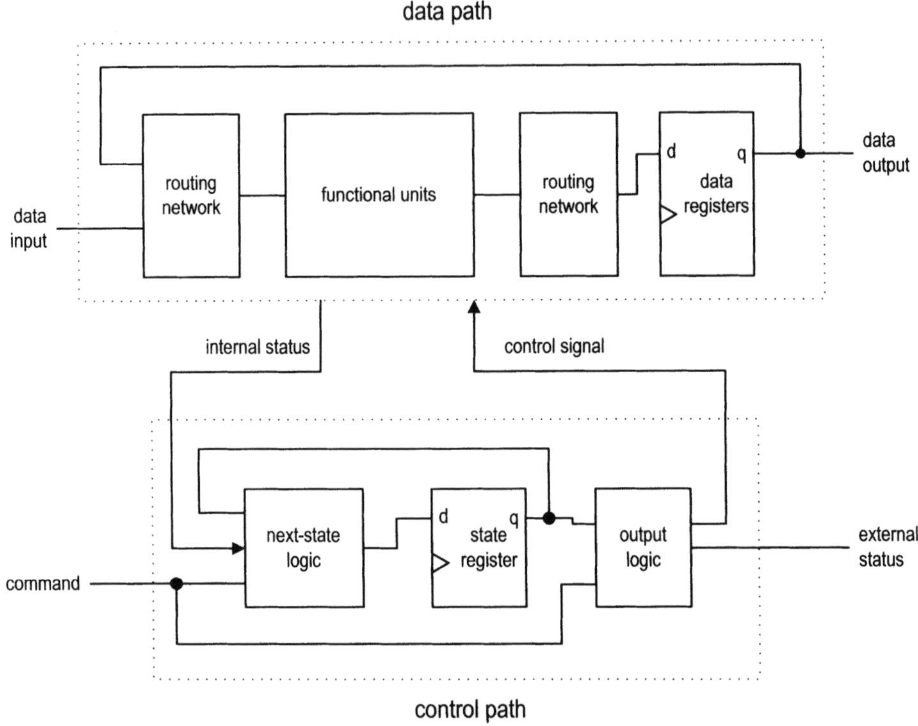

Figure 6.5 Block diagram of an FSMD.

tick can be asserted at any time, the FSM does not know how much time has elapsed when the first tick is detected in the `wait1_1` or `wait0_1` state. Thus, the waiting period in this design is between 20 and 30 ms but is not an exact interval. This deficiency can be overcome by applying the RT methodology. In this section, we use this improved debouncing circuit to illustrate the FSMD code development.

6.2.1 Debouncing circuit based on RT methodology

With the RT methodology, we can use an FSM to control the initiation of the timer to obtain the exact interval. The ASMD chart is shown in Figure 6.6. The circuit is expanded to include two output signals: `db_level`, which is the debounced output, and `db_tick`, which is a one-clock-cycle enable pulse asserted at the zero-to-one transition. The `zero` and `one` states mean that the `sw` input has been stabilized for '0' and '1', respectively. The `wait1` and `wait0` states are used to filter out short glitches. The `sw` signal must be stable for a certain amount of time or the transition will be treated as a glitch. The data path contains one register, `q`, which is 21 bits wide. Assume that the FSMD is originally in the `zero` state. When the `sw` input signal becomes '1', the FSMD moves to the `wait1` state and initializes `q` to "1 ··· 1". In the `wait1` state, the `q` decrements in each clock cycle. If `sw` remains as '1', the FSMD returns to this state repeatedly until `q` reaches "0 ··· 0" and then moves to the `one` state.

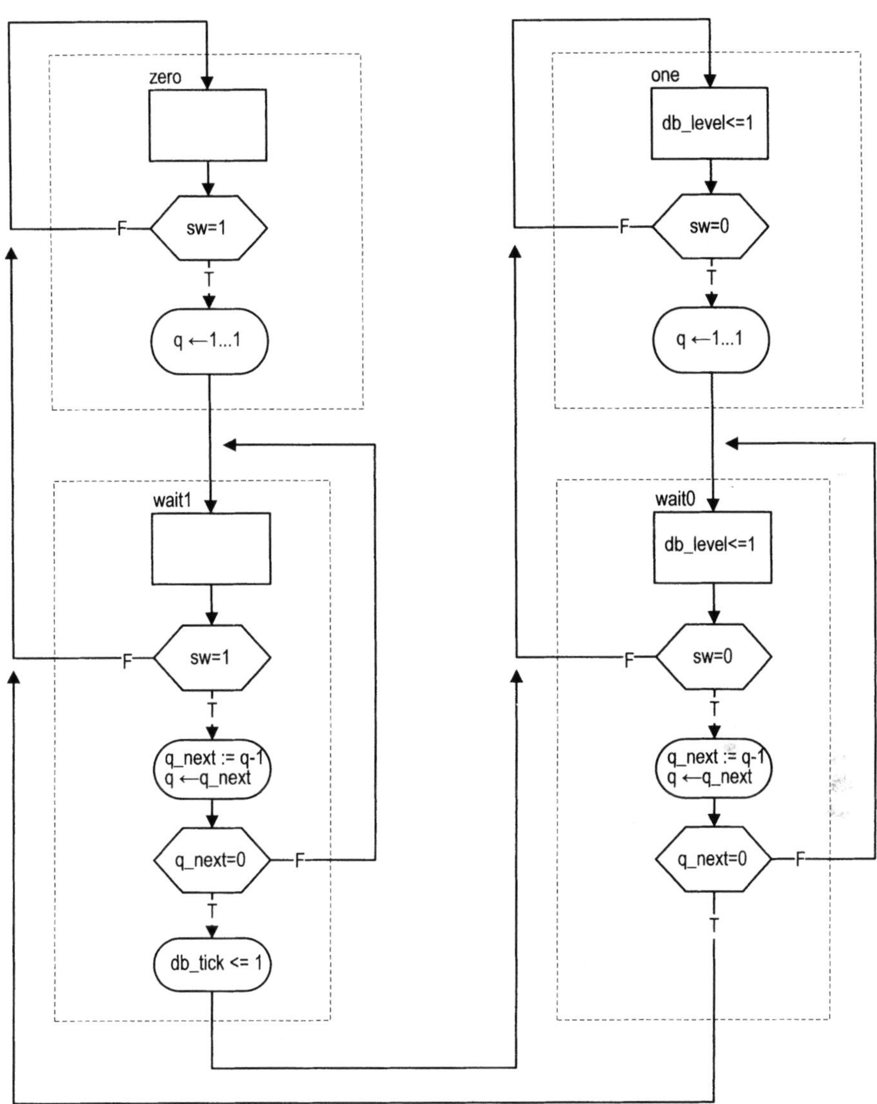

Figure 6.6 ASMD chart of a debouncing circuit.

Recall that the 50-MHz (i.e., 20-ns period) system clock is used on the prototyping board. Since the FSMD stays in the `wait1` state for 2^{21} clock cycles, it is about 40 ms (i.e., $2^{21}*20$ ns). We can modify the initial value of the q register to obtain the desired wait interval.

There are two ways to derive the HDL code, one with *explicit description* of the data path components and the other with *implicit description* of the data path components.

6.2.2 Code with explicit data path components

The first approach to FSMD code development is to separate the control FSM and the key data path components. From an ASMD chart, we first identify the key components in the data path and the associated control signals and then describe these components in individual code segments.

The key data path component of the debouncing circuit ASMD chart is a custom 21-bit decrement counter that can:

- Be initialized with a specific value
- Count downward or pause
- Assert a status signal when the counter reaches 0

We can create a binary counter with a `q_load` signal to load the initial value and a `q_dec` signal to enable the counting. The counter also generates a `q_zero` status signal, which is asserted when the counter reaches zero. The complete data path is composed of the q register and the next-state logic of the custom decrement counter. A comparison circuit is included to generate the `q_zero` status signal. The control path consists of an FSM, which takes the `sw` input and the `q_zero` status and asserts the control signals, `q_load` and `q_dec`, according to the desired action in the ASMD chart. The HDL code follows the data path specification and the ASMD chart, and is shown in Listing 6.1.

Listing 6.1 Debouncing circuit with an explicit data path component

```
library ieee;
use ieee.std_logic_1164.all;
use ieee.numeric_std.all;
entity debounce is
   port(
      clk, reset: in std_logic;
      sw: in std_logic;
      db_level, db_tick: out std_logic
   );
end debounce ;

architecture exp_fsmd_arch of debounce is
   constant N: integer:=21;  -- filter of 2^N * 20ns = 40ms
   type state_type is (zero, wait0, one, wait1);
   signal state_reg, state_next: state_type;
   signal q_reg, q_next: unsigned(N-1 downto 0);
   signal q_load, q_dec, q_zero: std_logic;
begin
   -- FSMD state & data registers
   process(clk,reset)
   begin
      if reset='1' then
         state_reg <= zero;
```

```
         q_reg <= (others=>'0');
      elsif (clk'event and clk='1') then
         state_reg <= state_next;
         q_reg <= q_next;
      end if;
   end process;

   -- FSMD data path (counter) next-state logic
   q_next <= (others=>'1') when q_load='1' else
             q_reg - 1 when q_dec='1' else
             q_reg;
   q_zero <= '1' when q_next=0 else '0';

   -- FSMD control path next-state logic
   process(state_reg,sw,q_zero)
   begin
      q_load <= '0';
      q_dec <= '0';
      db_tick <= '0';
      state_next <= state_reg;
      case state_reg is
         when zero =>
            db_level <= '0';
            if (sw='1') then
               state_next <= wait1;
               q_load <= '1';
            end if;
         when wait1=>
            db_level <= '0';
            if (sw='1') then
               q_dec <= '1';
               if (q_zero='1') then
                  state_next <= one;
                  db_tick <= '1';
               end if;
            else -- sw='0'
               state_next <= zero;
            end if;
         when one =>
            db_level <= '1';
            if (sw='0') then
               state_next <= wait0;
               q_load <= '1';
            end if;
         when wait0=>
            db_level <= '1';
            if (sw='0') then
               q_dec <= '1';
               if (q_zero='1') then
                  state_next <= zero;
               end if;
            else -- sw='1'
               state_next <= one;
```

```
            end if;
        end case;
    end process;
end exp_fsmd_arch;
```

6.2.3 Code with implicit data path components

An alternative coding style is to embed the RT operations within the FSM control path. Instead of explicitly defining the data path components, we just list RT operations with the corresponding FSM state. The code of the debouncing circuit is shown in Listing 6.2.

Listing 6.2 Debouncing circuit with an implicit data path component

```
architecture imp_fsmd_arch of debounce is
   constant N: integer:=21;  -- filter of 2^N * 20ns = 40ms
   type state_type is (zero, wait0, one, wait1);
   signal state_reg, state_next: state_type;
   signal q_reg, q_next: unsigned(N-1 downto 0);
begin
   -- FSMD state & data registers
   process(clk,reset)
   begin
      if reset='1' then
         state_reg <= zero;
         q_reg <= (others=>'0');
      elsif (clk'event and clk='1') then
         state_reg <= state_next;
         q_reg <= q_next;
      end if;
   end process;
   -- next-state logic & data path functional units/routing
   process(state_reg,q_reg,sw,q_next)
   begin
      state_next <= state_reg;
      q_next <= q_reg;
      db_tick <= '0';
      case state_reg is
         when zero =>
            db_level <= '0';
            if (sw='1') then
               state_next <= wait1;
               q_next <= (others=>'1');
            end if;
         when wait1=>
            db_level <= '0';
            if (sw='1') then
               q_next <= q_reg - 1;
               if (q_next=0) then
                  state_next <= one;
                  db_tick <= '1';
               end if;
            else -- sw='0'
               state_next <= zero;
```

```
               end if;
            when one =>
               db_level <= '1';
               if (sw='0') then
                  state_next <= wait0;
                  q_next <= (others=>'1');
               end if;
            when wait0=>
               db_level <= '1';
               if (sw='0') then
                  q_next <= q_reg - 1;
                  if (q_next=0) then
                     state_next <= zero;
                  end if;
               else -- sw='1'
                  state_next <= one;
               end if;
         end case;
      end process;
end imp_fsmd_arch;
```

The code consists of a memory segment and a combinational logic segment. The former contains the state register of the FSM and the data register of the data path. The latter basically specifies the next-state logic of the control path FSM. Instead of generating control signals, the next data register values are specified in individual states. The next-state logic of the data path, which consists of functional units and routing network, is created accordingly.

6.2.4 Comparison

Code with implicit data path components essentially follows the ASMD chart. We just convert the chart to an HDL description. Although this approach is simpler and more descriptive, we rely on synthesis software for data path construction and have less control. This can best be explained by an example. Consider the ASMD segment in Figure 6.7. The implicit description becomes

```
case
   when s1
      d1_next <= a * b;
      . . .
   when s2
      d2_next <= b * c;
      . . .
   when s3
      d3_next <= a * c;
      . . .
end case;
```

The synthesis software may infer three multipliers. Since a combinational multiplier is a complex circuit, it is more efficient to share the circuit. We can use explicit description to isolate the multiplier:

```
case
   when s1
```

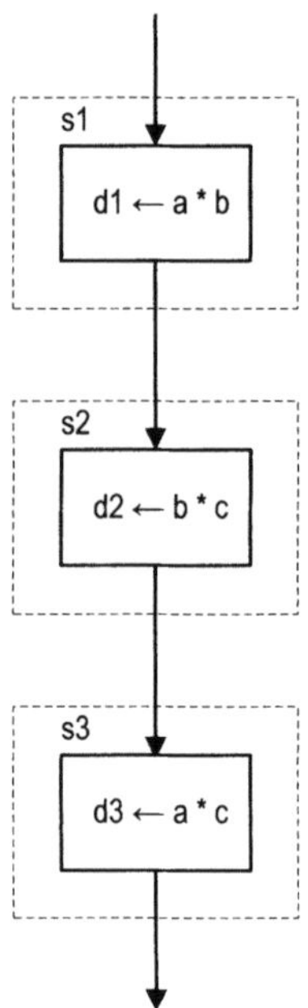

Figure 6.7 ASMD segment with sharing opportunity.

```
      in1 <= a;
      in2 <= b;
      d1_next <= m_out;
      . . .
   when s2
      in1 <= b;
      in2 <= c;
      d2_next <= m_out;
      . . .
   when s3
      in1 <= a;
      in2 <= c;
      d3_next <= m_out;
      . . .
end case;
-- explicit description of a single multiplier
m_out <= in1 * in2;
```

The code ensures that only one multiplier is inferred during synthesis. The implicit and explicit descriptions can be mixed for a complex FSMD design. We frequently isolate and extract complex data path components for code clarity and efficiency.

6.2.5 Testing circuit

The debouncing testing circuit discussed in Section 5.3.3 can be used to verify operation of the new design. Since the revised debouncing circuit's outputs include a one-clock-cycle tick signal, no edge detector is needed after the debouncing circuit. The revised block

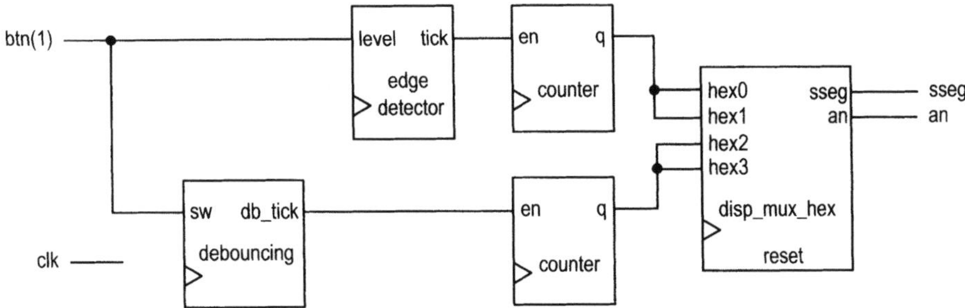

Figure 6.8 Debouncing testing circuit.

diagram is shown in Figure 6.8, and the corresponding code is shown in Listing 6.3.

Listing 6.3 Verification circuit for a debouncing circuit

```
library ieee;
use ieee.std_logic_1164.all;
use ieee.numeric_std.all;
entity debounce_test is
   port(
      clk: in std_logic;
      btn: in std_logic_vector(3 downto 0);
      an: out std_logic_vector(3 downto 0);
      sseg: out std_logic_vector(7 downto 0)
   );
end debounce_test;

architecture arch of debounce_test is
   signal q1_reg, q1_next: unsigned(7 downto 0);
   signal q0_reg, q0_next: unsigned(7 downto 0);
   signal b_count, d_count: std_logic_vector(7 downto 0);
   signal btn_reg: std_logic;
   signal db_tick, btn_tick, clr: std_logic;
begin
   -- instantiate debouncing circuit
   db_unit: entity work.debounce(fsmd_arch)
      port map(
         clk=>clk, reset=>'0', sw=>btn(1),
         db_level=> open, db_tick=>db_tick
      );
   -- instantiate hex display time-multiplxing circuit
   disp_unit: entity work.disp_hex_mux
      port map(
         clk=>clk, reset=>'0',
         hex3=>b_count(7 downto 4), hex2=>b_count(3 downto 0),
         hex1=>d_count(7 downto 4), hex0=>d_count(3 downto 0),
         dp_in=>"1011", an=>an, sseg=>sseg
      );

   --=================================================
   -- edge detection circuit for un-debounced input
```

```
--==================================================
process(clk)
begin
   if (clk'event and clk='1') then
      btn_reg <= btn(1);
   end if;
end process;
btn_tick <= (not btn_reg) and btn(1);

--==================================================
-- two counters
--==================================================
clr <= btn(0);
process(clk)
begin
   if (clk'event and clk='1') then
      q1_reg <= q1_next;
      q0_reg <= q0_next;
   end if;
end process;
-- next-state logic for the counter
q1_next <= (others=>'0') when clr='1' else
           q1_reg + 1 when btn_tick='1' else
           q1_reg;
q0_next <= (others=>'0') when clr='1' else
           q0_reg + 1 when db_tick='1' else
           q0_reg;
-- counter output
b_count <= std_logic_vector(q1_reg);
d_count <= std_logic_vector(q0_reg);
end arch;
```

6.3 DESIGN EXAMPLES

6.3.1 Fibonacci number circuit

The Fibonacci numbers constitute a sequence defined as

$$fib(i) = \begin{cases} 0 & \text{if } i = 0 \\ 1 & \text{if } i = 1 \\ fib(i-1) + fib(i-2) & \text{if } i > 1 \end{cases}$$

One way to calculate $fib(i)$ is to construct the function iteratively, from 0 to the desired i. This approach requires two temporary registers to store the two most recently calculated values (i.e., $fib(i-1)$ and $fib(i-2)$) and one index register to keep track of the number of iterations. The ASMD chart is shown in Figure 6.9, in which `t1` and `t0` are temporary storage registers and `n` is the index register. In addition to the regular data input and output signals, `i` and `f`, we include a command signal, `start`, which signals the beginning of operation, and two status signals: `ready`, which indicates that the circuit is idle and ready to take new input, and `done_tick`, which is asserted for one clock cycle when the operation

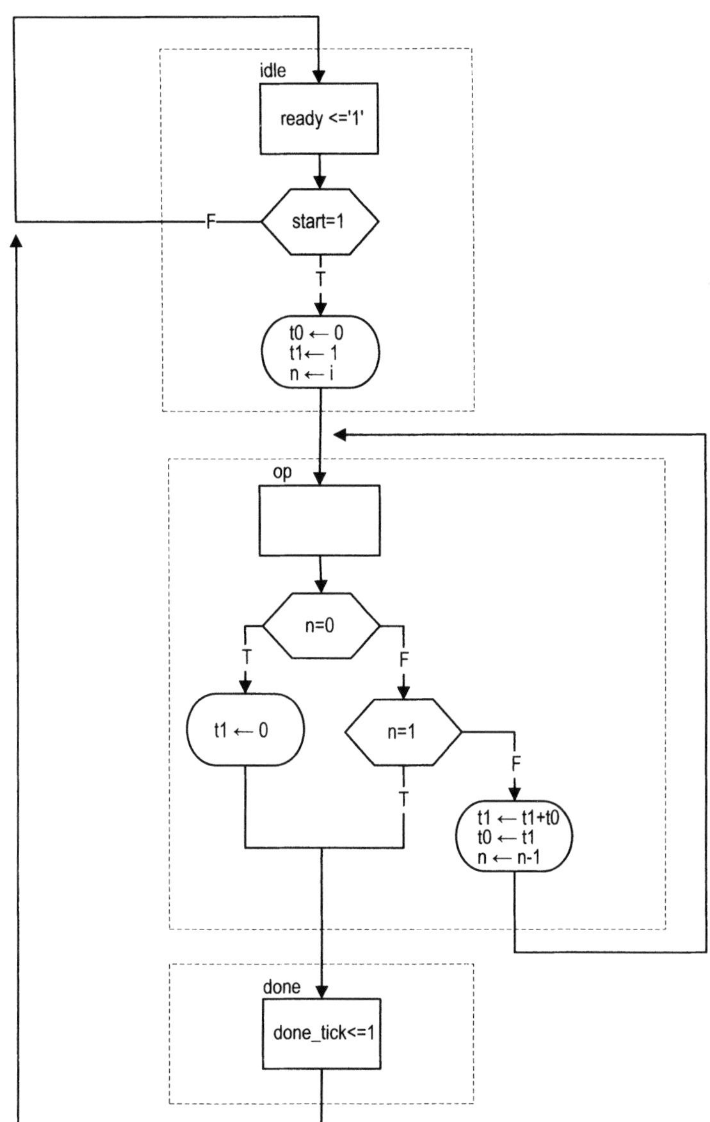

Figure 6.9 ASMD chart of a Fibonacci circuit.

is completed. Since this circuit, like many other FSMD designs, is probably a part of a larger system, these signals are needed to interface with other subsystems.

The ASMD chart has three states. The idle state indicates that the circuit is currently idle. When start is asserted, the FSMD moves to the op state and loads initial values to three registers. The t0 and t1 registers are loaded with 0 and 1, which represent $fib(0)$ and $fib(1)$, respectively. The n register is loaded with i, the desired number of iterations.

The main computation is iterated through the op state by three RT operations:

- t1 ← t1 + t0
- t0 ← t1
- n ← n - 1

The first two RT operations obtain a new value and store the two most recently calculated values in t1 and t0. The third RT operation decrements the iteration index. The iteration ended when n reaches 1 or its initial value is 0 (i.e., $fib(0)$). Unlike a regular flowchart, the operations in an ASMD block can be performed concurrently in the same clock cycle. We put all comparison and RT operations in the op state to reduce the computation time. Note that the new values of the t1 and t0 registers are loaded at the same time when the FSMD exits the op state (i.e., at the next rising edge of the clock). Thus, the original value of t1, not t1+t0, is stored to t0. The purpose of the done state is to generate the one-clock-cycle done_tick signal to indicate completion of the computation. This state can be omitted if this status signal is not needed.

The code follows the ASMD chart and is shown in Listing 6.4. Note that the Fibonacci function grows rapidly and the output signal should be wide enough to accommodate the desired result.

Listing 6.4 Fibonacci number circuit

```
library ieee;
use ieee.std_logic_1164.all;
use ieee.numeric_std.all;
entity fib is
   port(
      clk, reset: in std_logic;
      start: in std_logic;
      i: in std_logic_vector(4 downto 0);
      ready, done_tick: out std_logic;
      f: out std_logic_vector(19 downto 0)
   );
end fib;

architecture arch of fib is
   type state_type is (idle,op,done);
   signal state_reg, state_next: state_type;
   signal t0_reg, t0_next: unsigned(19 downto 0);
   signal t1_reg, t1_next: unsigned(19 downto 0);
   signal n_reg, n_next: unsigned(4 downto 0);
begin
   -- fsmd state and data registers
   process(clk,reset)
   begin
      if reset='1' then
         state_reg <= idle;
         t0_reg <= (others=>'0');
```

```
            t1_reg <= (others=>'0');
            n_reg <= (others=>'0');
         elsif (clk'event and clk='1') then
            state_reg <= state_next;
            t0_reg <= t0_next;
            t1_reg <= t1_next;
            n_reg <= n_next;
         end if;
      end process;
      -- fsmd next-state logic
      process(state_reg,n_reg,t0_reg,t1_reg,start,i,n_next)
      begin
         ready <='0';
         done_tick <= '0';
         state_next <= state_reg;
         t0_next <= t0_reg;
         t1_next <= t1_reg;
         n_next <= n_reg;
         case state_reg is
            when idle =>
               ready <= '1';
               if start='1' then
                  t0_next <= (others=>'0');
                  t1_next <= (0=>'1', others=>'0');
                  n_next <= unsigned(i);
                  state_next <= op;
               end if;
            when op =>
               if n_reg=0 then
                  t1_next <= (others=>'0');
                  state_next <= done;
               elsif n_reg=1 then
                  state_next <= done;
               else
                  t1_next <= t1_reg + t0_reg;
                  t0_next <= t1_reg;
                  n_next <= n_reg - 1;
              end if;
            when done =>
               done_tick <= '1';
               state_next <= idle;
         end case;
      end process;
      -- output
      f <= std_logic_vector(t1_reg);
   end arch;
```

6.3.2 Division circuit

Because of complexity, the division operator cannot be synthesized automatically. We use an FSMD to implement the long-division algorithm in this subsection. The algorithm is illustrated by the division of two 4-bit unsigned integers in Figure 6.10. The algorithm can

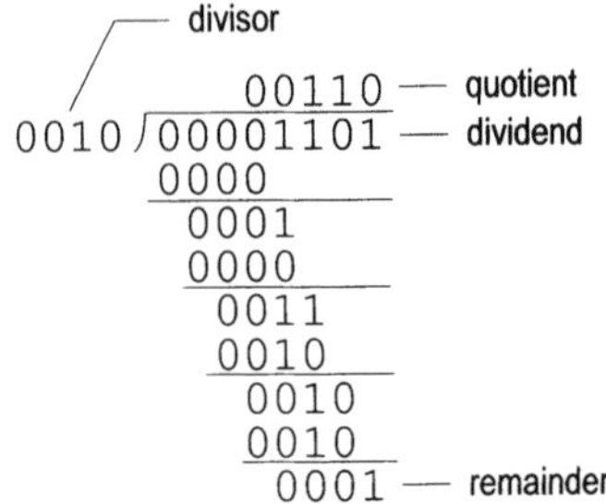

Figure 6.10 Long division of two 4-bit unsigned integers.

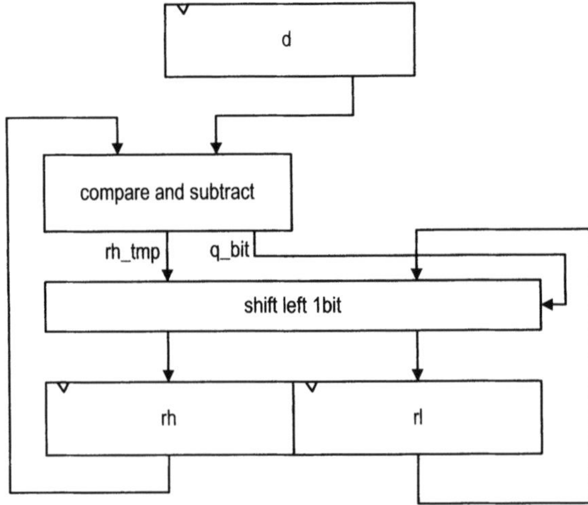

Figure 6.11 Sketch of division circuit's data path.

be summarized as follows:

1. Double the dividend width by appending 0's in front and align the divisor to the leftmost bit of the extended dividend.
2. If the corresponding dividend bits are greater than or equal to the divisor, subtract the divisor from the dividend bits and make the corresponding quotient bit 1. Otherwise, keep the original dividend bits and make the quotient bit 0.
3. Append one additional dividend bit to the previous result and shift the divisor to the right one position.
4. Repeat steps 2 and 3 until all dividend bits are used.

The sketch of the data path is shown in Figure 6.11. Initially, the divisor is stored in the `d` register and the extended dividend is stored in the `rh` and `rl` registers. In each iteration, the `rh` and `rl` registers are shifted to the left one position. This corresponds to shifting the divisor to the right of the previous algorithm. We can then compare `rh` and `d` and perform subtraction if `rh` is greater than or equal to `d`. When `rh` and `rl` are shifted to the left, the rightmost bit of `rl` becomes available. It can be used to store the current quotient bit. After we iterate through all dividend bits, the result of the last subtraction is stored in `rh` and becomes the remainder of the division, and all quotients are shifted into `rl`.

The ASMD chart of the division circuit is somewhat similar to that of the previous Fibonacci circuit. The FSMD consists of four states, `idle`, `op`, `last`, and `done`. To make the code clear, we extract the *compare and subtract* circuit to separate code segments. The main computation is performed in the `op` state, in which the dividend bits and divisor are compared and subtracted and then shifted left 1 bit. Note that the remainder should not be shifted in the last iteration. We create a separate state, `last`, to accommodate this special requirement. As in the preceding example, the purpose of the `done` state is to generate a one-clock-cycle `done_tick` signal to indicate completion of the computation. The code is shown in Listing 6.5.

Listing 6.5 Division circuit

```
library ieee;
use ieee.std_logic_1164.all;
use ieee.numeric_std.all;
entity div is
   generic(
      W: integer:=8;
      CBIT: integer:=4     -- CBIT=log2(W)+1
   );
   port(
       clk, reset: in std_logic;
       start: in std_logic;
       dvsr, dvnd: in std_logic_vector(W-1 downto 0);
       ready, done_tick: out std_logic;
       quo, rmd: out std_logic_vector(W-1 downto 0)
   );
end div;

architecture arch of div is
   type state_type is (idle,op,last,done);
   signal state_reg, state_next: state_type;
   signal rh_reg, rh_next: unsigned(W-1 downto 0);
   signal rl_reg, rl_next: std_logic_vector(W-1 downto 0);
   signal rh_tmp: unsigned(W-1 downto 0);
   signal d_reg, d_next: unsigned(W-1 downto 0);
   signal n_reg, n_next: unsigned(CBIT-1 downto 0);
   signal q_bit: std_logic;
begin
   -- fsmd state and data registers
   process(clk,reset)
   begin
      if reset='1' then
         state_reg <= idle;
         rh_reg <= (others=>'0');
         rl_reg <= (others=>'0');
         d_reg <= (others=>'0');
         n_reg <= (others=>'0');
      elsif (clk'event and clk='1') then
         state_reg <= state_next;
         rh_reg <= rh_next;
```

```
         rl_reg <= rl_next;
         d_reg <= d_next;
         n_reg <= n_next;
      end if;
   end process;

   -- fsmd next-state logic and data path logic
   process(state_reg,n_reg,rh_reg,rl_reg,d_reg,
           start,dvsr,dvnd,q_bit,rh_tmp,n_next)
   begin
      ready <='0';
      done_tick <= '0';
      state_next <= state_reg;
      rh_next <= rh_reg;
      rl_next <= rl_reg;
      d_next <= d_reg;
      n_next <= n_reg;
      case state_reg is
         when idle =>
            ready <= '1';
            if start='1' then
               rh_next <= (others=>'0');
               rl_next <= dvnd;                       -- dividend
               d_next <= unsigned(dvsr);              -- divisor
               n_next <= to_unsigned(W+1, CBIT); -- index
               state_next <= op;
            end if;
         when op =>
            -- shift rh and rl left
            rl_next <= rl_reg(W-2 downto 0) & q_bit;
            rh_next <= rh_tmp(W-2 downto 0) & rl_reg(W-1);
            --decrease index
            n_next <= n_reg - 1;
            if (n_next=1) then
               state_next <= last;
            end if;
         when last =>  -- last iteration
            rl_next <= rl_reg(W-2 downto 0) & q_bit;
            rh_next <= rh_tmp;
            state_next <= done;
         when done =>
            state_next <= idle;
            done_tick <= '1';
      end case;
   end process;

   -- compare and subtract
   process(rh_reg, d_reg)
   begin
      if rh_reg >= d_reg then
         rh_tmp <= rh_reg - d_reg;
         q_bit <= '1';
      else
```

```
            rh_tmp <= rh_reg;
            q_bit <= '0';
         end if;
      end process;

      -- output
      quo <= rl_reg;
      rmd <= std_logic_vector(rh_reg);
   end arch;
```

6.3.3 Binary-to-BCD conversion circuit

We discussed the BCD format in Section 4.5.2. In this format, a decimal number is represented as a sequence of 4-bit BCD digits. A binary-to-BCD conversion circuit converts a binary number to the BCD format. For example, the binary number "0010 0000 0000" becomes "0101 0001 0010" (i.e., 512_{10}) after conversion.

The binary-to-BCD conversion can be processed by a special BCD shift register, which is divided into 4-bit groups internally, each representing a BCD digit. Shifting a BCD sequence to the left requires adjustment if a BCD digit is greater than 9_{10} after shifting. For example, if a BCD sequence is "0001 0111" (i.e., 17_{10}), it should become "0011 0100" (i.e., 34_{10}) rather than "0010 1110". The adjustment requires subtracting 10_{10} (i.e., "1010") from the right BCD digit and adding 1 (which can be considered as a carry-out) to the next BCD digit. Note that subtracting 10_{10} is equivalent to adding 6_{10} for a 4-bit binary number. Thus, the foregoing adjustment can also be achieved by adding 6_{10} to the right BCD digit. The carry-out bit is generated automatically in this process.

In the actual implementation, it is more efficient to first perform the necessary adjustment on a BCD digit and then shift. We can check whether a BCD digit is greater than 4_{10} and, if this is the case, add 3_{10} to the digit. After all the BCD digits are corrected, we can then shift the entire register to the left one position. A binary-to-BCD conversion circuit can be constructed by shifting the binary input to a BCD shift register bit by bit, from MSB to LSB. Its operation can be summarized as follows:

1. For each 4-bit BCD digit in a BCD shift register, check whether the digit is greater than 4. If this is the case, add 3_{10} to the digit.
2. Shift the entire BCD register left one position and shift in the MSB of the input binary sequence to the LSB of the BCD register.
3. Repeat steps 1 and 2 until all input bits are used.

The conversion process of a 7-bit binary input, "111 1111" (i.e., 127_{10}), is demonstrated in Table 6.1.

The code of a 13-bit conversion circuit is shown in Listing 6.6. It uses a simple FSMD to control the overall operation. When the `start` signal is asserted, the binary input is stored into the p2s register. The FSM then iterates through the 13 bits, similar to the process described in previous examples. Four adjustment circuits are used to correct the four BCD digits. For clarity, they are isolated from the next-state logic and described in a separate code segment.

Listing 6.6 Binary-to-BCD conversion circuit

```
library ieee;
use ieee.std_logic_1164.all;
use ieee.numeric_std.all;
```

Table 6.1 Binary-to-BCD conversion example

Operation		Special BCD shift register			Binary input
		BCD digit 2	BCD digit 1	BCD digit 0	
Initial					111 1111
Bit 6	no adjustment shift left 1 bit			1 (1_{10})	11 1111
Bit 5	no adjustment shift left 1 bit			11 (3_{10})	1 1111
Bit 4	no adjustment shift left 1 bit			111 (7_{10})	1111
Bit 3	BCD digit 0 adjustment shift left 1 bit		1 (1_{10})	1010 0101 (5_{10})	111
Bit 2	BCD digit 0 adjustment shift left 1 bit		1 11 (3_{10})	1000 0001 (1_{10})	11
Bit 1	no adjustment shift left 1 bit		110 (6_{10})	0011 (3_{10})	1
Bit 0	BCD digit 1 adjustment shift left 1 bit	1 (1_{10})	1001 0010 (2_{10})	0011 0111 (7_{10})	

```
entity bin2bcd is
   port(
      clk: in std_logic;
      reset: in std_logic;
      start: in std_logic;
      bin: in std_logic_vector(12 downto 0);
      ready, done_tick: out std_logic;
      bcd3,bcd2,bcd1,bcd0: out std_logic_vector(3 downto 0)
   );
end bin2bcd ;

architecture arch of bin2bcd is
   type state_type is (idle, op, done);
   signal state_reg, state_next: state_type;
   signal p2s_reg, p2s_next: std_logic_vector(12 downto 0);
   signal n_reg, n_next: unsigned(3 downto 0);
   signal bcd3_reg, bcd2_reg, bcd1_reg, bcd0_reg:
          unsigned(3 downto 0);
   signal bcd3_next, bcd2_next, bcd1_next, bcd0_next:
          unsigned(3 downto 0);
   signal bcd3_tmp, bcd2_tmp, bcd1_tmp, bcd0_tmp:
```

```
            unsigned(3 downto 0);
begin
   -- state and data registers
   process (clk,reset)
   begin
      if reset='1' then
         state_reg <= idle;
         p2s_reg <= (others=>'0');
         n_reg <= (others=>'0');
         bcd3_reg <= (others=>'0');
         bcd2_reg <= (others=>'0');
         bcd1_reg <= (others=>'0');
         bcd0_reg <= (others=>'0');
      elsif (clk'event and clk='1') then
         state_reg <= state_next;
         p2s_reg <= p2s_next;
         n_reg <= n_next;
         bcd3_reg <= bcd3_next;
         bcd2_reg <= bcd2_next;
         bcd1_reg <= bcd1_next;
         bcd0_reg <= bcd0_next;
      end if;
   end process;

   -- fsmd next-state logic / data path operations
   process(state_reg,start,p2s_reg,n_reg,n_next,bin,
           bcd0_reg,bcd1_reg,bcd2_reg,bcd3_reg,
           bcd0_tmp,bcd1_tmp,bcd2_tmp,bcd3_tmp)
   begin
      state_next <= state_reg;
      ready <= '0';
      done_tick <= '0';
      p2s_next <= p2s_reg;
      bcd0_next <= bcd0_reg;
      bcd1_next <= bcd1_reg;
      bcd2_next <= bcd2_reg;
      bcd3_next <= bcd3_reg;
      n_next <= n_reg;
      case state_reg is
         when idle =>
            ready <= '1';
            if start='1' then
               state_next <= op;
               bcd3_next <= (others=>'0');
               bcd2_next <= (others=>'0');
               bcd1_next <= (others=>'0');
               bcd0_next <= (others=>'0');
               n_next <="1101";  -- index
               p2s_next <= bin;  -- input shift register
               state_next <= op;
            end if;
         when op =>
            -- shift in binary bit
```

```
               p2s_next <= p2s_reg(11 downto 0) & '0';
               -- shift 4 BCD digits
               bcd0_next <= bcd0_tmp(2 downto 0) & p2s_reg(12);
               bcd1_next <= bcd1_tmp(2 downto 0) & bcd0_tmp(3);
               bcd2_next <= bcd2_tmp(2 downto 0) & bcd1_tmp(3);
               bcd3_next <= bcd3_tmp(2 downto 0) & bcd2_tmp(3);
               n_next <= n_reg - 1;
               if (n_next=0) then
                   state_next <= done;
               end if;
            when done =>
               state_next <= idle;
               done_tick <= '1';
      end case;
   end process;

   -- data path function units
   -- four BCD adjustment circuits
   bcd0_tmp <= bcd0_reg + 3 when bcd0_reg > 4 else
               bcd0_reg;
   bcd1_tmp <= bcd1_reg + 3 when bcd1_reg > 4 else
               bcd1_reg;
   bcd2_tmp <= bcd2_reg + 3 when bcd2_reg > 4 else
               bcd2_reg;
   bcd3_tmp <= bcd3_reg + 3 when bcd3_reg > 4 else
               bcd3_reg;

   -- output
   bcd0 <= std_logic_vector(bcd0_reg);
   bcd1 <= std_logic_vector(bcd1_reg);
   bcd2 <= std_logic_vector(bcd2_reg);
   bcd3 <= std_logic_vector(bcd3_reg);
end arch;
```

6.3.4 Period counter

A period counter measures the period of a periodic input waveform. One way to construct the circuit is to count the number of clock cycles between two rising edges of the input signal. Since the frequency of the system clock is known, the period of the input signal can be derived accordingly. For example, if the frequency of the system clock is f and the number of clock cycles between two rising edges is N, the period of the input signal is $N * \frac{1}{f}$.

The design in this subsection measures the period in milliseconds. Its ASMD chart is shown in Figure 6.12. The period counter takes a measurement when the `start` signal is asserted. We use a rising-edge detection circuit to generate a one-clock-cycle tick, edge, to indicate the rising edge of the input waveform. After `start` is asserted, the FSMD moves to the `waite` state to wait for the first rising edge of the input. It then moves to the `count` state when the next rising edge of the input is detected. In the `count` state, we use two registers to keep track of the time. The `t` register counts for 50,000 clock cycles, from 0 to 49,999, and then wraps around. Since the period of the system clock is 20 ns, the `t` register takes 1 ms to circulate through 50,000 cycles. The `p` register counts in terms of milliseconds. It

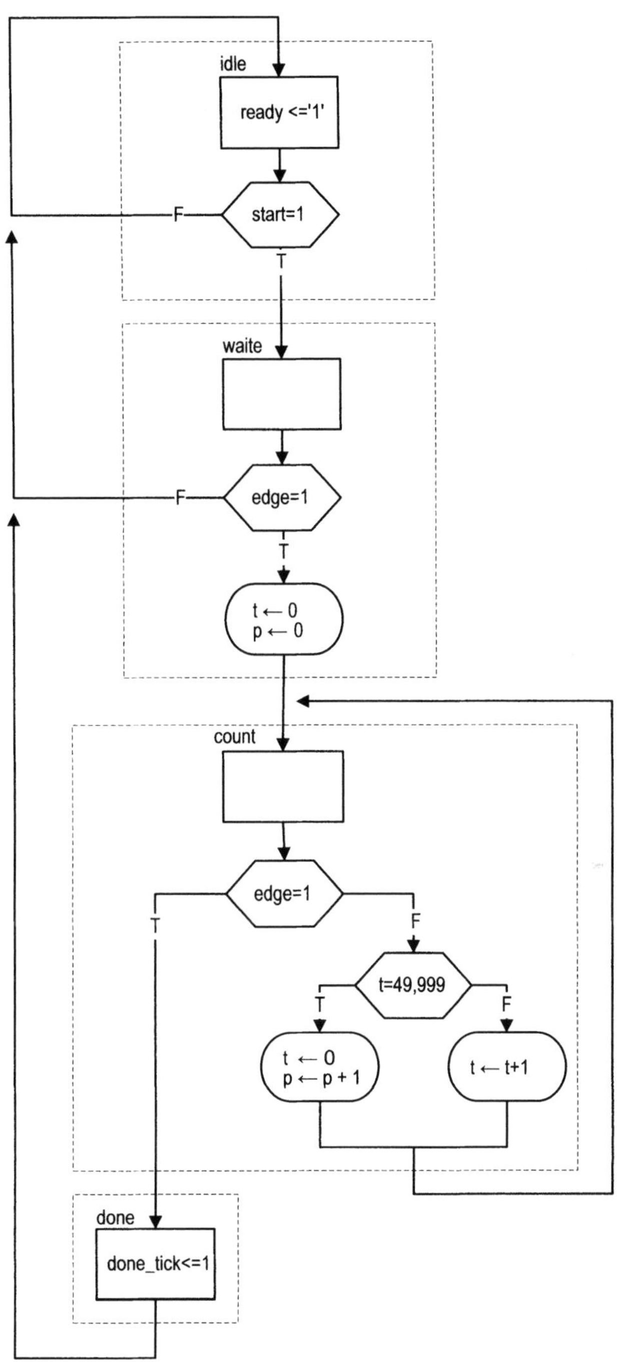

Figure 6.12 ASMD chart of a period counter.

is incremented once when the t register reaches 49,999. When the FSMD exits the count state, the period of the input waveform is stored in the p register and its unit is milliseconds. The FSMD asserts the done_tick signal in the done state, as in previous examples.

The code follows the ASMD chart and is shown in Listing 6.7. We use a constant, CLK_MS_COUNT, for the boundary of the millisecond counter. It can be replaced if a different measurement unit is desired.

Listing 6.7 Period counter

```
library ieee;
use ieee.std_logic_1164.all;
use ieee.numeric_std.all;
entity period_counter is
   port(
      clk, reset: in std_logic;
      start, si: in std_logic;
      ready, done_tick: out std_logic;
      prd: out std_logic_vector(9 downto 0)
   );
end period_counter;

architecture arch of period_counter is
   constant CLK_MS_COUNT: integer := 50000; -- 1 ms tick
   type state_type is (idle, waite, count, done);
   signal state_reg, state_next: state_type;
   signal t_reg, t_next: unsigned(15 downto 0);
   signal p_reg, p_next: unsigned(9 downto 0);
   signal delay_reg: std_logic;
   signal edge: std_logic;
begin
   -- state and data register
   process(clk,reset)
   begin
      if reset='1' then
         state_reg <= idle;
         t_reg <= (others=>'0');
         p_reg <= (others=>'0');
         delay_reg <= '0';
      elsif (clk'event and clk='1') then
         state_reg <= state_next;
         t_reg <= t_next;
         p_reg <= p_next;
         delay_reg <= si;
      end if;
   end process;

   -- edge detection circuit
   edge <= (not delay_reg) and si;

   -- fsmd next-state logic / data path operations
   process(start,edge,state_reg,t_reg,t_next,p_reg)
   begin
      ready <= '0';
      done_tick <= '0';
```

```
      state_next <= state_reg;
      p_next <= p_reg;
      t_next <= t_reg;
      case state_reg is
         when idle =>
            ready <= '1';
            if (start='1') then
               state_next <= waite;
            end if;
         when waite => -- wait for the first edge
            if (edge='1') then
               state_next <= count;
               t_next <= (others=>'0');
               p_next <= (others=>'0');
            end if;
         when count =>
            if (edge='1') then     -- 2nd edge arrived
               state_next <= done;
            else -- otherwise count
               if t_reg = CLK_MS_COUNT-1 then -- 1ms tick
                  t_next <= (others=>'0');
                  p_next <= p_reg + 1;
               else
                  t_next <= t_reg + 1;
               end if;
            end if;
         when done =>
            done_tick <= '1';
            state_next <= idle;
      end case;
   end process;
   prd <= std_logic_vector(p_reg);
end arch;
```

6.3.5 Accurate low-frequency counter

A frequency counter measures the frequency of a periodic input waveform. The common way to construct a frequency counter is to count the number of input pulses in a fixed amount of time, say, 1 second. Although this approach is fine for high-frequency input, it cannot measure a low-frequency signal accurately. For example, if the input is around 2 Hz, the measurement cannot tell whether it is 2.123 Hz or 2.567 Hz. Recall that the frequency is the reciprocal of the period (i.e., $frequency = \frac{1}{period}$). An alternative approach is to measure the period of the signal and then take the reciprocal to find the frequency. We use this approach to implement a low-frequency counter in this subsection.

This design example demonstrates how to use the previously designed parts to construct a large system. For simplicity, we assume that the frequency of the input is between 1 and 10 Hz (i.e., the period is between 100 and 1000 ms). The operation of this circuit includes three tasks:

1. Measure the period.
2. Find the frequency by performing a division operation.
3. Convert the binary number to BCD format.

We can use the period counter, division circuit, and binary-to-BCD converter to perform the three tasks and create another FSM as the master control to sequence and coordinate the operation of the three circuits. The block diagram is shown in Figure 6.13(a), and the ASM chart of the master control is shown in Figure 6.13(b). The FSM uses the `start` and `done_tick` signals of these circuits to initialize each task and to detect completion of the task. The code is shown in Listing 6.8.

Listing 6.8 Low-frequency counter

```
library ieee;
use ieee.std_logic_1164.all;
use ieee.numeric_std.all;
entity low_freq_counter is
   port(
      clk, reset: in std_logic;
      start: in std_logic;
      si: in std_logic;
      bcd3,bcd2,bcd1,bcd0: out std_logic_vector(3 downto 0)
   );
end low_freq_counter;

architecture arch of low_freq_counter is
   type state_type is (idle, count, frq, b2b);
   signal state_reg, state_next: state_type;
   signal prd: std_logic_vector(9 downto 0);
   signal dvsr, dvnd, quo: std_logic_vector(19 downto 0);
   signal prd_start, div_start, b2b_start: std_logic;
   signal prd_done_tick, div_done_tick, b2b_done_tick:
          std_logic;
begin
   --===============================================
   -- component instantiation
   --===============================================
   -- instantiate period counter
   prd_count_unit: entity work.period_counter
   port map(clk=>clk, reset=>reset, start=>prd_start, si=>si,
            ready=>open, done_tick=>prd_done_tick, prd=>prd);
   -- instantiate division circuit
   div_unit: entity work.div
   generic map(W=>20, CBIT=>5)
   port map(clk=>clk, reset=>reset, start=>div_start,
            dvsr=>dvsr, dvnd=>dvnd, quo=>quo, rmd=>open,
            ready=>open, done_tick=>div_done_tick);
   -- instantiate binary-to-BCD convertor
   bin2bcd_unit: entity work.bin2bcd
   port map
      (clk=>clk, reset=>reset, start=>b2b_start,
       bin=>quo(12 downto 0), ready=>open,
       done_tick=>b2b_done_tick,
       bcd3=>bcd3, bcd2=>bcd2, bcd1=>bcd1, bcd0=>bcd0);
   -- signal width extension
   dvnd <= std_logic_vector(to_unsigned(1000000, 20));
   dvsr <= "0000000000" & prd;

```

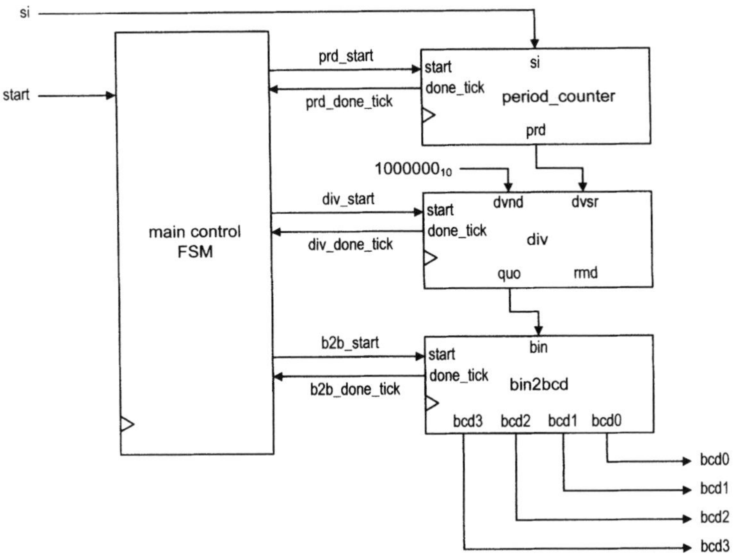

(a) Top-level block diagram

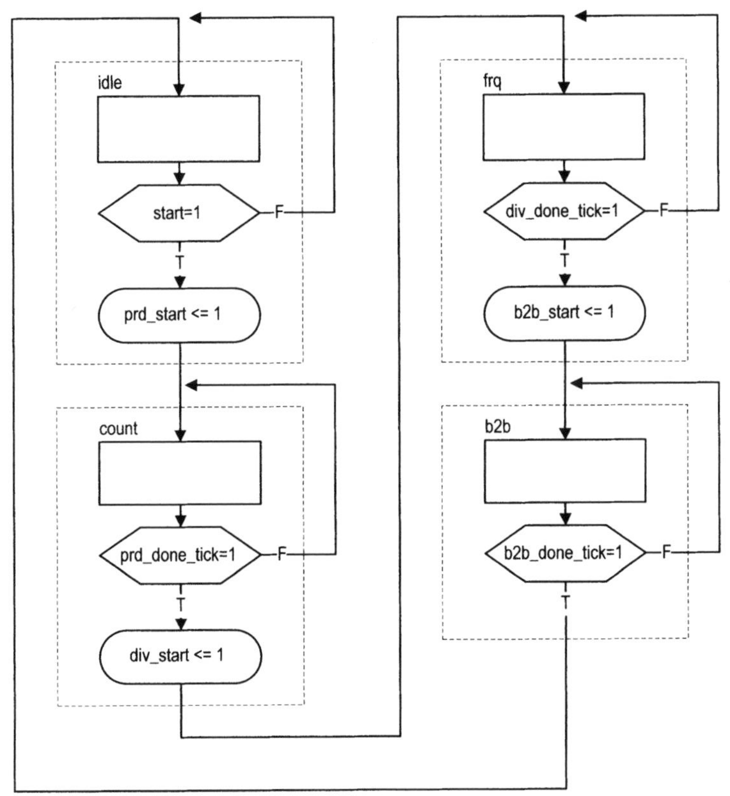

(b) ASM chart of main control

Figure 6.13 Accurate low-frequency counter.

```
--=====================================================
-- master FSM
--=====================================================
process(clk,reset)
begin
   if reset='1' then
      state_reg <= idle;
   elsif (clk'event and clk='1') then
      state_reg <= state_next;
   end if;
end process;

process(state_reg,start,
        prd_done_tick,div_done_tick,b2b_done_tick)
begin
   state_next <= state_reg;
   prd_start <='0';
   div_start <='0';
   b2b_start <='0';
   case state_reg is
      when idle =>
         if start='1' then
            state_next <= count;
            prd_start <='1';
         end if;
      when count =>
         if (prd_done_tick='1') then
            div_start <='1';
            state_next <= frq;
         end if;
      when frq =>
         if (div_done_tick='1') then
            b2b_start <='1';
            state_next <= b2b;
         end if;
      when b2b =>
         if (b2b_done_tick='1') then
            state_next <= idle;
         end if;
   end case;
end process;
end arch;
```

6.4 BIBLIOGRAPHIC NOTES

The bibliographic information for this chapter is similar to that for Chapter 3.

6.5 SUGGESTED EXPERIMENTS

6.5.1 Alternative debouncing circuit

Consider the alternative debouncing circuit in Experiment 5.5.2. Redesign the circuit using the RT methodology:

1. Derive the ASMD chart for the circuit.
2. Derive the HDL code based on the ASMD chart.
3. Replace the debouncing circuit in Section 6.2.5 with the alternative design and verify its operation.

6.5.2 BCD-to-binary conversion circuit

A BCD-to-binary conversion converts a BCD number to the equivalent binary representation. Assume that the input is an 8-bit signal in BCD format (i.e., two BCD digits) and the output is a 7-bit signal in binary representation. Follow the procedure in Section 6.3.3 to design a BCD-to-binary conversion circuit:

1. Derive the conversion algorithm and ASMD chart.
2. Derive the HDL code based on the ASMD chart.
3. Derive a testbench and use simulation to verify operation of the code.
4. Synthesize the circuit, program the FPGA, and verify its operation.

6.5.3 Fibonacci circuit with BCD I/O: design approach 1

To make the Fibonacci circuit more user friendly, we can modify the circuit to use the BCD format for the input and output. Assume that the input is an 8-bit signal in BCD format (i.e., two BCD digits) and the output is displayed as four BCD digits on the seven-segment LED display. Furthermore, the LED will display "9999" if the resulting Fibonacci number is larger than 9999 (i.e., overflow). The operation can be done in three steps: convert input to the binary format, compute the Fibonacci number, and convert the result back to the BCD format.

The first design approach is to follow the procedure in Section 6.3.5. We first construct three smaller subsystems, which are the BCD-to-binary conversion circuit, Fibonacci circuit, and binary-to-BCD conversion circuit, and then use a master FSM to control the overall operation. Design the circuit as follows:

1. Implement the BCD-to-binary conversion circuit in Experiment 6.5.2.
2. Modify the Fibonacci number circuit in Section 6.3.1 to include an output signal to indicate the overflow condition.
3. Derive the top-level block diagram and the master control FSM state diagram.
4. Derive the HDL code.
5. Derive a testbench and use simulation to verify operation of the code.
6. Synthesize the circuit, program the FPGA, and verify its operation.

6.5.4 Fibonacci circuit with BCD I/O: design approach 2

An alternative to the previous "subsystem approach" in Experiment 6.5.3 is to integrate the three subsystems into a single system and derive a customized FSMD for this particular application. The approach eliminates the overhead of the control FSM and provides opportunities to share registers among the three tasks. Design the circuit as follows:

1. Redesign the circuit of Experiment 6.5.3 using one FSMD. The design should eliminate all unnecessary circuits and states, such as the various `done_tick` signals and the `done` states, and exploit the opportunity to share and reuse the registers in different steps.
2. Derive the ASMD chart.
3. Derive the HDL code based on the ASMD chart.
4. Derive a testbench and use simulation to verify operation of the code.
5. Synthesize the circuit, program the FPGA and verify its operation.
6. Check the synthesis report and compare the number of LEs used in the two approaches.
7. Calculate the number of clock cycles required to complete the operation in the two approaches.

6.5.5 Auto-scaled low-frequency counter

The operation of the low-frequency counter in Section 6.3.5 is very restricted. The frequency range of the input signal is limited between 1 and 10 Hz. It loses accuracy when the frequency is beyond this range. Recall that the accuracy of this frequency counter depends on the accuracy of the period counter of Section 6.3.5, which counts in terms of millisecond ticks. We can modify the `t` counter to generate a microsecond tick (i.e., counting from 0 to 49) and increase the accuracy 1000-fold. This allows the range of the frequency counter to increase to 9999 Hz and still maintain at least four-digit accuracy.

Using a microsecond tick introduces more than four accuracy digits for low-frequency input, and the number must be shifted and truncated to be displayed on the seven-segment LED. An auto-scaled low-frequency counter performs the adjustment automatically, displays the four most significant digits, and places a decimal point in the proper place. For example, according to their range, the frequency measurements will be shown as "1.234", "12.34", "123.4", or "1234".

The auto-scaled low-frequency counter needs an additional BCD adjustment circuit. It first checks whether the most significant BCD digit (i.e., the four MSBs) of a BCD sequence is zero. If this is the case, the circuit shifts the BCD sequence to the left four positions and increments the decimal point counter. The operation is repeated until the most significant BCD digit is not "0000".

The complete auto-scaled low-frequency counter can be implemented as follows:

1. Modify the period counter to use the microsecond tick.
2. Extend the size of the binary-to-BCD conversion circuit.
3. Derive the ASMD chart for the BCD adjustment circuit and the HDL code.
4. Modify the control FSM to include the BCD adjustment in the last step.
5. Design a simple decoding circuit that uses the decimal point counter's output to activate the desired decimal point of the seven-segment LED display.
6. Derive a testbench and use simulation to verify operation of the code.
7. Synthesize the circuit, program the FPGA, and verify its operation.

6.5.6 Reaction timer

Eye–hand coordination is the ability of the eyes and hands to work together to perform a task. A reaction timer circuit measures how fast a human hand can respond after a person sees a visual stimulus. This circuit operates as follows:

1. The circuit has three input pushbuttons, corresponding to the `clear`, `start`, and `stop` signals. It uses a single discrete LED as the visual stimulus and displays relevant information on the seven-segment LED display.
2. A user pushes the `clear` button to force the circuit returning to the initial state, in which the seven-segment LED shows a welcome message, "HI," and the stimulus LED is off.
3. When ready, the user pushes the `start` button to initiate the test. The seven-segment LED goes off.
4. After a random interval between 2 and 15 seconds, the stimulus LED goes on and the timer starts to count upward. The timer increases every millisecond and its value is displayed in the format of "0.000" second on the seven-segment LED.
5. After the stimulus LED goes on, the user should try to push the `stop` button as soon as possible. The timer pauses counting once the `stop` button is asserted. The seven-segment LED shows the reaction time. It should be around 0.15 to 0.30 second for most people.
6. If the `stop` button is not pushed, the timer stops after 1 second and displays "1.000".
7. If the `stop` button is pushed before the stimulus LED goes on, the circuit displays "9.999" on the seven-segment LED and stops.

Design the circuit as follows:

1. Derive the ASMD chart.
2. Derive the HDL code based on the ASMD chart.
3. Synthesize the circuit, program the FPGA, and verify its operation.

6.5.7 Babbage difference engine emulation circuit

The Babbage difference engine is a mechanical digital computation device designed to tabulate a polynomial function. It was proposed by Charles Babbage, an English mathematician, in the nineteenth century. The engine is based on Newton's method of differences and avoids the need of multiplication. For example, consider a second-order polynomial $f(n) = 2n^2 + 3n + 5$. We can find the difference between $f(n)$ and $f(n-1)$:

$$f(n) - f(n-1) = 4n + 1$$

Assume that n is an integer and $n \geq 0$. The $f(n)$ can be defined recursively as

$$f(n) = \begin{cases} 5 & \text{if } n = 0 \\ f(n-1) + 4n + 1 & \text{if } n > 0 \end{cases}$$

This process can be repeated for the $4n + 1$ expression. Let $g(n) = 4n + 1$. We can find the difference between $g(n)$ and $g(n-1)$:

$$g(n) - g(n-1) = 4$$

The $g(n)$ can be defined recursively as

$$g(n) = \begin{cases} 5 & \text{if } n = 1 \\ g(n-1) + 4 & \text{if } n > 1 \end{cases}$$

and $f(n)$ can be rewritten as

$$f(n) = \begin{cases} 5 & \text{if } n = 0 \\ f(n-1) + g(n) & \text{if } n > 0 \end{cases}$$

Note that only additions are involved in the recursive definitions of $f(n)$ and $g(n)$.

Based on the definition of the last two recursive equations, we can derive an algorithm to compute $f(n)$. Two temporary registers are needed to keep track of the most recently calculated $f(n)$ and $g(n)$, and two additions are needed to update $f(n)$ and $g(n)$. Assume that n is a 6-bit input and interpreted as an unsigned integer. Design this circuit using the RT methodology:

1. Derive the ASMD chart.
2. Derive the HDL code based on the ASMD chart.
3. Derive a testbench and use simulation to verify operation of the code.
4. Synthesize the circuit, program the FPGA, and verify its operation.
5. Let $h(n) = n^3 + 2n^2 + 2n + 1$. Use the method above to find the recursive representation of $h(n)$ (note that three levels of recursive equations are needed for a three-order polynomial). Repeat steps 1 to 4.

PART II

I/O MODULES

CHAPTER 7

UART

7.1 INTRODUCTION

Universal asynchronous receiver and transmitter (UART) is a circuit that sends parallel data through a serial line. UARTs are frequently used in conjunction with the EIA (Electronic Industries Alliance) RS-232 standard, which specifies the electrical, mechanical, functional, and procedural characteristics of two data communication equipment. Because the voltage level defined in RS-232 is different from that of FPGA I/O, a voltage converter chip is needed between a serial port and an FPGA's I/O pins.

The S3 board has a RS-232 port with the standard nine-pin connector. The board contains the necessary voltage converter chip and configures the various RS-232's control signals to automatically generate acknowledgment for the PC's serial port. A standard straight-through serial cable can be used to connect the S3 board and PC's serial port. The S3 board basically handles the RS-232 standard and we only need to concentrate on the design of the UART circuit.

A UART includes a transmitter and a receiver. The transmitter is essentially a special shift register that loads data in parallel and then shifts it out bit by bit at a specific rate. The receiver, on the other hand, shifts in data bit by bit and then reassembles the data. The serial line is '1' when it is idle. The transmission starts with a *start bit*, which is '0', followed by *data bits* and an optional *parity bit*, and ends with *stop bits*, which are '1'. The number of data bits can be 6, 7, or 8. The optional parity bit is used for error detection. For odd parity, it is set to '0' when the data bits have an odd number of 1's. For even parity, it is set to '0' when the data bits have an even number of 1's. The number of stop bits can be 1, 1.5, or 2.

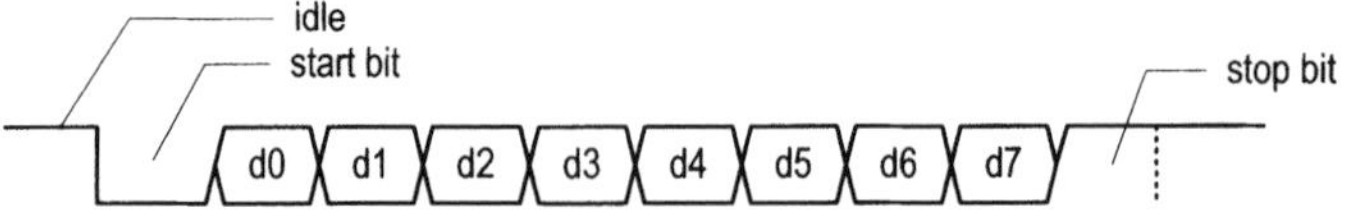

Figure 7.1 Transmission of a byte.

The transmission with 8 data bits, no parity, and 1 stop bit is shown in Figure 7.1. Note that the LSB of the data word is transmitted first.

No clock information is conveyed through the serial line. Before the transmission starts, the transmitter and receiver must agree on a set of parameters in advance, which include the baud rate (i.e., number of bits per second), the number of data bits and stop bits, and use of the parity bit. The commonly used baud rates are 2400, 4800, 9600, and 19,200 bauds.

We illustrate the design of the receiving and transmitting subsystems in the following sections. The design is customized for a UART with a 19,200 baud rate, 8 data bits, 1 stop bit, and no parity bit.

7.2 UART RECEIVING SUBSYSTEM

Since no clock information is conveyed from the transmitted signal, the receiver can retrieve the data bits only by using the predetermined parameters. We use an *oversampling scheme* to estimate the middle points of transmitted bits and then retrieve them at these points accordingly.

7.2.1 Oversampling procedure

The most commonly used sampling rate is 16 times the baud rate, which means that each serial bit is sampled 16 times. Assume that the communication uses N data bits and M stop bits. The oversampling scheme works as follows:

1. Wait until the incoming signal becomes '0', the beginning of the start bit, and then start the sampling tick counter.
2. When the counter reaches 7, the incoming signal reaches the middle point of the start bit. Clear the counter to 0 and restart.
3. When the counter reaches 15, the incoming signal progresses for one bit and reaches the middle of the first data bit. Retrieve its value, shift it into a register, and restart the counter.
4. Repeat step 3 N–1 more times to retrieve the remaining data bits.
5. If the optional parity bit is used, repeat step 3 one time to obtain the parity bit.
6. Repeat step 3 M more times to obtain the stop bits.

The oversampling scheme basically performs the function of a clock signal. Instead of using the rising edge to indicate when the input signal is valid, it utilizes sampling ticks to estimate the middle point of each bit. While the receiver has no information about the exact onset time of the start bit, the estimation can be off by at most $\frac{1}{16}$. The subsequent data bit retrievals are off by at most $\frac{1}{16}$ from the middle point as well. Because of the oversampling, the baud rate can only be a small fraction of the system clock rate, and thus this scheme is not appropriate for a high data rate.

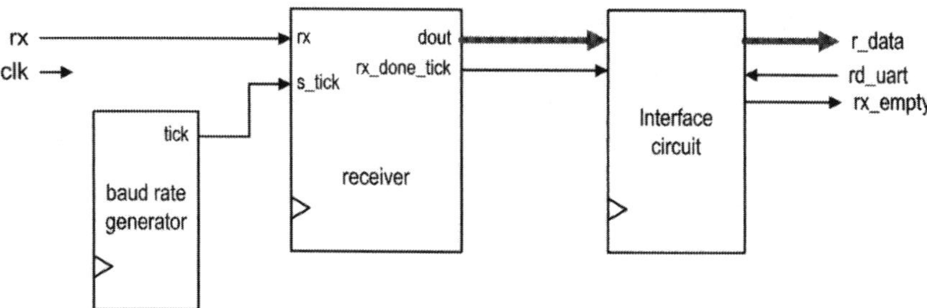

Figure 7.2 Conceptual block diagram of a UART receiving subsystem.

The conceptual block diagram of a UART receiving subsystem is shown in Figure 7.2. It consists of three major components:

- *UART receiver*: the circuit to obtain the data word via oversampling
- *Baud rate generator*: the circuit to generate the sampling ticks
- *Interface circuit*: the circuit that provides buffer and status between the UART receiver and the system that uses the UART

7.2.2 Baud rate generator

The baud rate generator generates a sampling signal whose frequency is exactly 16 times the UART's designated baud rate. To avoid creating a new clock domain and violating the synchronous design principle, the sampling signal should function as enable ticks rather than the clock signal to the UART receiver, as discussed in Section 4.3.2.

For the 19,200 baud rate, the sampling rate has to be 307,200 (i.e., 19,200∗16) ticks per second. Since the system clock rate is 50 MHz, the baud rate generator needs a mod-163 (i.e., $\frac{50*10^6}{307200}$) counter, in which the one-clock-cycle tick is asserted once every 163 clock cycles. The parameterized mod-m counter discussed in Section 4.3.2 can be used for this purpose by setting the `M` generic to 163.

7.2.3 UART receiver

With an understanding of the oversampling procedure, we can derive the ASMD chart accordingly, as shown in Figure 7.3. To accommodate future modification, two constants are used in the description. The `D_BIT` constant indicates the number of data bits, and the `SB_TICK` constant indicates the number of ticks needed for the stop bits, which is 16, 24, and 32 for 1, 1.5, and 2 stop bits, respectively. `D_BIT` and `SB_TICK` are assigned to 8 and 16 in this design.

The chart follows the steps discussed in Section 7.2.1 and includes three major states, `start`, `data`, and `stop`, which represent the processing of the start bit, data bits, and stop bit. The `s_tick` signal is the enable tick from the baud rate generator and there are 16 ticks in a bit interval. Note that the FSMD stays in the same state unless the `s_tick` signal is asserted. There are two counters, represented by the `s` and `n` registers. The `s` register keeps track of the number of sampling ticks and counts to 7 in the `start` state, to 15 in the `data` state, and to `SB_TICK` in the `stop` state. The `n` register keeps track of the number of data bits received in the `data` state. The retrieved bits are shifted into and reassembled in the `b`

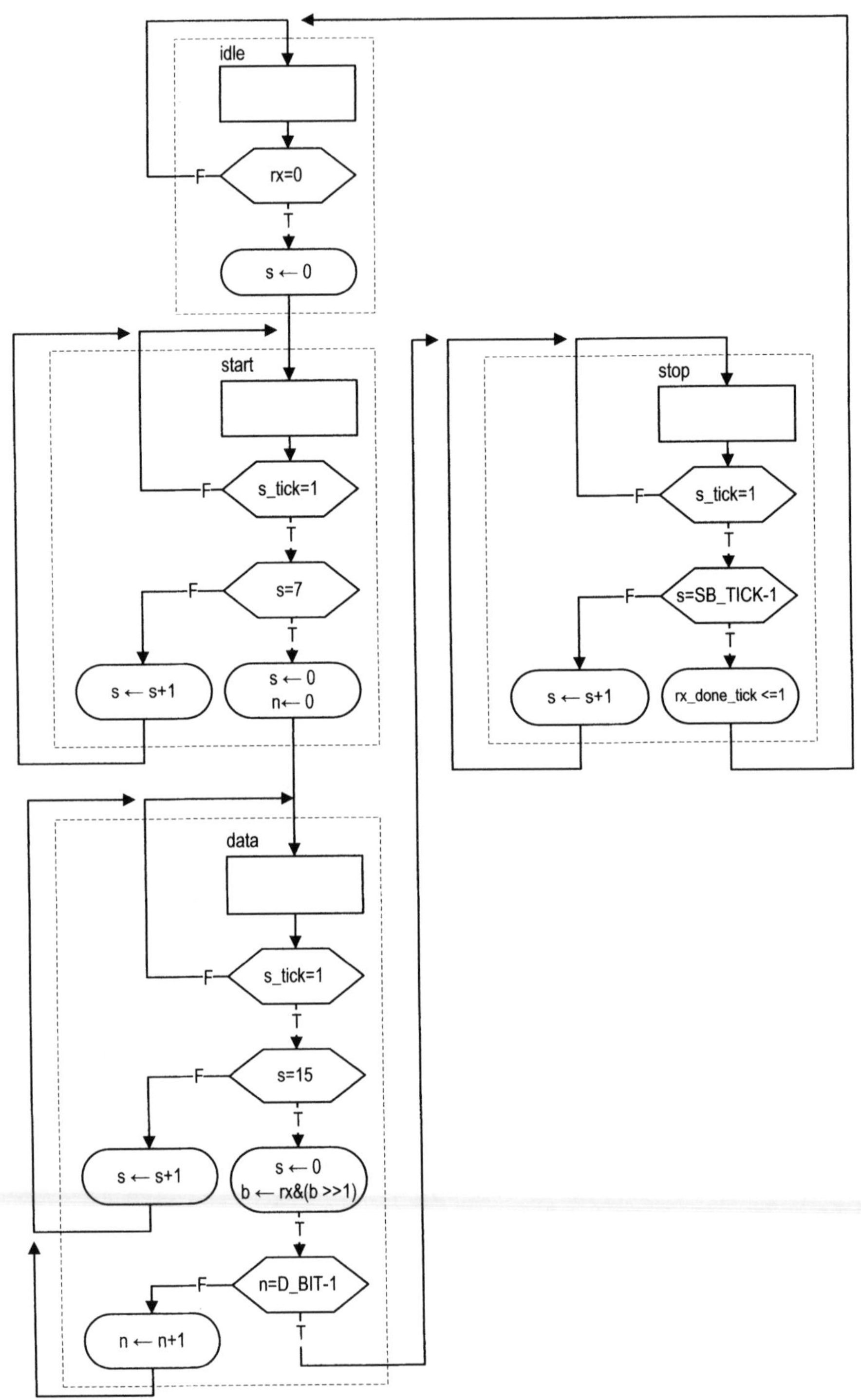

Figure 7.3 ASMD chart of a UART receiver.

register. A status signal, rx_done_tick, is included. It is asserted for one clock cycle after the receiving process is completed. The corresponding code is shown in Listing 7.1.

Listing 7.1 UART receiver

```
library ieee;
use ieee.std_logic_1164.all;
use ieee.numeric_std.all;
entity uart_rx is
   generic(
      DBIT: integer:=8;      -- # data bits
      SB_TICK: integer:=16   -- # ticks for stop bits
   );
   port(
      clk, reset: in std_logic;
      rx: in std_logic;
      s_tick: in std_logic;
      rx_done_tick: out std_logic;
      dout: out std_logic_vector(7 downto 0)
   );
end uart_rx ;

architecture arch of uart_rx is
   type state_type is (idle, start, data, stop);
   signal state_reg, state_next: state_type;
   signal s_reg, s_next: unsigned(3 downto 0);
   signal n_reg, n_next: unsigned(2 downto 0);
   signal b_reg, b_next: std_logic_vector(7 downto 0);
begin
   -- FSMD state & data registers
   process(clk,reset)
   begin
      if reset='1' then
         state_reg <= idle;
         s_reg <= (others=>'0');
         n_reg <= (others=>'0');
         b_reg <= (others=>'0');
      elsif (clk'event and clk='1') then
         state_reg <= state_next;
         s_reg <= s_next;
         n_reg <= n_next;
         b_reg <= b_next;
      end if;
   end process;
   -- next-state logic & data path functional units/routing
   process(state_reg,s_reg,n_reg,b_reg,s_tick,rx)
   begin
      state_next <= state_reg;
      s_next <= s_reg;
      n_next <= n_reg;
      b_next <= b_reg;
      rx_done_tick <='0';
      case state_reg is
         when idle =>
```

```
            if rx='0' then
               state_next <= start;
               s_next <= (others=>'0');
            end if;
         when start =>
            if (s_tick = '1') then
               if s_reg=7 then
                  state_next <= data;
                  s_next <= (others=>'0');
                  n_next <= (others=>'0');
               else
                  s_next <= s_reg + 1;
               end if;
            end if;
         when data =>
            if (s_tick = '1') then
               if s_reg=15 then
                  s_next <= (others=>'0');
                  b_next <= rx & b_reg(7 downto 1) ;
                  if n_reg=(DBIT-1) then
                     state_next <= stop ;
                  else
                     n_next <= n_reg + 1;
                  end if;
               else
                  s_next <= s_reg + 1;
               end if;
            end if;
         when stop =>
            if (s_tick = '1') then
               if s_reg=(SB_TICK-1) then
                  state_next <= idle;
                  rx_done_tick <='1';
               else
                  s_next <= s_reg + 1;
               end if;
            end if;
      end case;
   end process;
   dout <= b_reg;
end arch;
```

7.2.4 Interface circuit

In a large system, a UART is usually a peripheral circuit for serial data transfer. The main system checks its status periodically to retrieve and process the received word. The receiver's interface circuit has two functions. First, it provides a mechanism to signal the availability of a *new* word and to prevent the received word from being retrieved multiple times. Second, it can provide buffer space between the receiver and the main system. There are three commonly used schemes:

- A flag FF

- A flag FF and a one-word buffer
- A FIFO buffer

Note that the UART receiver asserts the `rx_ready_tick` signal one clock cycle after a data word is received.

The first scheme uses a *flag* FF to keep track of whether a new data word is available. The FF has two input signals. One is `set_flag`, which sets the flag FF to '1', and the other is `clr_flag`, which clears the flag FF to '0'. The `rx_ready_tick` signal is connected to the `set_flag` signal and sets the flag when a new data word arrives. The main system checks the output of the flag FF to see whether a new data word is available. It asserts the `clr_flag` signal one clock cycle after retrieving the word. The top-level block diagram is shown in Figure 7.4(a). To be consistent with other schemes, the flag FF's output is inverted to generate the final `rx_empty` signal, which indicates that no new word is available. In this scheme, the main system retrieves the data word directly from the shift register of the UART receiver and does not provide any additional buffer space. If the remote system initiates a new transmission before the main system consumes the old data word (i.e., the flag FF is still asserted), the old word will be overwritten, an error known as *data overrun*.

To provide some cushion, a one-word buffer can be added, as shown in Figure 7.4(b). When the `rx_ready_tick` signal is asserted, the received word is loaded to the buffer and the flag FF is set as well. The receiver can continue the operation without destroying the content of the last received word. Data overrun will not occur as long as the main system retrieves the word before a new word arrives. The code for this scheme is shown in Listing 7.2.

Listing 7.2 Interface with a flag FF and buffer

```
library ieee;
use ieee.std_logic_1164.all;
entity flag_buf is
   generic(W: integer:=8);
   port(
      clk, reset: in std_logic;
      clr_flag, set_flag: in std_logic;
      din: in std_logic_vector(W-1 downto 0);
      dout: out std_logic_vector(W-1 downto 0);
      flag: out std_logic
   );
end flag_buf;

architecture arch of flag_buf is
   signal buf_reg, buf_next: std_logic_vector(W-1 downto 0);
   signal flag_reg, flag_next: std_logic;
begin
   -- FF & register
   process(clk,reset)
   begin
      if reset='1' then
         buf_reg <= (others=>'0');
         flag_reg <= '0';
      elsif (clk'event and clk='1') then
         buf_reg <= buf_next;
         flag_reg <= flag_next;
      end if;
```

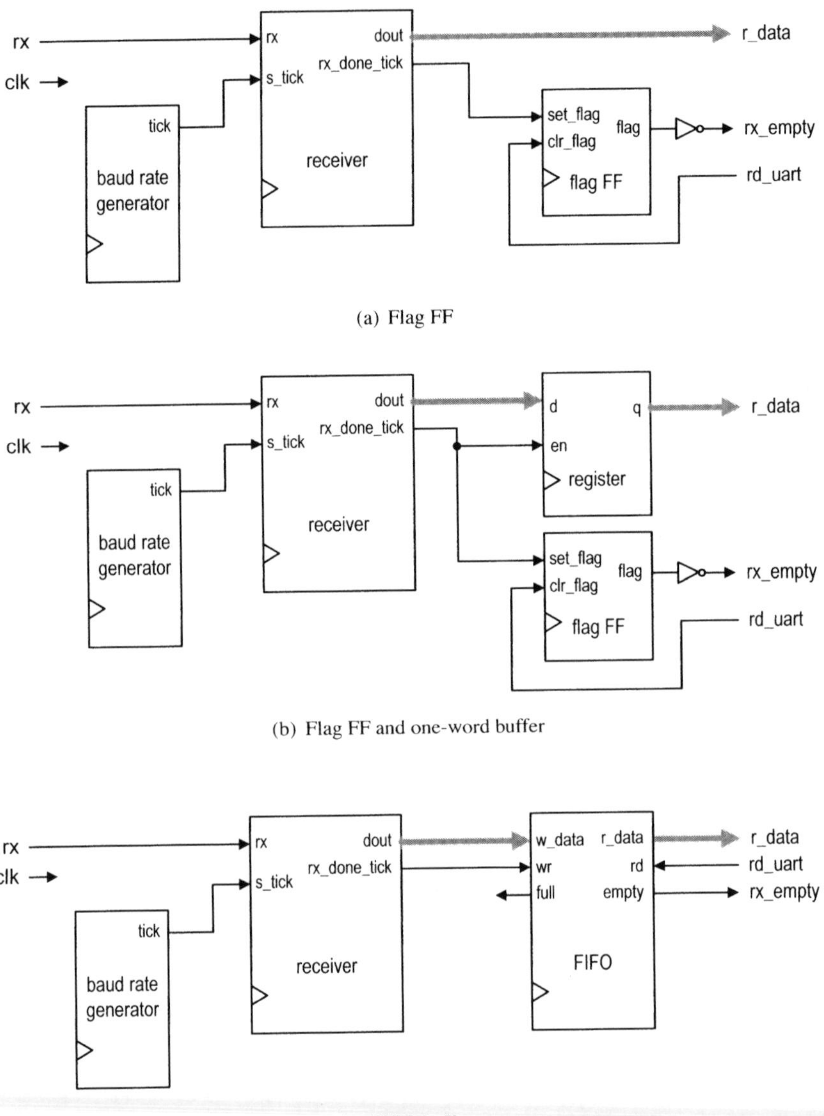

(a) Flag FF

(b) Flag FF and one-word buffer

(c) FIFO buffer

Figure 7.4 Interface circuit of a UART receiving subsystem.

```
   end process;
   -- next-state logic
   process(buf_reg,flag_reg,set_flag,clr_flag,din)
   begin
      buf_next <= buf_reg;
      flag_next <= flag_reg;
      if (set_flag='1') then
         buf_next <= din;
         flag_next <= '1';
      elsif (clr_flag='1') then
         flag_next <= '0';
      end if;
   end process;
   -- output logic
   dout <= buf_reg;
   flag <= flag_reg;
end arch;
```

The third scheme uses a FIFO buffer discussed in Section 4.5.3. The FIFO buffer provides more buffering space and further reduces the chance of data overrun. We can adjust the desired number of words in FIFO to accommodate the processing need of the main system. The detailed block diagram is shown in Figure 7.4(c).

The `rx_ready_tick` signal is connected to the `wr` signal of the FIFO. When a new data word is received, the `wr` signal is asserted one clock cycle and the corresponding data is written to the FIFO. The main system obtains the data from FIFO's read port. After retrieving a word, it asserts the `rd` signal of the FIFO one clock cycle to remove the corresponding item. The `empty` signal of the FIFO can be used to indicate whether any received data word is available. A data-overrun error occurs when a new data word arrives and the FIFO is full.

7.3 UART TRANSMITTING SUBSYSTEM

The organization of a UART transmitting subsystem is similar to that of the receiving subsystem. It consists of a UART transmitter, baud rate generator, and interface circuit. The interface circuit is similar to that of the receiving subsystem except that the main system sets the flag FF or writes the FIFO buffer, and the UART transmitter clears the flag FF or reads the FIFO buffer.

The UART transmitter is essentially a shift register that shifts out data bits at a specific rate. The rate can be controlled by one-clock-cycle enable ticks generated by the baud rate generator. Because no oversampling is involved, the frequency of the ticks is 16 times slower than that of the UART receiver. Instead of introducing a new counter, the UART transmitter usually shares the baud rate generator of the UART receiver and uses an internal counter to keep track of the number of enable ticks. A bit is shifted out every 16 enable ticks.

The ASMD chart of the UART transmitter is similar to that of the UART receiver. After assertion of the `tx_start` signal, the FSMD loads the data word and then gradually progresses through the `start`, `data`, and `stop` states to shift out the corresponding bits. It signals completion by asserting the `tx_done_tick` signal for one clock cycle. A 1-bit buffer, `tx_reg`, is used to filter out any potential glitch. The corresponding code is shown in Listing 7.3.

Listing 7.3 UART transmitter

```
library ieee;
use ieee.std_logic_1164.all;
use ieee.numeric_std.all;
entity uart_tx is
   generic(
      DBIT: integer:=8;      -- # data bits
      SB_TICK: integer:=16  -- # ticks for stop bits
   );
   port(
      clk, reset: in std_logic;
      tx_start: in std_logic;
      s_tick: in std_logic;
      din: in std_logic_vector(7 downto 0);
      tx_done_tick: out std_logic;
      tx: out std_logic
   );
end uart_tx ;

architecture arch of uart_tx is
   type state_type is (idle, start, data, stop);
   signal state_reg, state_next: state_type;
   signal s_reg, s_next: unsigned(3 downto 0);
   signal n_reg, n_next: unsigned(2 downto 0);
   signal b_reg, b_next: std_logic_vector(7 downto 0);
   signal tx_reg, tx_next: std_logic;
begin
   -- FSMD state & data registers
   process(clk,reset)
   begin
      if reset='1' then
         state_reg <= idle;
         s_reg <= (others=>'0');
         n_reg <= (others=>'0');
         b_reg <= (others=>'0');
         tx_reg <= '1';
      elsif (clk'event and clk='1') then
         state_reg <= state_next;
         s_reg <= s_next;
         n_reg <= n_next;
         b_reg <= b_next;
         tx_reg <= tx_next;
      end if;
   end process;
   -- next-state logic & data path functional units/routing
   process(state_reg,s_reg,n_reg,b_reg,s_tick,
           tx_reg,tx_start,din)
   begin
      state_next <= state_reg;
      s_next <= s_reg;
      n_next <= n_reg;
      b_next <= b_reg;
      tx_next <= tx_reg ;
```

```
         tx_done_tick <= '0';
         case state_reg is
            when idle =>
               tx_next <= '1';
               if tx_start='1' then
                  state_next <= start;
                  s_next <= (others=>'0');
                  b_next <= din;
               end if;
            when start =>
               tx_next <= '0';
               if (s_tick = '1') then
                  if s_reg=15 then
                     state_next <= data;
                     s_next <= (others=>'0');
                     n_next <= (others=>'0');
                  else
                     s_next <= s_reg + 1;
                  end if;
               end if;
            when data =>
               tx_next <= b_reg(0);
               if (s_tick = '1') then
                  if s_reg=15 then
                     s_next <= (others=>'0');
                     b_next <= '0' & b_reg(7 downto 1) ;
                     if n_reg=(DBIT-1) then
                        state_next <= stop ;
                     else
                        n_next <= n_reg + 1;
                     end if;
                  else
                     s_next <= s_reg + 1;
                  end if;
               end if;
            when stop =>
               tx_next <= '1';
               if (s_tick = '1') then
                  if s_reg=(SB_TICK-1) then
                     state_next <= idle;
                     tx_done_tick <= '1';
                  else
                     s_next <= s_reg + 1;
                  end if;
               end if;
         end case;
      end process;
      tx <= tx_reg;
   end arch;
```

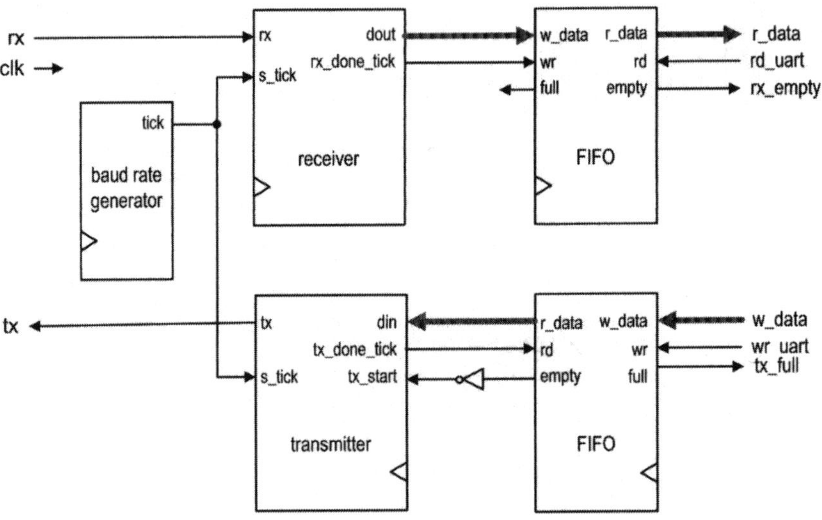

Figure 7.5 Block diagram of a complete UART.

7.4 OVERALL UART SYSTEM

7.4.1 Complete UART core

By combining the receiving and transmitting subsystems, we can construct the complete UART core. The top-level diagram is shown in Figure 7.5. The block diagram can be described by component instantiation, and the corresponding code is shown in Listing 7.4.

Listing 7.4 UART top-level description

```
library ieee;
use ieee.std_logic_1164.all;
use ieee.numeric_std.all;
entity uart is
   generic(
      -- Default setting:
      -- 19200 baud, 8 data bits, 1 stop bit, 2^2 FIFO
      DBIT: integer:=8;        -- # data bits
      SB_TICK: integer:=16;    -- # ticks for stop bits, 16/24/32
                               --   for 1/1.5/2 stop bits
      DVSR: integer:= 163;     -- baud rate divisor
                               -- DVSR = 50M/(16*baud rate)
      DVSR_BIT: integer:=8;    -- # bits of DVSR
      FIFO_W: integer:=2       -- # addr bits of FIFO
                               -- # words in FIFO=2^FIFO_W
   );
   port(
      clk, reset: in std_logic;
      rd_uart, wr_uart: in std_logic;
      rx: in std_logic;
      w_data: in std_logic_vector(7 downto 0);
      tx_full, rx_empty: out std_logic;
```

```
      r_data: out std_logic_vector(7 downto 0);
      tx: out std_logic
   );
end uart;

architecture str_arch of uart is
   signal tick: std_logic;
   signal rx_done_tick: std_logic;
   signal tx_fifo_out: std_logic_vector(7 downto 0);
   signal rx_data_out: std_logic_vector(7 downto 0);
   signal tx_empty, tx_fifo_not_empty: std_logic;
   signal tx_done_tick: std_logic;
begin
   baud_gen_unit: entity work.mod_m_counter(arch)
      generic map(M=>DVSR, N=>DVSR_BIT)
      port map(clk=>clk, reset=>reset,
               q=>open, max_tick=>tick);
   uart_rx_unit: entity work.uart_rx(arch)
      generic map(DBIT=>DBIT, SB_TICK=>SB_TICK)
      port map(clk=>clk, reset=>reset, rx=>rx,
               s_tick=>tick, rx_done_tick=>rx_done_tick,
               dout=>rx_data_out);
   fifo_rx_unit: entity work.fifo(arch)
      generic map(B=>DBIT, W=>FIFO_W)
      port map(clk=>clk, reset=>reset, rd=>rd_uart,
               wr=>rx_done_tick, w_data=>rx_data_out,
               empty=>rx_empty, full=>open, r_data=>r_data);
   fifo_tx_unit: entity work.fifo(arch)
      generic map(B=>DBIT, W=>FIFO_W)
      port map(clk=>clk, reset=>reset, rd=>tx_done_tick,
               wr=>wr_uart, w_data=>w_data, empty=>tx_empty,
               full=>tx_full, r_data=>tx_fifo_out);
   uart_tx_unit: entity work.uart_tx(arch)
      generic map(DBIT=>DBIT, SB_TICK=>SB_TICK)
      port map(clk=>clk, reset=>reset,
               tx_start=>tx_fifo_not_empty,
               s_tick=>tick, din=>tx_fifo_out,
               tx_done_tick=> tx_done_tick, tx=>tx);
   tx_fifo_not_empty <= not tx_empty;
end str_arch;
```

Xilinx specific

In the picoBlaze source file (discussed in Chapter 14), Xilinx supplies a customized UART module with similar functionality. Unlike our implementation, the module is described using low-level Xilinx primitives. It can be considered as a gate-level description that utilizes Xilinx-specific components. Since the designer has the expert knowledge of Xilinx devices and takes advantage of its architecture, its implementation is more efficient than the generic RT-level device-independent description of this chapter. It is instructive to compare the code complexity and the circuit size of the two descriptions.

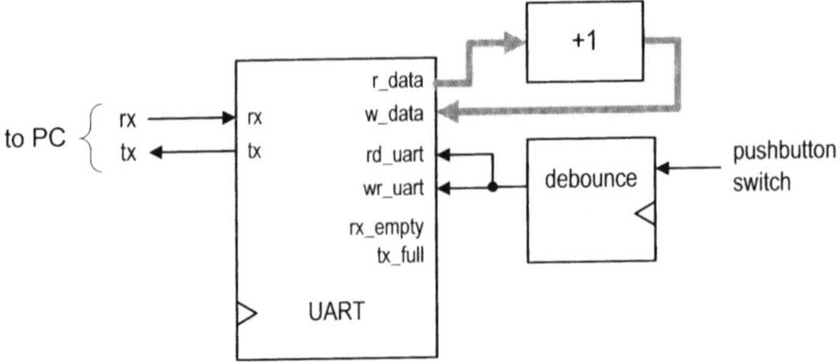

Figure 7.6 Block diagram of a UART verification circuit.

7.4.2 UART verification configuration

Verification circuit We use a loop-back circuit and a PC to verify the UART's operation. The block diagram is shown in Figure 7.6. In the circuit, the serial port of the S3 board is connected to the serial port of a PC. When we send a character from the PC, the received data word is stored in the UART receiver's four-word FIFO buffer. When retrieved (via the `r_data` port), the data word is incremented by 1 and then sent back to the transmitter (via the `w_data` port). The debounced pushbutton switch produces a single one-clock-cycle tick when pressed and it is connected to the `rd_uart` and `wr_uart` signals. When the tick is generated, it removes one word from the receiver's FIFO and writes the incremented word to the transmitter's FIFO for transmission. For example, we can first type `HAL` in the PC and the three data words are stored in the FIFO buffer of the UART receiver. We then can push the button on the S3 board three times. The three successive characters, `IBM`, will be transmitted back and displayed. The UART's `r_data` port is also connected to the eight LEDs of the S3 board, and its `tx_full` and `rx_empty` signals are connected to the two horizontal bars of the rightmost digit of the seven-segment display. The code is shown in Listing 7.5.

Listing 7.5 UART verification circuit

```
library ieee;
use ieee.std_logic_1164.all;
use ieee.numeric_std.all;
entity uart_test is
   port(
      clk, reset: in std_logic;
      btn: std_logic_vector(2 downto 0);
      rx: in std_logic;
      tx: out std_logic;
      led: out std_logic_vector(7 downto 0);
      sseg: out std_logic_vector(7 downto 0);
      an: out std_logic_vector(3 downto 0)
   );
end uart_test;

architecture arch of uart_test is
   signal tx_full, rx_empty: std_logic;
   signal rec_data,rec_data1: std_logic_vector(7 downto 0);
```

```
   signal btn_tick: std_logic;
begin
   -- instantiate uart
   uart_unit: entity work.uart(str_arch)
      port map(clk=>clk, reset=>reset, rd_uart=>btn_tick,
               wr_uart=>btn_tick, rx=>rx, w_data=>rec_data1,
               tx_full=>tx_full, rx_empty=>rx_empty,
               r_data=>rec_data, tx=>tx);
   -- instantiate debounce circuit
   btn_db_unit: entity work.debounce(fsmd_arch)
      port map(clk=>clk, reset=>reset, sw=>btn(0),
               db_level=>open, db_tick=>btn_tick);
   -- incremented data loop back
   rec_data1 <= std_logic_vector(unsigned(rec_data)+1);
   -- led display
   led <= rec_data;
   an <= "1110";
   sseg <= '1' & (not tx_full) & "11" & (not rx_empty) & "111";
end arch;
```

HyperTerminal of Windows On PC's side, Windows' HyperTerminal program can be used as a virtual terminal to interact with the S3 board. To be compatible with our customized UART, it has to be configured as 19,200 baud, 8 data bits, 1 stop bit, and no parity bit. The basic procedure is:

1. Select Start ≻ Programs ≻ Accessories ≻ Communications ≻ HyperTerminal. The HyperTerminal dialog appears.
2. Type a name for this connection, say `fpga_192`. Click OK. This connection can be saved and invoked later.
3. A Connect_to dialog appears. Press the Connecting Using field and select the desired serial port (e.g., COM1). Click OK.
4. The Port Setting dialog appears. Configure the port as follows:
   - Bits per second: `19200`
   - Data bits: `8`
   - Parity: `None`
   - Stop bits: `1`
   - Flow control: `None`

   Click OK.
5. Select File ≻ Properties ≻ Setting. Click ASCII Setup and check the Echo typed characters locally box. Click OK twice. This will allow the typed characters to be shown on the screen.

The HyperTerminal program is set up now and ready to communicate with the S3 board. We can type a few keys and observe the LEDs of the S3 board. Note that the received words are stored in the FIFO buffer and only the first received data word is displayed. After we press the pushbutton, the first data word will be removed from the FIFO and the incremented word will be looped back to the PC's serial port and displayed in the HyperTerminal window. The full and empty status of the respective FIFO buffers can be tested by consecutively receiving and transmitting more than four data words.

ASCII code In HyperTerminal, characters are sent in ASCII code, which is 7 bits and consists of 128 code words, including regular alphabets, digits, punctuation symbols, and nonprintable control characters. The characters and their code words (in hexadecimal format) are shown in Table 7.1. The nonprintable characters are shown enclosed in parentheses, such as (del). Several nonprintable characters may introduce special action when received:

- (nul): null byte, which is the all-zero pattern
- (bel): generate a bell sound, if supported
- (bs): backspace
- (ht): horizontal tab
- (nl): new line
- (vt): vertical tab
- (np): new page
- (cr): carriage return
- (esc): escape
- (sp): space
- (del): delete, which is also the all-one pattern

Since we use the PC's serial port to communicate with the S3 board in many experiments and projects, the following observations help us to manipulate and process the ASCII code:

- When the first hex digit in a code word is 0_{16} or 1_{16}, the corresponding character is a control character.
- When the first hex digit in a code word is 2_{16} or 3_{16}, the corresponding character is a digit or punctuation.
- When the first hex digit in a code word is 4_{16} or 5_{16}, the corresponding character is generally an uppercase letter.
- When the first hex digit in a code word is 6_{16} or 7_{16}, the corresponding character is generally a lowercase letter.
- If the first hex digit in a code word is 3_{16}, the lower hex digit represents the corresponding decimal digit.
- The upper- and lowercase letters differ in a single bit and can be converted to each other by adding or subtracting 20_{16} or inverting the sixth bit.

Note that the ASCII code uses only 7 bits, but a data word is normally composed of 8 bits (i.e., a byte). The PC uses an extended set in which the MSB is 1 and the characters are special graphics symbols. This code, however, is not part of the ASCII standard.

7.5 CUSTOMIZING A UART

The UART discussed in previous sections is customized for a particular configuration. The design and code can easily be modified to accommodate other required features:

- *Baud rate.* The baud rate is controlled by the frequency of the sampling ticks of the baud rate generator. The frequency can be changed by revising the `M` generic of the mod-m counter, which is represented as the `DVSR` constant in code.
- *Number of data bits.* The number of data bits can be changed by modifying the upper limit of the `n_reg` register, which is specified as the `DBIT` constant in code.
- *Parity bit.* A parity bit can be included by introducing a new state between the `data` and `stop` states in the ASMD chart in Figure 7.3.
- *Number of stop bits.* The number of stop bits can be changed by modifying the upper limit of the `s_reg` register in the `stop` state of the ASMD chart. The `SB_TICK` constant is used for this purpose. It can be 16, 24, or 32, which is for 1, 1.5, or 2 stop bits, respectively.

Table 7.1 ASCII codes

<table>
<tr><th>Code</th><th>Char</th><th>Code</th><th>Char</th><th>Code</th><th>Char</th><th>Code</th><th>Char</th></tr>
<tr><td>00</td><td>(nul)</td><td>20</td><td>(sp)</td><td>40</td><td>@</td><td>60</td><td>‘</td></tr>
<tr><td>01</td><td>(soh)</td><td>21</td><td>!</td><td>41</td><td>A</td><td>61</td><td>a</td></tr>
<tr><td>02</td><td>(stx)</td><td>22</td><td>"</td><td>42</td><td>B</td><td>62</td><td>b</td></tr>
<tr><td>03</td><td>(etx)</td><td>23</td><td>#</td><td>43</td><td>C</td><td>63</td><td>c</td></tr>
<tr><td>04</td><td>(eot)</td><td>24</td><td>$</td><td>44</td><td>D</td><td>64</td><td>d</td></tr>
<tr><td>05</td><td>(enq)</td><td>25</td><td>%</td><td>45</td><td>E</td><td>65</td><td>e</td></tr>
<tr><td>06</td><td>(ack)</td><td>26</td><td>&</td><td>46</td><td>F</td><td>66</td><td>f</td></tr>
<tr><td>07</td><td>(bel)</td><td>27</td><td>’</td><td>47</td><td>G</td><td>67</td><td>g</td></tr>
<tr><td>08</td><td>(bs)</td><td>28</td><td>(</td><td>48</td><td>H</td><td>68</td><td>h</td></tr>
<tr><td>09</td><td>(ht)</td><td>29</td><td>)</td><td>49</td><td>I</td><td>69</td><td>i</td></tr>
<tr><td>0a</td><td>(nl)</td><td>2a</td><td>*</td><td>4a</td><td>J</td><td>6a</td><td>j</td></tr>
<tr><td>0b</td><td>(vt)</td><td>2b</td><td>+</td><td>4b</td><td>K</td><td>6b</td><td>k</td></tr>
<tr><td>0c</td><td>(np)</td><td>2c</td><td>,</td><td>4c</td><td>L</td><td>6c</td><td>l</td></tr>
<tr><td>0d</td><td>(cr)</td><td>2d</td><td>-</td><td>4d</td><td>M</td><td>6d</td><td>m</td></tr>
<tr><td>0e</td><td>(so)</td><td>2e</td><td>.</td><td>4e</td><td>N</td><td>6e</td><td>n</td></tr>
<tr><td>0f</td><td>(si)</td><td>2f</td><td>/</td><td>4f</td><td>O</td><td>6f</td><td>o</td></tr>
<tr><td>10</td><td>(dle)</td><td>30</td><td>0</td><td>50</td><td>P</td><td>70</td><td>p</td></tr>
<tr><td>11</td><td>(dc1)</td><td>31</td><td>1</td><td>51</td><td>Q</td><td>71</td><td>q</td></tr>
<tr><td>12</td><td>(dc2)</td><td>32</td><td>2</td><td>52</td><td>R</td><td>72</td><td>r</td></tr>
<tr><td>13</td><td>(dc3)</td><td>33</td><td>3</td><td>53</td><td>S</td><td>73</td><td>s</td></tr>
<tr><td>14</td><td>(dc4)</td><td>34</td><td>4</td><td>54</td><td>T</td><td>74</td><td>t</td></tr>
<tr><td>15</td><td>(nak)</td><td>35</td><td>5</td><td>55</td><td>U</td><td>75</td><td>u</td></tr>
<tr><td>16</td><td>(syn)</td><td>36</td><td>6</td><td>56</td><td>V</td><td>76</td><td>v</td></tr>
<tr><td>17</td><td>(etb)</td><td>37</td><td>7</td><td>57</td><td>W</td><td>77</td><td>w</td></tr>
<tr><td>18</td><td>(can)</td><td>38</td><td>8</td><td>58</td><td>X</td><td>78</td><td>x</td></tr>
<tr><td>19</td><td>(em)</td><td>39</td><td>9</td><td>59</td><td>Y</td><td>79</td><td>y</td></tr>
<tr><td>1a</td><td>(sub)</td><td>3a</td><td>:</td><td>5a</td><td>Z</td><td>7a</td><td>z</td></tr>
<tr><td>1b</td><td>(esc)</td><td>3b</td><td>;</td><td>5b</td><td>[</td><td>7b</td><td>{</td></tr>
<tr><td>1c</td><td>(fs)</td><td>3c</td><td><</td><td>5c</td><td>\</td><td>7c</td><td>|</td></tr>
<tr><td>1d</td><td>(gs)</td><td>3d</td><td>=</td><td>5d</td><td>]</td><td>7d</td><td>}</td></tr>
<tr><td>1e</td><td>(rs)</td><td>3e</td><td>></td><td>5e</td><td>^</td><td>7e</td><td>~</td></tr>
<tr><td>1f</td><td>(us)</td><td>3f</td><td>?</td><td>5f</td><td>_</td><td>7f</td><td>(del)</td></tr>
</table>

- *Error checking*. Three types of errors can be detected in the UART receiving subsystem:
  - *Parity error*. If the parity bit is included, the receiver can check the correctness of the received parity bit.
  - *Frame error*. The receiver can check the received value in the `stop` state. If the value is not '1', the frame error occurs.
  - *Buffer overrun error*. This happens when the main system does not retrieve the received words in a timely manner. The UART receiver can check the value of the buffer's `flag_reg` signal or FIFO's `full` signal when the received word is ready to be stored (i.e., when the `rx_done_tick` signal is generated). Data overrun occurs if the `flag_reg` or `full` signal is still asserted.

7.6 BIBLIOGRAPHIC NOTES

Although the RS-232 standard is very old, it still provides a simple and reliable low-speed communication link between two devices. The *Wikipedia* Web site has a good overview article and several useful links on the subject (search with the keyword `RS232`). *Serial Port Complete* by Jan Axelson provides information on interfacing hardware devices to PC's serial port.

7.7 SUGGESTED EXPERIMENTS

7.7.1 Full-featured UART

The alternative to the customized UART is to include all features in design and to dynamically configure the UART as needed. Consider a full-featured UART that uses additional input signals to specify the baud rate, type of parity bit, and the numbers of data bits and stop bits. The UART also includes an error signal. In addition to the I/O signals of the `uart_top` design in Listing 7.4, the following signals are required:

- `bd_rate`: 2-bit input signal specifying the baud rate, which can be 1200, 2400, 4800, or 9600 baud
- `d_num`: 1-bit input signal specifying the number of data bits, which can be 7 or 8
- `s_num`: 1-bit input signal specifying the number of stop bits, which can be 1 or 2
- `par`: 2-bit input signal specifying the desired parity scheme, which can be no parity, even parity, or odd parity
- `err`: 3-bit output signal in which the bits indicate the existence of the parity error, frame error, and data overrun error

Derive this circuit as follows:

1. Modify the ASMD chart in Figure 7.3 to accommodate the required extensions.
2. Revise the UART receiver code according to the ASMD chart.
3. Revise the UART transmitter code to accommodate the required extensions.
4. Revise the top-level UART code and the verification circuit. Use the onboard switches for the additional input signals and three LEDs for the error signals. Synthesize the verification circuit.
5. Create different configurations in HyperTerminal and verify operation of the UART circuit.

7.7.2 UART with an automatic baud rate detection circuit

The most commonly used number of data bits of a serial connection is eight, which corresponds to a byte. When a regular ASCII code is used in communication (as we type in the HyperTerminal window), only seven LSBs are used and the MSB is '0'. If the UART is configured as 8 data bits, 1 stop bit, and no parity, the received word is in the form of `0_dddd_ddd0_1`, in which `d` is a data bit and can be '0' or '1'. Assume that there is sufficient time between the first word and subsequent transmissions. We can determine the baud rate by measuring the time interval between the first '0' and last '0'. Based on this observation, we can derive a UART with an automatic baud rate detection circuit. In this scheme, the transmitting system first sends an ASCII code for rate detection and then resumes normal operation afterward. The receiving subsystem uses the first word to determine a baud rate and then uses this rate for the baud rate generator for the remaining transmission.

Assume that UART configuration is 8 data bits, 1 stop bit, and no parity bit, and the baud rate can be 4800, 9600, or 19,200 baud. The revised UART receiver should have two operation modes. It is initially in the "detection mode" and waits for the first word. After the word is received and the baud rate is determined, the receiver enters "normal mode" and the UART operates in a regular fashion. Derive the UART as follows:

1. Draw the ASMD chart for the automatic baud rate detector circuit.
2. Derive the VHDL code for the ASMD chart. Use three LEDs on the S3 board to indicate the baud rate of the incoming signal.
3. Modify the UART to include three different baud rates: 4800, 9600, and 19,200. This can be achieved by using a register for the divisor of the baud rate generator and loading the value according to the desired baud rate.
4. Create a top-level FSMD to keep track of the mode and to control and coordinate operation of the baud rate detection circuit and the regular UART receiver. Use a pushbutton switch on the S3 board to force the UART into the detection mode.
5. Revise the top-level UART code and the verification circuit. Synthesize the verification circuit.
6. Create different configurations in HyperTerminal and verify operation of the UART.

7.7.3 UART with an automatic baud rate and parity detection circuit

In addition to the baud rate, we assume that the parity scheme also needs to be determined automatically, which can be no parity, even parity, or odd parity. Expand the previous automatic baud rate detection circuit to detect the parity configuration and repeat Experiment 7.7.2.

7.7.4 UART-controlled stopwatch

Consider the enhanced stopwatch in Experiment 4.7.6. Operation of the stopwatch is controlled by three switches on the S3 board. With the UART, we can use PC's HyperTerminal to send commands to and retrieve time from the stopwatch:

- When a `c` or `C` (for "clear") ASCII code is received, the stopwatch aborts current counting, is cleared to zero, and sets the counting direction to "up."
- When a `g` or `G` (for "go") ASCII code is received, the stopwatch starts to count.
- When a `p` or `P` (for "pause") ASCII code is received, counting pauses.
- When a `u` or `U` (for "up-down") ASCII code is received, the stopwatch reverses the direction of counting.

- When a `r` or `R` (for "receive") ASCII code is received, the stopwatch transmits the current time to the PC. The time should be displayed as "`DD.D`", where `D` is a decimal digit.
- All other codes will be ignored.

Design the new stopwatch, synthesize the circuit, connect it to a PC, and use HyperTerminal to verify its operation.

7.7.5 UART-controlled rotating LED banner

Consider the rotating LED banner circuit in Experiment 4.7.5. With the UART, we can use PC's HyperTerminal to control its operation and dynamically modify the digits in the banner:

- When a `g` or `G` (for "go") ASCII code is received, the LED banner rotates.
- When a `p` or `P` (for "pause") ASCII code is received, the LED banner pauses.
- When a `d` or `D` (for "direction") ASCII code is received, the LED banner reverses the direction of rotation.
- When a decimal-digit (i.e., 0, 1, ..., 9) ASCII code is received, the banner will be modified. The banner can be treated as a 10-word FIFO buffer. The new digit will be inserted at beginning (i.e., the leftmost position) of the banner and the rightmost digit will be shifted out and discarded.
- All other codes will be ignored.

Design the new rotating LED banner, synthesize the circuit, connect it to a PC, and use HyperTerminal to verify its operation.

CHAPTER 8

PS2 KEYBOARD

8.1 INTRODUCTION

PS2 port was introduced in IBM's Personal System/2 personnel computers. It is a widely supported interface for a keyboard and mouse to communicate with the host. The PS2 port contains two wires for communication purposes. One wire is for data, which is transmitted in a serial stream. The other wire is for the clock information, which specifies when the data is valid and can be retrieved. The information is transmitted as an 11-bit "packet" that contains a start bit, 8 data bits, an odd parity bit, and a stop bit. Whereas the basic format of the packet is identical for a keyboard and a mouse, the interpretation for the data bits is different. The FPGA prototyping board has a PS2 port and acts as a host. We discuss the keyboard interface in this chapter and cover the mouse interface in Chapter 9.

The communication of the PS2 port is bidirectional and the host can send a command to the keyboard or mouse to set certain parameters. For our purposes, the bidirectional communication is hardly required for the PS2 keyboard, and thus our discussion is limited to one direction, from the keyboard to the prototyping board. Bidirectional design will be examined in the mouse interface in Chapter 9.

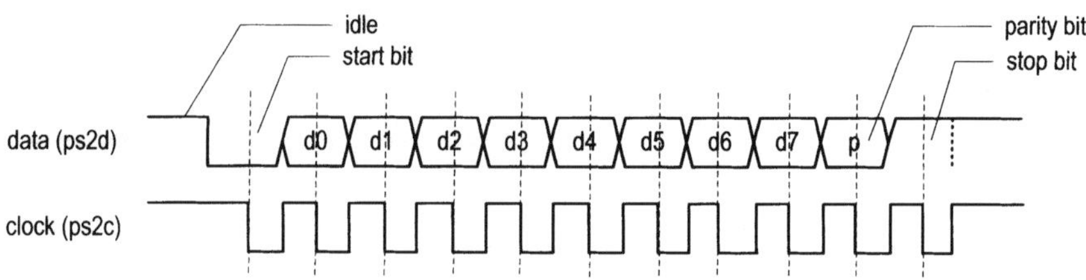

Figure 8.1 Timing diagram of a PS2 port.

8.2 PS2 RECEIVING SUBSYSTEM

8.2.1 Physical interface of a PS2 port

In addition to data and clock lines, the PS2 port includes connections for power (i.e., V_{cc}) and ground. The power is supplied by the host. In the original PS2 port, V_{cc} is 5 V and the outputs of the data and clock lines are open-collector. However, most current keyboards and mice can work well with 3.3 V. For an older keyboard and mouse, the 5-V supply can be obtained by switching the J2 jumper on the S3 board. The FPGA should still function properly since its I/O pins can tolerate 5-V input.

8.2.2 Device-to-host communication protocol

A PS2 device and its host communicate via packets. The basic timing diagram of transmitting a packet from a PS2 device to a host is shown in Figure 8.1, in which the data and clock signals are labeled ps2d and ps2c, respectively.

The data is transmitted in a serial stream, and its format is similar to that of a UART. Transmission begins with a start bit, followed by 8 data bits and an odd parity bit, and ends with a stop bit. Unlike a UART, the clock information is carried in a separate clock signal, ps2c. The falling edge of the ps2c signal indicates that the corresponding bit in the ps2d line is valid and can be retrieved. The clock period of the ps2c signal is between 60 and 100 μs (i.e., 10 kHz to 16.7 kHz), and the ps2d signal is stable at least 5 μs before and after the falling edge of the ps2c signal.

8.2.3 Design and code

The design of the PS2 port receiving subsystem is somewhat similar to that of a UART receiver. Instead of using the oversampling scheme, the falling-edge of the ps2c signal is used as the reference point to retrieve data. The subsystem includes a falling edge detection circuit, which generates a one-clock-cycle tick at the falling edge of the ps2c signal, and the receiver, which shifts in and assembles the serial bits.

The edge detection circuit discussed in Section 5.3.1 can be used to detect the falling edge and generate an enable tick. However, because of the potential noise and slow transition, a simple filtering circuit is added to eliminate glitches. Its code is

```
-- register
process (clk, reset)
   . . .
   filter_reg <= filter_next;
```

```
   . . .
end process;

-- 1-bit shifter
filter_next <= ps2c & filter_reg(7 downto 1);
-- "filter"
f_ps2c_next <= '1' when filter_reg="11111111" else
               '0' when filter_reg="00000000" else
               f_ps2c_reg;
```

The circuit is composed of an 8-bit shift register and returns a '1' or '0' when eight consecutive 1's or 0's are received. Any glitches shorter than eight clock cycles will be ignored (i.e., filtered out). The filtered output signal is then fed to the regular falling-edge detection circuit.

The ASMD chart of the receiver is shown in Figure 8.2. The receiver is initially in the `idle` state. It includes an additional control signal, `rx_en`, which is used to enable or disable the receiving operation. The purpose of the signal is to coordinate the bidirectional operation. It can be set to '1' for the keyboard interface.

After the first falling-edge tick and the `rx_en` signal are asserted, the FSMD shifts in the start bit and moves to the `dps` state. Since the received data is in fixed format, we shift in the remaining 10 bits in a single state rather than using separate `data`, `parity`, and `stop` states. The FSMD then moves to the `load` state, in which one extra clock cycle is provided to complete the shifting of the stop bit, and the `psrx_done_tick` signal is asserted for one clock cycle. The HDL code consists of the filtering circuit and an FSMD, which follows the ASMD chart. It is shown in Listing 8.1.

Listing 8.1 PS2 port receiver

```
library ieee;
use ieee.std_logic_1164.all;
use ieee.numeric_std.all;
entity ps2_rx is
   port (
      clk, reset: in  std_logic;
      ps2d, ps2c: in  std_logic;  -- key data, key clock
      rx_en: in std_logic;
      rx_done_tick: out  std_logic;
      dout: out std_logic_vector(7 downto 0)
   );
end ps2_rx;

architecture arch of ps2_rx is
   type statetype is (idle, dps, load);
   signal state_reg, state_next: statetype;
   signal filter_reg, filter_next:
          std_logic_vector(7 downto 0);
   signal f_ps2c_reg,f_ps2c_next: std_logic;
   signal b_reg, b_next: std_logic_vector(10 downto 0);
   signal n_reg,n_next: unsigned(3 downto 0);
   signal fall_edge: std_logic;
begin
   --=================================================
   -- filter and falling edge tick generation for ps2c
```

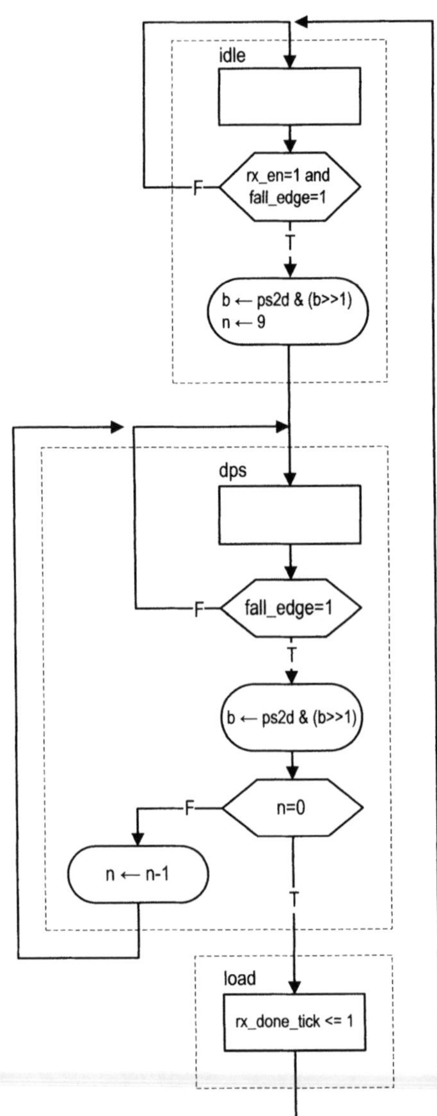

Figure 8.2 ASMD chart of the PS2 port receiver.

```
--=====================================================
process (clk, reset)
begin
   if reset='1' then
      filter_reg <= (others=>'0');
      f_ps2c_reg <= '0';
   elsif (clk'event and clk='1') then
      filter_reg <= filter_next;
      f_ps2c_reg <= f_ps2c_next;
   end if;
end process;

filter_next <= ps2c & filter_reg(7 downto 1);
f_ps2c_next <= '1' when filter_reg="11111111" else
               '0' when filter_reg="00000000" else
               f_ps2c_reg;
fall_edge <= f_ps2c_reg and (not f_ps2c_next);

--=====================================================
-- fsmd to extract the 8-bit data
--=====================================================
-- registers
process (clk, reset)
begin
   if reset='1' then
      state_reg <= idle;
      n_reg  <= (others=>'0');
      b_reg <= (others=>'0');
   elsif (clk'event and clk='1') then
      state_reg <= state_next;
      n_reg <= n_next;
      b_reg <= b_next;
   end if;
end process;
-- next-state logic
process(state_reg,n_reg,b_reg,fall_edge,rx_en,ps2d)
begin
   rx_done_tick <='0';
   state_next <= state_reg;
   n_next <= n_reg;
   b_next <= b_reg;
   case state_reg is
      when idle =>
         if fall_edge='1' and rx_en='1' then
            -- shift in start bit
            b_next <= ps2d & b_reg(10 downto 1);
            n_next <= "1001";
            state_next <= dps;
         end if;
      when dps =>  -- 8 data + 1 parity + 1 stop
         if fall_edge='1' then
         b_next <= ps2d & b_reg(10 downto 1);
            if n_reg = 0 then
```

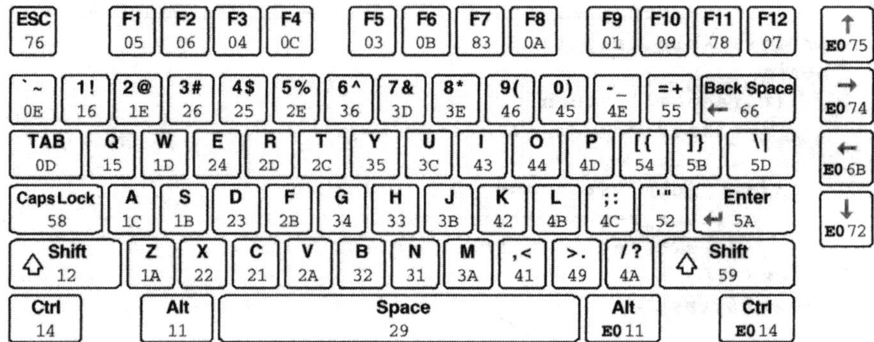

Figure 8.3 Scan code of the PS2 keyboard. (Courtesy of Xilinx, Inc. © Xilinx, Inc. 1994–2007. All rights reserved.)

```
                     state_next <=load;
                 else
                     n_next <= n_reg - 1;
                 end if;
              end if;
           when load =>
              -- 1 extra clock to complete the last shift
              state_next <= idle;
              rx_done_tick <='1';
        end case;
     end process;
     -- output
     dout <= b_reg(8 downto 1); -- data bits
  end arch;
```

There is no error detection circuit in the description. A more robust design should check the correctness of the start, parity, and stop bits and include a watchdog timer to prevent the keyboard from being locked in an incorrect state. This is left as an experiment at the end of the chapter.

8.3 PS2 KEYBOARD SCAN CODE

8.3.1 Overview of the scan code

A keyboard consists of a matrix of keys and an embedded microcontroller that monitors (i.e., scans) the activities of the keys and sends *scan code* accordingly. Three types of key activities are observed:

- When a key is pressed, the *make code* of the key is transmitted.
- When a key is held down continuously, a condition known as *typematic*, the make code is transmitted repeatedly at a specific rate. By default, a PS2 keyboard transmits the make code about every 100 ms after a key has been held down for 0.5 second.
- When a key is released, the *break code* of the key is transmitted.

The make code of the main part of a PS2 keyboard is shown in Figure 8.3. It is normally 1 byte wide and represented by two hexadecimal numbers. For example, the make code of the A key is 1C. This code can be conveyed by one packet when transmitted. The make codes of a handful of special-purpose keys, which are known as the *extended keys*, can have 2 to 4 bytes. A few of these keys are shown in Figure 8.3. For example, the make code of the upper arrow on the right is E0 75. Multiple packets are needed for the transmission. The break codes of the regular keys consist of F0 followed by the make code of the key. For example, the break code of the A key is F0 1C.

The PS2 keyboard transmits a sequence of codes according to the key activities. For example, when we press and release the A key, the keyboard first transmits its make code and then the break code:

```
1C F0 1C
```

If we hold the key down for awhile before releasing it, the make code will be transmitted multiple times:

```
1C 1C 1C ... 1C F0 1C
```

Multiple keys can be pressed at the same time. For example, we can first press the `shift` key (whose make code is 12) and then the A key, and release the A key and then release the `shift` key. The transmitted code sequence follows the make and break codes of the two keys:

```
12 1C F0 1C F0 12
```

The previous sequence is how we normally obtain an uppercase A. Note that there is no special code to distinguish the lower- and uppercase keys. It is the responsibility of the host device to keep track of whether the shift key is pressed and to determine the case accordingly.

8.3.2 Scan code monitor circuit

The scan code monitor circuit monitors the arrival of the received packets and displays the scan codes on a PC's HyperTerminal window. The basic design approach is to first split the received scan code into two 4-bit parts and treat them as two hexadecimal digits, and then convert the two digits to ASCII code words and send the words to a PC via the UART. The received scan codes should be displayed similar to the previous example sequences. The program is shown in Listing 8.2.

Listing 8.2 PS2 keyboard scan code monitor circuit

```
library ieee;
use ieee.std_logic_1164.all;
use ieee.numeric_std.all;
entity kb_monitor is
   port (
      clk, reset: in  std_logic;
      ps2d, ps2c: in  std_logic;
      tx: out  std_logic
   );
end kb_monitor;

architecture arch of kb_monitor is
   constant SP: std_logic_vector(7 downto 0):="00100000";
   -- blank space in ASCII
```

```
   type statetype is (idle, send1, send0, sendb);
   signal state_reg, state_next: statetype;
   signal scan_data, w_data: std_logic_vector(7 downto 0);
   signal scan_done_tick, wr_uart: std_logic;
   signal ascii_code: std_logic_vector(7 downto 0);
   signal hex_in: std_logic_vector(3 downto 0);
begin
   --=====================================================
   -- instantiation
   --=====================================================
   -- instantiate PS2 receiver
   ps2_rx_unit: entity work.ps2_rx(arch)
      port map(clk=>clk, reset=>reset, rx_en=>'1',
               ps2d=>ps2d, ps2c=>ps2c,
               rx_done_tick=>scan_done_tick,
               dout=>scan_data);

   -- instantiate UART
   uart_unit: entity work.uart(str_arch)
      port map(clk=>clk, reset=>reset, rd_uart=>'0',
               wr_uart=>wr_uart, rx=>'1', w_data=>w_data,
               tx_full=>open, rx_empty=>open, r_data=>open,
               tx=>tx);

   --=====================================================
   -- FSM to send 3 ASCII characters
   --=====================================================
   -- state registers
   process (clk, reset)
   begin
      if reset='1' then
         state_reg <= idle;
      elsif (clk'event and clk='1') then
         state_reg <= state_next;
      end if;
   end process;
   -- next-state logic
   process(state_reg, scan_done_tick, ascii_code)
   begin
      wr_uart <= '0';
      w_data <= SP;
      state_next <= state_reg;
      case state_reg is
         when idle => -- start when a scan code received
            if scan_done_tick='1' then
               state_next <= send1;
            end if;
         when send1 => -- send higher hex char
            w_data <= ascii_code;
            wr_uart <= '1';
            state_next <= send0;
         when send0 => -- send lower hex char
            w_data <= ascii_code;
```

```
            wr_uart <= '1';
            state_next <= sendb;
         when sendb => -- send blank space char
            w_data <= SP;
            wr_uart <= '1';
            state_next <= idle;
      end case;
   end process;

   --=====================================================
   -- scan code to ASCII display
   --=====================================================
   -- split the scan code into two 4-bit hex
   hex_in <= scan_data(7 downto 4) when state_reg=send1 else
             scan_data(3 downto 0);
   -- hex digit to ASCII code
   with hex_in select
      ascii_code <=
         "00110000" when "0000",  -- 0
         "00110001" when "0001",  -- 1
         "00110010" when "0010",  -- 2
         "00110011" when "0011",  -- 3
         "00110100" when "0100",  -- 4
         "00110101" when "0101",  -- 5
         "00110110" when "0110",  -- 6
         "00110111" when "0111",  -- 7
         "00111000" when "1000",  -- 8
         "00111001" when "1001",  -- 9
         "01000001" when "1010",  -- A
         "01000010" when "1011",  -- B
         "01000011" when "1100",  -- C
         "01000100" when "1101",  -- D
         "01000101" when "1110",  -- E
         "01000110" when others;  -- F
end arch;
```

An FSM is used to control the overall operation. The UART operation is initiated when a new scan code is received (as indicated by the assertion of `scan_done_tick`). The FSM circulates through the `send1`, `send0`, and `sendb` states, in which the ASCII codes of the upper hexadecimal digit, lower hexadecimal digit, and blank space are written to the UART. Recall that the UART has a FIFO of four words, and thus no overflow will occur. Note that the UART receiver is not used and the corresponding ports are mapped to constants or **open**.

8.4 PS2 KEYBOARD INTERFACE CIRCUIT

As discussed in Section 8.3.1, a sequence of packets is transmitted even for simple keyboard activities. It will be quite involved if we want to cover all possible combinations. In this section, we assume that only one regular key is pressed and released at a time and design a circuit that returns the make code of this key. This design provides a simple way to send a character or digit to the prototyping board and should be satisfactory for our purposes.

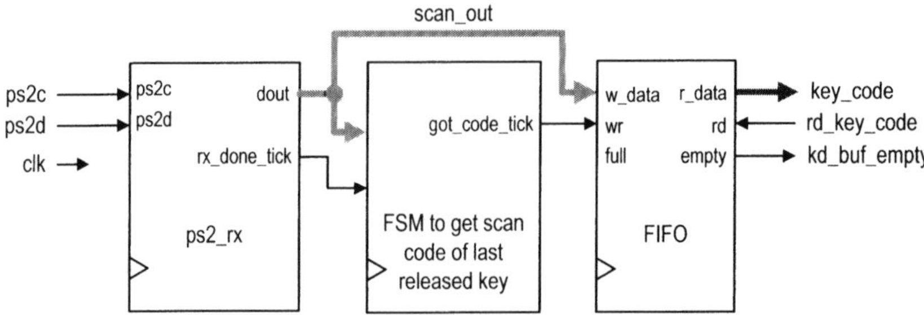

Figure 8.4 Block diagram of a last-released key circuit.

8.4.1 Basic design and HDL code

The keyboard circuit, as a UART, is a peripheral circuit of a large system and needs a mechanism to communicate with the main system. The flagging and buffering schemes discussed in Section 7.2.4 can be applied for the keyboard circuit as well. We use a four-word FIFO buffer as the interface in this design.

The top-level conceptual diagram is shown in Figure 8.4. It consists of the PS2 receiver, a FIFO buffer, and a control FSM. The basic idea is to use the FSM to keep track of the F0 packet of the break code. After it is received, the next packet should be the make code of this key and is written into the FIFO buffer. Note that this scheme cannot be applied to the extended keys since their make codes involve multiple packets. The corresponding HDL code is shown in Listing 8.3.

Listing 8.3 PS2 keyboard last-released key circuit

```
library ieee;
use ieee.std_logic_1164.all;
use ieee.numeric_std.all;
entity kb_code is
   generic(W_SIZE: integer:=2);  -- 2^W_SIZE words in FIFO
   port (
      clk, reset: in  std_logic;
      ps2d, ps2c: in  std_logic;
      rd_key_code: in std_logic;
      key_code: out std_logic_vector(7 downto 0);
      kb_buf_empty: out std_logic
   );
end kb_code;

architecture arch of kb_code is
   constant BRK: std_logic_vector(7 downto 0):="11110000";
   -- F0 (break code)
   type statetype is (wait_brk, get_code);
   signal state_reg, state_next: statetype;
   signal scan_out, w_data: std_logic_vector(7 downto 0);
   signal scan_done_tick, got_code_tick: std_logic;

begin
   --=================================================
   -- instantiation
```

```
--==========================================================
ps2_rx_unit: entity work.ps2_rx(arch)
   port map(clk=>clk, reset=>reset, rx_en=>'1',
            ps2d=>ps2d, ps2c=>ps2c,
            rx_done_tick=>scan_done_tick,
            dout=>scan_out);

fifo_key_unit: entity work.fifo(arch)
   generic map(B=>8, W=>W_SIZE)
   port map(clk=>clk, reset=>reset, rd=>rd_key_code,
            wr=>got_code_tick, w_data=>scan_out,
            empty=>kb_buf_empty, full=>open,
            r_data=>key_code);

--==========================================================
-- FSM to get the scan code after F0 received
--==========================================================
process (clk, reset)
begin
   if reset='1' then
      state_reg <= wait_brk;
   elsif (clk'event and clk='1') then
      state_reg <= state_next;
   end if;
end process;

process(state_reg, scan_done_tick, scan_out)
begin
   got_code_tick <='0';
   state_next <= state_reg;
   case state_reg is
      when wait_brk => -- wait for F0 of break code
         if scan_done_tick='1' and scan_out=BRK then
            state_next <= get_code;
         end if;
      when get_code => -- get the following scan code
         if scan_done_tick='1' then
            got_code_tick <='1';
            state_next <= wait_brk;
         end if;
   end case;
end process;
end arch;
```

The main part of the code is the FSM, which screens for the break code and coordinates the operation of two other modules. It checks the received packets in the `wait_brk` state continuously. When the `F0` packet is detected, it moves to the `get_code` state and waits for the next packet, which is the make code of the key. The FSM then asserts the `code_done_tick` signal for one clock cycle and returns to the `wait_brk` state.

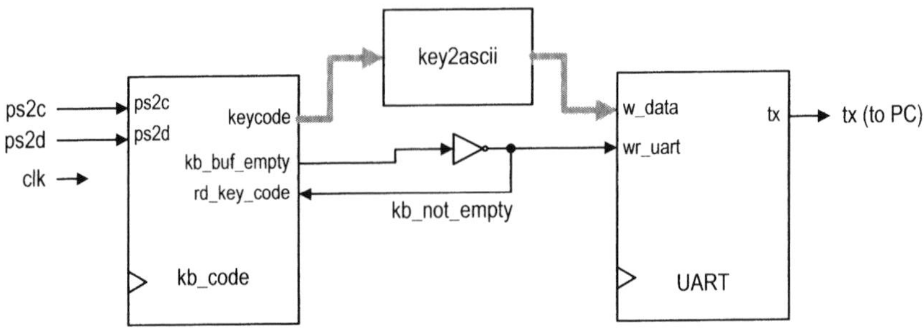

Figure 8.5 Block diagram of a keyboard verification circuit.

8.4.2 Verification circuit

We design a simple serial interface and decoding circuit to verify operation of the PS2 keyboard interface. The top-level block diagram is shown in Figure 8.5. The circuit converts a key's make code to the corresponding ASCII code and then sends the ASCII code to the UART. The corresponding character or digits can be displayed in the HyperTerminal window. The HDL code for the conversion circuit is shown in Listing 8.4.

Listing 8.4 Keyboard make code to ASCII code

```
library ieee;
use ieee.std_logic_1164.all;
use ieee.numeric_std.all;
entity key2ascii is
   port (
      key_code: in std_logic_vector(7 downto 0);
      ascii_code: out std_logic_vector(7 downto 0)
   );
end key2ascii;

architecture arch of key2ascii is
begin
   with key_code select
      ascii_code <=
         "00110000" when "01000101",  -- 0
         "00110001" when "00010110",  -- 1
         "00110010" when "00011110",  -- 2
         "00110011" when "00100110",  -- 3
         "00110100" when "00100101",  -- 4
         "00110101" when "00101110",  -- 5
         "00110110" when "00110110",  -- 6
         "00110111" when "00111101",  -- 7
         "00111000" when "00111110",  -- 8
         "00111001" when "01000110",  -- 9

         "01000001" when "00011100",  -- A
         "01000010" when "00110010",  -- B
         "01000011" when "00100001",  -- C
         "01000100" when "00100011",  -- D
         "01000101" when "00100100",  -- E
```

```
         "01000110" when "00101011",    -- F
         "01000111" when "00110100",    -- G
         "01001000" when "00110011",    -- H
         "01001001" when "01000011",    -- I
         "01001010" when "00111011",    -- J
         "01001011" when "01000010",    -- K
         "01001100" when "01001011",    -- L
         "01001101" when "00111010",    -- M
         "01001110" when "00110001",    -- N
         "01001111" when "01000100",    -- O
         "01010000" when "01001101",    -- P
         "01010001" when "00010101",    -- Q
         "01010010" when "00101101",    -- R
         "01010011" when "00011011",    -- S
         "01010100" when "00101100",    -- T
         "01010101" when "00111100",    -- U
         "01010110" when "00101010",    -- V
         "01010111" when "00011101",    -- W
         "01011000" when "00100010",    -- X
         "01011001" when "00110101",    -- Y
         "01011010" when "00011010",    -- Z

         "01100000" when "00001110",    -- `
         "00101101" when "01001110",    -- -
         "00111101" when "01010101",    -- =
         "01011011" when "01010100",    -- [
         "01011101" when "01011011",    -- ]
         "01011100" when "01011101",    -- \
         "00111011" when "01001100",    -- ;
         "00100111" when "01010010",    -- '
         "00101100" when "01000001",    -- ,
         "00101110" when "01001001",    -- .
         "00101111" when "01001010",    -- /

         "00100000" when "00101001",    -- (space)
         "00001101" when "01011010",    -- (enter, cr)
         "00001000" when "01100110",    -- (backspace)
         "00101010" when others;        -- *
end arch;
```

The complete code for the verification circuit follows the block diagram and is shown in Listing 8.5.

Listing 8.5 Keyboard verification circuit

```
library ieee;
use ieee.std_logic_1164.all;
use ieee.numeric_std.all;
entity kb_test is
   port (
      clk, reset: in  std_logic;
      ps2d, ps2c: in  std_logic;
      tx: out  std_logic
   );
```

```
end kb_test;

architecture arch of kb_test is
   signal scan_data, w_data: std_logic_vector(7 downto 0);
   signal kb_not_empty, kb_buf_empty: std_logic;
   signal key_code, ascii_code: std_logic_vector(7 downto 0);
begin
   kb_code_unit: entity work.kb_code(arch)
      port map(clk=>clk, reset=>reset, ps2d=>ps2d, ps2c=>ps2c,
               rd_key_code=>kb_not_empty, key_code=>key_code,
               kb_buf_empty=>kb_buf_empty);
   uart_unit: entity work.uart(str_arch)
      port map(clk=>clk, reset=>reset, rd_uart=>'0',
               wr_uart=>kb_not_empty, rx=>'1',
               w_data=>ascii_code, tx_full=>open,
               rx_empty=>open, r_data=>open, tx=>tx);
   key2a_unit: entity work.key2ascii(arch)
      port map(key_code=>key_code, ascii_code=>ascii_code);

   kb_not_empty <= not kb_buf_empty;
end arch;
```

8.5 BIBLIOGRAPHIC NOTES

Three articles, "PS/2 Mouse/Keyboard Protocol," "PS/2 Keyboard Interface," and "PS/2 Mouse Interface," by Adam Chapweske, provide detailed information on the PS2 keyboard and mouse interface. They can be found at the http://www.computer-engineering.org site. *Rapid Prototyping of Digital Systems: Quartus® II Edition* by James O. Hamblen et al. also contains a chapter on the PS2 port and the keyboard and mouse protocols.

8.6 SUGGESTED EXPERIMENTS

8.6.1 Alternative keyboard interface I

The interface circuit in Section 8.4 returns the make code of the last released key and thus ignores the typematic condition. An alternative approach is to consider the typematic condition. The keyboard interface circuit should return a key's make code repeatedly when it is held down and ignore the final break code. For simplicity, we assume that the extended keys are not used. Design the new interface circuit, resynthesize the verification circuit, and verify operation of the new interface circuit.

8.6.2 Alternative keyboard interface II

We can expand the interface circuit to distinguish whether the shift key is pressed so that both lower- and uppercase characters can be entered. The expanded circuit can be modified as follows:

- The keycode output should be extended from 8 bits to 9 bits. The extra bit indicates whether the shift key is held down.

- The FSM should add a special branch to process the make and break codes of the shift key and set the value of the corresponding bit accordingly.
- The width of the FIFO buffer should be extended to 9 bits.

Design the expanded interface circuit, modify the `key2ascii` circuit to handle both lower- and uppercase characters, resynthesize the verification circuit, and verify operation of the expanded interface circuit.

8.6.3 PS2 receiving subsystem with watchdog timer

There is no error-handling capability in the PS2 receiving subsystem in Section 8.2. The potential noise and glitches in the `ps2c` signal may cause the FSMD to be stuck in an incorrect state. One way to deal with this problem is to add a watchdog timer. The timer is initiated every time the `fall_edge_tick` signal is asserted in the `get_bit` state. The `time_out` signal is asserted if no subsequently falling edge arrives in the next 20 μs, and the FSMD returns to the `idle` state. Design the modified receiving subsystem, derive a testbench, and use simulation to verify its operation.

8.6.4 Keyboard-controlled stopwatch

Consider the enhanced stopwatch in Experiment 4.7.6. Operation of the stopwatch is controlled by three switches on the prototyping board. We can use the keyboard to send commands to the stopwatch:

- When the `C` (for "clear") key is pressed, the stopwatch aborts the current counting, is cleared to zero, and sets the counting direction to "up."
- When the `G` (for "go") key is pressed, the stopwatch starts to count.
- When the `P` (for "pause") key is pressed, the counting pauses.
- When the `U` (for "up-down") key is pressed, the stopwatch reverses the direction of counting.
- All other keys will be ignored.

Design the new stopwatch, synthesize the circuit, and verify its operation.

8.6.5 Keyboard-controlled rotating LED banner

Consider the rotating LED banner circuit in Experiment 4.7.5. We can use a keyboard to control its operation and dynamically modify the digits in the banner:

- When the `G` (for "go") key is pressed, the LED banner rotates.
- When the `P` (for "pause") key is pressed, the LED banner pauses.
- When the `D` (for "direction") key is pressed, the LED banner reverses the direction of rotation.
- When a decimal digit (i.e., 0, 1, ..., 9) key is pressed, the banner will be modified. The banner can be treated as a 10-word FIFO buffer. The new digit will be inserted at the beginning (i.e., the leftmost position) of the banner, and the rightmost digit will be shifted out and discarded.
- All other keys will be ignored.

Design the new rotating LED banner, synthesize the circuit, and verify its operation.

CHAPTER 9

PS2 MOUSE

9.1 INTRODUCTION

A computer mouse is designed mainly to detect two-dimensional motion on a surface. Its internal circuit measures the relative distance of movement and checks the status of the buttons. For a mouse with a PS2 interface, this information is packed in three packets and sent to the host through the PS2 port. In the *stream mode*, a PS2 mouse sends the packets continuously in a predesignated sampling rate.

Communication of the PS2 port is bidirectional and the host can send a command to the keyboard or mouse to set certain parameters. For our purposes, this functionality is hardly required for a keyboard, and thus the keyboard interface in Chapter 8 is limited to one direction, from the keyboard to the FPGA host. However, unlike the keyboard, a mouse is set to be in the non-steaming mode after power-up and does not send any data. The host must first send a command to the mouse to initialize the mouse and enable the stream mode. Thus, bidirectional communication of the PS2 port is needed for the PS2 mouse interface, and we must design a transmitting subsystem (i.e., from FPGA board to mouse) for the PS2 interface.

In this chapter, we provide a short overview of the PS2 mouse protocol, design a bidirectional PS interface, and derive a simple mouse interface.

Table 9.1 Mouse data packet format

byte 1	y_v	x_v	y_8	x_8	1	m	r	l
byte 2	x_7	x_6	x_5	x_4	x_3	x_2	x_1	x_0
byte 3	y_7	y_6	y_5	y_4	y_3	y_2	y_1	y_0

9.2 PS2 MOUSE PROTOCOL

9.2.1 Basic operation

A standard PS2 mouse reports the x-axis (right/left) and y-axis (up/down) movement and the status of the left button, middle button, and right button. The amount of each movement is recorded in a mouse's internal counter. When the data is transmitted to the host, the counter is cleared to zero and restarts the counting. The content of the counter represents a 9-bit signed integer in which a positive number indicates the right or up movement, and a negative number indicates the left or down movement.

The relationship between the physical distances is defined by the mouse's *resolution* parameter. The default value of resolution is four counts per millimeter. When a mouse moves continuously, the data is transmitted in a regular rate. The rate is defined by the mouse's *sampling rate* parameter. The default value of the sampling rate is 100 samples per second. If a mouse moves too fast, the amount of the movement during the sampling period may exceed the maximal range of the counter. The counter is set to the maximum magnitude in the appropriate direction. Two overflow bits are used to indicate the conditions.

The mouse reports the movement and button activities in 3 bytes, which are embedded in three PS2 packets. The detailed format of the 3-byte data is shown in Table 9.1. It contains the following information:

- $x_8, \ldots, x_0$: x-axis movement in 2's-complement format
- x_v: x-axis movement overflow
- $y_8, \ldots, y_0$: y-axis movement in 2's-complement format
- y_v: y-axis movement overflow
- l: left button status, which is '1' when the left button is pressed
- r: right button status, which is '1' when the right button is pressed
- m: optional middle button status, which is '1' when the middle button is pressed

During transmission, the byte 1 packet is sent first and the byte 3 packet is sent last.

9.2.2 Basic initialization procedure

The operation of a mouse is more complex than that of a keyboard. It has different operation modes. The most commonly used one is the *stream mode*, in which a mouse sends the movement data when it detects movement or button activity. If the movement is continuous, the data is generated at the designated sample rate.

During the operation, a host can send commands to a mouse to modify the default values of various parameters and set the operation mode, and a mouse may generate the status and send an acknowledgment. For our purposes, the default values are adequate, and the only task is to set the mouse to the stream mode.

The basic interaction sequence between a PS2 mouse and the FPGA host consists of the following:

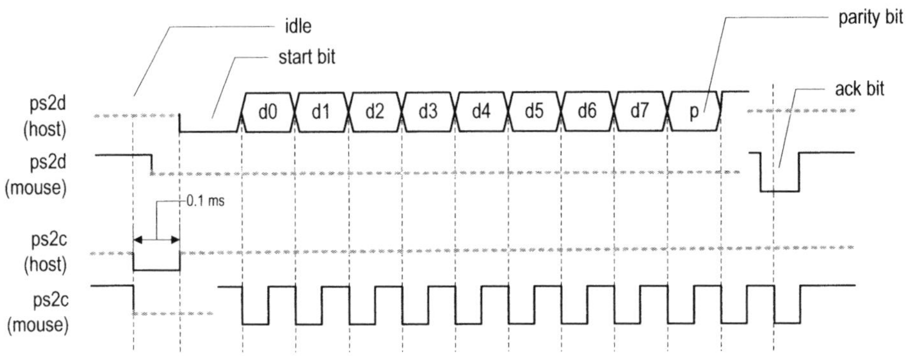

Figure 9.1 Host-to-device timing diagram of a PS2 port.

1. At power-on, a mouse performs a power-on test internally. The mouse sends 1-byte data `AA`, which indicates that the test is passed, and then 1-byte data `00`, which is the id of a standard PS2 mouse.
2. The FPGA host sends the command, `F4`, to enable the stream mode. The mouse will respond with `FE` to acknowledge acceptance of the command.
3. The mouse now enters the stream mode and sends normal data packets.

If a mouse is plugged into the FPGA prototyping board in advance, it performs the power-on test when the power of the board is turned on and sends the `AA 00` data immediately. The FPGA chip is not configured at this point and will not receive this data. Thus, we can usually ignore the power-on message in step 1. A minimal mouse interface circuit only needs to send the `F4` command, check the `FE` acknowledge, and enter the normal operation mode to process the mouse's regular data packet.

We can force the mouse to return to the initial state by sending the reset command:

1. The FPGA host sends the command, `FF`, to reset the mouse. The mouse will respond with `FE` to acknowledge acceptance of the command.
2. The mouse performs a power-on test internally and then sends `AA 00`. The stream mode will be disabled during the process.

Newer mouses add more functionality, such as a scrolling wheel and additional buttons, and thus send more information. Additional bytes are appended to the original 3-byte data to accommodate these new features.

9.3 PS2 TRANSMITTING SUBSYSTEM

9.3.1 Host-to-PS2-device communication protocol

Host-to-PS2-device communication protocol involves bidirectional data exchange. The mouse's data and clock lines actually are *open-collector* circuits. For our design purposes, we treat them as tri-state lines. The basic timing diagram of transmitting a packet from a host to a PS2 device is shown in Figure 9.1, in which the data and clock signals are labeled `ps2d` and `ps2c`. For clarity, the diagram is split into two parts to show which activities are generated by the host (i.e., the FPGA chip) and which activities are generated by the device (i.e., mouse). The basic operation sequence is as follows:

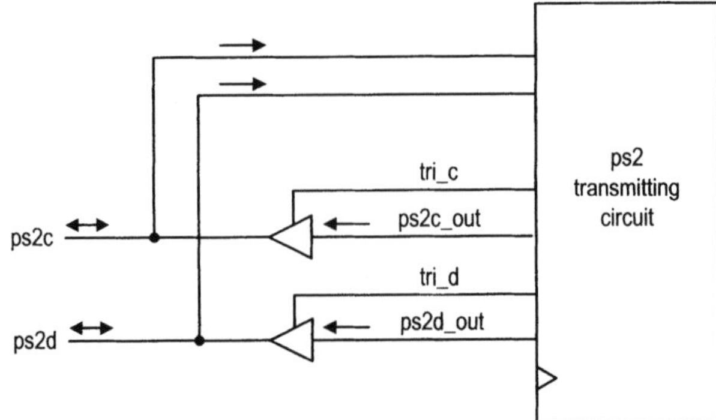

Figure 9.2 Tri-state buffers of the PS2 transmission subsystem.

1. The host forces the ps2c line to be '0' for at least 100 μs to inhibit any mouse activity. It can be considered that the host requests to send a packet.
2. The host forces the ps2d line to be '0' and disables the ps2c line (i.e., makes it high impedance). This step can be interpreted as the host sending a start bit.
3. The PS2 device now takes over the ps2c line and is responsible for future PS2 clock signal generation. After sensing the starting bit, the PS2 device generates a '1'-to-'0' transition.
4. Once detecting the transition, the host shifts out the least significant data bit over the ps2d line. It holds this value until the PS2 device generates a '1'-to-'0' transition in the ps2c line, which essentially acknowledges retrieval of the data bit.
5. Repeat step 4 for the remaining 7 data bits and 1 parity bit.
6. After sending the parity bit, the host disables the ps2d line (i.e., makes it high impedance). The PS2 device now takes over the ps2d line and acknowledges completion of the transmission by asserting the ps2d line to '0'. If desired, the host can check this value at the last '1'-to-'0' transition in the ps2c line to verify that the packet is transmitted successfully.

9.3.2 Design and code

Unlike the receiving subsystem, the ps2c and ps2d signals communicate in both directions. A tri-state buffer is needed for each signal. The tri-state interface is shown in Figure 9.2. The `tri_c` and `tri_d` signals are enable signals that control the tri-state buffers. When they are asserted, the corresponding `ps2c_out` and `ps2d_out` signals will be routed to the output ports.

To design the transmitting subsystem, we can follow the sequence of the preceding protocol to create an ASMD chart, as shown in Figure 9.3. The FSMD is initially in the `idle` state. To start the transmission, the host asserts the `wr_ps2` signal and places the data on the `din` bus. The FSMD loads `din`, along with the parity bit, `par` to the `shift_reg` register, loads the "1···1" to `c_reg`, and moves to the `rts` (for "request to send") state. In this state, the `ps2c_out` is set to '0' and the corresponding `tri_c` is asserted to enable the corresponding tri-state buffer. The `c_reg` is used as a 13-bit counter to generate a 164-μs delay. The FSMD then moves to the `start` state, in which the PS2 clock line is disabled and the data line is set to '1'. The PS2 device (i.e., mouse) now takes over and generates

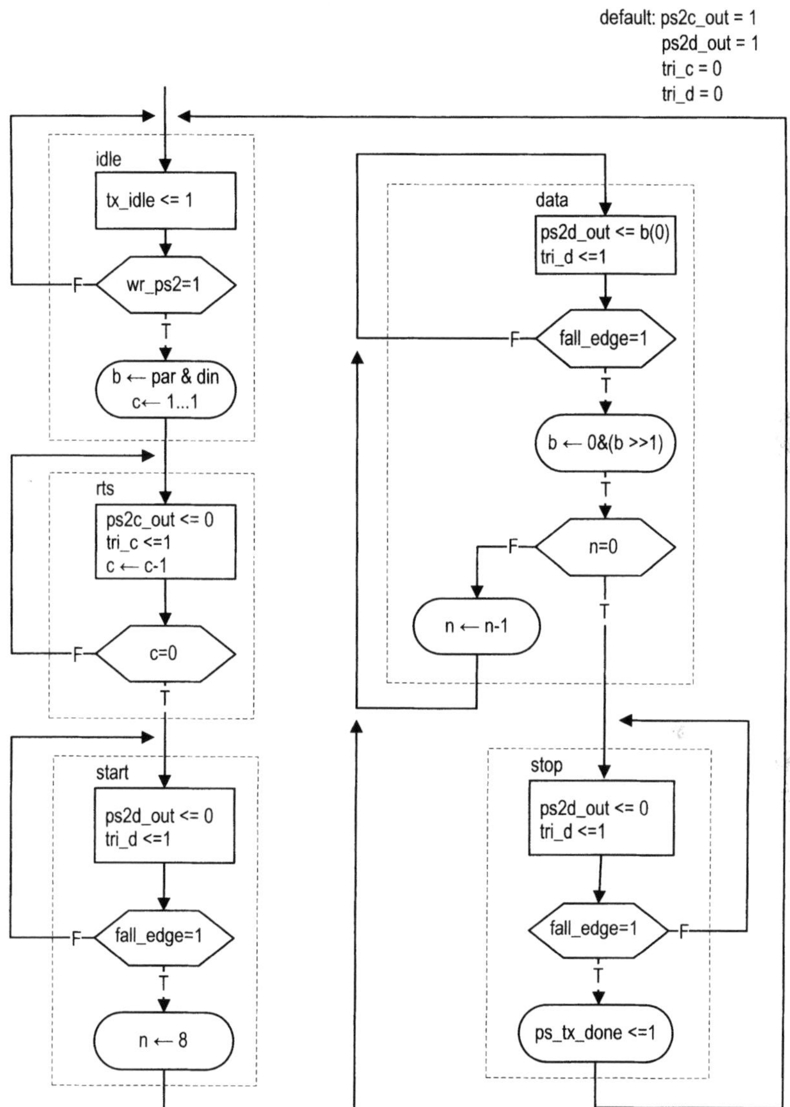

Figure 9.3 ASMD chart of the PS2 transmitting subsystem.

clock signal over the ps2c line. After detecting the falling edge of the ps2c signal through the fall_edge signal, the FSMD goes to the data state and shifts 8 data bits and 1 parity bit. The n register is used to keep track of the number of bits shifted. The FSMD then moves to the stop state, in which the data line is disabled. It returns to the idle state after sensing the last falling edge.

The FSMD also includes a tx_idle signal to indicate whether a transmission is in progress. This signal can be used to coordinate operation between the receiving and transmitting subsystems. The code follows the ASMD chart and is shown in Listing 9.1. A filtering circuit similar to that of Section 8.2 is used to generate the fall_edge signal.

Listing 9.1 PS2 port transmitter

```
library ieee;
use ieee.std_logic_1164.all;
use ieee.numeric_std.all;
entity ps2_tx is
   port (
      clk, reset: in  std_logic;
      din: in std_logic_vector(7 downto 0);
      wr_ps2: std_logic;
      ps2d, ps2c: inout std_logic;
      tx_idle: out std_logic;
      tx_done_tick: out std_logic
   );
end ps2_tx;

architecture arch of ps2_tx is
   type statetype is (idle, rts, start, data, stop);
   signal state_reg, state_next: statetype;
   signal filter_reg, filter_next: std_logic_vector(7 downto 0);
   signal f_ps2c_reg,f_ps2c_next: std_logic;
   signal fall_edge: std_logic;
   signal b_reg, b_next: std_logic_vector(8 downto 0);
   signal c_reg,c_next: unsigned(12 downto 0);
   signal n_reg,n_next: unsigned(3 downto 0);
   signal par: std_logic;
   signal ps2c_out, ps2d_out: std_logic;
   signal tri_c, tri_d: std_logic;
begin
   --=================================================
   -- filter and falling-edge tick generation for ps2c
   --=================================================
   process (clk, reset)
   begin
      if reset='1' then
         filter_reg <= (others=>'0');
         f_ps2c_reg <= '0';
      elsif (clk'event and clk='1') then
         filter_reg <= filter_next;
         f_ps2c_reg <= f_ps2c_next;
      end if;
   end process;
```

```
filter_next <= ps2c & filter_reg(7 downto 1);
f_ps2c_next <= '1' when filter_reg="11111111" else
               '0' when filter_reg="00000000" else
               f_ps2c_reg;
fall_edge <= f_ps2c_reg and (not f_ps2c_next);

--=================================================
-- fsmd
--=================================================
-- registers
process (clk, reset)
begin
   if reset='1' then
      state_reg <= idle;
      c_reg <= (others=>'0');
      n_reg  <= (others=>'0');
      b_reg <= (others=>'0');
   elsif (clk'event and clk='1') then
      state_reg <= state_next;
      c_reg <= c_next;
      n_reg <= n_next;
      b_reg <= b_next;
   end if;
end process;
-- odd parity bit
par <= not (din(7) xor din(6) xor din(5) xor din(4) xor
            din(3) xor din(2) xor din(1) xor din(0));
-- fsmd next-state logic and data path logic
process(state_reg,n_reg,b_reg,c_reg,wr_ps2,
        din,par,fall_edge)
begin
   state_next <= state_reg;
   c_next <= c_reg;
   n_next <= n_reg;
   b_next <= b_reg;
   tx_done_tick <='0';
   ps2c_out <= '1';
   ps2d_out <= '1';
   tri_c <= '0';
   tri_d <= '0';
   tx_idle <='0';
   case state_reg is
      when idle =>
         tx_idle <= '1';
         if wr_ps2='1' then
            b_next <= par & din;
            c_next <= (others=>'1'); -- 2^13-1
            state_next <= rts;
         end if;
      when rts =>  -- request to send
         ps2c_out <= '0';
         tri_c <= '1';
         c_next <= c_reg - 1;
```

```
            if (c_reg=0) then
               state_next <= start;
            end if;
         when start => -- assert start bit
            ps2d_out <= '0';
            tri_d <= '1';
            if fall_edge='1' then
               n_next <= "1000";
               state_next <= data;
            end if;
         when data => -- 8 data + 1 parity
            ps2d_out <= b_reg(0);
            tri_d <= '1';
            if fall_edge='1' then
               b_next <= '0' & b_reg(8 downto 1);
               if n_reg = 0 then
                   state_next <= stop;
               else
                   n_next <= n_reg - 1;
               end if;
            end if;
         when stop => -- assume floating high for ps2d
            if fall_edge='1' then
               state_next <= idle;
               tx_done_tick <='1';
            end if;
      end case;
   end process;
   -- tri-state buffers
   ps2c <= ps2c_out when tri_c ='1' else 'Z';
   ps2d <= ps2d_out when tri_d ='1' else 'Z';
end arch;
```

There is no error detection circuit in this code. A more robust design should check the correctness of the parity and acknowledgment bits and include a watchdog timer to prevent the mouse from being locked in an incorrect state.

9.4 BIDIRECTIONAL PS2 INTERFACE

9.4.1 Basic design and code

We can combine the receiving and transmitting subsystems to form a bidirectional PS2 interface. The top-level diagram is shown in Figure 9.4. We use the `tx_idle` and `rx_en` signals to coordinate the transmitting and receiving operations. Priority is given to the transmitting operation. When the transmitting subsystem is in operation, the `tx_idle` signal is deasserted, which, in turn, disables the receiving subsystem. The receiving subsystem can process input only when the transmitting subsystem is idle. The corresponding HDL code is shown in Listing 9.2.

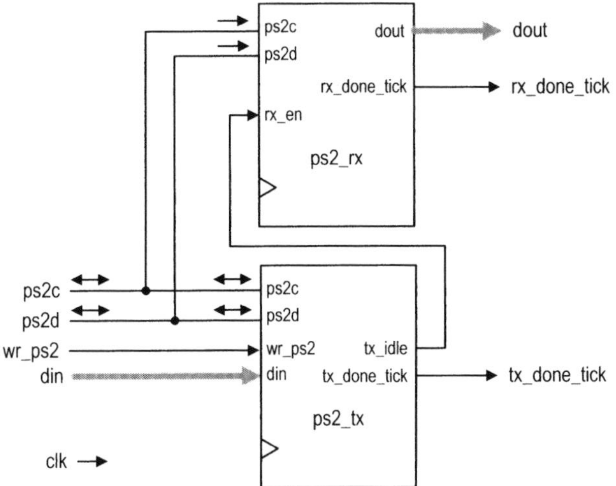

Figure 9.4 Top-level block diagram of a bidirectional PS2 interface.

Listing 9.2 Bidirectional PS2 interface

```
library ieee;
use ieee.std_logic_1164.all;
entity ps2_rxtx is
   port (
      clk, reset: in std_logic;
      wr_ps2: std_logic;
      din: in std_logic_vector(7 downto 0);
      dout: out std_logic_vector(7 downto 0);
      rx_done_tick: out  std_logic;
      tx_done_tick: out std_logic;
      ps2d, ps2c: inout std_logic
   );
end ps2_rxtx;

architecture arch of ps2_rxtx is
   signal tx_idle: std_logic;
begin
   ps2_tx_unit: entity work.ps2_tx(arch)
      port map(clk=>clk, reset=>reset, wr_ps2=>wr_ps2,
               din=>din, ps2d=>ps2d, ps2c=>ps2c,
               tx_idle=>tx_idle, tx_done_tick=>tx_done_tick);
   ps2_rx_unit: entity work.ps2_rx(arch)
      port map(clk=>clk, reset=>reset, rx_en=>tx_idle,
               ps2d=>ps2d, ps2c=>ps2c,
               rx_done_tick=>rx_done_tick, dout=>dout);
end arch;
```

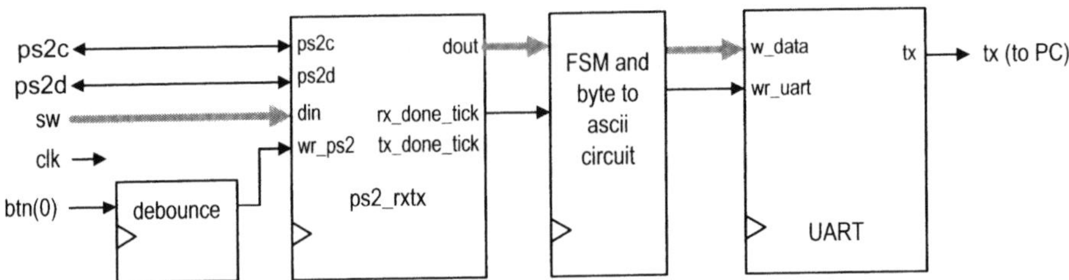

Figure 9.5 Block diagram of a mouse monitor circuit.

9.4.2 Verification circuit

We create a testing circuit to verify and monitor operation of the bidirectional interface. The block diagram is shown in Figure 9.5. A command is transmitted manually. We use the 8-bit switch to specify the data (i.e., the command from the host) and use a pushbutton to generate a one-clock-cycle tick to transmit the packet. The received packet data is first passed to the `byte-to-ascii` circuit, which converts the data into two ASCII characters plus a blank space. The characters are then transmitted via the UART and displayed in Windows HyperTerminal. The HDL code is shown in Listing 9.3.

Listing 9.3 Bidirectional PS2 interface monitor circuit

```
library ieee;
use ieee.std_logic_1164.all;
use ieee.numeric_std.all;
entity ps2_monitor is
   port (
      clk, reset: in  std_logic;
      sw: in std_logic_vector(7 downto 0);
      btn: in std_logic_vector(2 downto 0);
      ps2d, ps2c: inout  std_logic;
      tx: out  std_logic
   );
end ps2_monitor;

architecture arch of ps2_monitor is
   constant SP: std_logic_vector(7 downto 0):="00100000";
   -- blank space in ASCII
   type state_type is (idle, sendh, sendl, sendb);
   signal state_reg, state_next: state_type;
   signal rx_data, w_data: std_logic_vector(7 downto 0);
   signal psrx_done_tick: std_logic;
   signal wr_ps2, wr_uart: std_logic;
   signal ascii_code: std_logic_vector(7 downto 0);
   signal hex_in: std_logic_vector(3 downto 0);
begin
   --=========================================
   -- instantiation
   --=========================================
   btn_db_unit: entity work.debounce(fsmd_arch)
      port map(clk=>clk, reset=>reset, sw=>btn(0),
               db_level=>open, db_tick=>wr_ps2);
```

```
ps2_rxtx_unit: entity work.ps2_rxtx(arch)
   port map(clk=>clk, reset=>reset, wr_ps2=>wr_ps2,
            din=>sw, dout=>rx_data, ps2d=>ps2d,
            ps2c=>ps2c, rx_done_tick=>psrx_done_tick,
            tx_done_tick=>open);
-- only use the UART transmitter
uart_unit: entity work.uart(str_arch)
   generic map(FIFO_W=>4)
   port map(clk=>clk, reset=>reset, rd_uart=>'0',
            wr_uart=>wr_uart, rx=>'1', w_data=>w_data,
            tx_full=>open, rx_empty=>open, r_data=>open,
            tx=>tx);
--==============================================
-- FSM to send 3 ASCII characters
--==============================================
-- state registers
process (clk, reset)
begin
   if reset='1' then
      state_reg <= idle;
   elsif (clk'event and clk='1') then
      state_reg <= state_next;
   end if;
end process;
-- next-state logic
process(state_reg,psrx_done_tick,ascii_code)
begin
   wr_uart <= '0';
   w_data <= SP;
   state_next <= state_reg;
   case state_reg is
      when idle =>
         if psrx_done_tick='1' then
            state_next <= sendh;
         end if;
      when sendh => -- send higher hex char
         w_data <= ascii_code;
         wr_uart <= '1';
         state_next <= sendl;
      when sendl => -- send lower hex char
         w_data <= ascii_code;
         wr_uart <= '1';
         state_next <= sendb;
      when sendb => -- send blank space char
         w_data <= SP;
         wr_uart <= '1';
         state_next <= idle;
   end case;
end process;
--==============================================
-- scan code to ASCII display
--==============================================
-- split the scan code into two 4-bit hex
```

```
   hex_in <= rx_data(7 downto 4) when state_reg=sendh else
             rx_data(3 downto 0);
   -- hex digit to ASCII code
   with hex_in select
      ascii_code <=
         "00110000" when "0000",   -- 0
         "00110001" when "0001",   -- 1
         "00110010" when "0010",   -- 2
         "00110011" when "0011",   -- 3
         "00110100" when "0100",   -- 4
         "00110101" when "0101",   -- 5
         "00110110" when "0110",   -- 6
         "00110111" when "0111",   -- 7
         "00111000" when "1000",   -- 8
         "00111001" when "1001",   -- 9
         "01000001" when "1010",   -- A
         "01000010" when "1011",   -- B
         "01000011" when "1100",   -- C
         "01000100" when "1101",   -- D
         "01000101" when "1110",   -- E
         "01000110" when others;   -- F
end arch;
```

If a mouse is connected to the PS2 circuit, we can first issue the FF command to reset the mouse and then issue the F4 command to enable the stream mode. Windows HyperTerminal will show the mouse's acknowledge packets and subsequent mouse movement packets.

9.5 PS2 MOUSE INTERFACE

9.5.1 Basic design

The basic PS2 mouse interface creates another layer over the bidirectional PS2 circuit. Its two basic functions are to enable the stream mode and to reassemble the 3 data bytes. The output of the circuit are `xm` and `ym`, which are two 9-bit x- and y-axis movement signals; `btm`, which is the 3-bit button status signal; and `m_done_tick`, which is a one-clock-cycle status signal and is asserted when the assembled data is available.

The HDL code is shown in Listing 9.4. It is implemented by an FSMD with seven states. The `init1`, `init2`, and `init3` states are executed once after the `reset` signal is asserted. In these states, the FSMD issues the F4 command, waits for completion of the transmission, and then waits for the acknowledgment packet. The mouse is in the stream mode now. The FSMD then obtains and assembles the next three packets in the `pack1`, `pack2`, and `pack3` states, and activates the `m_done_tick` signal in the done state. The FSMD circulates these four states afterward.

Listing 9.4 Basic mouse interface circuit

```
library ieee;
use ieee.std_logic_1164.all;
use ieee.numeric_std.all;
entity mouse is
   port (
      clk, reset: in  std_logic;
```

```
      ps2d, ps2c: inout std_logic;
      xm, ym: out std_logic_vector(8 downto 0);
      btnm: out std_logic_vector(2 downto 0);
      m_done_tick: out std_logic
   );
end mouse;

architecture arch of mouse is
   constant STRM: std_logic_vector(7 downto 0):="11110100";
   -- stream command F4
   type state_type is (init1, init2, init3,
                       pack1, pack2, pack3, done);
   signal state_reg, state_next: state_type;
   signal rx_data: std_logic_vector(7 downto 0);
   signal rx_done_tick, tx_done_tick: std_logic;
   signal wr_ps2: std_logic;
   signal x_reg, y_reg: std_logic_vector(8 downto 0);
   signal x_next, y_next: std_logic_vector(8 downto 0);
   signal btn_reg, btn_next: std_logic_vector(2 downto 0);
begin
   -- instantiation
   ps2_rxtx_unit: entity work.ps2_rxtx(arch)
      port map(clk=>clk, reset=>reset, wr_ps2=>wr_ps2,
               din=>STRM, dout=>rx_data,
               ps2d=>ps2d, ps2c=>ps2c,
               rx_done_tick=>rx_done_tick,
               tx_done_tick=>tx_done_tick);
   -- state and data registers
   process (clk, reset)
   begin
      if reset='1' then
         state_reg <= init1;
         x_reg <= (others=>'0');
         y_reg <= (others=>'0');
         btn_reg <= (others=>'0');
      elsif (clk'event and clk='1') then
         state_reg <= state_next;
         x_reg <= x_next;
         y_reg <= y_next;
         btn_reg <= btn_next;
      end if;
   end process;
   -- next-state logic
   process(state_reg,rx_done_tick,tx_done_tick,
         x_reg,y_reg,btn_reg,rx_data)
   begin
      wr_ps2 <= '0';
      m_done_tick <= '0';
      x_next <= x_reg;
      y_next <= y_reg;
      btn_next <= btn_reg;
      state_next <= state_reg;
      case state_reg is
```

```
         when init1=>
            wr_ps2 <= '1';
            state_next <= init2;
         when init2=> -- wait for send to complete
            if tx_done_tick='1' then
               state_next <= init3;
            end if;
         when init3=> -- wait for acknowledge packet
            if rx_done_tick='1' then
               state_next <= pack1;
            end if;
         when pack1=> -- wait for 1st data packet
            if rx_done_tick='1' then
               state_next <= pack2;
               y_next(8) <= rx_data(5);
               x_next(8) <= rx_data(4);
               btn_next <=  rx_data(2 downto 0);
            end if;
         when pack2=> -- wait for 2nd data packet
            if rx_done_tick='1' then
               state_next <= pack3;
               x_next(7 downto 0) <= rx_data;
            end if;
         when pack3=> -- wait for 3rd data packet
            if rx_done_tick='1' then
               state_next <= done;
               y_next(7 downto 0) <= rx_data;
            end if;
         when done =>
            m_done_tick <= '1';
            state_next <= pack1;
      end case;
   end process;
   xm <= x_reg;
   ym <= y_reg;
   btnm <= btn_reg;
end arch;
```

This design provides only minimal functionalities. A more sophisticated circuit should have a robust method to initiate the stream mode and add additional buffer, similar to that in Section 7.2.4, to interact better with the external system.

9.5.2 Testing circuit

We use a simple testing circuit to demonstrate the use of the PS2 interface. The circuit uses a mouse to control the eight discrete LEDs of the prototyping board. Only one of the eight LEDs is lit and the position of that LED follows the x-axis movement of the mouse. The pressing of the left or right button places the lit LED to the leftmost or rightmost position.

The HDL code is shown in Listing 9.5. It uses a 10-bit counter to keep track of the current x-axis position. The counter is updated when a new data item is available (i.e., when the `m_done_tick` signal is asserted). The counter is set to 0 or maximum when the left or right mouse button is pressed. Otherwise, it adds the amount of the signed-extended x-axis movement. A decoding circuit uses the three MSBs of the counter to activate one of the LEDs.

Listing 9.5 Mouse-controlled LED circuit

```
library ieee;
use ieee.std_logic_1164.all;
use ieee.numeric_std.all;
entity mouse_led is
   port (
      clk, reset: in  std_logic;
      ps2d, ps2c: inout std_logic;
      led: out std_logic_vector(7 downto 0)
   );
end mouse_led;

architecture arch of mouse_led is
   signal p_reg, p_next: unsigned(9 downto 0);
   signal xm: std_logic_vector(8 downto 0);
   signal btnm: std_logic_vector(2 downto 0);
   signal m_done_tick: std_logic;

begin
   -- instantiation
   mouse_unit: entity work.mouse(arch)
      port map(clk=>clk, reset=>reset,
               ps2d=>ps2d, ps2c=>ps2c,
               xm=>xm, ym=>open, btnm=>btnm,
               m_done_tick=>m_done_tick);
   -- register
   process (clk, reset)
   begin
      if reset='1' then
         p_reg <= (others=>'0');
      elsif (clk'event and clk='1') then
         p_reg <= p_next;
      end if;
   end process;
   -- counter
   p_next <= p_reg when m_done_tick='0' else
             "0000000000" when btnm(0)='1' else --left button
             "1111111111" when btnm(1)='1' else --right button
             p_reg + unsigned(xm(8) & xm);

   with p_reg(9 downto 7) select
      led <= "10000000" when "000",
             "01000000" when "001",
             "00100000" when "010",
             "00010000" when "011",
             "00001000" when "100",
             "00000100" when "101",
             "00000010" when "110",
             "00000001" when others;
end arch;
```

9.6 BIBLIOGRAPHIC NOTES

The bibliographic information for this Chapter is similar to that for Chapter 8.

9.7 SUGGESTED EXPERIMENTS

The mouse is used mainly with a graphic video interface, which is discussed in Chapters 12 and 13. Many additional mouse-related experiments can be found in these chapters.

9.7.1 Keyboard control circuit

A host can issue a command to set certain parameters for a PS2 keyboard as well. For example, we can control the three LEDs of the keyboard by sending `ED 0X`. The `X` is a hexadecimal number with a format of "*0snc*", where s, n, and c are 1-bit values that control the Scroll, Num, and `Caps Lock` LEDs, respectively. We can incorporate this feature into the keyboard interface circuit of Section 8.4.1 and use a 3-bit switch to control the three keyboard LEDs. Design the expanded interface circuit, resynthesize the circuit, and verify its operation.

9.7.2 Enhanced mouse interface

For the mouse interface discussed in Section 9.5, we can alter the design to manually enable or disable the steam mode. This can be done by using two pushbuttons of the FPGA prototyping board. One button issues the reset command, FF, which disables the stream mode during operation, and the other button issues the `F4` command to enable the steam mode. Modify the original interface to incorporate this feature, and resynthesize the LED testing circuit to verify its operation.

9.7.3 Mouse-controlled seven-segment LED display

We can use the mouse to enter four decimal digits on the four-digit seven-segment LED display. The circuit functions as follows:

- Only one of the four decimal points of the LED display is lit. The lit decimal point indicates the location of the selected digit.
- The location of the selected digit follows the x-axis movement of the mouse.
- The content of the select seven-segment LED display is a decimal digit (i.e., 0, . . ., 9) and changes with the y-axis movement of the mouse.

Design and synthesize this circuit and verify its operation.

CHAPTER 10

EXTERNAL SRAM

10.1 INTRODUCTION

Random access memory (RAM) is used for massive storage in a digital system since a RAM cell is much simpler than an FF cell. A commonly used type of RAM is the asynchronous static RAM (SRAM). Unlike a register, in which the data is sampled and stored at an edge of a clock signal, accessing data from an asynchronous SRAM is more complicated. A read or write operation requires that the data, address, and control signals be asserted in a specific order, and these signals must be stable for a certain amount of time during the operation.

It is difficult for a synchronous system to access an SRAM directly. We usually use a *memory controller* as the interface, which takes commands from the main system synchronously and then generates properly timed signals to access the SRAM. The controller shields the main system from the detailed timing and makes the memory access appears like a synchronous operation. The performance of a memory controller is measured by the number of memory accesses that can be completed in a given period. While designing a simple memory controller is straightforward, achieving optimal performance involves many timing issues and is quite difficult.

The S3 board has two 256K-by-16 asynchronous SRAM devices, which total 1M bytes. In this chapter, we demonstrate the construction of a memory controller for these devices. Since the timing characteristics of each RAM device are different, the controller is applicable only to this particular device. However, the same design principle can be used for similar

SRAM devices. The Xilinx Spartan-3 device also contains smaller embedded memory blocks. The use of this memory is discussed in Chapter 11.

10.2 SPECIFICATION OF THE IS61LV25616AL SRAM

10.2.1 Block diagram and I/O signals

The S3 board has two IS61LV25616AL devices, which are 256K-by-16 SRAM manufactured by Integrated Silicon Solution, Inc. (ISSI). A simplified block diagram is shown in Figure 10.1(a). This device has an 18-bit address bus, `ad`, a bidirectional 16-bit data bus, `dio`, and five control signals. The data bus is divided into upper and lower bytes, which can be accessed individually. The five control signals are:

- `ce_n` (chip enable): disables or enables the chip
- `we_n` (write enable): disables or enables the write operation
- `oe_n` (output enable): disables or enables the output
- `lb_n` (lower byte enable): disables or enables the lower byte of the data bus
- `ub_n` (upper byte enable): disables or enables the upper byte of the data bus

All these signals are active low and the `_n` suffix is used to emphasize this property. The functional table is shown in Figure 10.1(b). The `ce_n` signal can be used to accommodate memory expansion, and the `we_n` and `oe_n` signals are used for write and read operations. The `lb_n` and `ub_n` signals are used to facilitate the byte-oriented configuration.

In the remainder of the chapter, we illustrate the design and timing issues of a memory controller. For clarity, we use one SRAM device and access the SRAM in 16-bit word format. This means that the `ce_n`, `lb_n`, and `ub_n` signals should always be activated (i.e., tied to '0'). The simplified functional table is shown in Figure 10.1(c).

10.2.2 Timing parameters

The timing characteristics of an asynchronous SRAM are quite complex and involve more than two dozen parameters. We concentrate only on a few key parameters that are relevant to our design.

The simplified timing diagrams for two types of read operations are shown in Figure 10.2(a) and (b). The relevant timing parameters are:

- t_{RC}: read cycle time, the minimal elapsed time between two read operations. It is about the same as t_{AA} for SRAM.
- t_{AA}: address access time, the time required to obtain stable output data after an address change.
- t_{OHA}: output hold time, the time that the output data remains valid after the address changes. This should not be confused with the hold time of an edge-triggered FF, which is a constraint for the `d` input.
- t_{DOE}: output enable access time, the time required to obtain valid data after `oe_n` is activated.
- t_{HZOE}: output enable to high-Z time, the time for the tri-state buffer to enter the high-impedance state after `oe_n` is deactivated.
- t_{LZOE}: output enable to low-Z time, the time for the tri-state buffer to leave the high-impedance state after `oe_n` is activated. Note that even when the output is no longer in the high-impedance state, the data is still invalid.

Values of these parameters for the IS61LV25616AL device are shown in Figure 10.2(c).

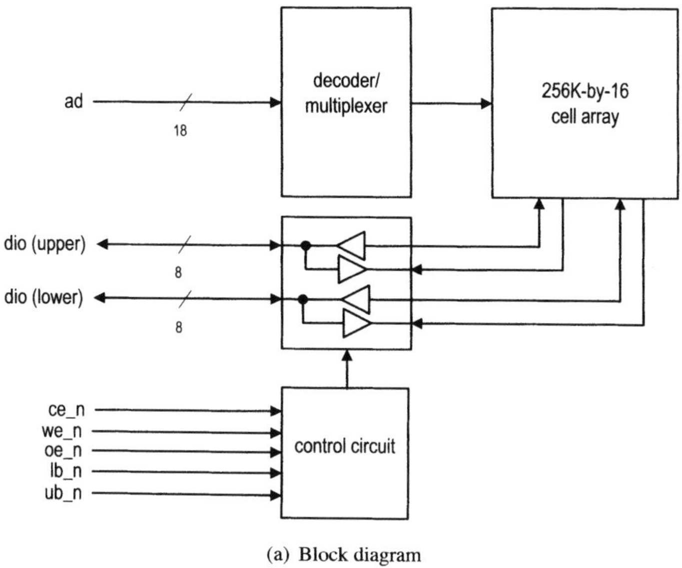

(a) Block diagram

Operation	ce_n	we_n	oe_n	lb_n	ub_n	dio (lower)	dio (upper)
disabled	1	-	-	-	-	Z	Z
	0	1	1	-	-	Z	Z
	0	-	-	1	1	Z	Z
read	0	1	0	0	1	data out	Z
	0	1	0	1	0	Z	data out
	0	1	0	0	0	data out	data out
write	0	0	-	0	1	data in	Z
	0	0	-	1	0	Z	data in
	0	0	-	0	0	data in	data in

(b) Functional table

Operation	we_n	oe_n	dio (16 bits)
output disabled	1	1	Z
read 16-bit word	1	0	data out
write 16-bit word	0	-	data in

(c) Simplified functional table

Figure 10.1 Block diagram and functional table of the ISSI 256K-by-16 SRAM.

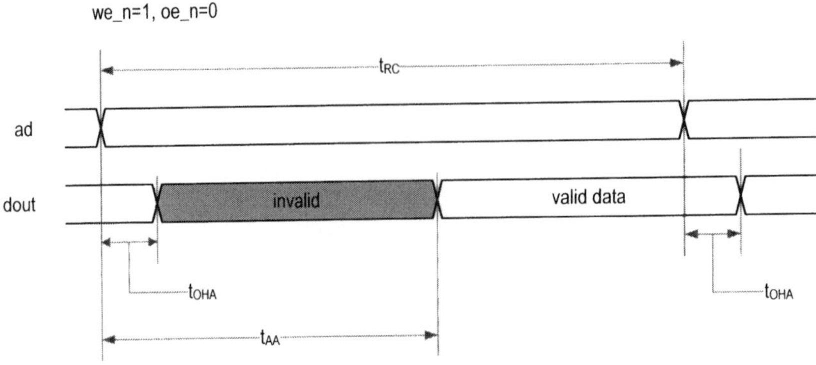

(a) Timing diagram of an address-controlled read cycle

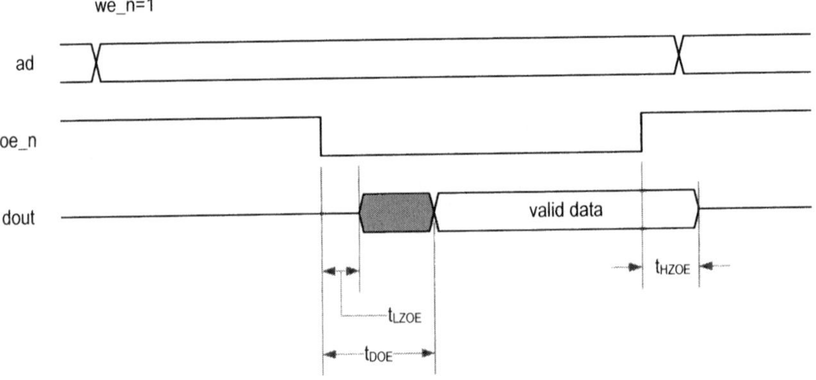

(b) Timing diagram of an oe_n-controlled read cycle

parameter		min	max
t_{RC}	read cycle time	10	–
t_{AA}	address access time	–	10
t_{OHA}	output hold time	2	–
t_{DOE}	output enable access time	–	4
t_{HZOE}	output enable to high-Z time	–	4
t_{LZOE}	output enable to low-Z time	0	–

(c) Timing parameters (in ns)

Figure 10.2 Timing diagrams and parameters of a read operation.

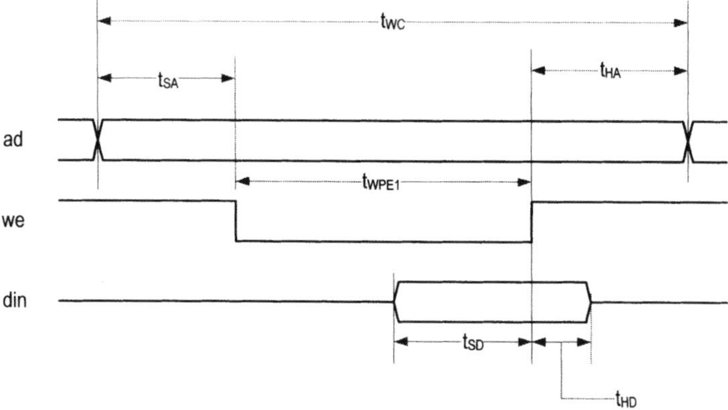

(a) Timing diagram of a write cycle

parameter		min	max
t_{WC}	write cycle time	10	–
t_{SA}	address setup time	0	–
t_{HA}	address hold time	0	–
t_{PWE1}	we_n pulse width	8	–
t_{SD}	data setup time	6	–
t_{HD}	data hold time	0	–

(b) Timing parameter (in ns)

Figure 10.3 Timing diagram and parameters of a write operation.

The simplified timing diagram for a we_n-controlled write operation is shown in Figure 10.3(a). The relevant timing parameters are:

- t_{WC}: write cycle time, the minimal elapsed time between two write operations.
- t_{SA}: address setup time, the minimal time that the address must be stable before we_n is activated.
- t_{HA}: address hold time, the minimal time that the address must be stable after we_n is deactivated.
- t_{PWE1}: we_n pulse width, the minimal time that we_n must be asserted.
- t_{SD}: data setup time, the minimal time that data must be stable before the latching edge (the edge in which we_n moves from '0' to '1').
- t_{HD}: data hold time, the minimal time that data must be stable after the latching edge.

The values of these parameters for the IS61LV25616AL device are shown in Figure 10.3(b). The complete timing information can be found in the data sheet of the IS61LV25616AL device.

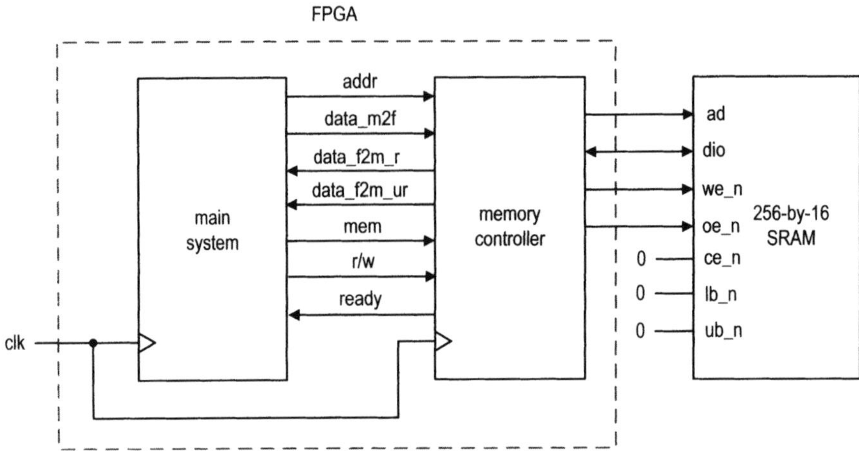

Figure 10.4 Role of an SRAM memory controller.

10.3 BASIC MEMORY CONTROLLER

10.3.1 Block diagram

The role of a memory controller and its I/O signals are shown in Figure 10.4. The signals to the SRAM side are discussed in Section 10.2.1. The signals to the main system side are:

- `mem`: is asserted to '1' to initiate a memory operation.
- `rw`: specifies whether the operation is a read ('1') or write ('0') operation.
- `addr`: is the 18-bit address.
- `data_f2s`: is the 16-bit data to be written to the SRAM (the `_f2s` suffix stands for FPGA to SRAM).
- `data_s2f_r`: is the 16-bit registered data retrieved from the SRAM (the `_s2f` suffix stands for SRAM to FPGA).
- `data_s2f_ur`: is the 16-bit unregistered data retrieved from SRAM.
- `ready`: is a status signal indicating whether the controller is ready to accept a new command. This signal is needed since a memory operation may take more than one clock cycle.

The memory controller basically provides a "synchronous wrap" around the SRAM. When the main system wants to access the memory, it places the address and data (for a write operation) on the bus and activates the command (i.e., the `mem` and `rw` signals). At the rising edge of the clock, all signals are sampled by the memory controller and the desired operation is performed accordingly. For a read operation, the data becomes available after one or two clock cycles.

The block diagram of a memory controller is shown in Figure 10.5. Its data path contains one address register, which stores the address, and two data registers, which store the data from each direction. Since the data bus, `dio`, is a bidirectional signal, a tri-state buffer is needed. The control path is an FSM, which follows the timing diagrams and specifications in Figures 10.2 and 10.3 to generate a proper control sequence.

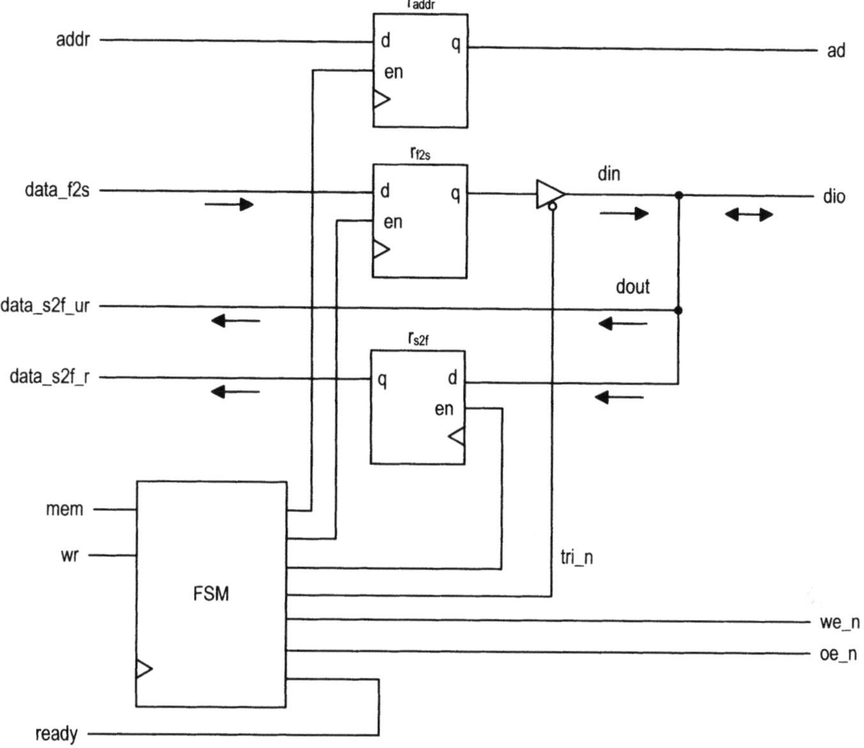

Figure 10.5 Block diagram of a memory controller.

10.3.2 Timing requirement

Although the timing diagrams appear to be complicated at first glance, the control sequences are fairly simple. Let us first consider a read cycle. The `we_n` should be deactivated during the entire operation. Its basic operation sequence is:

1. Place the address on the `ad` bus and activate the `oe_n` signal. These two signals must be stable for the entire operation.
2. Wait for at least t_{AA}. The data from the SRAM becomes available after this interval.
3. Retrieve the data from `dio` and deactivate the `oe_n` signal.

We use the `we_n`-controlled write cycle in our design, as shown in Figure 10.3(a). The basic operation sequence is:

1. Place the address on the `ad` bus and data on the `dio` bus and activate the `we_n` signal. These signals must be stable for the entire operation.
2. Wait for at least t_{PWE1}.
3. Deactivate the `we_n` signal. The data is latched to the SRAM at the '0'-to-'1' transition edge.
4. Remove the data from the `dio` bus.

Note that t_{HD} (data hold time after write ends) is 0 ns for this SRAM, which implies that it is theoretically possible to remove the data and deactivate `we_n` simultaneously. However, because of the variations in propagation delays, this condition cannot be guaranteed in a real circuit. To achieve proper latching, we need to ensure that the we_n signal is always deactivated first.

10.3.3 Register file versus SRAM

We discuss the design of a register file in Section 4.2.3. Its basic storage elements are D FFs and thus it is completely synchronous. Although a memory controller wraps the SRAM in a synchronous interface, there are several differences:

- A register file usually has one write port and multiple read ports.
- The read and write ports of a register file can be accessed at the same time (i.e., the read and write operations can be done at the same time).
- Writing to a register takes only one clock cycle.
- Data from a register's read ports is always available and the read operation involves no clock or additional control signals.

In summary, a register file is faster and more flexible. However, due to the circuit size of an FF, a register file is feasible only for small storage.

10.4 A SAFE DESIGN

With the block diagram of Figure 10.5, the remaining task is to derive the controller. Our first scheme uses a "safe" design, which means that the design provides large timing margins and does not impose any stringent timing constraints. The control signals are generated directly from the FSM. The controller uses two clock cycles (i.e., 40 ns) to complete memory access and requires three clock cycles (i.e., 60 ns) for back-to-back operations.

10.4.1 ASMD chart

The ASMD chart for this controller is shown in Figure 10.6. The FSM has five states and is initially in the idle state. It starts the memory operation when the mem signal is activated. The rw signal determines whether it is a read or write operation.

For a read operation, the FSM moves to the rd1 state. The memory address, addr, is sampled and stored in the addr_reg register at the transition. The oe_n signal is activated in the rd1 and rd2 states. At the end of the read cycle, the FSM returns to the idle state. The retrieved data is stored in the data_s2f_reg register at the transition, and the oe_n signal is deactivated afterward. Note that the block diagram of Figure 10.5 has two read ports. The data_s2f_r signal is a registered output and becomes available *after* the FSM exits the r2 state. The data remains unchanged until the end of the next read cycle. The data_s2f_ur signal is connected directly to the SRAM's dio bus. Its data should become valid at the end of the rd2 state but will be removed after the FSM enters the idle state. In some applications, the main system samples and stores the memory readout in its own register, and the unregistered output allows this action to be completed one clock cycle earlier.

For a write operation, the FSM moves to the wr1 state. The memory address, addr, and data, data_f2s, are sampled and stored in the addr_reg and data_f2s_reg registers at the transition. The we_n and tri_n signals are both activated in the wr1 state. The latter enables the tri-state buffer to put the data over the SRAM's dio bus. When the FSM moves to the wr2 state, we_n is deactivated but tri_n remains asserted. This ensures that the data is properly latched to the SRAM when we_n changes from'0' to '1'. At the end of the write

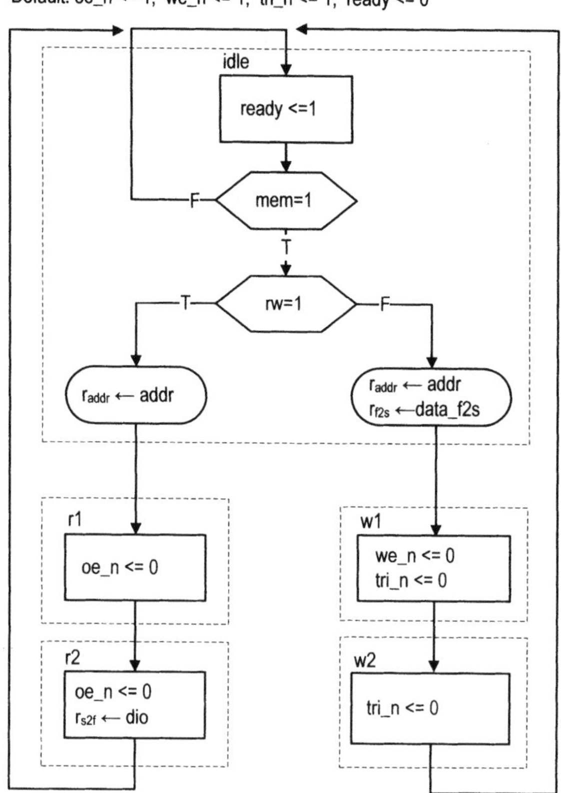

Figure 10.6 ASMD chart of a safe SRAM controller.

cycle, the FSM returns to the `idle` state and `tri_n` is deactivated to remove data from the `dio` bus.

10.4.2 Timing analysis

To ensure correct operation of a memory controller, we must verify that the design meets various timing requirements. Recall that the FSM is controlled by a 50-MHz clock signal and thus stays in each state for 20 ns.

During the read cycle, `oe_n` is asserted for two states, totaling 40 ns, which provides a 30-ns margin over the 10-ns t_{AA}. Although it appears that `oe_n` can be deasserted in the `rd2` state, this imposes a more stringent timing constraint. This issue is explained in Section 10.5.3. The data is stored in the `data_s2f` register when the FSM moves from the `rd2` state to the `idle` state. Although `oe_n` is deasserted at the transition, the data remains valid for a small interval because of the FPGA's pad delay and the t_{HZOE} delay of the SRAM chip. It can be sampled properly by the clock edge.

During the write cycle, `we_n` is asserted in the `wr1` state, and the 20-ns interval exceeds the 8-ns t_{PWE1} requirement. The `tri_n` signal remains asserted in the `wr2` state and thus ensures that the data is still stable during the '0'-to-'1' transition edge of the `we_n` signal.

In terms of performance, both read and write operations take two clock cycles to complete. During the read operation, the unregistered data (i.e., `data_s2f_ur`) is available at the end of the second clock cycle (i.e., just before the rising edge of the second clock cycle) and the registered data (i.e., `data_s2f_r`) is available right after the rising edge of the second clock cycle. Although a memory operation can be done in two clocks, the main system cannot access memory at this rate. Both read and write operations must return to the `idle` state after completion. The main system must wait for another clock cycle to issue a new memory operation, and thus the back-to-back memory access takes three clock cycles.

10.4.3 HDL implementation

The HDL code can be derived by following the block diagram in Figure 10.5 and the ASMD chart in Figure 10.6. The memory controller must generate fast, glitch-free control signals. One method is to modify the output logic to include *look-ahead output buffers* for the Moore output signals. This scheme adds a buffer (i.e., D FF) for each output signal to remove glitches and reduce clock-to-output delay. To compensate the one clock cycle delay introduced by the buffer, we "look ahead" at the state's future value (i.e., the `state_next` signal) and use it to replace the state's current value (i.e., the `state_reg` signal) in the FSM's output logic.

The complete HDL code is shown in Listing 10.1. To facilitate future expansion, we label the S3 board's two SRAM chips as `a` and `b` and add an `_a` suffix to the SRAM's I/O signals in port declaration. Note that tri-state buffers are required for the bidirectional data signal `dio_a`.

Listing 10.1 SRAM controller with three-cycle back-to-back operation

```
library ieee;
use ieee.std_logic_1164.all;
entity sram_ctrl is
   port(
      clk, reset: in std_logic;
      -- to/from main system
      mem: in std_logic;
      rw: in std_logic;
      addr: in std_logic_vector(17 downto 0);
      data_f2s: in std_logic_vector(15 downto 0);
      ready: out std_logic;
      data_s2f_r, data_s2f_ur:
            out std_logic_vector(15 downto 0);
      -- to/from chip
      ad: out std_logic_vector(17 downto 0);
      we_n, oe_n: out std_logic;
      -- SRAM chip a
      dio_a: inout std_logic_vector(15 downto 0);
      ce_a_n, ub_a_n, lb_a_n: out std_logic
   );
end sram_ctrl;

architecture arch of sram_ctrl is
   type state_type is (idle, rd1, rd2, wr1, wr2);
   signal state_reg, state_next: state_type;
   signal data_f2s_reg, data_f2s_next:
```

```
         std_logic_vector(15 downto 0);
   signal data_s2f_reg, data_s2f_next:
         std_logic_vector(15 downto 0);
   signal addr_reg, addr_next: std_logic_vector(17 downto 0);
   signal we_buf, oe_buf, tri_buf: std_logic;
   signal we_reg, oe_reg, tri_reg: std_logic;
begin
   -- state & data registers
   process(clk,reset)
   begin
      if (reset='1') then
         state_reg <= idle;
         addr_reg <= (others=>'0');
         data_f2s_reg <= (others=>'0');
         data_s2f_reg <= (others=>'0');
         tri_reg <= '1';
         we_reg <= '1';
         oe_reg <= '1';
      elsif (clk'event and clk='1') then
         state_reg <= state_next;
         addr_reg <= addr_next;
         data_f2s_reg <= data_f2s_next;
         data_s2f_reg <= data_s2f_next;
         tri_reg <= tri_buf;
         we_reg <= we_buf;
         oe_reg <= oe_buf;
      end if;
   end process;
   -- next-state logic
   process(state_reg,mem,rw,dio_a,addr,data_f2s,
           data_f2s_reg,data_s2f_reg,addr_reg)
   begin
      addr_next <= addr_reg;
      data_f2s_next <= data_f2s_reg;
      data_s2f_next <= data_s2f_reg;
      ready <= '0';
      case state_reg is
         when idle =>
            if mem='0' then
               state_next <= idle;
            else
               addr_next <= addr;
               if rw='0' then --write
                  state_next <= wr1;
                  data_f2s_next <= data_f2s;
               else -- read
                  state_next <= rd1;
               end if;
            end if;
            ready <= '1';
         when wr1 =>
            state_next <= wr2;
         when wr2 =>
```

```
            state_next <= idle;
         when rd1 =>
            state_next <= rd2;
         when rd2=>
            data_s2f_next <= dio_a;
            state_next <= idle;
      end case;
   end process;
   -- "look-ahead" output logic
   process(state_next)
   begin
      tri_buf <= '1';  -- default
      we_buf <= '1';
      oe_buf <= '1';
      case state_next is
         when idle =>
         when wr1 =>
            tri_buf <= '0';
            we_buf <= '0';
         when wr2 =>
            tri_buf <= '0';
         when rd1 =>
            oe_buf <= '0';
         when rd2=>
            oe_buf <= '0';
      end case;
   end process;
   -- to main system
   data_s2f_r <= data_s2f_reg;
   data_s2f_ur <= dio_a;
   -- to SRAM
   we_n <= we_reg;
   oe_n <= oe_reg;
   ad <= addr_reg;
   --i/o for SRAM chip a
   ce_a_n <='0';
   ub_a_n <='0';
   lb_a_n <='0';
   dio_a <= data_f2s_reg when tri_reg='0' else (others=>'Z');
end arch;
```

To minimize the off-chip pad delay (discussed in Section 10.5.1), the corresponding FPGA's I/O pins should be configured properly. This can be done by adding additional information in the constraint file. A typical line is

```
NET "ad<17>"  LOC = "L3" | IOSTANDARD = LVCMOS33 | SLEW=FAST ;
```

10.4.4 Basic testing circuit

We use two circuits to verify operation of the SRAM controller. The first one is a basic testing circuit that allows us manually to perform a single read or write operation. In addition to the SRAM chip I/O signals, the circuit has the following signals:

- sw. It is 8 bits wide and used as data or address input.

- `led`. It is 8 bits wide and used to display the retrieved data.
- `btn(0)`. When it is asserted, the current value of `sw` is loaded to a data register. The output of the register is used as the data input for the write operation.
- `btn(1)`. When it is asserted, the controller uses the value of `sw` as a memory address and performs a write operation.
- `btn(2)`. When it is asserted, the controller uses the value of `sw` as a memory address and performs a read operation. The readout is routed to the `led` signal.

During a write operation, we first specify the data value and load it to the internal register and then specify the address and initiate the write operation. During a read operation, we specify the address and initiate the read operation. The retrieved data is displayed in eight discrete LEDs. The complete HDL code is shown in Listing 10.2.

Listing 10.2 Basic SRAM testing circuit

```
library ieee;
use ieee.std_logic_1164.all;
use ieee.numeric_std.all;
entity ram_ctrl_test is
  port(
      clk, reset: in std_logic;
      sw: in std_logic_vector(7 downto 0);
      btn: in std_logic_vector(2 downto 0);
      led: out std_logic_vector(7 downto 0);
      ad: out std_logic_vector(17 downto 0);
      we_n, oe_n: out std_logic;
      dio_a: inout std_logic_vector(15 downto 0);
      ce_a_n, ub_a_n, lb_a_n: out std_logic
  );
end ram_ctrl_test;

architecture arch of ram_ctrl_test is
   constant ADDR_W: integer:=18;
   constant DATA_W: integer:=16;
   signal addr: std_logic_vector(ADDR_W-1 downto 0);
   signal data_f2s, data_s2f:
          std_logic_vector(DATA_W-1 downto 0);
   signal mem, rw: std_logic;
   signal data_reg: std_logic_vector(7 downto 0);
   signal db_btn: std_logic_vector(2 downto 0);

begin
   ctrl_unit: entity work.sram_ctrl
      port map(
         clk=>clk, reset=>reset,
         mem=>mem, rw =>rw, addr=>addr, data_f2s=>data_f2s,
         ready=>open, data_s2f_r=>data_s2f,
         data_s2f_ur=>open, ad=>ad,
         we_n=>we_n, oe_n=>oe_n, dio_a=>dio_a,
         ce_a_n=>ce_a_n, ub_a_n=>ub_a_n, lb_a_n=>lb_a_n);

    debounce_unit0: entity work.debounce
      port map(
         clk=>clk, reset=>reset, sw=>btn(0),
```

```
         db_level=>open, db_tick=>db_btn(0));
   debounce_unit1: entity work.debounce
      port map(
         clk=>clk, reset=>reset, sw=>btn(1),
         db_level=>open, db_tick=>db_btn(1));
   debounce_unit2: entity work.debounce
      port map(
         clk=>clk, reset=>reset, sw=>btn(2),
         db_level=>open, db_tick=>db_btn(2));

   --data registers
   process(clk)
   begin
      if (clk'event and clk='1') then
         if (db_btn(0)='1') then
            data_reg <= sw;
         end if;
      end if;
   end process;
   -- address
   addr <= "0000000000" & sw;
   -- command
   process(db_btn,data_reg)
   begin
      data_f2s <= (others=>'0');
      if db_btn(1)='1' then -- write
         mem <= '1';
         rw <= '0';
         data_f2s <= "00000000" & data_reg;
      elsif db_btn(2)='1' then -- read
         mem <= '1';
         rw <= '1';
      else
         mem <= '0';
         rw <= '1';
      end if;
   end process;
   -- output
   led <= data_s2f(7 downto 0);
end arch;
```

10.4.5 Comprehensive SRAM testing circuit

The second circuit performs comprehensive testing. It verifies operation of the SRAM controller and checks the integrity of the SRAM chip as well. This circuit has three functions:

- Write testing data patterns to the entire SRAM at the maximal rate.
- Read the entire SRAM at the maximal rate, check the retrieved data against the original patterns, and record the number of erroneous readouts.
- Inject erroneous data.

These functions can be initiated by three debounced pushbuttons.

The ASMD chart is shown in Figure 10.7. It contains three branches, corresponding to

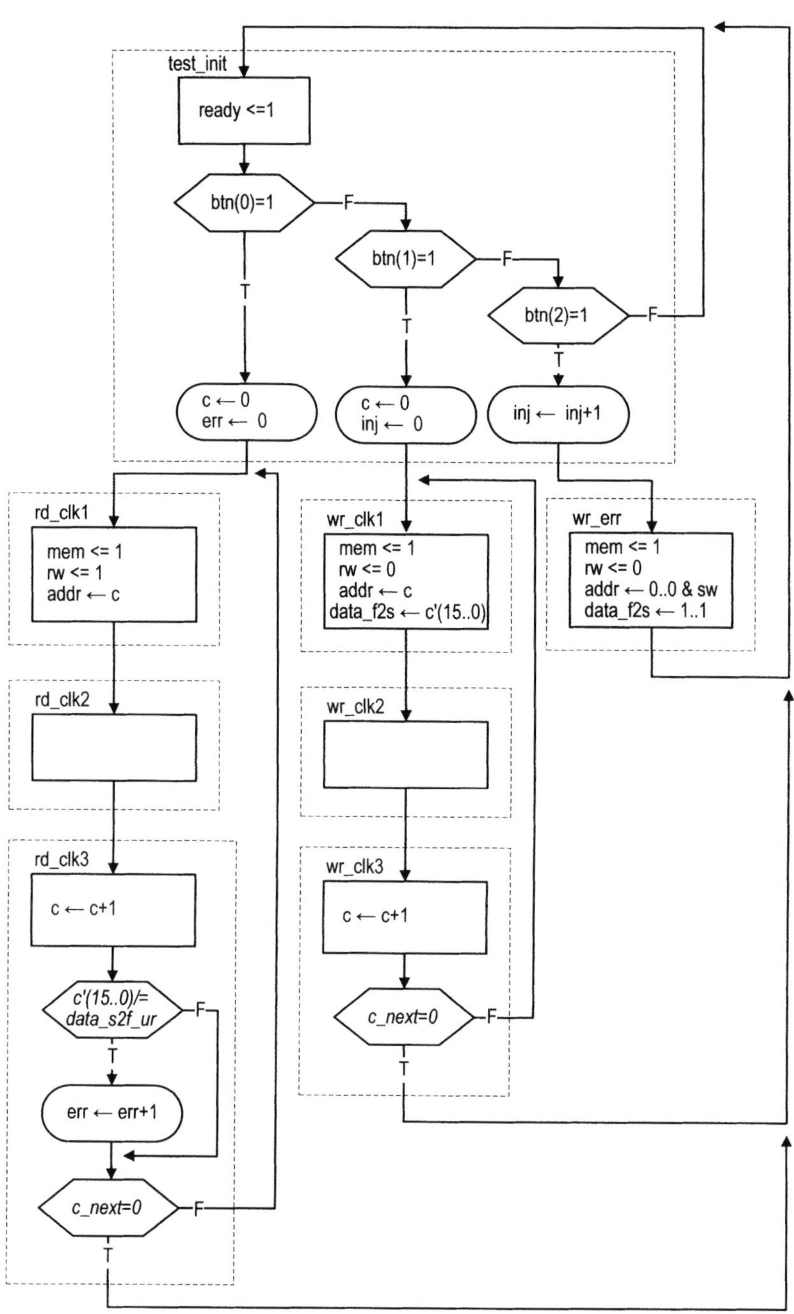

Figure 10.7 ASMD chart of a comprehensive SRAM testing circuit.

three functions. The middle branch writes the test patterns to the SRAM. The `wr_clk1`, `wr_clk2`, and `wr_clk3` states correspond to the `idle`, `wr1`, and `wr2` states of the SRAM controller. The FSMD uses the 18-bit `c` register as a counter to loop through this branch 2^{18} times. The content of the `c` register is used as an address and the reversed 16 LSBs are used as data during a write operation. The FSMD writes all memory locations while looping through this branch. The left branch reads data from the SRAM. The three states correspond to the `idle`, `rd1`, and `rd2` states of the SRAM controller. The FSMD again loops through the branch 2^{18} times. The retrieved data is compared with the original test patterns, and the `err` register is used to keep track of the number of mismatches. The right branch performs a single write operation. It uses the 8-bit switch to form a memory address and writes an erroneous pattern to that address. The `inj` counter is used to keep track of the number of injected errors. The complete HDL code is shown in Listing 10.3.

Listing 10.3 Comprehensive SRAM testing circuit

```
library ieee;
use ieee.std_logic_1164.all;
use ieee.numeric_std.all;
entity sram_test is
  port(
      clk, reset: in std_logic;
      sw: in std_logic_vector(7 downto 0);
      btn: in std_logic_vector(2 downto 0);
      led: out std_logic_vector(7 downto 0);
      an: out std_logic_vector(3 downto 0);
      sseg: out std_logic_vector(7 downto 0);
      ad: out std_logic_vector(17 downto 0);
      we_n, oe_n: out std_logic;
      dio_a: inout std_logic_vector(15 downto 0);
      ce_a_n, ub_a_n, lb_a_n: out std_logic
  );
end sram_test;

architecture arch of sram_test is
   constant ADDR_W: integer:=18;
   constant DATA_W: integer:=16;
   signal addr: std_logic_vector(ADDR_W-1 downto 0);
   signal data_f2s, data_s2f:
          std_logic_vector(DATA_W-1 downto 0);
   signal mem, rw: std_logic;
   type state_type is (test_init, rd_clk1, rd_clk2, rd_clk3,
                       wr_err, wr_clk1, wr_clk2, wr_clk3);
   signal state_reg, state_next: state_type;
   signal c_next, c_reg: unsigned(ADDR_W-1 downto 0);
   signal c_std: std_logic_vector(ADDR_W-1 downto 0);
   signal inj_next, inj_reg: unsigned(7 downto 0);
   signal err_next, err_reg: unsigned(15 downto 0);
   signal db_btn: std_logic_vector(2 downto 0);

begin
   --============================================
   -- component instantiation
   --============================================
```

```
ctrl_unit: entity work.sram_ctrl
port map(
   clk=>clk, reset=>reset,
   mem=>mem, rw =>rw, addr=>addr,
   data_f2s=>data_f2s, ready=>open,
   data_s2f_r=>open, data_s2f_ur=>data_s2f,
   ad=>ad, dio_a=>dio_a,
   we_n=>we_n, oe_n=>oe_n,
   ce_a_n=>ce_a_n, ub_a_n=>ub_a_n, lb_a_n=>lb_a_n);

 debounce_unit0: entity work.debounce
    port map(
       clk=>clk, reset=>reset, sw=>btn(0),
       db_level=>open, db_tick=>db_btn(0));
 debounce_unit1: entity work.debounce
    port map(
       clk=>clk, reset=>reset, sw=>btn(1),
       db_level=>open, db_tick=>db_btn(1));
 debounce_unit2: entity work.debounce
    port map(
       clk=>clk, reset=>reset, sw=>btn(2),
       db_level=>open, db_tick=>db_btn(2));
 disp_unit: entity work.disp_hex_mux
   port map(
      clk=>clk, reset=>'0',dp_in=>"1111",
      hex3=>std_logic_vector(err_reg(15 downto 12)),
      hex2=>std_logic_vector(err_reg(11 downto 8)),
      hex1=>std_logic_vector(err_reg(7 downto 4)),
      hex0=>std_logic_vector(err_reg(3 downto 0)),
      an=>an, sseg=>sseg);

--==================================================
-- FSMD
--==================================================
-- state & data registers
process(clk,reset)
begin
   if (reset='1') then
      state_reg <= test_init;
      c_reg <= (others=>'0');
      inj_reg <= (others=>'0');
      err_reg <= (others=>'0');
   elsif (clk'event and clk='1') then
      state_reg <= state_next;
      c_reg <= c_next;
      inj_reg <= inj_next;
      err_reg <= err_next;
  end if;
end process;
c_std <= std_logic_vector(c_reg);
-- fsmd next-state logic / data path operations
process(state_reg,sw,db_btn,c_reg,c_std,
        c_next,inj_reg,err_reg,data_s2f)
```

```
begin
   c_next <= c_reg;
   inj_next <= inj_reg;
   err_next <= err_reg;
   addr <= (others=>'0');
   rw <= '1';
   mem <= '0';
   data_f2s <= (others=>'0');
   case state_reg is
      when test_init =>
         if db_btn(0)='1' then
            state_next <= rd_clk1;
            c_next <=(others=>'0');
            err_next <=(others=>'0');
         elsif db_btn(1)='1' then
            state_next <= wr_clk1;
            c_next <=(others=>'0');
            inj_next <=(others=>'0'); -- clear injected err
         elsif db_btn(2)='1' then
            state_next <= wr_err;
            inj_next <= inj_reg + 1;
         else
            state_next <= test_init;
         end if;
      when wr_err => -- write 1 err; done in next 2 clocks
         state_next <= test_init;
         mem <= '1';
         rw <= '0';
         addr <= "0000000000" & sw;
         data_f2s <= (others=>'1');
      when wr_clk1 => -- in idle state of sram_ctrl
         state_next <= wr_clk2;
         mem <= '1';
         rw <= '0';
         addr <= c_std;
         data_f2s <= not c_std(DATA_W-1 downto 0);
      when wr_clk2 => -- in wr1 state of sram_ctrl
         state_next <= wr_clk3;
      when wr_clk3 => -- in wr2 state of sram_ctrl
         c_next <= c_reg + 1;
         if c_next=0 then
            state_next <= test_init;
         else
            state_next <= wr_clk1;
         end if;
      when rd_clk1 => -- in idle state of sram_ctrl
         state_next <= rd_clk2;
         mem <= '1';
         rw <= '1';
         addr <= c_std;
      when rd_clk2 => -- in rd1 state of sram_ctrl
         state_next <= rd_clk3;
      when rd_clk3 => -- in rd2 state of sram_ctrl
```

```
               -- compare readout; must use unregistered output
               if (not c_std(DATA_W-1 downto 0))/=data_s2f then
                  err_next <= err_reg + 1;
               end if;
               c_next <= c_reg + 1;
               if c_next=0 then
                  state_next <= test_init;
               else
                  state_next <= rd_clk1;
               end if;
         end case;
      end process;
      led <= std_logic_vector(inj_reg);
   end arch;
```

Note that the number of write–read mismatches is connected to the seven-segment LED display and shown as a four-digit hexadecimal number, and the number of injected errors is connected to the eight discrete LEDs.

We can use this circuit as follows:

- Perform the read function. Since the SRAM is not written yet, it is in the initial "power-on" state. The seven-segment LED display should show a large number of mismatches.
- Perform the write function.
- Perform the read function. The number of mismatches should be zero if both the SRAM controller and the SRAM device work properly.
- Inject error data a few times (to different memory locations).
- Perform the read function again. The number of mismatches should be the same as the number of injected errors.

10.5 MORE AGGRESSIVE DESIGN

Although the previous memory controller functions properly, it does not have optimal performance. While both the read and write cycles are 10 ns of the SRAM device, the back-to-back memory access of this controller takes 60 ns (i.e., three clock cycles). In this section, we study the timing issue in more detail, examine several more aggressive designs and their potential problems, and discuss some FPGA features that help to remedy the problems.

10.5.1 Timing issues

Timing issues on asynchronous SRAM There are two subtle timing issues in designing a high-performance asynchronous SRAM controller. The first issue is deactivation of the `we_n` signal. The '0'-to-'1' transition of `we_n` functions somewhat like a clock edge of an FF, in which the data is latched and stored to the internal memory element. Note that the data hold time (t_{HD}) is zero for this SRAM. Although it appears that it is fine to deactivate `we_n` and remove data at the same time, this approach is not reliable because of the variations in propagation delays. We must ensure that `we_n` is deactivated *before* data is removed from the bus.

The second issue is the potential conflict on the data bus, `dio`. Recall that the data bus is a bidirectional bus. The controller places data on the bus during a write operation, and the

SRAM places data on the bus during a read operation. A condition known as `fighting` occurs if the controller and SRAM place data on the bus at the same time. This condition should be avoided to ensure reliable operation.

Estimation of propagation delay Designing a good memory controller requires having a good understanding about the propagation delays of various signals. However, it is a difficult task. First, during synthesis, an RT-level description is optimized and mapped to logic cells and wire interconnects. The final implementation may not resemble the block diagram depicted by the initial description, and thus it is difficult to estimate the propagation delay from the initial description.

Second, a memory operation involves *off-chip* data access. Additional propagation delay is introduced when a signal propagates through the FPGA's I/O pads. The delay, sometimes known as *pad delay*, is usually much larger than the internal wiring delay and its exact value depends on a variety of factors, including the type of FPGA device, the location of the output register (in LE or IOB), the I/O standards, the slew rate, the driver strength, and external loading.

It requires intimate knowledge of the FPGA device and the synthesis software to perform a good timing analysis and to estimate the propagation delays of various signals.

10.5.2 Alternative design I

The first alternative design is targeted to reduce the back-to-back operation overhead. Instead of always returning to the `idle` state, the memory controller can check the `mem` signal at the end of current memory operation (i.e., in the `rd2` or `wr2` state) and determine what to do next. It initiates a new memory operation immediately if there is a pending request.

The revised ASMD chart for this controller is shown in Figure 10.8. In the `rd2` and `wr2` states, the `mem` and `rw` signals are examined and the FSMD may move directly to the `rd1` or `wr1` state if another memory operation is required.

Timing analysis Most of the original timing analysis in Section 10.4.2 can still be applied to this design. However, skipping the `idle` state introduces subtle new complications when different types of back-to-back memory operations are performed. The issue is the potential fighting on the data bus.

Let us consider a write operation performed immediately after a read operation. During the read operation, the signal flows from the SRAM to the FPGA. To facilitate this operation, the tri-state buffer of the SRAM should be "turned on" (i.e., passing signal) and the tri-state buffer of the FPGA should be "turned off" (i.e., high impedance). During the write operation, the signal flows from the FPGA to the SRAM, and the roles of the two tri-state buffers are reversed. Note that a small delay is required to turn on or off a tri-state buffer. In the SRAM chip, these delays are specified by t_{HZOE} (`oe_n` to high-impedance time) and t_{LZOE} (`oe_n` to low-impedance time) in Figure 10.2.

In the original SRAM controller, both tri-state buffers are turned off in the `idle` state. The state provides enough time for the data bus to settle to the high-impedance condition. The new design requires the two tristate buffers to reverse directions simultaneously during back-to-back operations. For example, when moving from the `rd2` state to the `wr1` state, the FSMD generates signals to turn off the SRAM's tri-state buffer and to turn on the FPGA's tri-state buffer. A problem may occur in this transition if the SRAM's tri-state buffer is turned off too slowly or the FPGA's tri-state buffer is turned on too quickly. In a small interval, both buffers may allow data to be placed on the bus and fighting occurs. Similarly, fighting may occur when a read operation is performed immediately after a write operation.

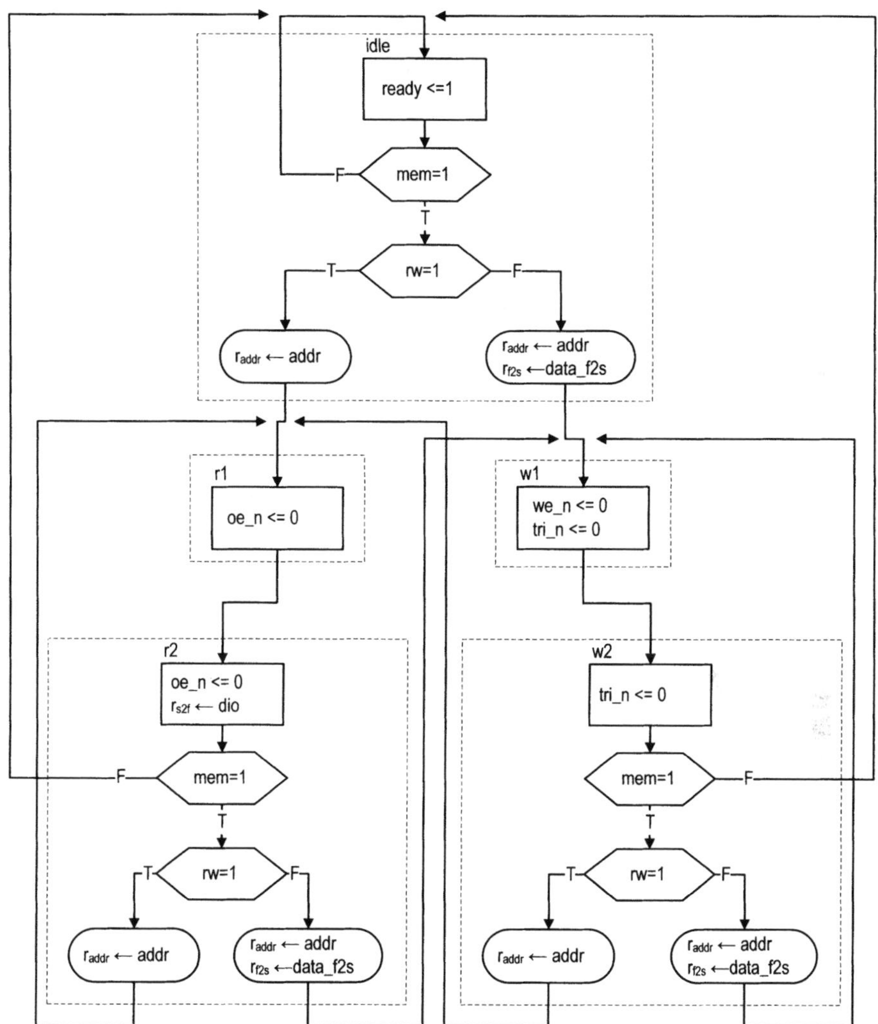

Figure 10.8 ASMD chart of SRAM controller design I.

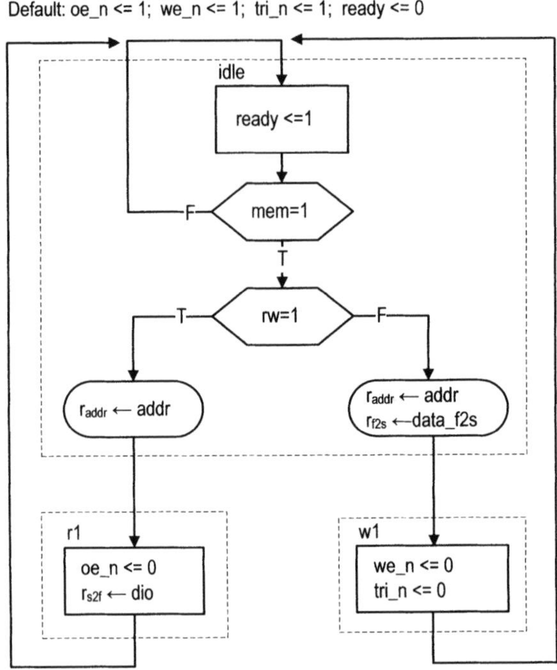

Figure 10.9 ASMD chart of SRAM controller design II.

Since the interval tends to be very small, the fighting should not cause severe damage to the devices but may introduce a large transient current which makes the design less reliable. We must do a detailed timing analysis to examine whether fighting occurs, and may even need to fine-tune the timing to fix the problem. As discussed in Section 10.5.1, it is a difficult task.

10.5.3 Alternative design II

Timing analysis in Section 10.4.2 shows that the initial design provides a large safety margin. In this controller, a memory operation takes two clock cycles, which amount to 40 ns. Since the read and write cycles of the SRAM are each 10 ns, we naturally wonder whether it is possible to reduce the operation time to a single 20-ns clock cycle. This can be done by eliminating the `rd2` and `wr2` states in the ASMD chart. The second alternative design uses this approach. The revised ASMD chart is shown in Figure 10.9. It takes one clock cycle to complete the memory access and requires two clock cycles to complete the back-to-back operations.

Timing analysis Reducing a state from the original controller imposes much tighter timing constraints for both read and write operations. Let us first consider the read operation. During operation, the address signal first propagates through the FPGA's I/O pads to the SRAM's address bus, and the retrieved data then propagates back through the I/O pads to FPGA's internal logic. All of this must be completed within a 20-ns clock cycle. In addition to the 10-ns SRAM address access time (i.e., t_{AA}), the cycle must accommodate two pad delays. The pad delay of a Spartan-3 device can range from 4 ns to more than 10 ns. Therefore, we need to "fine-tune" the synthesis to achieve this margin.

Unlike the read operation, a write operation is "one-way" and only needs to propagate the address, data, and control signals to the SRAM chip. If we assume that the signals experience similar pad delays, the absolute value of the delay is a lesser issue. Instead, the key is the *order* of signals being activated and deactivated. As discussed in Section 10.5.1, `we_n` must be deactivated before data to latch the data properly to the SRAM. In the original design, this is achieved by including the second state in the write operation, `wr2`, in which `we_n` is deactivated but the data is still available (i.e., `tri_n` is still active). In the revised controller, the `we_n` and `tri_n` signals are deactivated simultaneously at the end of the `wr1` state. Due to the variations in the internal logic and pad delays, normal synthesis cannot guarantee that `we_n` is deactivated before the data is removed from the external data bus. Again, for a reliable design, we need to fine-tune the synthesis to satisfy this goal.

10.5.4 Alternative design III

We can combine the features from the two preceding revisions to derive the third alternative design. This new controller eliminates the second clock cycle in the read and write operations and allows back-to-back operation without first returning to the `idle` state. This is the most aggressive design. The revised ASMD chart is shown in Figure 10.10. It combines the modifications from the previous two ASMD charts. The revised design takes one clock cycle to complete the memory access and one clock cycle to complete back-to-back operations.

Note that the `we_n` signal must be asserted for a fraction of the clock period and cannot be shown in the ASMD chart. We use the `we_tmp` in the `wr1` state and later derive `we_n` from this signal.

Timing analysis Since the new design combines the features of the two previous designs, all the timing issues discussed in the two preceding subsections must be considered for this design as well. One additional issue is generation of the `we_n` signal. During back-to-back write operations, the ASMD stays on the `wr1` state. In the original design, the `we_n` signal is a Moore output. It will be asserted to '0' continuously in this case. The controller does not function properly since the data is latched to the SRAM at the '0'-to-'1' transition of the `we_n` signal. To solve the problem, the `we_n` signal must be asserted in only a fraction of the clock period.

One possible way to solve the problem is to assert the signal only at the first half of the clock, which is 10 ns and can satisfy the t_{WPE1} requirement in theory. Intuitively, we are tempted to do this by gating the `we_tmp` signal with the clock signal, `clk`:

```
we_n <= we_tmp or (not clk);
```

However, this is not a reliable solution because of the potential glitches and delay variation. A better alternative is discussed in the next subsection.

10.5.5 Advanced FPGA features$^{Xilinx\ specific}$

The memory controller examples in this section illustrate the limitations of the FSM-based controller and synchronous design methodology. Basically, an FSM cannot generate a control sequence that is "finer" than the period of its clock signal. The operation of these alternative designs relies on factors that cannot be specified by an RT-level HDL description.

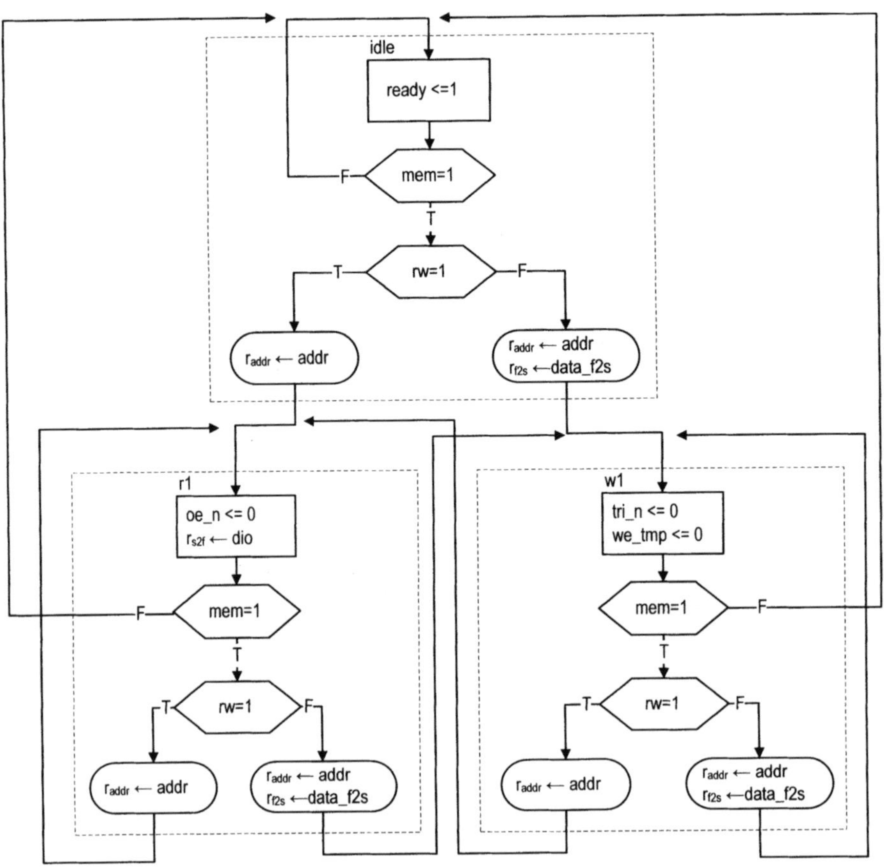

Figure 10.10 ASMD chart of SRAM controller design III.

Due to the variations in propagation delays, the synthesized circuits are not reliable and may or may not work.

There are some ad hoc features to obtain better control. These features are usually device and software dependent. For example, the digital clock manager (DCM) circuit and input/output block (IOB) of the Spartan-3 device can help to remedy some of the previously discussed problems. Detailed discussion of DCM and IOB is beyond the scope of this book. In this subsection, we sketch a few ideas and illustrate how to apply these features to obtain a more reliable controller.

DCM A Spartan-3 FPGA device contains up to eight *digital clock managers* (DCMs). As its name indicates, a DCM is a circuit that manipulates the system clock signal. It can multiply or divide the frequency or shift the phase of the incoming clock signal to generate new clock signals.

One way to obtain a "finer" control sequence is to use a faster clock. Since implementation of a memory controller is fairly simple, the circuit itself can operate at a faster clock rate. For example, we can isolate the memory controller and drive it with a DCM-generated 200-MHz clock signal, whose period is only 5 ns. Consider the write operation of the ASMD chart in Figure 10.6. In the new controller, each state lasts only 5 ns. To satisfy the 10-ns `we_n` requirement, we need to expand the `wr1` state to two states and assert the `we_n` signal in these states. The complete write operation now requires four states. However, because of the faster clock rate, the four clock cycles amount to only 20 ns, which is much better than the original 60-ns design.

A simple application of clock phase shift is discussed in the next subsection.

IOB An *input/output block* (IOB) of a Spartan-3 FPGA device provides a programmable interface between an I/O pin and the device's internal logic. It contains several storage registers and tri-state buffers as well as analog driver circuits that can be configured to provide different slew rates and driver strength and to support a variety of I/O standards.

To minimize the off-chip pad delay discussed in Section 10.5.3, we can put the output registers of the memory controller to the FFs inside the IOBs and configure the driver with the proper slew rate and strength. This can be done by specifying the desired condition and configuration in the constraint file.

An IOB also contains a *double data rate* (DDR) register, which has two clocks and two inputs. Conceptually, we can think that the two inputs are sampled independently by the two clocks and the sampled values are stored in the same register. The DDR register and DCM can be combined to generate a control signal whose width is a fraction of a clock signal, as the `we_n` signal discussed in Section 10.5.4. The block diagram is shown in Figure 10.11(a). The regular output register is replaced with a DDR register. The top portion of the DDR consists of the *we_tmp* signal and the original clock signals, `clk`. The bottom input of the DDR is tied to '1' and the clock is connected to the out-of-phase clock signal, `clk180`, which is generated by a DCM. The '1' is always loaded at the rising edge of the `clk180` signal, which corresponds to the falling edge of the `clk` signal. It essentially deactivates the second half of the *we_n* signal. The timing diagram is shown in Figure 10.11(b). This approach generates a clean half-cycle signal and is far more reliable than the clock gating scheme discussed in Section 10.5.4.

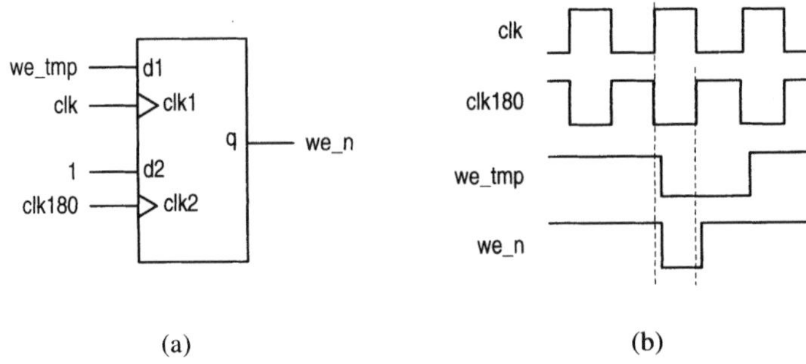

Figure 10.11 Generating a half-cycle signal with DDR.

10.6 BIBLIOGRAPHIC NOTES

The data sheet published by ISSI provides detailed information for the IS61LV25616AL SRAM device. The Xilinx application note, *XAPP462 Using Digital Clock Managers (DCMs) in Spartan-3 FPGAs*, discusses the use of DCM, and the data sheet, *DS099 Spartan-3 FPGA Family: Complete Data Sheet*, explains the architecture and configuration of the IOB and the DDR register.

10.7 SUGGESTED EXPERIMENTS

10.7.1 Memory with a 512K-by-16 configuration

There are two 256K-by-16 SRAM chips, and their I/O connections are shown in the manual of the S3 board. We can expand them to form a 512K-by-16 SRAM.

1. Derive a scheme to combine the two chips.
2. Follow the procedure in Section 10.4 to design a memory controller for the 512K-by-16 SRAM. Derive the HDL description.
3. Modify the testing circuit in Section 10.4.5 for the new controller and derive the HDL description.
4. Synthesize the testing circuit and verify operation of the controller and SRAM chips.

10.7.2 Memory with a 1M-by-8 configuration

Repeat Experiment 10.7.1 but configure the two chips as a 1M-by-8 SRAM. The `lb_n` and `ub_n` signals can be used for this purpose.

10.7.3 Memory with an 8M-by-1 configuration

A single bit of the 256K-by-16 SRAM can be written as follows:

- Read a 16-bit word.
- Modify the designated bit in the word.
- Write the 16-bit word back.

Repeat Experiment 10.7.1 but configure the two chips as an 8M-by-1 SRAM.

10.7.4 Expanded memory testing circuit

The memory testing circuit in Section 10.4.5 conducts exhaustive back-to-back read and back-to-back write tests. We can expand the circuit to include an exhaustive "read-after-write" test, in which the testing circuit issues write and read operations alternately for the entire memory space. To make the test more effective, the writing and reading addresses should be different. For example, we can make the read operation retrieve the data written 16 positions earlier (i.e., if the current writing address is `c`, the reading address will be `c-16`). Create a modified ASMD chart, derive an HDL description, synthesize the circuit, and verify its operation.

10.7.5 Memory controller and testing circuit for alternative design I

Derive the HDL code for alternative design I in Section 10.5.2 and create an expanded testing circuit similar to the one in Experiment 10.7.4. Synthesize the testing circuit and examine whether any error occurs during operation.

10.7.6 Memory controller and testing circuit for alternative design II

Repeat the process in Experiment 10.7.5 for alternative design II discussed in Section 10.5.3.

10.7.7 Memory controller and testing circuit for alternative design III

Repeat the process in Experiment 10.7.5 for alternative design III discussed in Section 10.5.4.

10.7.8 Memory controller with DCM

Study the application note on DCM and follow the discussion in Section 10.5.5 to drive the safe memory controller discussed in Section 10.4 with a higher clock rate (150 MH or even 200 MHz). Derive an ASMD chart and HDL code, and create a new testing circuit. Synthesize the circuit and verify operation of the memory controller and the SRAM.

10.7.9 High-performance memory controller

Study the documentation of the DCM and the IOB, and apply these features to reconstruct alternative design III discussed in Section 10.5.4. Create a new testing circuit. Synthesize the circuit and verify operation of the memory controller and the SRAM.

CHAPTER 11

XILINX SPARTAN-3 SPECIFIC MEMORY

11.1 INTRODUCTION

A digital system frequently requires memory for storage. To facilitate this need, most FPGA devices contain dedicated embedded memory modules. While these modules cannot replace the massive external memory devices, they are useful for applications that require small or intermediate-sized memory.

Although the basic internal structure of memory modules is similar, there are many subtle differences in their I/O interfaces. It is usually difficult for synthesis software to extract the desired features from the code and to infer a matching memory module from the underlying device library. In Xilinx ISE, we can use *HDL instantiation*, the Core Generator program, or the *behavioral HDL inference template* to incorporate an embedded memory module into a design. The third one is semi-device independent and we use this method in this book. In this chapter, we briefly examine Spartan-3 memory modules and the first two methods and provide detailed descriptions of several key behavioral HDL templates.

11.2 EMBEDDED MEMORY OF SPARTAN-3 DEVICE

11.2.1 Overview

There are two types of embedded memory in a Spartan-3 device: distributed RAM and block RAM. A *distributed RAM* is constructed from the logic cell's look-up table (LUT). The LUT can be configured as a 16-by-1 synchronous RAM, and multiple LUTs can be cascaded to form a wider and deeper memory module. The Spartan-3 XC3S200 device of the S3 board can provide up to 30K bits of distributed memory, which is small compared to a block RAM or external memory. Furthermore, since the distributed RAM uses the logic cells, it competes for resources with the normal logic. Thus, it is feasible only for applications that require relatively small storage.

A *block RAM* is a special memory module embedded in an FPGA device and is separated from the regular logic cells. It can be thought of as a fast SRAM wrapped by a synchronous, configurable interface. Each block RAM consists of 16K (2^{14}) data bits plus optional 2K parity bits. It can be organized in different widths, from 16K by 1 (i.e., 2^{14} by 2^0) to 512 by 32 (i.e., 2^9 by 2^5). The Spartan-3 XC3S200 device has 12 block RAMs, totaling 172K data bits. These block RAMs can be used for intermediate-sized applications, such as a FIFO, a large look-up table, or an intermediate-sized local memory. In comparison, the external SRAM chips of the S3 board have a capacity of 8M bits.

Both the distributed RAM and block RAM are already "wrapped" with a synchronous interface, and thus no additional memory controller circuit is needed. They are very flexible and can be configured to perform single- and dual-port access and to support various types of buffering and clocking schemes. Detailed discussion is beyond the scope of this book. We only examine several commonly used configurations, including a synchronous single-port RAM, a synchronous dual-port RAM, and a ROM in Section 11.4.

11.2.2 Comparison

The Spartan-3 device and the S3 board provide several options for storage elements. It is a good idea to keep in mind the relative capacities of these options:

- *XC3S200's FFs* (for registers): about 4.5K bits, embedded in logic cells and I/O buffers
- *XC3S200's distributed RAM*: 30K bits, constructed from the logic cells
- *XC3S200's block RAM*: 172K bits, configured as twelve 16K-bit modules
- *External SRAM*: 8M bits, configured as two 256K-by-16 SRAM chips

This helps us to decide which option is most suitable for an application at hand.

11.3 METHOD TO INCORPORATE MEMORY MODULES

Although memory modules have similar internal structure, there are many subtle differences in their interfaces, such as the numbers of read and write ports, clocking scheme, data and address buffering, enable and reset signals, and initial values. Although it is possible to describe the desired module behaviors in HDL code, the synthesis software may or may not recognize the designer's intention. Therefore, the HDL code cannot always infer the proper memory module and is normally not portable. In Xilinx ISE, there are three methods to incorporate an embedded memory module into a design:

- HDL instantiation
- The Core Generator program
- The behavioral HDL inference template

The first two are specific for Xilinx devices and the third is a semi-device-independent behavioral description. Because of the clarity of the behavioral description, we use the third method in this book. We provide a brief overview of the three methods in this section.

11.3.1 Memory module via HDL component instantiation

We have used HDL component instantiation in many earlier design examples to include predesigned modules or to create a hierarchy. Instantiating a Xilinx memory module is similar except that there is no HDL description for the architecture body. We must check the manual to find the exact entity name and the associated generics and I/O port definitions. This is a tedious process and is particularly error-prone for memory modules because of the large number of configurations and options.

The instantiation code for many Xilinx components can be obtained directly from ISE by selecting Edit ≻ Language Templates. The following are segments of a 16K-by-1 dual-port RAM:

```
-- RAMB16_S1_S1: Virtex-II/II-Pro,
-- Spartan-3/3E 16k x 1 Dual-Port RAM
-- Xilinx  HDL Language Template version 8.1i
RAMB16_S1_S1_inst : RAMB16_S1_S1
generic map(
   init_a => "0",
   init_b => "0",
   srval_a => "0",
   srval_b => "0",
   write_mode_a => "WRITE_FIRST",
   write_mode_b => "WRITE_FIRST",
   sim_collision_check => "ALL",
   init_00 => x"0 ... 0",
   ...
   init_3f => x"0 ... 0"
),
port map(
   doa => doa,        -- port a 1-bit data output
   dob => dob,        -- port b 1-bit data output
   addra => addra,    -- port a 14-bit address input
   addrb => addrb,    -- port b 14-bit address input
   clka => clka,      -- port a clock
   clkb => clkb,      -- port b clock
   dia => dia,        -- port a 1-bit data input
   dib => dib,        -- port b 1-bit data input
   ena => ena,        -- port a ram enable input
   enb => enb,        -- port b ram enable input
   ssra => ssra,      -- port a synchronous set/reset input
   ssrb => ssrb,      -- port b synchronous set/reset input
   wea => wea,        -- port a write enable input
   web => web         -- port b write enable input
);
```

Although the code is readily available, we must study the manual carefully to find the right component and proper configuration parameters.

11.3.2 Memory module via Core Generator

To simplify the instantiation process, Xilinx provides a utility program, known as Core Generator (Coregen), to generate Xilinx-specific components. This utility can be invoked from the ISE environment by selecting Project ≻ New Source. After the New Source

Wizard dialog appears, we select IP (Coregen & Architecture Wizard) to invoke the Coregen program. The program guides the users through a series of questions and then generates several files. The file with the .xco extension is a text file that contains the information necessary to construct the desired memory component. The file with the .vhd extension contains the "wrapper" code for simulation purpose. This file cannot be used to instantiate the desired component and is ignored during the synthesis process.

Although using the Coregen program is more convenient than direct HDL instantiation, it is not within the HDL framework and can lead to a compatibility problem when a design is not done in the Xilinx ISE environment.

11.3.3 Memory module via HDL inference

Although it is not possible to develop a device-independent HDL description, the synthesis program of ISE, known as XST, provides a collection of behavioral HDL templates to infer memory modules from Xilinx FPGA devices. These templates are done by behavioral descriptions and contain no device-specific component instantiation. They are easy to understand and can be simulated without an additional HDL library. However, while the description does not explicitly refer to any Xilinx component, the code may not be recognized by other third-party synthesis software, and the desired memory module cannot always be inferred. Thus, these templates can best be described as "semi-portable" and "semi-device-independent" behavioral descriptions. Templates for commonly used memory modules are discussed in Section 11.4.

On the downside, the template approach is based on the ability of the XST software to recognize the template and infer the proper memory module accordingly. The software may change during upgrade or misinterpret some code. It is a good idea to check the XST synthesis report to ensure that the desired memory module is inferred correctly.

11.4 HDL TEMPLATES FOR MEMORY INFERENCE

To use behavioral HDL description to infer the Xilinx memory module, the XST's templates should be followed closely. To avoid misinterpretation, we should refrain from creating our own "innovative" code. The codes in the following subsections are all based on templates of the *XST v8.1i Manual*. They are the same as the original templates except that generics are used for the width of address bits and the width of data bits, and the `numeric_std` package is used to replace the proprietary `std_logic_unsigned` package. It is a good practice to confine the memory description in a separate HDL module so that the module can easily be identified and replaced when needed. In this section, we discuss the behavioral HDL templates for six configurations, including two for single-port RAMs, two for dual-port RAMs, and two for ROMs.

11.4.1 Single-port RAM

The embedded memory of a Spartan-3 device is already wrapped with a synchronous interface similar to that in Section 10.3. Its write operation is always synchronous. At the rising edge of the clock, the address, input data, and relevant control signals, such as `we` (i.e., write enable), are sampled. If `we` is asserted, a write operation is performed (i.e., the input data is stored into the memory location designated by the address signal).

The read operation can be asynchronous or synchronous. For *asynchronous read*, the address signal is used directly to access the RAM array. After the address signal changes, the data becomes available after a short delay. For *synchronous read*, the address signal is sampled at the rising edge of the clock and stored in a register. The registered address is then used to access the RAM array. Because of the register, the availability of data is delayed and is synchronized by the clock signal. Due to the internal structure, asynchronous read operation can only be realized by the distributed RAM.

Single-port RAM with asynchronous read The template for the single-port RAM with asynchronous read is shown in Listing 11.1. It is modified after the `rams_04` entity of the *XST Manual*.

Listing 11.1 Template for a single-port RAM with asynchronous read

```
-- single-port RAM with asynchronous read
-- modified from XST 8.1i rams_04
library ieee;
use ieee.std_logic_1164.all;
use ieee.numeric_std.all;
entity xilinx_one_port_ram_async is
   generic(
      ADDR_WIDTH: integer:=8;
      DATA_WIDTH: integer:=1
   );
   port(
      clk: in std_logic;
      we: in std_logic;
      addr: in std_logic_vector(ADDR_WIDTH-1 downto 0);
      din: in std_logic_vector(DATA_WIDTH-1 downto 0);
      dout: out std_logic_vector(DATA_WIDTH-1 downto 0)
    );
end xilinx_one_port_ram_async;

architecture beh_arch of xilinx_one_port_ram_async  is
   type ram_type is array (2**ADDR_WIDTH-1 downto 0)
        of std_logic_vector (DATA_WIDTH-1 downto 0);
   signal ram: ram_type;
begin
   process (clk)
   begin
      if (clk'event and clk = '1') then
         if (we='1') then
            ram(to_integer(unsigned(addr))) <= din;
         end if;
      end if;
   end process;
   dout <= ram(to_integer(unsigned(addr)));
end beh_arch;
```

The code is very similar to the register file discussed in Section 4.2.3 except that the read and write operations use the same address. It contains a user-defined two-dimensional array data type for storage and uses dynamic indexing to access the element in the array. The code shows that the write operation is controlled by the clock signal and the read operation depends only on the address. Since asynchronous read can be realized only by the distributed RAM, this configuration is only recommended for applications that require small storage.

Single-port RAM with synchronous read The template for the single-port RAM with synchronous read is shown in Listing 11.2. It is modified after the `rams_07` entity of the *XST Manual.*

Listing 11.2 Template for a single-port RAM with synchronous read

```
-- single-port RAM with synchronous read
-- modified from XST 8.1i rams_07
library ieee;
use ieee.std_logic_1164.all;
use ieee.numeric_std.all;
entity xilinx_one_port_ram_sync is
   generic(
      ADDR_WIDTH: integer:=12;
      DATA_WIDTH: integer:=8
   );
   port(
      clk: in std_logic;
      we: in std_logic;
      addr: in std_logic_vector(ADDR_WIDTH-1 downto 0);
      din: in std_logic_vector(DATA_WIDTH-1 downto 0);
      dout: out std_logic_vector(DATA_WIDTH-1 downto 0)
    );
end xilinx_one_port_ram_sync;

architecture beh_arch of xilinx_one_port_ram_sync is
   type ram_type is array (2**ADDR_WIDTH-1 downto 0)
        of std_logic_vector (DATA_WIDTH-1 downto 0);
   signal ram: ram_type;
   signal addr_reg: std_logic_vector(ADDR_WIDTH-1 downto 0);
begin
   process (clk)
   begin
      if (clk'event and clk = '1') then
         if (we='1') then
            ram(to_integer(unsigned(addr))) <= din;
         end if;
         addr_reg <= addr;
      end if;
   end process;
   dout <= ram(to_integer(unsigned(addr_reg)));
end beh_arch;
```

Note that the `addr` signal is now sampled and stored to the `addr_reg` register at the rising edge of the clock, and the memory array (the `ram` signal) is accessed via the `addr_reg` signal. The data is available only after the `addr_reg` is updated and thus implicitly synchronized to the `clk` signal.

Synthesis report During synthesis, a proper RAM module should be inferred from the code template. We can check the synthesis report to confirm the inference of the RAM module. For example, consider the instantiation of a 4K-by-8 RAM (2^{12}-by-2^3) with synchronous read:

```
unit_4K_by_8: entity work.xilinx_one_port_sram_sync
   generic map(ADDR_WIDTH=>12, DATA_WIDTH=>8)
   port map(clk=>clk, we=>we, addr=>addr,
            din=>din,dout=>dout);
```

The inference of RAM should be indicated in the HDL Synthesis section of the synthesis report:

```
===========================================================
*                       HDL Synthesis                     *
===========================================================
. . .
Found 4096x8-bit single-port block RAM for signal <ram>.
---------------------------------------------------------
| mode            | write-first              |        |
| aspect ratio    | 4096-word x 8-bit        |        |
| clock           | connected to signal <clk>  | rise |
| write enable    | connected to signal <we>   | high |
| address         | connected to signal <addr> |      |
| data in         | connected to signal <din>  |      |
| data out        | connected to signal <dout> |      |
| ram_style       | Auto                       |      |
---------------------------------------------------------
Summary:
inferred   1 RAM(s).
```

The number of block RAMs used should be reported in the Final Report section of the synthesis report:

```
Device utilization summary:
Selected Device : 3s200ft256-5
 . . .
 Number of BRAMs:    2  out of     12    16%
 . . .
```

As we expected, a 4K-by-8 single-port block RAM is inferred and two block RAMs are used to realize the circuit.

11.4.2 Dual-port RAM

A dual-port RAM includes a second port for memory access. Ideally, the second port should be able to conduct read or write operation independently and have its own set of address, data input and output, and control signals. To be compatible with older versions of XST, we consider a configuration with the second port that can conduct a read operation only. In this book, the main application of the dual-port configuration is for video memory, which requires one write port and one read port. Thus, this configuration does not impose a serious limitation for our purposes. As in a single-port RAM, the read operation of a dual-port RAM can be asynchronous or synchronous.

Dual-port RAM with asynchronous read The template for the dual-port RAM with asynchronous read is shown in Listing 11.3. It is modified after the `rams_09` entity of the *XST Manual*.

Listing 11.3 Template for a dual-port RAM with asynchronous read

```
-- dual-port RAM with asynchronous read
-- modified from XST 8.1i rams_09
library ieee;
use ieee.std_logic_1164.all;
use ieee.numeric_std.all;
entity xilinx_dual_port_ram_async is
   generic(
      ADDR_WIDTH: integer:=6;
      DATA_WIDTH:integer:=8
   );
   port(
      clk: in std_logic;
      we: in std_logic;
      addr_a: in std_logic_vector(ADDR_WIDTH-1 downto 0);
      addr_b: in std_logic_vector(ADDR_WIDTH-1 downto 0);
      din_a: in std_logic_vector(DATA_WIDTH-1 downto 0);
      dout_a: out std_logic_vector(DATA_WIDTH-1 downto 0);
      dout_b: out std_logic_vector(DATA_WIDTH-1 downto 0)
   );
end xilinx_dual_port_ram_async;

architecture beh_arch of xilinx_dual_port_ram_async is
   type ram_type is array (0 to 2**ADDR_WIDTH-1)
        of std_logic_vector (DATA_WIDTH-1 downto 0);
   signal ram: ram_type;
begin
   process(clk)
   begin
     if (clk'event and clk = '1') then
        if (we = '1') then
           ram(to_integer(unsigned(addr_a))) <= din_a;
        end if;
     end if;
   end process;
   dout_a <= ram(to_integer(unsigned(addr_a)));
   dout_b <= ram(to_integer(unsigned(addr_b)));
end beh_arch;
```

The write operation is similar to that of the single-port RAM, but the code includes a second output port, `dout_b`, which retrieves data from the second address, `addr_b`. As in a single-port RAM with asynchronous read, the dual-port version can be realized only by distributed RAM, and thus its size is limited. Note that if we ignore the `dout_a` port, it is the same as the single-read-port register file of Listing 4.6.

Dual-port RAM with synchronous read The template for the dual-port RAM with synchronous read is shown in Listing 11.4. It is modified after the `rams_11` entity of the *XST Manual*.

Listing 11.4 Template for a dual-port RAM with synchronous read

```
-- dual-port RAM with synchronous read
-- modified from XST 8.1i rams_11
library ieee;
use ieee.std_logic_1164.all;
use ieee.numeric_std.all;
entity xilinx_dual_port_ram_sync is
   generic(
      ADDR_WIDTH: integer:=6;
      DATA_WIDTH:integer:=8
   );
   port(
      clk: in std_logic;
      we: in std_logic;
      addr_a: in std_logic_vector(ADDR_WIDTH-1 downto 0);
      addr_b: in std_logic_vector(ADDR_WIDTH-1 downto 0);
      din_a: in std_logic_vector(DATA_WIDTH-1 downto 0);
      dout_a: out std_logic_vector(DATA_WIDTH-1 downto 0);
      dout_b: out std_logic_vector(DATA_WIDTH-1 downto 0)
   );
end xilinx_dual_port_ram_sync;

architecture beh_arch of xilinx_dual_port_ram_sync is
   type ram_type is array (0 to 2**ADDR_WIDTH-1)
        of std_logic_vector (DATA_WIDTH-1 downto 0);
   signal ram: ram_type;
   signal addr_a_reg, addr_b_reg:
          std_logic_vector(ADDR_WIDTH-1 downto 0);
begin
   process(clk)
   begin
     if (clk'event and clk = '1') then
        if (we = '1') then
           ram(to_integer(unsigned(addr_a))) <= din_a;
        end if;
        addr_a_reg <= addr_a;
        addr_b_reg <= addr_b;
     end if;
   end process;
   dout_a <= ram(to_integer(unsigned(addr_a_reg)));
   dout_b <= ram(to_integer(unsigned(addr_b_reg)));
end beh_arch;
```

The code is similar to Listing 11.3 except that the two addresses are first stored in two registers and the registered outputs are used to access memory.

11.4.3 ROM

Despite its name, a ROM (read-only memory) is a combinational circuit and has no internal state. Its output depends only on its input (i.e., address). There is no real embedded ROM in a Spartan-3 device, but it can be emulated by a combinational circuit or a single-port RAM with the write operation disabled. The content of the ROM can be expressed as a constant in the HDL code and the values are loaded to the RAM when the device is programmed. Since the ROM is based in a RAM, the read operation can be asynchronous or synchronous.

ROM with asynchronous read A real ROM is a combinational circuit and thus should not have a buffer or a clock signal. To be consistent with the terms used in this section, we call it a *ROM with asynchronous read*. The template of this type of ROM is shown by an example in Listing 11.5. The code is to implement the hex-to-seven segment LED encoder, similar to that in Listing 3.12. The address of the ROM functions as the 4-bit hexadecimal input and its content is the corresponding LED patterns. The content of the ROM is defined by the HEX2LED_ROM constant and is essentially the truth table of this circuit.

Listing 11.5 Template for a ROM with asynchronous read

```
library ieee;
use ieee.std_logic_1164.all;
use ieee.numeric_std.all;
entity rom_template is
   port(
      addr: in std_logic_vector(3 downto 0);
      data: out std_logic_vector(6 downto 0)
   );
end rom_template;

architecture arch of rom_template is
   constant ADDR_WIDTH: integer:=4;
   constant DATA_WIDTH: integer:=7;
   type rom_type is array (0 to 2**ADDR_WIDTH-1)
        of std_logic_vector(DATA_WIDTH-1 downto 0);
   -- ROM definition
   constant HEX2LED_ROM: rom_type:=(  -- 2^4-by-7
      "0000001",  -- addr 00
      "1001111",  -- addr 01
      "0010010",  -- addr 02
      "0000110",  -- addr 03
      "1001100",  -- addr 04
      "0100100",  -- addr 05
      "0100000",  -- addr 06
      "0001111",  -- addr 07
      "0000000",  -- addr 08
      "0000100",  -- addr 09
      "0001000",  -- addr 10
      "1100000",  -- addr 11
      "0110001",  -- addr 12
      "1000010",  -- addr 13
      "0110000",  -- addr 14
      "0111000"   -- addr 15
   );
begin
   data <= HEX2LED_ROM(to_integer(unsigned(addr)));
end arch;
```

Note that the memory row is defined in ascending order:

```
... array (0 to 2**ADDR_WIDTH-1) of ...
```

and the first row of the HEX2LED_ROM constant corresponds to the address 00 of the ROM. The rows defined in the HEX2LED_ROM table must be reversed if the rom_type data type is defined in descending order:

```
... array (2**ADDR_WIDTH-1 downto 0) of ...
```

Since there is no address or data buffer in this circuit, the ROM cannot be realized by a block RAM. It is actually synthesized as a combinational circuit with the logic cells. The code can be considered as another form of a selected signal assignment or case statement. This type of ROM is feasible only for a small table. This code template is very general and is not specific to Xilinx devices.

ROM with synchronous read For a large table, it is better to utilize a block RAM to realize the ROM. Since the read operation of a block RAM is controlled and synchronized by a clock signal, the ROM requires a clock signal as well. The template for the ROM with synchronous read is shown in Listing 11.6. It is modified after the rams_21c entity of the *XST Manual*, and the hex-to-seven segment LED encoder is used for demonstration.

Listing 11.6 Template for a ROM with synchronous read

```
-- ROM with synchronous read
-- modified from XST 8.1i rams_21c
library ieee;
use ieee.std_logic_1164.all;
use ieee.numeric_std.all;
entity xilinx_rom_sync_template is
   port(
      clk: in std_logic;
      addr: in std_logic_vector(3 downto 0);
      data: out std_logic_vector(6 downto 0)
   );
end xilinx_rom_sync_template;

architecture arch of xilinx_rom_sync_template is
   constant ADDR_WIDTH: integer:=4;
   constant DATA_WIDTH: integer:=7;
   type rom_type is array (0 to 2**ADDR_WIDTH-1)
        of std_logic_vector(DATA_WIDTH-1 downto 0);
   -- ROM definition
   constant HEX2LED_ROM: rom_type:=(  -- 2^4-by-7
      "0000001",  -- addr 00
      "1001111",  -- addr 01
      "0010010",  -- addr 02
      "0000110",  -- addr 03
      "1001100",  -- addr 04
      "0100100",  -- addr 05
      "0100000",  -- addr 06
      "0001111",  -- addr 07
      "0000000",  -- addr 08
      "0000100",  -- addr 09
      "0001000",  -- addr 10
      "1100000",  -- addr 11
      "0110001",  -- addr 12
      "1000010",  -- addr 13
```

```
      "0110000",   -- addr 14
      "0111000"    -- addr 15
   );
   signal addr_reg: std_logic_vector(ADDR_WIDTH-1 downto 0);
begin
   -- addr register to infer block RAM
   process (clk)
   begin
      if (clk'event and clk = '1') then
        addr_reg <= addr;
      end if;
   end process;
   data <= HEX2LED_ROM(to_integer(unsigned(addr_reg)));
end arch;
```

The code is similar to that of the single-port RAM with synchronous read but with a predefined constant. Note that operation of this ROM depends on the clock signal, and its timing is different from that of a normal ROM. Artificial inclusion of the clock signal is necessary to infer a block RAM for the ROM implementation. During synthesis, the software automatically determines whether to use regular logic cells or block RAMs to realize this circuit.

11.5 BIBLIOGRAPHIC NOTES

Two Xilinx application notes, *XAPP464 Using Look-Up Tables as Distributed RAM in Spartan-3 Generation FPGAs* and *XAPP463 Using Block RAM in Spartan-3 Generation FPGAs*, provide detailed information on the distributed RAM and block RAM. Chapter 2 of the *XST User Guide v8.1i*, titled *HDL Coding Techniques*, includes about two dozen HDL code templates to infer various memory configurations.

The comprehensive ISE tutorial, *ISE In-Depth Tutorial*, includes a section on the Core Generator program. Although the program is simple, we need to know the module's basic functionalities and its relevant parameters to create a proper instance.

11.6 SUGGESTED EXPERIMENTS

11.6.1 Block-RAM-based FIFO

In Section 4.5.3, we design a FIFO buffer that uses a register file for storage. To increase its capacity, we can replace the register file with a block RAM-based dual-port RAM module. Derive the HDL code for the new design. Synthesize the verification circuit discussed in Section 4.5.3 with the new FIFO buffer and verify its operation. Note that due to the synchronous read, the behavior of the new FIFO is not completely identical to that of the original FIFO.

11.6.2 Block-RAM-based stack

We discuss the function of a stack in Experiment 4.7.7. To increase its capacity, we can replace the register file with a block RAM-based dual-port RAM module. Repeat the experiment.

11.6.3 ROM-based sign-magnitude adder

We can implement any n-input, m-output function with a 2^n-by-m ROM. Consider the sign-magnitude adder discussed in Section 3.7.2 and assume that a and b are 4-bit input signals. Design this circuit as follows:

1. Write a program in a conventional programming language, such as C or Java, to generate a 2^8-by-4 truth table for this circuit.
2. Follow the ROM template in Listing 11.5 to derive the HDL code. Cut and paste the table to the code.
3. Synthesize the circuit and verify its operation.
4. Check the synthesis report and compare the sizes (in terms of the number of logic cells) of the original implementation and the ROM-based implementation.
5. Expand a and b to 8-bit input signals and repeat steps 1 to 4.

11.6.4 ROM based $\sin(x)$ function

One way to implement a sinusoidal function, $\sin(x)$, is to use a look-up table. Assume that the desired implementation requires 10-bit input resolution [i.e., there are 1024 (2^{10}) points between the input range of 0 and 2π] and 8-bit output resolution [i.e., there are 256 (2^8) points between the output range of –1 and +1]. Let the input and output be the 10-bit x signal and the 8-bit y signal. The relationship between x and y is

$$\frac{y}{2^7} = \sin\left(2\pi\frac{x}{2^{10}}\right)$$

Because of the symmetry of the sin function, we only need to construct a 2^8-by-7 table for the first quadrant (i.e., between 0 and $\frac{\pi}{2}$) and use simple pre- and postprocessing circuits to obtain the values in other quadrants. Design this circuit as follows:

1. Write a program in a conventional programming language to generate the 2^8-by-7 table for the first quadrant.
2. Follow the ROM template in Listing 11.6 to derive the HDL code for the look-up table. Cut and paste the table to the code.
3. Derive the complete HDL code.
4. Derive a testbench to generate the sinusoidal output for three complete periods. This can be done by using a 10-bit counter to generate the 10-bit ROM address for $3 * 2^{10}$ clock cycles. In ModelSim, we can display the y signal in Analog format to emulate the effect of a digital-to-analog converter.

11.6.5 ROM-based $\sin(x)$ and $\cos(x)$ functions

In many communication modulation schemes, the $\sin(x)$ and $\cos(x)$ functions are needed at the same time. Assume that the format of the input and output is similar to that in Experiment 11.6.4. The new circuit has two outputs, y_s and y_c:

$$\frac{y_s}{2^7} = \sin\left(2\pi\frac{x}{2^{10}}\right)$$
$$\frac{y_c}{2^7} = \cos\left(2\pi\frac{x}{2^{10}}\right)$$

Although we can follow the previous procedure and create a new ROM for the $\cos(x)$ function, a better alternative is to share the same ROM for both $\sin(x)$ and $\cos(x)$ functions.

This is based on the observations that $\cos(x)$ is only a phase shift of $\sin(x)$ and that the FPGA's block RAM can provide dual-port access.

Note that this circuit requires essentially a "dual-port ROM." No HDL behaviorial template is given for this type of memory. We need to experiment with HDL codes and to check the synthesis report to ensure that only one block RAM is inferred. It may be necessary to use the Core Generator program or direct HDL component instantiation to achieve this goal.

Construct this special ROM and derive the HDL code for the pre- and postprocessing circuits. Use a testbench similar to that in Experiment 11.6.4 to verify the circuit's operation.

CHAPTER 12

VGA CONTROLLER I: GRAPHIC

12.1 INTRODUCTION

VGA (video graphics array) is a video display standard introduced in the late 1980s in IBM PCs and is widely supported by PC graphics hardware and monitors. We discuss the design of a basic eight-color 640-by-480 resolution interface for CRT (cathode ray tube) monitors in this book. CRT synchronization and basic graphic processing are examined in this chapter, and text generation is discussed in Chapter 13.

12.1.1 Basic operation of a CRT

The conceptual sketch of a monochrome CRT monitor is shown in Figure 12.1. The electron gun (cathode) generates a focused electron beam, which traverses a vacuum tube and eventually hits the phosphorescent screen. Light is emitted at the instant that electrons hit a phosphor dot on the screen. The intensity of the electron beam and the brightness of the dot are determined by the voltage level of the external video input signal, labeled `mono` in Figure 12.1. The `mono` signal is an analog signal whose voltage level is between 0 and 0.7 V.

A vertical deflection coil and a horizontal deflection coil outside the tube produce magnetic fields to control how the electron beam travels and to determine where on the screen the electrons hit. In today's monitors, the electron beam traverses (i.e., scans) the screen systematically in a fixed pattern, from left to right and from top to bottom, as shown in Figure 12.2.

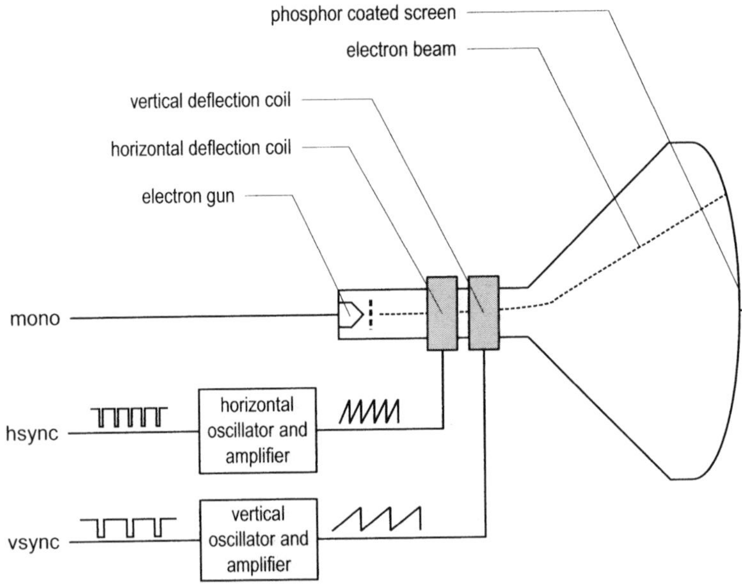

Figure 12.1 Conceptual diagram of a CRT monitor.

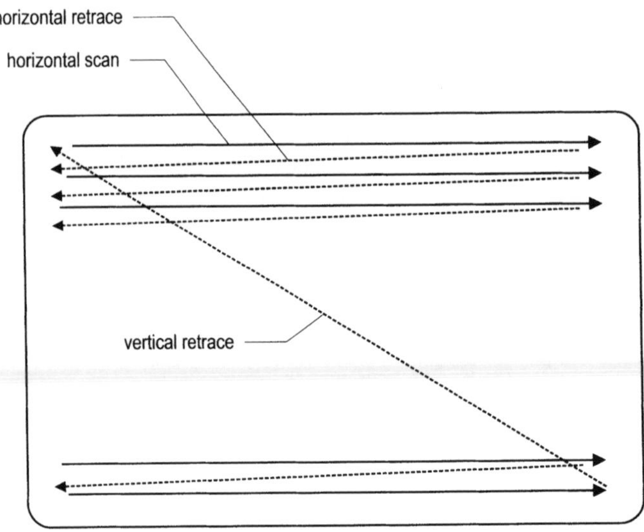

Figure 12.2 CRT scanning pattern.

Table 12.1 Three-bit VGA color combinations

Red (R)	Green (G)	Blue (B)	Resulting color
0	0	0	black
0	0	1	blue
0	1	0	green
0	1	1	cyan
1	0	0	red
1	0	1	magenta
1	1	0	yellow
1	1	1	white

The monitor's internal oscillators and amplifiers generate sawtooth waveforms to control the two deflection coils. For example, the electron beam moves from the left edge to the right edge as the voltage applied to the horizontal deflection coil gradually increases. After reaching the right edge, the beam returns rapidly to the left edge (i.e., *retraces*) when the voltage changes to 0. The relationship between the sawtooth waveform and the scan is shown in Figure 12.4. Two external synchronization signals, `hsync` and `vsync`, control generation of the sawtooth waveforms. These signals are digital signals. The relationship between the `hsync` signal and the horizontal sawtooth is also shown in Figure 12.4. Note that the "1" and "0" periods of the `hsync` signal correspond to the rising and falling ramps of the sawtooth waveform.

The basic operation of a color CRT is similar except that it has three electron beams, which are projected to the red, green, and blue phosphor dots on the screen. The three dots are combined to form a pixel. We can adjust the voltage levels of the three video input signals to obtain the desired pixel color.

12.1.2 VGA port of the S3 board

The VGA port has five active signals, including the horizontal and vertical synchronization signals, `hsync` and `vsync`, and three video signals for the red, green, and blue beams. It is physically connected to a 15-pin D-subminiature connector. A video signal is an analog signal and the video controller uses a digital-to-analog converter to convert the digital output to the desired analog level. If a video signal is represented by an N-bit word, it can be converted to 2^N analog levels. The three video signals can generate 2^{3N} different colors. This is also known as *3N-bit color* since a color is defined by $3N$ bits. In the S3 board, 1-bit word is used for each video signal, and this leads to only eight (i.e., 2^3) possible colors. The possible color combinations are shown in Table 12.1. If we use the same 1-bit signal to drive the video signals, they become either "000" or "111" and the monitor functions as a black-and-white monochrome monitor.

12.1.3 Video controller

A video controller generates the synchronization signals and outputs data pixels serially. A simplified block diagram of a VGA controller is shown in Figure 12.3. It contains a synchronization circuit, labeled `vga_sync`, and a pixel generation circuit.

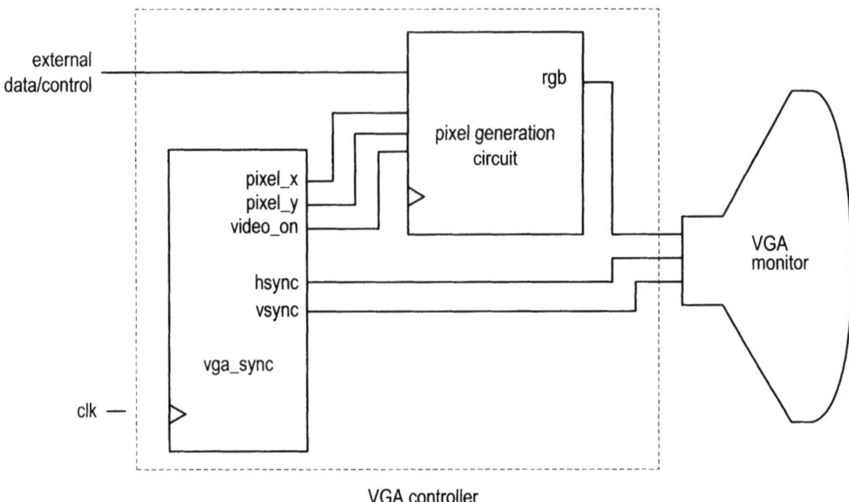

Figure 12.3 Simplified block diagram of a VGA controller.

The vga_sync circuit generates the timing and synchronization signals. The hsync and vsync signals are connected to the VGA port to control the horizontal and vertical scans of the monitor. The two signals are decoded from the internal counters, whose outputs are the pixel_x and pixel_y signals. The pixel_x and pixel_y signals indicate the relative positions of the scans and essentially specify the location of the current pixel. The vga_sync circuit also generates the video_on signal to indicate whether to enable or disable the display. The design of this circuit is discussed in Section 12.2.

The pixel generation circuit generates the three video signals, which are collectively referred to as the rgb signal. A color value is obtained according to the current coordinates of the pixel (the pixel_x and pixel_y signals) and the external control and data signals. This circuit is more involved and is discussed in the second half of this chapter and Chapter 13.

12.2 VGA SYNCHRONIZATION

The video synchronization circuit generates the hsync signal, which specifies the required time to traverse (scan) a row, and the vsync signal, which specifies the required time to traverse (scan) the entire screen. Subsequent discussions are based on a 640-by-480 VGA screen with a 25-MHz *pixel rate*, which means that 25M pixels are processed in a second. Note that this resolution is also know as the *VGA mode*.

The screen of a CRT monitor usually includes a small black border, as shown at the top of Figure 12.4. The middle rectangle is the visible portion. Note that the coordinate of the vertical axis increases downward. The coordinates of the top-left and bottom-right corners are (0,0) and (639,479), respectively.

12.2.1 Horizontal synchronization

A detailed timing diagram of one horizontal scan is shown in Figure 12.4. A period of the hsync signal contains 800 pixels and can be divided into four regions:

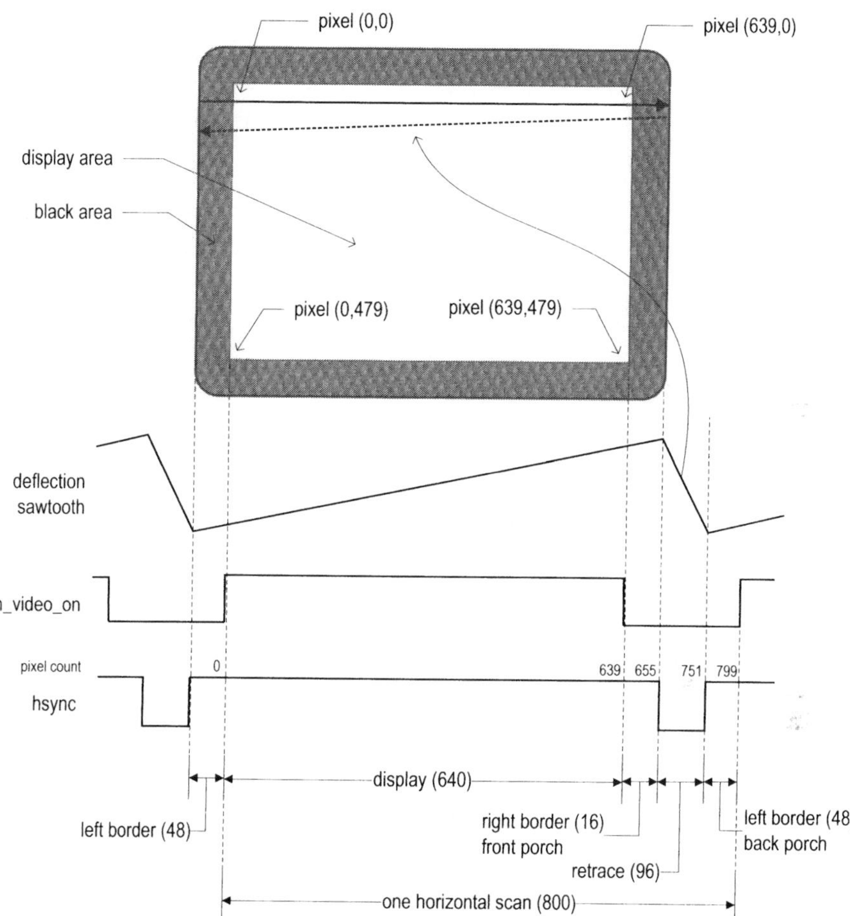

Figure 12.4 Timing diagram of a horizontal scan.

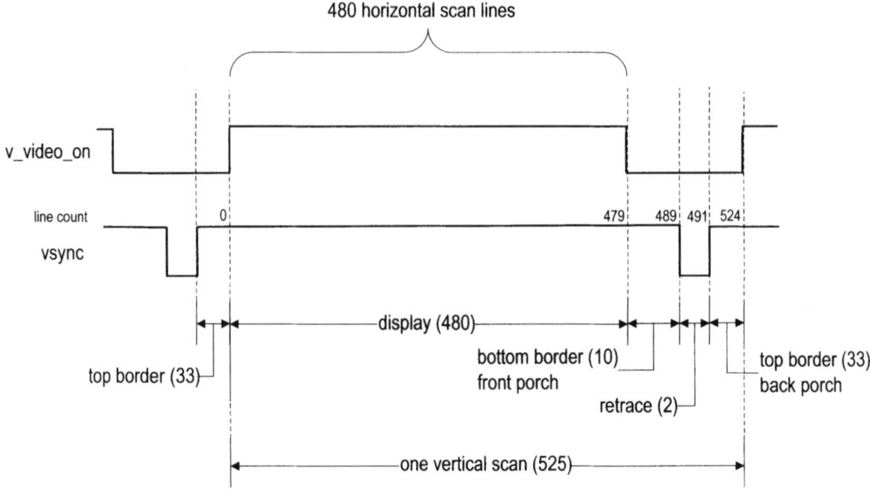

Figure 12.5 Timing diagram of a vertical scan.

- *Display*: region where the pixels are actually displayed on the screen. The length of this region is 640 pixels.
- *Retrace*: region in which the electron beams return to the left edge. The video signal should be disabled (i.e., black), and the length of this region is 96 pixels.
- *Right border*: region that forms the right border of the display region. It is also know as the *front porch* (i.e., porch before retrace). The video signal should be disabled, and the length of this region is 16 pixels.
- *Left border*: region that forms the left border of the display region. It is also know as the *back porch* (i.e., porch after retrace). The video signal should be disabled, and the length of this region is 48 pixels.

Note that the lengths of the right and left borders may vary for different brands of monitors.

The `hsync` signal can be obtained by a special mod-800 counter and a decoding circuit. The counts are marked on the top of the `hsync` signal in Figure 12.4. We intentionally start the counting from the beginning of the display region. This allows us to use the counter output as the horizontal (x-axis) coordinate. This output constitutes the `pixel_x` signal. The `hsync` signal goes low when the counter's output is between 656 and 751.

Note that the CRT monitor should be black in the right and left borders and during retrace. We use the `h_video_on` signal to indicate whether the current horizontal coordinate is in the displayable region. It is asserted only when the pixel count is smaller than 640.

12.2.2 Vertical synchronization

During the vertical scan, the electron beams move gradually from top to bottom and then return to the top. This corresponds to the time required to refresh the entire screen. The format of the `vsync` signal is similar to that of the `hsync` signal, as shown in Figure 12.5. The time unit of the movement is represented in terms of horizontal scan lines. A period of the `vsync` signal is 525 lines and can be divided into four regions:

- *Display*: region where the horizontal lines are actually displayed on the screen. The length of this region is 480 lines.

- *Retrace*: region that the electron beams return to the top of the screen. The video signal should be disabled, and the length of this region is 2 lines.
- *Bottom border*: region that forms the bottom border of the display region. It is also know as the *front porch* (i.e., porch before retrace). The video signal should be disabled, and the length of this region is 10 lines.
- *Top border*: region that forms the top border of the display region. It is also know as the *back porch* (i.e., porch after retrace). The video signal should be disabled, and the length of this region is 33 lines.

As in the horizontal scan, the lengths of the top and bottom borders may vary for different brands of monitors.

The `vsync` signal can be obtained by a special mod-525 counter and a decoding circuit. Again, we intentionally start counting from the beginning of the display region. This allows us to use the counter output as the vertical (y-axis) coordinate. This output constitutes the `pixel_y` signal. The `vsync` signal goes low when the line count is 490 or 491.

As in the horizontal scan, we use the `v_video_on` signal to indicate whether the current vertical coordinate is in the displayable region. It is asserted only when the line count is smaller than 480.

12.2.3 Timing calculation of VGA synchronization signals

As mentioned earlier, we assume that the pixel rate is 25 MHz. It is determined by three parameters:

- p: the number of pixels in a horizontal scan line. For 640-by-480 resolution, it is

$$p = 800 \, \frac{pixels}{line}$$

- l: the number of lines in a screen (i.e., a vertical scan). For 640-by-480 resolution, it is

$$l = 525 \, \frac{lines}{screen}$$

- s: the number of screens per second. For flickering-free operation, we can set it to

$$s = 60 \, \frac{screens}{second}$$

The s parameter specifies how fast the screen should be refreshed. For a human eye, the refresh rate must be at least 30 screens per second to make the motion appear to be continuous. To reduce flickering, the monitor usually has a much higher rate , such as the 60 screens per second specification above. The pixel rate can be calculated by the three parameters:

$$\text{pixel rate} = p * l * s \approx 25M \, \frac{pixels}{second}$$

The pixel rate for other resolutions and refresh rates can be calculated in a similar fashion. Clearly, the rate increases as the resolution and refresh rate grow.

12.2.4 HDL implementation

The function of the `vga_sync` circuit is discussed in Section 12.1.3. If the frequency of the system clock is 25 MHz, the circuit can be implemented by two special counters: a mod-800 counter to keep track of the horizontal scan and a mod-525 counter to keep track of the vertical scan.

Since our designs generally use the 50-MHz oscillator of the prototyping board, the system clock rate is twice the pixel rate. Instead of creating a separate 25-MHz clock domain and violating the synchronous design methodology, we can generate a 25-MHz enable tick to enable or pause the counting. The tick is also routed to the p_tick port as an output signal to coordinate operation of the pixel generation circuit.

The HDL code is shown in Listing 12.1. It consists of a mod-2 counter to generate the 25-MHz enable tick and two counters for the horizontal and vertical scans. We use two status signals, h_end and v_end, to indicate completion of the horizontal and vertical scans. The values of various regions of the horizontal and vertical scans are defined as constants. They can be easily modified if a different resolution or refresh rate is used. To remove potential glitches, output buffers are inserted for the hsync and vsync signals. This leads to a one-clock-cycle delay. We should add a similar buffer for the rgb signal in the pixel generation circuit to compensate for the delay.

Listing 12.1 VGA synchronization circuit

```
library ieee;
use ieee.std_logic_1164.all;
use ieee.numeric_std.all;
entity vga_sync is
   port(
      clk, reset: in std_logic;
      hsync, vsync: out std_logic;
      video_on, p_tick: out std_logic;
      pixel_x, pixel_y: out std_logic_vector (9 downto 0)
    );
end vga_sync;

architecture arch of vga_sync is
   -- VGA 640-by-480 sync parameters
   constant HD: integer:=640; --horizontal display area
   constant HF: integer:=16 ; --h. front porch
   constant HB: integer:=48 ; --h. back porch
   constant HR: integer:=96 ; --h. retrace
   constant VD: integer:=480; --vertical display area
   constant VF: integer:=10;  --v. front porch
   constant VB: integer:=33;  --v. back porch
   constant VR: integer:=2;   --v. retrace
   -- mod-2 counter
   signal mod2_reg, mod2_next: std_logic;
   -- sync counters
   signal v_count_reg, v_count_next: unsigned(9 downto 0);
   signal h_count_reg, h_count_next: unsigned(9 downto 0);
   -- output buffer
   signal v_sync_reg, h_sync_reg: std_logic;
   signal v_sync_next, h_sync_next: std_logic;
   -- status signal
   signal h_end, v_end, pixel_tick: std_logic;
begin
   -- registers
   process (clk,reset)
```

```
begin
   if reset='1' then
      mod2_reg <= '0';
      v_count_reg <= (others=>'0');
      h_count_reg <= (others=>'0');
      v_sync_reg <= '0';
      h_sync_reg <= '0';
   elsif (clk'event and clk='1') then
      mod2_reg <= mod2_next;
      v_count_reg <= v_count_next;
      h_count_reg <= h_count_next;
      v_sync_reg <= v_sync_next;
      h_sync_reg <= h_sync_next;
   end if;
end process;
-- mod-2 circuit to generate 25 MHz enable tick
mod2_next <= not mod2_reg;
-- 25 MHz pixel tick
pixel_tick <= '1' when mod2_reg='1' else '0';
-- status
h_end <=  -- end of horizontal counter
   '1' when h_count_reg=(HD+HF+HB+HR-1) else --799
   '0';
v_end <=  -- end of vertical counter
   '1' when v_count_reg=(VD+VF+VB+VR-1) else --524
   '0';
-- mod-800 horizontal sync counter
process (h_count_reg,h_end,pixel_tick)
begin
   if pixel_tick='1' then  -- 25 MHz tick
      if h_end='1' then
         h_count_next <= (others=>'0');
      else
         h_count_next <= h_count_reg + 1;
      end if;
   else
      h_count_next <= h_count_reg;
   end if;
end process;
-- mod-525 vertical sync counter
process (v_count_reg,h_end,v_end,pixel_tick)
begin
   if pixel_tick='1' and h_end='1' then
      if (v_end='1') then
         v_count_next <= (others=>'0');
      else
         v_count_next <= v_count_reg + 1;
      end if;
   else
      v_count_next <= v_count_reg;
   end if;
end process;
-- horizontal and vertical sync, buffered to avoid glitch
```

```
      h_sync_next <=
         '1' when (h_count_reg>=(HD+HF))                  --656
             and (h_count_reg<=(HD+HF+HR-1)) else --751
         '0';
      v_sync_next <=
         '1' when (v_count_reg>=(VD+VF))                  --490
             and (v_count_reg<=(VD+VF+VR-1)) else --491
         '0';
      -- video on/off
      video_on <=
         '1' when (h_count_reg<HD) and (v_count_reg<VD) else
         '0';
      -- output signal
      hsync <= h_sync_reg;
      vsync <= v_sync_reg;
      pixel_x <= std_logic_vector(h_count_reg);
      pixel_y <= std_logic_vector(v_count_reg);
      p_tick <= pixel_tick;
   end arch;
```

12.2.5 Testing circuit

To verify operation of the synchronization circuit, we can connect the rgb signal to three switches. The entire visible region should be turned on with a single color. We can go through the eight possible combinations and check the colors defined in Table 12.1. The HDL code is shown in Listing 12.2. As mentioned in Section 12.2.4, an output buffer is added for the rgb signal.

Listing 12.2 VGA synchronization testing circuit

```
library ieee;
use ieee.std_logic_1164.all;
entity vga_test is
   port (
      clk, reset: in std_logic;
      sw: in std_logic_vector(2 downto 0);
      hsync, vsync: out  std_logic;
      rgb: out std_logic_vector(2 downto 0)
   );
end vga_test;

architecture arch of vga_test is
   signal rgb_reg: std_logic_vector(2 downto 0);
   signal video_on: std_logic;
begin
   -- instantiate VGA sync circuit
   vga_sync_unit: entity work.vga_sync
      port map(clk=>clk, reset=>reset, hsync=>hsync,
               vsync=>vsync, video_on=>video_on,
               p_tick=>open, pixel_x=>open, pixel_y=>open);
   -- rgb buffer
   process (clk,reset)
   begin
```

```
         if reset='1' then
            rgb_reg <= (others=>'0');
         elsif (clk'event and clk='1') then
            rgb_reg <= sw;
         end if;
      end process;
      rgb <= rgb_reg when video_on='1' else "000";
   end arch;
```

12.3 OVERVIEW OF THE PIXEL GENERATION CIRCUIT

The pixel generation circuit generates the 3-bit `rgb` signal for the VGA port. The external control and data signals specify the content of the screen, and the `pixel_x` and `pixel_y` signals from the `vga_sync` circuit provide the current coordinates of the pixel. For our discussion purposes, we divided this circuit into three broad categories:

- Bit-mapped scheme
- Tile-mapped scheme
- Object-mapped scheme

In a *bit-mapped scheme*, a *video memory* is used to store the data to be displayed on the screen. Each pixel of the screen is mapped directly to a memory word, and the `pixel_x` and `pixel_y` signals form the address. A graphics processing circuit continuously updates the screen and writes relevant data to the video memory. A retrieval circuit continuously reads the video memory and routes the data to the `rgb` signal. This is the scheme used in today's high-performance video controller. For 640-by-480 resolution, there are about 310k (i.e., 640∗480) pixels on a screen. This translates to 310k memory bits for a monochrome display and 930k memory bits (i.e., 3 bits per pixel) for a 3-bit color display. A bit-mapped example is discussed in Section 12.5.

To reduce the memory requirement, one alternative is to use a *tile-mapped scheme*. In this scheme, we group a collection of bits to form a *tile* and treat each tile as a display unit. For example, we can define an 8-by-8 square of pixels (i.e., 64 pixels) as a tile. The 640-by-480 pixel-oriented screen becomes an 80-by-60 tile-oriented screen. Only 4800 (i.e., 80∗60) words are needed for the *tile memory*. The number of bits in a word depends on the number of tile patterns. For example, if there are 32 tile patterns, each word should contain 5 bits, and the size of the tile memory is about 24k bits (i.e., 5∗4800). The tile-mapped scheme usually requires a ROM to store the tile patterns. We call it *pattern memory*. Assume that monochrome patterns are used in the previous example. Each 8-by-8 tile pattern requires 64 bits, and the entire 32 patterns need 2K (i.e., 8∗8∗32) bits. The overall memory requirement is about 26k bits, which is much smaller than the 310k bits of the bit-mapped scheme. The text display discussed in Chapter 13 is based on this scheme.

For some applications, the video display can be very simple and contains only a few objects. Instead of wasting memory to store a mostly blank screen, we can generate these objects using simple object generation circuits. We call this approach an *object-mapped scheme*. An object-mapped example is discussed in Section 12.4.

The three schemes can be mixed together to generate a full screen. For example, we can use a bit-mapped scheme to generate the background and use an object-mapped scheme to produce the main objects. We can also use a bit-mapped scheme for one portion of a screen and tile-mapped text for another part of the screen.

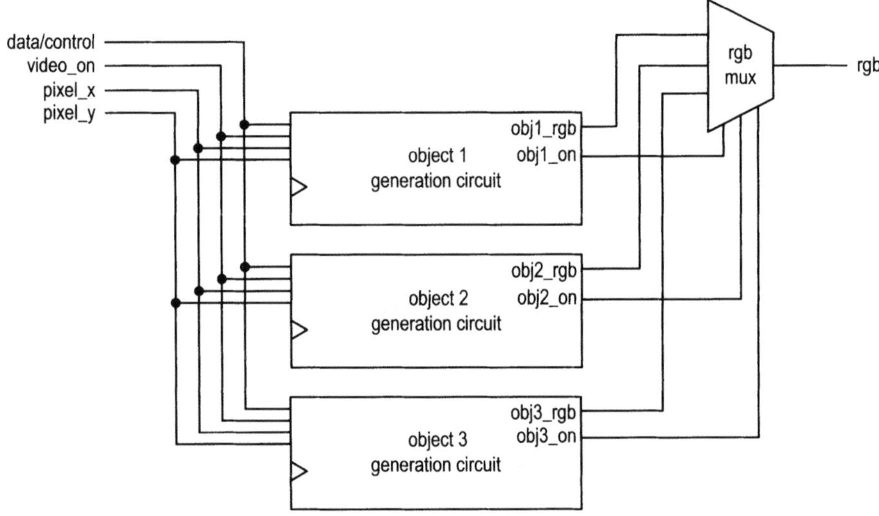

Figure 12.6 Conceptual diagram of object-mapped pixel generation.

12.4 GRAPHIC GENERATION WITH AN OBJECT-MAPPED SCHEME

The conceptual diagram of an object-mapped pixel generation circuit that contains three objects is shown in Figure 12.6. The diagram consists of three object generation circuits and a special selecting and routing circuit, labeled `rgb mux`. An object generation circuit performs the following tasks:

- It keeps the coordinates of the current object and compares it with the current scan location provided by the `pixel_x` and `pixel_y` signals.
- If the current scan location falls within the region, it asserts the `obj_i_on` signal to indicate that the current scan location is within the region of the ith object and the object should be "turned on."
- It specifies the desired color in the `obj_i_rgb` signal.

The `rgb mux` circuit performs multiplexing according to an internal prioritizing scheme. It examines various `obj_i_on` signals and determines which `obj_i_rgb` signal is to be routed to the `rgb` output. The prioritizing scheme prioritizes the order of the displays when multiple `obj_i_on` signals are asserted at the same time. It corresponds to selecting an object for the foreground.

We use a simplified ping-pong-like game to illustrate the various graphic generation schemes. The design is constructed as follows:

1. Create a simple still screen with rectangular objects.
2. Add a round object.
3. Introduce animation.
4. Add text for scores and information.
5. Create a top-level control circuit.

The first three steps are discussed in this section, and the last two steps are discussed in Chapter 13.

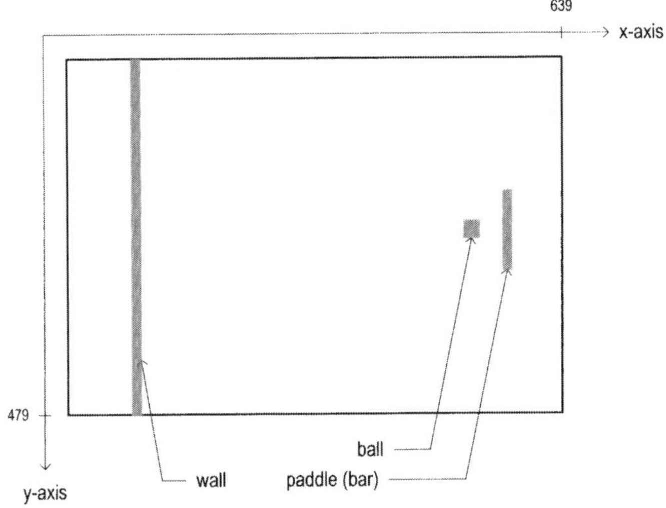

Figure 12.7 Still screen of the pong game.

12.4.1 Rectangular objects

A rectangular object can be described by its boundary coordinates on the screen. The still screen of the game is shown in Figure 12.7. It has three objects: a wall, which is shown as a narrow stripe on the left; a paddle, which is shown as a short vertical bar on the right; and a square ball. The coordinates of the displayable area of the screen is also shown. Note that the y-axis increases downward.

Let us first examine generation of the wall stripe. For clarity, we define constants for the relevant boundaries and sizes in code. The code segment for the wall is

```
constant WALL_X_L: integer:=32;
constant WALL_X_R: integer:=35;
...
-- pixel within wall
wall_on <=
   '1' when (WALL_X_L<=pix_x) and (pix_x<=WALL_X_R) else
   '0';
-- wall rgb output
wall_rgb <= "001"; -- blue
```

The wall is a four-pixel-wide vertical stripe between columns 32 and 35, which as defined as `WALL_X_L` and `WALL_X_R`, representing the left and right x-coordinates of the wall, respectively. The object has two output signals, `wall_on` and `wall_rgb`. The `wall_on` signal, which indicates that the wall object should be turned on, is asserted when the current horizontal scan is within its region. Since the stripe covers the entire vertical column, there is no need for the y-axis boundaries. The `wall_rgb` signal indicates that the color of the wall is "001" (blue).

The code segment for the bar (paddle) is

```
-- bar left, right boundary
constant BAR_X_L: integer:=600;
constant BAR_X_R: integer:=603;
```

```
-- bar top, bottom boundary
constant BAR_Y_SIZE: integer:=72;
constant BAR_Y_T: integer:=MAX_Y/2-BAR_Y_SIZE/2; --204
constant BAR_Y_B: integer:=BAR_Y_T+BAR_Y_SIZE-1;
...
-- pixel within bar
bar_on <=
   '1' when (BAR_X_L<=pix_x) and (pix_x<=BAR_X_R) and
            (BAR_Y_T<=pix_y) and (pix_y<=BAR_Y_B) else
   '0';
-- bar rgb output
bar_rgb <= "010"; --green
```

The code is similar to that of the wall segment except that it includes the y-axis boundaries. The desired vertical length of the bar is 72 pixels, which is defined by BAR_Y_SIZE. Since we wish to place the bar in the middle, the top boundary of the bar, which is BAR_Y_T, is one half of the maximal y-value (i.e., 480/2) minus one half of the bar length. The bottom boundary of the bar is the top boundary plus the bar length. Generation of the bar_on signal is similar to that of the wall_on signal except that the vertical scan must be within the bar's y-axis boundaries as well.

The code for the ball can be constructed in a similar fashion. The final code segment is the selection and multiplexing circuit, which examines the on signals of three objects and routes the corresponding rgb signal to output. The code is

```
process(video_on,wall_on,bar_on,sq_ball_on,
        wall_rgb,bar_rgb,ball_rgb)
begin
   if video_on='0' then
       graph_rgb <= "000"; --blank
   else
      if wall_on='1' then
         graph_rgb <= wall_rgb;
      elsif bar_on='1' then
         graph_rgb <= bar_rgb;
      elsif sq_ball_on='1' then
         graph_rgb <= ball_rgb;
      else
         graph_rgb <= "110"; -- yellow background
      end if;
   end if;
end process;
```

The circuit first checks whether the video_on is asserted, and if this is the case, examines the three on signals in turn. When an on signal is asserted, it indicates that the scan is within its region, and the corresponding rgb signal is passed to the output. If no signal is asserted, the scan is in the "background" and the output is assigned to be "110" (yellow).

The complete HDL code is shown in Listing 12.3.

Listing 12.3 Pixel-generation circuit for the pong game screen

```
library ieee;
use ieee.std_logic_1164.all;
use ieee.numeric_std.all;
entity pong_graph_st is
```

```
   port(
      video_on: in std_logic;
      pixel_x,pixel_y: in std_logic_vector(9 downto 0);
      graph_rgb: out std_logic_vector(2 downto 0)
   );
end pong_graph_st;

architecture sq_ball_arch of pong_graph_st is
   -- x, y coordinates (0,0) to (639,479)
   signal pix_x, pix_y: unsigned(9 downto 0);
   constant MAX_X: integer:=640;
   constant MAX_Y: integer:=480;
   ----------------------------------------------
   -- vertical stripe as a wall
   ----------------------------------------------
   -- wall left, right boundary
   constant WALL_X_L: integer:=32;
   constant WALL_X_R: integer:=35;
   ----------------------------------------------
   -- right vertical bar
   ----------------------------------------------
   -- bar left, right boundary
   constant BAR_X_L: integer:=600;
   constant BAR_X_R: integer:=603;
   -- bar top, bottom boundary
   constant BAR_Y_SIZE: integer:=72;
   constant BAR_Y_T: integer:=MAX_Y/2-BAR_Y_SIZE/2; --204
   constant BAR_Y_B: integer:=BAR_Y_T+BAR_Y_SIZE-1;
   ----------------------------------------------
   -- square ball
   ----------------------------------------------
   constant BALL_SIZE: integer:=8;
   -- ball left, right boundary
   constant BALL_X_L: integer:=580;
   constant BALL_X_R: integer:=BALL_X_L+BALL_SIZE-1;
   -- ball top, bottom boundary
   constant BALL_Y_T: integer:=238;
   constant BALL_Y_B: integer:=BALL_Y_T+BALL_SIZE-1;
   ----------------------------------------------
   -- object output signals
   ----------------------------------------------
   signal wall_on, bar_on, sq_ball_on: std_logic;
   signal wall_rgb, bar_rgb, ball_rgb:
          std_logic_vector(2 downto 0);

begin
   pix_x <= unsigned(pixel_x);
   pix_y <= unsigned(pixel_y);
   ----------------------------------------------
   -- (wall) left vertical stripe
   ----------------------------------------------
   -- pixel within wall
   wall_on <=
```

```
      '1' when (WALL_X_L<=pix_x) and (pix_x<=WALL_X_R) else
      '0';
   -- wall rgb output
   wall_rgb <= "001"; -- blue
   ----------------------------------------------
   -- right vertical bar
   ----------------------------------------------
   -- pixel within bar
   bar_on <=
      '1' when (BAR_X_L<=pix_x) and (pix_x<=BAR_X_R) and
               (BAR_Y_T<=pix_y) and (pix_y<=BAR_Y_B) else
      '0';
   -- bar rgb output
   bar_rgb <= "010"; --green
   ----------------------------------------------
   -- square ball
   ----------------------------------------------
   -- pixel within squared ball
   sq_ball_on <=
      '1' when (BALL_X_L<=pix_x) and (pix_x<=BALL_X_R) and
               (BALL_Y_T<=pix_y) and (pix_y<=BALL_Y_B) else
      '0';
   ball_rgb <= "100";   -- red
   ----------------------------------------------
   -- rgb multiplexing circuit
   ----------------------------------------------
   process(video_on,wall_on,bar_on,sq_ball_on,
           wall_rgb, bar_rgb, ball_rgb)
   begin
      if video_on='0' then
          graph_rgb <= "000"; --blank
      else
         if wall_on='1' then
            graph_rgb <= wall_rgb;
         elsif bar_on='1' then
            graph_rgb <= bar_rgb;
         elsif sq_ball_on='1' then
            graph_rgb <= ball_rgb;
         else
            graph_rgb <= "110"; -- yellow background
         end if;
      end if;
   end process;
end sq_ball_arch;
```

After deriving the pixel generation circuit, we can combine it with the VGA synchronization circuit to construct the complete video interface. The top-level HDL code is shown in Listing 12.4. Note that the `graph_rgb` signal is routed to output through an output buffer. It is loaded when the `pixel_tick` signal is asserted. This synchronizes the `rgb` output with the buffered `hsync` and `vsync` signals.

Listing 12.4 Complete circuit for a still pong game screen

```
library ieee;
```

```
use ieee.std_logic_1164.all;
entity pong_top_st is
   port (
      clk,reset: in std_logic;
      hsync, vsync: out  std_logic;
      rgb: out std_logic_vector(2 downto 0)
   );
end pong_top_st;

architecture arch of pong_top_st is
   signal pixel_x, pixel_y: std_logic_vector (9 downto 0);
   signal video_on, pixel_tick: std_logic;
   signal rgb_reg, rgb_next: std_logic_vector(2 downto 0);
begin
   -- instantiate VGA sync
   vga_sync_unit: entity work.vga_sync
      port map(clk=>clk, reset=>reset,
               video_on=>video_on, p_tick=>pixel_tick,
               hsync=>hsync, vsync=>vsync,
               pixel_x=>pixel_x, pixel_y=>pixel_y);
   -- instantiate graphic generator
   pong_grf_st_unit: entity work.pong_graph_st(sq_ball_arch)
      port map (video_on=>video_on,
                pixel_x=>pixel_x, pixel_y=>pixel_y,
                graph_rgb=>rgb_next);
   -- rgb buffer
   process (clk)
   begin
      if (clk'event and clk='1') then
         if (pixel_tick='1') then
            rgb_reg <= rgb_next;
         end if;
      end if;
   end process;
   rgb <= rgb_reg;
end arch;
```

12.4.2 Non-rectangular object

Direct checking of the boundaries of a non-rectangular object is very difficult. An alternative is to specify the object pattern in a bit map and generate the rgb and on signals according to the map. This can best be explained by an example. Assume that we want to have a round ball in the pong game screen. The bit map of a circle within an 8-by-8 pixel square is shown in Figure 12.8. The circle object can be generated as follows:

- Check whether the scan coordinates are within the 8-by-8 pixel square.
- If this is the case, obtain the corresponding pixel from the bit map.
- Use the retrieved bit to generate the rgb and on signals for the circle object.

To implement this scheme, we need to include a *pattern ROM* to store the bit map and an address mapping circuit to convert the scan coordinates to the ROM's row and column.

To accommodate the change, the ball portion from Listing 12.3 must be modified. First, we define a pattern ROM for the circle. It can be done by declaring a two-dimensional

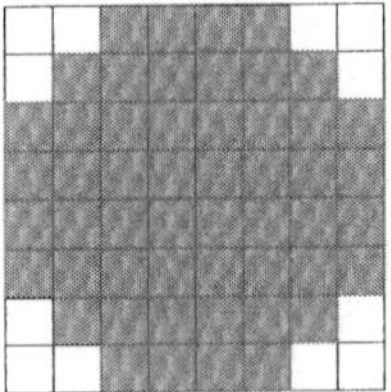

Figure 12.8 Bit map of a circle.

constant, as in the ROM template of Listing 11.5. To facilitate future animation, we also use signals to replace constants for the square ball boundaries. The revised architecture declaration portion becomes

```
constant BALL_SIZE: integer:=8;
-- ball left, right boundary
signal ball_x_l, ball_x_r: unsigned(9 downto 0);
-- ball top, bottom boundary
signal ball_y_t, ball_y_b: unsigned(9 downto 0);
--==============================================
-- round ball image ROM
--==============================================
type rom_type is array (0 to 7) of std_logic_vector(0 to 7);
-- ROM definition
constant BALL_ROM: rom_type :=
(
   "00111100", --   ****
   "01111110", --  ******
   "11111111", -- ********
   "11111111", -- ********
   "11111111", -- ********
   "11111111", -- ********
   "01111110", --  ******
   "00111100"  --   ****
);
signal rom_addr, rom_col: unsigned(2 downto 0);
signal rom_data: std_logic_vector(7 downto 0);
signal rom_bit: std_logic;
-- new signal to indicate whether the scan coordinates
-- are within the round ball region
signal rd_ball_on: std_logic;
```

Second, we expand the ball generation segment to include the mapping of the circle bit map:

```
-- pixel within square ball
sq_ball_on <=
   '1' when (ball_x_l<=pix_x) and (pix_x<=ball_x_r) and
            (ball_y_t<=pix_y) and (pix_y<=ball_y_b) else
   '0';
-- map current pixel location to ROM addr/col
rom_addr <= pix_y(2 downto 0) - ball_y_t(2 downto 0);
rom_col <= pix_x(2 downto 0) - ball_x_l(2 downto 0);
```

```
rom_data <= BALL_ROM(to_integer(rom_addr));
rom_bit <= rom_data(to_integer(rom_col));
rd_ball_on <=
   '1' when (sq_ball_on='1') and (rom_bit='1') else
   '0';
-- ball rgb output
ball_rgb <= "100";   -- red
```

The first statement checks whether the current scan coordinates are within the square ball region and asserts the `sq_ball_on` signal accordingly. This part is the same as Listing 12.3 except that signals are used for boundaries. The second part obtains the corresponding ROM bit according to the current scan coordinates. If the scan coordinates are within the square ball region, subtracting the three LSBs from the top boundary (i.e., `ball_y_t`) provides the corresponding ROM row (i.e., `rom_addr`), and subtracting the three LSBs from the left boundary (i.e., `ball_x_l`) provides the corresponding ROM column (i.e., `rom_col`). The bit can then be retrieved by two indexing operations. It is then combined with the `sq_ball_on` signal to generate the `rd_ball_on` signal. This design just assigns a monochrome color (i.e., "100" red) for the round ball region. We can duplicate the pattern ROM three times to store the `rgb` value for each pixel and generate a multiple-color ball.

Finally, we need to make a minor modification in the multiplexing circuit to substitute the `sq_ball_on` signal with the `rd_ball_on` signal:

```
process ...
   ...
     elsif rd_ball_on='1' then
       graph_rgb <= ball_rgb;
   ...
end process;
```

These modifications are incorporated into the animated graph in the next subsection.

12.4.3 Animated object

When an object changes its location gradually in each scan, it creates the illusion of motion and becomes *animated*. To achieve this, we can use registers to store the boundaries of an object and update its value in each scan. In the pong game, the paddle is controlled by two pushbuttons and can move up and down, and the ball can move and bounce in all directions. We illustrate how to create animation for these two objects in this subsection.

While the VGA controller is driven by a 25-MHz pixel rate, the screen of the VGA monitor is refreshed only 60 times per second. The boundary registers only need to be updated at this rate. We create a 60-Hz enable tick, `refr_tick`, which is asserted one clock cycle every $\frac{1}{60}$ second.

Let us first examine the design of the paddle. To accommodate the changing y-axis coordinates, we replace the constants with two signals, `bar_y_t` and `bar_y_b`, to represent the top and bottom boundaries, and create a register, `bar_y_reg`, to store the current y-axis location of the top boundary. If one of the pushbuttons is pressed, `bar_y_reg` either increases or decreases a fixed amount when the `refr_tick` signal is asserted. The amount is defined by a constant, `BAR_V`, which stands for the bar velocity. We assume that assertion of the `btn(1)` and `btn(0)` signals causes the paddle to move up and down, respectively, and that the paddle stops moving when it reaches the top or the bottom of the screen. The code segment for updating `bar_y_reg` is

```
-- new bar y-position
process(bar_y_reg,bar_y_b,bar_y_t,refr_tick,btn)
begin
   bar_y_next <= bar_y_reg; -- default, no move
   if refr_tick='1' then
      if btn(1)='1' and bar_y_b<(MAX_Y-1-BAR_V) then
      -- button 1 asserted and bar not reach bottom yet
         bar_y_next <= bar_y_reg + BAR_V; -- move down
      elsif btn(0)='1' and bar_y_t > BAR_V then
      -- button 0 asserted and bar not reach top yet
         bar_y_next <= bar_y_reg - BAR_V; -- move up
      end if;
   end if;
end process;
```

The design of the ball is more involved. We have to replace the four boundary constants with four signals and create two registers, ball_x_reg and ball_y_reg, to store the current x- and y-axis coordinates of the left and top boundaries. The ball usually moves at a constant velocity (i.e., at a constant speed and in the same direction). It may change direction when hitting the wall, the paddle, or the bottom or top of the screen. We decompose the velocity into an x-component and a y-component, whose values can be either a positive constant value, BALL_V_P, or a negative constant value, BALL_V_N. The current values of the two components are stored in the x_delta_reg and y_delta_reg registers. The code segment for updating ball_x_reg and ball_y_reg is

```
-- new ball position
ball_x_next <=
   ball_x_reg + x_delta_reg when refr_tick='1' else
   ball_x_reg ;
ball_y_next <=
   ball_y_reg + y_delta_reg when refr_tick='1' else
   ball_y_reg ;
```

and the code segment for updating x_delta_reg and y_delta_reg is

```
-- new ball velocity
process(x_delta_reg,y_delta_reg,ball_y_t,ball_x_l,ball_x_r,
        ball_y_t,ball_y_b,bar_y_t,bar_y_b)
begin
   x_delta_next <= x_delta_reg; --default, no change
   y_delta_next <= y_delta_reg; --default, no change
   if ball_y_t < 1 then -- reach top
      y_delta_next <= BALL_V_P; --down
   elsif ball_y_b > (MAX_Y-1) then --reach bottom
      y_delta_next <= BALL_V_N; --up
   elsif ball_x_l <= WALL_X_R  then --reach wall
      x_delta_next <= BALL_V_P; --bounce back (to right)
   elsif (BAR_X_L<=ball_x_r) and (ball_x_r<=BAR_X_R) then
      -- reach x-coordinate of bar
      if (bar_y_t<=ball_y_b) and (ball_y_t<=bar_y_b) then
         -- within y-range of bar, hit
         x_delta_next <= BALL_V_N; --bounce back (to left)
      end if;
   end if;
end process;
```

Note that if the paddle bar misses the ball, the ball continues moving to right and eventually wraps around.

The complete code is shown in Listing 12.5.

Listing 12.5 Pixel-generation circuit for the animated pong game

```
library ieee;
use ieee.std_logic_1164.all;
use ieee.numeric_std.all;
entity pong_graph_animate is
   port(
        clk, reset: std_logic;
        btn: std_logic_vector(1 downto 0);
        video_on: in std_logic;
        pixel_x,pixel_y: in std_logic_vector(9 downto 0);
        graph_rgb: out std_logic_vector(2 downto 0)
   );
end pong_graph_animate;

architecture arch of pong_graph_animate is
   signal refr_tick: std_logic;
   -- x, y coordinates (0,0) to (639,479)
   signal pix_x, pix_y: unsigned(9 downto 0);
   constant MAX_X: integer:=640;
   constant MAX_Y: integer:=480;
   ----------------------------------------------
   -- vertical stripe as a wall
   ----------------------------------------------
   -- wall left, right boundary
   constant WALL_X_L: integer:=32;
   constant WALL_X_R: integer:=35;
   ----------------------------------------------
   -- right paddle bar
   ----------------------------------------------
   -- bar left, right boundary
   constant BAR_X_L: integer:=600;
   constant BAR_X_R: integer:=603;
   -- bar top, bottom boundary
   signal bar_y_t, bar_y_b: unsigned(9 downto 0);
   constant BAR_Y_SIZE: integer:=72;
   -- reg to track top boundary (x position is fixed)
   signal bar_y_reg, bar_y_next: unsigned(9 downto 0);
   -- bar moving velocity when a button is pressed
   constant BAR_V: integer:=4;
   ----------------------------------------------
   -- square ball
   ----------------------------------------------
   constant BALL_SIZE: integer:=8; -- 8
   -- ball left, right boundary
   signal ball_x_l, ball_x_r: unsigned(9 downto 0);
   -- ball top, bottom boundary
   signal ball_y_t, ball_y_b: unsigned(9 downto 0);
   -- reg to track left, top boundary
   signal ball_x_reg, ball_x_next: unsigned(9 downto 0);
```

```
   signal ball_y_reg, ball_y_next: unsigned(9 downto 0);
   -- reg to track ball speed
   signal x_delta_reg, x_delta_next: unsigned(9 downto 0);
   signal y_delta_reg, y_delta_next: unsigned(9 downto 0);
   -- ball velocity can be pos or neg
   constant BALL_V_P: unsigned(9 downto 0)
            :=to_unsigned(2,10);
   constant BALL_V_N: unsigned(9 downto 0)
            :=unsigned(to_signed(-2,10));
   ----------------------------------------------
   -- round ball image ROM
   ----------------------------------------------
   type rom_type is array (0 to 7)
        of std_logic_vector(0 to 7);
   -- ROM definition
   constant BALL_ROM: rom_type :=
   (
      "00111100", --   ****
      "01111110", --  ******
      "11111111", -- ********
      "11111111", -- ********
      "11111111", -- ********
      "11111111", -- ********
      "01111110", --  ******
      "00111100"  --   ****
   );
   signal rom_addr, rom_col: unsigned(2 downto 0);
   signal rom_data: std_logic_vector(7 downto 0);
   signal rom_bit: std_logic;
   ----------------------------------------------
   -- object output signals
   ----------------------------------------------
   signal wall_on, bar_on, sq_ball_on, rd_ball_on: std_logic;
   signal wall_rgb, bar_rgb, ball_rgb:
          std_logic_vector(2 downto 0);
begin
   -- registers
   process (clk,reset)
   begin
      if reset='1' then
         bar_y_reg <= (others=>'0');
         ball_x_reg <= (others=>'0');
         ball_y_reg <= (others=>'0');
         x_delta_reg <= ("0000000100");
         y_delta_reg <= ("0000000100");
      elsif (clk'event and clk='1') then
         bar_y_reg <= bar_y_next;
         ball_x_reg <= ball_x_next;
         ball_y_reg <= ball_y_next;
         x_delta_reg <= x_delta_next;
         y_delta_reg <= y_delta_next;
      end if;
   end process;
```

```
   pix_x <= unsigned(pixel_x);
   pix_y <= unsigned(pixel_y);
   -- refr_tick: 1-clock tick asserted at start of v-sync
   --       i.e., when the screen is refreshed (60 Hz)
   refr_tick <= '1' when (pix_y=481) and (pix_x=0) else
                '0';
   ----------------------------------------------
   -- (wall) left vertical stripe
   ----------------------------------------------
   -- pixel within wall
   wall_on <=
      '1' when (WALL_X_L<=pix_x) and (pix_x<=WALL_X_R) else
      '0';
   -- wall rgb output
   wall_rgb <= "001"; -- blue
   ----------------------------------------------
   -- right vertical bar
   ----------------------------------------------
   -- boundary
   bar_y_t <= bar_y_reg;
   bar_y_b <= bar_y_t + BAR_Y_SIZE - 1;
   -- pixel within bar
   bar_on <=
      '1' when (BAR_X_L<=pix_x) and (pix_x<=BAR_X_R) and
               (bar_y_t<=pix_y) and (pix_y<=bar_y_b) else
      '0';
   -- bar rgb output
   bar_rgb <= "010"; --green
   -- new bar y-position
   process(bar_y_reg,bar_y_b,bar_y_t,refr_tick,btn)
   begin
      bar_y_next <= bar_y_reg; -- no move
      if refr_tick='1' then
         if btn(1)='1' and bar_y_b<(MAX_Y-1-BAR_V) then
            bar_y_next <= bar_y_reg + BAR_V; -- move down
         elsif btn(0)='1' and bar_y_t > BAR_V then
            bar_y_next <= bar_y_reg - BAR_V; -- move up
         end if;
      end if;
   end process;

   ----------------------------------------------
   -- square ball
   ----------------------------------------------
   -- boundary
   ball_x_l <= ball_x_reg;
   ball_y_t <= ball_y_reg;
   ball_x_r <= ball_x_l + BALL_SIZE - 1;
   ball_y_b <= ball_y_t + BALL_SIZE - 1;
   -- pixel within ball
   sq_ball_on <=
      '1' when (ball_x_l<=pix_x) and (pix_x<=ball_x_r) and
               (ball_y_t<=pix_y) and (pix_y<=ball_y_b) else
```

```
      '0';
   -- map current pixel location to ROM addr/col
   rom_addr <= pix_y(2 downto 0) - ball_y_t(2 downto 0);
   rom_col <= pix_x(2 downto 0) - ball_x_l(2 downto 0);
   rom_data <= BALL_ROM(to_integer(rom_addr));
   rom_bit <= rom_data(to_integer(rom_col));
   -- pixel within ball
   rd_ball_on <=
      '1' when (sq_ball_on='1') and (rom_bit='1') else
      '0';
   -- ball rgb output
   ball_rgb <= "100";   -- red
   -- new ball position
   ball_x_next <= ball_x_reg + x_delta_reg
                     when refr_tick='1' else
                  ball_x_reg ;
   ball_y_next <= ball_y_reg + y_delta_reg
                     when refr_tick='1' else
                  ball_y_reg ;
   -- new ball velocity
   process(x_delta_reg,y_delta_reg,ball_y_t,ball_x_l,ball_x_r,
           ball_y_t,ball_y_b,bar_y_t,bar_y_b)
   begin
      x_delta_next <= x_delta_reg;
      y_delta_next <= y_delta_reg;
      if ball_y_t < 1 then -- reach top
         y_delta_next <= BALL_V_P;
      elsif ball_y_b > (MAX_Y-1) then   -- reach bottom
         y_delta_next <= BALL_V_N;
      elsif ball_x_l <= WALL_X_R  then -- reach wall
         x_delta_next <= BALL_V_P;      -- bounce back
      elsif (BAR_X_L<=ball_x_r) and (ball_x_r<=BAR_X_R) then
         -- reach x of right bar
         if (bar_y_t<=ball_y_b) and (ball_y_t<=bar_y_b) then
            x_delta_next <= BALL_V_N; --hit, bounce back
         end if;
      end if;
   end process;
   --------------------------------------------
   -- rgb multiplexing circuit
   --------------------------------------------
   process(video_on,wall_on,bar_on,rd_ball_on,
           wall_rgb, bar_rgb, ball_rgb)
   begin
      if video_on='0' then
          graph_rgb <= "000"; --blank
      else
         if wall_on='1' then
            graph_rgb <= wall_rgb;
         elsif bar_on='1' then
            graph_rgb <= bar_rgb;
         elsif rd_ball_on='1' then
            graph_rgb <= ball_rgb;
```

```
            else
               graph_rgb <= "110"; -- yellow background
            end if;
         end if;
      end process;
   end arch;
```

As in the still screen, we can combine the synchronization circuit and create the top-level description. The HDL code is shown in Listing 12.6.

Listing 12.6 Complete circuit for the animated pong game screen

```
library ieee;
use ieee.std_logic_1164.all;
entity pong_top_an is
   port (
      clk,reset: in std_logic;
      btn: in std_logic_vector (1 downto 0);
      hsync, vsync: out  std_logic;
      rgb: out std_logic_vector(2 downto 0)
   );
end pong_top_an;

architecture arch of pong_top_an is
   signal pixel_x, pixel_y: std_logic_vector (9 downto 0);
   signal video_on, pixel_tick: std_logic;
   signal rgb_reg, rgb_next: std_logic_vector(2 downto 0);
begin
   -- instantiate VGA sync
   vga_sync_unit: entity work.vga_sync
      port map(clk=>clk, reset=>reset,
               video_on=>video_on, p_tick=>pixel_tick,
               hsync=>hsync, vsync=>vsync,
               pixel_x=>pixel_x, pixel_y=>pixel_y);
   -- instantiate graphic generator
   pong_graph_an_unit: entity work.pong_graph_animate
      port map (clk=>clk, reset=>reset,
                btn=>btn, video_on=>video_on,
                pixel_x=>pixel_x, pixel_y=>pixel_y,
                graph_rgb=>rgb_next);
   -- rgb buffer
   process (clk)
   begin
      if (clk'event and clk='1') then
         if (pixel_tick='1') then
            rgb_reg <= rgb_next;
         end if;
      end if;
   end process;
   rgb <= rgb_reg;
end arch;
```

Note that there is no other control mechanism is this code. The ball simply moves and bounces continuously. A top-level control circuit is discussed in Chapter 13.

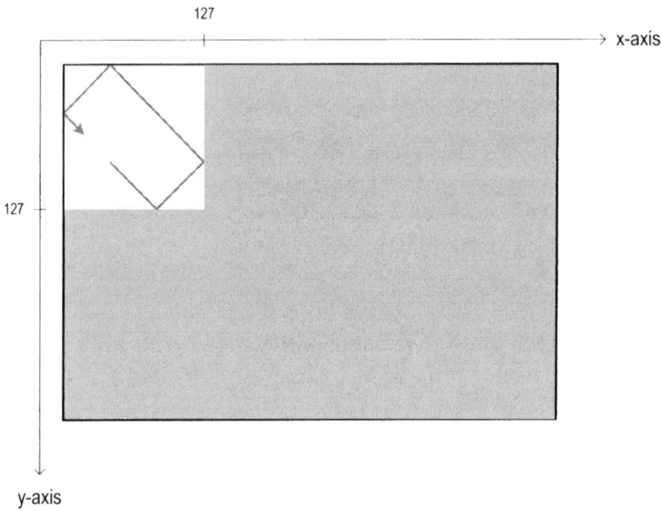

Figure 12.9 Dot trace shown in a 128-by-128 bit map.

12.5 GRAPHIC GENERATION WITH A BIT-MAPPED SCHEME

The bit-mapped scheme maps each pixel to a word in video memory. There are about 310k pixels in a 640-by-480 screen. This translates to 310k and 930k bits for monochrome and color displays, respectively. The actual size of the video memory can be much larger since the memory address must be properly aligned for fast access. For example, to map the pixel's current coordinates to a memory location, we can concatenate the pixel's x-coordinate, which is 10 bits (i.e., $\lceil \log_2(640) \rceil$), and the pixel's y-coordinate, which is 9 bits (i.e., $\lceil \log_2(480) \rceil$). This approach requires no additional circuit to translating the pixel's coordinates to a memory address but introduces some unused "holes" in memory. The memory size is increased from 310k words to 512K (i.e., 2^{10+9}) words.

For the S3 board, memory is available from the external SRAM chips and FPGA's embedded block RAMs, as discussed in Chapters 10 and 11. Recall that the total capacity of the Spartan 3S200 device's block RAM is only about 192K bits. It is not large enough for a full-screen bit-mapped display. We must use the external SRAM, which is 8M bits, for this purpose.

In this section, we use a small 128-by-128 (2^7-by-2^7) area of the screen to illustrate the design of the bit-mapped scheme. The screen has 16K (2^{14}) pixels in this area and requires a 16K-by-3 video memory for color display. This can be implemented by three embedded block RAMs. The small area is at the top-left corner of the screen and displays the trace of a bouncing one-pixel dot, as shown in Figure 12.9. The circuit uses a 3-bit switch to specify the color of the trace and a pushbutton switch to randomly select the origin of the trace. When the pushbutton switch is pressed, the dot starts to move, like the bouncing ball in Section 12.4.3. The trace forms a rectangle after the dot hits the four sides of the small area. A new trace is generated each time the pushbutton switch is pressed.

12.5.1 Dual-port RAM implementation

A conceptual block diagram of this circuit is shown in Figure 12.10. The video memory is a

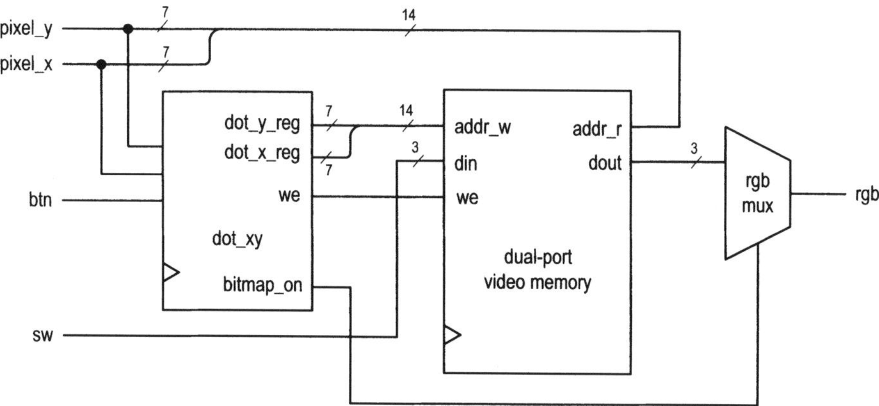

Figure 12.10 Conceptual block diagram of a dot trace circuit.

synchronous 16K-by-3 (i.e., 2^{14}-by-3) dual-port RAM. The dual-port module discussed in Listing 11.4 can be used for this purpose. The seven LSBs of the pixel's y-coordinate form the seven MSBs of the memory address, and the seven LSBs of the pixel's x-coordinate form the seven LSBs of the memory address. The `dot_xy` circuit keeps track of the current location of the dot and generates its current y- and x-coordinates, which are concatenated as the write address. The 3-bit external switch input, `sw`, is the `rgb` value, which is connected to the memory's `din_a` port. The seven LSBs of `pixel_y` and the seven LSBs of `pixel_x` form the read address. The data is retrieved continuously and the corresponding readout is routed to the rgb multiplexing circuit.

The complete code of the dot trace pixel generation circuit is shown in Listing 12.7. We use two registers, `dot_x_reg` and `dot_y_reg`, to keep track of the dot's current x- and y-coordinates and use two registers, `v_x_reg` and `v_y_reg`, to keep track of the current horizontal and vertical velocities. Computation of the dot's coordinates and velocities is similar to that of the bouncing ball in Section 12.4.3. In addition to regular updates, the `dot_x_next` and `dot_y_next` signals obtain the values of the seven LSBs of `pix_x` and `pix_y` when the pushbutton switch is pressed. Since these signals change much faster than a human's perception, the new origin appears to be random.

Listing 12.7 Pixel-generation circuit for a 128-by-128 bit map

```
library ieee;
use ieee.std_logic_1164.all;
use ieee.numeric_std.all;
entity bitmap_gen is
   port(
        clk, reset: std_logic;
        btn: std_logic_vector(1 downto 0);
        sw: std_logic_vector(2 downto 0);
        video_on: in std_logic;
        pixel_x,pixel_y: in std_logic_vector(9 downto 0);
        bit_rgb: out std_logic_vector(2 downto 0)
   );
end bitmap_gen;
```

```
architecture dual_port_ram_arch of bitmap_gen is
   signal pix_x, pix_y: unsigned(9 downto 0);
   signal refr_tick: std_logic;
   signal load_tick: std_logic;
   --------------------------------------------
   -- video sram
   --------------------------------------------
   signal we: std_logic;
   signal addr_r, addr_w: std_logic_vector(13 downto 0);
   signal din, dout: std_logic_vector(2 downto 0);
   --------------------------------------------
   -- dot location and velocity
   --------------------------------------------
   constant MAX_X: integer:=128;
   constant MAX_Y: integer:=128;
   -- dot velocity can be pos or neg
   constant DOT_V_P: unsigned(6 downto 0)
            :=to_unsigned(1,7);
   constant DOT_V_N: unsigned(6 downto 0)
            :=unsigned(to_signed(-1,7));
   -- reg to keep track of dot location
   signal dot_x_reg, dot_x_next: unsigned(6 downto 0);
   signal dot_y_reg, dot_y_next: unsigned(6 downto 0);
   -- reg to keep track of dot velocity
   signal v_x_reg, v_x_next: unsigned(6 downto 0);
   signal v_y_reg, v_y_next: unsigned(6 downto 0);
   --------------------------------------------
   -- object output signals
   --------------------------------------------
   signal bitmap_on: std_logic;
   signal bitmap_rgb: std_logic_vector(2 downto 0);
begin
   -- instantiate debounce circuit for a button
   debounce_unit: entity work.debounce
      port map(clk=>clk, reset=>reset, sw=>btn(0),
               db_level=>open, db_tick=>load_tick);
   -- instantiate dual-port video RAM (2^12-by-7)
   video_ram: entity work.xilinx_dual_port_ram_sync
      generic map(ADDR_WIDTH=>14, DATA_WIDTH=>3)
      port map(clk=>clk, we=>we,
               addr_a=>addr_w, addr_b=>addr_r,
               din_a=>din, dout_a=>open, dout_b=>dout);
   -- video ram interface
   addr_w <= std_logic_vector(dot_y_reg & dot_x_reg);
   addr_r <=
      std_logic_vector(pix_y(6 downto 0) & pix_x(6 downto 0));
   we <= '1';
   din <= sw;
   bitmap_rgb <= dout;
   -- registers
   process (clk,reset)
   begin
      if reset='1' then
```

```
         dot_x_reg <= (others=>'0');
         dot_y_reg <= (others=>'0');
         v_x_reg <= DOT_V_P;
         v_y_reg <= DOT_V_P;
      elsif (clk'event and clk='1') then
         dot_x_reg <= dot_x_next;
         dot_y_reg <= dot_y_next;
         v_x_reg <= v_x_next;
         v_y_reg <= v_y_next;
      end if;
   end process;
   -- misc. signals
   pix_x <= unsigned(pixel_x);
   pix_y <= unsigned(pixel_y);
   refr_tick <= '1' when (pix_y=481) and (pix_x=0) else
                '0';
   -- pixel within bit map area
   bitmap_on <=
      '1' when (pix_x<=127) and (pix_y<=127) else
      '0';
   -- dot position
   -- "randomly" load dot location when btn(0) pressed
   dot_x_next <=
       pix_x(6 downto 0) when load_tick='1' else
       dot_x_reg + v_x_reg when refr_tick='1' else
       dot_x_reg ;
   dot_y_next <=
       pix_y(6 downto 0) when load_tick='1' else
       dot_y_reg + v_y_reg when refr_tick='1' else
   dot_y_reg ;
   -- dot x velocity
   process(v_x_reg,dot_x_reg)
   begin
      v_x_next <= v_x_reg;
      if dot_x_reg =1 then                -- reach left
         v_x_next <= DOT_V_P;             -- bounce back
      elsif dot_x_reg=(MAX_X-2) then      -- reach right
         v_x_next <= DOT_V_N;             -- bounce back
      end if;
   end process;
   -- dot y velocity
   process(v_y_reg,dot_y_reg)
   begin
      v_y_next <= v_y_reg;
      if dot_y_reg =1 then                   -- reach top
         v_y_next <= DOT_V_P;
      elsif dot_y_reg = (MAX_Y-2) then       -- reach bottom
         v_y_next <= DOT_V_N;
      end if;
   end process;
   -- rgb multiplexing circuit
   process(video_on,bitmap_on,bitmap_rgb)
   begin
```

```
      if video_on='0' then
         bit_rgb <= "000"; --blank
      else
         if bitmap_on='1' then
            bit_rgb <= bitmap_rgb;
         else
            bit_rgb <= "110"; -- yellow background
         end if;
      end if;
   end process;
end dual_port_ram_arch;
```

The HDL code for the top-level system is shown in Listing 12.8.

Listing 12.8 Complete circuit for a bit-mapped screen

```
library ieee;
use ieee.std_logic_1164.all;
entity dot_top is
   port (
      clk,reset: in std_logic;
      btn: in std_logic_vector (1 downto 0);
      sw: in std_logic_vector (2 downto 0);
      hsync, vsync: out  std_logic;
      rgb: out std_logic_vector(2 downto 0)
   );
end dot_top;

architecture arch of dot_top is
   signal pixel_x, pixel_y: std_logic_vector(9 downto 0);
   signal video_on, pixel_tick: std_logic;
   signal rgb_reg, rgb_next: std_logic_vector(2 downto 0);
begin
   -- instantiate VGA sync circuit
   vga_sync_unit: entity work.vga_sync
      port map(clk=>clk, reset=>reset,
               hsync=>hsync, vsync=>vsync,
               video_on=>video_on, p_tick=>pixel_tick,
               pixel_x=>pixel_x, pixel_y=>pixel_y);
   -- instantiate bit-mapped pixel generator
   bitmap_unit: entity work.bitmap_gen
      port map(clk=>clk, reset=>reset, btn=>btn, sw=>sw,
               video_on=>video_on, pixel_x=>pixel_x,
               pixel_y=>pixel_y, bit_rgb=>rgb_next);
   -- rgb buffer
   process (clk)
   begin
      if (clk'event and clk='1') then
         if (pixel_tick='1') then
            rgb_reg <= rgb_next;
         end if;
      end if;
   end process;
   rgb <= rgb_reg;
```

```
end arch;
```

12.5.2 Single-port RAM implementation

Although a dual-port memory is ideal, it is not always available. Using regular single-port memory, such as the S3 board's external SRAM, for the video memory requires careful coordination between the write and read operations to avoid interruption on data retrieval. For demonstration purposes, we configure the embedded block RAM as a single-port synchronous SRAM and redesign the previous dot trace circuit.

In the dot trace circuit, the dot's coordinates are updated once every screen scan. Thus, the video memory can be written at this rate as well. We can do this during the vertical retrace since the video is off in this period and writing video memory does not interfere with the screen data retrieval. Note that the `refr_tick` signal is asserted when `pixel_y` is 481. The video is off in this location, and writing video memory will not interfere with the screen data retrieval. We use this signal as the write enable signal, `we`, for the single-port RAM. The single-port RAM module discussed in Listing 11.2 can be used for this purpose. The memory portion of Listing 12.7 now becomes

```
-- instantiate video sram
video_ram: entity work.xilinx_one_port_ram_sync
   generic map(ADDR_WIDTH=>14, DATA_WIDTH=>3)
   port map(clk=>clk, we=>we, addr=>addr,
            din=>din, dout=>dout);
-- video ram interface
addr_w <=std_logic_vector(dot_y_reg & dot_x_reg);
addr_r <=
   std_logic_vector(pix_y(6 downto 0) & pix_x(6 downto 0));
addr <= addr_w when refr_tick='1' else addr_r;
we <= refr_tick;
din <= sw;
bitmap_rgb <= dout;
```

The dot trace circuit updates one pixel in a screen scan. The required memory bandwidth for writing is 60*3 bits per second, which is rather low. Thus, the previous design is fairly straightforward. The design of memory interface becomes much more difficult when a large memory bandwidth is required (i.e., when a large portion of the screen is updated at a rapid rate).

12.6 BIBLIOGRAPHIC NOTES

Rapid Prototyping of Digital Systems by James O. Hamblen et al. contains timing information for monitors with different resolutions and refresh rates.

12.7 SUGGESTED EXPERIMENTS

12.7.1 VGA test pattern generator

A VGA test pattern generator produces two simple patterns to verify operation of a VGA monitor. The first pattern divides the screen evenly into eight vertical stripes, each displaying a unique color. The second pattern is similar but the screen is divided into eight horizontal stripes. A 1-bit switch is used to select the pattern.

Design a pixel generating circuit for this pattern generator and then combine it with the synchronization circuit in a top-level module. Synthesize and verify operation of the circuit.

12.7.2 SVGA mode synchronization circuit

The specification for the super VGA (SVGA) mode with 72-Hz refresh rate is

- *resolution*: 800-by-600 pixels
- *pixel rate*: 50 MHz
- *horizontal display region*: 800 pixels
- *horizontal right border*: 64 pixels
- *horizontal left border*: 56 pixels
- *horizontal retrace*: 120 pixels
- *vertical display region*: 600 lines
- *vertical bottom border*: 23 lines
- *vertical top border*: 37 lines
- *vertical retrace*: 6 lines

We wish to create a dual-mode synchronization circuit that can support both VGA and SVGA modes. The mode can be selected by a switch. Construct the circuit as follows:

1. Modify the horizontal and vertical synchronization counters of Listing 12.1 to accommodate both modes.
2. Design a pixel-generating circuit that draws a 100-pixel grid on the screen (i.e., draw a vertical line every 100 pixels and draw a horizontal line every 100 pixels).
3. Derive a top-level module. Synthesize and verify operation of the two modes.

12.7.3 Visible screen adjustment circuit

Due to the internal timing error of a monitor, the visible portion of the screen may not always be centered. We can adjust the location of the visible portion by slightly modifying the widths surrounding black border areas. In a horizontal scan line, there are 64 pixels for the right and left border regions. To move the visible portion horizontally, we can add a certain number of pixels to one border region and subtract the same number from the opposite border region. We can adjust the visible portion vertically in a similar fashion. Design a screen adjustment circuit as follows:

1. Expand the VGA synchronization circuit to include this feature. Use a switch to select the vertical or horizontal mode, and use two pushbuttons to move the visible screen to left/up and right/down.
2. Modify the testing circuit in Section 12.2.5 to incorporate the new synchronization circuit.
3. Synthesize and verify operation of the circuit.

12.7.4 Ball-in-a-box circuit

The ball-in-a-box circuit displays a bouncing ball inside a square box. The square box is centered on the screen and its size is 256-by-256 pixels. The ball is an 8-by-8 round ball. When the ball hits the wall, the ball bounces back and the wall flashes (i.e., changes color briefly). The ball can travel at four different speeds, which are selected by two slide

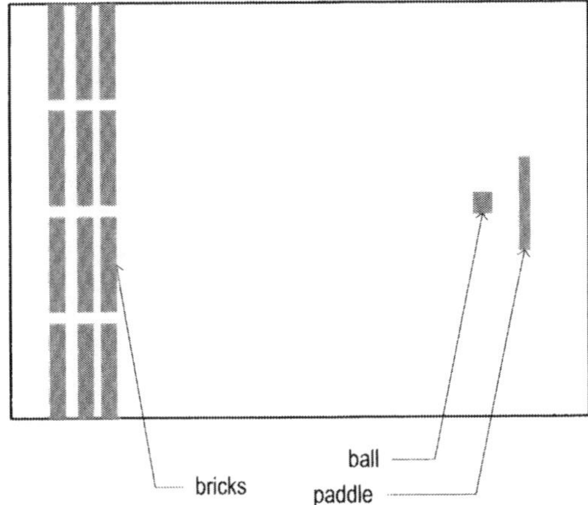

Figure 12.11 Screen of the breakout game.

switches, and its direction changes randomly when a pushbutton switch is pressed. Derive the HDL code and then synthesize and verify operation of the circuit.

12.7.5 Two-balls-in-a-box circuit

We can expand the circuit in Experiment 12.7.4 to include two balls inside the box. When two balls collide, the new directions of the two balls should follow the laws of physics. Derive the HDL code and then synthesize and verify operation of the circuit.

12.7.6 Two-player pong game

The two-player pong game replaces the left wall with another paddle, which is controlled by the second player. To better accommodate two players, we can use the keyboard interface of Section 8.4 as the input device. Four keys can be defined to control vertical movements of the two paddles. Derive the HDL code and then synthesize and verify operation of the circuit.

12.7.7 Breakout game

The breakout game is a somewhat like the pong game. In this game, the left wall is replaced by several layers of "bricks." When the ball hits a brick, the ball bounces back and the brick disappears. The basic screen is shown in Figure 12.11. As in the code of Listing 12.5, we assume that the game runs continuously. Derive the HDL code and then synthesize and verify operation of the circuit.

12.7.8 Full-screen dot trace

We can implement the full-screen dot trace circuit of Section 12.5 using the external SRAM chip as follows:

1. Modify the SRAM controller in Chapter 10 to configure the SRAM chip as a 2^{19}-by-8 memory.

2. Follow the discussion in Section 12.5.2 to incorporate the new memory module in the circuit. Note that accessing the external memory requires two clock cycles.
3. Synthesize and verify operation of the circuit.

12.7.9 Mouse pointer circuit

The mouse interface is discussed in Section 9.5. The mouse pointer circuit uses a mouse to control the movement of a small 16-by-16 square on the screen. It functions as follows:

- The square moves according to the movement of the mouse.
- The pointer wraps around when it reaches a border.
- The pointer changes color when the left button of the mouse is pressed. It circulates through the eight colors defined in Table 12.1.

Synthesize and verify operation of the circuit.

12.7.10 Small-screen mouse scribble circuit

Mouse scribble circuit keeps track of the trace of the mouse movement in a 128-by-128 screen, somewhat similar to the dot trace circuit discussed in Section 12.5. Its specification is as follows:

- The 3-bit switch determines the color of the trace.
- Clicking the left button of the mouse turns on and off the trace alternately.
- Clicking the right button of the mouse clears the screen.

Synthesize and verify operation of the circuit.

12.7.11 Full-screen mouse scribble circuit

Repeat Experiment 12.7.10, but use the full screen. An external SRAM module similar to that in Experiment 12.7.8 is needed for this circuit.

CHAPTER 13

VGA CONTROLLER II: TEXT

13.1 INTRODUCTION

A tile-mapped pixel generation scheme is discussed in Section 12.3. A tile can be considered as a "super pixel." Whereas a pixel is defined by a 3-bit word in a bit-mapped scheme, a tile is mapped to a predesigned pattern. One method of constructing a text display is to treat the characters as tiles and design the pixel generation circuit with the tile-mapped scheme. We discuss this method in this chapter and apply it to add scores and rules to the pong game.

13.2 TEXT GENERATION

13.2.1 Character as a tile

When applying a tile-mapped scheme, we treat each character as a tile. In a bit-mapped scheme, the value of a pixel represents a 3-bit color. On the other hand, the value of a tile represents the code of a specific pattern. For the text display, we use the 7-bit ASCII code for the character tiles.

The patterns of the tiles constitute the *font* of the character set. A variety of fonts are available. We choose an 8-by-16 (i.e., 8-column-by-16-row) font similar to the one used in early IBM PC. In this font, each character is represented as an 8-by-16 pixel pattern. The pattern for the letter "A" is shown in Figure 13.1(a).

The character patterns are stored in a ROM and each pattern requires $2^4 * 8$ bits. The pattern memory is known as *font ROM*. The original font set consists of 256 patterns,

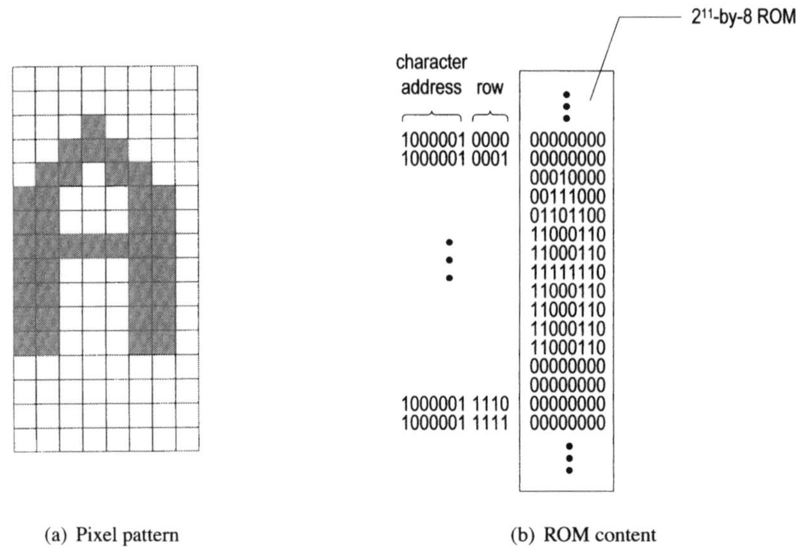

(a) Pixel pattern

(b) ROM content

Figure 13.1 Font pattern for the letter A.

including digits, upper- and lowercase letters, punctuation symbols, and many special-purpose graphic symbols. We implement only the first half [i.e., 128 (2^7)] of the patterns and exclude most graphic symbols. To accommodate this set, $2^7 * 2^4 * 8$ ROM bits are needed. It is usually configured as a 2^{11}-by-8 ROM.

When we use these 8-by-16 characters (i.e., tiles) in a 640-by-480 resolution screen, 80 (i.e., $\frac{640}{8}$) tiles can be fitted into a horizontal line and 30 (i.e., $\frac{480}{16}$) tiles can be fitted into a vertical line. In other words, the screen can be treated as an 80-by-25 tile screen. We can put characters on the screen using these scaled coordinates.

13.2.2 Font ROM

Our font set implements the 128 characters of the ASCII code, listed in Table 7.1. The 128 (2^7) character patterns can be accommodated by a 2^{11}-by-8 font ROM. In this ROM, the seven MSBs of the 11-bit address are used to identify the character, and the four LSBs of the address are used to identify the row within a character pattern. The address and ROM content for the letter "A" are shown in Figure 13.1(b).

In the ASCII table, the first column (ASCII codes 00_{16} to $1F_{16}$) are nonprintable control characters. The font ROM uses these codes to implement special graphic symbols. For example, the 06_{16} code will generate a spade pattern, ♠, on the screen. Note that the 00_{16} code is reserved for a blank tile.

The 2^{11}-by-8 font ROM can fit neatly into a single block RAM of the Spartan-3 device. We use the ROM template of Listing 11.6 to ensure that a block RAM will be inferred during synthesis. Part of the HDL code is shown in Listing 13.1. The complete code has 2^{11} rows in constant definition and the file can be downloaded from the companion Web site.

Listing 13.1 Partial code of the font ROM

```
library ieee;
use ieee.std_logic_1164.all;
use ieee.numeric_std.all;
entity font_rom is
   port(
      clk: in std_logic;
      addr: in std_logic_vector(10 downto 0);
      data: out std_logic_vector(7 downto 0)
   );
end font_rom;

architecture arch of font_rom is
   constant ADDR_WIDTH: integer:=11;
   constant DATA_WIDTH: integer:=8;
   signal addr_reg: std_logic_vector(ADDR_WIDTH-1 downto 0);
   type rom_type is array (0 to 2**ADDR_WIDTH-1)
        of std_logic_vector(DATA_WIDTH-1 downto 0);
   -- ROM definition
   constant ROM: rom_type:=(   -- 2^11-by-8
   -- code x00 (blank space)
   "00000000", -- 0
   "00000000", -- 1
   "00000000", -- 2
   "00000000", -- 3
   "00000000", -- 4
   "00000000", -- 5
   "00000000", -- 6
   "00000000", -- 7
   "00000000", -- 8
   "00000000", -- 9
   "00000000", -- a
   "00000000", -- b
   "00000000", -- c
   "00000000", -- d
   "00000000", -- e
   "00000000", -- f
   -- code x01 (smiley face)
   "00000000", -- 0
   "00000000", -- 1
   "01111110", -- 2  ******
   "10000001", -- 3 *      *
   "10100101", -- 4 * *  * *
   "10000001", -- 5 *      *
   "10000001", -- 6 *      *
   "10111101", -- 7 * **** *
   "10011001", -- 8 *  **  *
   "10000001", -- 9 *      *
   "10000001", -- a *      *
   "01111110", -- b  ******
   "00000000", -- c
   "00000000", -- d
   "00000000", -- e
```

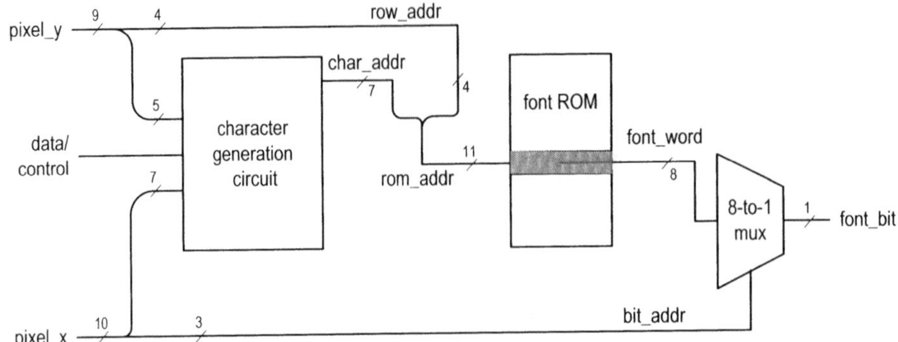

Figure 13.2 Two-stage text generation circuit.

```
      "00000000", -- f
      -- code x02
      . . .
      );
begin
   -- addr register to infer block RAM
   process (clk)
   begin
      if (clk'event and clk = '1') then
        addr_reg <= addr;
      end if;
   end process;
   data <= ROM(to_integer(unsigned(addr_reg)));
end arch;
```

Note that the block RAM-based ROM implementation introduces one-clock-cycle delay, as discussed in Section 11.4.3.

13.2.3 Basic text generation circuit

The pixel generation circuit generates the pixel values according to the current pixel coordinates (provided by the `pixel_x` and `pixel_y` signals) and the external data and control signals. Pixel generation based on a tile-mapped scheme involves two stages. The first stage uses the upper bits of the `pixel_x` and `pixel_y` signals to generate a tile's code, and the second stage uses this code and lower bits to generate the pixel's value.

The text generation circuit follows this method, and the basic diagram is shown in Figure 13.2. The screen is treated as a grid of 80-by-30 tiles, each containing an 8-by-16 font pattern. In the first stage, the `pixel_x(9 downto 3)` and `pixel_y(8 downto 4)` signals provides the x- and y-coordinates of the current tile location. The character generation circuit uses these coordinates, combined with other external data, to generate the value of this tile (labeled `char_addr`), which corresponds to a character's ASCII code. In the second stage, the ASCII code becomes the seven MSBs of the address of the font ROM and specifies the location of the current pattern. It is concatenated with the four LSBs of the screen's y-coordinate [i.e., `pixel_y(3 downto 0)`, labeled `row_addr`] to form the complete address (labeled `rom_addr`) of the font ROM. The output of the font ROM (labeled `font_word`) corresponds to an 8-bit row in the pattern. The three LSBs of the screen's x-coordinate [i.e., pixel_x(2 downto 0), labeled bit_addr] specify the desired pixel location, and an 8-to-1 multiplexer routes the pixel to the output.

13.2.4 Font display circuit

We use a simple font display circuit to verify operation of the font ROM and display all font patterns on the screen. The 128 patterns are arranged in four rows, which correspond to the four columns of the ASCII table in Table 7.1. We can obtain each pattern by using the proper x- and y-coordinates to generate the desired ASCII code, which is labeled the char_addr signal. The code segment is

```
char_addr <= pixel_y(5 downto 4) & pixel_x(7 downto 3);
```

The pixel_x(7 downto 3) signal forms the five LSBs of the ASCII code, and thus 32 (2^5) consecutive font patterns will be displayed in a row. The pixel_y(5 downto 4) signal forms the two MSBs of the ASCII code, and thus four consecutive rows will be displayed. Since the upper bits of the pixel_x and pixel_y signals are left unspecified, the 32-by-4 region will be displayed repetitively on the screen. An additional code segment is included to turn on the display for the top-left portion of the screen only. The complete code is shown in Listing 13.2.

Listing 13.2 Pixel generation of a font display circuit

```
library ieee;
use ieee.std_logic_1164.all;
use ieee.numeric_std.all;
entity font_test_gen is
   port(
      clk: in std_logic;
      video_on: in std_logic;
      pixel_x, pixel_y: std_logic_vector(9 downto 0);
      rgb_text: out std_logic_vector(2 downto 0)
   );
end font_test_gen;

architecture arch of font_test_gen is
   signal rom_addr: std_logic_vector(10 downto 0);
   signal char_addr: std_logic_vector(6 downto 0);
   signal row_addr: std_logic_vector(3 downto 0);
   signal bit_addr: std_logic_vector(2 downto 0);
   signal font_word: std_logic_vector(7 downto 0);
   signal font_bit, text_bit_on: std_logic;
begin
   -- instantiate font ROM
   font_unit: entity work.font_rom
      port map(clk=>clk, addr=>rom_addr, data=>font_word);
   -- font ROM interface
   char_addr<=pixel_y(5 downto 4) & pixel_x(7 downto 3);
   row_addr<=pixel_y(3 downto 0);
   rom_addr <= char_addr & row_addr;
   bit_addr<=pixel_x(2 downto 0);
   font_bit <= font_word(to_integer(unsigned(not bit_addr)));
   -- "on" region limited to top-left corner
   text_bit_on <=
```

```
      font_bit when pixel_x(9 downto 8)="00" and
                    pixel_y(9 downto 6)="0000" else
      '0';
   -- rgb multiplexing circuit
   process(video_on,font_bit,text_bit_on)
   begin
      if video_on='0' then
          rgb_text <= "000"; --blank
      else
        if text_bit_on='1' then
            rgb_text <= "010"; -- green
        else
            rgb_text <= "000"; -- black
        end if;
      end if;
   end process;
end arch;
```

The key part of the code is the font ROM interface. For clarity, we define the following signals for the font ROM, as shown in Figure 13.2:

- `char_addr`: 7 bits, the ASCII code of the character
- `row_addr`: 4 bits, the row number in a particular font pattern
- `rom_addr`: 11 bits, the address of the font ROM; the concatenation of `char_addr` and `row_addr`
- `bit_addr`: 3 bits, the column number in a particular font pattern
- `font_word`: 8 bits, a row of pixels of the font pattern specified by `rom_addr`
- `font_bit`: 1 bit, one pixel of `font_word` specified by `bit_addr`

The connection of these signals follows the diagram in Figure 13.2. The routing of the `font_bit` signal is done by a multiplexer, coded as an array with dynamic index:

```
font_bit <= font_word(to_integer(unsigned(not bit_addr)));
```

Note that a row (i.e., a word) in the font ROM is defined with a descending order [i.e., `(7 downto 0)`]. Since the screen's x-coordinate is defined in an ascending fashion, in which the numbers increases from left to right, the order of the retrieved bits must be reversed. This is achieved by the **not** operator in the expression.

We need to combine the synchronization circuit and create the top-level description. The HDL code is shown in Listing 13.3.

Listing 13.3 Top-level description of a font display circuit

```
library ieee;
use ieee.std_logic_1164.all;
use ieee.numeric_std.all;
entity font_test_top is
   port(
      clk, reset: in std_logic;
      hsync, vsync: out  std_logic;
      rgb: out std_logic_vector(2 downto 0)
   );
end font_test_top;

architecture arch of font_test_top is
   signal pixel_x, pixel_y: std_logic_vector(9 downto 0);
```

```
   signal video_on, pixel_tick: std_logic;
   signal rgb_reg, rgb_next: std_logic_vector(2 downto 0);
begin
   -- instantiate VGA sync circuit
   vga_sync_unit: entity work.vga_sync
      port map(clk=>clk, reset=>reset, hsync=>hsync,
               vsync=>vsync, video_on=>video_on,
               pixel_x=>pixel_x, pixel_y=>pixel_y,
               p_tick=>pixel_tick);
   -- instantiate font ROM
   font_gen_unit: entity work.font_test_gen
      port map(clk=>clk, video_on=>video_on,
               pixel_x=>pixel_x, pixel_y=>pixel_y,
               rgb_text=>rgb_next);
   -- rgb buffer
   process (clk)
   begin
      if (clk'event and clk='1') then
         if (pixel_tick='1') then
            rgb_reg <= rgb_next;
         end if;
      end if;
   end process;
   rgb <= rgb_reg;
end arch;
```

There is subtle timing issue in this circuit. Because of the block RAM implementation, the font ROM's output suffers a one-clock-cycle delay. However, since the pixel_tick signal is asserted every two clock cycles, the pixel_x signal is remained unchanged within this interval and the corresponding bit (i.e., font_bit) can be retrieved properly. The rgb multiplexing circuit can use this data, and the desired value is stored to the rgb_reg register in a timely manner.

13.2.5 Font scaling

In the tile-mapped scheme, we can scale a tile pattern to larger sizes by "enlarging" the screen pixels. For example, we can scale the 8-by-16 font to the 16-by-32 font by enlarging the original pixel four times (i.e., expanding one pixel to four pixels). To perform the scaling, we just need to shift pixel coordinates to the right 1 bit and discard the LSBs of the pixel_x and pixel_y signals. This can best be explained by an example. Let us repeat the previous font displaying circuit with enlarged 16-by-32 fonts. The screen can now be treated as a grid of 40-by-15 tiles. The new font addresses become

```
row_addr<=pixel_y(4 downto 1);
bit_addr<=pixel_x(3 downto 1);
char_addr<=pixel_y(6 downto 5) & pixel_x(8 downto 4);
```

The first two statements imply that the same font_bit value will be obtained when pixel_x(0) and pixel_y(0) are "00", "01", "10", and "11", and this effectively enlarges the original pixel to four pixels. The text_bit_on condition also needs to be modified to accommodate a larger region:

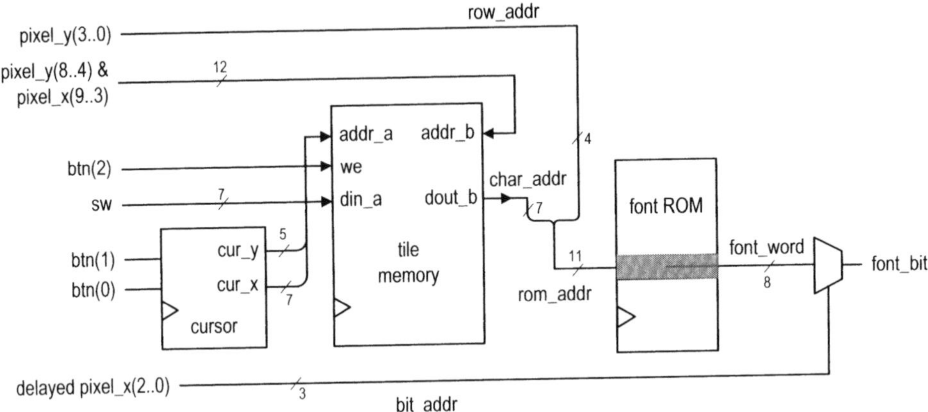

Figure 13.3 Text generation circuit with tile memory.

```
text_bit_on <=
   font_bit when pixel_x(9)="0" and
                 pixel_y(9 downto 7)="000" else
   '0';
```

We can apply this scheme to scale up the font even further. Note that the enlarged fonts may appear jagged because they simply magnify the original pattern and introduce no new detail.

13.3 FULL-SCREEN TEXT DISPLAY

A full-screen text display, as the name indicates, uses the entire screen to display text characters. The character generation circuit now contains a *tile memory* that stores the ASCII code of each tile. The design of the tile memory is similar to the video memory of the bit-mapped circuit in Section 12.5. For easy memory access, we can concatenate the x- and y-coordinates of a tile to form the address. This translates to 12 bits for the 80-by-30 (i.e., 2^7-by-2^5) tile screen. Since each tile contains a 7-bit ASCII code, a 2^{12}-by-7 memory module is required. A synchronous dual-port RAM can be used for this purpose. A circuit with tile memory is shown in Figure 13.3.

Because accessing tile memory requires another clock cycle, retrieving a font pattern is now increased to two clock cycles. This prolonged delay introduces a subtle timing problem. Because the `pixel_x` signal is updated every two clock cycles, its value has incremented when the `font_word` value becomes available. Thus, when the bit is retrieved by the statements

```
bit_addr<=pixel_x(2 downto 0);
font_bit <= font_word(to_integer(unsigned(not bit_addr)));
```

the incremented `bit_addr` is used and an incorrect font bit will be selected and routed to the output. One way to overcome the problem is to pass the `pixel_x` signal through two buffers and use this delayed signal in place of the `pixel_x` signal.

We use a simple circuit to demonstrate the design of the full-screen tile-mapped scheme. The circuit reads an ASCII code from a 7-bit switch and places it in the marked location of the 80-by-30 tile screen. The conceptual diagram is shown in Figure 13.3. A cursor is included to mark the current location of entry, where the color is reversed. The cursor block keeps track of the current location of the cursor. The circuit uses three pushbutton switches for control. Two buttons move the cursor right and down, respectively. The third button is for the write operation. When it is pressed, the current value of the 7-bit switch is written to the tile memory. The HDL code is shown in Listing 13.4.

Listing 13.4 Pixel generation of a full-screen text display

```
library ieee;
use ieee.std_logic_1164.all;
use ieee.numeric_std.all;
entity text_screen_gen is
   port(
      clk, reset: std_logic;
      btn: std_logic_vector(2 downto 0);
      sw: std_logic_vector(6 downto 0);
      video_on: in std_logic;
      pixel_x, pixel_y: in std_logic_vector(9 downto 0);
      text_rgb: out std_logic_vector(2 downto 0)
   );
end text_screen_gen;

architecture arch of text_screen_gen is
   -- font ROM
   signal char_addr: std_logic_vector(6 downto 0);
   signal rom_addr: std_logic_vector(10 downto 0);
   signal row_addr: std_logic_vector(3 downto 0);
   signal bit_addr: unsigned(2 downto 0);
   signal font_word: std_logic_vector(7 downto 0);
   signal font_bit: std_logic;
   -- tile RAM
   signal we: std_logic;
   signal addr_r, addr_w: std_logic_vector(11 downto 0);
   signal din, dout: std_logic_vector(6 downto 0);
   -- 80-by-30 tile map
   constant MAX_X: integer:=80;
   constant MAX_Y: integer:=30;
   -- cursor
   signal cur_x_reg, cur_x_next: unsigned(6 downto 0);
   signal cur_y_reg, cur_y_next: unsigned(4 downto 0);
   signal move_x_tick, move_y_tick: std_logic;
   signal cursor_on: std_logic;
   -- delayed pixel count
   signal pix_x1_reg, pix_y1_reg: unsigned(9 downto 0);
   signal pix_x2_reg, pix_y2_reg: unsigned(9 downto 0);
   -- object output signals
   signal font_rgb, font_rev_rgb:
            std_logic_vector(2 downto 0);
begin
   -- instantiate debounce circuit for two buttons
   debounce_unit0: entity work.debounce
      port map(clk=>clk, reset=>reset, sw=>btn(0),
               db_level=>open, db_tick=>move_x_tick);
```

```
 debounce_unit1: entity work.debounce
    port map(clk=>clk, reset=>reset, sw=>btn(1),
             db_level=>open, db_tick=>move_y_tick);
-- instantiate font ROM
font_unit: entity work.font_rom
   port map(clk=>clk, addr=>rom_addr, data=>font_word);
-- instantiate dual-port tile RAM (2^12-by-7)
video_ram: entity work.xilinx_dual_port_ram_sync
   generic map(ADDR_WIDTH=>12, DATA_WIDTH=>7)
   port map(clk=>clk, we=>we,
            addr_a=>addr_w, addr_b=>addr_r,
            din_a=>din, dout_a=>open, dout_b=>dout);
-- registers
process (clk)
begin
  if (clk'event and clk='1') then
      cur_x_reg <= cur_x_next;
      cur_y_reg <= cur_y_next;
      pix_x1_reg <= unsigned(pixel_x); -- 2-clock delay
      pix_x2_reg <= pix_x1_reg;
      pix_y1_reg <= unsigned(pixel_y);
      pix_y2_reg <= pix_y1_reg;
  end if;
end process;
-- tile RAM write
addr_w <=std_logic_vector(cur_y_reg & cur_x_reg);
we <= btn(2);
din <= sw;
-- tile RAM read
-- use undelayed coordinates to form tile RAM address
addr_r <=pixel_y(8 downto 4) & pixel_x(9 downto 3);
char_addr <= dout;
-- font ROM
row_addr<=pixel_y(3 downto 0);
rom_addr <= char_addr & row_addr;
-- use delayed coordinate to select a bit
bit_addr<=pix_x2_reg(2 downto 0);
font_bit <= font_word(to_integer(not bit_addr));
-- new cursor position
cur_x_next <=
   (others=>'0') when move_x_tick='1' and -- wrap around
                      cur_x_reg=MAX_X-1 else
   cur_x_reg + 1  when move_x_tick='1' else
   cur_x_reg ;
cur_y_next <=
   (others=>'0') when move_y_tick='1' and -- wrap around
                      cur_y_reg=MAX_Y-1 else
   cur_y_reg + 1  when move_y_tick='1' else
   cur_y_reg;
-- object signals
-- green over black and reversed video for curser
font_rgb <="010" when font_bit='1' else "000";
font_rev_rgb <="000" when font_bit='1' else "010";
```

```
   -- use delayed coordinates for comparison
   cursor_on <='1' when pix_y2_reg(8 downto 4)=cur_y_reg and
                        pix_x2_reg(9 downto 3)=cur_x_reg else
             '0';
   -- rgb multiplexing circuit
   process(video_on,cursor_on,font_rgb,font_rev_rgb)
   begin
      if video_on='0' then
         text_rgb <= "000"; --blank
      else
         if cursor_on='1' then
            text_rgb <= font_rev_rgb;
         else
            text_rgb <= font_rgb;
         end if;
      end if;
   end process;
end arch;
```

The font ROM interface signals are similar to those in Listing 13.2 except that the char_addr is obtained from the read port of the tile memory. To facilitate the font ROM access delay, we creat two delayed signals, pix_x2_reg and pix_y2_reg, from the current x- and y-coordinates, pixel_x and pixel_y. Note that the undelayed signals, pixel_x and pixel_y, are used to form the address to access the font ROM, but the delayed signal, pix_x2_reg, is used to obtain the font bit. The instantiation and interface of the dual-port tile RAM is similar to those of the video RAM in Listing 12.7.

The cursor_on signal is used to identify the current cursor location. The colors of the font pattern are reversed in this location. Because the font bits are delayed by two clocks, we use the delayed coordinates, pix_x2_reg and pix_y2_reg, for comparison.

The delayed font bits also introduce one pixel delay for the final rgb signal. This implies the overall visible portion of the VGA monitor is shifted to right by one pixel. To correct the problem, we should revise the vga_sync circuit and use the delayed pix_x2_reg and pix_y2_reg signals to generate the hsync and vsync signals. Since the shift has little effect on the overall video quality, we do not make this modification.

The top-level code combines the text pixel generation circuit and the synchronization circuit and is shown in Listing 13.5.

Listing 13.5 Top-level system of a full-screen text display

```
library ieee;
use ieee.std_logic_1164.all;
entity text_screen_top is
   port(
      clk,reset: in std_logic;
      btn: in std_logic_vector (2 downto 0);
      sw: in std_logic_vector (6 downto 0);
      hsync, vsync: out  std_logic;
      rgb: out std_logic_vector(2 downto 0)
   );
end text_screen_top;

architecture arch of text_screen_top is
   signal pixel_x, pixel_y: std_logic_vector(9 downto 0);
```

```
   signal video_on, pixel_tick: std_logic;
   signal rgb_reg, rgb_next: std_logic_vector(2 downto 0);
begin
   -- instantiate VGA sync circuit
   vga_sync_unit: entity work.vga_sync
      port map(clk=>clk, reset=>reset,
               hsync=>hsync, vsync=>vsync,
               video_on=>video_on, p_tick=>pixel_tick,
               pixel_x=>pixel_x, pixel_y=>pixel_y);
   -- instantiate full-screen text generator
   text_gen_unit: entity work.text_screen_gen
      port map(clk=>clk, reset=>reset, btn=>btn, sw=>sw,
               video_on=>video_on, pixel_x=>pixel_x,
               pixel_y=>pixel_y, text_rgb=>rgb_next);
   -- rgb buffer
   process (clk)
   begin
      if (clk'event and clk='1') then
         if (pixel_tick='1') then
            rgb_reg <= rgb_next;
         end if;
      end if;
   end process;
   rgb <= rgb_reg;
end arch;
```

13.4 THE COMPLETE PONG GAME

We create a free-running graphic circuit for the pong game in Section 12.4.3. In this section, we add a text interface to display scores and messages, and design a top-level control FSM that integrates the graphic and text subsystems and coordinates the overall circuit operation. The rules and operations of the complete game are:

- When the game starts, it displays the text of the rule.
- After a player presses a button, the game starts.
- The player scores a point each time hitting the ball with the paddle.
- When the player misses the ball, the game pauses and a new ball is provided. Three balls are provided in each session.
- The score and the number of remaining balls are displayed on the top of the screen.
- After three misses, the game is ended and displays the end-of-game message.

In the following subsections, we first discuss the text subsystem, graphic subsystem, and auxiliary counters, and then derive a top-level FSM to coordinate and control the overall operation. The conceptual diagram is shown in Figure 13.4.

13.4.1 Text subsystem

The text subsystem of the pong game consists of four text messages:

- Display the score as "`Scores: DD`" and the number of remaining balls as"`Ball: D`" in 16-by-32 font on top of the screen.

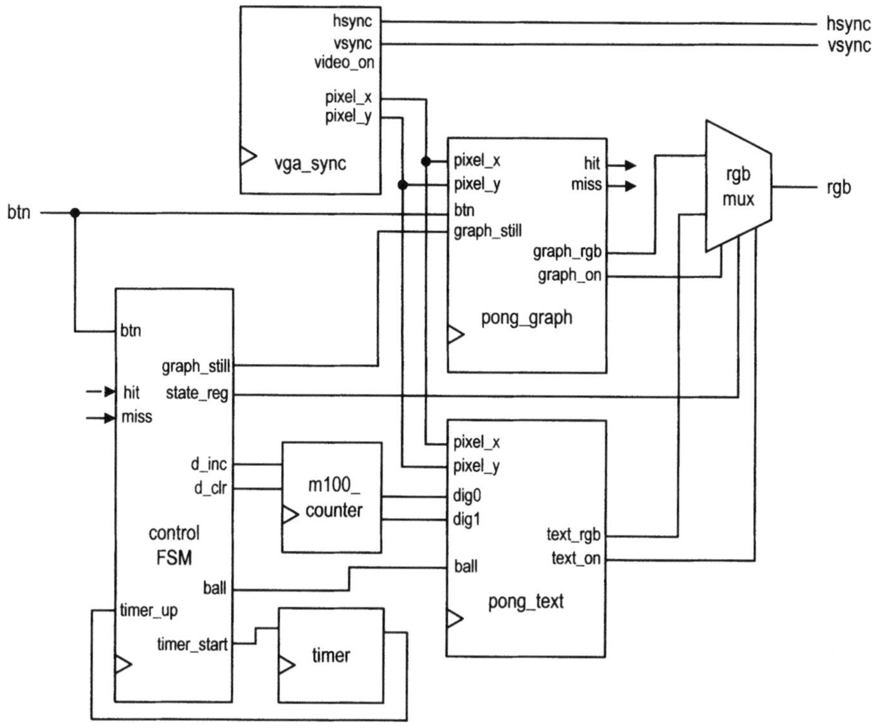

Figure 13.4 Top-level block diagram of the complete pong game.

- Display the rule message "`Rules: Use two buttons to move paddle up or down.`" in regular font at the beginning of the game.
- Display the "`PONG`" logo in 64-by-128 font on the background.
- Display the end-of-game message "`Game Over`" in 32-by-64 font at the end of the game.

A sketch of the first three messages is shown in Figure 13.5. The end-of-game message is overlapped with the rule message and not included.

Since these messages use different font sizes and are displayed at different occasions, they cannot be treated as a single screen. We treat each text message as an individual object and generate the on status signal and the font ROM address. For example, the logo message segment is

```
logo_on <=
   '1' when pix_y(9 downto 7)=2 and
      (3<= pix_x(9 downto 6) and pix_x(9 downto 6)<=6) else
   '0';
row_addr_l <= std_logic_vector(pix_y(6 downto 3));
bit_addr_l <= std_logic_vector(pix_x(5 downto 3));
with pix_x(8 downto 6) select
  char_addr_l <=
     "1010000" when "011", -- P x50
     "1001111" when "100", -- O x4f
     "1001110" when "101", -- N x4e
```

Figure 13.5 Text of the pong game.

```
           "1000111" when others; --G x47
```

The `logo_on` signal indicates that the current scan is in the logo region and the corresponding text should be "turned on." The other statements specify the message content and the font ROM connections to generate the scaled 32-by-64 characters. The other three segments are similar. A separate multiplexing circuit examines various on signals and routes one set of addresses to the font ROM.

The text subsystem receives the score and the number of remaining balls via the `ball`, `dig0`, and `dig1` ports. It outputs the `rgb` information via the `rgb_text` port and outputs the on status information via the 4-bit `text_on` port, which is the concatenation of four individual on signals. The complete code is shown in Listing 13.6.

Listing 13.6 Text subsystem for the pong game

```
library ieee;
use ieee.std_logic_1164.all;
use ieee.numeric_std.all;
entity pong_text is
   port(
      clk, reset: in std_logic;
      pixel_x, pixel_y: in std_logic_vector(9 downto 0);
      dig0, dig1: in std_logic_vector(3 downto 0);
      ball: in std_logic_vector(1 downto 0);
      text_on: out std_logic_vector(3 downto 0);
      text_rgb: out std_logic_vector(2 downto 0)
   );
end pong_text;

architecture arch of pong_text is
   signal pix_x, pix_y: unsigned(9 downto 0);
   signal rom_addr: std_logic_vector(10 downto 0);
   signal char_addr, char_addr_s, char_addr_l, char_addr_r,
          char_addr_o: std_logic_vector(6 downto 0);
   signal row_addr, row_addr_s, row_addr_l,row_addr_r,
          row_addr_o: std_logic_vector(3 downto 0);
   signal bit_addr, bit_addr_s, bit_addr_l,bit_addr_r,
          bit_addr_o: std_logic_vector(2 downto 0);
```

```
signal font_word: std_logic_vector(7 downto 0);
signal font_bit: std_logic;
signal score_on, logo_on, rule_on, over_on: std_logic;
signal rule_rom_addr: unsigned(5 downto 0);
type rule_rom_type is array (0 to 63) of
    std_logic_vector (6 downto 0);
-- rule text ROM definition
constant RULE_ROM: rule_rom_type :=
(
   -- row 1
   "1010010", -- R
   "1010101", -- U
   "1001100", -- L
   "1000101", -- E
   "0111010", -- :
   "0000000", --
   "0000000", --
   "0000000", --
   "0000000", --
   "0000000", --
   "0000000", --
   "0000000", --
   "0000000", --
   "0000000", --
   "0000000", --
   "0000000", --
   -- row 2
   "1010101", -- U
   "1110011", -- s
   "1100101", -- e
   "0000000", --
   "1110100", -- t
   "1110111", -- w
   "1101111", -- o
   "0000000", --
   "1100010", -- b
   "1110101", -- u
   "1110100", -- t
   "1110100", -- t
   "1101111", -- o
   "1101110", -- n
   "1110011", -- s
   "0000000", --
   -- row 3
   "1110100", -- t
   "1101111", -- o
   "0000000", --
   "1101101", -- m
   "1101111", -- o
   "1110110", -- v
   "1100101", -- e
   "0000000", --
   "1110000", -- p
```

```
         "1100001", -- a
         "1100100", -- d
         "1100100", -- d
         "1101100", -- l
         "1100101", -- e
         "0000000", --
         "0000000", --
         -- row 4
         "1110101", -- u
         "1110000", -- p
         "0000000", --
         "1100001", -- a
         "1101110", -- n
         "1100100", -- d
         "0000000", --
         "1100100", -- d
         "1101111", -- o
         "1110111", -- w
         "1101110", -- n
         "0101110", -- .
         "0000000", --
         "0000000", --
         "0000000", --
         "0000000"  --
      );
begin
   pix_x <= unsigned(pixel_x);
   pix_y <= unsigned(pixel_y);
   -- instantiate font ROM
   font_unit: entity work.font_rom
      port map(clk=>clk, addr=>rom_addr, data=>font_word);

   ---------------------------------------------------------
   -- score region
   --   - display score and ball at top left
   --   - text: "Score:DD Ball:D"
   --   - scale to 16-by-32 font
   ---------------------------------------------------------
   score_on <=
      '1' when pix_y(9 downto 5)=0 and
               pix_x(9 downto 4)<16 else
      '0';
   row_addr_s <= std_logic_vector(pix_y(4 downto 1));
   bit_addr_s <= std_logic_vector(pix_x(3 downto 1));
   with pix_x(7 downto 4) select
     char_addr_s <=
        "1010011" when "0000", -- S x53
        "1100011" when "0001", -- c x63
        "1101111" when "0010", -- o x6f
        "1110010" when "0011", -- r x72
        "1100101" when "0100", -- e x65
        "0111010" when "0101", -- : x3a
        "011" & dig1 when "0110", -- digit 10
```

```
        "011" & dig0 when "0111", -- digit 1
        "0000000" when "1000",
        "0000000" when "1001",
        "1000010" when "1010", -- B x42
        "1100001" when "1011", -- a x61
        "1101100" when "1100", -- l x6c
        "1101100" when "1101", -- l x6c
        "0111010" when "1110", -- :
        "01100" & ball when others;

   ------------------------------------------------
   -- logo region:
   --    - display logo "PONG" at top center
   --    - used as background
   --    - scale to 64-by-128 font
   ------------------------------------------------
   logo_on <=
      '1' when pix_y(9 downto 7)=2 and
         (3<= pix_x(9 downto 6) and pix_x(9 downto 6)<=6) else
      '0';
   row_addr_l <= std_logic_vector(pix_y(6 downto 3));
   bit_addr_l <= std_logic_vector(pix_x(5 downto 3));
   with pix_x(8 downto 6) select
     char_addr_l <=
        "1010000" when "011", -- P x50
        "1001111" when "100", -- O x4f
        "1001110" when "101", -- N x4e
        "1000111" when others; --G x47
   ------------------------------------------------
   -- rule region
   --    - display rule at center
   --    - 4 lines, 16 characters each line
   --    - rule text:
   --         Rule:
   --         Use two buttons
   --         to move paddle
   --         up and down
   ------------------------------------------------
   rule_on <= '1' when pix_x(9 downto 7) = "010" and
                       pix_y(9 downto 6)=  "0010"  else
              '0';
   row_addr_r <= std_logic_vector(pix_y(3 downto 0));
   bit_addr_r <= std_logic_vector(pix_x(2 downto 0));
   rule_rom_addr <= pix_y(5 downto 4) & pix_x(6 downto 3);
   char_addr_r <= RULE_ROM(to_integer(rule_rom_addr));
   ------------------------------------------------
   -- game over region
   --    - display "Game Over" at center
   --    - scale to 32-by-64 fonts
   ------------------------------------------------
   over_on <=
      '1' when pix_y(9 downto 6)=3 and
         5<= pix_x(9 downto 5) and pix_x(9 downto 5)<=13 else
```

```
      '0';
   row_addr_o <= std_logic_vector(pix_y(5 downto 2));
   bit_addr_o <= std_logic_vector(pix_x(4 downto 2));
   with pix_x(8 downto 5) select
     char_addr_o <=
        "1000111" when "0101", -- G x47
        "1100001" when "0110", -- a x61
        "1101101" when "0111", -- m x6d
        "1100101" when "1000", -- e x65
        "0000000" when "1001", --
        "1001111" when "1010", -- O x4f
        "1110110" when "1011", -- v x76
        "1100101" when "1100", -- e x65
        "1110010" when others; -- r x72
   ---------------------------------------------
   -- mux for font ROM addresses and rgb
   ---------------------------------------------
   process(score_on,logo_on,rule_on,pix_x,pix_y,font_bit,
           char_addr_s,char_addr_l,char_addr_r,char_addr_o,
           row_addr_s,row_addr_l,row_addr_r,row_addr_o,
           bit_addr_s,bit_addr_l,bit_addr_r,bit_addr_o)
   begin
      text_rgb <= "110";  -- yellow background
      if score_on='1' then
         char_addr <= char_addr_s;
         row_addr <= row_addr_s;
         bit_addr <= bit_addr_s;
         if font_bit='1' then
            text_rgb <= "001";
         end if;
      elsif rule_on='1' then
         char_addr <= char_addr_r;
         row_addr <= row_addr_r;
         bit_addr <= bit_addr_r;
         if font_bit='1' then
            text_rgb <= "001";
         end if;
      elsif logo_on='1' then
         char_addr <= char_addr_l;
         row_addr <= row_addr_l;
         bit_addr <= bit_addr_l;
         if font_bit='1' then
            text_rgb <= "011";
         end if;
      else -- game over
         char_addr <= char_addr_o;
         row_addr <= row_addr_o;
         bit_addr <= bit_addr_o;
         if font_bit='1' then
            text_rgb <= "001";
         end if;
      end if;
   end process;
```

```
   text_on <= score_on & logo_on & rule_on & over_on;
   --------------------------------------------------
   -- font ROM interface
   --------------------------------------------------
   rom_addr <= char_addr & row_addr;
   font_bit <= font_word(to_integer(unsigned(not bit_addr)));
end arch;
```

The structure of each segment is similar. Because the messages are short, they are coded with the regular ROM template. Since no clock signal is used, a distributed RAM or combinational logic should be inferred. Generation of the two-digit score depends on the two 4-bit external signals, dig0 and dig1. Note that the ASCII codes for the digits 0, 1, ..., 9, are 30_{16}, 31_{16}, ..., 39_{16}. We can generate the char_addr signal simply by concatenating "011" in front of dig0 and dig1.

13.4.2 Modified graphic subsystem

To accommodate the new top-level controller, the graphic circuit in Section 12.4.3 requires several modifications:

- Add a gra_still (for "still graphics") control signal. When it is asserted, the vertical bar is placed in the middle and the ball is placed at the center of the screen without movement.
- Add the hit and miss status signals. The hit signal is asserted for one clock cycle when the paddle hits the ball. The miss signal is asserted when the paddle misses the ball and the ball reaches the right border.
- Add a graph_on signal to indicate the on status of the graph subsystem.

The modified portion of the code is shown in Listing 13.7.

Listing 13.7 Modified portion of a graph subsystem for the pong game

```
   . . .
   -- new ball position
   ball_x_next <=
      to_unsigned((MAX_X)/2,10) when gra_still='1' else
      ball_x_reg + ball_vx_reg when refr_tick='1' else
      ball_x_reg ;
   ball_y_next <=
      to_unsigned((MAX_Y)/2,10) when gra_still='1' else
      ball_y_reg + ball_vy_reg when refr_tick='1' else
      ball_y_reg ;
   -- new ball velocity
   process(ball_vx_reg,ball_vy_reg,ball_y_t,ball_x_l,ball_x_r,
           ball_y_t,ball_y_b,bar_y_t,bar_y_b,gra_still)
   begin
      hit <='0';
      miss <='0';
      ball_vx_next <= ball_vx_reg;
      ball_vy_next <= ball_vy_reg;
      if gra_still='1' then                --initial velocity
         ball_vx_next <= BALL_V_N;
         ball_vy_next <= BALL_V_P;
      elsif ball_y_t < 1 then              -- reach top
```

```
            ball_vy_next <= BALL_V_P;
         elsif ball_y_b > (MAX_Y-1) then    -- reach bottom
            ball_vy_next <= BALL_V_N;
         elsif ball_x_l <= WALL_X_R  then -- reach wall
            ball_vx_next <= BALL_V_P;     -- bounce back
         elsif (BAR_X_L<=ball_x_r) and (ball_x_r<=BAR_X_R) and
               (bar_y_t<=ball_y_b) and (ball_y_t<=bar_y_b) then
               -- reach x of right bar, a hit
               ball_vx_next <= BALL_V_N; -- bounce back
               hit <= '1';
         elsif (ball_x_r>MAX_X) then        -- reach right border
            miss <= '1';                    -- a miss
         end if;
      end process;
      . . .
      graph_on <= wall_on or bar_on or rd_ball_on;
      . . .
```

13.4.3 Auxiliary counters

The top-level design requires two small utility modules, m100_counter and timer, to facilitate the counting. The m100_counter module is a two-digit decade counter that counts from 00 to 99 and is used to keep track of the scores of the game. Two control signals, d_inc and d_clr, increment and clear the counter, respectively. The code is shown in Listing 13.8.

Listing 13.8 Two-digit decade counter

```
library ieee;
use ieee.std_logic_1164.all;
use ieee.numeric_std.all;
entity m100_counter is
   port(
      clk, reset: in std_logic;
      d_inc, d_clr: in std_logic;
      dig0,dig1: out std_logic_vector (3 downto 0)
   );
end m100_counter;

architecture arch of m100_counter is
   signal dig0_reg, dig1_reg: unsigned(3 downto 0);
   signal dig0_next, dig1_next: unsigned(3 downto 0);
begin
   -- registers
   process (clk,reset)
   begin
      if reset='1' then
         dig1_reg <= (others=>'0');
         dig0_reg <= (others=>'0');
      elsif (clk'event and clk='1') then
         dig1_reg <= dig1_next;
         dig0_reg <= dig0_next;
      end if;
```

```
   end process;
   -- next-state logic for the decimal counter
   process(d_clr,d_inc,dig1_reg,dig0_reg)
   begin
      dig0_next <= dig0_reg;
      dig1_next <= dig1_reg;
      if (d_clr='1') then
         dig0_next <= (others=>'0');
         dig1_next <= (others=>'0');
      elsif (d_inc='1') then
         if dig0_reg=9 then
            dig0_next <= (others=>'0');
            if dig1_reg=9 then -- 10th digit
               dig1_next <= (others=>'0');
            else
               dig1_next <= dig1_reg + 1;
            end if;
         else -- dig0 not 9
            dig0_next <= dig0_reg + 1;
         end if;
      end if;
   end process;
   dig0 <= std_logic_vector(dig0_reg);
   dig1 <= std_logic_vector(dig1_reg);
end arch;
```

The `timer` module uses the 60-Hz tick, `timer_tick`, to generate a 2-second interval. Its purpose is to pause the video for a small interval between transitions of the screens. It starts counting when the `timer_start` signal is asserted and activates the `timer_up` signal when the 2-second interval is up. The code is shown in Listing 13.9.

Listing 13.9 Two-second timer

```
library ieee;
use ieee.std_logic_1164.all;
use ieee.numeric_std.all;
entity timer is
   port(
      clk, reset: in std_logic;
      timer_start, timer_tick: in std_logic;
      timer_up: out std_logic
   );
end timer;

architecture arch of timer is
   signal timer_reg, timer_next: unsigned(6 downto 0);
begin
   -- registers
   process (clk, reset)
   begin
      if reset='1' then
         timer_reg <= (others=>'1');
      elsif (clk'event and clk='1') then
         timer_reg <= timer_next;
```

```
         end if;
      end process;
      -- next-state logic
      process(timer_start,timer_reg,timer_tick)
      begin
         if (timer_start='1') then
            timer_next <= (others=>'1');
         elsif timer_tick='1' and timer_reg/=0 then
            timer_next <= timer_reg - 1;
         else
            timer_next <= timer_reg;
         end if;
      end process;
      -- output logic
      timer_up <='1' when timer_reg=0 else '0';
   end arch;
```

13.4.4 Top-level system

The top-level system of the pong game consists of the previously designed modules, including video synchronization circuit, graphic subsystem, text subsystem, and utility counters, as well as a control FSM and an rgb multiplexing circuit. The block diagram is shown in Figure 13.4.

The control FSM monitors overall system operation and coordinates the activities of the text and graphic subsystems. Its ASMD chart is shown in Figure 13.6. The FSM has four states and operates as follows:

- Initially, the FSM is in the `newgame` state. The game starts when a button is pressed and the FSM moves to the `play` state.
- In the `play` state, the FSM checks the `hit` and `miss` signals continuously. When the `hit` signal is activated, the `d_inc` signal is asserted for one clock cycle to increment the score counter. When the `miss` signal is asserted, the FSM activates the 2-second timer, decrements the number of the balls by 1, and examines the number of remaining balls. If it is zero, the game is ended and the FSM moves to the `over` state. Otherwise, the FSM moves to the `newball` state.
- The FSM waits in the `newball` state until the 2-second interval is up (i.e., when the `timer_up` signal is asserted) and a button is pressed. It then moves to the `play` state to continue the game.
- The FSM stays in the `over` state until the 2-second interval is up. It then moves to the `newgame` state for a new game.

The `rgb` multiplexing circuit routes the `text_rgb` or `graph_rgb` signals to output according to the `text_on` and `graphic_on` signals. The key segment is

```
if (text_on(3)='1') or
   (state_reg=newgame and text_on(1)='1') or
   (state_reg=over and text_on(0)='1') then
   rgb_next <= text_rgb;
elsif graph_on='1' then -- display graph
  rgb_next <= graph_rgb;
elsif text_on(2)='1' then -- display logo
  rgb_next <= text_rgb;
```

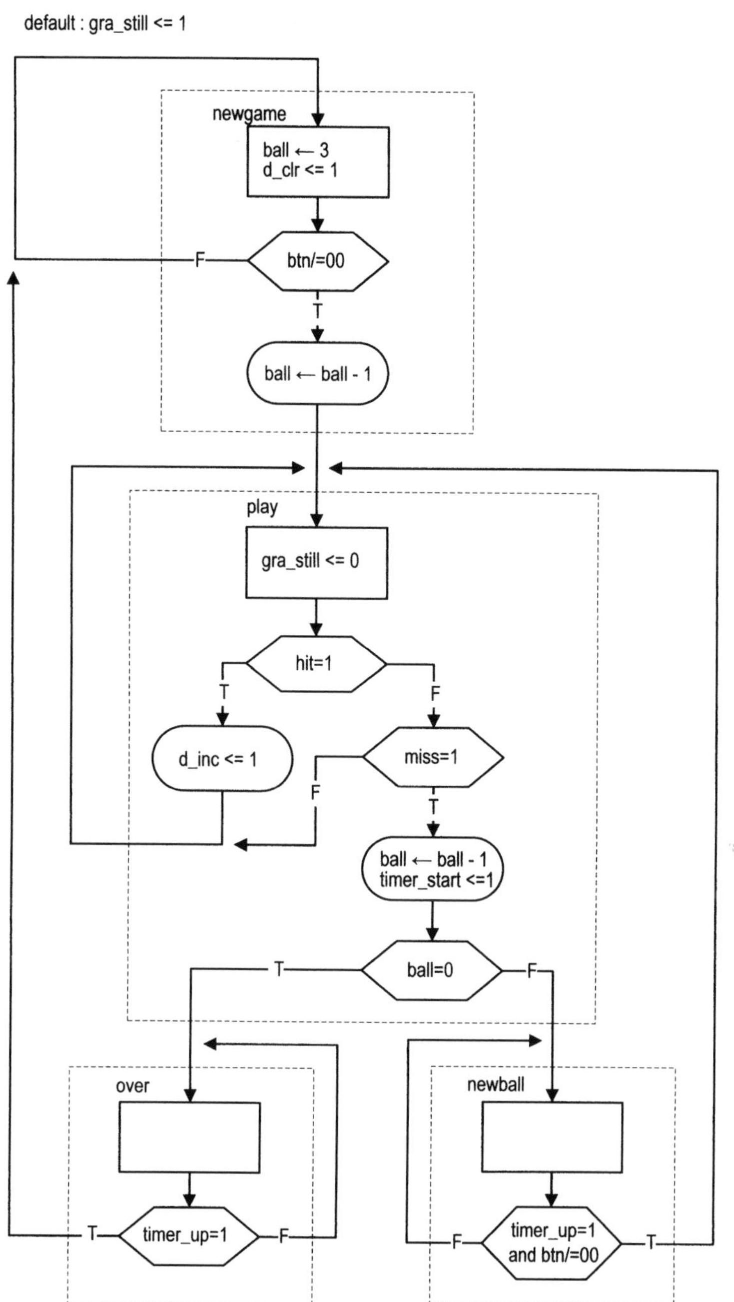

Figure 13.6 ASMD chart of the pong controller.

```
else
  rgb_next <= "110"; -- yellow background
end if;
```

The `text_on(3)='1'` expression is the condition for the scores, which is always displayed. The `text_on(1)='1'` expression is the condition for the rule, which is displayed only when the FSM is in the `newgame` state. Similarly, the end-of-game message, whose status is indicated by the `text_on(0)` signal, is displayed only when the FSM is in the `over` state. The logo, whose status is indicated by the `text_on(2)` signal, is used as part of the background and is displayed only when no other on signal is asserted.

The complete code is shown in Listing 13.10.

Listing 13.10 Top-level system for the pong game

```
library ieee;
use ieee.std_logic_1164.all;
use ieee.numeric_std.all;
entity pong_top is
   port(
      clk, reset: in std_logic;
      btn: in std_logic_vector (1 downto 0);
      hsync, vsync: out std_logic;
      rgb: out   std_logic_vector (2 downto 0)
   );
end pong_top;

architecture arch of pong_top is
   type state_type is (newgame, play, newball, over);
   signal video_on, pixel_tick: std_logic;
   signal pixel_x, pixel_y: std_logic_vector (9 downto 0);
   signal graph_on, gra_still, hit, miss: std_logic;
   signal text_on: std_logic_vector(3 downto 0);
   signal graph_rgb, text_rgb: std_logic_vector(2 downto 0);
   signal rgb_reg, rgb_next: std_logic_vector(2 downto 0);
   signal state_reg, state_next: state_type;
   signal dig0, dig1: std_logic_vector(3 downto 0);
   signal d_inc, d_clr: std_logic;
   signal timer_tick, timer_start, timer_up: std_logic;
   signal ball_reg, ball_next: unsigned(1 downto 0);
   signal ball: std_logic_vector(1 downto 0);
begin
   -- instantiate video synchronization unit
   vga_sync_unit: entity work.vga_sync
      port map(clk=>clk, reset=>reset,
               hsync=>hsync, vsync=>vsync,
               pixel_x=>pixel_x, pixel_y=>pixel_y,
               video_on=>video_on, p_tick=>pixel_tick);
   -- instantiate text module
   ball <= std_logic_vector(ball_reg);  --type conversion
   text_unit: entity work.pong_text
      port map(clk=>clk, reset=>reset,
               pixel_x=>pixel_x, pixel_y=>pixel_y,
               dig0=>dig0, dig1=>dig1, ball=>ball,
               text_on=>text_on, text_rgb=>text_rgb);
```

```
   -- instantiate graph module
   graph_unit: entity work.pong_graph
      port map(clk=>clk, reset=>reset, btn=>btn,
               pixel_x=>pixel_x, pixel_y=>pixel_y,
               gra_still=>gra_still,hit=>hit, miss=>miss,
               graph_on=>graph_on,rgb=>graph_rgb);
   -- instantiate 2-sec timer
   timer_tick <=  -- 60-Hz tick
      '1' when pixel_x="0000000000" and
               pixel_y="0000000000" else
      '0';
   timer_unit: entity work.timer
      port map(clk=>clk, reset=>reset,
               timer_tick=>timer_tick,
               timer_start=>timer_start,
               timer_up=>timer_up);
   -- instantiate 2-digit decade counter
   counter_unit: entity work.m100_counter
      port map(clk=>clk, reset=>reset,
               d_inc=>d_inc, d_clr=>d_clr,
               dig0=>dig0, dig1=>dig1);
   -- registers
   process (clk,reset)
   begin
      if reset='1' then
         state_reg <= newgame;
         ball_reg <= (others=>'0');
         rgb_reg <= (others=>'0');
      elsif (clk'event and clk='1') then
         state_reg <= state_next;
         ball_reg <= ball_next;
         if (pixel_tick='1') then
           rgb_reg <= rgb_next;
         end if;
      end if;
   end process;
   -- fsmd next-state logic
   process(btn,hit,miss,timer_up,state_reg,
           ball_reg,ball_next)
   begin
      gra_still <= '1';
      timer_start <='0';
      d_inc <= '0';
      d_clr <= '0';
      state_next <= state_reg;
      ball_next <= ball_reg;
      case state_reg is
         when newgame =>
            ball_next <= "11";     -- three balls
            d_clr <= '1';          -- clear score
            if (btn /= "00") then -- button pressed
               state_next <= play;
               ball_next <= ball_reg - 1;
```

```
            end if;
         when play =>
            gra_still <= '0';    -- animated screen
            if hit='1' then
               d_inc <= '1';     -- increment score
            elsif miss='1' then
               if (ball_reg=0) then
                  state_next <= over;
               else
                  state_next <= newball;
               end if;
               timer_start <= '1';  -- 2-sec timer
               ball_next <= ball_reg - 1;
            end if;
         when newball =>
            -- wait for 2 sec and until button pressed
            if  timer_up='1' and (btn /= "00") then
              state_next <= play;
            end if;
         when over =>
            -- wait for 2 sec to display game over
            if timer_up='1' then
                state_next <= newgame;
            end if;
       end case;
   end process;
   -- rgb multiplexing circuit
   process(state_reg,video_on,graph_on,graph_rgb,
           text_on,text_rgb)
   begin
      if video_on='0' then
         rgb_next <= "000"; -- blank the edge/retrace
      else
         -- display score, rule or game over
         if (text_on(3)='1') or
            (state_reg=newgame and text_on(1)='1') or -- rule
            (state_reg=over and text_on(0)='1') then
            rgb_next <= text_rgb;
         elsif graph_on='1'  then -- display graph
           rgb_next <= graph_rgb;
         elsif text_on(2)='1'  then -- display logo
           rgb_next <= text_rgb;
         else
           rgb_next <= "110"; -- yellow background
         end if;
      end if;
   end process;
   rgb <= rgb_reg;
end arch;
```

13.5 BIBLIOGRAPHIC NOTES

Several other character fonts are available. *Rapid Prototyping of Digital Systems* by James O. Hamblen et al. uses a compact 64-character 8-by-8 font set. The tile-mapped scheme is not limited to the text display. It is widely used in the early video game. The article "Computer Graphics During the 8-bit Computer Game Era" by Steven Collins (*ACM SIGGRAPH*, May 1998) provides a comprehensive review of the history and design techniques of the tile-based game.

13.6 SUGGESTED EXPERIMENTS

13.6.1 Rotating banner

A rotating banner on the monitor screen moves a line from right to left and then wraps around. It is similar to the Window's Marquee screen saver. Let the text on the banner be "Hello, FPGA World." The banner should be displayed in four different font sizes and can travel at four different speeds. The font size and speed are controlled by four switches. Derive the HDL description and then synthesize and verify operation of the circuit.

13.6.2 Underline for the cursor

The full-screen text display circuit in Section 13.3 uses reversed color to indicate the current cursor location. Modify the design to use an underline to indicate the cursor location. Derive the HDL description and then synthesize and verify operation of the circuit.

13.6.3 Dual-mode text display

It is sometimes better for text to be displayed on a "vertical" screen. This can be done by turning the monitor 90 degrees and resting it on its side. Design this circuit as follows:

1. Modify the full-screen text display circuit in Section 13.3 for a vertical screen.
2. Merge the normal and vertical designs to create a "dual-mode" text display. Use a switch to select the desired mode.
3. Derive the HDL description and then synthesize and verify operation of the circuit.

13.6.4 Keyboard text entry

Instead of switches and buttons, it is more natural to use a keyboard to enter text. We can use the four arrow keys to move the cursor and use the regular keys to enter the characters. Use the keyboard interface discussed in Section 8.4 to design the new circuit. Derive the HDL description and then synthesize and verify operation of the circuit.

13.6.5 UART terminal

The UART terminal receives input from the UART port and displays the received characters on a monitor. When connected to the PC's serial port, it should echo the text on Window's HypterTerminal. The detailed specifications are:

- A cursor is used to indicate the current location.
- The screen starts a new line when a "carriage return" code ($0d_{16}$) is received.

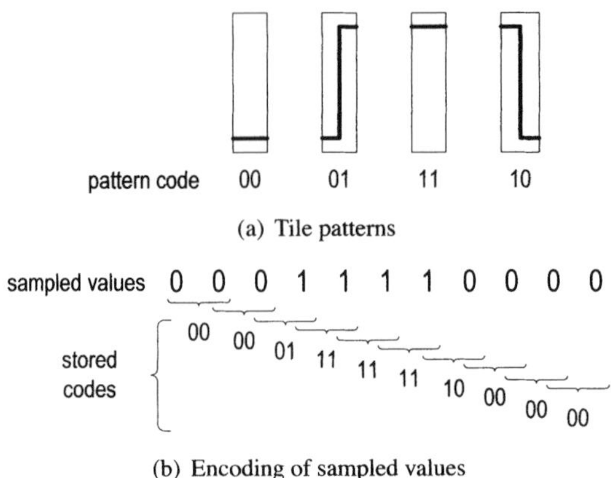

Figure 13.7 Tile patterns and encoding of square wave.

- A line wraps around (i.e., starts a new line) after 80 characters.
- When the cursor reaches the bottom of the screen (i.e., the last line), the first line will be discarded and all other lines move up (i.e., scroll up) one position.

Derive the HDL description and then synthesize and verify operation of the circuit.

13.6.6 Square wave display

We can draw a square wave by using four simple tile patterns shown in Figure 13.7(a). Follow the procedure of a full-screen text display in Section 13.3 to design a full-screen wave editor:

1. Let the tile size be 8 columns by 64 rows. Create a pattern ROM for the four patterns.
2. Calculate the number of tiles on a 640-by-480 resolution screen and derive the proper configuration for the tile memory.
3. Use three pushbuttons for control and a 2-bit switch to enter the pattern.
4. Derive the HDL description and then synthesize and verify operation of the circuit.

13.6.7 Simple four-trace logic analyzer

A logic analyzer displays the waveforms of a collection of digital signals. We want to design a simple logic analyzer that captures the waveforms of four input signals in "free-running" mode. Instead of using a trigger pattern, data capture is initiated with activation of a pushbutton switch. For simplicity, we assume that the frequencies of the input waveform are between 10 kHz and 100 kHz. The circuit can be designed as follows:

1. Use a sampling tick to sample the four input signals. Make sure to select a proper rate so that the desired input frequency range can be displayed properly on the screen.
2. For a point in the sampled signal, its value can be encoded as a tile pattern by including the value of the previous point. For example, if the sampled sequence of one signal is "00001111000", the tile patterns become "00 00 00 01 11 11 11 10 00 00", as shown in Figure 13.7(b).
3. Follow the procedure of the preceding square wave experiment to design the tile memory and video interface to display the four waveforms being stored .
4. Derive the HDL description and then synthesize the circuit.

To verify operation of the circuit, we can connect four external signals via headers around the prototyping board. Alternatively, we can create a top-level test module that includes a 4-bit counter (say, a mod-10 counter around 50 kHz) and the logic analyzer, resynthesize the circuit, and verify its operation.

13.6.8 Complete two-player pong game

The free-running two-player pong game is described in Experiment 12.7.6. Follow the procedure of the pong game in Section 13.4 to derive the complete system. This should include the design of a new text display subsystem and the design of a top-level FSM controller. Derive the HDL description and then synthesize and verify operation of the circuit.

13.6.9 Complete breakout game

The free-running breakout game is described in Experiment 12.7.7. Follow the procedure of the pong game in Section 13.4 to derive the complete system. This should include the design of a new text display subsystem and the design of a top-level FSM controller. Derive the HDL description and then synthesize and verify operation of the circuit.

PART III

PICOBLAZE MICROCONTROLLER *XILINX SPECIFIC*

CHAPTER 14

PICOBLAZE OVERVIEW

14.1 INTRODUCTION

The *PicoBlaze* processor is a compact 8-bit microcontroller core for Xilinx FPGA devices. It is provided as a cell-level HDL description (which is known as *soft core*) and can be synthesized along with other logic. PicoBlaze is optimized for efficiency and occupies only about 200 logic cells, which amount to less than 5% resource of a 3S200 device. While not intended as a high-performance processor, it is compact and flexible and can be used for simple data processing and control, particularly for non-time-critical "house-keeping" and I/O operations. The PicoBlaze processor can be easily integrated into a larger system and adds another dimension of flexibility in an FPGA-based design.

Although the detailed coverage of assembly language programming and microcontrollers is beyond the scope of this book, this part provides a comprehensive overview of PicoBlaze's organization and instruction set, and illustrates the general assembly program development and I/O interface through a set of examples. We review PicoBlaze's organization and instruction set in this chapter, introduce assembly language programming in Chapter 15, and discuss the general I/O interface and interrupt interface in Chapters 16 and 17.

14.2 CUSTOMIZED HARDWARE AND CUSTOMIZED SOFTWARE

14.2.1 From special-purpose FSMD to general-purpose microcontroller

The RT-level design and FSMD discussed in Chapter 6 provide a general methodology to convert a sequential algorithm to customized hardware. The rearranged block diagram is shown in Figure 14.1(a). In an FSMD, all components, including the number of registers, the routing of registers' input and output, the number and types of functional units, and the control FSM, are tailored to the target application. The data path may contain multiple function units and multiple routing paths, as shown in the diagram.

An alternative is to keep the same hardware but use *customized software* for different applications. The transformation can be done as follows. First, we can replace the customized data path with a fixed configuration, as shown in the top of Figure 14.1(b). The data registers and customized routing networks are replaced by a register file, which has a fixed number of registers and contains only two read ports and one write port. The customized function units are replaced with an *ALU* (arithmetic and logic unit), which can only perform a set of predefined functions. The data path now can perform RT operations in the following format only:

$$\texttt{rd} \leftarrow \texttt{r1 op r2}$$

where `r1`, `r2`, and `rd` are the addresses of two source registers and one destination register, and `op` is one of the available ALU functions.

Second, we can replace the customized FSM with a *programmable state machine*, as shown in the bottom of Figure 14.1(b). Recall that operation of an FSM consists of three parts:

- The state register keeps track of the current state.
- The output logic activates certain output signals according to the current state.
- The next-state logic determines the new state.

The programmable state machine modifies these operations as follows:

- It replaces the state register with the *program counter*. The content of the program counter represents the current state of the control path.
- In an FSM, each state activates certain output signals to control operation of the data path. The programmable state machine encodes these output patterns into *instructions* and stores them in a memory module, known as *program memory* or *instruction memory*. A memory address corresponds to a state (i.e., a value) of the program counter. During execution, the instruction pointed by the program counter is retrieved from the memory and decoded to generate the control signals. The instruction memory and decoding logic function as a sophisticated output logic circuit.
- In an FSM, there is no limitation on where to go next. From a given state, the FSM can check the input condition and move to one of many possible next states. In a programmable state machine, the next state is usually the value of the current state plus 1 (i.e., the program counter is incremented by 1), which reflects the nature of the sequential execution. The sequential execution may be altered only by several special instructions, such as a *jump* instruction, in which the program counter is loaded with a different value. The incrementor and the associated multiplexing logic function as a simple next-state logic circuit.

After we replace the data path with a register file and an ALU and replace the dedicated FSM with a programmable state machine, customizing the system corresponds to developing a new sequence of instructions (i.e., develop a *software program*) and loads the instructions

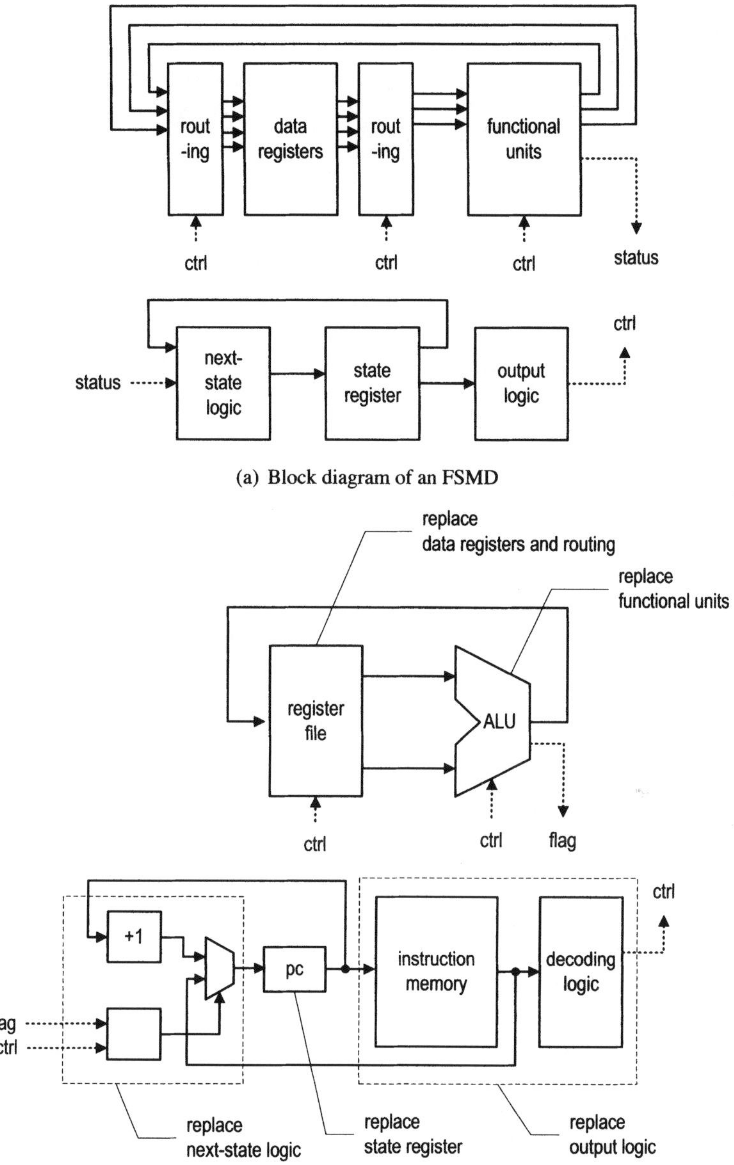

(a) Block diagram of an FSMD

(b) Simplified block diagram of a microcontroller

Figure 14.1 Diagrams of an FSMD and a microcontroller.

to the instruction memory. The organization of the FSMD is now the same for different applications and becomes a *general-purpose* hardware platform. The platform constitutes the basic skeleton of the PicoBlaze microcontroller.

14.2.2 Application of microcontroller

In a customized FSMD, the data path can be created to accommodate an individual application's needs. It may contain multiple customized functional units and parallel routing paths, and can complete complex computation in a single state (i.e., one clock cycle). On the other hand, the PicoBlaze microcontroller can only perform one predefined RT operation (i.e., an instruction) at a time. It may need many instructions to perform the same task and thus require much more time.

Many tasks can be done by either a customized FSMD or a microcontroller. The trade-off is between the hardware complexity, performance and ease of development. There is no exact rule on which one to choose. Because developing software is usually easier than creating customized hardware, the microcontroller option is generally preferable for non-time-critical applications. We can determine the feasibility of this option by examining the computation complexity. PicoBlaze requires two clock cycles to complete an instruction. If the system clock is 50 MHz, 25 million instructions can be perform in one second. For a task (or a collection of tasks), we can examine how frequent a request is issued and how fast the task must be completed, and then estimate the number of available instructions. For example, assume that a keyboard interface generates a new input data every 1 ms and the data must be processed within this interval. Within the 1-ms period, PicoBlaze can complete 25,000 instructions. The PicoBlaze controller will be a viable option if the required processing can be done by using less than 25,000 instructions. In general, the microcontroller is suitable for many non-time-critical I/O-interface or "house-keeping" tasks.

14.3 OVERVIEW OF PICOBLAZE

14.3.1 Basic organization

PicoBlaze is a compact 8-bit microcontroller with the following characteristics:

- 8-bit data width
- 8-bit ALU with the carry and zero flags
- 16 8-bit general-purpose registers
- 64-byte data memory
- 18-bit instruction width
- 10-bit instruction address, which supports a program up to 1024 instructions
- 31-word call/return stack
- 256 input ports and 256 output ports
- 2 clock cycles per instruction
- 5 clock cycles for interrupt handling

PicoBlaze is based on the skeleton described in Figure 14.1(b) and adds several enhancements to make it more versatile. The expanded diagram is shown in Figure 14.2. To reduce clutter, only the main data flow is shown. The sizes of main storage components are listed in round brackets. The processor makes several enhancements over the original skeleton:

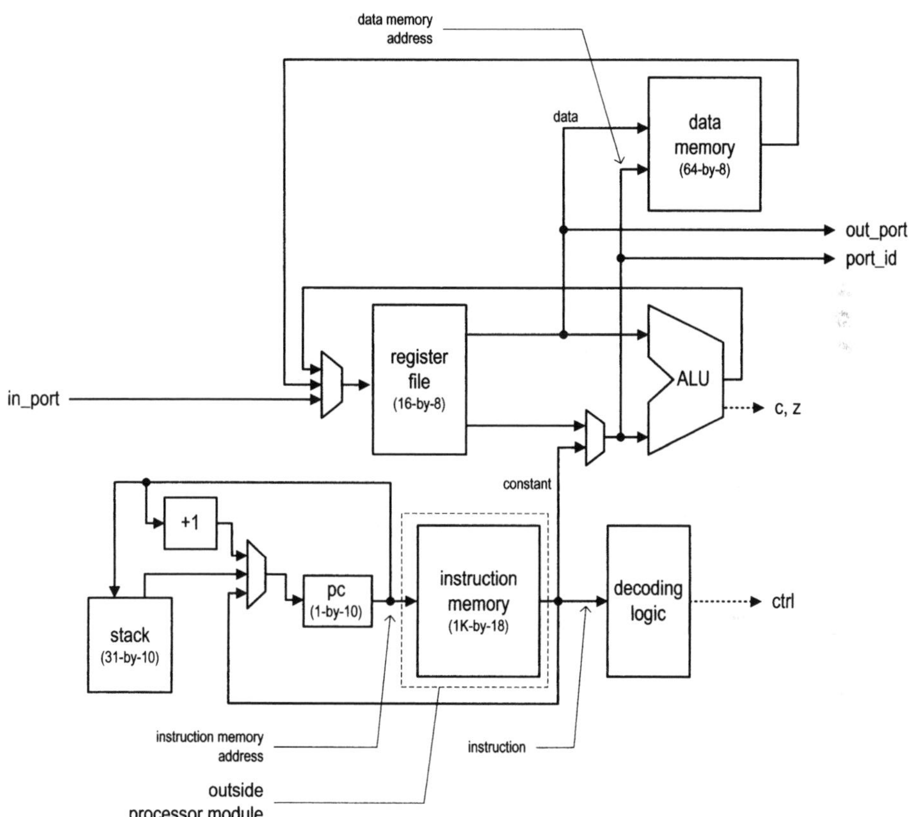

Figure 14.2 Block diagram of PicoBlaze.

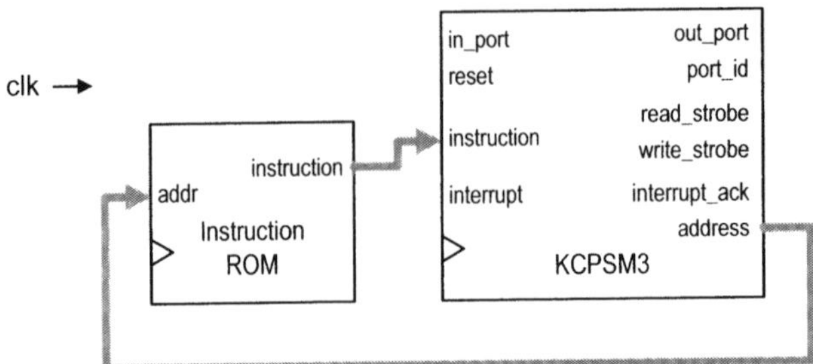

Figure 14.3 Top-level diagram of PicoBlaze.

- *Add a 64-word data memory.* It is known as *scratch RAM* in Xilinx literature but we call it *data RAM*. The data RAM can be considered as a reservoir to store additional data. Note that there is no direct path between the data RAM and ALU. Data must be fetched to a register for processing and then stored back to the data RAM.
- *Add an immediate constant field in some instructions.* This allows a constant, rather than the content of a register, to be used in ALU and other operations. The two-to-one multiplexer before the ALU's bottom input is used to select the register output or the constant field.
- *Add a 31-word stack to support the call/return functions.* We discuss the call and return procedure in more detail in Section 14.5.8.
- *Add paths to input and output external data.* An 8-bit `port_id` signal is used to identify a port and thus up to 256 input ports and 256 output ports can be supported. The I/O interface is discussed in detail in Chapter 16.
- *Add an interrupt handling circuit* (not shown in the diagram). The interrupt mechanism is discussed in detail in Chapter 17.

14.3.2 Top-level HDL modules

During synthesis, a PicoBlaze system is organized as two top-level HDL modules, as shown in Figure 14.3. The `KCPSM3` module is the PicoBlaze processor. `KCPSM3`, which stands for *constant (K) coded programmable state machine*, reflects the original name of the PicoBlaze processor. It has following input and output signals:

- `clk` (input, 1 bit): system clock signal
- `reset` (input, 1 bit): reset signal
- `address` (output, 10 bits): address of the instruction memory, which specifies the location of the instruction to be retrieved
- `instruction` (input, 18 bits): fetched instruction
- `port_id` (output, 8 bits): address of the input or output port
- `in_port` (input, 8 bits): input data from I/O peripherals
- `read_storbe` (output, 1 bit): strobe associated with the input operation
- `out_port` (output, 8 bits): output data to I/O peripherals
- `write_storbe` (output, 1 bit): strobe associated with the output operation
- `interrupt` (input, 1 bit): interrupt request from I/O peripherals
- `interrupt_ack` (output, 1 bit): interrupt acknowledgement to I/O peripherals

The second module is for the instruction memory. During the development, we usually store the compiled assembly code to memory in advance and configure it as a ROM in HDL code. It is thus known as an *instruction ROM*.

14.4 DEVELOPMENT FLOW

While developing a system based on a conventional microcontroller, we examine the required functionalities and select a processor with the proper computation capability and adequate I/O interface. Additional chips are frequently needed to perform special functions. One advantage of using a soft-core microcontroller is that we can have both a customized circuit and a microcontroller developed and implemented in the same FPGA device. A large application usually includes many different tasks. In an FPGA platform, we can implement the time-critical tasks in a customized circuit (i.e., "hardware") for performance and realize the remaining house-keeping and low-speed I/O functions in a microcontroller (i.e., "software").

The basic PicoBlaze-based development flow is shown in Figure 14.4. It consists of the following steps:

1. Determine the software–hardware partition.
2. Develop the assembly program for the software portion.
3. Compile the assembly program to generate an instruction ROM. The ROM is an HDL file.
4. Perform instruction-set-level simulation.
5. Derive HDL code for the hardware portion. The hardware includes customized circuits to perform special I/O and time-critical functions and customized circuits to interface with PicoBlaze.
6. Create the top-level HDL code that combines the codes for the PicoBlaze core, the instruction ROM, and customized hardware.
7. Develop a testbench and perform HDL simulation for the entire system.
8. Synthesize and implement the HDL code and program the FPGA chip on the prototyping board.

The subsequent chapters explain these steps in detail.

The step 9 shown in the dotted line is not a part of the normal development flow. It reloads the instruction memory after the entire system is synthesized. This step is discussed in Section 15.5.3.

14.5 INSTRUCTION SET

PicoBlaze has 57 instructions. The instructions have five general formats. We organize the instructions according to the nature of their operations and divide them into following categories:

- Logical instructions
- Arithmetic instructions
- Compare and test instructions
- Shift and rotate instructions
- Data movement instructions
- Program flow control instructions
- Interrupt related instructions

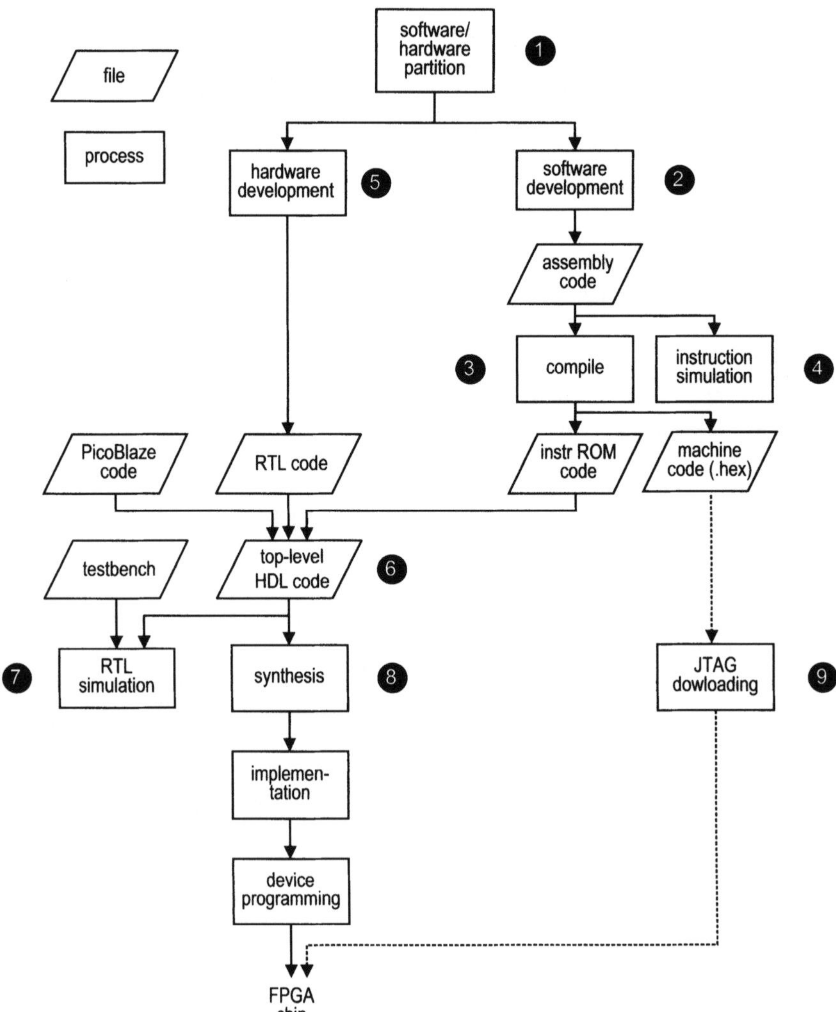

Figure 14.4 Development flow of a system with PicoBlaze.

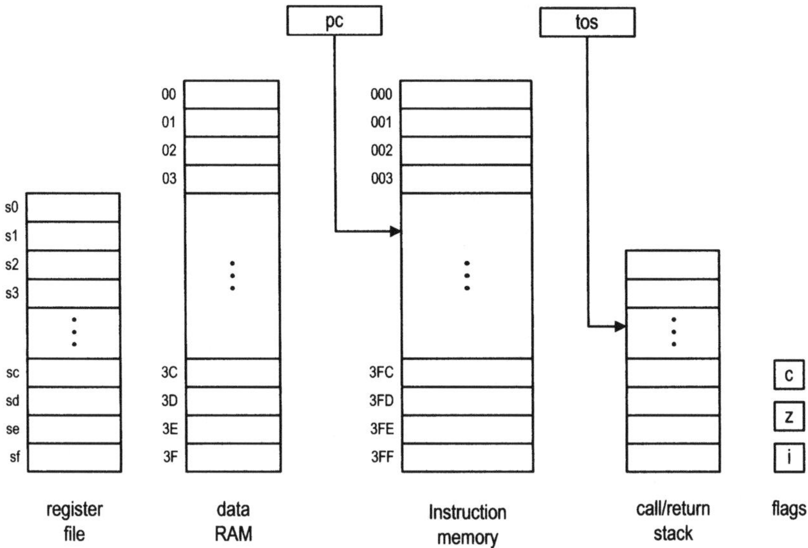

Figure 14.5 PicoBlaze programming model.

In this section, we first examine the program model and instruction format, and then list and explain each instruction.

14.5.1 Programming model

From an assembly programming point of view, PicoBlaze contains 16 8-bit registers, a 64-byte data RAM, three flags (for zero, carry and interrupt), the program counter and the top-of-stack pointer. The model, sometimes known as the instruction set architecture, is shown in Figure 14.5. After an instruction is executed, the contents of these components are modified explicitly or implicitly. The operations associated with each instruction are discussed in Section 14.5.3.

We use the following notations for these memory components and some constant definitions:

- `sX`, `sY`: each representing one of the 16 general-purpose registers, where `X` and `Y` take on hexadecimal values from `0` to `f`
- `pc`: program counter
- `tos`: top-of-stack pointer of the call/return stack
- `c`, `z`, `i`: carry, zero, and interrupt flags
- `KK`: 8-bit constant value or port id, which is usually expressed as two hexadecimal digits
- `SS`: 6-bit constant data memory address, which is usually expressed as two hexadecimal digits
- `AAA`: 10-bit constant instruction memory address, which is usually expressed as three hexadecimal digits

14.5.2 Instruction format

In an assembly program, we generally follow the conventions used in our HDL code, in which a keyword (an instruction mnemonic) is in a boldface font and a constant is in capital letters. PicoBalze's instructions have five formats:

- **op** sX, sY: *register-register format.* The **op** term specifies the operation. The sX and sY terms are the two operands and sX also serves as the destination register. It performs the sX ← sX **op** sY operation.
- **op** sX, KK: *register-constant format.* This format is similar to the register-register format except that the second operand is replaced by an immediate constant. It performs the sX ← sX **op** KK operation.
- **op** sX: *single-register format.* This format is used in shift and rotate instructions, which involve only one operand. It performs the sX ← **op** sX operation.
- **op** AAA: *single-address format.* This format is used in jump and call instructions. The AAA term is an address of the instruction memory. If the specified condition is met, AAA is loaded into the program counter.
- **op**: *zero-operand format.* This format is used in some miscellaneous instructions that do not involve any operand.

There are two assembler programs for PicoBlaze: *KCPSM3* from Xilinx and *PBlazeIDE* from Mediatronix. The two programs use different mnemonics for several instructions. In the following subsections, the alternative mnemonics used in PBlazeIDE are shown in round brackets.

14.5.3 Logical instructions

There are six logical instructions, which support the and, or, and xor operations. An instruction performs bitwise logical operation between two registers or one register and a constant. The carry flag, c, is always cleared. The zero flag, z, reflects the result of the operation. The mnemonics, brief descriptions, and pseudo operations of these instructions are:

- **and** sX, sY
  - bitwise and operation
  - pseudo operation:

    ```
    sX ← sX and sY;
    c ← 0;
    ```

- **and** sX, KK
  - bitwise and operation
  - pseudo operation:

    ```
    sX ← sX and KK;
    c ← 0;
    ```

- **or** sX, sY
  - bitwise or operation
  - pseudo operation:

    ```
    sX ← sX or sY;
    c ← 0;
    ```

- **or** sX, KK
  - bitwise or operation

- pseudo operation:

  ```
  sX ← sX or KK;
  c ← 0;
  ```

- **xor** sX, sY
  - bitwise xor operation
  - pseudo operation:

    ```
    sX ← sX xor sY;
    c ← 0;
    ```

- **xor** sX, KK
  - bitwise xor operation
  - pseudo operation:

    ```
    sX ← sX xor KK;
    c ← 0;
    ```

14.5.4 Arithmetic instructions

There are eight arithmetic instructions, which support addition and subtraction with or without the carry flag. The carry flag, c, and the zero flag, z, reflect the result of operation. The mnemonics, brief descriptions, and pseudo operations of these instructions are:

- **add** sX, sY
  - add without the carry flag
  - pseudo operation:

    ```
    sX ← sX + sY;
    ```

- **add** sX, KK
  - add without the carry flag
  - pseudo operation:

    ```
    sX ← sX + KK;
    ```

- **addcy** sX, sY (**addc** sX, sY)
  - add with the carry flag
  - pseudo operation:

    ```
    sX ← sX + sY + c;
    ```

- **addcy** sX, KK (**addc** sX, KK)
  - add with the carry flag
  - pseudo operation:

    ```
    sX ← sX + KK + c;
    ```

- **sub** sX, sY
  - subtract without the carry flag
  - pseudo operation:

    ```
    sX ← sX - sY;
    ```

- **sub** sX, KK
  - subtract without the carry flag
  - pseudo operation:

    ```
    sX ← sX - KK;
    ```

- **subcy** sX, sY (**subc** sX, sY)
  - subtract with the carry flag (flag functioning as a borrow bit)
  - pseudo operation:

```
sX ← sX - sY - c;
```

- **subcy** sX, KK (**subc** sX, KK)
  - subtract with the carry flag (flag functioning as a borrow bit)
  - pseudo operation:

```
sX ← sX - KK - c;
```

14.5.5 Compare and test instructions

The compare and test instructions examine two registers or one register and constant, and set the carry and zero flags accordingly. The contents of the registers remain intact. These instructions are usually used in conjunction with a conditional jump or call instruction, whose operation is based on the values of the flags.

A compare instruction performs subtraction operation. The result is used to set the carry and zero flags and not stored to any register. The mnemonics, brief descriptions, and pseudo operations of the two instructions are:

- **compare** sX, sY (**comp** sX, sY)
  - compare two registers and set the flags
  - pseudo operation:

```
if sX=sY then z ← 1 else z ← 0;
if sY>sX then c ← 1 else c ← 0;
```

- **compare** sX, KK (**comp** sX, KK)
  - compare a register and a constant and set the flags
  - pseudo operation:

```
if sX=KK then z ← 1 else z ← 0;
if KK>sX then c ← 1 else c ← 0;
```

A test instruction performs an and operation. The result is used to set the flags and not stored in any register. If the result is 0, the zero flag is set to 1. The result is also fed to an eight-input xor circuit to obtain the odd parity. If there are odd number of 1's in the result, the carry flag is set to 1. The mnemonics, brief descriptions, and pseudo operations of the two instructions are shown below. The t is the 8-bit temporary result and will be discarded.

- **test** sX, sY
  - test two registers and set the flags
  - pseudo operation:

```
t ← sX and sY;
if t=0 then z ← 1 else z ← 0;
c ← t(7) xor t(6) xor ··· xor t(0);
```

- **test** sX, KK
  - test a register and a constant and set the flags
  - pseudo operation:

```
t ← sX and KK;
if t=0 then z ← 1 else z ← 0;
c ← t(7) xor t(6) xor ··· xor t(0);
```

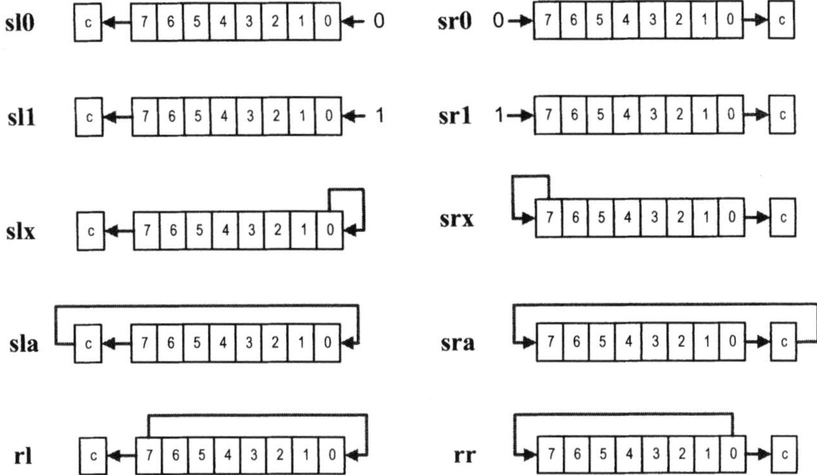

Figure 14.6 Illustration of shift and rotate instructions.

14.5.6 Shift and rotate instructions

There are four shift-left instructions, four shift-right instructions, and two rotate instructions. These instructions use the single-register format and have only one operand. The graphical representations of these instructions are shown in Figure 14.6. The mnemonics, brief descriptions, and pseudo operations of these instructions are shown below. The & symbol means to concatenate two operands.

- **sl0** sX
  - shift a register left 1 bit and shift 0 into the LSB
  - pseudo operation:

```
sX ← sX(6..0) & 0;
c ← sX(7);
```

- **sl1** sX
  - shift a register left 1 bit and shift 1 into the LSB
  - pseudo operation:

```
sX ← sX(6..0) & 1;
c ← sX(7);
```

- **slx** sX
  - shift a register left 1 bit and shift sX(0) into the LSB
  - pseudo operation:

```
sX ← sX(6..0) & sX(0);
c ← sX(7);
```

- **sla** sX
  - shift a register left 1 bit and shift c into the LSB
  - pseudo operation:

```
sX ← sX(6..0) & c;
c ← sX(7);
```

- **sr0** sX
  - shift a register right 1 bit and shift 0 into the MSB
  - pseudo operation:

```
sX ← 0 & sX(7..1);
c ← sX(0);
```

- **sr1** sX
  - shift a register right 1 bit and shift 1 into the MSB
  - pseudo operation:

```
sX ← 1 & sX(7..1);
c ← sX(0);
```

- **srx** sX
  - shift a register right 1 bit and shift `sX(7)` into the MSB
  - pseudo operation:

```
sX ← sX(7) & sX(7..1);
c ← sX(0);
```

- **sra** sX
  - shift a register right 1 bit and shift `c` into the MSB
  - pseudo operation:

```
sX ← c & sX(7..1);
c ← sX(0);
```

- **rl** sX
  - rotate a register left 1 bit
  - pseudo operation:

```
sX ← sX(6..0) & sX(7);
c ← sX(7);
```

- **rr** sX
  - rotate a register right 1 bit
  - pseudo operation:

```
sX ← sX(0) & sX(7..1);
c ← sX(0);
```

14.5.7 Data movement instructions

In PicoBlaze, the computation is done via the registers and ALU. The data RAM supplies additional storage and the I/O ports provide paths to peripherals. There are several instructions to move data between the registers, data RAM, and I/O ports. The instructions can be divided into three categories:

- *Between registers*: the **load** instruction
- *Between a register and data RAM*: the **fetch** and **store** instructions
- *Between a register and an I/O port*: the **input** and **output** instructions

The mnemonics, brief descriptions, and pseudo operations of the data movement instructions are shown below. The `RAM[ ]` notation represents the content of the data RAM. Note that in some instructions, the *indirect address* notation, as in `(sY)`, is used in mnemonic to emphasize that the content of the `sY` register is used.

- **load** sX, sY
  - move data between two registers
  - pseudo operation:

    sX ← sY;
- **load** sX, KK
  - move a constant to a register
  - pseudo operation:

    sX ← KK;
- **fetch** sX, (sY) (**fetch** sX, sY)
  - move data from the data RAM to a register
  - pseudo operation:

    sX ← RAM[(sY)];
- **fetch** sX, SS
  - move data from the data RAM to a register
  - pseudo operation:

    sX ← RAM[SS];
- **store** sX, (sY) (**store** sX, sY)
  - move data from a register to the data RAM
  - pseudo operation:

    RAM[(sY)] ← sX;
- **store** sX, SS
  - move data from a register to the data RAM
  - pseudo operation:

    RAM[SS] ← sX;
- **input** sX, (sY) (**in** sX, sY)
  - move data from the input port to a register
  - pseudo operation:

    port_id ← sY;
    sX ← in_port;
- **input** sX, KK (**in** sX, KK)
  - move data from the input port to a register
  - pseudo operation:

    port_id ← KK;
    sX ← in_port;
- **output** sX, (sY) (**out** sX, sY)
  - move data from a register to the output port
  - pseudo operation:

    port_id ← sY;
    out_port ← sX;
- **output** sX, KK (**out** sX, KK)
  - move data from a register to the output port
  - pseudo operation:

    port_id ← KK;
    out_port ← sX;

There is no explicit instruction to move data to or from the instruction memory. However, many instructions include a field for an immediate constant. Since the constant is part of the instruction and stored in the instruction memory, it can be considered as data that is implicitly moved from the instruction memory to a register.

14.5.8 Program flow control instructions

In PicoBlaze, the program counter indicates where to fetch the instruction. By default, the execution proceeds to the next address in the instruction memory and the program counter is implicitly incremented (i.e., pc ← pc + 1). The **jump**, **call** and **return** instructions can explicitly load a value to the program counter and modify the program flow. These instructions can be executed unconditionally or conditionally based on the values of the carry and zero flags.

A **jump** instruction loads new value to the program counter if the corresponding condition is met. The program execution changes the regular flow and branches to the new address. The program flow continues normally after this point. The mnemonics, brief descriptions, and pseudo operations of these instructions are shown below. Recall that AAA is for the 10-bit instruction memory address and pc is for the program counter.

- **jump** AAA
  - unconditionally jump
  - pseudo operation:

    `pc ← AAA;`
- **jump c**, AAA
  - jump if the carry flag is set
  - pseudo operation:

    `if c=1 then pc ← AAA else pc ← pc + 1;`
- **jump nc**, AAA
  - jump if the carry flag is not set
  - pseudo operation:

    `if c=0 then pc ← AAA else pc ← pc + 1;`
- **jump z**, AAA
  - jump if the zero flag is set
  - pseudo operation:

    `if z=1 then pc ← AAA else pc ← pc + 1;`
- **jump nz**, AAA
  - jump if the zero flag is not set
  - pseudo operation:

    `if z=0 then pc ← AAA else pc ← pc + 1;`

The **call** and **return** instructions are used to implement a software function. When a function is *called*, the processor suspends the current execution and branches to the corresponding routine. When the routine computation is completed, the processor *returns* to the suspended point and continues the execution. Like a **jump** instruction, a **call** instruction loads a new value to the program counter if the corresponding condition is met. In addition, it also saves the current value of the program counter in a special buffer, known as the *stack*. The new address represents the starting point of a routine. The routine should include a **return** instruction in the end. The **return** instruction obtains the saved value from the

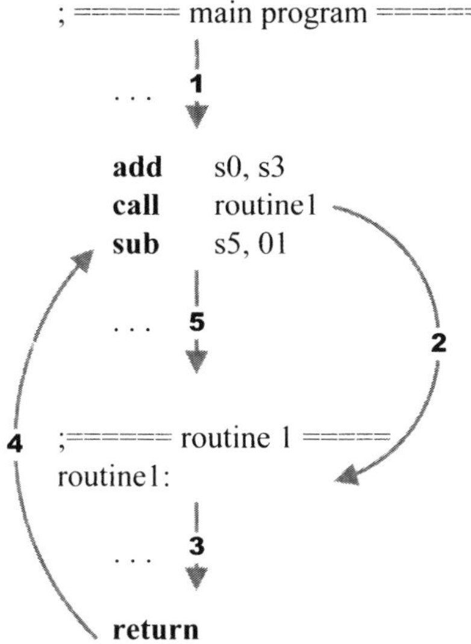

Figure 14.7 Representative flow of a subroutine call.

stack, increments the value by 1, and loads it to the program counter. This allows the execution to return to the instruction that immediately follows the original **call** instruction. A representative program flow is shown in Figure 14.7.

PicoBlaze allows nested function calls, which means that a function can be called within another function. To support this feature, a stack, which is a *last-in-first-out* buffer, is used to store the program counter's values. In this buffer, the address of the newest call is pushed to the top of the stack (i.e., the "last-in"). Assume that this routine does not contain other function call inside. It will be completed first and the saved returned address is on the top of the stack. It should be popped from the stack (i.e., "first-out") to resume the previous execution. PicoBlaze provides a 31-word stack for the nested call and return operations.

The mnemonics, brief descriptions, and pseudo operations of the **call** and **return** instructions are shown below. Recall that and `tos` is for the top-of-stack pointer. The `STACK[ ]` notation represents the content of the stack.

- **call** `AAA`
  - unconditionally call subroutine
  - pseudo operation:

```
tos ← tos + 1;
STACK[tos] ← pc;
pc ← AAA;
```

- **call c**, `AAA`
  - call subroutine if the carry flag is set
  - pseudo operation:

```
if c=1 then
   tos ← tos + 1;
   STACK[tos] ← pc;
   pc ← AAA;
else
```

```
        pc ← pc + 1;
```

- **call nc**, AAA
  - call subroutine if the carry flag is not set
  - pseudo operation:

```
if c=0 then
    tos ← tos + 1;
    STACK[tos] ← pc;
    pc ← AAA;
else
    pc ← pc + 1;
```

- **call z**, AAA
  - call subroutine if the zero flag is set
  - pseudo operation:

```
if z=1 then
    tos ← tos + 1;
    STACK[tos] ← pc;
    pc ← AAA;
else
    pc ← pc + 1;
```

- **call nz**, AAA
  - call subroutine if the zero flag is not set
  - pseudo operation:

```
if z=0 then
    tos ← tos + 1;
    STACK[tos] ← pc;
    pc ← AAA;
else
    pc ← pc + 1;
```

- **return (ret)**
  - unconditionally return
  - pseudo operation:

```
pc ← STACK[tos] + 1;
tos ← tos - 1;
```

- **return c (ret c)**
  - return if the carry flag is set
  - pseudo operation:

```
if c=1 then
    pc ← STACK[tos] + 1;
    tos ← tos - 1;
else
    pc ← pc + 1;
```

- **return nc (ret nc)**
  - return if the carry flag is not set
  - pseudo operation:

```
if c=0 then
    pc ← STACK[tos] + 1;
    tos ← tos - 1;
```

```
else
   pc ← pc + 1;
```

- **return z (ret z)**
  - return if the zero flag is set
  - pseudo operation:

```
if z=1 then
   pc ← STACK[tos] + 1;
   tos ← tos - 1;
else
   pc ← pc + 1;
```

- **return nz (ret nz)**
  - return if the zero flag is not set
  - pseudo operation:

```
if z=0 then
   pc ← STACK[tos] + 1;
   tos ← tos - 1;
else
   pc ← pc + 1;
```

14.5.9 Interrupt related instructions

Interrupt is another mechanism to alter program execution and its detail is discussed in Chapter 17. Unlike the **jump** and **call** instructions, it is initiated from an external request. When the interrupt flag is enabled and the interrupt request is asserted, PicoBlaze completes execution of the current instruction, saves the address of the next instruction in the call/return stack, preserves the carry and zero flags, disables the interrupt flag, and loads the program counter with 3FF, which is the starting address of the interrupt service routine. PicoBlaze has two return-from-interrupt instructions, which resume the operation from the interrupted location. It also has two instructions that enable and disable the interrupt request by setting or clearing the interrupt flag, `i`. The mnemonics, brief descriptions and pseudo operations of these instructions are:

- **returni disable (reti disable)**
  - return from interrupt service routine and keep the interrupt flag disabled
  - pseudo operation:

```
pc ← STACK[tos];
tos ← tos - 1;
i ← 0;
c ← preserved c;
z ← preserved z;
```

- **returni enable (reti enable)**
  - return from interrupt service routine and keep the interrupt flag enabled
  - pseudo operation:

```
pc ← STACK[tos];
tos ← tos - 1;
i ← 1;
c ← preserved c;
z ← preserved z;
```

- **enable interrupt (eint)**
  - enable interrupt request
  - pseudo operation:

    ```
    i ← 1;
    ```

- **disable interrupt (dint)**
  - disable interrupt request
  - pseudo operation:

    ```
    i ← 0;
    ```

Note that the interrupt mechanism saves the address of the next instruction. When a **returni** instruction is executed, the address saved on the top of the stack (i.e., `STACK[tos]`) is restored. This is different from a regular **return** instruction, in which the incremented address (i.e., `STACK[tos]+1`) is restored.

14.6 ASSEMBLER DIRECTIVES

An *assembler directive* looks like an instruction in an assembly program. However, it is not part of the microcontroller's instruction set but is used to help program development. As its name suggests, a directive "directs" the assembler to perform a specific task, such as defining a constant or reserving data space. The KCPSM3 and PBlazeIDE assemblers have somewhat different directives and they are discussed in the following subsections.

14.6.1 The KCPSM3 directives

The mnemonics, descriptions, and examples of key directives used in the KCPSM3 assembler are:

- **address**
  - The directive specifies the subsequent code to be put to a specific address in the instruction ROM.
  - Example:

    ```
    address 3FF
    ```

- **namereg**
  - The directive gives a symbolic name for a register. It makes code more descriptive.
  - Example:

    ```
    namereg s5, index
    ```

- **constant**
  - The directive gives a symbolic name for a constant. It makes code more descriptive.
  - Example:

    ```
    constant max, F0
    ```

14.6.2 The PBlazeIDE directives

The mnemonics, descriptions, and examples of key directives used in the PBlazeIDE assembler are shown below. Note that a $ sign is needed for a number in hexadecimal format.

- **org**
  - The directive specifies the subsequent code to be put to a specific address in the instruction ROM (i.e., "originate" from this address).
  - Example:

```
org   $3FF
```

- **equ**
  - The directive "equates" a symbol to a value or register. It gives a symbolic name for a constant or a register.
  - Example:

```
max     equ    128/8
index   equ    s5
```

- **dsin, dsout, dsio**
  - These directives equate a symbolic name for an I/O port id. The corresponding port can be defined as input, output, or both input and output. The difference between these directives and **equ** is that PBlazeIDE generates "port indicators" for these directives on the simulation screen. The I/O activities can be displayed and simulated via these indicators.
  - Example:

```
keyboard  dsin   $0E
switch    dsin   $0F
led       dsout  $15
```

- **vhdl**
  - This directive generates instruction ROM in VHDL format. The detail is discussed in Chapter 15.
  - Example:

```
vhdl "template.vhd", "target.vhd", "ROM"
```

14.7 BIBLIOGRAPHIC NOTES

The PicoBlaze's manual from Xilinx, *PicoBlaze 8-bit Embedded Microcontroller User Guide*, provides detailed information about this microcontroller, including the hardware organization, instruction set, development process, and the KCPSM3 and PBlazeIDE assemblers. Ken Chapman, the designer of PicoBlaze, describes the derivation of this microcontroller in article "Creating Embedded Microcontrollers," which is available in the *TechXclusives* section of Xilinx Web site.

The KCPSM3 assembler, PicoBlaze HDL code, and instruction ROM HDL template can be downloaded from the Xilinx Web site. Searching with the "PicoBlaze" keyword will lead to the downloading page. The PBlazeIDE assembler can be downloaded from the Mediatronix Web site, `http://www.mediatronix.com`. The site also provides more detailed information about the software.

CHAPTER 15

PICOBLAZE ASSEMBLY CODE DEVELOPMENT

15.1 INTRODUCTION

Because of its simplicity, PicoBlaze cannot effectively support high-level programming languages and the code is generally developed in assembly language. In this chapter, we provide an overview of code development, which is illustrated in a bottom-up fashion. We first introduce the segments of frequently used data and control operations and then examine the use of a subroutine and finally outline the derivation of overall program structure.

15.2 USEFUL CODE SEGMENTS

The PicoBlaze microcontroller contains instructions for byte-oriented data manipulation and simple conditional branch. In this section, we illustrate how to construct code to perform bit and multiple-byte operations and to realize frequently used high-level language control constructs.

15.2.1 KCPSM3 conventions

The KCPSM3 assembler uses the following conventions in an assembly program:

- Use a "`:`" sign after a symbolic address in code, as in "`done:`".
- Use a "`;`" sign before a comment.
- Use `HH` for a constant, in which `H` is a hexadecimal digit.

An example of a code segment follows:

```
    ; this is a demo segment
    test s0, 82          ;compare s0 with 1000_0010
    jump z, clr_s1       ;if MSB of s0 is 0, go to clr_s1
    load s1, FF          ;no, load 1111_1111 to s1
clr_s1:
    load s1, 01          ;load 0000_0001 to s1
```

15.2.2 Bit manipulation

PicoBlaze's instruction set is primarily for byte-oriented operations. Bit-oriented operations are frequently needed to control low-level I/O activities, such as testing, setting, and clearing a 1-bit flag signal.

To manipulate a single bit, we first define a *mask* to isolate and preserve (i.e., mask) the unrelated bits and then apply the designated operation on the desired bits (i.e., unmasked bits). We can set, clear, and toggle (i.e., invert) some bits of a data byte by performing **or**, **and**, and **xor** instructions with a proper mask. The following code segment shows how to set, clear, and toggle the second LSB of the s0 register:

```
    constant SET_MASK, 02     ;mask=0000_0010
    constant CLR_MASK, FD     ;mask=1111_1101
    constant TOG_MASK, 02     ;mask=0000_0010

    or  s0, SET_MASK          ;set 2nd LSB to 1
    and s0, CLR_MASK          ;clear 2nd LSB to 0
    xor s0, TOG_MASK          ;toggle 2nd LSB
```

The toggle operation is based on the observation that for any Boolean variable x, $x \oplus 0 = x$ and $x \oplus 1 = x'$. The same principle can be applied to multiple bits. For example, we can clear the upper nibble (i.e., four MSBs) by using

```
    and s0, 0F                ;mask=0000_1111
```

We can also apply the concept of the and mask to the **test** instruction to check a single bit. For example, the following code segment tests the MSB of the s0 register and branches to a proper routine accordingly:

```
    test s0, 80          ;mask=1000_0000
    jump nz, msb_set     ;MSB is 1, branch to msb_set
    ;code for MSB not set
    jump done
msb_set:
    ;code for MSB set
    ...
done:
    ...
```

A single bit can be extracted by applying the previous code. For example, the following code segment extracts the MSB of the s0 register and stores it in the s1 register:

```
    load s1, 00
    test s0, 80          ;mask=1000_0000, extract MSB
    jump z, done         ;yes, MSB is 0
    load s1, 01          ;no, load 1 to s1
```

```
done:
    ...
```

15.2.3 Multiple-byte manipulation

A microcontroller sometimes needs to handle wide, multiple-byte data, such as a large counter. Since the data width of PicoBlaze is 8 bits, processing this type of data requires a mechanism to propagate information between two successive instructions. PicoBlaze uses the carry flag for this purpose. For the arithmetic instructions, there are two versions for addition and subtraction, one with carry and one without carry, as in the **add** and **addcy** instructions. For the shift and rotate instructions, carry can be shifted into the MSB or LSB of a register, and vice versa.

Assume that x and y are 24-bit data and each occupies three registers. The following code segment illustrates the use of carry in multiple-byte addition:

```
namereg s0, x0   ;least significant byte of x
namereg s1, x1   ;middle byte of x
namereg s2, x2   ;most significant byte of x
namereg s3, y0   ;least significant byte of y
namereg s4, y1   ;middle byte of y
namereg s5, y2   ;most significant byte of y

;add: {x2,x1,x0} + {y2,y1,y0}
add x0, y0       ;add least significant bytes
addcy x1, y1     ;add middle bytes with carry
addcy x2, y2     ;add most significant bytes with carry
```

The first instruction performs normal addition of the least significant bytes and stores the carry-out bit into the carry flag. The second instruction then includes the carry flag when adding the middle bytes. Similarly, the third instruction uses the carry flag from the previous addition to obtain the result for the most significant bytes.

The incrementing and subtraction of multiple bytes can be achieved in a similar fashion:

```
;increment: {x2,x1,x0} + 1
add x0, 01       ;inc least significant byte
addcy x1, 00     ;add carry to middle byte
addcy x2, 00     ;add carry to most significant byte

;subtract: {x2,x1,x0} - {y2,y1,y0}
sub x0, y0       ;sub least significant byte
subcy x1, y1     ;sub middle byte with borrow
subcy x2, y2     ;sub most significant byte with borrow
```

Multiple-byte data can be shifted by including the carry flag in the individual shift instruction. For example, the **sla** instruction shifts data left one position and shifts the carry flag into LSB. The code for shifting a 3-byte data left can be written as

```
;shift {x2,x1,x0} via carry
sl0 x0           ;0 to LSB of x0, MSB of x0 to carry
sla x1           ;carry to LSB of x1, MSB of x1 to carry
sla x2           ;carry to LSB of x2, MSB of x2 to carry
```

15.2.4 Control structure

A high-level programming language usually contains various control constructs to alter the execution sequence. These include the if-then-else, case, and for-loop statements. On the other hand, PicoBlaze provides only simple conditional and unconditional **jump** instructions. Despite its simplicity, we can use them with a **test** or **compare** instruction to implement the high-level control constructs. The following examples illustrate the construction of the if-then-else, case, and for-loop statements.

Let us first consider the if-then-else statement:

```
if (s0==s1) {
   /* then-branch statements */
}
else {
   /* else-branch statements */
}
```

The corresponding assembly code segment is

```
   compare s0, s1
   jump nz, else_branch
   ;code for then branch
   ...
   jump if_done
else_branch:
   ;code for else branch
   ...
if_done:
   ;code following if statement
   ...
```

The code uses the **compare** instruction to check the `s0==s1` condition and to set the zero flag. The following **jump** instruction examines the flag and jumps to the else branch if the flag is not set.

The case statement can be considered as a multiway jump, in which the execution is transferred according to the value of the selection expression. The following statement uses the `s0` variable as the selection expression and jumps to the corresponding branch:

```
switch (s0) {
   case value1:
      /* case value1 statements */
      break;
   case value2:
      /* case value2 statements */
      break;
   case value3:
      /* case value3 statements */
      break;
   default:
      /* default statements */
}
```

The multiway jump can be implemented by a hardware feature known as "index address mode" in some processors. However, since PicoBlaze does not support this feature, the case statement has to be constructed as a sequence of if-then-else statements. In other words, the previous case statement is treated as:

```
if (s0==value1) {
   /* case value1 statements */
}
else if (s0==value2) {
   /* case value2 statements */
}
else if (s0==value3) {
   /* case value3 statements */
}
else{
   /* default statements */
}
```

The corresponding assembly code segment becomes

```
   constant value1, ...
   constant value2, ...
   constant value3, ...

   compare s0, value1     ;test value1
   jump nz, case_2        ;not equal to value1, jump
   ;code for case 1
   ...
   jump case_done
case_2:
   compare s0, value2     ;test value2
   jump nz, case_3        ;not equal to value2, jump
   ;code for case 2
   ...
   jump case_done
case_3:
   compare s0, value3     ;test value3
   jump default           ;not equal to value3, jump
   ;code for case 3
   ...
   jump case_done
default:
   ;code for default case
   ...
case_done:
   ;code following case statement
   ...
```

The for-loop statement executes a segment of the code repetitively. The loop statement can be implemented by using a counter to keep track of the iteration number. For example, consider the following:

```
for(i=MAX, i=0, i-1) {
   /* loop body statements */
}
```

The assembly code segment is

```
namereg s0, i          ;loop index
constant MAX, ...      ;loop boundary
```

```
    load i, MAX          ;load loop index
loop_body:
    ;code for loop body
    ...
    sub i, 01            ;dec loop index?
    jump nz, loop_body   ;done?
    ;code following for loop
    ...
```

15.3 SUBROUTINE DEVELOPMENT

A subroutine, such as a function in C, implements a section of a larger program. It is coded to perform a specific task and can be used repetitively. Using subroutines allows us to divide a program into small, manageable parts and thus greatly improve the reliability and readability of a program. It is the base of modern programming practice and is supported by all high-level programming languages.

PicoBlaze uses the **call** and **return** instructions to implement the subroutine. The **call** instruction saves the current content of the program counter and transfers the program execution to the starting address of a subroutine. A subroutine ends with a **return** instruction, which restores the saved program counter and resumes the previous execution. A representative flow is shown in Figure 14.7. Note that PicoBlaze only saves and restores the content of the program counter during a function call and return. We have to manage the register and data RAM use manually to ensure that the original system state is not altered after a subroutine call.

The following multiplication example illustrates the development of subroutines. We assume that the inputs are two 8-bit numbers in unsigned integer format and the output is a 16-bit product. The algorithm is based on a simple shift-and-add method. This method iterates through 8 bits of multiplier. In each iteration, the multiplicand is shifted left one position. If the corresponding multiplier bit is '1', the shifted multiplicand is added to the partial product. The assembly code is shown in Listing 15.1. The multiplicand and multiplier are stored in the s3 and s4 registers. The individual bit of multiplier is obtained by repetitively shifting s4 to the right, which moves the LSB to the carry flag. Note that instead of actually shifting the multiplicand to the left, we shift the partial product, which consists of 2 bytes and is stored in s5 and s6, to the right.

Listing 15.1 Software integer multiplication

```
;=========================================================
;routine: mult_soft
;  function: 8-bit unsigned multiplier using
;            shift-and-add algorithm
;  input register:
;     s3: multiplicand
;     s4: multiplier
;  output register:
;     s5: upper byte of product
;     s6: lower byte of product
;  temp register: i
;=========================================================
mult_soft:
   load s5, 00                ;clear s5
```

```
    load i, 08                    ;initialize loop index
mult_loop:
    sr0 s4                        ;shift LSB to carry
    jump nc, shift_prod           ;LSB is 0
    add s5, s3                    ;LSB is 1
shift_prod:
    sra s5                        ;shift upper byte right,
                                  ;carry to MSB, LSB to carry
    sra s6                        ;shift lower byte right,
                                  ;LSB of s5 to MSB of s6
    sub i, 01                     ;dec loop index
    jump nz, mult_loop            ;repeat until i=0
    return
```

Because of the primitive nature of the assembly language, thorough documentation is instrumental. A subroutine should include a descriptive header and detailed comments. A representative header is shown in Listing 15.1. It consists of a short function description and the use of registers. The latter shows how the registers are allocated and is crucial to preventing conflict in a large program.

15.4 PROGRAM DEVELOPMENT

Developing a complete assembly program consists of the following steps:

1. Derive the pseudo code of the *main program*.
2. Identify tasks in the main program and define them as subroutines. If needed, continue refining the complex subroutines and divide them into smaller routines.
3. Determine the register and data RAM use.
4. Derive assembly code for the subroutines.

Steps 1, 2, and 4 basically follow a *divide-and-conquer* approach and are applicable for any software development. A microcontroller-based application is normally for a simple embedded system, in which the processor monitors the I/O activities continuously and responds accordingly. Its main program usually has the following structure:

```
    call initilaization_routine
forever:
    call task1_routine
    call task2_routine
    ...
    call taskn_routine
    jump forever
```

Step 3 is unique for assembly code development. Unlike a high-level language program, in which the compiler automatically allocates storage to variables, we must manually manage the data storage in assembly code. PicoBlaze has 16 registers and 64 bytes of data RAM to store data. The registers can be considered as fast storage, in which the data can be manipulated directly. The data RAM, on the other hand, is "auxiliary" storage. Its data needs to be transferred to a register for processing. For example, if we want to increment a data item located in the RAM, it must first be loaded into a register, incremented there, and then stored back to the RAM.

Because of the limited space for data storage, its use has to be planned carefully in advance, particularly when the code is complex and involves nested subroutines. To assist

00	lower byte of a
01	unused
02	lower byte of b
03	unused
04	lower byte of a^2
05	upper byte of a^2
06	lower byte of b^2
07	upper byte of b^2
08	lower byte of $a^2 + b^2$
09	upper byte of $a^2 + b^2$
0A	carry of $a^2 + b^2$

Figure 15.1 Data RAM memory allocation.

coding, we can first identify the needed *global storage* or *local storage*. The former keeps data that is needed in the entire program. The latter provides space to store intermediate results, and the data will be discarded after the required computation is completed.

15.4.1 Demonstration example

The development process can best be explained by an example. Let us consider a program that uses the previous multiplication subroutine. It reads two inputs, a and b, from the switch, calculates $a^2 + b^2$, and displays the result on eight discrete LEDs. Since the I/O interface is to be discussed in Chapter 16, we limit the I/O to a single input port, the 8-bit switch, and a single output port, the 8-bit LEDs. We assume that a and b are obtained from the upper nibble (i.e., the four MSBs) and the lower nibble (i.e., the four LSBs) of the switch. The main program is

```
    call clear_data_ram
forever:
    call read_switch
    call square
    call write_led
    jump forever
```

The subroutines are defined as follows:

- `clr_data_mem`: clears data memory at system initialization
- `read_switch`: obtains the two nibbles from the switch and stores their values to the data RAM
- `square`: uses the multiplication subroutine to calculate $a^2 + b^2$
- `write_led`: writes the eight LSBs of the calculated result to the LED port

For demonstration purposes, we create two smaller routines, `get_upper_nibble` and `get_lower_nibble`, within the `read_switch` routine to obtain the upper nibble and lower nibble from a register.

The next step in development is to plan the register and data RAM use. For global storage, we introduce a global register, `sw_in`, to store the input value of switch and allocate 11 bytes of data RAM to store the inputs and result of the `square` routine. Allocation of the data RAM is shown in Figure 15.1. Note that the addresses 01 and 03 are not actually used. They are reserved to simplify the seven-segment LED display code, which is discussed in Chapter 16. All remaining registers are used as local storage. For program clarity, we define three symbolic names, data, addr, and i, as temporary registers for data, port and memory address, and loop index.

The last step is to derive the assembly code for the subroutines. The complete code is shown in Listing 15.2. The clr_data_mem uses a loop to clear data memory. The i register is the loop index and initialized with 64 (i.e., 40_{16}). The index is decremented in each loop and 0 is loaded to the corresponding data RAM address. The write_led routine fetches the eight LSBs of the calculated result from the data RAM and outputs them to the LED port.

The read_switch routine includes two smaller routines. The get_upper_nibble routine shifts the data register right four times to move the upper nibble to the four LSBs. The get_lowe_nibble routine clears the four MSBs of the data register to 0's and thus removes the upper nibble. The "glue instructions" of read_switch input the switch values, set up the input for the two nibble routines, and store the result in the data RAM.

The square routine fetches data from the data RAM, utilizes the mult_soft routine to calculate a^2 and b^2, performs addition, and stores the result back to the data RAM.

Listing 15.2 Square program with simple nibble input

```
;===========================================================
; square circuit with simple I/O interface
;===========================================================
;program operation:
;   - read switch to a (4 MSBs) and b (4 LSBs)
;   - calculate a*a + b*b
;   - display data on 8 leds

;===========================================================
; data constant
;===========================================================
constant UP_NIBBLE_MASK, 0F   ;00001111

;===========================================================
; data ram address alias
;===========================================================
constant a_lsb, 00
constant b_lsb, 02
constant aa_lsb, 04
constant aa_msb, 05
constant bb_lsb, 06
constant bb_msb, 07
constant aabb_lsb, 08
constant aabb_msb, 09
constant aabb_cout, 0A

;===========================================================
; register alias
;===========================================================
;commonly used local variables
namereg s0, data   ;reg for temporary data
namereg s1, addr   ;reg for temporary mem & i/o port addr
namereg s2, i      ;general-purpose loop index
;global variables
namereg sf, sw_in
```

```
;=================================================================
; port alias
;=================================================================
;---------------input port definitions---------------------
constant sw_port, 01 ;8-bit switches
;---------------output port definitions--------------------
constant led_port, 05

;=================================================================
; main program
;=================================================================
;calling hierarchy:
;
;main
;   - clr_data_mem
;   - read_switch
;       - get_upper_nibble
;       - get_lower_nibble
;   - square
;       - mult_soft
;   - write_led
;

   call clr_data_mem
forever:
   call read_switch
   call square
   call write_led
   jump forever

;=================================================================
;routine: clr_data_mem
;  function: clear data ram
;  temp register: data, i
;=================================================================
clr_data_mem:
   load i, 40              ;unitize loop index to 64
   load data, 00
clr_mem_loop:
   store data, (i)
   sub i, 01               ;dec loop index
   jump nz, clr_mem_loop   ;repeat until i=0
   return

;=================================================================
;routine: read switch
;  function: obtain two nibbles from input
;  input register: sw_in
;  temp register: data
;=================================================================
read_switch:
   input sw_in, sw_port    ;read switch input
```

```
   load data, sw_in
   call get_lower_nibble
   store data, a_lsb        ;store a to data ram
   load data, sw_in
   call get_upper_nibble
   store data, b_lsb        ;store b to data ram

;=========================================================
;routine: get_lower_nibble
;  function: get lower 4 bits of data
;  input register: data
;  output register: data
;=========================================================
get_lower_nibble:
   and data, UP_NIBBLE_MASK ;clear upper nibble
   return

;=========================================================
;routine: get_upper_nible
;  function: get upper 4 bits of data
;  input register: data
;  output register: data
;=========================================================
get_upper_nibble:
   sr0 data                 ;right shift 4 times
   sr0 data
   sr0 data
   sr0 data
   return

;=========================================================
;routine: write_led
;  function: output 8 LSBs of result to 8 leds
;  temp register: data
;=========================================================
write_led:
   fetch data, aabb_lsb
   output data, led_port
   return

;=========================================================
;routine: square
;  function: calculate a*a + b*b
;     data/result stored in ram started w/ SQ_BASE_ADDR
;  temp register: s3, s4, s5, s6, data
;=========================================================
square:
   ;calculate a*a
   fetch s3, a_lsb           ;load a
   fetch s4, a_lsb           ;load a
   call mult_soft            ;calculate a*a
   store s6, aa_lsb          ;store lower byte of a*a
   store s5, aa_msb          ;store upper byte of a*a
```

```
      ; calculate b*b
      fetch s3, b_lsb              ;load b
      fetch s4, b_lsb              ;load b
      call mult_soft               ;calculate b*b
      store s6, bb_lsb             ;store lower byte of b*b
      store s5, 07                 ;store upper byte of b*b
      ; calculate a*a+b*b
      fetch data, aa_lsb           ;get lower byte of a*a
      add data, s6                 ;add lower byte of a*a+b*b
      store data, aabb_lsb         ;store lower byte of a*a+b*b
      fetch data, aa_msb           ;get upper byte of a*a
      addcy data, s5               ;add upper byte of a*a+b*b
      store data, aabb_msb         ;store upper byte of a*a+b*b
      load data, 00                ;clear data, but keep carry
      addcy data, 00               ;get carry-out from previous +
      store data, aabb_cout        ;store carry-out of a*a+b*b
      return

;=================================================================
;routine: mult_soft
;  function: 8-bit unsigned multiplier using
;            shift-and-add algorithm
;  input register:
;     s3: multiplicand
;     s4: multiplier
;  output register:
;     s5: upper byte of product
;     s6: lower byte of product
;  temp register: i
;=================================================================
mult_soft:
   load s5, 00                     ;clear s5
   load i, 08                      ;initialize loop index
mult_loop:
   sr0 s4                          ;shift lsb to carry
   jump nc, shift_prod             ;lsb is 0
   add s5, s3                      ;lsb is 1
 shift_prod:
   sra s5                          ;shift upper byte right,
                                   ;carry to MSB, LSB to carry
   sra s6                          ;shift lower byte right,
                                   ;lsb of s5 to MSB of s6
   sub i, 01                       ;dec loop index
   jump nz, mult_loop              ;repeat until i=0
   return
```

15.4.2 Program documentation

Developing an assembly program is a tedious process. The use of symbolic names and good documentation can make the code clear and reduce many unnecessary errors. It also helps future revision and maintenance. For the KCPSM3 assembler, we can use the **constant** directive to assign a symbolic name (alias) to a data constant, a memory address, or a port id, and use the **namereg** directive to assign a symbolic name to a register.

A representative main program header is shown in Listing 15.2. It contains the following segments:

- *General program description*: provides a general description for the purpose, operation, and I/O of the program
- *Data constants*: declares symbolic names for constants
- *Data RAM address alias*: declares symbolic names for data RAM addresses
- *Register alias*: declares symbolic names for registers
- *Port alias*: declares symbolic names for I/O ports
- *Program calling hierarchy*: illustrates the calling structure and subroutines

The aliases and directives have no effect on the final machine code. When the assembly code is processed, they are replaced with the actual constant values. However, using aliases can greatly enhance the readability of the assembly code and reduce unnecessary errors. The following code segment further illustrates the impact of the alias and documentation. The purpose of this segment is to obtain values for variables a, b, and c, and store them in proper data RAM locations. The location is specified by the UART input, which is the ASCII code of character a, b, or c. The segment with aliases and proper comments is

```
;constant alias
   constant ASCII_a, 61             ;ASCII code for a
   constant ASCII_b, 62             ;ASCII code for b
   constant ASCII_c, 63             ;ASCII code for c
;data ram address alias
   constant a_addr, 02
   constant b_addr, 04
   constant c_addr, 06
;register alias
   namereg s0, data                 ;reg for temporary data
   namereg s1, addr                 ;reg for temporary addr
   namereg sF, sw_in                ;switch input
;port alias
   constant sw_port, 01             ;switch input
   constant uart_rx_port, 02        ;UART input

;assembly code with alias
   ;get input
   input sw_in, sw_port             ;get switch
   input data, uart_rx_port         ;get char
   ;check received char
   compare data, ASCII_a            ;check ASCII a
   jump nz, chk_ascii_b             ;no, check next
   store  sw_in, a_addr             ;yes, store a to data ram
   jump done
chk_ascii_b:
   compare data, ASCII_b            ;check ASCII b
   jump nz, chk_ascii_c             ;no, check next
   store sw_in, b_addr              ;yes, store b to data ram
   jump done
chk_ascii_c:
   compare data, ASCII_c            ;check ASCII c
   jump nz, ascii_err               ;no, error
```

```
    store sw_in, c_addr              ;yes, store b to data ram
    jump done
ascii_err:
    ...
done:
    ...
```

If we use hard literals and strip the comments, the code becomes

```
;assembly code with no alias or comments
    input sf, 01
    input s0, 02
    compare s0, 61
    jump nz, addr1
    store sf, 02
    jump addr4
addr1:
    compare s0, 62
    jump nz, addr2
    store sf, 04
    jump addr4
addr2:
    compare s0, 63
    jump nz, addr3
    store sf, 06
    jump addr4
addr3:
    ...
addr4:
    ...
```

While the functionality of this code segment is the same, it is very difficult to comprehend, debug, or modify.

15.5 PROCESSING OF THE ASSEMBLY CODE

PicoBlaze-based development flow is reviewed in Section 14.4. After the assembly code is developed, it is then compiled (translated) to machine instruction in step 3. The instruction-set-level simulation can also be performed to verify the correctness of the code, as in step 4. The two steps and the direct downloading process (step 9) are discussed in detail in this section.

Xilinx provides an assembler known as *KCPSM3* for compiling in step 3 and downloading utility programs in step 9. The programs, HDL codes for the PicoBlaze processor, and relevant template files can be downloaded from the Xilinx's web site. A program known as *PBlazeIDE* from Mediatronix can perform the instruction-set-level simulation in step 4. It can also be used as an assembler. PBlazeIDE can be downloaded from Mediatronix's Web site.

15.5.1 Compiling with KCSPM3

Assembler is the software that translates the instruction mnemonics to machine instructions, which are represented as 0's and 1's, and substitutes the aliases and symbolic branch addresses with actual values. The machine instructions are then downloaded to the instruction memory of a microcontroller. Since PicoBlaze is embedded inside FPGA, the instruction ROM becomes an HDL ROM module with the compiled assembly code. The ROM will be instantiated later in the top-level HDL code and synthesized along with PicoBlaze and the I/O interface circuit.

Xilinx provides the *KCPSM3* assembler for this task. It is a command-line, DOS-based program. KCPSM3 basically takes an assembly program, along with the necessary template files, and generates the HDL code for the instruction ROM. The procedure of compiling an assembly program is as follows:

1. Create a directory for the project and copy `kcpsm3.exe`, `ROM_form.vhd`, `ROM_form.v`, and `ROM_form.coe` to the directory. The latter three are code templates used by KCPSM3.
2. Create the assembly program and save it as plain text file with an extension of `.psm`. Any PC-based editor, such as Notepad, can be used for this purpose.
3. Invoke a DOS window by selecting Start ≻ Programs ≻ Accessories ≻ Command Prompt. In the DOS window, navigate to the project directory.
4. Type `kcpsm3 myfile.psm` to run the program.
5. Correct syntax errors if necessary and recompile.
6. After successful compiling, the file containing the instruction ROM, `myfile.vhd`, is generated.

In addition to the HDL file, KCPSM3 also generates files that are suitable for block RAM initialization and other utilities. The file with the `.hex` extension can be used for JTAG downloading, which is discussed in Section 15.5.3, and the file with the `.fmt` extension is a reformatted `.psm` file for "pretty printing."

15.5.2 Simulation by PBlazeIDE

As the name indicates, instruction-set-level simulation simulates the operation of a PicoBlaze system instruction by instruction. The *PBlazeIDE* program can be used for this purpose. PBlazeIDE is a Windows-based program with an integrated development environment, which includes a text editor, an assembler, and an instruction-set-level simulator.

PBlazeIDE uses slightly different instruction mnemonics and directives, as discussed in Section 14.5. Thus, the code written for by KCPSM3 cannot be used directly by PBlazeIDE, and vice versa. The mnemonic differences are summarized in Table 15.1, and the directive examples are shown in Table 15.2. Note that the PBlazeIDE assembler uses both decimal and hexadecimal format for constants. A hexadecimal number is started with a $ sign, as in `$1A`.

The procedure of using PBlazeIDE for KCPSM3 code is as follows:

1. Compile the assembly code with KCPSM3.
2. Launch PBlazeIDE.
3. Select Settings ≻ PicoBlaze 3. This specifies the version 3 of PicoBlaze, which is used in the Spartan-3 device.
4. Select File ≻ Import and a dialog window appears. Select the corresponding `.fmt` file. The "import" function converts the KCPSM3 code to the PBlazeIDE code. The formatted program is easier for conversion. The converted file may sometimes need minor manual editing.
5. Manually specify the **dsin, dsout**, and **dsio** directives for I/O ports. When one of these directives is used, a port indicator will be added to the simulation screen to show the activities of the port.

Table 15.1 Mnemonic differences between KCPSM3 and PBlazeIDE

KCPSM3	PBlazeIDE
addcy	**addc**
subcy	**subc**
compare	**comp**
store sX, (sY)	**store** sX, sY
fetch sX, (sY)	**fetch** sX, sY
input sX, (sY)	**in** sX, sY
input sX, KK	**in** sX, $KK
output sX, (sY)	**out** sX, sY
output sX, KK	**out** sX, $KK
return	**ret**
returni	**reti**
enable interrupt	**eint**
disable interrupt	**dint**

Table 15.2 Directive examples of KCPSM3 and PBlazeIDE

Function	KCPSM3	PBlazeIDE
code location	**address** 3FF	**org** $3FF
constant	**constant** MAX, 3F	MAX **equ** $3F
register alias	**namereg** addr, s2	addr **equ** s2
port alias	**constant** in_port, 00	in_port **dsin** $00
	constant out_port, 10	out_port **dsout** $10
	constant bi_port, 0F	bi_port **dsio** $0F

6. Enter the simulation mode by selecting Simulate ≻ Simulate. Perform simulation.
7. If the assembly code needs to be revised, it must be done outside PBlazeIDE. Simply close the current file, invoke an external editor to edit the original .psm file, save the file, and restart from step 1. If the file is edited within PBlazeIDE, it cannot be converted back to KCPSM3 code.

A representative simulation screenshot is shown in Figure 15.2. The simulator displays the assembly code in the central window and highlights the next instruction to be executed. The instruction address, instruction code, and breakpoints are shown next to the code. The current state of PicoBlaze is shown at the left, which includes the status of the flags, the content of the registers, and the content of the data RAM. The values of the program counter and stack pointer as well as some execution statistics are shown in the bottom row.

The emulated I/O ports created by the **dsin**, **dsout**, and **dsio** directives are shown at the right. There are an input port, `switch`, and an output port, `led`, on this particular screen. Since PBlazeIDE has no information about I/O behavior, the input port data must be entered and modified manually during simulation.

During simulation, the assembly program can be executed continuously, by one step, by one instruction, or to pause at a specific breakpoint. The simulation action is controlled by the commands of the Simulate menu or the icons on the top:

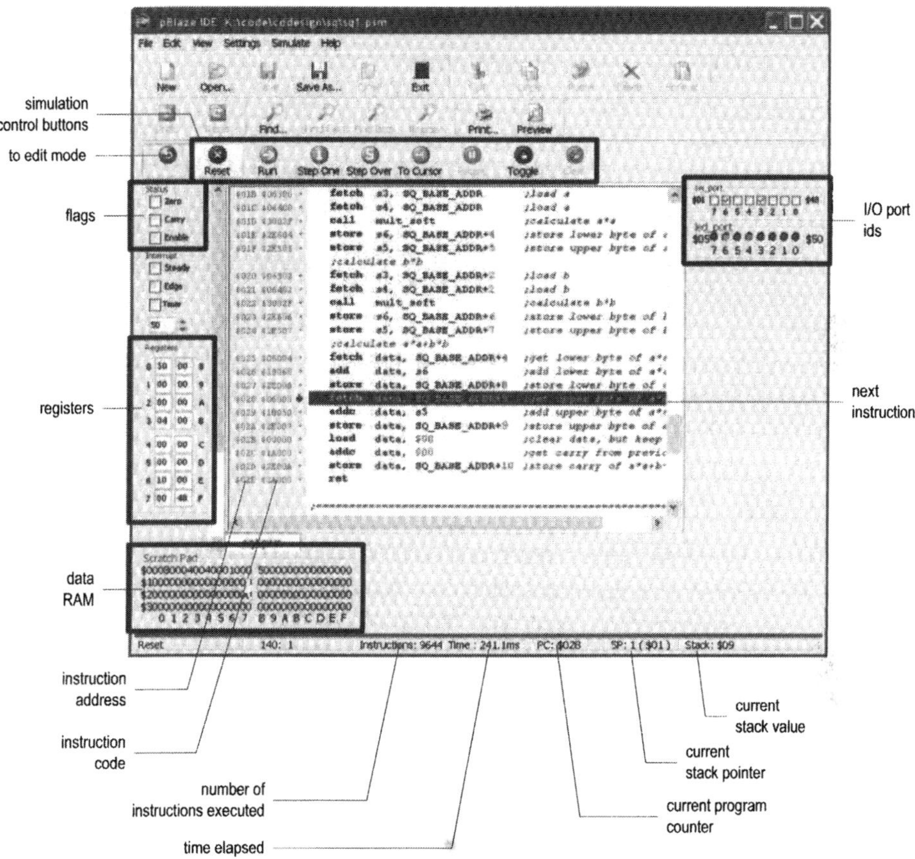

Figure 15.2 Screenshot of pBlazeIDE in simulation mode.

- Reset: clears the program counter and stack pointer
- Run: runs the program continuously until a breakpoint
- Single step: executes one instruction
- Step over: executes the entire subroutine for a **call** instruction and executes one instruction for other instructions
- Run to cursor: runs the program to the current cursor position
- Pause: pauses the simulation
- Toggle breakpoint: sets or clears a breakpoint at the current cursor position
- Remove all breakpoints: clears all breakpoints

15.5.3 Reloading code via the JTAG port

After the instruction ROM HDL is generated, we can continue steps 6 and 8 in Figure 14.4 to synthesize the entire code and download the configuration file to the FPGA chips. Note that the synthesis flow must be repeated each time the assembly code is modified.

Since synthesis is a complex process, it requires a significant amount of computation time. When the I/O configuration is fixed, resynthesizing the entire circuit after each assembly program modification is not really needed. It is possible to reload the machine code to the ROM, which is implemented by a block RAM, by using the FPGA's JTAG interface. This corresponds to the dotted line of step 9 in Figure 14.4. The basic procedure is as follows:

1. Replace the original ROM template with one that contains the JTAG interface circuit.
2. Use KCPSM3 to compile the assembly code as usual.
3. Synthesize the top-level HDL code and program the FPGA chip.
4. In subsequent assembly program modifications, compile the program as usual. Recall that a file in `hex` format (ended with the `.hex` extension) is generated.
5. Use the Xilinx utility to embed the `.hex` file to a JTAG programming file and download the file to the FPGA's block RAM via the JTAG interface.

The detailed procedure and the relevant programs and templates can be found in the `JTAG_loader` directory of the downloaded `KCPSM` file.

15.5.4 Compiling by PBlazeIDE

As discussed earlier, PBlazeIDE is an integrated program that contains an assembler and editor. If the program is developed with PBlazeIDE mnemonics, PBlazeIDE can replace the KCPSM3 assembler. The instruction ROM VHDL file is generated by a directive. If the HDL file is needed, simply include the **vhdl** directive in the assembly code. Its syntax is

```
vhdl "ROM_form.vhd", "rom_target.vhd", "rom_entity_name"
```

The `"ROM_form.vhd"` term specifies a VHDL template file, which is the same file as that discussed in Section 15.5.1. It should be copied to the directory where the assembly program file resides. The `"rom_target.vhd"` term specifies the name of the generated ROM VHDL file, and the `"rom_entity_name"` term indicates the desired entity name of the previously generated VHDL file. The VHDL file is generated automatically when PBlazeIDE is switched from the edit mode to the simulation mode.

Note that since PBlazeIDE does not generate a `hex` file, the reloading scheme discussed in Section 15.5.3 cannot be applied directly.

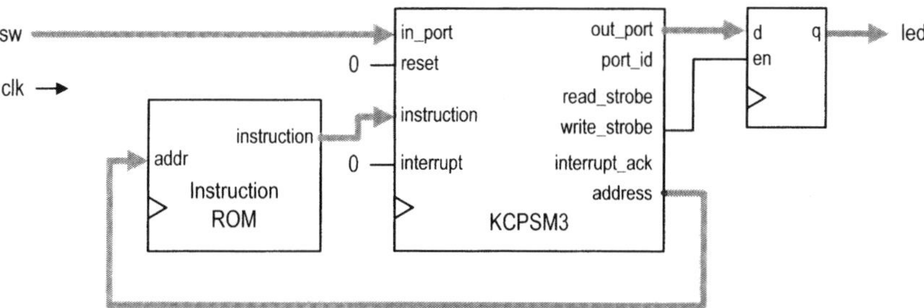

Figure 15.3 PicoBlaze with a simple I/O interface.

15.6 SYNTHESES WITH PICOBLAZE

After generating the HDL file for the instruction ROM, we can combine it with PicoBlaze to synthesize the entire system in an FPGA chip. Unlike a normal microcontroller, PicoBlaze has no built-in I/O peripherals. The I/O interface is created and customized as needed. The circuit is described in HDL code. Since the focus in this chapter is assembly program development, we use a simple I/O configuration, which contains only one switch input port and one led output port, for synthesis. The development of more sophisticated I/O interface is discussed in detail in Chapters 16 and 17.

The top-level block diagram of this design is shown in Figure 15.3. It contains the PicoBlaze processor, which is labeled `kcpsm3`, the instruction ROM, and a register. The register functions as a buffer for the eight LEDs. When PicoBlaze executes the **output** instruction, it places the data on `out_port` and asserts the `write_strobe` signal, which enables the register and stores the data in the register. The `sw` signal is connected to `in_port`. When PicoBlaze executes the **input** instruction, it retrieves the value of the `sw` signal and stores it in an internal register. The corresponding HDL code is shown in Listing 15.3. It consists of instantiations of the PicoBlaze processor and instruction ROM, and a segment for the output buffer. The `kcpsm3` entity is the name of the PicoBlaze processor, and its code is stored in an HDL file of the same name. The `sio_rom` entity is from the previously generated instruction ROM file.

Listing 15.3 PicoBlaze with a simple I/O configuration

```
library ieee;
use ieee.std_logic_1164.all;
use ieee.numeric_std.all;
entity pico_sio is
   port(
      clk, reset: in std_logic;
      sw: in std_logic_vector(7 downto 0);
      led: out std_logic_vector(7 downto 0)
   );
end pico_sio;

architecture arch of pico_sio is
   -- KCPSM3/ROM signals
   signal address: std_logic_vector(9 downto 0);
   signal instruction: std_logic_vector(17 downto 0);
   signal port_id: std_logic_vector(7 downto 0);
```

```
   signal in_port, out_port: std_logic_vector(7 downto 0);
   signal write_strobe: std_logic;
   -- register signals
   signal led_reg: std_logic_vector(7 downto 0);

begin
   -- =============================================================
   --  KCPSM and ROM instantiation
   -- =============================================================
   proc_unit: entity work.kcpsm3
      port map(
         clk=>clk, reset=>reset,
         address=>address, instruction=>instruction,
         port_id=>open, write_strobe=>write_strobe,
         out_port=>out_port, read_strobe=>open,
         in_port=>in_port, interrupt=>'0',
         interrupt_ack=>open);
   rom_unit: entity work.sio_rom
      port map(
          clk => clk, address=>address,
          instruction=>instruction);
   -- =============================================================
   --  output interface
   -- =============================================================
   --output register
   process (clk)
   begin
      if (clk'event and clk='1') then
         if write_strobe='1' then
            led_reg <= out_port;
         end if;
      end if;
   end process;
   led <= led_reg;
   -- =============================================================
   --  input interface
   -- =============================================================
   in_port <= sw;
end arch;
```

15.7 BIBLIOGRAPHIC NOTES

The bibliographic information for this chapter is similar to that for Chapter 14. The procedure of reloading compiled code via JTAG port is explained in the article, "PicoBlaze JTAG Loader Quick User Guide," by Kris Chaplin and Ken Chapman, which appears in the `JTAG_loader` directory of the downloaded `KCPSM` file.

15.8 SUGGESTED EXPERIMENTS

15.8.1 Signed multiplication

The subroutine in Listing 15.1 assumes that the inputs are in unsigned integer format. Modify the subroutine to perform the signed multiplication, in which the two inputs and output are interpreted as signed integers, and use simulation to verify its operation.

15.8.2 Multi-byte multiplication

The subroutine in Listing 15.1 assumes that the inputs are 8 bits wide. Some application may need more precision and we want to extend the subroutine to take 16-bit unsigned inputs. An operand now requires two registers and the result needs four registers. Develop the subroutine and use simulation to verify its operation.

15.8.3 Barrel shift function

PicoBlaze can only shift or rotate a single bit. A "barrel" shifting function can perform the shift and rotate operation for multiple bits. This function has three input registers. The first register contains data to be shifted or rotated; the second register specifies the amount, which is between 0 and 7; and the third register indicates the types of operation, which can be shift left, shift right, rotate left, or rotate right. We assume that 0 will be shifted in for the two shift operations. Develop the subroutine and use simulation to verify its operation.

15.8.4 Reverse function

A reverse function reverses the bit order of an input. For example, if the input is "01010011", the output becomes "11001010". We can use the 8-bit switch as input and the 8-bit discrete LEDs as output. Derive and simulate the assembly code, obtain the instruction ROM and create the top-level HDL code, synthesize the system, and verify its operation.

15.8.5 Binary-to-BCD conversion

Binary-to-BCD conversion is discussed in Section 6.3.3. This function can be implemented by using assembly code as well. Assume that the input is an 8-bit binary number and the output is a two-digit 8-bit BCD number. If the input exceeds 99, the output generates a special overflow pattern, "11111111". We can use the 8-bit switch as input and the 8-bit discrete LEDs as output. Derive and simulate the assembly code, obtain the instruction ROM and create the top-level HDL code, synthesize the system, and verify its operation.

15.8.6 BCD-to-binary conversion

Repeat Experiment 15.8.5, but develop the assembly code and circuit for BCD-to-binary conversion.

15.8.7 Heartbeat circuit

A "heartbeat circuit" is discussed in Experiment 4.7.4. We can create a similar pattern using the eight discrete LEDs as well. Derive and simulate the assembly code, obtain the instruction ROM and create the top-level HDL code, synthesize the system, and verify its operation.

15.8.8 Rotating LED circuit

We want to design a circuit that rotates a simple LED pattern to the left or right at four different speeds. The four patterns are "00000001", "00000011", "00001111", and "00001101". The pattern, direction, and rotation speed can be selected from the 8-bit switch (only 5 bits are used). The speed should be properly chosen so that all four patterns are visually observable. Derive and simulate the assembly code, obtain the instruction ROM and create the top-level HDL code, synthesize the system, and verify its operation.

15.8.9 Discrete LED dimmer

The concept of PWM and LED dimmer are discussed in Experiment 4.7.2. In this experiment, we want to use eight discrete LEDS to show the various degrees of the brightness. This can be done by changing the "on" fraction of an LED. The "on" fraction of the eight LEDS will be $\frac{8}{8}, \frac{7}{8}, \frac{6}{8}, \ldots, \frac{1}{8}$. Derive and simulate the assembly code, obtain the instruction ROM and create the top-level HDL code, synthesize the system, and verify its operation.

CHAPTER 16

PICOBLAZE I/O INTERFACE

16.1 INTRODUCTION

To interact with the external environment, a regular microcontroller chip consists of a variety of built-in I/O peripherals, such as a UART, SPI (serial peripheral interface), timer, etc. When starting a new development, we select a microcontroller chip according to the I/O requirements of the application and may sometimes need to use additional chips to realize less commonly used functions.

Unlike a regular microcontroller, PicoBlaze has no built-in I/O peripherals. It just provides a simple generic input and output structure for an I/O interface. I/O peripherals are constructed as needed and thus are customized to each application. PicoBlaze uses the **input** and **output** instructions to transfer data between its internal registers and I/O ports, and its interface consists of the following signals:

- `port_id`: an 8-bit signal that specifies the port id (i.e., port address) of an **input** or **output** instruction
- `in_port`: an 8-bit signal where PicoBlaze obtains input data during operation of an **input** instruction
- `out_port`: an 8-bit signal where PicoBlaze places output data during operation of an **output** instruction
- `read_strobe`: a 1-bit signal that is asserted in the second clock cycle of an **input** instruction
- `write_strobe`: a 1-bit signal that is asserted in the second clock cycle of an **output** instruction

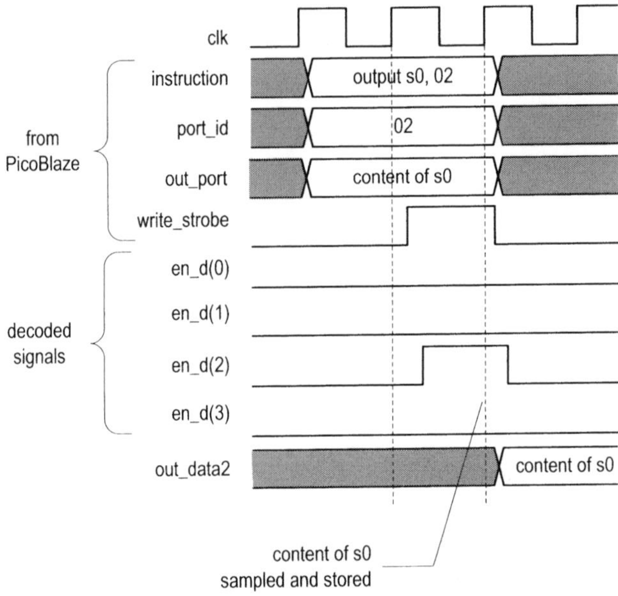

Figure 16.1 Timing diagram of an **output** instruction.

Although there are only two 8-bit ports to input and output data, the 8-bit port_id signal can be used to distinguish different peripherals, and thus it is said that PicoBlaze can support up to 256 (i.e., 2^8) input ports and 256 output ports.

In the remaining chapter, we examine the detailed I/O timing of PicoBlaze and illustrate the I/O interface development by adding a series of peripherals for the square circuit of Chapter 15.

16.2 OUTPUT PORT

16.2.1 Output instruction and timing

The **output** instruction writes data to the output port. It has two forms:

```
output sX, (sY)
output sX, port_name
```

In the first form, the port id is stored in the sY register. In the second form, the port id is specified explicitly by port_name, which is a two-digit hexadecimal number or a previously defined symbolic constant. The output data is always stored in the sX register.

The timing diagram of an **output** instruction,

```
output s0, 02
```

is shown in the top five traces of Figure 16.1. Recall that each PicoBlaze instruction takes two clock cycles. When the instruction is executed, the content of s0 is placed on out_port and 02 is placed on port_id for two clock cycles. The write_strobe signal is asserted in the second clock cycle. It can be used as an enable tick to store data in an output register or to initiate the designated peripheral operation.

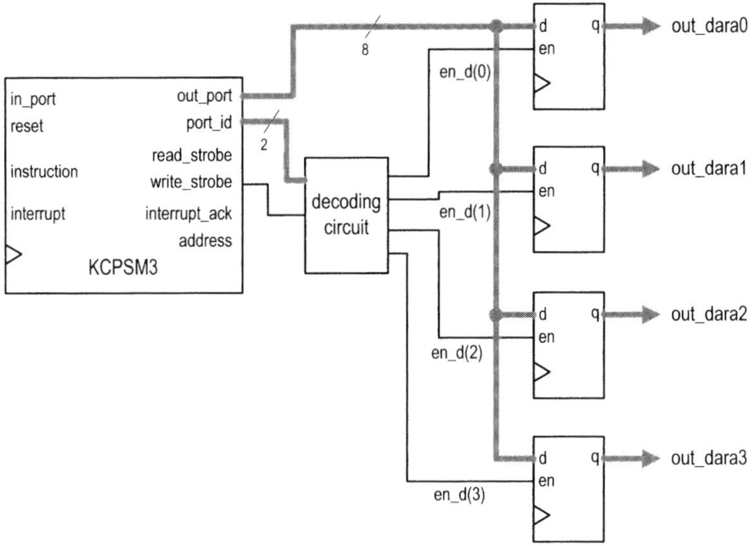

Figure 16.2 Output decoding of four output registers.

Table 16.1 Truth table of a decoding circuit

input			**output**
`write_strobe`	`port_id(1)`	`port_id(0)`	`en_d`
0	–	–	0000
1	0	0	0001
1	0	1	0010
1	1	0	0100
1	1	1	1000

16.2.2 Output interface

The output interface between PicoBlaze and an output peripheral usually consists of a decoding circuit and necessary output buffers, which are normally an array of registers. The decoding circuit decodes the port id and generates an enable tick accordingly. After the **output** instruction, the data will be stored in the designated buffer.

To illustrate the construction, let us consider a PicoBlaze interface with four output buffers. We assign 00_{16}, 01_{16}, 02_{16}, and 03_{16} as their port ids. Note that the six MSBs of the port addresses are identical and only two LSBs are needed to distinguish a port. The block diagram is shown in Figure 16.2. The key is the decoding circuit, whose function table is shown in Table 16.1. It is a 2-to-2^2 decoder. In the second clock cycle of an **output** instruction, `write_strobe` is asserted and 1 bit of the 4-bit `en_d` signal is asserted accordingly. The one-clock-cycle enable tick activates the corresponding output register to retrieve data from the `out_port` signal. The decoding timing diagram of the instruction

```
output s0, 02
```

is shown at the bottom of Figure 16.1. During the second clock cycle of the **output** instruction, the `en_d(2)` signal is asserted and the data value on `out_port` is stored in the corresponding buffer at the rising edge of the next clock.

Once understanding the basic operation, we can derive the HDL code accordingly. The code segment is

```
process(write_strobe,port_id)
begin
   if write_strobe='0' then
      en_d <= "0000";
   else
      case port_id(1 downto 0) is
         when "00" =>
            en_d <= "0001";
         when "01" =>
            en_d <= "0010";
         when "10" =>
            en_d <= "0100";
         when others =>
            en_d <= "1000";
      end case;
   end if;
end process;
```

This scheme is very general and can be applied to any number of output ports.

The choice of the port address is somewhat arbitrary. We use the binary code in the previous example. If the number of the output port is smaller than eight, one-hot code can be used to simplify the decoding circuit. For example, we can define the four previous port ids as 01_{16} (i.e., 00000001_2), 02_{16} (i.e., 00000010_2), 04_{16} (i.e., 00000100_2), and 08_{16} (i.e., 00001000_2). The decoding logic can be simplified to

```
process(write_strobe,port_id)
begin
   if write_strobe='0' then
      en_d <= "0000";
   else
      en_d <= port_id(3 downto 0);
   end if;
end process;
```

Note that no decoding logic is needed if there is only a single output port. The `write_strobe` signal can be connected to the register's enable signal, as shown in Figure 15.3.

As discussed in Section 15.4.2, it is good practice to use symbolic aliases for I/O ports and declare its binary address in the header. For example, the initial output port address assignment can be declared as

```
;--------------output port definitions--------------
constant out_port_a, 00
constant out_port_b, 01
constant out_port_c, 02
constant out_port_d, 04
```

If the assignment is changed, we need to modify the header but keep the remaining assembly code intact. Using a clear header also allows us easily to identify the port ids when the companion HDL code is developed.

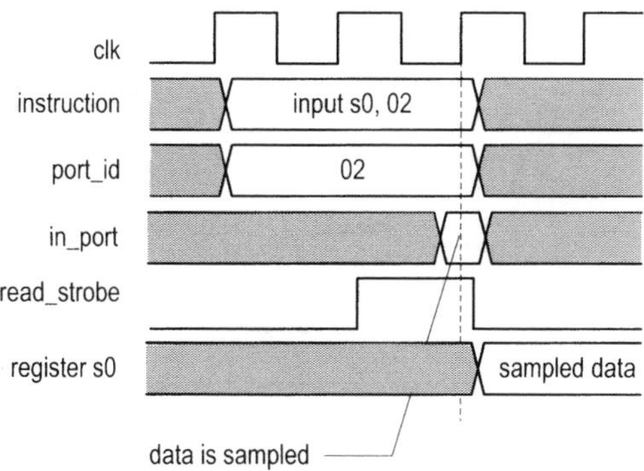

Figure 16.3 Timing diagram of an **input** instruction.

16.3 INPUT PORT

16.3.1 Input instruction and timing

The **input** instruction reads data from the input port. Similar to the **output** instruction, it has two forms:

```
input sX, (sY)
input sX, port_name
```

The `sY` register or `port_name` specifies the read port id. The retrieved data is stored in the `sX` register.

The timing diagram of an **input** instruction,

```
input s0, 02
```

is shown in Figure 16.3. When the instruction is executed, `02` is placed on `port_id`. After two clock cycles, `in_port` will be sampled at the rising edge of the clock and its value is stored in the `s0` register. The external circuit must ensure that the input data is stable during the sampling edge to avoid timing violation.

As in the **output** instruction, the `read_strobe` signal is asserted in the second clock cycle. The function of the `read_strobe` signal is less obvious and is discussed in the next subsection.

16.3.2 Input interface

The input interface between PicoBlaze and input peripherals usually consists of a multiplexing circuit, which uses `port_id` as the selection signal to route the desired value to `in_port`. Sometimes, a decoding circuit similar to the one in the output interface is also necessary to signal the completion of the data access.

For the purpose of input interface design, an input port can be classified as a *continuous-access* or *single-access port*. For a continuous-access port, the data is presented continuously, such as the switch input of Section 15.4.1. On the other hand, the availability of data of a single-access port is triggered by a single discrete event, such as receiving a character in an UART buffer. The flag FF and buffers discussed in Section 7.2.4 are in this category. After the data is retrieved, we must remove it from the buffer to prevent the same data from

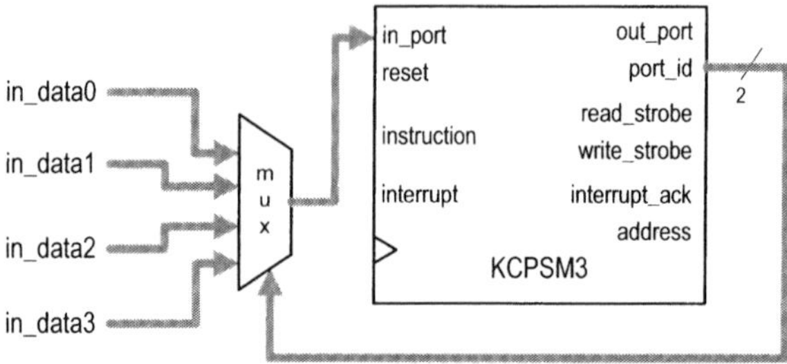

Figure 16.4 Block diagram of four continuous-access ports.

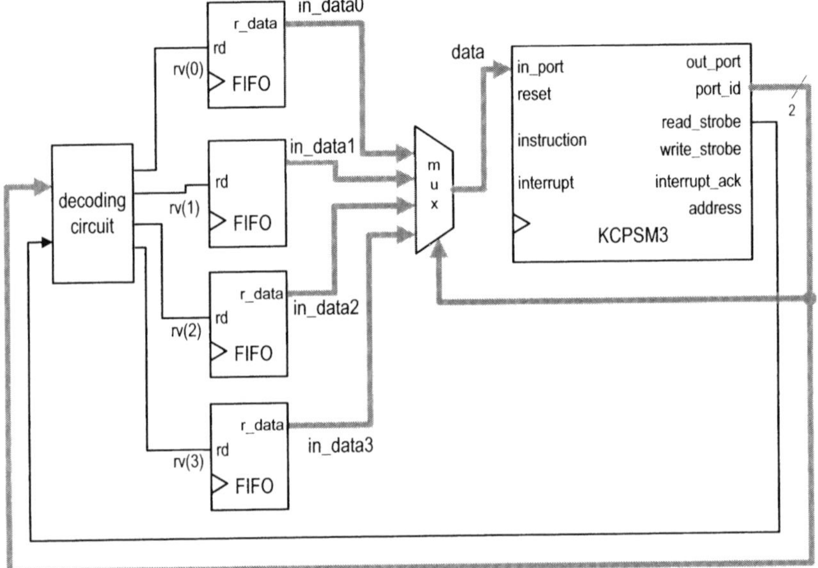

Figure 16.5 Block diagram of four single-access ports.

being processed again. This is usually done by utilizing a one-clock-cycle tick to clear the flag FF or remove a word from a FIFO buffer.

The interface for continuous-access ports involves only a multiplexing circuit. Consider an interface with four such ports. The block diagram is shown in Figure 16.4.

The interface for single-access ports needs a mechanism to remove the retrieved data from the buffer in the end of an **input** instruction. This can be done by using a decoding circuit that decodes the `port_id` and `read_strobe` signals. The circuit is identical to the decoding circuit of the output interface except that `write_strobe` is replaced by `read_strobe`. The decoded output can be considered as a "removal" signal, which is asserted for one clock cycle and removes the previously retrieved data. Consider an interface with four FIFOs. The diagram of the complete decoding and multiplexing circuit is shown in Figure 16.5. The `rv` signal is the decoded removal signal. In the end of an **input** instruction, 1 bit of this 4-bit signal is asserted and the corresponding FIFO performs a read operation, in which the first word is removed from the buffer. Assume that 00_{16}, 01_{16}, 02_{16}, and 03_{16} are assigned as the port ids. The HDL code segment for the interface is

```
-- multiplexing circuit
with port_id(1 downto 0) select
   data <= in_data0 when "00",
           in_data1 when "01",
           in_data2 when "10",
           in_data3 when others;
-- decoding circuit
process(reade_strobe,port_id)
begin
   if read_strobe='0' then
      rv <= "0000";
   else
      case port_id(1 downto 0) is
         when "00" =>
            rv <= "0001";
         when "01" =>
            rv <= "0010";
         when "10" =>
            rv <= "0100";
         when others =>
            rv <= "1000";
      end case;
   end if;
end process;
```

In a real application, it is likely that the input interface contains both continuous- and single-access ports. A decoding circuit is only needed for single-access ports.

16.4 SQUARE PROGRAM WITH A SWITCH AND SEVEN-SEGMENT LED DISPLAY INTERFACE

To demonstrate the construction of the PicoBlaze I/O interface, we add more versatile input and output peripherals to the square routine of Chapter 15. Recall that the square routine calculates $a^2 + b^2$, where a and b are 8-bit unsigned integers.

We use the 8-bit switch and a pushbutton to enter the values of a and b. The pushbutton generates a one-clock-cycle tick when pressed. The tick indicates that the current value of the switch should be loaded. The values of a and b are loaded alternately; i.e., the first pressing loads a, the second pressing loads b, the third pushing loads a, and so on. A second pushbutton is also included to clear the PicoBlaze's data RAM and relevant registers.

We use four seven-segment LEDs to display the inputs and computed results. The LEDs are arranged as four hexadecimal numbers. Since the range of $a^2 + b^2$ is up to 17 bits, the decimal point of the leftmost LED is used for the MSB. The three lower bits of the switch select what to display, which can be a, b, a^2, b^2, or $a^2 + b^2$.

In summary, the interface consists of the following:

- *Switch*: provides the values of a and b and selects the content of the LED display
- *Pushbutton 0*: loads the a and b alternatively when pressed
- *Pushbutton 1*: clears data RAM and relevant registers when pressed
- *Seven-segment LED*: displays the selected 17-bit value in four hexadecimal digits

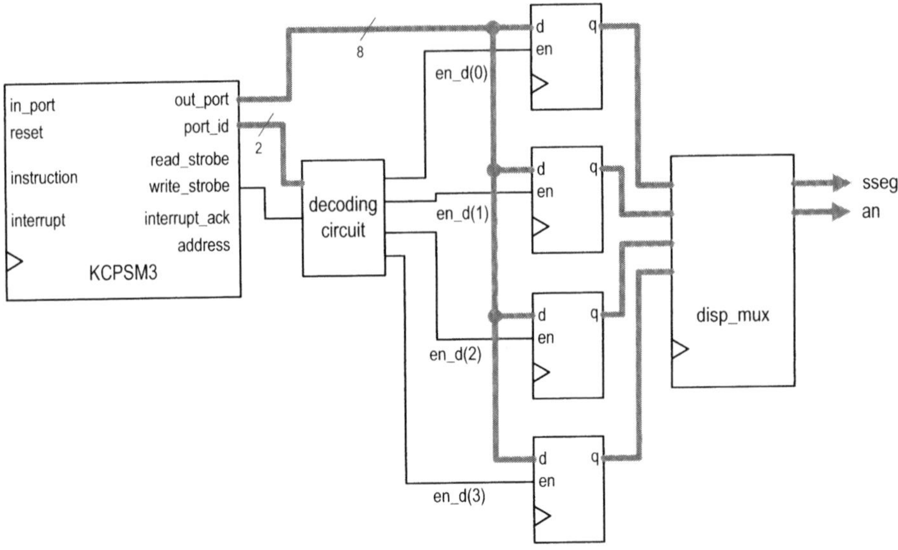

Figure 16.6 Output interface of a square circuit.

16.4.1 Output interface

Recall that the four seven-segment LEDs on the prototyping board share the same input pins, and a time-multiplexing circuit is required. For a PicoBlaze-based design, the multiplexing can be done by either an external circuit or a software routine. We use the external-circuit approach, which is simpler for assembly code development, in this section and discuss the software approach in Chapter 17. The LED time-multiplexing circuit designed in Section 4.5.1 can be used for this purpose. This circuit shields the timing and appears as four independent seven-segment LEDs for external system. The block diagram of the PicoBlaze output interface is shown in Figure 16.6. The interface consists of four 8-bit output ports, each port representing a seven-segment LED pattern.

In the assembly code, the four LED patterns are stored in PicoBlaze's data RAM with symbolic addresses of `led0`, `led1`, `led2`, and `led3`. The corresponding code segment is

```
...
;data RAM address alias
constant led0, 10
constant led1, 11
constant led2, 12
constant led3, 13
...
;output port definitions
constant sseg0_port, 00      ;7-seg led 0
constant sseg1_port, 01      ;7-seg led 1
constant sseg2_port, 02      ;7-seg led 2
constant sseg3_port, 03      ;7-seg led 3
...
disp_led:
   fetch data, led0
   output data, sseg0_port
```

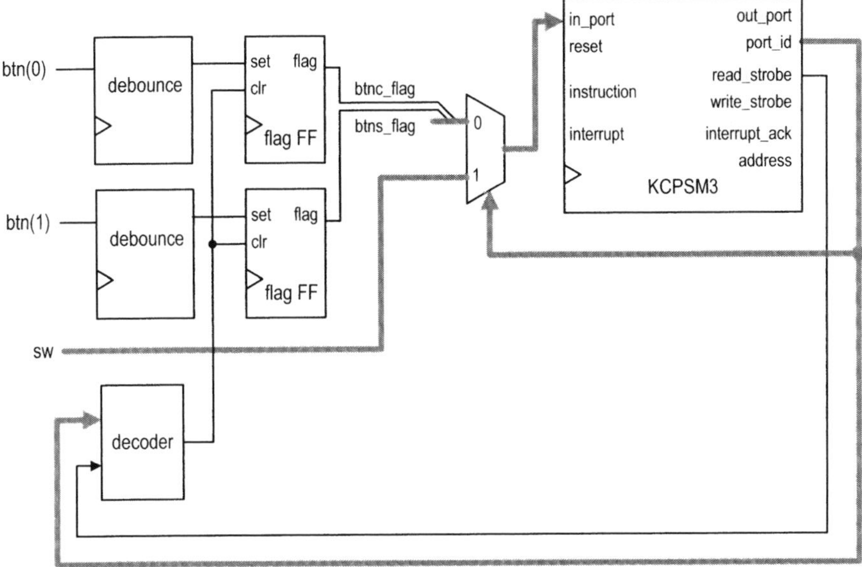

Figure 16.7 Input interface of a square circuit.

```
fetch data, led1
output data, sseg1_port
fetch data, led2
output data, sseg2_port
fetch data, led3
output data, sseg3_port
return
```

16.4.2 Input interface

The input interface consists of an 8-bit switch and two 1-bit pushbuttons. The former is a continuous-access port since the value is always present. The latter is a single-access port since pressing a button leads to only a single event (e.g., loading a to the register once rather than continuously). Because of the mechanical glitches, a debouncing circuit is needed to generate a clean one-clock-cycle tick. Since PicoBlaze's port can take up 8-bit data, inputs from the two pushbuttons can be grouped together as a single input port. The block diagram of the input interface is shown in Figure 16.7. The interface consists of two debouncing circuits, a two-to-one multiplexer, a decoding circuit, and two flag FFs. The function of the two flag FFs is discussed in Section 7.2.4. They provide a mechanism to set and clear the "button-pressing event." When a button is pressed, the debouncing circuit's output sets the flag. It remains asserted until it is retrieved by the PicoBlaze's **input** instruction, which sets the selection signal of the multiplexer to route the desired value to PicoBlaze's input port, and activates the clear signal. For clarity, we name the pushbutton 1 as the s button (for setting the value) and pushbutton 0 as the c button (for clearing the data RAM).

The pseudo code to process the input is

```
;input the button flags
;if c=1 then
```

```
;   call the clearing-ram routine
; if s=1 then
;   input switch value
;   store it to data ram
;   toggle a/b address offset
```

Since the s button inputs the values of a and b alternately, we use a global register, switch_a_b, to keep track of which one is being read currently. The register serves as the data RAM address offset, which can be 0 or 2, and its value toggles when the s button is pressed. The corresponding assembly code subroutine is

```
;input port definitions
constant rd_flag_port, 00   ;2 flags (xxxxxxsc):
constant sw_port, 01        ;8-bit switch
...
proc_btn:
   input s3, rd_flag_port  ;get flag
   ;check and process c button
   test s3, 01             ;check c button flag
   jump z, chk_btns        ;flag not set
   call init               ;flag set, clear
   jump proc_btn_done
chk_btns:
   ;check and process s button
   test s3, 02             ;check s button flag
   jump z, proc_btn_done   ;flag not set
   input data, sw_port     ;get switch
   load addr, a_lsb        ;get addr of a
   add addr, switch_a_b    ;add offset
   store data, (addr)      ;write data to ram
   ;update current disp position
   xor switch_a_b, 02      ;toggle between 00, 02
proc_btn_done:
   return
```

16.4.3 Assembly code development

After designing the I/O interface, we can derive the assembly program. The development follows the divide-and-conquer approach discussed in Chapter 15 and partitions the main program into several subroutines. The main program is

```
   call init               ;initialization
forever:
   ;main loop body
   call proc_btn           ;check & process buttons
   call square             ;calculate square
   call load_led_pttn      ;store led patterns to ram
   call disp_led           ;output led pattern
   jump forever
```

The complete code is shown in Listing 16.1.

The square subroutine is from Chapter 15, and the proc_btn and disp_led subroutines are discussed in the previous two subsections. The init subroutine performs system initialization. It uses a loop to load 0's to data RAM (i.e., clear the RAM) and sets the switch_a_b register to 0 (i.e., read a). The `load_led_pttn` subroutine reads the switch input, retrieves the desired values from the data RAM, converts the values to seven-segment LED patterns, and stores them to the corresponding locations in the data RAM. These patterns are then written to the output ports in the subsequent `disp_led` routine. The `load_led_pttn` routine consists of the `get_upper_nibble` and `get_lower_nibble` routines to extract the two hexadecimal digits and the `hex_to_led` routine to convert a hexadecimal digit to the corresponding seven-segment LED pattern.

The program requires more storage. In addition to the data RAM and registers required for the `square` subroutine, this program utilizes a new global register `switch_a_b` to keep track of whether a or b is being read, and 4 bytes in data RAM, whose addresses are labeled `led0`, `led1`, `led2`, and `led3`, to store four seven-segment LED patterns.

Listing 16.1 Square program with a switch and seven-segment LED interface

```
;=========================================================
; square circuit with 7-seg LED interface
;=========================================================
;program operation:
;   - read a and b from switch
;   - calculate a*a + b*b
;   - display data on 7-seg led

;=========================================================
; data RAM address alias
;=========================================================
constant a_lsb, 00
constant b_lsb, 02
constant aa_lsb, 04
constant aa_msb, 05
constant bb_lsb, 06
constant bb_msb, 07
constant aabb_lsb, 08
constant aabb_msb, 09
constant aabb_cout, 0A
constant led0, 10
constant led1, 11
constant led2, 12
constant led3, 13

;=========================================================
; register alias
;=========================================================
;commonly used local variables
namereg s0, data        ;reg for temporary data
namereg s1, addr        ;reg for temporary mem & i/o port addr
namereg s2, i           ;general-purpose loop index
;global variables
namereg sf, switch_a_b  ;ram offset for current switch input

;=========================================================
; port alias
;=========================================================
;--------------input port definitions---------------------
```

```
constant rd_flag_port, 00   ;2 flags (xxxxxxsc):
constant sw_port, 01        ;8-bit switch
;------------output port definitions-----------------
constant sseg0_port, 00     ;7-seg led 0
constant sseg1_port, 01     ;7-seg led 1
constant sseg2_port, 02     ;7-seg led 2
constant sseg3_port, 03     ;7-seg led 3

;=====================================================
; main program
;=====================================================
;calling hierarchy:
;
;main
;   - init
;   - proc_btn
;        - init
;   - square
;        - mult_soft
;   - load_led_pttn
;        - get_lower_nibble
;        - get_upper_nibble
;        - hex_to_led
;   - disp_led
;
; =====================================================

   call init                 ;initialization
forever:
   ;main loop body
   call proc_btn             ;check & process buttons
   call square               ;calculate square
   call load_led_pttn        ;store led patterns to ram
   call disp_led             ;output led pattern
   jump forever

;=====================================================
;routine: init
;   function: perform initialization, clear register/ram
;   output register:
;      switch_a_b: cleared to 0
;   temp register: data, i
;=====================================================
init:
   ;clear memory
   load i, 40                ;unitize loop index to 64
   load data, 00
clr_mem_loop:
   store data, (i)
   sub i, 01                 ;dec loop index
   jump nz, clr_mem_loop     ;repeat until i=0
   ;clear register
   load switch_a_b, 00
```

```
   return

;==========================================================
;routine: proc_btn
;  function: check two buttons and process the display
;  input reg:
;     switch_a_b: ram offset (0 for a and 2 for b)
;  output register:
;     s3: store input port flag
;     switch_a_b: may be toggled
;  temp register used: data, addr
;==========================================================
proc_btn:
   input s3, rd_flag_port  ;get flag
   ;check and process c button
   test s3, 01             ;check c button flag
   jump z, chk_btns        ;flag not set
   call init               ;flag set, clear
   jump proc_btn_done
chk_btns:
   ;check and process s button
   test s3, 02             ;check s button flag
   jump z, proc_btn_done   ;flag not set
   input data, sw_port     ;get switch
   load addr, a_lsb        ;get addr of a
   add addr, switch_a_b    ;add offset
   store data, (addr)      ;write data to ram
   ;update current disp position
   xor switch_a_b, 02      ;toggle between 00, 02
proc_btn_done:
   return

;==========================================================
;routine: load_led_pttn
;  function: read 3 LSBs of switch input and convert the
;            desired values to four led patterns and
;            load them to ram
;            switch: 000:a; 001:b; 010:a^2; 011:b^2;
;                    others: a^2 + b^2
;  temp register used: data, addr
;    s6: data from sw input port

;==========================================================
load_led_pttn:
   input s6, sw_port       ;get switch
   sl0 s6                  ;*2 to obtain addr offset
   compare s6, 08          ;sw>100?
   jump c, sw_ok           ;no
   load s6, 08             ;yes, sw error, make default
sw_ok:
   ;process byte 0, lower nibble
   load addr, a_lsb
   add addr, s6            ;get lower addr
```

```
    fetch data, (s6)          ;get lower byte
    call get_lower_nibble     ;get lower nibble
    call hex_to_led           ;convert to led pattern
    store data, led0
    ;process byte 0, upper nibble
    fetch data, (addr)
    call get_upper_nibble
    call hex_to_led
    store data, led1
    ;process byte 1, lower nibble
    add addr, 01              ;get upper addr
    fetch data, (addr)
    call get_lower_nibble
    call hex_to_led
    store data, led2
    ;process byte 1, upper nibble
    fetch data, (addr)
    call get_upper_nibble
    call hex_to_led
    ;check for sw=100 to process carry as led dp
    compare s6, 08            ;display final result?
    jump nz, led_done         ;no
    add addr, 01              ;get carry addr
    fetch s6, (addr)          ;s6 to store carry
    test s6, 01               ;carry=1?
    jump z, led_done          ;no
    and data, 7F              ;yes, assert msb (dp) to 0
led_done:
    store data, led3
    return

;=================================================================
;routine: disp_led
;  function: output four led patterns
;  temp register used: data
;=================================================================
disp_led:
    fetch data, led0
    output data, sseg0_port
    fetch data, led1
    output data, sseg1_port
    fetch data, led2
    output data, sseg2_port
    fetch data, led3
    output data, sseg3_port
    return

;=================================================================
;routine: hex_to_led
;  function: convert a hex digit to 7-seg led pattern
;  input register: data
;  output register: data
;=================================================================
```

```
hex_to_led:
   compare data, 00
   jump nz, comp_hex_1
   load data, 81           ;7-seg pattern 0
   jump hex_done
comp_hex_1:
   compare  data, 01
   jump nz, comp_hex_2
   load data, CF           ;7-seg pattern 1
   jump hex_done
comp_hex_2:
   compare data, 02
   jump nz, comp_hex_3
   load data, 92           ;7-seg pattern 2
   jump hex_done
comp_hex_3:
   compare data, 03
   jump nz, comp_hex_4
   load data, 86           ;7-seg pattern 3
   jump hex_done
comp_hex_4:
   compare data, 04
   jump nz, comp_hex_5
   load data, CC           ;7-seg pattern 4
   jump hex_done
comp_hex_5:
   compare data, 05
   jump nz, comp_hex_6
   load data, A4           ;7-seg pattern 5
   jump hex_done
comp_hex_6:
   compare data, 06
   jump nz, comp_hex_7
   load data, A0           ;7-seg pattern 6
   jump hex_done
comp_hex_7:
   compare data, 07
   jump nz, comp_hex_8
   load data, 8F           ;7-seg pattern 7
   jump hex_done
comp_hex_8:
   compare data, 08
   jump nz, comp_hex_9
   load data, 80           ;7-seg pattern 8
   jump hex_done
comp_hex_9:
   compare data, 09
   jump nz, comp_hex_a
   load data, 84           ;7-seg pattern 9
   jump hex_done
comp_hex_a:
   compare data, 0A
   jump nz, comp_hex_b
```

```
   load data, 88          ;7-seg pattern a
   jump hex_done
comp_hex_b:
   compare data, 0B
   jump nz, comp_hex_c
   load data, E0          ;7-seg pattern b
   jump hex_done
comp_hex_c:
   compare data, 0C
   jump nz, comp_hex_d
   load data, B1          ;7-seg pattern C
   jump hex_done
comp_hex_d:
   compare data, 0D
   jump nz, comp_hex_e
   load data, C2          ;7-seg pattern d
   jump hex_done
comp_hex_e:
   compare data, 0E
   jump nz, comp_hex_f
   load data, B0          ;7-seg pattern E
   jump hex_done
comp_hex_f:
   load data, B8          ;7-seg pattern F
hex_done:
   return

;=========================================================
;routine: get_lower_nibble
;  function: get lower 4 bits of data
;  input register: data
;  output register: data
;=========================================================
get_lower_nibble:
   and data, 0F           ;clear upper nibble
   return

;=========================================================
;routine: get_upper_nibble
;  function: get upper 4 bits of in_data
;  input register: data
;  output register: data
;=========================================================
get_upper_nibble:
   sr0 data               ;right shift 4 times
   sr0 data
   sr0 data
   sr0 data
   return

;=========================================================
;routine: square
;  function: calculate a*a + b*b
```

```
;      data/result stored in ram started w/ SQ_BASE_ADDR
;   temp register: s3, s4, s5, s6, data
;===============================================================
square:
    ;calculate a*a
    fetch s3, a_lsb          ;load a
    fetch s4, a_lsb          ;load a
    call mult_soft           ;calculate a*a
    store s6, aa_lsb         ;store lower byte of a*a
    store s5, aa_msb         ;store upper byte of a*a
    ;calculate b*b
    fetch s3, b_lsb          ;load b
    fetch s4, b_lsb          ;load b
    call mult_soft           ;calculate b*b
    store s6, bb_lsb         ;store lower byte of b*b
    store s5, bb_msb         ;store upper byte of b*b
    ;calculate a*a+b*b
    fetch data, aa_lsb       ;get lower byte of a*a
    add data, s6             ;add lower byte of a*a+b*b
    store data, aabb_lsb     ;store lower byte of a*a+b*b
    fetch data, aa_msb       ;get upper byte of a*a
    addcy data, s5           ;add upper byte of a*a+b*b
    store data, aabb_msb     ;store upper byte of a*a+b*b
    load data, 00            ;clear data, but keep carry
    addcy data, 00           ;get carry from previous +
    store data, aabb_cout    ;store carry of a*a+b*b
    return

;===============================================================
;routine: mult_soft
;   function: 8-bit unsigned multiplier using
;             shift-and-add algorithm
;   input register:
;      s3: multiplicand
;      s4: multiplier
;   output register:
;      s5: upper byte of product
;      s6: lower byte of product
;   temp register: i
;===============================================================
mult_soft:
    load s5, 00              ;clear s5
    load i, 08               ;initialize loop index
mult_loop:
    sr0  s4                  ;shift lsb to carry
    jump nc, shift_prod      ;lsb is 0
    add s5, s3               ;lsb is 1
shift_prod:
    sra s5                   ;shift upper byte right,
                             ;carry to MSB, LSB to carry
    sra s6                   ;shift lower byte right,
                             ;lsb of s5 to MSB of s6
    sub i, 01                ;dec loop index
```

```
jump nz, mult_loop          ;repeat until i=0
return
```

16.4.4 VHDL code development

The complete HDL code simply combines the PicoBlaze processor, instruction ROM, the input interface and peripherals shown in Figure 16.7, and the output interface and peripherals shown in Figure 16.6. It is shown in Listing 16.2.

Listing 16.2 PicoBlaze with a switch and seven-segment LED interface

```
library ieee;
use ieee.std_logic_1164.all;
use ieee.numeric_std.all;
entity pico_btn is
   port(
      clk, reset: in std_logic;
      sw: in std_logic_vector(7 downto 0);
      btn: in std_logic_vector(1 downto 0);
      an: out std_logic_vector(3 downto 0);
      sseg: out std_logic_vector(7 downto 0)
   );
end pico_btn;

architecture arch of pico_btn is
   -- KCPSM3/ROM signals
   signal address: std_logic_vector(9 downto 0);
   signal instruction: std_logic_vector(17 downto 0);
   signal port_id: std_logic_vector(7 downto 0);
   signal in_port, out_port: std_logic_vector(7 downto 0);
   signal write_strobe, read_strobe: std_logic;
   signal interrupt, interrupt_ack: std_logic;
   signal kcpsm_reset: std_logic;
   -- I/O port signals
   -- output enable
   signal en_d: std_logic_vector(3 downto 0);
   -- four-digit seven-segment led display
   signal ds3_reg, ds2_reg: std_logic_vector(7 downto 0);
   signal ds1_reg, ds0_reg: std_logic_vector(7 downto 0);
   -- two pushbuttons
   signal btnc_flag_reg, btnc_flag_next: std_logic;
   signal btns_flag_reg, btns_flag_next: std_logic;
   signal set_btnc_flag, set_btns_flag: std_logic;
   signal clr_btn_flag: std_logic;
begin
   -- =====================================================
   --    I/O modules
   -- =====================================================
   disp_unit: entity work.disp_mux
      port map(
         clk=>clk, reset=>'0',
         in3=>ds3_reg, in2=>ds2_reg, in1=>ds1_reg,
         in0=>ds0_reg, an=>an, sseg=>sseg);
```

```
btnc_db_unit: entity work.debounce
   port map(
      clk=>clk, reset=>reset, sw=>btn(0),
      db_level=>open, db_tick=>set_btnc_flag);
btns_db_unit: entity work.debounce
   port map(
      clk=>clk, reset=>reset, sw=>btn(1),
      db_level=>open, db_tick=>set_btns_flag);
-- ==================================================
--  KCPSM and ROM instantiation
-- ==================================================
proc_unit: entity work.kcpsm3
   port map(
      clk=>clk, reset =>kcpsm_reset,
      address=>address, instruction=>instruction,
      port_id=>port_id, write_strobe=>write_strobe,
      out_port=>out_port, read_strobe=>read_strobe,
      in_port=>in_port, interrupt=>interrupt,
      interrupt_ack=>interrupt_ack);
rom_unit: entity work.btn_rom
   port map(
       clk => clk, address=>address,
       instruction=>instruction);
-- unused inputs on processor
kcpsm_reset <= '0';
interrupt <= '0';
-- ==================================================
--  output interface
-- ==================================================
--    outport port id:
--      0x00: ds0
--      0x01: ds1
--      0x02: ds2
--      0x03: ds3
-- ==================================================
-- registers
process (clk)
begin
   if (clk'event and clk='1') then
      if en_d(0)='1' then ds0_reg <= out_port; end if;
      if en_d(1)='1' then ds1_reg <= out_port; end if;
      if en_d(2)='1' then ds2_reg <= out_port; end if;
      if en_d(3)='1' then ds3_reg <= out_port; end if;
   end if;
end process;
-- decoding circuit for enable signals
process(port_id,write_strobe)
begin
   en_d <= (others=>'0');
   if write_strobe='1' then
      case port_id(1 downto 0) is
         when "00" => en_d <="0001";
         when "01" => en_d <="0010";
```

```
            when "10" => en_d <="0100";
            when others => en_d <="1000";
         end case;
      end if;
   end process;
   --===========================================================
   --  input interface
   --===========================================================
   --     input port id
   --       0x00: flag
   --       0x01: switch
   --===========================================================
   -- input register (for flags)
   process(clk)
   begin
      if (clk'event and clk='1') then
         btnc_flag_reg <= btnc_flag_next;
         btns_flag_reg <= btns_flag_next;
      end if;
   end process;

   btnc_flag_next <= '1' when set_btnc_flag='1' else
                     '0' when clr_btn_flag='1' else
                      btnc_flag_reg;
   btns_flag_next <= '1' when set_btns_flag='1' else
                     '0' when clr_btn_flag='1' else
                      btns_flag_reg;
   -- decoding circuit for clear signals
   clr_btn_flag <='1' when read_strobe='1' and
                           port_id(0)='0' else
                  '0';
   -- input multiplexing
   process(port_id,btns_flag_reg,btnc_flag_reg,sw)
   begin
      case port_id(0) is
         when '0' =>
            in_port <= "000000" &
                       btns_flag_reg & btnc_flag_reg;
         when others =>
            in_port <= sw;
      end case;
   end process;
end arch;
```

16.5 SQUARE PROGRAM WITH A COMBINATIONAL MULTIPLIER AND UART CONSOLE

In this section, we add two more I/O peripherals to the previous design. One is a combinational multiplier, which accelerates the multiplication, and the other is an UART, which provides a communication link to a PC.

16.5.1 Multiplier interface

Since PicoBlaze does not contain a hardware multiplier, the multiplication is done by a software routine, mult_soft. It uses a shift-and-add algorithm to iterate through the 8-bit multiplier and requires about 60 instructions in the worst-case scenario. An alternative is to utilize the Spartan-3 device's built-in combinational multiplier.

Since PicoBlaze provides no mechanism to use a coprocessor, the multiplier must be configured as an I/O peripheral. We can create an 8-bit combinational multiplier that takes two 8-bit operands and returns a 16-bit product. To facilitate this peripheral, the PicoBlaze's interface requires two additional output ports and buffers for the two operands and two additional input ports for the 16-bit product. The assembly routine now only needs to pass the operands to the output ports and then retrieve the results from the input ports. The code becomes

```
;input port definitions
constant mult_prod0_port, 03 ;multiplication product 8 LSBs
constant mult_prod1_port, 04 ;multiplication product 8 MSBs
;output port definitions
constant mult_src0_port, 05  ;multiplier operand 0
constant mult_src1_port, 06  ;multiplier operand 1
...
mult_hard:
   output s3, mult_src0_port
   output s4, mult_src1_port
   input s5, mult_prod1_port
   input s6, mult_prod0_port
   return
```

Note that the combinational multiplier can complete the computation with one instruction (i.e., two clock cycles), and thus no additional timing mechanism is needed in the code. This routine can be used in place of the previous mult_soft routine.

16.5.2 UART interface

With the UART interface, information can be entered and displayed in Windows HyperTerminal, which is more flexible and versatile than switches and LEDs. We use it as a simple control console for the square routine. A representative screen is shown in Figure 16.8. The console generates an SQ> prompt and a user can respond with a lowercase a, b, c, or d character. The a and b characters are used to input values for a and b of the square routine. When the key is pressed, the value of the 8-bit switch is read and stored into the corresponding data RAM location. The c character is used to clear the data RAM and reinitialize the program. Its function is identical to that of the c button. The d character leads to a "data RAM dump," in which the 64 bytes of the data RAM are displayed on screen. This allows us to observe the various values of the square routine and the four seven-segment LED patterns. An Error message is returned for all other characters.

The UART module designed in Section 7.4 can be used for this purpose. Since the transmission and receiving FIFO buffers provide a storage and flagging mechanism, no additional circuit is needed. We need only expand the decoding and multiplexing circuits to accommodate the additional I/O ports. The UART interface block diagram is sketched in Figure 16.9, in which the other I/O peripherals are omitted to reduce clutter. PicoBlaze's output port, out_port, is connected to w_data of UART. The decoded enable signal is connected to wr_uart, and the data is written to UART transmitting FIFO when it is

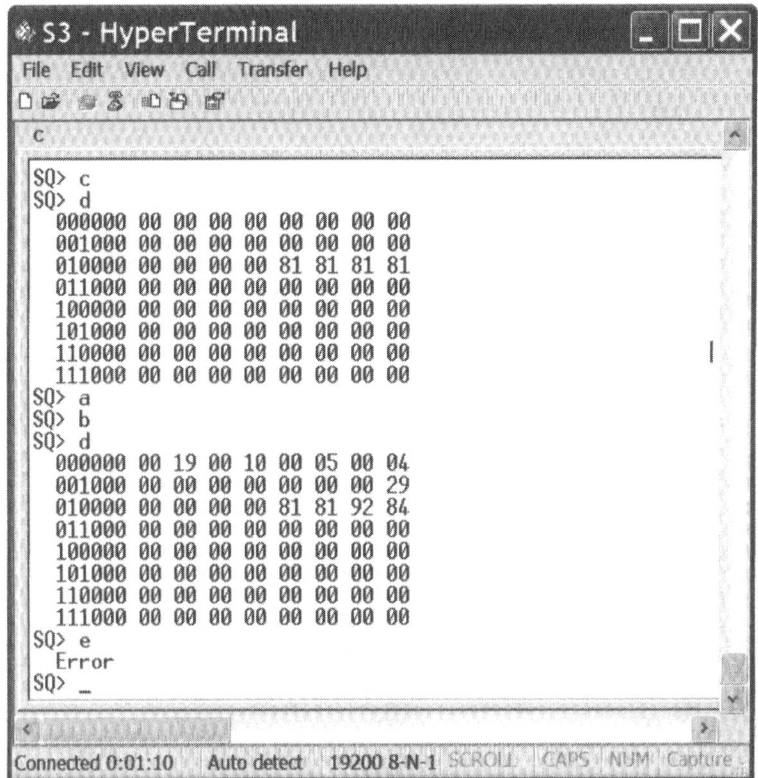

Figure 16.8 Representative console screen.

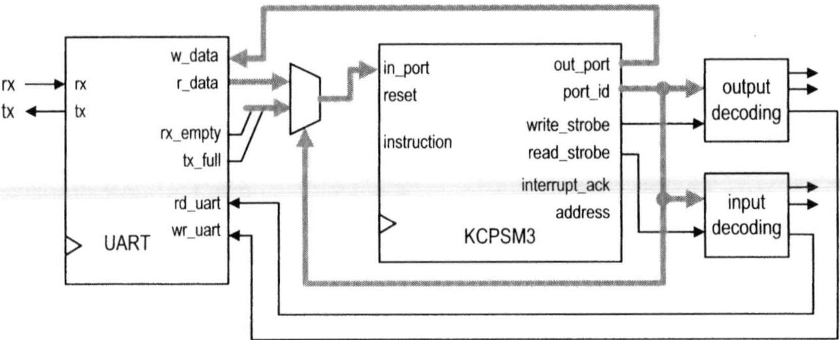

Figure 16.9 UART I/O interface.

asserted. Similarly, r_data of UART is routed to PicoBlaze's input multiplexing circuit, and the decoded clear signal is connected to rd_uart. When the UART receiving FIFO port is specified in an **input** instruction, the receiving FIFO's output is routed to PicoBlaze's input port, in_port, and the decoded remove signal is asserted one clock cycle to remove one word from the receiving FIFO. The UART interface also needs to route the two status signals, rx_empty and tx_full, to PicoBlaze's input multiplexing circuit. The assembly program needs to check the status before reading or writing the UART's FIFOs. Since the signals are only 2 bits wide, they can be grouped with the previous s and c buttons in the same input port.

16.5.3 Assembly code development

Since the previous assembly code is developed in a modular fashion, we can expand the program by adding a routine, proc_uart, to process UART transactions. The main program becomes

```
    call init                 ;initialization
forever:
    ;main loop body
    call proc_btn             ;check & process buttons
    call proc_uart            ;check & process uart rx
    call square               ;calculate square
    call load_led_pttn        ;store led patterns to ram
    call disp_led             ;output led pattern
    jump forever
```

Because of the complexity of the required console operation, the proc_uart is quite involved. The pseudo code of this routine is

```
;    if (no character in UART receiving FIFO) then
;       return
;    input characters from FIFO
;    if (characters is a) then
;       input switch value
;       store it to data ram
;       display prompt
;       return
;    if (characters is b) then
;       input switch value
;       store it to data ram
;       display prompt
;       return
;    if (characters is c) then
;       perform initialization
;       return
;    if (characters is d) then
;       dump data ram
;       return
;    display error message
;    return
```

We follow the modular development approach and further divide this routine into simpler routines. A key low-level routine is tx_one_byte, which transmits 1 byte via the UART port. Its code is

```
;input port definitions
constant rd_flag_port, 00
; 4 flags (xxxxtrsc):
;    t: uart tx full,  r: uart rx not empty
;    s: s button flag, c: c button flag
;output port definitions
constant uart_tx_port, 04      ;uart receiver port
;register alias
namereg sd, tx_data            ;data to be tx by uart
...
tx_one_byte:
   input s6, rd_flag_port
   test s6, 08                    ;check uart_tx_full
   jump nz, tx_one_byte           ;yes, keep on waiting
   output tx_data, uart_tx_port ;no, write to uart tx fifo
   return
```

Since PicoBlaze's processing speed is much higher than the UART's transmission speed, we must prevent buffer overflow. The routine keeps on checking the status of the transmitting FIFO buffer, and writes data only when the buffer is not full.

The task of dumping data RAM requires the most work. It displays the data RAM address and contents as an 8-by-8 table, which lists the byte address first and then the 8 bytes of data in hexadecimal format, as in

```
001000 00 0F 00 09 00 04 00 03
010000 00 00 FF 1D 00 00 00 19
 . . .
111000 00 00 00 00 00 FF FF FF
```

The routine consists of three major routines: `disp_ram_addr`, which sends ASCII codes to display the 5-bit base address in binary format; `disp_ram_data`, which sends ASCII codes to display 8 bytes of data; and `hex_to_ascii`, which converts a hexadecimal digit to the corresponding ASCII code.

The complete code is shown in Listing 16.3. It includes detailed comments to explain operation of the subroutines. The unmodified subroutines of Listing 16.1 are omitted.

Listing 16.3 Square program with a UART console

```
;=========================================================
; square circuit with UART and multiplier interface
;=========================================================
;program operation:
;   - read a and b from switch
;   - calculate a*a + b*b
;   - display data on HyperTerminal and 7-seg led

;=========================================================
; data constants
;=========================================================
;selected ASCII codes
constant ASCII_0,  30
constant ASCII_1,  31
constant ASCII_2,  32
constant ASCII_3,  33
constant ASCII_a,  61
```

```
constant ASCII_b,  62
constant ASCII_c,  63
constant ASCII_d,  64
constant ASCII_o,  6F
constant ASCII_r,  72
constant ASCII_E,  45
constant ASCII_S,  53
constant ASCII_Q,  51
constant ASCII_D_U,44    ; uppercase D
constant ASCII_GT, 3E    ; >
constant ASCII_SP, 20    ; space
constant ASCII_CR, 0D    ; carriage return
constant ASCII_LF, 0A    ; line feed

;==========================================================
; data RAM address alias
;==========================================================
constant a_lsb, 00
constant b_lsb, 02
constant aa_lsb, 04
constant aa_msb, 05
constant bb_lsb, 06
constant bb_msb, 07
constant aabb_lsb, 08
constant aabb_msb, 09
constant aabb_cout, 0A
constant led0, 10
constant led1, 11
constant led2, 12
constant led3, 13

;==========================================================
; register alias
;==========================================================
;commonly used local variables
namereg s0, data         ;reg for temporary data
namereg s1, addr         ;reg for temporary mem & i/o port addr
namereg s2, i            ;general-purpose loop index
;global variables
namereg sc, switch_a_b   ;ram offset for current switch input
namereg sd, tx_data      ;data to be tx by uart

;==========================================================
; port alias
;==========================================================
;-------------input port definitions---------------------
constant rd_flag_port, 00
; 4 flags (xxxxtrsc):
;    t: uart tx full
;    r: uart rx not empty
;    s: s button flag
;    c: c button flag
constant sw_port,         01    ;8-bit switches
```

```
constant uart_rx_port,     02    ;uart receiver port
constant mult_prod0_port, 03    ;multiplication product 8 LSBs
constant mult_prod1_port, 04    ;multiplication product 8 MSBs
;---------------output port definitions---------------
constant sseg0_port,       00    ;7-seg led 0
constant sseg1_port,       01    ;7-seg led 1
constant sseg2_port,       02    ;7-seg led 2
constant sseg3_port,       03    ;7-seg led 3
constant uart_tx_port,     04    ;uart receiver port
constant mult_src0_port, 05     ;multiplier operand 0
constant mult_src1_port, 06     ;multiplier operand 1

;=====================================================
; main program
;=====================================================
;calling hierarchy:
;
;main
;   - init
;        - tx_prompt
;             - tx_one_byte
;   - proc_btn
;        - init
;   - proc_uart
;        - tx_prompt
;        - init
;        - proc_uart_err
;             - tx_one_byte
;        - dump_mem
;             - tx_prompt
;             - disp_ram_addr
;                 - tx_one_byte
;             - disp_ram_data
;                 - tx_one_byte
;                 - get_upper_nibble
;                 - get_lower_nibble
;                 - hex_to_ascii
;   - square
;        - mult_hard
;   - load_led_pttn
;        - get_lower_nibble
;        - get_upper_nibble
;        - hex_to_led
;   - disp_led
;
;=====================================================
    call init                  ;initialization
forever:
    ;main loop body
    call proc_btn              ;check & process buttons
    call proc_uart             ;check & process uart rx
    call square                ;calculate square
    call load_led_pttn         ;store led patterns to ram
```

```
   call disp_led             ;output led pattern
   jump forever

;=========================================================
;routine: init
;  function: perform initialization, clear register/ram
;  output register:
;     switch_a_b: cleared to 0
;  temp register: data, i
;=========================================================
init:
   ;clear memory
   load i, 40                ;unitize loop index to 64
   load data, 00
clr_mem_loop:
   store data, (i)
   sub i, 01                 ;dec loop index
   jump nz, clr_mem_loop     ;repeat until i=0
   ;clear register
   load switch_a_b, 00
   call tx_prompt
   return

;=========================================================
;routine: proc_uart
;  function: read uart input char:
;     a or b: read a or b from switch;
;     c: clear;   d: dump/display data ram  other: error
;  input reg: s3 (input port flag)
;  temp register used: data
;     s4: store received uart char or 00 (no uart input)
;=========================================================
proc_uart :
   test s3, 04               ;check uart rx status
   jump z, uart_rx_done      ;go to done if rx empty
   ;process received char
   input s4, uart_rx_port    ;get char
   ;check if received char is a
   compare s4, ASCII_a       ;check ASCII a
   jump nz, chk_ascii_b      ;no, check next
   input data, sw_port       ;get switch
   store data, a_lsb         ;write a to data ram
   call tx_prompt            ;new prompt line
   jump uart_rx_done
chk_ascii_b:
   ;check if received char is b
   compare s4, ASCII_b       ;check ASCII b
   jump nz, chk_ascii_c      ;no, check next
   input data, sw_port       ;get switch
   store data, b_lsb         ;write b to data ram
   call tx_prompt            ;new prompt line
   jump uart_rx_done
chk_ascii_c:
```

```
   ;check if received char is c
   compare s4, ASCII_c      ;check ASCII c
   jump nz, chk_ascii_d     ;no check next
   call init                ;clear
   jump uart_rx_done
chk_ascii_d:
   ;check if received char is d
   compare s4, ASCII_d         ;check ASCII d
   jump nz, ascii_undefined
   call dump_mem            ;dump/display ram
   jump uart_rx_done
ascii_undefined:
   ;undefined char
   call proc_uart_error
uart_rx_done:
   return

;==========================================================
;routine: proc_uart_error
;   function: display "Error" for unknown uart char
;==========================================================
proc_uart_error:
   load tx_data, ASCII_LF
   call tx_one_byte         ;transmit LF
   load tx_data, ASCII_CR
   call tx_one_byte         ;transmit CR
   load tx_data, ASCII_SP
   call tx_one_byte         ;transmit SP
   call tx_one_byte         ;transmit SP
   load tx_data, ASCII_E
   call tx_one_byte         ;transmit E
   load tx_data, ASCII_r
   call tx_one_byte         ;transmit r
   load tx_data, ASCII_r
   call tx_one_byte         ;transmit r
   load tx_data, ASCII_o
   call tx_one_byte         ;transmit o
   load tx_data, ASCII_r
   call tx_one_byte         ;transmit r
   call tx_prompt
   return

;==========================================================
;routine: dump_mem
;   function: when d received, dump 64 bytes of ram as
;      001000 XX XX XX XX XX XX XX XX
;      010000 XX XX XX XX XX XX XX XX
;      . . .
;      111000 XX XX XX XX XX XX XX XX
;   temp register used:
;      s3: as outer loop index
;      s4: ram base address
;==========================================================
```

```
dump_mem:
    load s3, 00                  ;addr used as loop index
 dump_loop:
    ;loop body
    load s4, s3                  ;get ram base addr (xxx000)
    sl0 s4
    sl0 s4
    sl0 s4
    call disp_ram_addr
    call disp_ram_data
    add s3, 01                   ;inc loop index
    compare s3, 08
    jump nz, dump_loop           ;loop not reach 8 yet
    call tx_prompt               ;new prompt
    return

;==========================================================
;routine: tx_prompt
;  function: generate prompt "SQ>"
;  temp register: tx_data
;==========================================================
tx_prompt:
    load tx_data, ASCII_LF
    call tx_one_byte             ;transmit LF
    load tx_data, ASCII_CR
    call tx_one_byte             ;transmit CR
    load tx_data, ASCII_S
    call tx_one_byte             ;transmit S
    load tx_data, ASCII_Q
    call tx_one_byte             ;transmit Q
    load tx_data, ASCII_GT
    call tx_one_byte             ;transmit >
    load tx_data, ASCII_SP
    call tx_one_byte             ;transmit SP
    return

;==========================================================
;routine: disp_ram_addr
;  function: display 6-bit ram addr
;     bbb000
;  input register:
;     s4: base address
;  temp register:
;     i, s7: 1-bit mask
;==========================================================
disp_ram_addr:
    ;new line
    load tx_data, ASCII_LF
    call tx_one_byte             ;transmit LF
    load tx_data, ASCII_CR
    call tx_one_byte             ;transmit CR
    load tx_data, ASCII_SP
    call tx_one_byte             ;transmit SP
```

```
    call tx_one_byte          ;transmit SP
    ;initialize the loop index and mask
    load i, 06                ;addr used as loop index
    load s7, 20               ;set mask to 0010_0000
tx_loop:
    ;loop body
    load tx_data, ASCII_1     ;load default ASCII 1
    test s7, s4               ;check the bit
    jump nz, tx_01            ;the bit is 1
    load tx_data, ASCII_0;    ;the bit is 0, load ASCII 0
tx_01:
    call tx_one_byte          ;transmit the ASCII 1 or 0
    ;update loop index and mask
    sr0 s7                    ;shift mask bit
    sub  i, 01                ;dec loop index
    jump nz, tx_loop          ;loop not reach 0 yet
    ;done with loop, send ASCII space
    load tx_data, ASCII_SP    ;load ASCII SP
    call tx_one_byte          ;transmit SP
    return

;==========================================================
;routine: disp_ram_data
;  function: 8-byte data in form of
;      00 11 22 33 44 55 66 77 88
;  input register:
;      s4: ram base address (xxx000)
;  temp register: i, addr, data
;==========================================================
disp_ram_data:
    ;initialize the loop index and mask
    load i, 08                ;addr used as loop index
d_ram_loop:
    ;loop body
    load addr, s4
    add addr, i
    sub addr, 01              ;calculate addr offset
    ;send upper nibble
    fetch data, (addr)
    call get_upper_nibble
    call hex_to_ascii         ;convert to ascii
    load tx_data, data
    call tx_one_byte
    ;send lower nibble
    fetch data, (addr)
    call get_lower_nibble
    call hex_to_ascii         ;convert to ascii
    load tx_data, data
    call tx_one_byte
    ;send a space
    load tx_data, ASCII_SP;
    call tx_one_byte          ;transmit SP
    sub i, 01                 ;dec loop index
```

```
    jump nz, d_ram_loop      ;loop not reach 0 yet
    return

;==========================================================
; routine: hex_to_ascii
;   function: convert a hex number to ascii code
;             add 30 for 0-9, add 37 for A-F
;   input register: data
;==========================================================
hex_to_ascii:
    compare data, 0a
    jump c, add_30           ;0 to 9, offset 30
    add data, 07             ;a to f, extra offset 07
add_30:
    add data, 30
    return

;==========================================================
; routine: tx_one_byte
;   function: wait until uart tx fifo not full;
;             then write a byte to fifo
;   input register: tx_data
;   temp register:
;      s6: read port flag
;==========================================================
tx_one_byte:
    input s6, rd_flag_port
    test s6, 08                  ;check uart_tx_full
    jump nz, tx_one_byte         ;yes, keep on waiting
    output tx_data, uart_tx_port ;no, write to uart tx fifo
    return

;==========================================================
; routine: square
;   function: calculate a*a + b*b
;      data/result stored in ram started w/ SQ_BASE_ADDR
;   temp register: s3, s4, s5, s6, data
;==========================================================
square:
    ;calculate a*a
    fetch s3, a_lsb          ;load a
    fetch s4, a_lsb          ;load a
    call mult_hard           ;calculate a*a
    store s6, aa_lsb         ;store lower byte of a*a
    store s5, aa_msb         ;store upper byte of a*a
    ;calculate b*b
    fetch s3, b_lsb          ;load b
    fetch s4, b_lsb          ;load b
    call mult_hard           ;calculate b*b
    store s6, bb_lsb         ;store lower byte of b*b
    store s5, bb_msb         ;store upper byte of b*b
    ;calculate a*a+b*b
    fetch data, aa_lsb       ;get lower byte of a*a
```

```
    add data, s6              ;add lower byte of a*a+b*b
    store data, aabb_lsb      ;store lower byte of a*a+b*b
    fetch data, aa_msb        ;get upper byte of a*a
    addcy data, s5            ;add upper byte of a*a+b*b
    store data, aabb_msb      ;store upper byte of a*a+b*b
    load data, 00             ;clear data, but keep carry
    addcy data, 00            ;get carry from previous +
    store data, aabb_cout     ;store carry of a*a+b*b
    return

;=============================================================
;routine: mult_hard
;  function: 8-bit unsigned multiplication using
;               external combinational multiplier;
;  input register:
;     s3: multiplicand
;     s4: multiplier
;  output register:
;     s5: upper byte of product
;     s6: lower byte of product
;  temp register:
;=============================================================
mult_hard:
    output s3, mult_src0_port
    output s4, mult_src1_port
    input s5, mult_prod1_port
    input s6, mult_prod0_port
    return

;=============================================================
;The following are the same as the previous Listing:
;  proc_btn, load_led_pttn, disp_led
;  hex_to_led, get_lower_nibble, get_upper_nibble
;  ...
;=============================================================
```

16.5.4 VHDL code development

The new square circuit adds a UART and a combinational multiplier to an I/O interface. The former is the module discussed in Section 7.4, and the latter can be inferred from the HDL's * operator. The decoding and multiplexing parts of HDL code in Listing 16.2 can be expanded to accommodate the two new peripherals. The complete VHDL code is shown in Listing 16.4. The detailed I/O port address assignment can be found in the header section of Listing 16.3.

Listing 16.4 PicoBlaze with UART console and multiplier interface

```
library ieee;
use ieee.std_logic_1164.all;
use ieee.numeric_std.all;
entity pico_uart is
   port(
      clk, reset: in std_logic;
```

```
      sw: in std_logic_vector(7 downto 0);
      btn: in std_logic_vector(3 downto 0);
      rx: in std_logic;
      an: out std_logic_vector(3 downto 0);
      sseg: out std_logic_vector(7 downto 0);
      tx: out  std_logic
   );
end pico_uart;

architecture arch of pico_uart is
   -- KCPSM3/ROM signals
   signal address: std_logic_vector(9 downto 0);
   signal instruction: std_logic_vector(17 downto 0);
   signal port_id: std_logic_vector(7 downto 0);
   signal in_port, out_port: std_logic_vector(7 downto 0);
   signal write_strobe, read_strobe: std_logic;
   signal interrupt, interrupt_ack: std_logic;
   signal kcpsm_reset: std_logic;
   -- I/O port signals
   -- output enable
   signal en_d: std_logic_vector(6 downto 0);
   -- four-digit seven-segment led display
   signal ds3_reg, ds2_reg: std_logic_vector(7 downto 0);
   signal ds1_reg, ds0_reg: std_logic_vector(7 downto 0);
   -- two pushbuttons
   signal btnc_flag_reg, btnc_flag_next: std_logic;
   signal btns_flag_reg, btns_flag_next: std_logic;
   signal set_btnc_flag, set_btns_flag: std_logic;
   signal clr_btn_flag: std_logic;
   -- uart
   signal w_data: std_logic_vector(7 downto 0);
   signal rd_uart, rx_not_empty, rx_empty: std_logic;
   signal wr_uart, tx_full: std_logic;
   signal rx_char: std_logic_vector(7 downto 0);
   -- multiplier
   signal m_src0_reg, m_src1_reg: std_logic_vector(7 downto 0);
   signal prod: std_logic_vector(15 downto 0);
begin
   --=====================================================
   --  I/O modules
   --=====================================================
   disp_unit: entity work.disp_mux
      port map(
         clk=>clk, reset=>'0',
         in3=>ds3_reg, in2=>ds2_reg, in1=>ds1_reg,
         in0=>ds0_reg, an=>an, sseg=>sseg);
   uart_unit: entity work.uart(str_arch)
      port map(
         clk=>clk, reset=>reset, rd_uart=>rd_uart,
         wr_uart=>wr_uart, rx=>rx,
         w_data=>out_port, tx_full=>tx_full,
         rx_empty=>rx_empty, r_data=>rx_char, tx=>tx);
   btnc_db_unit: entity work.debounce
```

```
      port map(
         clk=>clk, reset=>reset, sw=>btn(0),
         db_level=>open, db_tick=>set_btnc_flag);
   btns_db_unit: entity work.debounce
      port map(
         clk=>clk, reset=>reset, sw=>btn(1),
         db_level=>open, db_tick=>set_btns_flag);
   -- combinational multiplier
   prod <= std_logic_vector
            (unsigned(m_src0_reg) * unsigned(m_src1_reg));
   -- =====================================================
   --  KCPSM and ROM instantiation
   -- =====================================================
   proc_unit: entity work.kcpsm3
      port map(
         clk=>clk, reset =>kcpsm_reset,
         address=>address, instruction=>instruction,
         port_id=>port_id, write_strobe=>write_strobe,
         out_port=>out_port, read_strobe=>read_strobe,
         in_port=>in_port, interrupt=>interrupt,
         interrupt_ack=>interrupt_ack);
   rom_unit: entity work.uart_rom
      port map(
          clk => clk, address=>address,
          instruction=>instruction);
   -- unused inputs on processor
   kcpsm_reset <= '0';
   interrupt <= '0';
   -- =====================================================
   --  output interface
   -- =====================================================
   --     outport port id:
   --       0x00: ds0
   --       0x01: ds1
   --       0x02: ds2
   --       0x03: ds3
   --       0x04: uart_tx_fifo
   --       0x05: m_src0
   --       0x06: m_src1
   -- =====================================================
   -- registers
   process (clk)
   begin
      if (clk'event and clk='1') then
         if en_d(0)='1' then ds0_reg <= out_port; end if;
         if en_d(1)='1' then ds1_reg <= out_port; end if;
         if en_d(2)='1' then ds2_reg <= out_port; end if;
         if en_d(3)='1' then ds3_reg <= out_port; end if;
         if en_d(5)='1' then m_src0_reg <= out_port; end if;
         if en_d(6)='1' then m_src1_reg <= out_port; end if;
      end if;
   end process;
   -- decoding circuit for enable signals
```

```
process(port_id,write_strobe)
begin
   en_d <= (others=>'0');
   if write_strobe='1' then
      case port_id(2 downto 0) is
         when "000" => en_d <="0000001";
         when "001" => en_d <="0000010";
         when "010" => en_d <="0000100";
         when "011" => en_d <="0001000";
         when "100" => en_d <="0010000";
         when "101" => en_d <="0100000";
         when others => en_d <="1000000";
      end case;
   end if;
end process;
wr_uart <= en_d(4);
--=====================================================
--  input interface
--=====================================================
--    input port id
--      0x00: flag
--      0x01: switch
--      0x02: uart_rx_fifo
--      0x03: prod lower byte
--      0x04: prod upper byte
--=====================================================
-- input register (for flags)
process(clk)
begin
   if (clk'event and clk='1') then
      btnc_flag_reg <= btnc_flag_next;
      btns_flag_reg <= btns_flag_next;
   end if;
end process;

btnc_flag_next <= '1' when set_btnc_flag='1' else
                  '0' when clr_btn_flag='1' else
                   btnc_flag_reg;
btns_flag_next <= '1' when set_btns_flag='1' else
                  '0' when clr_btn_flag='1' else
                   btns_flag_reg;
-- decoding circuit for clear signals
clr_btn_flag <='1' when read_strobe='1' and
                        port_id(2 downto 0)="000" else
                '0';
rd_uart <= '1' when read_strobe='1' and
                    port_id(2 downto 0)="010" else
           '0';
-- input multiplexing
rx_not_empty <= not rx_empty;
process(port_id,tx_full,rx_not_empty,
        btns_flag_reg,btnc_flag_reg,sw,rx_char,prod)
begin
```

```
         case port_id(2 downto 0) is
            when "000" =>
               in_port <= "0000" & tx_full & rx_not_empty &
                          btns_flag_reg & btnc_flag_reg;
            when "001" =>
               in_port <= sw;
            when "010" =>
               in_port <= rx_char;
            when "011" =>
               in_port <=prod(7 downto 0);
            when others =>
               in_port <= prod(15 downto 8);
         end case;
      end process;
end arch;
```

16.6 BIBLIOGRAPHIC NOTES

The basic bibliographic information for this chapter is similar to that for Chapter 14. The downloaded kcpsm file contains a comprehensive UART and timer design example. The Xilinx Web site has pages for "PicoBlaze Forum" and "PicoBlaze User Resources," where additional PicoBlaze examples are available.

16.7 SUGGESTED EXPERIMENTS

16.7.1 Low-frequency counter I

An accurate low-frequency counter is discussed in Section 6.3.5. We can treat the period counter, division circuit, and binary-to-BCD conversion circuit as three I/O modules, and replace the top-level FSM with PicoBlaze. Design the I/O interface, derive the assembly and HDL codes, compile and synthesize the circuit, and verify its operation.

16.7.2 Low-frequency counter II

We can reduce the hardware of the frequency counter of Experiment 16.7.1 by replacing the division circuit and binary-to-BCD conversion circuit with software subroutines. Redesign the I/O interface, derive the assembly and HDL codes, compile and synthesize the circuit, and verify its operation.

16.7.3 Auto-scaled low-frequency counter

An auto-scaled low-frequency counter is discussed in Experiment 6.5.5. We can use PicoBlaze to perform all non-time-critical functions. Redesign the circuit with PicoBlaze and minimal external hardware. Derive the assembly and HDL codes, compile and synthesize the circuit, and verify its operation.

16.7.4 Basic reaction timer with a software timer

The reaction timer is discussed in Experiment 6.5.6. We can redesign the circuit using PicoBlaze. One task of the design is to keep track of the elapsed time interval. This can be done by a software counting routine. Recall that a 50-MHz clock is used on the prototyping board and each instruction takes two clock cycles. We can create a counting loop to record the number of instructions executed and derive the time interval accordingly. Since the interval is at least in the millisecond range, multiple registers are needed for this purpose. Design the I/O interface, derive the assembly and HDL codes, compile and synthesize the circuit, and verify its operation.

16.7.5 Basic reaction timer with a hardware timer

We can repeat Experiment 16.7.4 with a customized hardware timer. The timer should be treated as an I/O peripheral. PicoBlaze can output a command to clear, start, or pause the timer, and can input the counter's content. Design the I/O interface, derive the assembly and HDL codes, compile and synthesize the circuit, and verify its operation.

16.7.6 Enhanced reaction timer

An enhanced reaction timer keeps track of the last four response times and the fastest response time, and displays the data on Windows HyperTerminal. We can design a console similar to that of Section 16.5. There should be three commands:

- `c`: clears all data
- `f`: displays the fastest response
- `r`: displays the time of the last four responses
- All other characters: displays "error"

Expand the design in Experiment 16.7.4 or 16.7.5 to include this feature. Derive the assembly and HDL codes, compile and synthesize the circuit, and verify its operation.

16.7.7 Small-screen mouse scribble circuit

A small-screen mouse scribble circuit is discussed in Experiment 12.7.10. We can use PicoBlaze to monitor the activities of the mouse and update the video memory accordingly. Design the I/O interface, derive the assembly and HDL codes, compile and synthesize the circuit, and verify its operation.

16.7.8 Full-screen mouse scribble circuit

A full-screen mouse scribble circuit is discussed in Experiment 12.7.11. We can use PicoBlaze to monitor the activities of the mouse and update the video memory accordingly. Design the I/O interface, derive the assembly and HDL codes, compile and synthesize the circuit, and verify its operation.

16.7.9 Enhanced rotating banner

A VGA rotating banner circuit is discussed in Experiment 13.6.1. Instead of a fixed message, we can enhance this circuit by using a keyboard to enter the message dynamically. Assume that the message buffer is 20 characters long and its characters are updated in a first-in-first-out fashion. Redesign the circuit with PicoBlaze. Design the I/O interface, derive the assembly and HDL codes, compile and synthesize the circuit, and verify its operation.

16.7.10 Pong game

The complete pong game is discussed in Section 13.4. Some functions of the design can be implemented by PicoBlaze:

- Top-level control FSM
- Top-level two-second timer and two-digit decade counter
- The circuit that updates the paddle position, ball position, and ball velocities in Listing 12.5

Modify the original circuit, design the I/O interface, derive the assembly and HDL codes, compile and synthesize the circuit, and verify its operation.

16.7.11 Text editor

A UART terminal is discussed in Experiment 13.6.5. We can use PicoBlaze to obtain data and commands from the UART and update the tile memory accordingly. Design the I/O interface, derive the assembly and HDL codes, compile and synthesize the circuit, and verify its operation.

CHAPTER 17

PICOBLAZE INTERRUPT INTERFACE

17.1 INTRODUCTION

During normal program execution, a microcontroller *polls* the I/O peripherals (i.e., checks the status signals) and determines the course of action accordingly. An I/O peripheral is passive and waits for its turn. The *interrupt* is a mechanism that allows an external I/O peripheral to initiate the operation. It, as the name shows, interrupts normal program execution and starts a service routine for the I/O peripheral. For a microcontroller, the interrupt is usually reserved for a time-critical peripheral operation, which must be processed immediately. The PicoBlaze microcontroller provides support for simple interrupt-handling capability. In this chapter, we examine the PicoBlaze's interrupt mechanism and use an example to illustrate software and interface development.

17.2 INTERRUPT HANDLING IN PICOBLAZE

Interrupt handling is a coordinated effort between hardware and software. When an external peripheral needs service through interrupt, it asserts the `interrupt` signal of PicoBlaze. If the interrupt service is enabled, PicoBlaze completes execution of the current instruction, activates the `interrupt_ack` signal to acknowledge the acceptance of the interrupt request, and then implicitly executes the **call** 3FF instruction. When the instruction is executed, the current content of the program counter is saved in stack and the 3FF address is loaded to the programmer counter. Note that the 3FF address is the last location in the instruction

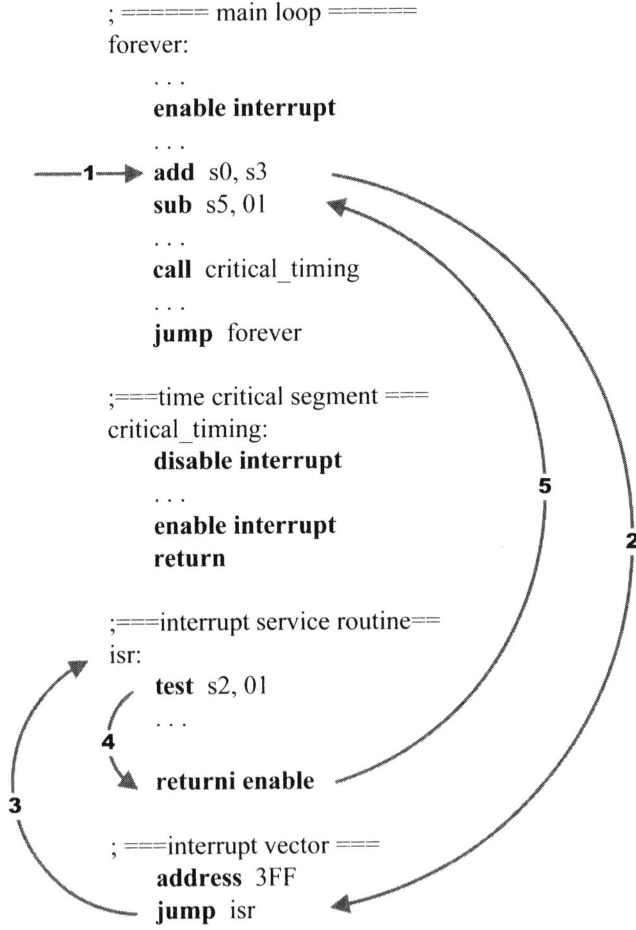

Figure 17.1 Interrupted flow.

memory and serves as the starting point of the interrupt service routine. It usually contains a **jump** instruction, which leads to the body of the service routine. The service should be ended with a **returni** instruction to return to the interrupted point and resume the previous execution.

17.2.1 Software processing

Four instructions are associated with interrupt, as discussed in Section 14.5.9. The **enable interrupt** and **disable interrupt** instructions enable and disable the interrupt request, and the two return-from-interrupt instructions, **returni enable** and **returni disable**, return execution to the interrupted point.

A typical program segment with interrupt service routine is shown in Figure 17.1. It generally consists of the following segments:

- *An initial* **enable interrupt** *instruction*: used to enable the interrupt service. This is needed since the interrupt request is disabled by default.

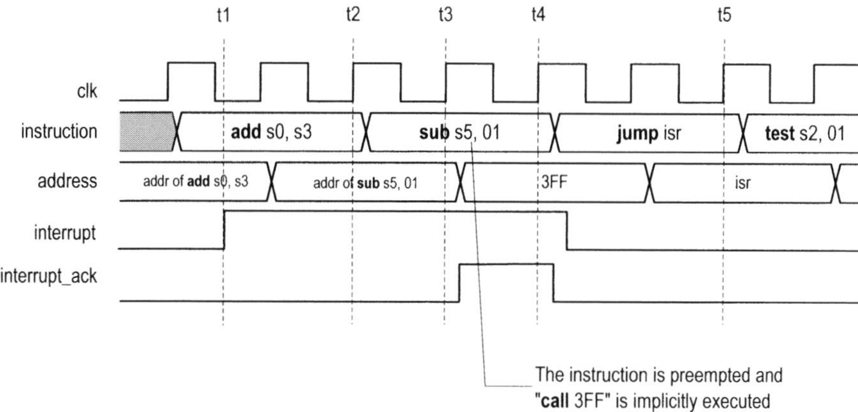

Figure 17.2 Timing diagram of an interrupt event.

- *A* **jump** *instruction in the end of the instruction memory* (i.e., 3FF): leads to the interrupt service routine.
- *Interrupt service routine*: the code that actually performs the requested service. The routine should be ended with a **returni** instruction.

A representative flow of an interrupt event is shown in Figure 17.1. We assume that the external I/O assert the `interrupt` signal in the middle of the **add** `s0,s3` instruction. PicoBlaze performs the following steps in sequence:

1. Completes execution of the current execution.
2. Saves the content of the program counter, clears the interrupt flag, `i`, to zero, preserves the zero and carry flags, and loads the program counter with `3FF`.
3. Executes the **jump** `isr` instruction in the `3FF` address.
4. Performs the service routine.
5. Executes the **returni** instruction, in which the saved program counter and flags are restored.
6. Resumes the interrupted program and executes the **sub** `s5,01` instruction.

17.2.2 Timing

The detailed timing diagram of the previous interrupt event is shown in Figure 17.2. The basic sequence is:

- At `t1`: The external interrupt interface asserts the `interrupt` signal. PicoBlaze continues the normal operation to complete execution of the current **add** `s0,s3` instruction.
- At `t2`: PicoBlaze recognizes the interrupt and aborts the next instruction (**sub** `s5,01`) and implicitly executes the **call** `3FF` instruction.
- At `t3`: PicoBlaze asserts the `interrupt_ack` signal. It also saves the address of the **sub** `s5,01` instruction, preserves the zero and carry flags, and clears the interrupt flag to 0.
- At `t4`: PicoBlaze loads and executes the instruction in address `3FF`, **jump** `isr`. The external interrupt interface circuit acknowledges the `interrupt_ack` signal and deasserts the `interrupt` signal.

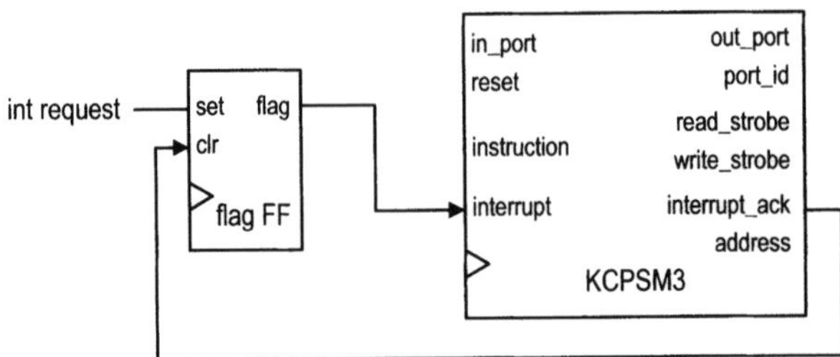

Figure 17.3 Interrupt interface with a single request.

- At `t5`: PicoBlaze starts the interrupt service routine.

Note that it requires up to five clock cycles from the time that the `interrupt` signal is asserted to the time that the first instruction of interrupt service routine is executed.

17.3 EXTERNAL INTERFACE

The nature of the interrupt request is similar to that of a single-access port discussed in Section 16.3.2. After the request is accepted, it must be cleared so that the same request will not be processed multiple times. The flag FF discussed in Section 7.2.4 can be used for this purpose.

17.3.1 Single interrupt request

If there is only one I/O peripheral in a PicoBlaze system that can generate an interrupt request, we just need a single flag FF in the interrupt interface circuit, as shown in Figure 17.3. When the service is required, the external I/O circuit asserted the `int request` signal for one clock cycle, which sets the flag FF to '1' and activates the `interrupt` input of PicoBlaze. If the interrupt is enabled in PicoBlaze, it acknowledges acceptance of the request by asserting the `interrupt_ack` signal for one clock cycle, which clears the flag FF to '0'.

17.3.2 Multiple interrupt requests

Processing a PicoBlaze system with two or more interrupt requests is more involved. The PicoBlaze microcontroller must determine which peripheral issues the request and clear the corresponding flag FF after the request is accepted. This needs the coordination of the hardware interface and the interrupt service routine.

The interrupt interface with two requests is shown in Figure 17.4. The two individual requests, `int request0` and `int request1`, are connected to two flag FFs, and the output signals of the FFs are passed to an or gate to generate the final interrupt request signal. In addition, the two signals are also routed to the input multiplexer. If at least one request is asserted, the `interrupt` signal of PicoBlaze is asserted. When PicoBlaze senses the request, it does not know which peripheral or whether both peripherals issue the request. The interrupt service routine must first input the two request signals and check their values according to the assigned priority, and then perform the corresponding service.

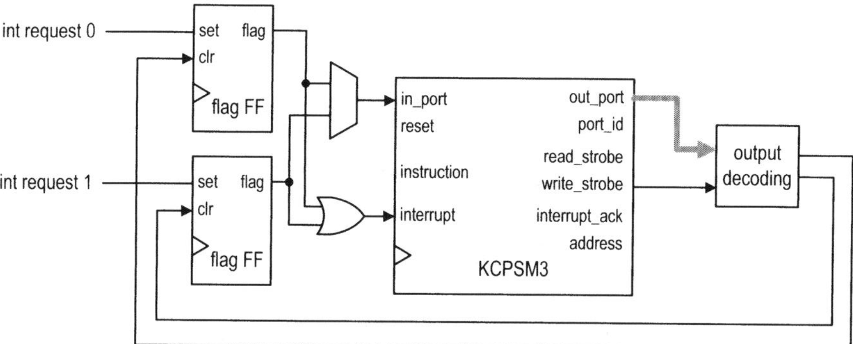

Figure 17.4 Interrupt interface with two requests.

In addition, PicoBlaze also needs to clear the corresponding flag FF. The `interrupt_ack` signal cannot be used for this purpose because it is not known which peripheral's request is accepted when the `interrupt_ack` signal asserted. Instead, we need to use a special output decoding circuit to generate a clear tick. The `clr` signal of each flag FF is assigned to a unique port id. In the interrupt service routine, we add an **output** instruction after determining which interrupt request is accepted. The instruction does not actually output any data. It is used to generate a single-clock-cycle tick to clear the corresponding flag FF.

To reduce the software overhead and increase response speed, we can design an *interrupt controller* to facilitate the process. This approach is discussed in Experiment 17.7.5.

17.4 SOFTWARE DEVELOPMENT CONSIDERATIONS

17.4.1 Interrupt as an alternative scheduling scheme

Recall that a microcontroller-based application usually follows a simple polling program structure:

```
     call initialization_routine
forever:
     call task1_routine;
     call task2_routine;
      . . .
     call taskn_routine;
     jump forever;
```

Some tasks may involve I/O operations. During execution, the microcontroller checks the I/O status in turn and takes actions accordingly. The program structure implicitly implements a *round-robin* schedule, in which each task waits in turn to be executed. This scheme can work properly if the loop interval is short enough so that each I/O request can be checked and processed in a timely manner. In some applications, there may exist one or two time-critical I/O requests that require immediate attention. The interrupt mechanism provides a way to alter the original schedule and gives certain tasks higher priorities.

Since an interrupt can occur at any time, the original loop must consider the frequency of interrupt and the required service time of each interrupt request. This can be complicated if there are multiple interrupt requests and the service routine is involved.

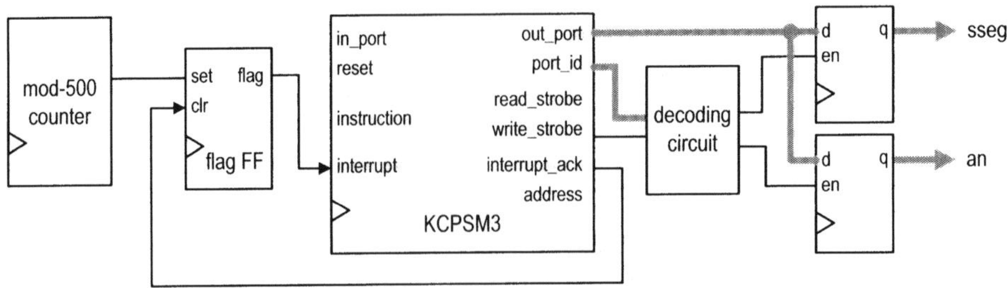

Figure 17.5 Interrupt interface with a timer.

17.4.2 Development of an interrupt service routine

The interrupt service routine is somewhat like a subroutine. It suspends normal program execution, performs an independent task, and then resumes the previous execution. However, unlike a subroutine call, an interrupt can occur any time. To resume execution later, the service routine must save the *current state* (also known as the *context*) of the PicoBlaze processor. In other words, the service routine must save all registers used in service routine computation and then restore them before returning to normal execution. This process is known as *context switching*.

Since PicoBlaze is a compact 8-bit microcontroller, the hardware support for context switching and scheduling is very limited. We should use the polling scheme in general and keep the interrupt structure simple and straightforward. Instead of worrying about context switching, we can allocate several dedicated registers to be used exclusively in the interrupt service routine.

17.5 DESIGN EXAMPLE

The square circuit of Chapter 16 uses a seven-segment LED display to show the values of input operands and result. We use the predesigned LED multiplexing module, `disp_mux`, for this purpose. The design of this module is discussed in Section 4.5.1. It consists of a large counter to generate slow enable pulses and a multiplexing circuit to route the input patterns.

To save hardware, we can implement this functionality in software and let PicoBlaze control the 4-bit enable signal, `an`, and the 8-bit LED signal, `sseg`, of the four-digit LED display directly. To generate a visually continuous pattern, the enable pulse and LED patterns must be refreshed at a constant rate, as shown in Figure 4.6. While using pure software to keep track of time is possible, the code is tedious and error-prone. We use a dedicated hardware timer and PicoBlaze's interrupt facility to perform the task. The required hardware and software modifications are illustrated in the following subsections.

17.5.1 Interrupt interface

The block diagram of the timer and interrupt interface, as well as the new output buffers, is shown in Figure 17.5. The timer is a mod-500 counter and generates a single-clock-cycle tick every 500 clock cycles. Since the 50-MHz clock is used for the timer, the period of the tick is 0.01 ms. Because there is only one interrupt request, we use the flag FF scheme discussed in Section 17.3.1 for the interrupt interface. The tick sets the flag FF and activates the `interrupt` signal of PicoBlaze.

17.5.2 Interrupt service routine development

To keep track of the elapsed time, PicoBlaze counts the number of timer ticks. As discussed in Section 17.4.2, we want to keep the interrupt service routine simple and use two dedicated registers, `count_msb` and `count_lsb`, for this task. The two registers are cascaded as a 16-bit register and are incremented each time the interrupt service routine is called. They can count to 0.6 second (i.e., $2^{16} * 0.01$ ms). The interrupt-related code segment is

```
    namereg se, count_msb   ;timer tick count 8 MSBs
    namereg sf, count_lsb   ;timer tick count 8 LSBs
    ...
;interrupt service routine
int_service_routine:
    add count_lsb, 01       ;inc 16-bit counter
    addcy count_msb, 00
    returni enable

;interrupt vector
    address 3FF
    jump int_service_routine
```

17.5.3 Assembly code development

With the timing information available, we can derive a new subroutine, `display_mux_out`, for the LED display. This routine replaces the `disp_led` routine used in Chapter 16. Two new output buffers are needed to store the an and `sseg` signals, as shown in Figure 17.5. The main task of the subroutine is to store the an pattern, which can be "1110", "1101", "1011", or "0111", and the corresponding seven-segment LED pattern to the registers periodically. As discussed in Section 4.5.1, the refreshing rate should be around from a few hundred to a few thousand hertz. In our code we update these registers every 2^{10} ticks, which is about 10 ms. We also use a register, `led_pos`, to keep track of the current display position (i.e., one of the four LED displays).

To incorporate the new interrupt feature into Listing 16.3, the code is modified as follows:

- Add new port and register definitions.
- Replace the original `disp_led` routine with the `display_mux_out` routine.
- Add the **enable interrupt** instruction in the `init` routine to enable interrupt handling.
- Initialize the `led_pos`, `count_msb`, and `count_lsb` registers in the `init` routine.
- Add the interrupt service routine.

The modified portion of the assembly code is shown in Listing 17.1.

Listing 17.1 Square program with interrupt interface

```
...
;register alias
namereg sb, led_pos     ;led disp position (0, 1, 2 or 3)
namereg se, count_msb   ;timer tick count 8 MSBs
namereg sf, count_lsb   ;timer tick count 8 LSBs
...
```

```
;output port definitions
constant an_port, 00
constant sseg_port, 01
...
; main program
   call init                  ;initialization
forever:
   ;main loop body
   call proc_btn              ;check & process buttons
   call square                ;calculate square
   call load_led_pttn         ;store led patterns to ram
   call display_mux_out       ; multiplex led patterns
   jump forever

;==========================================================
;routine: init
;==========================================================
init:
   enable interrupt
   ...
   load led_pos, 00
   load count_msb, 00
   load count_lsb, 00
   return

;==========================================================
;routine: display_mux_out
;  function: generate enable pulse & led pattern
;            for 4-digit 7-segment led display
;  input register:
;     count_msb, count_lsb: timer count
;     led_pos: current led position
;  output register:
;     led_pos: updated led position
;  tmp register: data, addr
;==========================================================
display_mux_out:
   compare count_msb, 02   ;count=00000100_00000000
   jump c, mux_out_done
   ;clear time counter (count > 20)
   load count_lsb, 00
   load count_msb, 00
   ;update 7-segment led position
   add led_pos, 01
   compare led_pos, 04
   jump nz, gen_an_signal
   load led_pos, 00         ;led_pos wraps around
gen_an_signal:
   ;generate 4-bit anode enable signal
   load data, 0E             ;xxxx_1110
   compare led_pos, 00
   jump z, shift_an_0
   compare led_pos, 01
```

```
    jump z, shift_an_1
    compare led_pos, 02
    jump z, shift_an_2
    sl1 data                  ;shift 1110 3 times
 shift_an_2:
    sl1 data                  ;shift 1110 2 times
 shift_an_1:
    sl1 data                  ;shift 1110 1 times
 shift_an_0:
    output data, an_port
    ;output 7-seg led pattern
    load addr, led0
    add addr, led_pos
    fetch data, (addr)
    output data, sseg_port
mux_out_done:
    return

;=========================================================
;routine: interrupt service routine
;   function: increment 16-bit counter
;   input register:
;       count_msb, count_lsb: timer count
;   output register:
;       count_msb, count_lsb: incremented
;=========================================================
int_service_routine:
    add count_lsb, 01         ;inc 16-bit counter
    addcy count_msb, 00
    returni enable

;=========================================================
;interrupt vector
;=========================================================
    address 3FF
    jump int_service_routine

;=========================================================
;The following are the same as the previous Listing:
;   proc_btn, load_led_pttn,
;   hex_to_led, get_lower_nibble, get_upper_nibble
;   square, mult_soft
;   ...
;=========================================================
```

17.5.4 VHDL code development

The I/O interface of the interrupt-based square circuit includes three parts. The input interface is similar to that in Section 16.4. The output interface consists of a decoding circuit and two output registers for the an and sseg signals, as shown on the right of Figure 17.5. The interrupt interface consists of a timer and a flag FF, as shown on the left of Figure 17.5. The HDL code basically follows the block diagram and is shown in Listing 17.2.

Listing 17.2 PicoBlaze-based square circuit with interrupt

```
library ieee;
use ieee.std_logic_1164.all;
use ieee.numeric_std.all;
entity pico_int is
   port(
      clk, reset: in std_logic;
      sw: in std_logic_vector(7 downto 0);
      btn: in std_logic_vector(1 downto 0);
      an: out std_logic_vector(3 downto 0);
      sseg: out std_logic_vector(7 downto 0)
   );
end pico_int;

architecture arch of pico_int is
   -- KCPSM3/ROM signals
   signal address: std_logic_vector(9 downto 0);
   signal instruction: std_logic_vector(17 downto 0);
   signal port_id: std_logic_vector(7 downto 0);
   signal in_port, out_port: std_logic_vector(7 downto 0);
   signal write_strobe, read_strobe: std_logic;
   signal interrupt, interrupt_ack: std_logic;
   -- I/O port signals
   -- output enable
   signal en_d: std_logic_vector(1 downto 0);
   -- four-digit seven-segment led display
   signal sseg_reg: std_logic_vector(7 downto 0);
   signal an_reg: std_logic_vector(3 downto 0);
   -- two pushbuttons
   signal btnc_flag_reg, btnc_flag_next: std_logic;
   signal btns_flag_reg, btns_flag_next: std_logic;
   signal set_btnc_flag, set_btns_flag: std_logic;
   signal clr_btn_flag: std_logic;
   -- interrupt-related signals
   signal timer_reg, timer_next: unsigned(8 downto 0);
   signal ten_us_tick: std_logic;
   signal timer_flag_reg, timer_flag_next: std_logic;
begin
   --=========================================================
   -- I/O modules
   --=========================================================
   btnc_db_unit: entity work.debounce
      port map(
         clk=>clk, reset=>reset, sw=>btn(0),
         db_level=>open, db_tick=>set_btnc_flag);
   btns_db_unit: entity work.debounce
      port map(
         clk=>clk, reset=>reset, sw=>btn(1),
         db_level=>open, db_tick=>set_btns_flag);
   --=========================================================
```

```
-- KCPSM and ROM instantiation
--=================================================
proc_unit: entity work.kcpsm3
   port map(
      clk=>clk, reset =>reset,
      address=>address, instruction=>instruction,
      port_id=>port_id, write_strobe=>write_strobe,
      out_port=>out_port, read_strobe=>read_strobe,
      in_port=>in_port, interrupt=>interrupt,
      interrupt_ack=>interrupt_ack);
rom_unit: entity work.int_rom
   port map(
       clk => clk, address=>address,
       instruction=>instruction);
--=================================================
-- output interface
--=================================================
--    outport port id:
--      0x00: an
--      0x01: ssg
--=================================================
-- registers
process (clk)
begin
   if (clk'event and clk='1') then
      if en_d(0)='1' then
         an_reg <= out_port(3 downto 0);
      end if;
      if en_d(1)='1' then sseg_reg <= out_port; end if;
   end if;
end process;
an <= an_reg;
sseg <= sseg_reg;
-- decoding circuit for enable signals
process(port_id,write_strobe)
begin
   en_d <= (others=>'0');
   if write_strobe='1' then
      case port_id(0) is
         when '0' => en_d <="01";
         when others => en_d <="10";
      end case;
   end if;
end process;
--=================================================
-- input interface
--=================================================
--    input port id
--      0x00: flag
--      0x01: switch
--=================================================
-- input register (for flags)
process(clk)
```

```
begin
   if (clk'event and clk='1') then
      btnc_flag_reg <= btnc_flag_next;
      btns_flag_reg <= btns_flag_next;
   end if;
end process;

btnc_flag_next <= '1' when set_btnc_flag='1' else
                  '0' when clr_btn_flag='1' else
                   btnc_flag_reg;
btns_flag_next <= '1' when set_btns_flag='1' else
                  '0' when clr_btn_flag='1' else
                   btns_flag_reg;
-- decoding circuit for clear signals
clr_btn_flag <='1' when read_strobe='1' and
                        port_id(0)='0' else
               '0';
-- input multiplexing
process(port_id,btns_flag_reg,btnc_flag_reg,sw)
begin
   case port_id(0) is
      when '0' =>
         in_port <= "000000" &
                     btns_flag_reg & btnc_flag_reg;
      when others =>
         in_port <= sw;
   end case;
end process;
--=====================================================
--  interrupt interface
--=====================================================
-- 10 us counter
process(clk)
begin
   if (clk'event and clk='1') then
      timer_reg <= timer_next;
   end if;
end process;
timer_next <= (others=>'0') when timer_reg=499 else
              timer_reg+1;
ten_us_tick <= '1' when timer_reg=499 else '0';
-- 10 us tick flag
process(clk)
begin
   if (clk'event and clk='1') then
      timer_flag_reg <= timer_flag_next;
   end if;
end process;
timer_flag_next <= '1' when ten_us_tick='1' else
                   '0' when interrupt_ack='1' else
                   timer_flag_reg;
-- interrupt request
interrupt <= timer_flag_reg;
```

```
end arch;
```

17.6 BIBLIOGRAPHIC NOTES

The bibliographic information for this chapter is similar to that for Chapters 14 to 16.

17.7 SUGGESTED EXPERIMENTS

17.7.1 Alternative timer interrupt service routine

The interrupt service routine in Listing 17.1 uses two dedicated registers to record the number of timer ticks. The two registers thus cannot be used for other computation. An alternative is to use 2 bytes of the data RAM for this purpose and use the registers only temporarily in the service routine. Since interrupt can occur anytime, we must save and restore the corresponding registers. For example, if the `s0` and `s1` registers are used in the service routine for computation, their contents must be saved when the service routine is invoked and then restored later when the computation is completed. Derive the assembly and HDL codes, compile and synthesize the circuit, and verify its operation.

17.7.2 Programmable timer

We can replace the mod-500 counter of Section 17.5 with a general mod-m counter and thus make the timer "programmable." The new timer operates as follows:

- m is a 12-bit unsigned number.
- The four LSBs of m is "1111".
- The timer has an 8-bit register to store the eight MSBs of m. The register is treated as a new output port of PicoBlaze.
- A new pushbutton controls the loading of the register. When it is pressed, PicoBlaze inputs the value from the 8-bit switch and outputs the value to the timer's register.

Design the new I/O interface, derive the assembly and HDL codes, and compile and synthesize the circuit. Load different values in the timer and observe what happens to the LED display.

17.7.3 Set-button interrupt service routine

In the square circuit discussed in Section 16.4, the `s` button is used to load the a and b operands from the 8-bit switch. Its status is polled continuously in the main loop. We can revise this portion of the code and use an interrupt mechanism to perform this task. The interrupt service routine involves several temporary registers, and they must be saved and restored properly, as discussed in Experiment 17.7.1. Design the new I/O interface, derive the assembly and HDL codes, compile and synthesize the circuit, and verify its operation.

17.7.4 Interrupt interface with two requests

Assume that we want to implement both the timer interrupt request of Listing 17.1 and the set-button interrupt request of Experiment 17.7.3 in a PicoBlaze system. Follow the

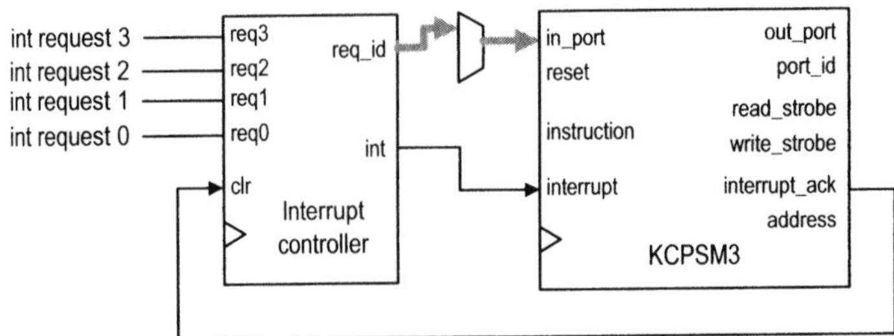

Figure 17.6 Interrupt interface with a four-request interrupt handler.

discussion in Section 17.3.2 to design the new interrupt interface and interrupt service routine. Derive the assembly and HDL codes, compile and synthesize the circuit, and verify its operation.

17.7.5 Four-request interrupt controller

An interrupt controller helps the processor to process multiple interrupt requests. The block diagram of a four-request interrupt controller is shown in Figure 17.6. The interrupt controller should contain four flag FFs and a special priority encoding circuit. If one or more interrupt requests are activated, the controller determines which request has the highest priority, places its 2-bit code on the `req_id` port, and asserts the `int` signal. When PicoBlaze asserts the `interrupt_ack` signal, the controller clears the corresponding flag. For simplicity, we assume that `int_request_3` has the highest priority and `int_request_0` has the lowest priority.

Derive HDL code for the interrupt controller and repeat Experiment 17.7.4 using the new controller (the two unused interrupt requests can be tied to '0').

APPENDIX A
SAMPLE VHDL TEMPLATES

A.1 GENERAL VHDL CONSTRUCTS

A.1.1 Overall code structure

Listing A.1 Overall code structure

```
library ieee;
use ieee.std_logic_1164.all;
use ieee.numeric_std.all;

-- entity declaration
entity bin_counter is
   -- optional generic declaration
   generic(N: integer := 8);
   -- port declaration
   port(
      clk, reset: in std_logic;                 -- clock & reset
      load, en, syn_clr: in std_logic;          -- input control
      d: in std_logic_vector(N-1 downto 0);     -- input data
      max_tick: out std_logic;                  -- output status
      q: out std_logic_vector(N-1 downto 0)     -- output data
   );
end bin_counter;
```

```
-- architecture body
architecture demo_arch of bin_counter is
   -- constant declaration
   constant MAX: integer := (2**N-1);
   -- internal signal declaration
   signal r_reg: unsigned(N-1 downto 0);
   signal r_next: unsigned(N-1 downto 0);
begin
   --============================================
   -- component instantiation
   --============================================
   -- no instantiation in this code

   --============================================
   -- memory elements
   --============================================
   -- register
   process(clk,reset)
   begin
      if (reset='1') then
         r_reg <= (others=>'0');
      elsif (clk'event and clk='1') then
         r_reg <= r_next;
      end if;
   end process;

   --============================================
   -- combinational circuits
   --============================================
   -- next-state logic
   r_next <= (others=>'0') when syn_clr='1' else
             unsigned(d)    when load='1' else
             r_reg + 1      when en ='1'  else
             r_reg;
   -- output logic
   q <= std_logic_vector(r_reg);
   max_tick <= '1' when r_reg=MAX else '0';
end demo_arch;
```

A.1.2 Component instantiation

Listing A.2 Component instantiation template

```
library ieee;
use ieee.std_logic_1164.all;
entity counter_inst is
   port(
      clk, reset: in  std_logic;
      load16, en16, syn_clr16: in std_logic;
      d: in std_logic_vector(15 downto 0);
      max_tick8, max_tick16: out std_logic;
```

```
      q: out std_logic_vector(15 downto 0)
   );
end counter_inst;

architecture structure_arch of counter_inst is
begin
   -- instantiation of 16-bit counter, all ports used
   counter_16_unit: entity work.bin_counter(demo_arch)
      generic map(N=>16)
      port map(clk=>clk, reset=>reset,
               load=>load16, en=>en16, syn_clr=>syn_clr16,
               d=>d, max_tick=>max_tick16, q=>q);
   -- instantiation of free-running 8-bit counter
   -- with only the max_tick signal
   counter_8_unit: entity work.bin_counter
      port map(clk=>clk, reset=>reset,
               load=>'0', en=>'1', syn_clr=>'0',
               d=>"00000000", max_tick=>max_tick8, q=>open);
end structure_arch;
```

A.2 COMBINATIONAL CIRCUITS

A.2.1 Arithmetic operations

Listing A.3 Arithmetic operations

```
library ieee;
use ieee.std_logic_1164.all;
use ieee.numeric_std.all;
entity arith_demo is
   port(
      a, b: in std_logic_vector(7 downto 0);
      diff, inc: out std_logic_vector(7 downto 0)
   );
end arith_demo;

architecture arch of arith_demo is
   signal au, bu, diffu: unsigned(7 downto 0);
begin
   --=============================================
   -- convert inputs to unsigned/signed internally
   -- and then convert the result back
   --=============================================
   au <= unsigned(a);
   bu <= unsigned(b);
   diffu <= au - bu when (au > bu) else
            bu - au;
   diff <= std_logic_vector(diffu);

   --=============================================
   -- convert multiple times in a statement
```

```
   --=========================================
   inc <= std_logic_vector(unsigned(a) + 1);
end arch;
```

A.2.2 Fixed-amount shift operations

Listing A.4 Fixed-amount shift operations

```
library ieee;
use ieee.std_logic_1164.all;
entity fixed_shift_demo is
   port(
      a: in std_logic_vector(7 downto 0);
      sh1, sh2, sh3, rot, swap: out
            std_logic_vector(7 downto 0)
   );
end fixed_shift_demo;

architecture arch of fixed_shift_demo is
begin
   -- shift left 3 positions
   sh1 <= a(4 downto 0) & "000" ;
   -- shift right 3 positions (logical shift)
   sh2 <= "000" & a(7 downto 3);
   -- shift right 3 positions and shifting in sign bit
   -- (arithmetic shift)
   sh3 <= a(7) & a(7) & a(7)& a(7 downto 3);
   -- rotate right 3 positions
   rot <= a(2 downto 0) & a(7 downto 3);
   -- swap two nibbles
   swap <= a(3 downto 0) & a(7 downto 4);
end arch;
```

A.2.3 Routing with concurrent statements

Listing A.5 Routing with concurrent statements

```
library ieee;
use ieee.std_logic_1164.all;
entity decoder1 is
   port(
      a: in std_logic_vector(1 downto 0);
      en: in std_logic;
      y1, y2: out std_logic_vector(3 downto 0)
   );
end decoder1;

architecture concurrent_arch of decoder1 is
   signal s: std_logic_vector(2 downto 0);
begin
   --=========================================
```

```
   -- conditional signal assignment statement
   --=========================================
   y1 <= "0000" when (en='0') else
         "0001" when (a="00") else
         "0010" when (a="01") else
         "0100" when (a="10") else
         "1000";        -- a="11"

   --=========================================
   -- selected signal assignment statement
   --=========================================
   s <= en & a;
   with s select
      y2 <= "0000" when "000"|"001"|"010"|"011",
            "0001" when "100",
            "0010" when "101",
            "0100" when "110",
            "1000" when others;    -- s="111"
end concurrent_arch;
```

A.2.4 Routing with if and case statements

Listing A.6 If and case statement templates

```
library ieee;
use ieee.std_logic_1164.all;
entity decoder2 is
   port(
      a: in std_logic_vector(1 downto 0);
      en: in std_logic;
      y1, y2: out std_logic_vector(3 downto 0)
   );
end decoder2;

architecture seq_arch of decoder2 is
   signal s: std_logic_vector(2 downto 0);
begin
   --=========================================
   -- if statement
   --=========================================
   process(en,a)
   begin
      if (en='0') then
         y1 <= "0000";
      elsif (a="00") then
         y1 <= "0001";
      elsif (a="01")then
         y1 <= "0010";
      elsif (a="10")then
         y1 <= "0100";
      else
         y1 <= "1000";
```

```
      end if;
   end process;

   --==========================================
   -- case statement
   --==========================================
   s <= en & a;
   process(s)
   begin
      case s is
         when "000"|"001"|"010"|"011" =>
            y2 <= "0001";
         when "100" =>
            y2 <= "0001";
         when "101" =>
            y2 <= "0010";
         when "110" =>
            y2 <= "0100";
         when others =>
            y2 <= "1000";
      end case;
   end process;
end seq_arch;
```

A.2.5 Combinational circuit using process

Listing A.7 Combinational circuit using process

```
library ieee;
use ieee.std_logic_1164.all;
entity comb_proc is
   port(
      a, b: in std_logic_vector(1 downto 0);
      data_in: std_logic_vector(7 downto 0);
      xa_out, xb_out: out std_logic_vector(7 downto 0);
      ya_out, yb_out: out std_logic_vector(7 downto 0)
   );
end comb_proc;

architecture arch of comb_proc is
begin
   --==========================================
   -- without default output signal assignment
   --==========================================
   -- must include else branch
   -- output signal must be assigned in all branches
   process(a,b,data_in)
   begin
      if a > b then
         xa_out <= data_in;
         xb_out <= (others=>'0');
      elsif a < b then
```

```
         xa_out <= (others=>'0');
         xb_out <= data_in;
      else  -- a=b
         xa_out <= (others=>'0');
         xb_out <= (others=>'0');
     end if;
   end process;
   --==========================================
   -- with default output signal assignment
   --==========================================
   process(a,b,data_in)
   begin
      ya_out <= (others=>'0');
      yb_out <= (others=>'0');
      if a > b then
         ya_out <= data_in;
      elsif a < b then
         yb_out <= data_in;
      end if;
   end process;
end arch;
```

A.3 MEMORY COMPONENTS

A.3.1 Register template

Listing A.8 Register template

```
library ieee;
use ieee.std_logic_1164.all;
entity reg_template is
   port(
      clk, reset: in std_logic;
      en: in std_logic;
      q1_next, q2_next, q3_next: in
            std_logic_vector(7 downto 0);
      q1_reg, q2_reg, q3_reg: out
            std_logic_vector(7 downto 0)
   );
end reg_template;

architecture arch of reg_template is
begin
   --==========================================
   -- register without reset
   --==========================================
   process(clk)
   begin
      if (clk'event and clk='1') then
         q1_reg <= q1_next;
      end if;
```

```
   end process;

   --==============================================
   -- register with asynchronous reset
   --==============================================
   process(clk,reset)
   begin
      if (reset='1') then
         q2_reg <=(others=>'0');
      elsif (clk'event and clk='1') then
         q2_reg <= q2_next;
      end if;
   end process;

   --==============================================
   -- register with enable and asynchronous reset
   --==============================================
   process(clk,reset)
   begin
      if (reset='1') then
         q3_reg <=(others=>'0');
      elsif (clk'event and clk='1') then
         if (en='1') then
            q3_reg <= q3_next;
         end if;
      end if;
   end process;
end arch;
```

A.3.2 Register file

Listing A.9 Register file

```
library ieee;
use ieee.std_logic_1164.all;
use ieee.numeric_std.all;
entity reg_file is
   generic(
      B: integer:=8; -- number of bits
      W: integer:=2  -- number of address bits
   );
   port(
      clk, reset: in std_logic;
      wr_en: in std_logic;
      w_addr, r_addr: in std_logic_vector (W-1 downto 0);
      w_data: in std_logic_vector (B-1 downto 0);
      r_data: out std_logic_vector (B-1 downto 0)
   );
end reg_file;

architecture arch of reg_file is
   type reg_file_type is array (2**W-1 downto 0) of
```

```
         std_logic_vector(B-1 downto 0);
   signal array_reg: reg_file_type;
begin
   process(clk,reset)
   begin
      if (reset='1') then
         array_reg <= (others=>(others=>'0'));
      elsif (clk'event and clk='1') then
         if wr_en='1' then
            array_reg(to_integer(unsigned(w_addr))) <= w_data;
         end if;
      end if;
   end process;
   -- read port
   r_data <= array_reg(to_integer(unsigned(r_addr)));
end arch;
```

A.4 REGULAR SEQUENTIAL CIRCUITS

Listing A.10 Sequential circuit template

```
library ieee;
use ieee.std_logic_1164.all;
use ieee.numeric_std.all;
entity bin_counter is
   generic(N: integer := 8);
   port(
      clk, reset: in std_logic;
      load, en, syn_clr: in std_logic;
      d: in std_logic_vector(N-1 downto 0);
      max_tick: out std_logic;
      q: out std_logic_vector(N-1 downto 0)
   );
end bin_counter;

architecture demo_arch of bin_counter is
   constant MAX: integer := (2**N-1);
   signal r_reg: unsigned(N-1 downto 0);
   signal r_next: unsigned(N-1 downto 0);

begin
   --============================================
   -- register
   --============================================
   process(clk,reset)
   begin
      if (reset='1') then
         r_reg <= (others=>'0');
      elsif (clk'event and clk='1') then
         r_reg <= r_next;
      end if;
```

```
   end process;
   --=============================================
   -- next-state logic
   --=============================================
   r_next <= (others=>'0') when syn_clr='1' else
             unsigned(d)   when load='1' else
             r_reg + 1     when en ='1'  else
             r_reg;
   --=============================================
   -- output logic
   --=============================================
   q <= std_logic_vector(r_reg);
   max_tick <= '1' when r_reg=MAX else '0';
end demo_arch;
```

A.5 FSM

Listing A.11 FSM template

```
-- code for the FSM in Figure A.1
library ieee;
use ieee.std_logic_1164.all;
entity fsm_eg is
   port(
      clk, reset: in std_logic;
      a, b: in std_logic;
      y0, y1: out std_logic
   );
end fsm_eg;

architecture two_seg_arch of fsm_eg is
   type eg_state_type is (s0, s1, s2);
   signal state_reg, state_next: eg_state_type;
begin
   --=============================================
   -- state register
   --=============================================
   process(clk,reset)
   begin
      if (reset='1') then
         state_reg <= s0;
      elsif (clk'event and clk='1') then
         state_reg <= state_next;
      end if;
   end process;
   --=============================================
   -- next-state/output logic
   --=============================================
   process(state_reg,a,b)
   begin
      state_next <= state_reg;  -- default back to same state
```

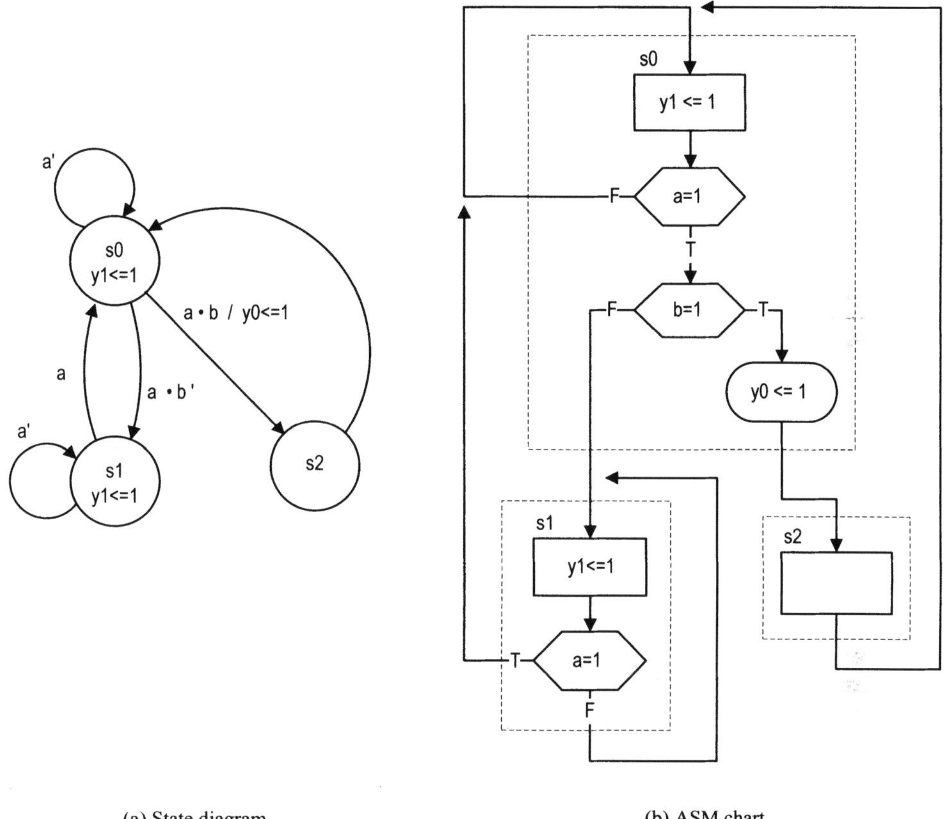

(a) State diagram

(b) ASM chart

Figure A.1 State diagram and ASM chart of an FSM template.

```
      y0 <= '0';    -- default 0
      y1 <= '0';    -- default 0
      case state_reg is
         when s0 =>
            if a='1' then
               if b='1' then
                  state_next <= s2;
                  y0 <= '1';
               else
                  state_next <= s1;
               end if;
            -- no else branch, use default
            end if;
         when s1 =>
            y1 <= '1';
            if (a='1') then
               state_next <= s0;
            -- no else branch, use default
            end if;
         when s2 =>
            state_next <= s0;
      end case;
   end process;
end two_seg_arch;
```

A.6 FSMD

Listing A.12 FSMD template

```
-- code for the FSMD shown in Figure A.2
library ieee;
use ieee.std_logic_1164.all;
use ieee.numeric_std.all;
entity fib is
    port(
        clk, reset: in std_logic;
        start: in std_logic;
        i: in std_logic_vector(4 downto 0);
        ready, done_tick: out std_logic;
        f: out std_logic_vector(19 downto 0)
    );
end fib;

architecture arch of fib is
   type state_type is (idle,op,done);
   signal state_reg, state_next: state_type;
   signal t0_reg, t0_next, t1_reg, t1_next:
          unsigned(19 downto 0);
   signal n_reg, n_next: unsigned(4 downto 0);
begin
   --=====================================
```

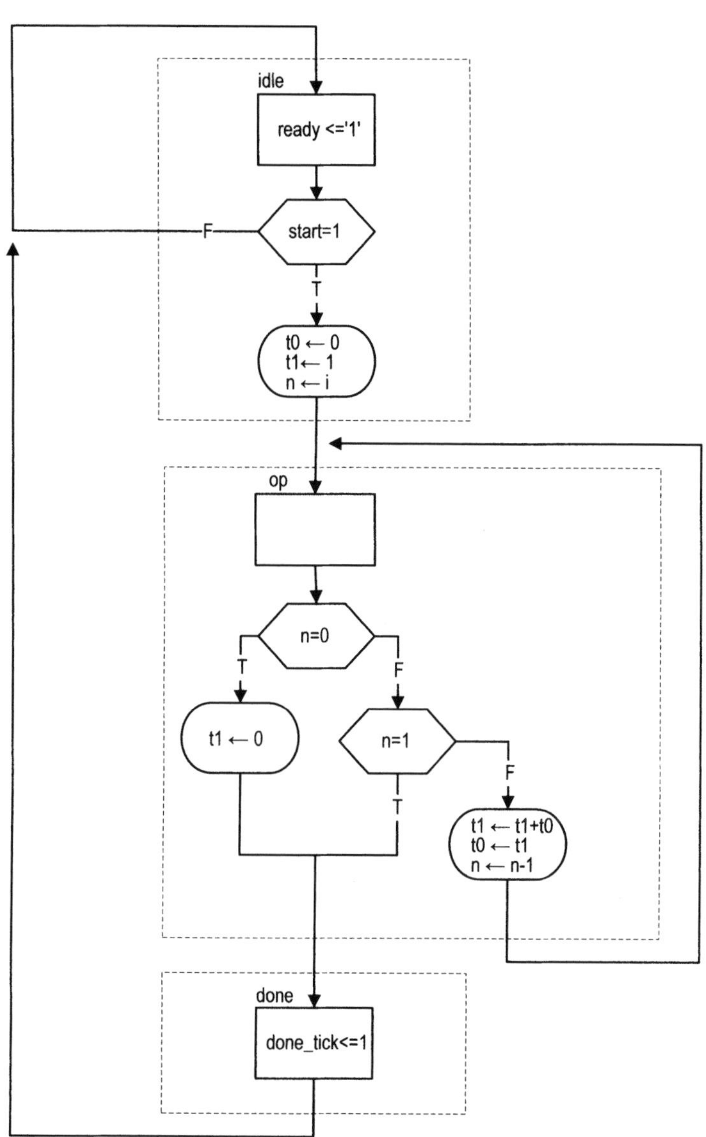

Figure A.2 ASMD chart of an FSMD template.

```
-- state and data registers
--=============================================
process(clk,reset)
begin
   if reset='1' then
      state_reg <= idle;
      t0_reg <= (others=>'0');
      t1_reg <= (others=>'0');
      n_reg <= (others=>'0');
   elsif (clk'event and clk='1') then
      state_reg <= state_next;
      t0_reg <= t0_next;
      t1_reg <= t1_next;
      n_reg <= n_next;
   end if;
end process;
--=============================================
-- next-state logic and data path functional units
--=============================================
process(state_reg,n_reg,t0_reg,t1_reg,start,i,n_next)
begin
   ready <='0';
   done_tick <= '0';
   state_next <= state_reg; -- default back to same state
   t0_next <= t0_reg;       -- default keep previous value
   t1_next <= t1_reg;       -- default keep previous value
   n_next <= n_reg;         -- default keep previous value
   case state_reg is
      when idle =>
         ready <= '1';
         if start='1' then
            t0_next <= (others=>'0');
            t1_next <= (0=>'1', others=>'0');
            n_next <= unsigned(i);
            state_next <= op;
         end if;
      when op =>
         if n_reg=0 then
            t1_next <= (others=>'0');
            state_next <= done;
         elsif n_reg=1 then
            state_next <= done;
         else
            t1_next <= t1_reg + t0_reg;
            t0_next <= t1_reg;
            n_next <= n_reg - 1;
         end if;
      when done =>
         done_tick <= '1';
         state_next <= idle;
   end case;
end process;
-- output
```

```
    f <= std_logic_vector(t1_reg);
end arch;
```

A.7 S3 BOARD CONSTRAINT FILE (S3.UCF)

```
#==========================================================
#    Pin assignment for Xilinx
#    Spartan-3 Starter board
#==========================================================

#==========================================================
# clock and reset
#==========================================================
NET "clk"    LOC = "T9" ;
NET "reset"  LOC = "L14";

#==========================================================
# buttons & switches
#==========================================================
# 4 push buttons
NET "btn<0>"   LOC = "M13";
NET "btn<1>"   LOC = "M14";
NET "btn<2>"   LOC = "L13";
#NET "btn<3>"  LOC = "L14";  #btn<3> also used as reset

# 8 slide switches
NET "sw<0>"  LOC = "F12";
NET "sw<1>"  LOC = "G12";
NET "sw<2>"  LOC = "H14";
NET "sw<3>"  LOC = "H13";
NET "sw<4>"  LOC = "J14";
NET "sw<5>"  LOC = "J13";
NET "sw<6>"  LOC = "K14";
NET "sw<7>"  LOC = "K13";

#==========================================================
# RS232
#==========================================================
NET "rx"  LOC = "T13" | DRIVE=8 | SLEW=SLOW;
NET "tx"  LOC = "R13" | DRIVE=8 | SLEW=SLOW;

#==========================================================
# 4-digit time-multiplexed 7-segment LED display
#==========================================================
# digit enable
NET "an<0>"  LOC = "D14";
NET "an<1>"  LOC = "G14";
NET "an<2>"  LOC = "F14";
NET "an<3>"  LOC = "E13";

# 7-segment led segments
```

```
NET "sseg<7>"  LOC = "P16"; # decimal point
NET "sseg<6>"  LOC = "E14"; # segment a
NET "sseg<5>"  LOC = "G13"; # segment b
NET "sseg<4>"  LOC = "N15"; # segment c
NET "sseg<3>"  LOC = "P15"; # segment d
NET "sseg<2>"  LOC = "R16"; # segment e
NET "sseg<1>"  LOC = "F13"; # segment f
NET "sseg<0>"  LOC = "N16"; # segment g

#=========================================================
# 8 discrete LEDs
#=========================================================
NET "led<0>"  LOC = "K12";
NET "led<1>"  LOC = "P14";
NET "led<2>"  LOC = "L12";
NET "led<3>"  LOC = "N14";
NET "led<4>"  LOC = "P13";
NET "led<5>"  LOC = "N12";
NET "led<6>"  LOC = "P12";
NET "led<7>"  LOC = "P11";

#=========================================================
# VGA outputs
#=========================================================
NET "rgb<2>"  LOC = "R12" | DRIVE=8 | SLEW=FAST;
NET "rgb<1>"  LOC = "T12" | DRIVE=8 | SLEW=FAST;
NET "rgb<0>"  LOC = "R11" | DRIVE=8 | SLEW=FAST;
NET "vsync"   LOC = "T10" | DRIVE=8 | SLEW=FAST;
NET "hsync"   LOC = "R9"  | DRIVE=8 | SLEW=FAST;

#=========================================================
# PS2 port
#=========================================================
NET "ps2c" LOC="M16" | DRIVE=8 |SLEW=SLOW;
NET "ps2d" LOC="M15" | DRIVE=8 |SLEW=SLOW;

#=========================================================
# two SRAM chips
#=========================================================
# shared 18-bit memory address
NET "ad<17>"  LOC="L3" | IOSTANDARD = LVCMOS33 | SLEW=FAST;
NET "ad<16>"  LOC="K5" | IOSTANDARD = LVCMOS33 | SLEW=FAST;
NET "ad<15>"  LOC="K3" | IOSTANDARD = LVCMOS33 | SLEW=FAST;
NET "ad<14>"  LOC="J3" | IOSTANDARD = LVCMOS33 | SLEW=FAST;
NET "ad<13>"  LOC="J4" | IOSTANDARD = LVCMOS33 | SLEW=FAST;
NET "ad<12>"  LOC="H4" | IOSTANDARD = LVCMOS33 | SLEW=FAST;
NET "ad<11>"  LOC="H3" | IOSTANDARD = LVCMOS33 | SLEW=FAST;
NET "ad<10>"  LOC="G5" | IOSTANDARD = LVCMOS33 | SLEW=FAST;
NET "ad<9>"   LOC="E4" | IOSTANDARD = LVCMOS33 | SLEW=FAST;
NET "ad<8>"   LOC="E3" | IOSTANDARD = LVCMOS33 | SLEW=FAST;
NET "ad<7>"   LOC="F4" | IOSTANDARD = LVCMOS33 | SLEW=FAST;
NET "ad<6>"   LOC="F3" | IOSTANDARD = LVCMOS33 | SLEW=FAST;
NET "ad<5>"   LOC="G4" | IOSTANDARD = LVCMOS33 | SLEW=FAST;
```

```
NET "ad<4>"     LOC="L4" | IOSTANDARD = LVCMOS33 | SLEW=FAST;
NET "ad<3>"     LOC="M3" | IOSTANDARD = LVCMOS33 | SLEW=FAST;
NET "ad<2>"     LOC="M4" | IOSTANDARD = LVCMOS33 | SLEW=FAST;
NET "ad<1>"     LOC="N3" | IOSTANDARD = LVCMOS33 | SLEW=FAST;
NET "ad<0>"     LOC="L5" | IOSTANDARD = LVCMOS33 | SLEW=FAST;

# shared oe, we
NET "oe_n"      LOC="K4" | IOSTANDARD = LVCMOS33 | SLEW=FAST;
NET "we_n"      LOC="G3" | IOSTANDARD = LVCMOS33 | SLEW=FAST;

# sram chip 1 data, ce, ub, lb
NET "dio_a<15>" LOC="R1" | IOSTANDARD=LVCMOS33 | SLEW=FAST;
NET "dio_a<14>" LOC="P1" | IOSTANDARD=LVCMOS33 | SLEW=FAST;
NET "dio_a<13>" LOC="L2" | IOSTANDARD=LVCMOS33 | SLEW=FAST;
NET "dio_a<12>" LOC="J2" | IOSTANDARD=LVCMOS33 | SLEW=FAST;
NET "dio_a<11>" LOC="H1" | IOSTANDARD=LVCMOS33 | SLEW=FAST;
NET "dio_a<10>" LOC="F2" | IOSTANDARD=LVCMOS33 | SLEW=FAST;
NET "dio_a<9>"  LOC="P8" | IOSTANDARD=LVCMOS33 | SLEW=FAST;
NET "dio_a<8>"  LOC="D3" | IOSTANDARD=LVCMOS33 | SLEW=FAST;
NET "dio_a<7>"  LOC="B1" | IOSTANDARD=LVCMOS33 | SLEW=FAST;
NET "dio_a<6>"  LOC="C1" | IOSTANDARD=LVCMOS33 | SLEW=FAST;
NET "dio_a<5>"  LOC="C2" | IOSTANDARD=LVCMOS33 | SLEW=FAST;
NET "dio_a<4>"  LOC="R5" | IOSTANDARD=LVCMOS33 | SLEW=FAST;
NET "dio_a<3>"  LOC="T5" | IOSTANDARD=LVCMOS33 | SLEW=FAST;
NET "dio_a<2>"  LOC="R6" | IOSTANDARD=LVCMOS33 | SLEW=FAST;
NET "dio_a<1>"  LOC="T8" | IOSTANDARD=LVCMOS33 | SLEW=FAST;
NET "dio_a<0>"  LOC="N7" | IOSTANDARD=LVCMOS33 | SLEW=FAST;
NET "ce_a_n"    LOC="P7" | IOSTANDARD=LVCMOS33 | SLEW=FAST;
NET "ub_a_n"    LOC="T4" | IOSTANDARD=LVCMOS33 | SLEW=FAST;
NET "lb_a_n"    LOC="P6" | IOSTANDARD=LVCMOS33 | SLEW=FAST;

# sram chip 2 data, ce, ub, lb
NET "dio_b<15>" LOC="N1" | IOSTANDARD=LVCMOS33 | SLEW=FAST;
NET "dio_b<14>" LOC="M1" | IOSTANDARD=LVCMOS33 | SLEW=FAST;
NET "dio_b<13>" LOC="K2" | IOSTANDARD=LVCMOS33 | SLEW=FAST;
NET "dio_b<12>" LOC="C3" | IOSTANDARD=LVCMOS33 | SLEW=FAST;
NET "dio_b<11>" LOC="F5" | IOSTANDARD=LVCMOS33 | SLEW=FAST;
NET "dio_b<10>" LOC="G1" | IOSTANDARD=LVCMOS33 | SLEW=FAST;
NET "dio_b<9>"  LOC="E2" | IOSTANDARD=LVCMOS33 | SLEW=FAST;
NET "dio_b<8>"  LOC="D2" | IOSTANDARD=LVCMOS33 | SLEW=FAST;
NET "dio_b<7>"  LOC="D1" | IOSTANDARD=LVCMOS33 | SLEW=FAST;
NET "dio_b<6>"  LOC="E1" | IOSTANDARD=LVCMOS33 | SLEW=FAST;
NET "dio_b<5>"  LOC="G2" | IOSTANDARD=LVCMOS33 | SLEW=FAST;
NET "dio_b<4>"  LOC="J1" | IOSTANDARD=LVCMOS33 | SLEW=FAST;
NET "dio_b<3>"  LOC="K1" | IOSTANDARD=LVCMOS33 | SLEW=FAST;
NET "dio_b<2>"  LOC="M2" | IOSTANDARD=LVCMOS33 | SLEW=FAST;
NET "dio_b<1>"  LOC="N2" | IOSTANDARD=LVCMOS33 | SLEW=FAST;
NET "dio_b<0>"  LOC="P2" | IOSTANDARD=LVCMOS33 | SLEW=FAST;
NET "ce_b_n"    LOC="N5" | IOSTANDARD=LVCMOS33 | SLEW=FAST;
NET "ub_b_n"    LOC="R4" | IOSTANDARD=LVCMOS33 | SLEW=FAST;
NET "lb_b_n"    LOC="P5" | IOSTANDARD=LVCMOS33 | SLEW=FAST;

#==================================================
```

```
# Timing constraint of S3 50-MHz onboard oscillator
# name of the clock signal is clk
#==========================================================
NET "clk" TNM_NET = "clk";
TIMESPEC "TS_clk" = PERIOD "clk" 40 ns HIGH 50 %;
```

REFERENCES

1. P. J. Ashenden, *The Designer's Guide to VHDL*, 2nd ed., Morgan Kaufmann, 2001.
2. J. Axelson, *Serial Port Complete*, 2nd ed., Lakeview Research, 2007.
3. L. Bening and H. D. Foster, *Principles of Verifiable RTL Design*, 2nd ed., Springer-Verlag, 2001.
4. J. Bergeron, *Writing Testbenches: Functional Verification of HDL Models*, Springer-Verlag, 2003.
5. K. Chapman, "Creating Embedded Microcontrollers," *TechXclusives* at www.xilinx.com.
6. A. Chapweske, "PS/2 Mouse/Keyboard Protocol," http://www.computer-engineering.org.
7. A. Chapweske, "PS/2 Keyboard Interface," http://www.computer-engineering.org.
8. A. Chapweske, "PS/2 Mouse Interface," http://www.computer-engineering.org.
9. P. P. Chu, *RTL Hardware Design Using VHDL: Coding for Efficiency, Portability, and Scalability*, Wiley-IEEE Press, 2006.
10. M. D. Ciletti, *Advanced Digital Design with the Verilog HDL*, Prentice Hall, 2003.
11. M. D. Ciletti, *Starter's Guide to Verilog 2001*, Prentice Hall, 2003.
12. C. E. Cummings, "Coding and Scripting Techniques for FSM Designs with Synthesis-Optimized, Glitch-Free Outputs," SNUG (*Synopsys Users Group Conference*), Boston, 2000.
13. D. D. Gajski, *Principles of Digital Design*, Prentice Hall, 1997.
14. J. O. Hamblen et al., *Rapid Prototyping of Digital Systems: Quartus® II Edition*, Springer, 2005.
15. IEEE, *IEEE Standard for Verilog Hardware Description Language (IEEE Std 1364-2001)*, Institute of Electrical and Electronics Engineers, 2001.
16. IEEE, *IEEE Standard VHDL Language Reference Manual (IEEE Std 1076-2001)*, Institute of Electrical and Electronics Engineers, 2001.

FPGA Prototyping by VHDL Examples. By Pong P. Chu

17. IEEE, *IEEE Standard for VHDL Register Transfer Level (RTL) Synthesis (IEEE Std 1076.6-1999)*, Institute of Electrical and Electronics Engineers, 2000.

18. IEEE, *IEEE Standard VHDL Synthesis Packages (IEEE Std 1076.3-1997)*, Institute of Electrical and Electronics Engineers, 1997.

19. IEEE, *IEEE Standard Multivalue Logic System for VHDL Model Interoperability (IEEE Std 1164-1993)*, Institute of Electrical and Electronics Engineers, 1993.

20. Integrated Silicon Solution, "Data Sheet of IS61LV25616AL SRAM," Integrated Silicon Solution, Inc.

21. R. H. Katz and G. Borriello, *Contemporary Logic Design*, 2nd ed., Prentice Hall, 2004.

22. M. Keating and P. Bricaud, *Methodology Manual for System-on-a-Chip Designs*, 3rd ed., Springer-Verlag, 2002.

23. C. M. Maxfield, *The Design Warrior's Guide to FPGAs*, Newnes, 2004.

24. Mentor Graphics, *ModelSim Tutorial*, Mentor Graphics Corporation.

25. S. Palnitkar, *Verilog HDL*, 2nd ed., Prentice Hall, 2003.

26. D. A. Patterson and J. L. Hennessy, *Computer Organization and Design: The Hardware/Software Interface*, 3rd ed., Morgan Kaufmann, 2004.

27. J. M. Rabaey, *Digital Integrated Circuits*, 2nd ed., Prentice Hall, 2002.

28. J. F. Wakerly, *Digital Design: Principles and Practices*, Prentice Hall, 2002.

29. W. Wolf, *FPGA-Based System Design*, Prentice Hall, 2004.

30. Xilinx, *DS099 Spartan-3 FPGA Family: Complete Data Sheet*, Xilinx, Inc.

31. Xilinx, *ISE 8.1i Quick Start Tutorial*, Xilinx, Inc.

32. Xilinx, *ISE In-Depth Tutorial*, Xilinx, Inc.

33. Xilinx, *PicoBlaze 8-bit Embedded Microcontroller User Guide*, Xilinx, Inc.

34. Xilinx, *Spartan-3 Starter Kit Board User Guide*, Xilinx, Inc.

35. Xilinx, *XAPP462 Using Digital Clock Managers (DCMs) in Spartan-3 FPGAs*, Xilinx, Inc.

36. Xilinx, *XAPP463 Using Block RAM in Spartan-3 Generation FPGAs*, Xilinx, Inc.

37. Xilinx, *XAPP464 Using Look-Up Tables as Distributed RAM in Spartan-3 Generation FPGAs*, Xilinx, Inc.

38. Xilinx, *XST User Guide v8.1i*, Xilinx, Inc.

INDEX

Printed and bound by CPI Group (UK) Ltd, Croydon, CR0 4YY

21/08/2024

14543916-0001